Animal Behaviour

Animal Behaviour

Charlotte Uhlenbroek

SECOND EDITION

DORLING KINDERSLEY

Senior Art Editor Sharon Spencer
Senior Editor Miezan van Zyl
Project Art Editor Francis Wong
Project Editor Salima Hirani
Senior Production Editor Andy Hilliard
Senior Production Controller Meskerem Berhane
Jacket Designer Surabhi Wadhwa
Managing Editor Angeles Gavira Guerrero
Managing Art Editor Michael Duffy
Publishing Director Georgina Dee
Art Director Maxine Pedliham
Managing Director Liz Gough

DK INDIA

Senior Art Editor Mahua Sharma
DTP Coordinator Tarun Sharma
Project Art Editor Rupanki Arora Kaushik
DTP Designer Anurag Trivedi
Designer Aarushi Dhawan
Creative Technical Support Vijay Kandwal
Assistant Designers Tanya Varkey, Shaarang Bhanot
Senior Jackets Coordinator Priyanka Sharma Saddi
Senior DTP Designer Harish Aggarwal
Picture Researcher Suemdha Chopra
Managing Art Director Sudakshina Basu

FIRST EDITION

DORLING KINDERSLEY

Senior Art Editors Maxine Lea, Ina Stradins
Senior Editors Peter Frances, Angeles Gavira Guerrero
Project Art Editors Alison Gardner, Samantha Richiardi, Hugh Schermuly, Francis Wong, Steve Woosnam-Savage
Project Editors Rob Houston, Nathan Joyce, Cathy Meeus, Ruth O'Rourke, Gill Pitts, David Summers, Rebecca Warren, Victoria Wiggins
Designers Sonia Barbate, Julian Barford, Mark Lloyd
Editors Polly Boyd, Tamlyn Calitz, Salima Hirani, Ben Hoare, Claire Tennant-Scull, Miezan van Zyl, Ed Wilson
Production Editor Tony Phipps
Creative Technical Support Adam Brackenbury, John Goldsmid
Researcher Verity Greenwood
Indexers Hilary Bird, Richard Bird
Jacket Designers Lee Ellwood, Duncan Turner
Production Inderjit Bhullar
Illustrators Peter Bull, Kevin Jones, Richard Tibbetts
Picture Researcher Laura Barwick
Cartographer John Plumer
Managing Editor Sarah Larter
Senior Managing Art Editor Philip Ormerod
Reference Publisher Jonathan Metcalf
Art Director Bryn Walls

DK INDIA

Art Director Shefali Upadhyay
Editor Aakriti Singal
Designer Neerja Rawat
DTP Designer Dheeraj Arora

This edition published in 2025
First published in Great Britain as *Animal Life* in 2008 by
Dorling Kindersley Limited
20 Vauxhall Bridge Road,
London SW1V 2SA

The authorised representative in the EEA is
Dorling Kindersley Verlag GmbH. Arnulfstr.
124 80636 Munich, Germany

Copyright © 2008, 2025
Dorling Kindersley Limited
A Penguin Random House Company
10 9 8 7 6 5 4 3 2 1
001–345206–Jun/2025

All rights reserved.
No part of this publication may be reproduced, stored in or introduced into a retrieval system, or transmitted, in any form, or by any means (electronic, mechanical, photocopying, recording, or otherwise), without the prior written permission of the copyright owner.

A CIP catalogue record for this book is available from the British Library.
ISBN: 978-0-2417-1991-6

Printed and bound in China

www.dk.com

This book was made with Forest Stewardship Council™ certified paper – one small step in DK's commitment to a sustainable future. Learn more at www.dk.com/uk/information/sustainability

---

Editor in Chief Dr. Charlotte Uhlenbroek

Second Edition: Contributors

Frances Dipper
Chris Mattison
George McGavin
Sean Rands
Marianne Taylor
Andy Wakefield

First Edition: Contributors

Richard Beatty
Dr. Frances Dipper
Dr. Kim Dennis-Bryan
Professor Tim Halliday
Rob Hume
Chris Mattison
Dr. George C. McGavin
Dr. Sanjida O'Connell
Dr. Douglas Palmer
Steve Parker
Dr. Katie Parson
Dr. Sean Rands
Dr. Graham Scott
Dr. Charlotte Uhlenbroek
Dr. Elizabeth White
John Woodward

Consultants

Dr. Juliet Clutton-Brock
Dr. Frances Dipper
Professor Tim Halliday
Rob Hume
Chris Mattison
Dr. George C. McGavin

American Museum of Natural History

Chief consultant: Dr. Christopher J. Raxworthy
Dr. George F. Barrowclough
Dr. Randall T. Schuh
Dr. Mark E. Siddall
Dr. John S. Sparks
Dr. Robert S. Voss

Animal data
The behaviour profiles in this book contain summary information about the animals being described. This information usually covers a species, but in some cases it refers to a group, such as family or genus.

SIZE In most cases (and unless otherwise stated), this refers to the length of the adult animal, with the following dimensions given for different groups:

Mammals: head and body
Birds: tip of bill to tip of tail
Reptiles, Amphibians, and Fishes: head and body, including tail
Invertebrates: head and body, including tail but not including antennae

DISTRIBUTION Occurrence, including both habitat and geographical distribution.

08 **Foreword**

Animal Kingdom
10

- 12 **What is an animal?**
- 14 **Evolution**
- 16 **Animal history**
- 20 **Classification**
- 24 **Animal groups**
  - 26 Arthropod groups
  - 28 Vertebrate groups
  - 30 Fish groups
  - 32 Amphibian groups
  - 34 Reptile groups
  - 36 Bird groups
  - 38 Mammal groups

Animal Anatomy
42

- 44 **Skeletons and muscles**
  - 46 Water skeletons
  - 47 Horny skeletons
  - 48 Chalky skeletons
  - 50 Bony skeletons
- 52 **Movement**
  - 54 Walking and running
  - 56 Climbing and leaping
  - 58 Burrowing, slithering, and sliding
  - 60 Flying and gliding
  - 62 Swimming
- 64 **Body coverings**
  - 66 Skin
  - 68 Scales
  - 70 Feathers
  - 71 Fur, hair, and bristles
- 72 **Body systems**
  - 74 Breathing
  - 76 Circulation
  - 77 Digestion
  - 78 Fluids and temperature control
  - 80 Brains, nerves, and hormones
- 82 **Senses**
  - 84 Touch and vibration
  - 86 Taste and smell
  - 88 Vision
  - 92 Hearing
  - 94 Echolocation
  - 96 Electricity and magnetism

CONTENTS

Animal Behaviour

98

102 LIVING SPACE
- **104** Home ranges and territories
- **116** Migration
- **130** Animal architects

146 HUNTING AND FEEDING
- **150** Feeding on plants
- **162** Omnivores
- **170** Predation
- **218** Scavenging
- **228** Feeding relationships

242 DEFENCE
- **244** Weapons and threats
- **264** Camouflage and deception
- **280** Group defence

292 SEX AND REPRODUCTION
- **296** Reproducing without a mate
- **300** Finding a mate
- **308** Sexual rivalry
- **320** Courtship
- **334** Mating

346 BIRTH AND DEVELOPMENT
- **348** Life stories
- **364** Raising young
- **376** Play and learning

388 SOCIETY

410 COMMUNICATION
- **412** Pheromones and smell
- **416** Visual signals
- **424** Sound
- **430** Touch, vibration, electricity

438 INTELLIGENCE

454 Glossary

462 Index

478 Acknowledgments

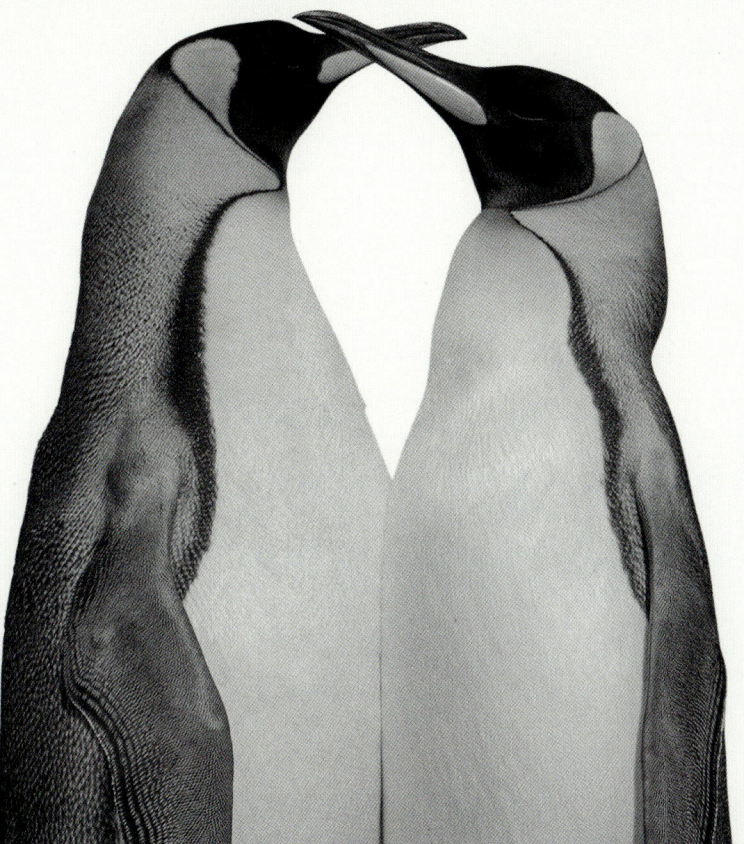

FOREWORD

To discover the rich diversity of animals' behaviour is both enthralling and key to understanding the world we live in. I'm delighted to present a new edition of this book, which, like the first edition, is a dynamic exploration of animal behaviour packed with extraordinary images and informative, lively text. It covers a huge range of stories, including many new discoveries such as the solicitous maternal care shown by a species of jumping spider that nurses its spiderlings with droplets of nutritious milk, and the architectural wonder of ancient networks of termite tunnels and mounds that cover a mind-blowing 230,000 square km (88,800 square miles) in Brazil.

The essentials of animal life are simple – find food, defend yourself, reproduce, and disperse – but the ways in which animals do these things are exceedingly varied. Whether it is a pack of African wild dogs working closely together to bring down prey more than twice their weight, a golden mole swimming beneath the surface of the sand to detect the tiny seismic vibrations of its insect prey, or a forked-tailed drongo tricking other animals to hand over food, the wealth of different strategies reflects the diversity of animals and the huge range of physical and social environments in which they live.

An animal's behaviour depends largely on its form and evolutionary history, and the first two parts of this book describe the major groups of animals and their evolution, anatomy, and senses. The main part of the book then looks at animals in action. It is divided into eight sections that look at different aspects of animals' lives. It is not a complete catalogue of all animal behaviour – that would run to millions of pages and is expanding all the time – rather it's a carefully-selected overview of our current knowledge of animal behaviour, including both typical and unusual behaviours, classic studies and new research.

It is an exciting time to be writing about animal behaviour. Advances in neurobiology, anatomy, and physiology have revolutionized our understanding of how animals do the things they do. The rapidly expanding field of ecology is revealing the complex web of relationships between different species and the maturation of long-term studies of social behaviour is providing intimate views of animal societies and relationships over time. Some discoveries, such as symbolic communication in bonobos, or Asian elephants burying their dead, are blurring the boundaries between human and animal behaviour. While other studies, such as those on the fringed jumping spider, are forcing us to revise our understanding of intelligence. Meanwhile, technological innovations have transformed research in recent decades providing a rapidly expanding window into the lives of creatures and taking us into realms utterly alien to our experience, such as the use of polarized light and magnetism to navigate, electricity to hunt, or minute vibrations to communicate.

This book reflects the remarkable body of work carried out by researchers who have devoted years, often whole lifetimes, to the patient observation of animals in the field and in the lab and to designing ingenious experiments to learn why animals behave in the ways they do. Some species have been very well studied and we know a great deal about their behaviour; others are barely known and as yet we only have tantalizing glimpses into their lives. At a time when so many species are under threat, our knowledge of animals' behaviour is increasingly critical to our efforts to protect them in the face of habitat destruction, climate change and pollution.

Written by a team of leading zoologists and illustrated with images that jump off the page, I hope this book will captivate and inspire readers and make all of us more determined to protect the precious animal life of our planet.

CHARLOTTE UHLENBROEK

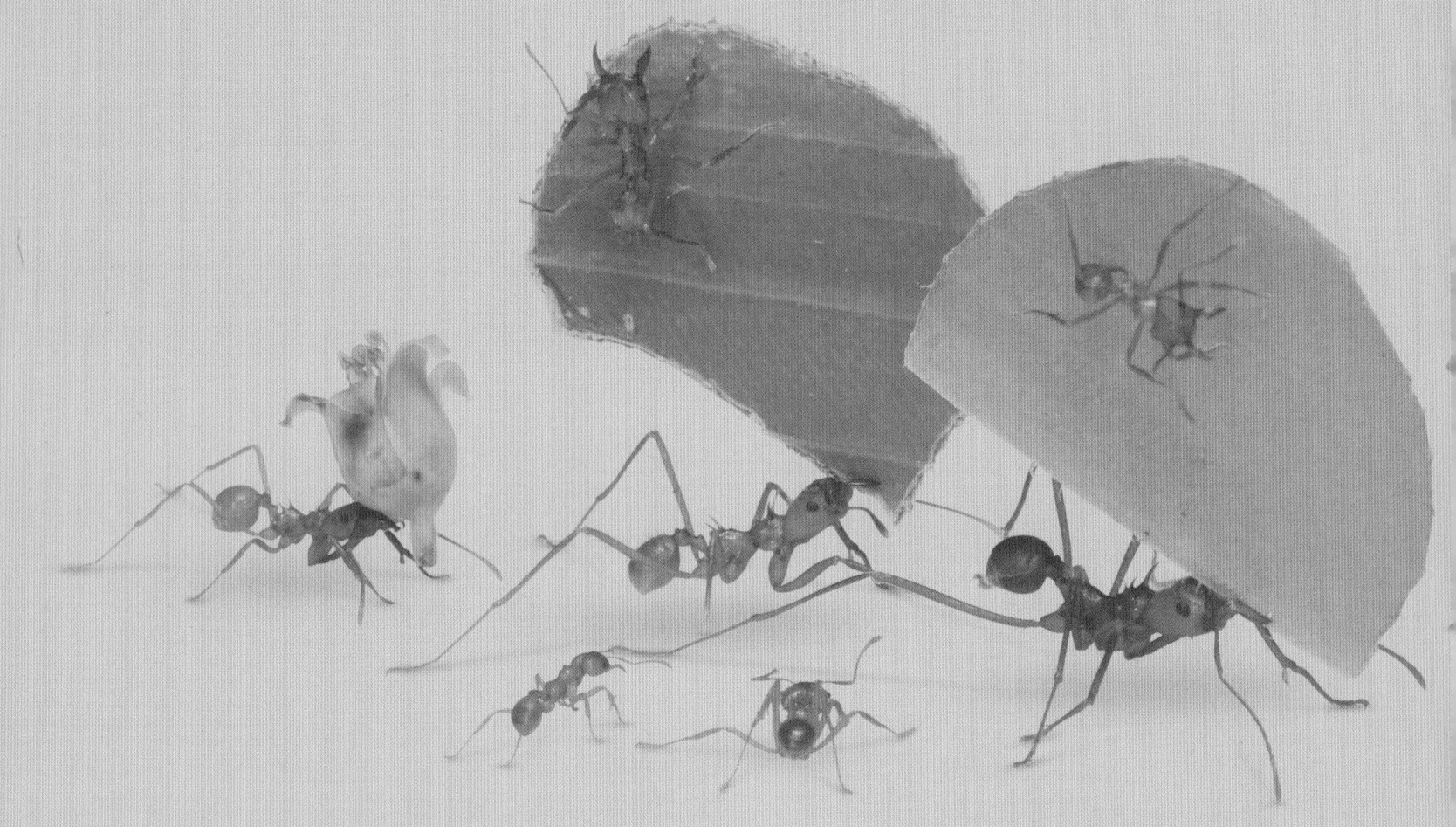

Animal Kingdom

What is an animal ?

There are at least two million living species of animals on Earth. They range from microscopic worms to huge whales, but they all share a few key characteristics that, when combined, distinguish them from all other forms of life. These defining characteristics include both physiological features and the behaviour that makes animals so intriguing.

Life on Earth is traditionally divided into at least five "kingdoms". Two of these, consisting mostly of bacteria and protists, are mainly microscopic, so we are rarely aware of them. The other three are more familiar – fungi, plants, and animals. The essential differences between fungi and plants are not always very obvious at first sight, but most animals are easy to recognize by the way they move and react to their environment. Some aquatic animals move very little, and may look rather like plants, but animals and plants function in very different ways.

Species diversity Scientists believe that there may be more than ten million species of animals, although fewer than two million have been described scientifically. Of these, less than 5 per cent are vertebrates, such as mammals, birds, and fishes. The arthropods make up by far the largest group of animals on Earth.

ENERGY AND FOOD

Plants, and many bacteria and protists, use the energy of sunlight to make food. They combine carbon dioxide with water to form a sugar called glucose – a simple carbohydrate – in a process known as photosynthesis. The glucose stores energy, which plants use to fuel their growth. They can also convert glucose into other carbohydrates, such as the tough cellulose that reinforces their structure. As they take up the water they need, plants also acquire dissolved chemicals such as nitrates and phosphates, which they turn into proteins. Animals cannot make their own food from simple chemicals. A few, such as reef corals, live in partnership with organisms that can produce food like this, but most get their nourishment by eating plants or other living things. They digest the living tissue to break it down into simpler ingredients, such as glucose, and use these to fuel and build their own bodies. Their need to find food is one reason why animals have evolved mobility and senses.

Mobile feeders Gerenuks are superbly adapted to reach the most succulent young shoots on trees. Standing on their hind legs, they can stretch their long, muscular necks in among the branches.

UNIQUE EMBRYOS

Some simple creatures, such as jellyfish, sea anemones, and corals, can multiply asexually by growing buds that turn into new animals. Many insects and other invertebrates, such as water fleas and some aphids, can develop from unfertilized eggs – a process known as parthenogenesis. In both cases the young are clones of their parent.

However, most animals produce single-celled eggs, each fertilized by the sperm cell of another individual to create a "zygote" that contains the DNA of both parents. This single fertilized cell develops into a ball of cells called a blastula, which is unique to animals. Through a process of cell division, the blastula becomes a multicellular embryo (see p.347). Having inherited a mixture of genes from each parent, the embryos produced in this way are genetically different (except in the case of identical twins). Combined with gene mutation and natural selection (see pp.14–15), this genetic mixing creates the variation that has enabled animals to evolve into such a dazzling variety of species.

Multicellular Animals are built up from many microscopic cells that, unlike those of plants or fungi, do not have rigid cell walls. In all animals, except sponges, the cells are organized into different types of living tissue such as muscles and nerves. These tissues may form specialized organs such as the heart, brain, and lungs. The body plan usually becomes fixed early in life, but when some animals, such as butterflies, become adults their bodies undergo a radical rebuild, called metamorphosis (see p.354).

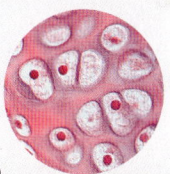

Feeding Nearly all animals obtain nutrition from other living organisms or from the remains of dead organisms. Parasitic worms that live inside other animals absorb simple nutrients through their skins. Other animals have ways of ingesting food into gut cavities, which are specialized for digesting it and turning it into useful nutrients such as glucose. Some aquatic animals simply filter food particles from the water, but most animals have well-defined, mobile mouths that they can use to seize and even chew their food.

Gas exchange All animals need oxygen to turn carbohydrate food into energy, a process that releases carbon dioxide. This is the reverse of photosynthesis, which produces oxygen, so animals are oxygen consumers not producers. They exchange gases through thin-walled gills in water (as in fishes), through their moist skins (as in some amphibians), through branched tube systems (insects), or through lungs. Many types of animal have bloodstreams of some description that carry these gases around the body, along with food, such as blood sugar.

Sensory systems Nearly all animals, except sponges, have networks of nerve cells that respond to external stimuli. Touch a simple animal like a sea anemone (a cnidarian), and it will twitch. More complex animals have sense organs that react to light, sound, pressure, scent, taste, and even electricity. They also have brains that can memorize and recognize the stimuli, enabling many animals to learn by experience. Most of these sensory organs are concentrated at the head of a typical animal, near its mouth.

Mobility A very distinctive feature of animals is their mobility. Some aquatic animals, such as mussels, spend their adult lives attached to rocks and may not move visibly, but they do pump water through their bodies. Mussels also open and close their shells as the tide rises and falls. Most other animals are able to slither, crawl, swim, walk, run, and even fly. Combined with their senses and memories, this enables them to seek out food, escape enemies, and find breeding partners. In other words, they display behaviour.

Evolution

British naturalist Charles Darwin's definition of evolution was "descent with modification", a term he used to describe how successive generations of a species adapt to their changing environments over time to eventually form entirely new species.

WHAT IS EVOLUTION?

Evolution is the process of change in the inherited characteristics of populations of animals over time. The crux of the theory is that all life today has evolved and diverged from simple ancestors that lived in the seas over 3 billion years ago. This means that all animals are related to each other. Accumulated evidence from biology, genetics, and fossils supports evolution as the unifying theory that directs our understanding of life and its history.

Peppered moth variation These three moths are members of the same species. The variations originally occurred as a result of genetic mutations. Natural selection led to the darkest moth becoming more abundant, as this moth was better able to blend into the trees the moths rest on during the day, which were blackened by industrial pollution.

MACROEVOLUTION AND MICROEVOLUTION

The large-scale pattern of change is known as "macroevolution". Macroevolution refers to large-scale changes such as the evolution of limbed vertebrates from those with fins. Other examples of macroevolution are the emergence of the shelled egg, freeing some land-living, four-limbed animals from dependence upon water for reproduction, and the divergence of egg-laying reptiles into other major groups, including turtles and crocodiles. This occurs as a result of small-scale descent with modification, known as "microevolution". For example, since their introduction to the United States of America, house sparrow populations in the north and south of the continent have developed differences, with the northern variant becoming bigger, probably as an adaptation to the colder climate.

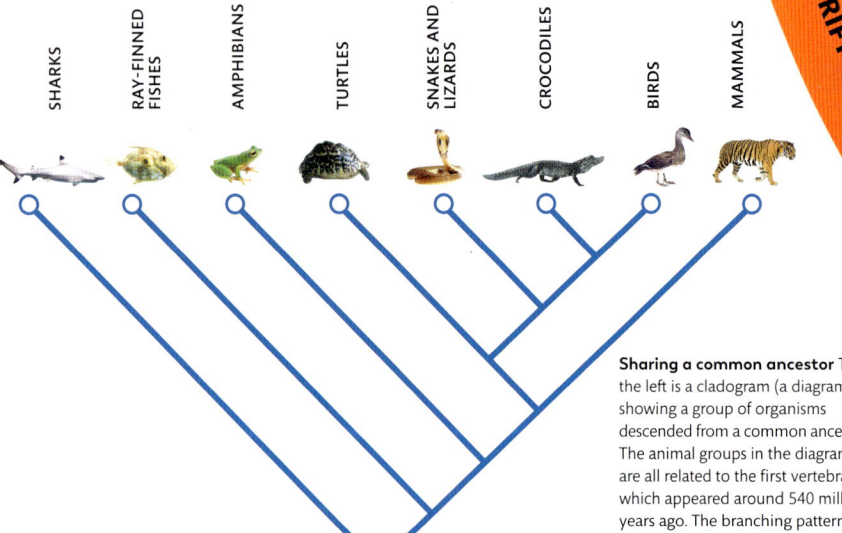

Sharing a common ancestor To the left is a cladogram (a diagram showing a group of organisms descended from a common ancestor). The animal groups in the diagram are all related to the first vertebrate, which appeared around 540 million years ago. The branching patterns occur as a result of divergent evolution. These branching patterns form a "family tree" (or phylogeny).

Natural selection This mechanism is often described as "the survival of the fittest". This species of butterfly varies in colour and reproduces in large numbers, not all of which survive, due to limited resources in the environment. Predators eat more of the purples, as they are less camouflaged than the yellows. The surviving yellows produce more of their own kind. With continued predator preference over time, the yellow butterflies become dominant.

Genetic drift Randomly occurring change in the genetic make-up of a population over time is known as genetic drift. For example, a forest fire wipes out most of the purple butterflies in the population. The next generation contains the genes of the lucky survivors, not necessarily the "fitter" ones. Despite being unlikely, it is even possible for a series of chance events to lead to the total loss of the purple population.

Gene flow Gene flow (or migration) results from the movement of genes from one population to another. For instance, genes are carried from one population and introduced to another by the migration of an adult

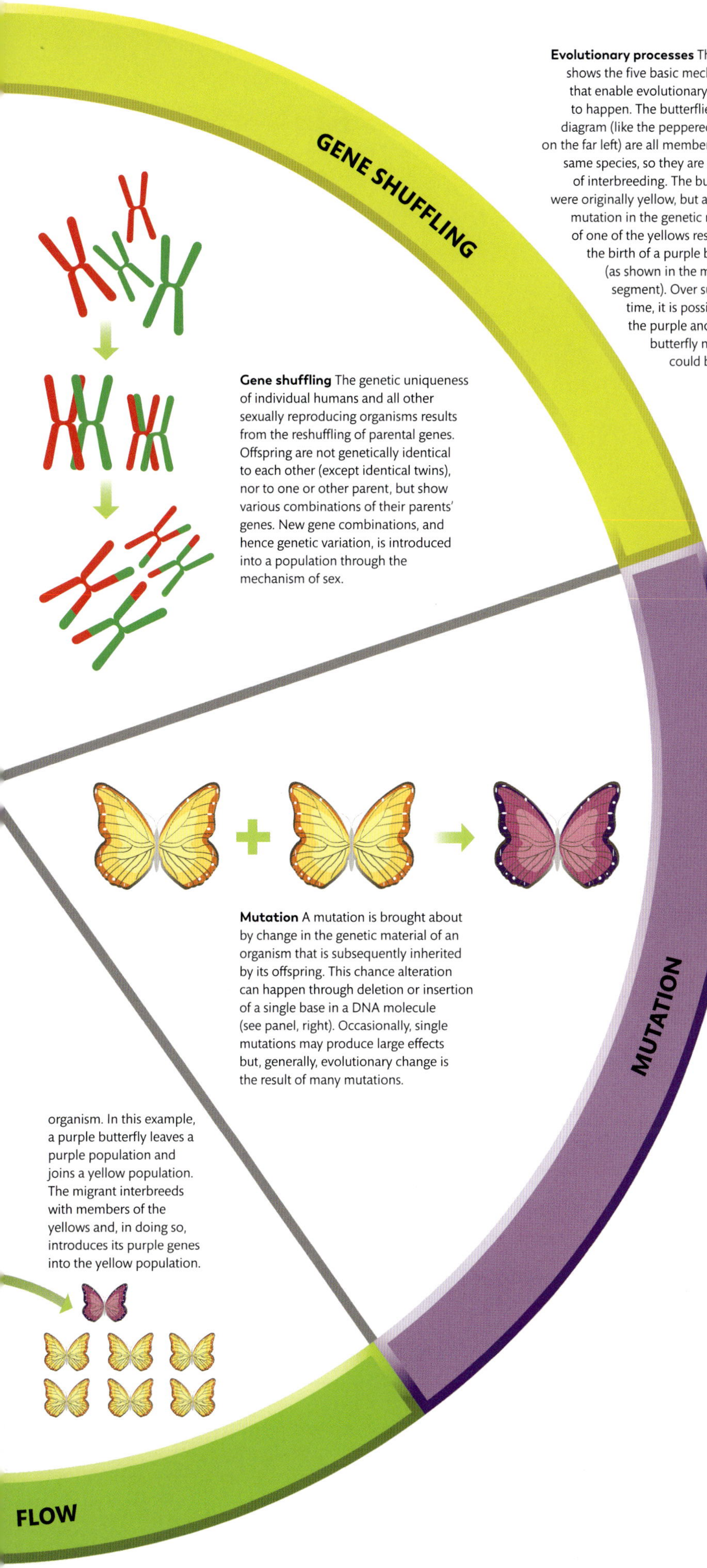

EVOLUTION

Evolutionary processes This chart shows the five basic mechanisms that enable evolutionary change to happen. The butterflies in the diagram (like the peppered moths on the far left) are all members of the same species, so they are capable of interbreeding. The butterflies were originally yellow, but a chance mutation in the genetic material of one of the yellows resulted in the birth of a purple butterfly (as shown in the mutation segment). Over sufficient time, it is possible that the purple and yellow butterfly numbers could be even.

ANATOMY DNA AND GENES

Every life form is made up of a specific series of molecules, and the order of molecules is contained in a chemical code. This code is extremely complex and is encased in spiral-shaped molecules of deoxyribonucleic acid (DNA). Chemicals, known as bases, link each molecule of DNA. There are four different kinds – adenine, cytosine, guanine, and thymine. They are always linked up in pairs – adenine always fuses with thymine, and cytosine with guanine. The sequence of these bases makes up the cell's genetic code. The code found in each human cell consists of 20,000–25,000 separate instructions. Each of these instructions is known as a gene, and each gene is responsible for controlling particular characteristics. For example, there is a single gene that is responsible for the colour of eyes. Genetics is the study of how these characteristics are inherited and is one of the central pillars of biology.

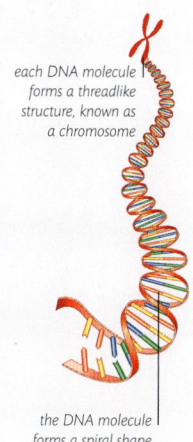

each DNA molecule forms a threadlike structure, known as a chromosome

the DNA molecule forms a spiral shape (a double helix), and is linked by the 4 different bases

Gene shuffling The genetic uniqueness of individual humans and all other sexually reproducing organisms results from the reshuffling of parental genes. Offspring are not genetically identical to each other (except identical twins), nor to one or other parent, but show various combinations of their parents' genes. New gene combinations, and hence genetic variation, is introduced into a population through the mechanism of sex.

Mutation A mutation is brought about by change in the genetic material of an organism that is subsequently inherited by its offspring. This chance alteration can happen through deletion or insertion of a single base in a DNA molecule (see panel, right). Occasionally, single mutations may produce large effects but, generally, evolutionary change is the result of many mutations.

organism. In this example, a purple butterfly leaves a purple population and joins a yellow population. The migrant interbreeds with members of the yellows and, in doing so, introduces its purple genes into the yellow population.

FLOW

GENE SHUFFLING

MUTATION

SPECIATION

Among other meanings, a species can be defined as a group of similar organisms that can interbreed to produce fertile offspring. Speciation is the process whereby new species evolve from a single ancestral species. This occurs for a number of reasons, such as geographical isolation arising from habitat fragmentation. If a small population is isolated from the main group and its members can only share genes with each other, over time they will evolve independently to the point where, if they came back in contact with the original group, they could not interbreed.

Darwin's finches Isolated gene pools in islands such as the Galapagos create unique traits. This woodpecker finch has evolved to use tools to catch prey.

DIVERGENT EVOLUTION

Over vast periods of time, repeated speciation has led to evolutionary divergence, where new descendent species become significantly different from their common ancestors. For instance, all life on land has diverged from water-living ancestors, and all living species of mammal have diverged from a common ancestral mammal that lived alongside the dinosaurs. These series of changes arise as a product of Earth's dynamic environments, which vary from place to place and from time to time.

CONVERGENT EVOLUTION

Sometimes, different organisms will evolve similar characteristics to adapt to the environment that they inhabit. For example, the similarity in body forms of whales, seals, and penguins is the result of similar adaptations to similar ways of life. The common factor is the adaptation of a streamlined body shape, with reduced limbs for a more efficient swimming motion. In a similar way, wings have evolved independently in birds and bats for flight.

Coevolution and mutual dependency Some flowers rely on hummingbirds for pollination, while some hummingbirds rely on specific flowers for nectar. They have coevolved in terms of shape and colour to accommodate each other's survival.

NEOPROTOZOIC				
PRECAMBRIAN	CAMBRIAN		ORDOVICIAN	SILURIAN
550	500		450	

AIR **LAND** **SEA**

Animal history

The evolution and expansion of animal life on Earth is a remarkable story. From microscopic beginnings billions of years ago, animal life evolved in the protective and supportive medium of ocean water. Fossilized remains show us that the earliest multicellular animals may have evolved around 890 million years ago (MYA). However, the fossil record is by no means complete. We know surprisingly little about the origins of some groups, such as sharks and rays, but with each new fossil discovery, we move a step closer to answering the questions that have puzzled palaeontologists for years.

DIVERSIFICATION AND PROLIFERATION

Early in the Cambrian, marine invertebrates underwent a period of expansion and diversification. Many familiar living invertebrate groups evolved in this period, along with now extinct groups. The first vertebrate animals also evolved in the Cambrian. These diversified into several fish-related groups, some of which are now extinct. After the arthropods moved into the terrestrial environments, they proliferated and rapidly diversified. By late Devonian times, tetrapod (four-limbed) vertebrates had left the water and the next stage in vertebrate evolution had begun. The airways were the last environment for animal life to conquer, with insects first achieving this in the Carboniferous period. Many animal groups have members that have evolved and adapted to life in each environment. For example, reptiles first evolved on land, then evolved water-living members before finally taking to the air.

EXTINCTION EVENTS

The history of animal evolution was not one of simple expansion and diversification. As animal groups evolved and died away, changing environments and events impacted upon their evolution, sometimes disastrously. There were several major extinction events that reset the evolutionary clock. The most devastating of these – the Permian–Triassic extinction – wiped out 96 per cent of all marine species.

ORDOVICIAN–SILURIAN EXTINCTION 440 MYA
One third of all brachiopod and bryozoan families, and many groups of conodonts and trilobites were rendered extinct. Overall, around 100 families of marine invertebrates were wiped out.

Earliest terrestrial arthropod groups (centipedes, millipedes, and others) evolve around 450 MYA.

HOW THIS CHART WORKS
This chart separates animal life into three major habitats – sea, land, and air. The major animal groups are individually coloured. Their relative abundance through time is represented by an expanding and contracting band. The evolution of each group is signified by tie lines that link them to their ancestral group. The three invertebrate bands are shown on a separate scale to the vertebrates due to the difficulty in estimating their numbers (they are thought to account for 97 per cent of all species). The size of their strands are relative to each other.

- Invertebrates
- Birds
- Mammals
- Reptiles
- Amphibians
- Bony fishes
- Sharks and rays
- Jawless fishes

MAWSONITES

EVOLUTION OF ANIMAL LIFE
Complex multicellular organisms began to appear in the Ediacaran period, around 630 MYA. This fossil of a *Mawsonites* species is thought to be an early jellyfish or a primitive worm.

Earliest jawed fishes evolve around 450 MYA.

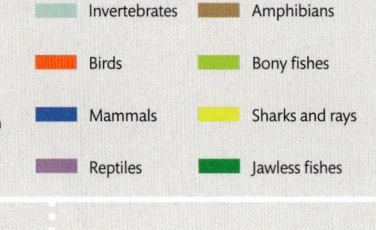
ESTONIOCERAS NAUTILUS

OLENELLUS TRILOBITE

The Cambrian "Explosion", around 540 MYA, saw the evolution of groups of marine invertebrates, and also the evolution of the first vertebrates.

Evolution of coral

Primitive nautiloids (marine cephalopods) become abundant around 475 MYA.

Coral reefs become widespread in the mid-Ordovician period, around 470 MYA.

FAVOSITES CORAL

PALEOZOIC

DEVONIAN	CARBONIFEROUS	PERMIAN
400	350	300

LATE DEVONIAN EXTINCTION 365 MYA
This event mostly affected marine organisms. Coral reefs, brachiopods, and trilobites were all severely reduced in number. Most terrestrial animals were unscathed, but some early amphibians were wiped out.

ARCHIMYLACRIS

Late Carboniferous insects begin to appear around 320 MYA, including roaches and dragonflies. *Archimylacris* was an early cockroach with folded wings.

AERIAL INVERTEBRATES

ACANTHOSTEGA

Evolving from fishes, the first tetrapods (four-legged vertebrates) rose up out of the water and started colonizing the land around 370 MYA. *Acanthostega* had both lungs and gills, eight digits on each limb, and webbed feet.

Amniote ancestors are thought to branch out from the amphibians around 340 MYA.

This fossil of *Westlothiana lizziae* was hailed as the first true reptile due to its superficial reptilelike features, but it is now thought to be an amniote ancestor (345 MYA).

WESTLOTHIANA LIZZIAE

The amniotes split into two groups around 315 MYA – the synapsids (eventually leading to living mammals) and the sauropsids (eventually leading to living reptiles).

REPTILES

AMPHIBIANS

Earliest known scorpions evolve around 418 MYA.

Early land snails evolve in the Carboniferous, around 320 MYA.

Arthropods continue to diversify. *Graeophonus* was a true spider relative.

GRAEOPHONUS "SPIDER"

TERRESTRIAL INVERTEBRATES

CHEIRACANTHUS JAWED FISH

Acanthodians (early jawed fishes), such as *Cheiracanthus*, expand early in the Devonian period, around 410 MYA.

HELIOCOPRION TOOTH SPIRAL

Colossal early Permian sharks, such as *Heliocoprion*, become the dominant predators in the seas, around 298 MYA.

BONY FISHES

SHARKS AND RAYS

JAWLESS FISHES

PTERASPIS JAWLESS FISH

Early jawless fishes are common around 405 MYA. *Pteraspis* had a distinctive flattened head, enclosed by massive bony plates.

Extensive development of Carboniferous coral reefs, around 350 MYA.

MARINE INVERTEBRATES

CONTINUED OVERLEAF »

MESOZOIC

TRIASSIC	JURASSIC
250 200	150

The first true flies evolve in the mid-Triassic.

The earliest known moth – *Archaeolepis mane*, evolves around 190 MYA.

Pterodactylus was a pterosaur – the only non-avian reptiles to develop powered flight. Their wings were formed of membranes of skin.

PTERODACTYLUS

Birds evolve around 155 MYA. *Archaeopteryx* had more in common with dinosaurs than modern birds.

ARCHAEOPTERYX

CYNOGNATHUS

Cynodonts were a group of synapsids, which are thought to be direct ancestors of mammals. *Cynognathus* was a carnivorous doglike cynodont.

Mammals continue to diversify. *Amblotherium* was a small, primitive insectivore.

AMBLOTHERIUM

Compsognathus was one of the smallest dinosaurs to have existed. It was chicken-sized, but extremely agile. It mostly preyed on insects.

HERRERASAURUS

Dinosaurs evolve around 230 MYA.

Post-extinction expansion of dinosaurs and other reptile groups, around 200 MYA.

COMPSOGNATHUS

SEA TURTLE

The first marine turtles evolve around 215 MYA.

Large marine predators thrived around 175 MYA. *Ichthyosaurus* had strengthening bones around its eyes, enabling it to dive very deep.

ICHTHYOSAURUS

Bony fishes rapidly expand and diversify after the Permian–Triassic extinction. *Lepidotus* was a common bottom-dwelling fish with thickly-enamelled scales.

LEPIDOTUS BONY FISH

Triassic recovery in the seas. Reefs emerge again with new kinds of coral.

PERMIAN–TRIASSIC EXTINCTION 250 MYA
Earth's most severe extinction event, affecting all animal groups. 96 per cent of marine species were wiped out, and around 70 per cent of terrestrial vertebrates.

TRIASSIC–JURASSIC EXTINCTION 210 MYA
23 per cent of both marine and non-marine families were wiped out, including sponges, gastropods, bivalves, cephalopods, brachiopods, insects, and vertebrates.

ERYON SPINY LOBSTER

Cretaceous spiny lobsters, such as *Eryon*, were common in shallow waters. The family still exists today, but they have adapted to the ocean depths.

» **EVOLUTION CONTINUED**

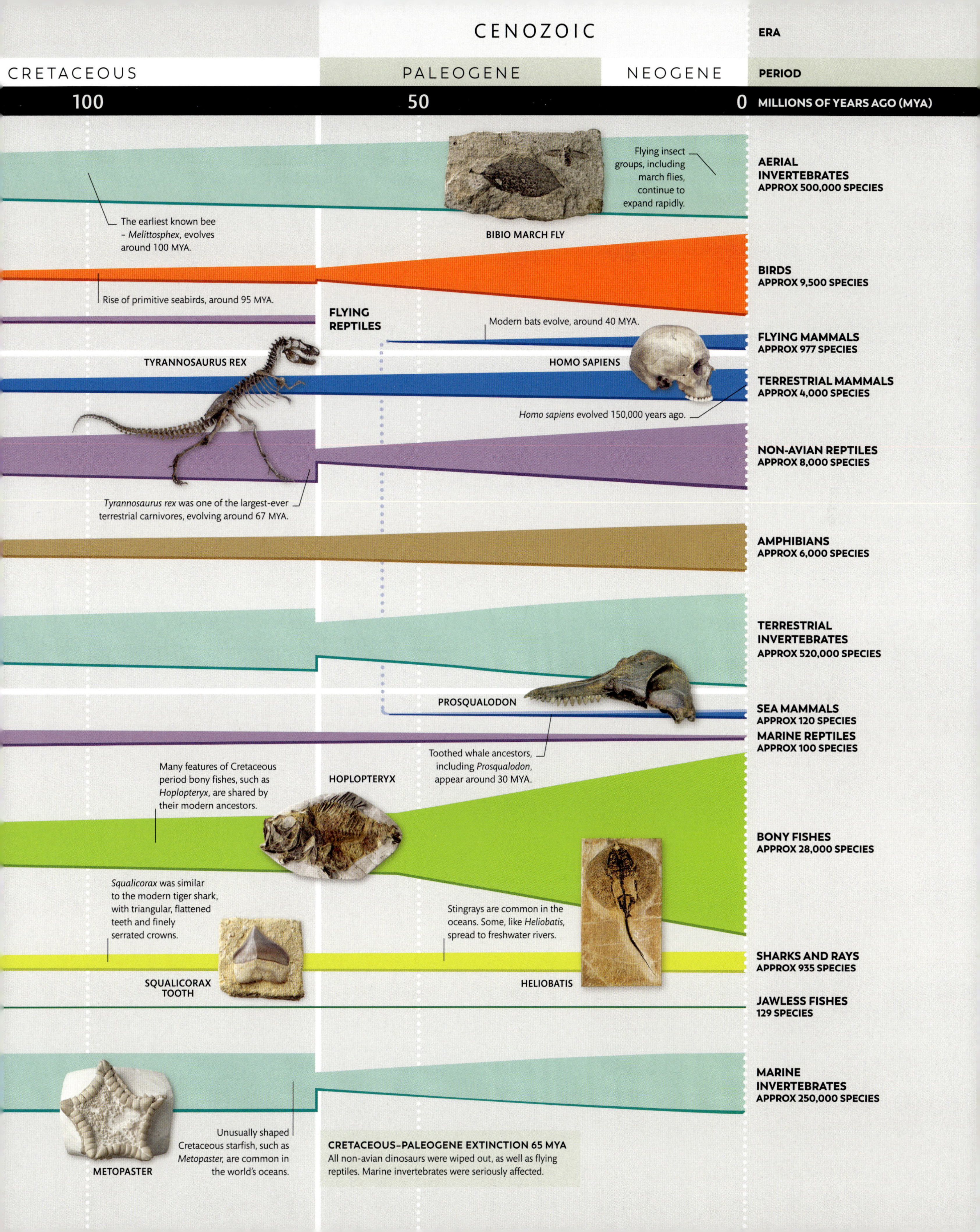

ERA		CENOZOIC	
PERIOD	CRETACEOUS	PALEOGENE	NEOGENE
MILLIONS OF YEARS AGO (MYA)	100	50	0

AERIAL INVERTEBRATES
APPROX 500,000 SPECIES

The earliest known bee – *Melittosphex*, evolves around 100 MYA.

Flying insect groups, including march flies, continue to expand rapidly.

BIBIO MARCH FLY

BIRDS
APPROX 9,500 SPECIES

Rise of primitive seabirds, around 95 MYA.

FLYING MAMMALS
APPROX 977 SPECIES

FLYING REPTILES

Modern bats evolve, around 40 MYA.

TERRESTRIAL MAMMALS
APPROX 4,000 SPECIES

TYRANNOSAURUS REX

HOMO SAPIENS

Homo sapiens evolved 150,000 years ago.

NON-AVIAN REPTILES
APPROX 8,000 SPECIES

Tyrannosaurus rex was one of the largest-ever terrestrial carnivores, evolving around 67 MYA.

AMPHIBIANS
APPROX 6,000 SPECIES

TERRESTRIAL INVERTEBRATES
APPROX 520,000 SPECIES

PROSQUALODON

SEA MAMMALS
APPROX 120 SPECIES

MARINE REPTILES
APPROX 100 SPECIES

Many features of Cretaceous period bony fishes, such as *Hoplopteryx*, are shared by their modern ancestors.

HOPLOPTERYX

Toothed whale ancestors, including *Prosqualodon*, appear around 30 MYA.

BONY FISHES
APPROX 28,000 SPECIES

Squalicorax was similar to the modern tiger shark, with triangular, flattened teeth and finely serrated crowns.

Stingrays are common in the oceans. Some, like *Heliobatis*, spread to freshwater rivers.

SHARKS AND RAYS
APPROX 935 SPECIES

SQUALICORAX TOOTH

HELIOBATIS

JAWLESS FISHES
129 SPECIES

Unusually shaped Cretaceous starfish, such as *Metopaster*, are common in the world's oceans.

METOPASTER

CRETACEOUS–PALEOGENE EXTINCTION 65 MYA
All non-avian dinosaurs were wiped out, as well as flying reptiles. Marine invertebrates were seriously affected.

MARINE INVERTEBRATES
APPROX 250,000 SPECIES

Classification

Before 1650, the study of living organisms was much more localized than it is today. However, when the early explorers started to send home vast collections of exotic plants and animals previously unknown to science, it soon became evident that, without some sort of ordered system, the situation would rapidly become chaotic.

ORDER FROM CHAOS

John Ray (1628–1705) was the first person to attempt to classify the natural world. He organized organisms based on their form and structure, or morphology, using lengthy names that incorporated a brief anatomical description. But it was Carl Linnaeus (1707–1778) who devised the system of classification that we still use today. Like Ray, Linnaeus made use of morphological features, but used them to group things together rather than to describe them. He set up formal categories on the basis of shared morphological features, creating a hierarchy of increasing exclusiveness that extends from kingdom to species (see diagram, right). Over time, scientists have expanded the system, adding levels such as domain and cohort, and sub-dividing others into infra-, super-, and sub- categories to accommodate our increasing knowledge of different animals. Despite these revisions, the Linnaean system has remained fundamentally the same since its inception 250 years ago.

NOMENCLATURE

In formulating his hierarchical system, Linnaeus also streamlined the names of individual organisms – species were previously referred to by a common name or descriptive anatomical phrase. He adopted Latin as the universal language of taxonomy, and gave each taxon a unique two-word name, called a binomial, by combining the genus and species names. *Homo sapiens*, for example, is the scientific name for humans. What makes the name unique is the species part – all humans carry the generic name *Homo*, including fossil humans such as *Homo habilis*, but only modern humans are referred to as *Homo sapiens*, or "knowing man". Binomial names can still be descriptive but, more crucially, the unique name avoids confusion.

Linnaean system The Linnaean classification system is shown here in its original form. To demonstrate how this system works, the highlighted boxes trace the systematic position of the Indian rhinoceros, from the broadest grouping of kingdom to the narrowest grouping of species, which comprises only Indian rhinoceroses.

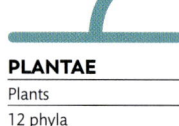
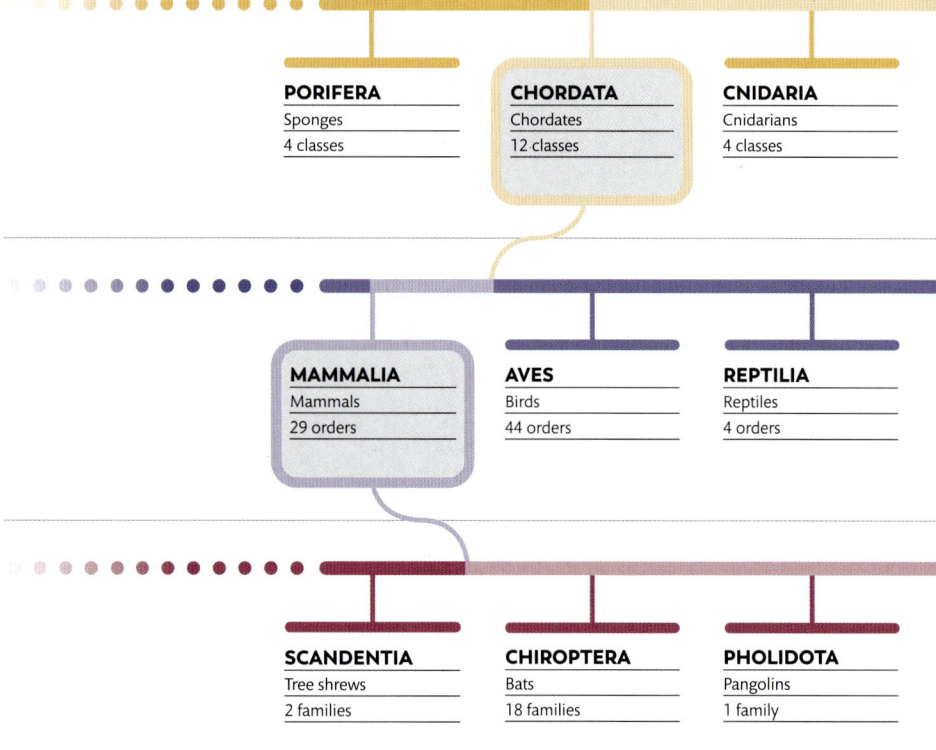

PLANTAE — Plants — 12 phyla

PORIFERA — Sponges — 4 classes
CHORDATA — Chordates — 12 classes
CNIDARIA — Cnidarians — 4 classes

MAMMALIA — Mammals — 29 orders
AVES — Birds — 44 orders
REPTILIA — Reptiles — 4 orders

SCANDENTIA — Tree shrews — 2 families
CHIROPTERA — Bats — 18 families
PHOLIDOTA — Pangolins — 1 family

Carl Linnaeus This Swedish botanist, who was often referred to as the father of taxonomy, published the first edition of the *Systema Naturae*, his classification of living organisms, in 1735. The resulting system remains in use today.

> "Nature does not proceed by **leaps and bounds.**"
> Carl Linnaeus

RHINOCEROS — One-horned rhinoceroses — 2 species

RHINOCEROS UNICORNIS — Indian rhinoceros
RHINOCEROS SONDAICUS — Javan rhinoceros

Misleading names The common name "robin" is applied to very different birds, but using their Latin names readily distinguishes them. The American robin (left) is *Turdus migratorius*, while the European robin (right) is *Erithacus rubecula*.

FUNGI	ANIMALIA	BACTERIA	PROTOCTISTA
Fungi	Animals	Bacteria	Protoctists
3 phyla	35 phyla	14 phyla	30 phyla

KINGDOM
This is the highest level of Linnaeus's hierarchy. Each contains living organisms that work in fundamentally the same way. Initially, there were only two kingdoms, plant and animal, but today there are at least five.

PLATYHELMINTHES	NEMATODA	MOLLUSCA	ARTHROPODA
Flatworms	Roundworms	Molluscs	Arthropods
3 classes	2 classes	7 classes	17 classes

PHYLUM
A major subdivision of the animal kingdom, made up of classes. Phylum Chordata, for example, comprises all animals that possess a precursor of the backbone, called a notochord, at some time during their lives.

AMPHIBIA	CHONDRICHTHYES	OSTEICHTHYES	MYXINI
Amphibians	Cartilaginous fishes	Bony fishes	Hagfishes
3 orders	c.13 orders	45 orders	1 order

CLASS
A taxonomic level made up of orders and their respective subgroups. Class Mammalia, for example, comprises those chordates that have a single jaw bone (the dentary), fur, and mammary glands.

CARNIVORA	PERISSODACTYLA	PRIMATES	LAGOMORPHA
Carnivores	Odd-toed ungulates	Primates	Lagomorphs
18 families	3 families	16 families	2 families

ORDER
More exclusive are the different orders into which a class is subdivided. Each order contains one or more families and their subgroups. The Perissodactyla, for example, are plant-eating mammals that walk on an odd number of toes.

EQUIDAE	TAPIRIDAE	RHINOCEROTIDAE
Horses	Tapirs	Rhinoceroses
1 genus	1 genus	4 genera

FAMILY
A family is a subdivision of an order, and it contains one or more genera and their subgroups. Family Rhinocerotidae, for example, comprises those perissodactyls (odd-toed ungulates) that have horns on their noses.

DICERORHINUS	CERATOTHERIUM	DICEROS
Sumatran rhinoceros	White rhinoceros	Black rhinoceros
1 species	1 species	1 species

GENUS
Aristotle (384–322 BCE) was the first to use the term genus to group things together. It was later adopted by Linnaeus to identify a subdivision of a family. The genus Rhinoceros contains the one-horned rhinoceroses.

SPECIES
This group comprises similar individuals able to interbreed in the wild. Indian rhinoceroses, for example, breed only with one another and not with other types of rhinoceros. Their species name unicornis refers to the single horn.

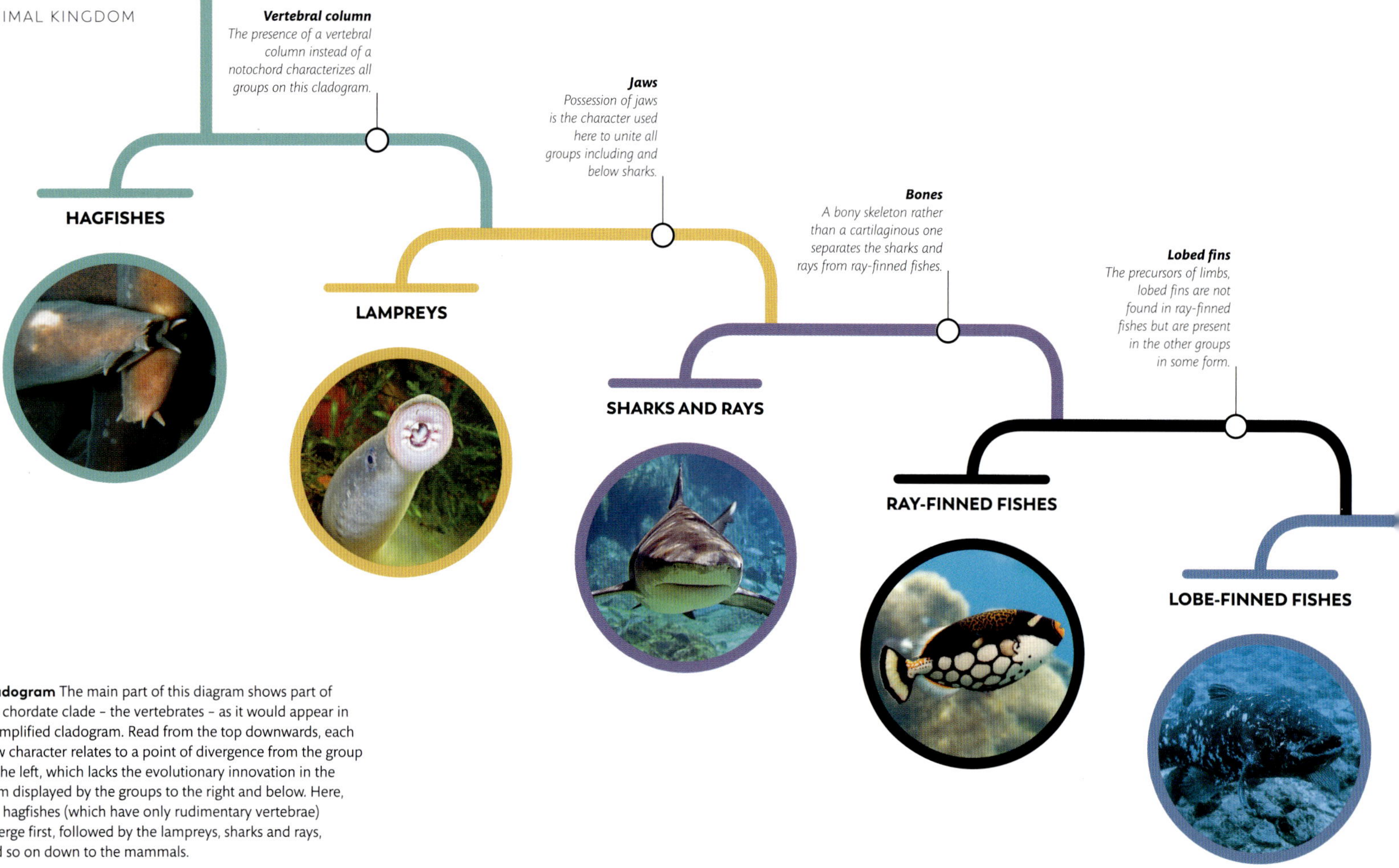

Vertebral column
The presence of a vertebral column instead of a notochord characterizes all groups on this cladogram.

Jaws
Possession of jaws is the character used here to unite all groups including and below sharks.

Bones
A bony skeleton rather than a cartilaginous one separates the sharks and rays from ray-finned fishes.

Lobed fins
The precursors of limbs, lobed fins are not found in ray-finned fishes but are present in the other groups in some form.

HAGFISHES

LAMPREYS

SHARKS AND RAYS

RAY-FINNED FISHES

LOBE-FINNED FISHES

Cladogram The main part of this diagram shows part of the chordate clade – the vertebrates – as it would appear in a simplified cladogram. Read from the top downwards, each new character relates to a point of divergence from the group to the left, which lacks the evolutionary innovation in the form displayed by the groups to the right and below. Here, the hagfishes (which have only rudimentary vertebrae) diverge first, followed by the lampreys, sharks and rays, and so on down to the mammals.

PHYLOGENETIC CLASSIFICATION

A relatively new system for classifying living organisms, which arose in the 1950s, is called phylogenetics, or cladistics. Based on the work of German entomologist Willi Hennig (1913–1976), it unites organisms in groups called clades on the basis of morphology (form and structure) and genetic characters. The system assumes that a character shared by a group of organisms but not by others indicates they have a closer evolutionary relationship to each other and therefore a more recent ancestor in common. Like the Linnaean system (see pp.20–21) this method of classification is hierarchical, but, unlike those created by Linnaeus, the groupings are used to construct taxonomic trees using evolutionary relationships.

PRIMITIVE AND DERIVED CHARACTERS

The characters that are important in cladistic classification are referred to as "derived" because they are altered in some way from what is considered the ancestral "primitive" condition. They also need to be present in at least two groups, or taxa, to be informative about relationships. For example, in the rhinoceroses, the character of a hairy body is found only in the Sumatran rhino (*Dicerorhinus sumatrensis*) and therefore it tells you nothing about its relationship with the rest of the rhino species, whereas a single horn (see character 4 in the diagram, opposite) is unique to both the Indian (*Rhinoceros unicornis*) and Javan (*Rhinoceros sondaicus*) rhinoceroses, suggesting they inherited it from an ancestor they shared in the past. Derived characters, such as a single horn, that are unique to particular taxa, are referred to as synapomorphies. Although, for simplicity, only single characters are shown in the rhinoceros diagram opposite, the number of characters used to create a cladistic hierarchy, or cladogram, is usually very large – so large that it takes a computer to analyse the data and generate the cladogram.

COMMON ANCESTRY

Cladistics assumes that the more derived characters species have in common, the more closely related they are to each other than to anything else. This being the case, it also then follows that they have a more recent ancestor in common than they do with other taxa. This can be confirmed by examining the fossil record for taxa or characters once a cladogram has been generated. Brothers, for example, share more characters with each other than they do with their cousins because they have the same parents, parents being their common ancestors. They also have features in common with their cousins because they share the same grandparents, so the whole family would be placed within the same clade, but with the cousins branching off earlier from the line leading to the brothers. In the same way, rhinoceroses form a clade within the odd-toed ungulates.

CASE STUDY **GENETICS**

Until recently, cladistics was based on morphological characters, because investigation of evolutionary history involves looking at fossils in which DNA is not preserved. Today, cladistics is being used increasingly to examine the relationships of living animals. For these organisms, relationships can be established using DNA analysis. Such work has led to major revisions in some of the "traditional" groupings. For example, whales are now grouped with even-toed ungulates and more specifically with hippopotamuses.

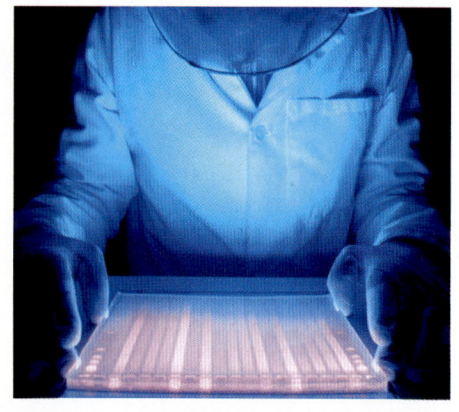

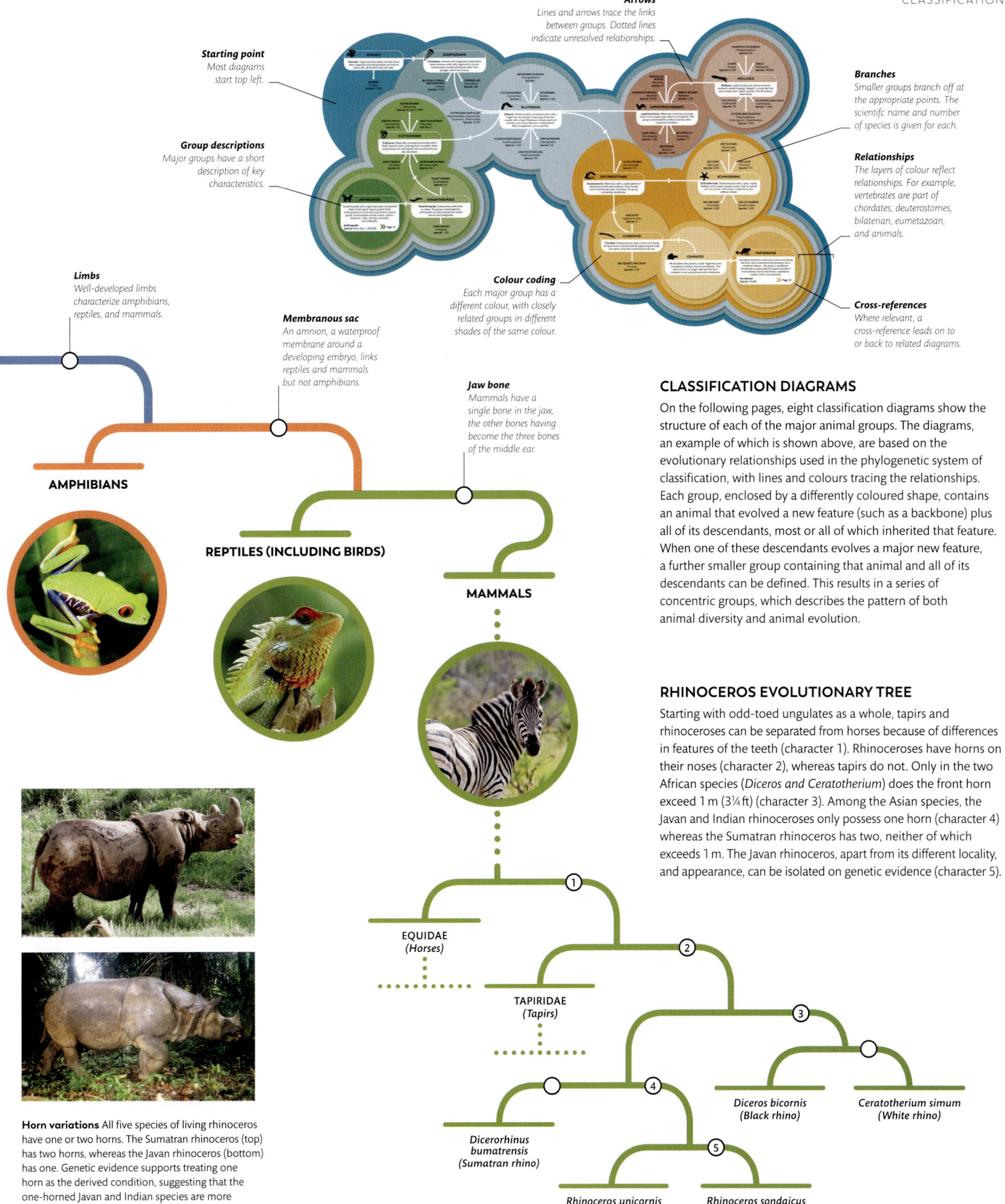

CLASSIFICATION DIAGRAMS

On the following pages, eight classification diagrams show the structure of each of the major animal groups. The diagrams, an example of which is shown above, are based on the evolutionary relationships used in the phylogenetic system of classification, with lines and colours tracing the relationships. Each group, enclosed by a differently coloured shape, contains an animal that evolved a new feature (such as a backbone) plus all of its descendants, most or all of which inherited that feature. When one of these descendants evolves a major new feature, a further smaller group containing that animal and all of its descendants can be defined. This results in a series of concentric groups, which describes the pattern of both animal diversity and animal evolution.

RHINOCEROS EVOLUTIONARY TREE

Starting with odd-toed ungulates as a whole, tapirs and rhinoceroses can be separated from horses because of differences in features of the teeth (character 1). Rhinoceroses have horns on their noses (character 2), whereas tapirs do not. Only in the two African species (*Diceros* and *Ceratotherium*) does the front horn exceed 1 m (3¼ ft) (character 3). Among the Asian species, the Javan and Indian rhinoceroses only possess one horn (character 4) whereas the Sumatran rhinoceros has two, neither of which exceeds 1 m. The Javan rhinoceros, apart from its different locality, and appearance, can be isolated on genetic evidence (character 5).

Horn variations All five species of living rhinoceros have one or two horns. The Sumatran rhinoceros (top) has two horns, whereas the Javan rhinoceros (bottom) has one. Genetic evidence supports treating one horn as the derived condition, suggesting that the one-horned Javan and Indian species are more closely related to each other than to the others.

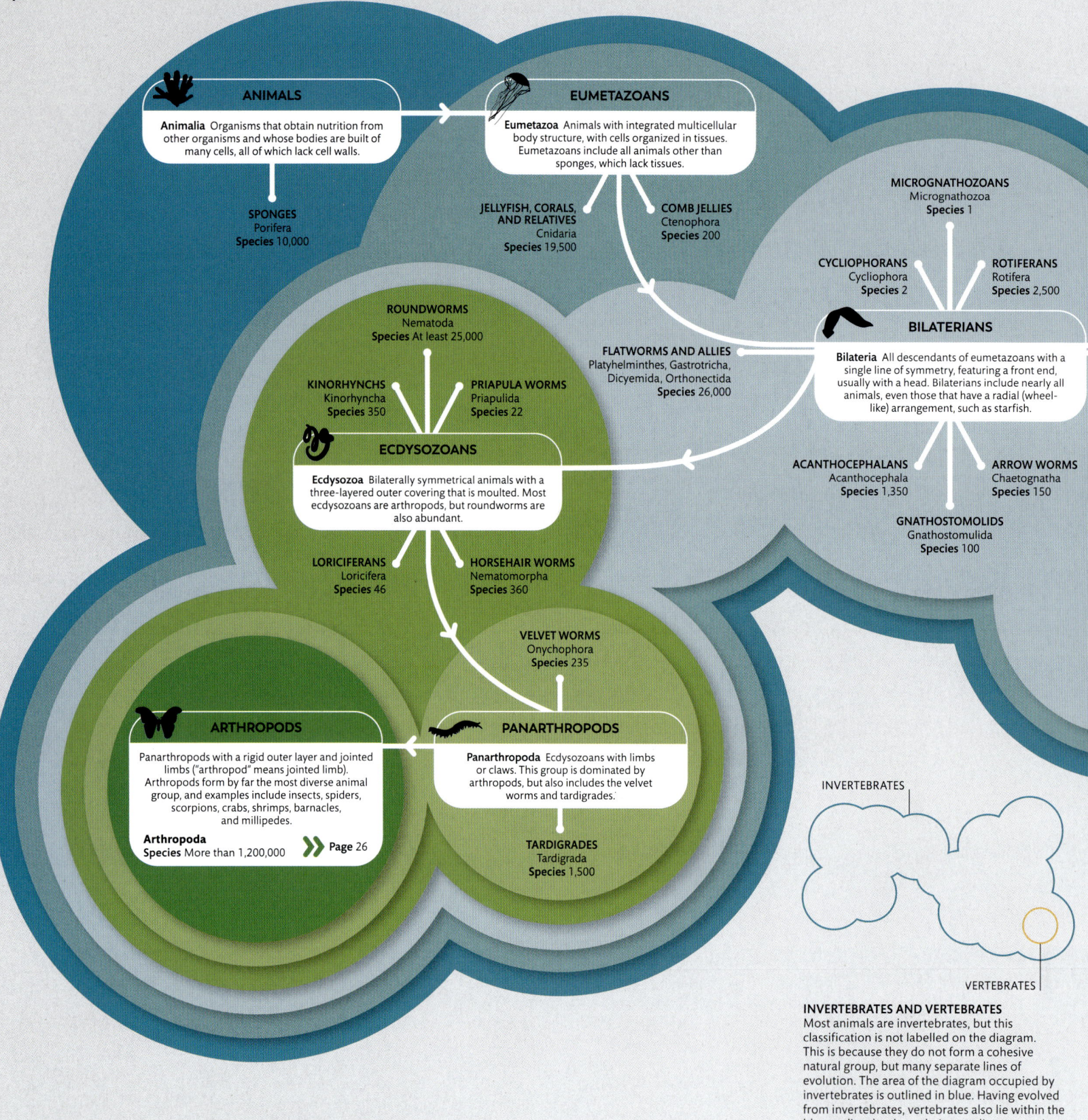

Animal groups

Over one and a half million animal species have been identified, but the total is probably several million. The vast majority of these are invertebrates – animals without a backbone – from simple sponges and jellyfish to sophisticated honey bees. The vast array of invertebrate groups occupies most of the animal evolutionary tree. Although relatively few vertebrates have been identified, they comprise a diverse group ranging in size from tiny frogs less than 8 mm (⅜ in) long to the blue whale, at more than 30 m (98 ft) long, the largest animal to have ever lived.

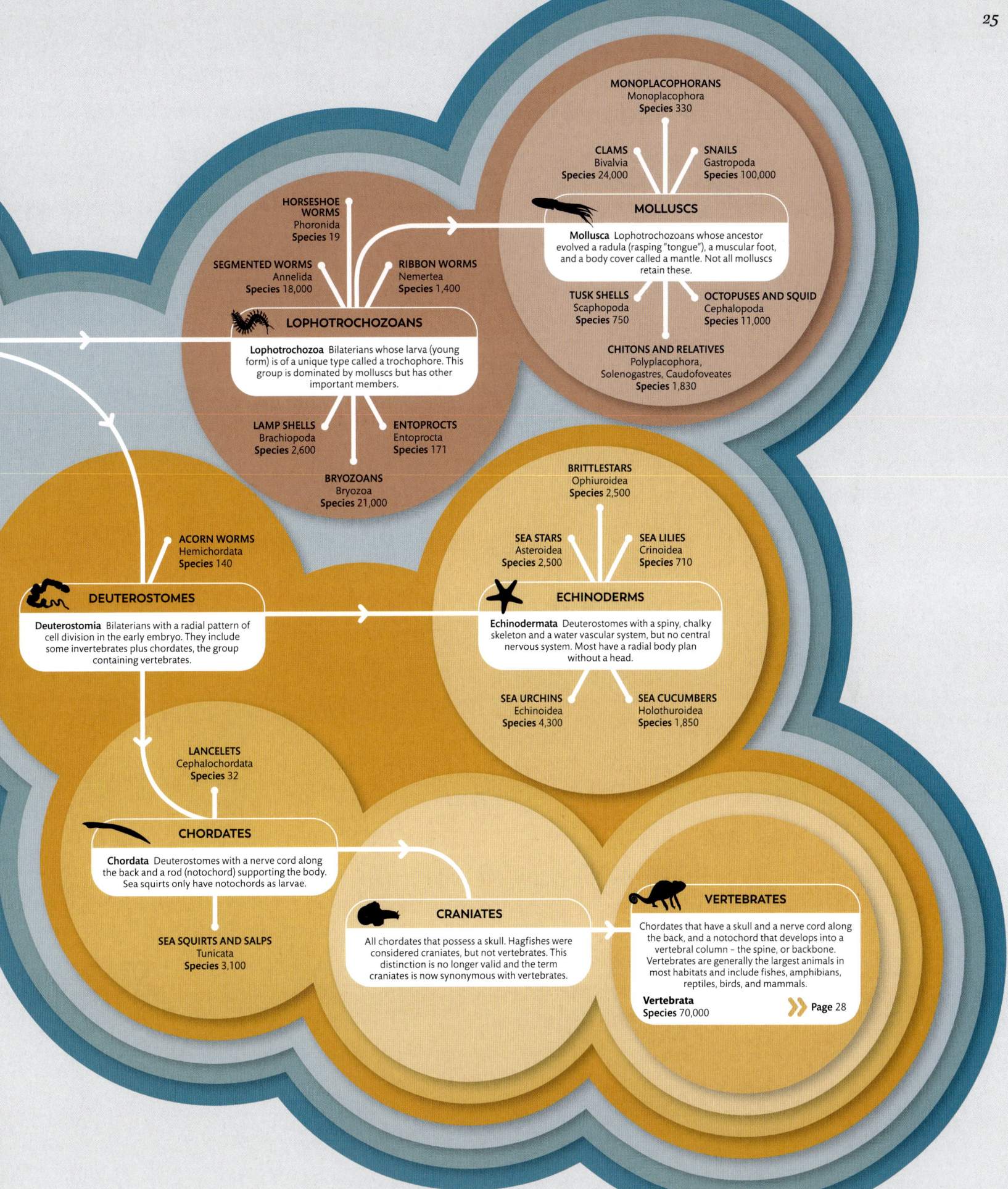

ARTHROPODS

Arthropoda Segmented animals with pairs of jointed limbs and a rigid exoskeleton. Body segments are aggregated or fused into functional units, the most universal being a head.

SEA SPIDERS
Pycnogonida
Species 1,400

CHELICERATES

Chelicerata Arthropods with bodies divided into two main sections. They have no antennae, and the first pair of limbs takes the form of pincerlike mouthparts (chelicerae).

MUSSEL AND SEED SHRIMPS
Ostracoda
Species 17,000

CEPHALOCARIDANS
Cephalocarida
Species 12

MILLIPEDES
Diplopoda
Species 13,900

CENTIPEDES
Chilopoda
Species 3,500

MYRIAPODS

Myriapoda Arthropods with a head and trunk. The head has one pair of antennae and simple eyes. Trunk segments have one pair of legs, but may be fused into double segments.

HORSESHOE CRABS
Merostomata
Species 4

CRUSTACEANS

Crustacea Arthropods with three body sections. Their heads have jaws, two pairs of antennae, and one pair of eyes. They have two-branched limbs and, typically, gills to breathe.

SYMPHYLANS
Symphyla
Species 235

PAUROPODS
Pauropoda
Species 1,000

SPIDERS
Araneae
Species 52,300

SCORPIONS
Scorpiones
Species 2,800

WATER FLEAS AND RELATIVES
Branchiopoda
Species 1,700

BARNACLES, COPEPODS, AND RELATIVES
Maxillopoda
Species 14,000

MITES
Acariformes
Species 22,700

ARACHNIDS

Arachnida Mainly terrestrial chelicerates with pairs of simple eyes. Food is typically liquefied outside the body, and they breathe through book lungs or tracheae, or both.

TANTULOCARIDS
Tantulocarida
Species 39

REMIPEDES
Remipedia
Species 29

TICKS AND RELATIVES
Parasitiformes
Species 6,300

7 OTHER ORDERS
Species 5,300

HARVESTMEN
Opiliones
Species 6,800

MALACOSTRACANS

Malacostraca Includes the larger shrimp- and crablike crustaceans. The thorax has an upper shell and eight limb-bearing segments; the abdomen has six limb-bearing segments.

DECAPODS

Decapoda Eucaridans that use the front three pairs of limbs for feeding and the back five pairs for walking. One pair of walking legs may have pincers.

EUCARIDANS

Eucarida Malacostracans with the upper shell fused to all segments of the thorax. The eyes of eucaridans are always stalked.

MANTIS SHRIMPS
Stomatopoda
Species 520

SYNCARIDANS
Syncarida
Species 250

WOODLICE, AMPHIPODS, AND RELATIVES
Peracarida
Species 26,500

KRILL
Euphausiacea
Species 90

Arthropod groups

Arthropods appeared in the seas more than 540 million years ago. There are four main groups of living species: chelicerates, myriapods, crustaceans, and hexapods. The relationship between these groups has been the subject of debate. For example, the once common view that hexapods and myriapods are most closely related to each other has been challenged by studies that suggest that hexapods are more closely related to crustaceans.

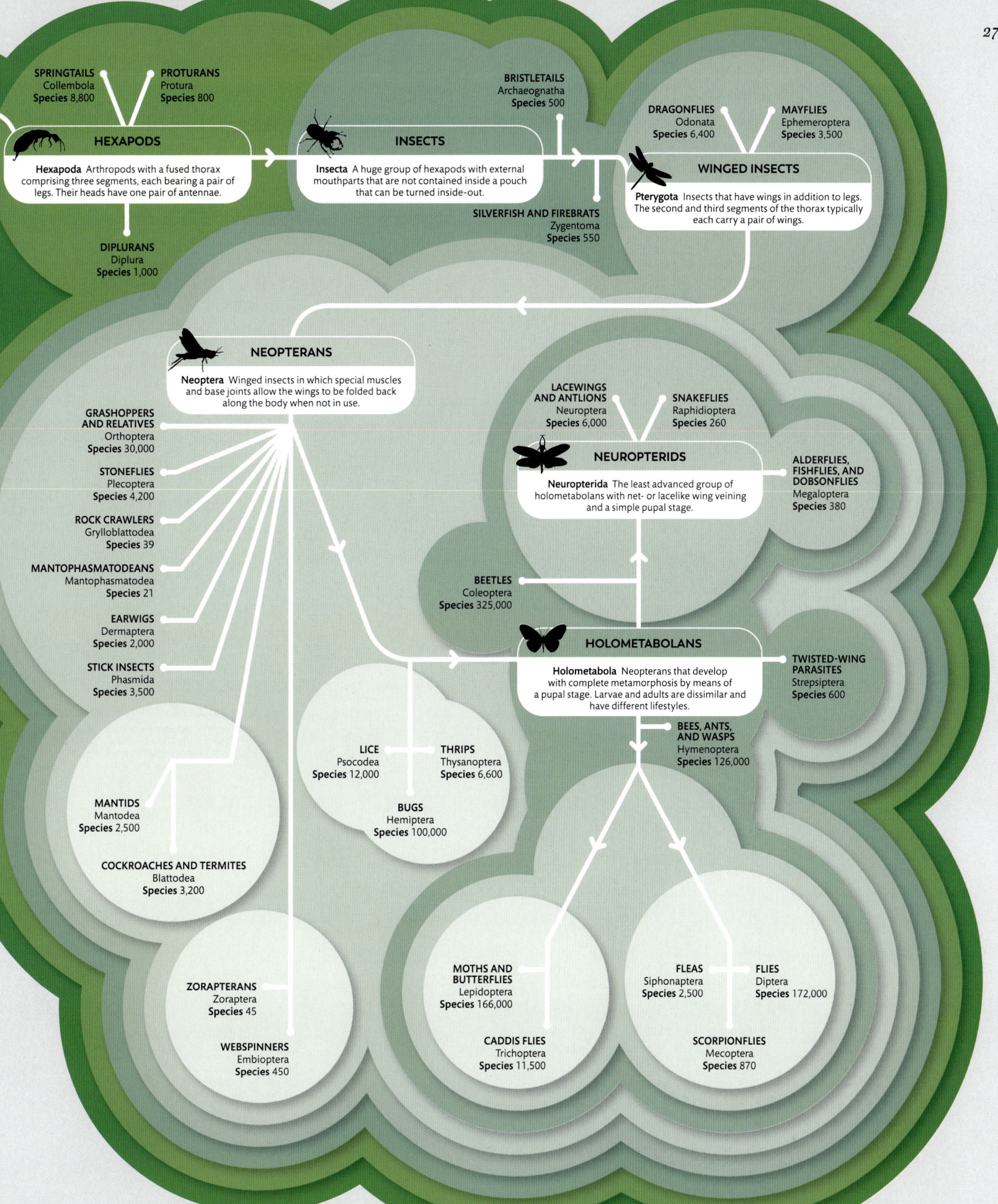

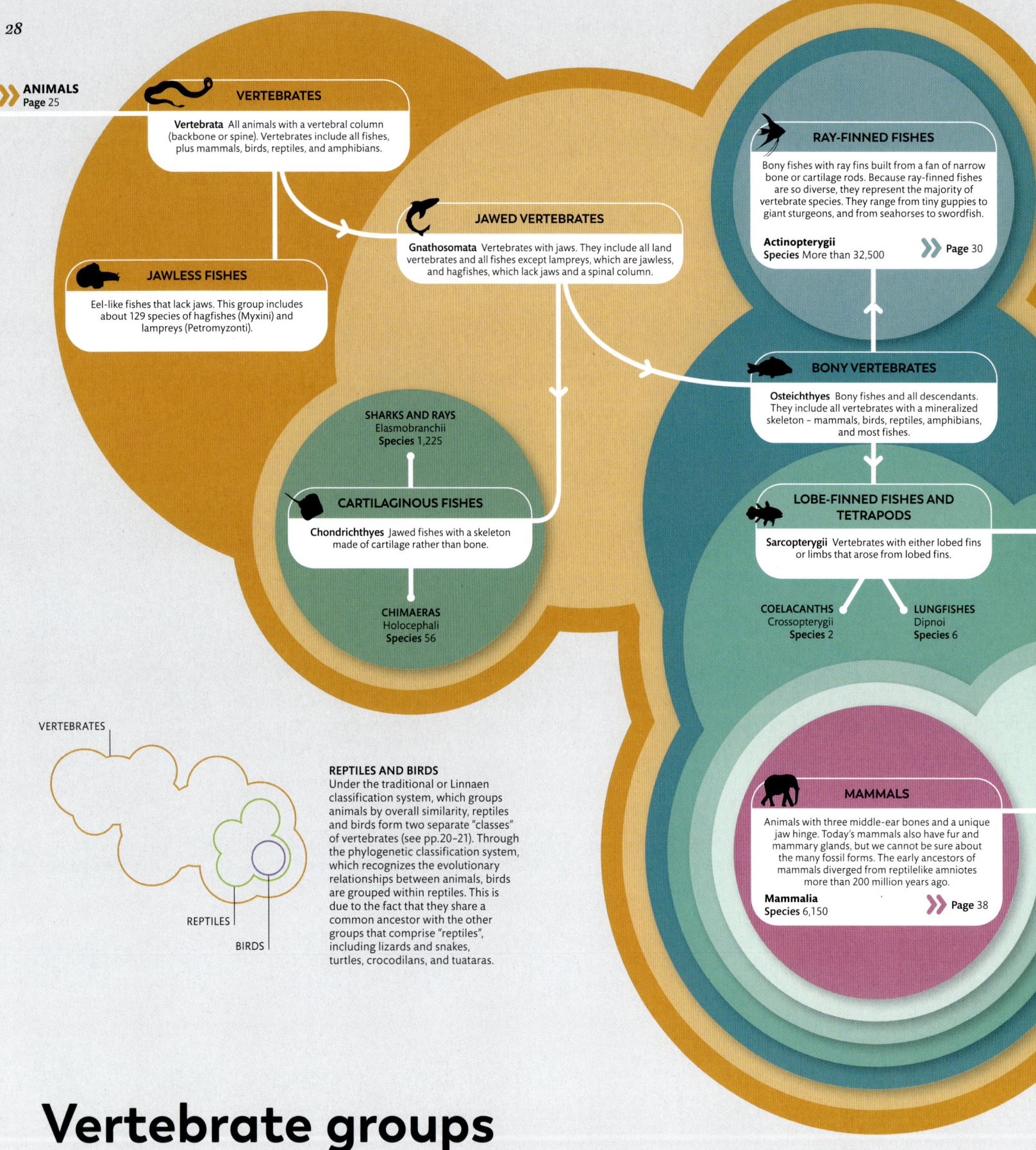

Vertebrate groups

Although vertebrates are a very diverse group of animals, only about 70,000 species have been identified – a tiny fraction of all animal species. The first vertebrates were primitive fishes, and fishes make up more than half of all living vertebrate species. This evolutionary tree has tetrapods at its centre, and it was the earliest tetrapods that first grew limbs and left the water for land. These are the common ancestors from which the vast array of amphibians, reptiles, birds, and mammals evolved, populating the land, taking to the sky, and, in some cases, returning to the sea.

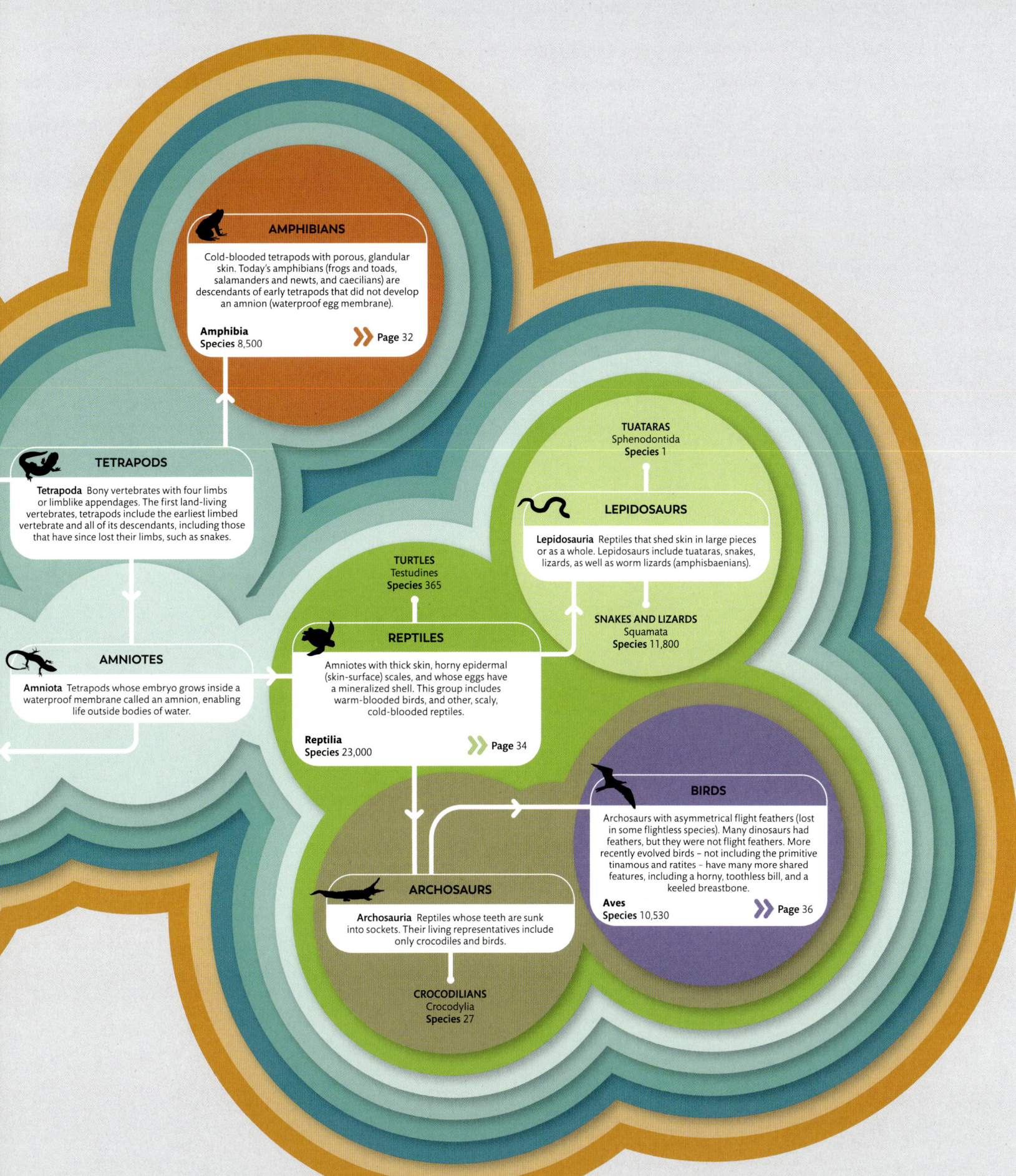

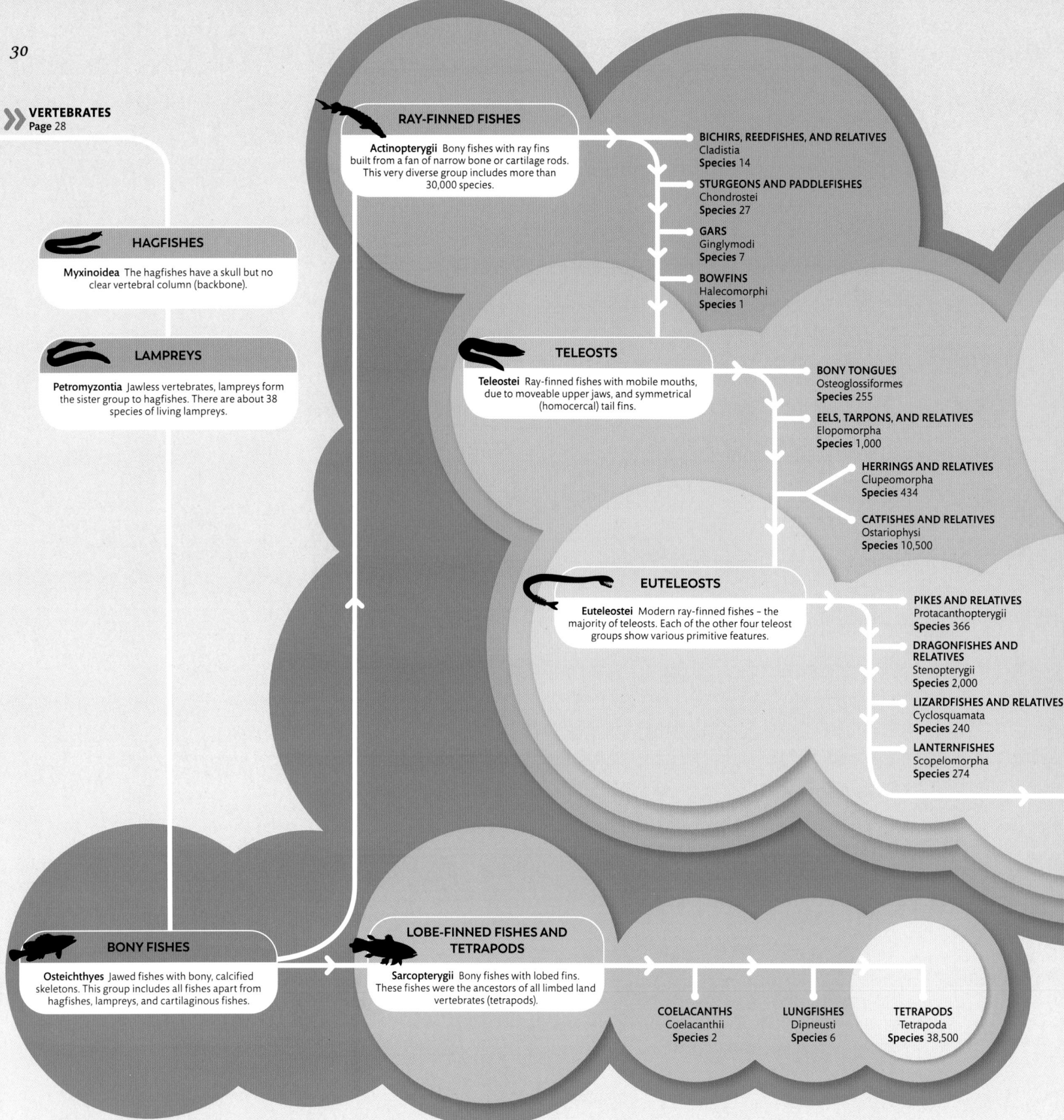

Fish groups

The earliest fishes evolved from primitive jawed vertebrates more than 500 million years ago, and from these, two main groups emerged. Cartilaginous fishes remain largely unchanged as modern-day sharks, rays and skates, and chimaeras. Bony fishes diverged into lobe-finned fishes and ray-finned fishes. The former gave rise to tetrapods, the first limbed vertebrates and the ancestors of amphibians, reptiles, birds, and mammals. Ray-finned fishes evolved into a diverse group that includes more than half of all vertebrate species, and the vast majority of living fishes.

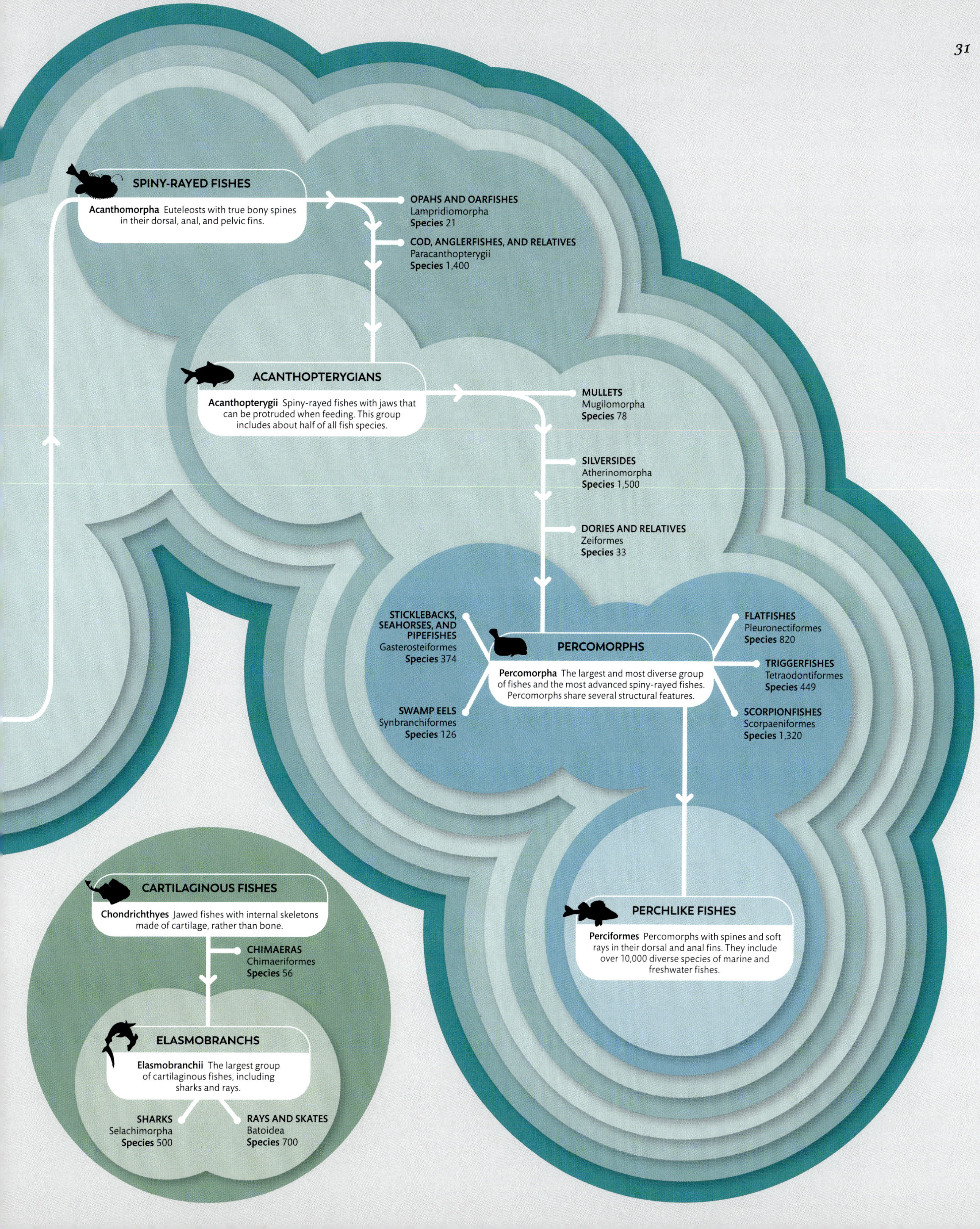

SPINY-RAYED FISHES

Acanthomorpha Euteleosts with true bony spines in their dorsal, anal, and pelvic fins.

OPAHS AND OARFISHES
Lampridiomorpha
Species 21

COD, ANGLERFISHES, AND RELATIVES
Paracanthopterygii
Species 1,400

ACANTHOPTERYGIANS

Acanthopterygii Spiny-rayed fishes with jaws that can be protruded when feeding. This group includes about half of all fish species.

MULLETS
Mugilomorpha
Species 78

SILVERSIDES
Atherinomorpha
Species 1,500

DORIES AND RELATIVES
Zeiformes
Species 33

STICKLEBACKS, SEAHORSES, AND PIPEFISHES
Gasterosteiformes
Species 374

PERCOMORPHS

Percomorpha The largest and most diverse group of fishes and the most advanced spiny-rayed fishes. Percomorphs share several structural features.

FLATFISHES
Pleuronectiformes
Species 820

TRIGGERFISHES
Tetraodontiformes
Species 449

SCORPIONFISHES
Scorpaeniformes
Species 1,320

SWAMP EELS
Synbranchiformes
Species 126

PERCHLIKE FISHES

Perciformes Percomorphs with spines and soft rays in their dorsal and anal fins. They include over 10,000 diverse species of marine and freshwater fishes.

CARTILAGINOUS FISHES

Chondrichthyes Jawed fishes with internal skeletons made of cartilage, rather than bone.

CHIMAERAS
Chimaeriformes
Species 56

ELASMOBRANCHS

Elasmobranchii The largest group of cartilaginous fishes, including sharks and rays.

SHARKS
Selachimorpha
Species 500

RAYS AND SKATES
Batoidea
Species 700

AMPHIBIANS

Amphibia Cold-blooded tetrapods. Most produce eggs that hatch into larvae then metamorphose into adults. Their porous and glandular skin is kept moist.

SALAMANDERS AND FROGS

Batrachia All amphibians other than the limbless caecilians. The group includes all types of newts and salamanders and frogs and toads.

TAILED AND NEW ZEALAND FROGS
Leiopelmatidae
Species 5

FROGS AND TOADS

Anura Tailless amphibians usually with large hind limbs adapted for jumping and swimming. Most lay eggs that hatch into tadpoles, which metamorphose into adults.

CALLING FROGS

Lalagobatrachia All frogs other than tailed and New Zealand frogs. They communicate by calling and most have vocal sacs.

MEXICAN BURROWING TOAD
Rhinophrynidae
Species 1

TONGUELESS FROGS
Pipidae
Species 41

SPADEFOOT TOADS AND RELATIVES
Pelobatidae
Species 5

MIDWIFE TOADS
Alytidae
Species 12

FIRE-BELLIED TOADS
Bombinatoridae
Species 8

CAECILIANS

Gymnophiona Limbless, wormlike amphibians that burrow in soil or live in rivers. Some species lay eggs, producing larvae; others give birth to live young.

POISON-DART FROGS
Dendrobatidae
Species 198

TRUE TOADS
Bufonidae
Species 609

GLASS FROGS
Centrolenidae
Species 157

HYLOIDES

TREE FROGS
Hylidae
Species 722

SOUTHERN FROGS
Cycloramphidae
Species 36

14 OTHER FAMILIES

FROG OR TOAD?
There is no clear distinction between frogs and toads. Together they make up a group called the anurans. "True toads" are members of a smaller group, called the Bufonidae, but the name "toad" is often used for any anuran that has dry, warty skin and spends most of its life on land. Frogs have smooth, moist skin and spend a lot of their time in water. Most anurans undergo a radical metamorphosis from aquatic tadpoles to terrestrial adults.

Amphibian groups

Amphibians have existed for at least 230 million years, when they evolved from fishes. It is not clear whether the three main groups – caecilians, salamanders and newts, and frogs and toads – are descended from a common ancestor or whether they evolved from different groups.

Amphibians are often erroneously seen as an intermediate group between fishes and reptiles. In fact, they evolved adaptations for living in moist habitats around fresh water. This diagram represents a hypothesis of amphibian relationships, and not all families are shown here.

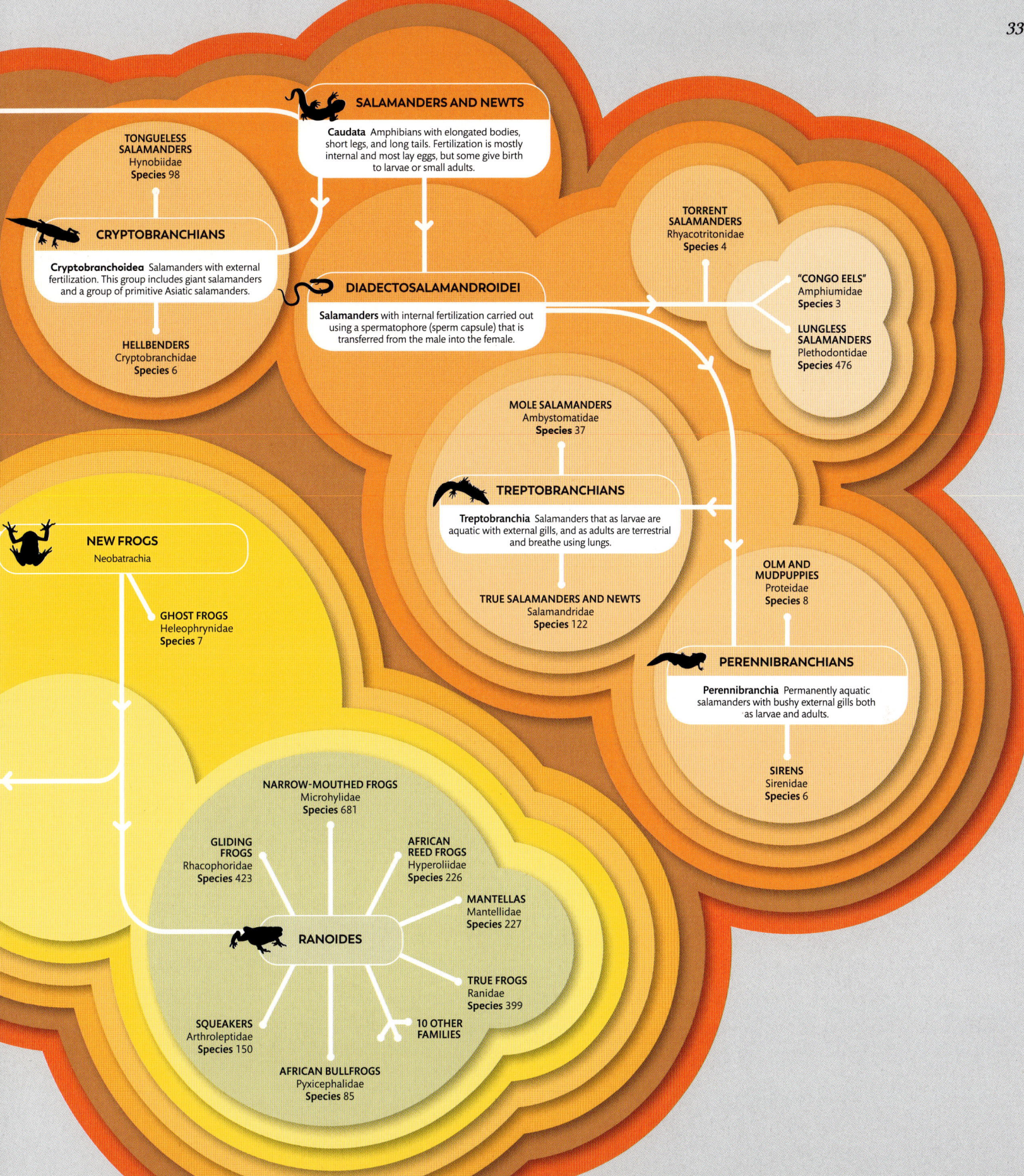

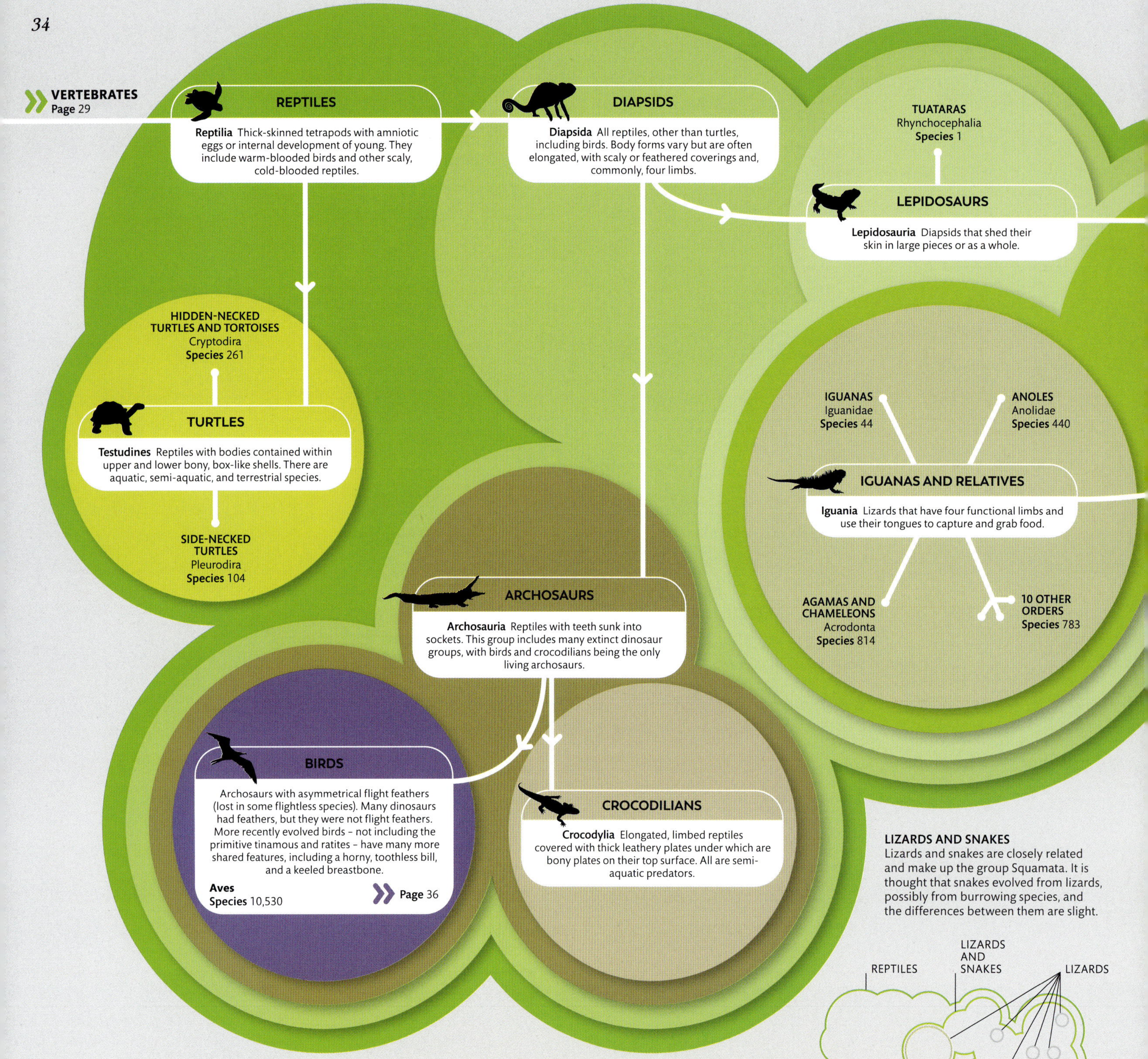

VERTEBRATES
Page 29

REPTILES
Reptilia Thick-skinned tetrapods with amniotic eggs or internal development of young. They include warm-blooded birds and other scaly, cold-blooded reptiles.

DIAPSIDS
Diapsida All reptiles, other than turtles, including birds. Body forms vary but are often elongated, with scaly or feathered coverings and, commonly, four limbs.

TUATARAS
Rhynchocephalia
Species 1

LEPIDOSAURS
Lepidosauria Diapsids that shed their skin in large pieces or as a whole.

HIDDEN-NECKED TURTLES AND TORTOISES
Cryptodira
Species 261

TURTLES
Testudines Reptiles with bodies contained within upper and lower bony, box-like shells. There are aquatic, semi-aquatic, and terrestrial species.

SIDE-NECKED TURTLES
Pleurodira
Species 104

IGUANAS
Iguanidae
Species 44

ANOLES
Anolidae
Species 440

IGUANAS AND RELATIVES
Iguania Lizards that have four functional limbs and use their tongues to capture and grab food.

AGAMAS AND CHAMELEONS
Acrodonta
Species 814

10 OTHER ORDERS
Species 783

ARCHOSAURS
Archosauria Reptiles with teeth sunk into sockets. This group includes many extinct dinosaur groups, with birds and crocodilians being the only living archosaurs.

BIRDS
Archosaurs with asymmetrical flight feathers (lost in some flightless species). Many dinosaurs had feathers, but they were not flight feathers. More recently evolved birds – not including the primitive tinamous and ratites – have many more shared features, including a horny, toothless bill, and a keeled breastbone.
Aves
Species 10,530
» Page 36

CROCODILIANS
Crocodylia Elongated, limbed reptiles covered with thick leathery plates under which are bony plates on their top surface. All are semi-aquatic predators.

LIZARDS AND SNAKES
Lizards and snakes are closely related and make up the group Squamata. It is thought that snakes evolved from lizards, possibly from burrowing species, and the differences between them are slight.

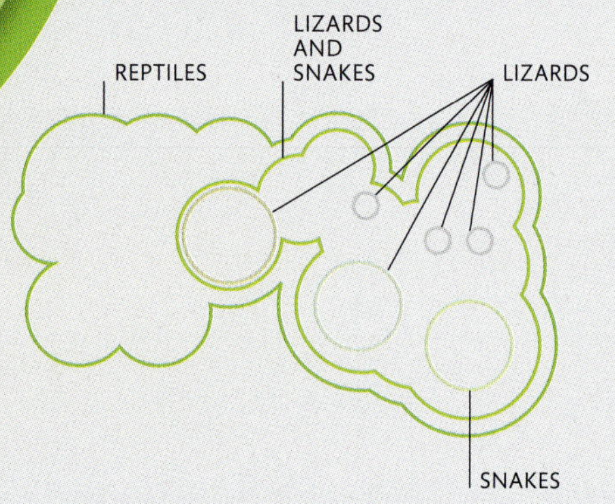

REPTILES
LIZARDS AND SNAKES
LIZARDS
SNAKES

Reptile groups

The oldest groups of reptiles are the turtles and archosaurs, which first appeared about 220 million years ago. Archosaurs include crocodilians and birds, which are feathered reptiles, but also the extinct dinosaurs. Lepidosaurs include the tuataras, relics of a once widespread group of lizardlike reptiles, and the squamates, a huge group that includes all lizards and snakes. This diagram represents one hypothesis of reptile relationships. Controversy surrounds the relations between squamates and the placement of turtles. Not all families are shown here.

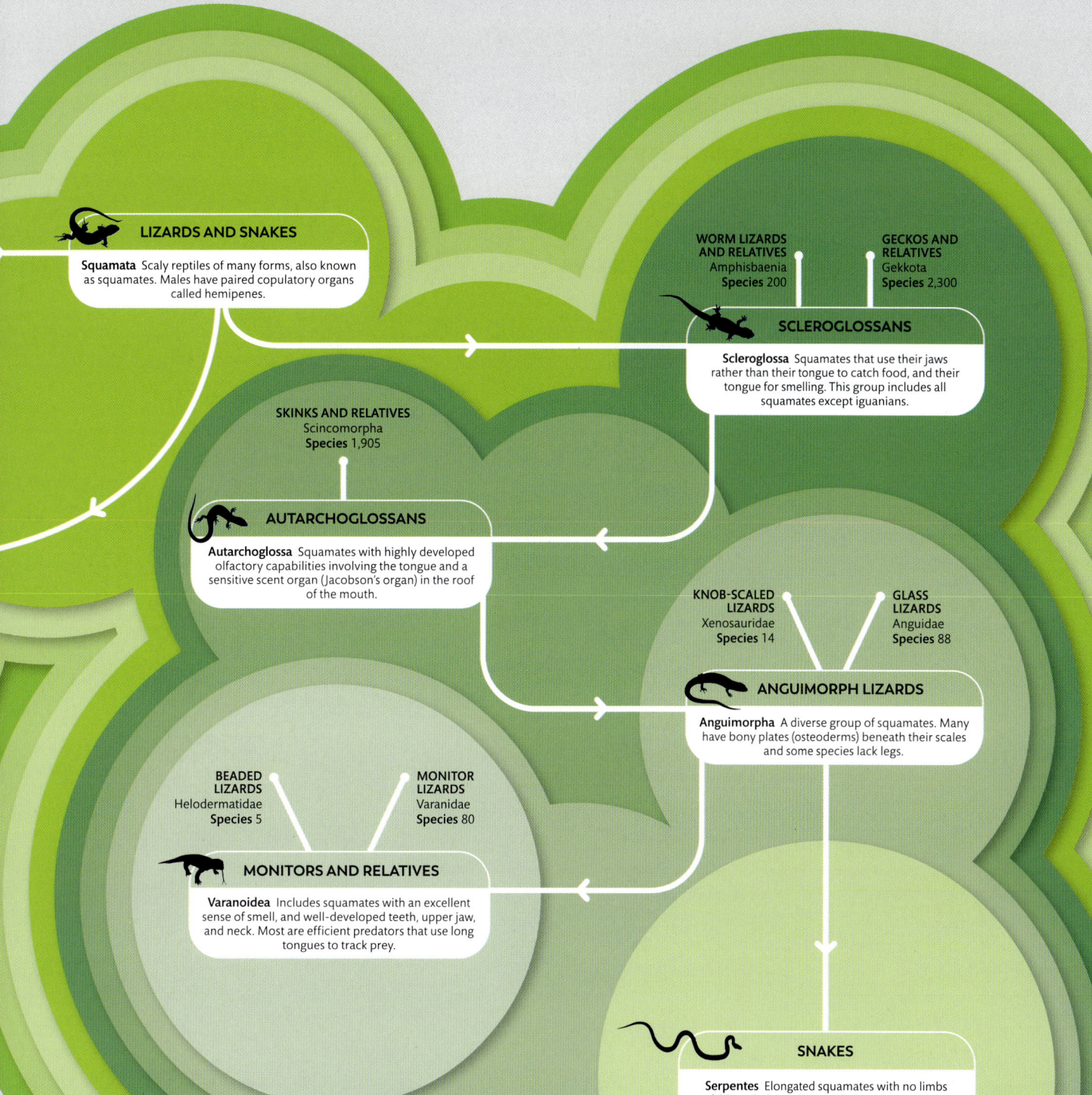

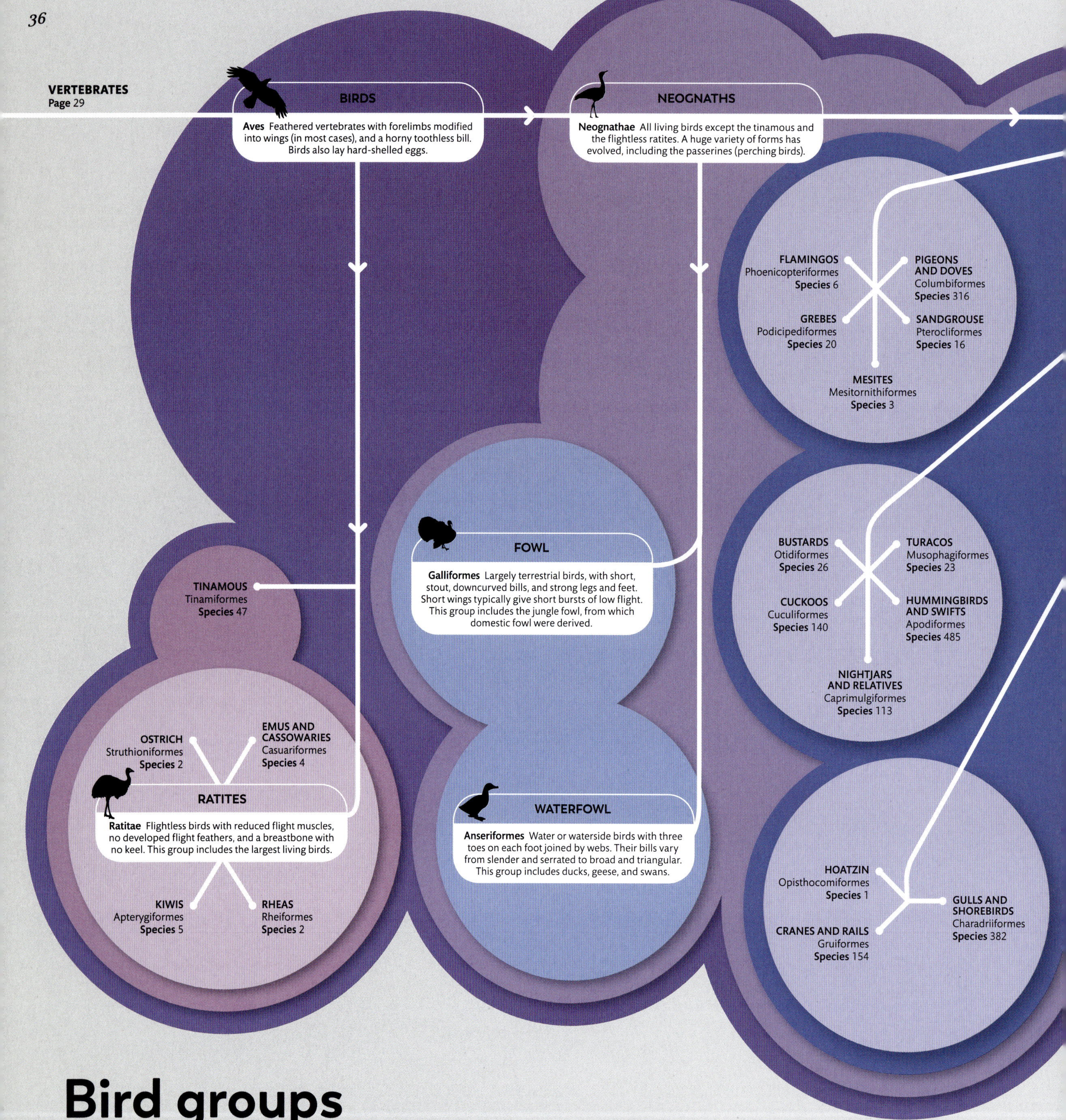

VERTEBRATES
Page 29

BIRDS
Aves Feathered vertebrates with forelimbs modified into wings (in most cases), and a horny toothless bill. Birds also lay hard-shelled eggs.

NEOGNATHS
Neognathae All living birds except the tinamous and the flightless ratites. A huge variety of forms has evolved, including the passerines (perching birds).

FLAMINGOS
Phoenicopteriformes
Species 6

PIGEONS AND DOVES
Columbiformes
Species 316

GREBES
Podicipediformes
Species 20

SANDGROUSE
Pteroclciformes
Species 16

MESITES
Mesitornithiformes
Species 3

TINAMOUS
Tinamiformes
Species 47

FOWL
Galliformes Largely terrestrial birds, with short, stout, downcurved bills, and strong legs and feet. Short wings typically give short bursts of low flight. This group includes the jungle fowl, from which domestic fowl were derived.

BUSTARDS
Otidiformes
Species 26

TURACOS
Musophagiformes
Species 23

CUCKOOS
Cuculiformes
Species 140

HUMMINGBIRDS AND SWIFTS
Apodiformes
Species 485

NIGHTJARS AND RELATIVES
Caprimulgiformes
Species 113

OSTRICH
Struthioniformes
Species 2

EMUS AND CASSOWARIES
Casuariformes
Species 4

RATITES
Ratitae Flightless birds with reduced flight muscles, no developed flight feathers, and a breastbone with no keel. This group includes the largest living birds.

WATERFOWL
Anseriformes Water or waterside birds with three toes on each foot joined by webs. Their bills vary from slender and serrated to broad and triangular. This group includes ducks, geese, and swans.

HOATZIN
Opisthocomiformes
Species 1

CRANES AND RAILS
Gruiformes
Species 154

GULLS AND SHOREBIRDS
Charadriiformes
Species 382

KIWIS
Apterygiformes
Species 5

RHEAS
Rheiformes
Species 2

Bird groups

Birds number over 10,000 species, ranging from the primitive tinamous and ratites to perching birds, the most recently evolved group. Outward appearances make some groupings such as penguins and hummingbirds obvious, but birds within other groups, such as the cranes and rails, may appear to have little in common. DNA studies have helped to resolve some of the relationships, producing dramatically revised groupings. However, the exact nature of some relationships are yet to be resolved and not all orders are represented here.

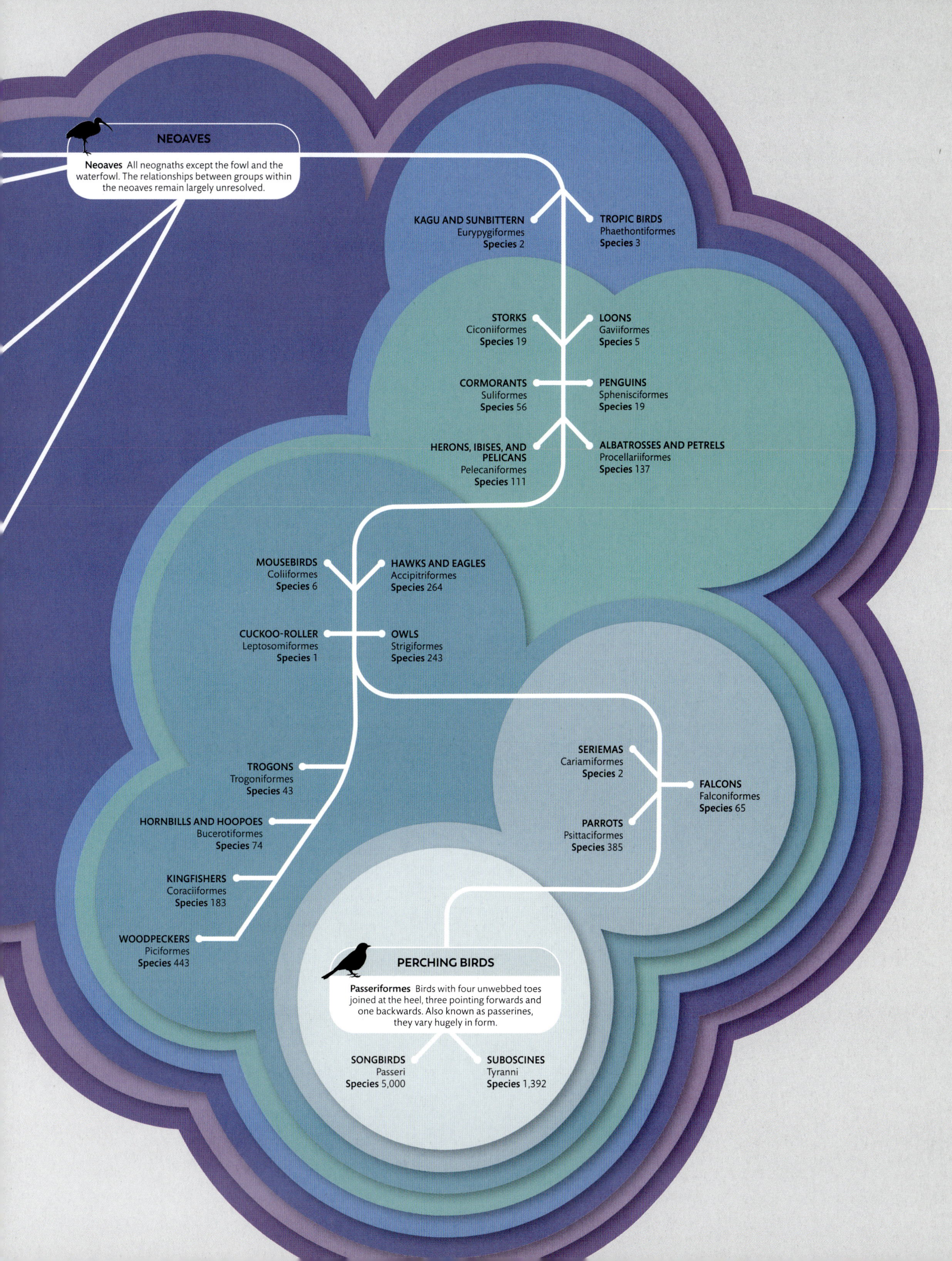

NEOAVES

Neoaves All neognaths except the fowl and the waterfowl. The relationships between groups within the neoaves remain largely unresolved.

KAGU AND SUNBITTERN
Eurypygiformes
Species 2

TROPIC BIRDS
Phaethontiformes
Species 3

STORKS
Ciconiiformes
Species 19

LOONS
Gaviiformes
Species 5

CORMORANTS
Suliformes
Species 56

PENGUINS
Sphenisciformes
Species 19

HERONS, IBISES, AND PELICANS
Pelecaniformes
Species 111

ALBATROSSES AND PETRELS
Procellariiformes
Species 137

MOUSEBIRDS
Coliiformes
Species 6

HAWKS AND EAGLES
Accipitriformes
Species 264

CUCKOO-ROLLER
Leptosomiformes
Species 1

OWLS
Strigiformes
Species 243

TROGONS
Trogoniformes
Species 43

SERIEMAS
Cariamiformes
Species 2

FALCONS
Falconiformes
Species 65

HORNBILLS AND HOOPOES
Bucerotiformes
Species 74

PARROTS
Psittaciformes
Species 385

KINGFISHERS
Coraciiformes
Species 183

WOODPECKERS
Piciformes
Species 443

PERCHING BIRDS

Passeriformes Birds with four unwebbed toes joined at the heel, three pointing forwards and one backwards. Also known as passerines, they vary hugely in form.

SONGBIRDS
Passeri
Species 5,000

SUBOSCINES
Tyranni
Species 1,392

VERTEBRATES Page 28

MAMMALS
Mammalia Characteristics of this group include a lower jaw comprising a single bone, and skin that contains glands (including mammary glands) and is usually covered with hair.

LIVE-BEARING MAMMALS
Theria Mammals that produce live young, at various stages of development. This group includes both the placental and marsupial (pouched) mammals.

PLACENTAL MAMMALS
Placentalia Live-bearing mammals with young that develop in the uterus attached to a placenta, which allows nutrients and waste to pass between a mother and her offspring.

ANTEATERS, ARMADILLOS, AND SLOTHS
Xenarthra
Species 39

EGG-LAYING MAMMALS
Prototheria The only mammals that reproduce by laying soft-shelled eggs. Their body temperature is maintained at a lower level than that of most other mammals.

PLATYPUS AND ECHIDNAS
Monotremata
Species 5

OPOSSUMS
Didelphimorphia
Species 125

BANDICOOTS
Peramelemorphia
Species 22

MARSUPIALS
Marsupialia Live-bearing mammals that have a pouch (marsupium) in which the young are nurtured on milk to complete their development.

KANGAROOS AND RELATIVES
Diprotodontia
Species 155

4 OTHER ORDERS
Species 80

LAURASIATHERIANS
Laurasiatheria The most diverse group of placental mammals, ranging from whales to bats, cats to rhinoceroses.

BATS
Chiroptera
Species 1,400

HEDGEHOGS AND SHREWS
Eulipotyphla
Species 566

SKUNKS
Mephitidae
Species 12

RACCOONS
Procyonidae
Species 18

WEASELS
Mustelidae
Species 70

RED PANDA
Ailuridae
Species 1

WALRUS
Odobenidae
Species 1

CIVETS
Viverridae
Species 33

PANGOLINS
Pholidota
Species 8

CARNIVORES
Carnivora Mainly meat-eating mammals with well-developed canine teeth and powerful cheek teeth with a scissorlike action, called carnassials.

EARED SEALS
Otariidae
Species 16

TRUE SEALS
Phocidae
Species 18

MALAGASY CARNIVORES
Eupleridae
Species 10

CATTLE AND ANTELOPES
Bovidae
Species 143

CAMELS AND LLAMAS
Camelidae
Species 4

BEARS
Ursidae
Species 8

DOGS
Canidae
Species 36

CATS
Felidae
Species 40

MONGOOSES
Herpestidae
Species 33

HYENAS
Hyaenidae
Species 4

DEER
Cervidae
Species 55

EVEN-TOED HOOVED MAMMALS AND WHALES
Cetartiodactyla Laurasiatherians with a uniquely-shaped hock bone, known as the astragulus or talus, including the terrestrial ancestors of modern whales.

PIGS
Suidae
Species 18

WHALES AND DOLPHINS
Cetacea
Species 83

GIRAFFES
Giraffidae
Species 9

HIPPOPOTAMUSES
Hippopotamidae
Species 2

Mammal groups

The primitive egg-laying mammals were the first group to diverge, followed by the marsupials. The placental mammals divided into three broad groups, the laurasiatherians, afrotherians, and euarchontoglires, plus the anteaters and relatives, before evolving into the diverse array of forms and sizes we see today. Although many of the traditional mammal groups, such as primates and carnivores, appear on this diagram, others are less familiar. These include the even-toed hooved mammals and whales, which have been combined quite recently using genetic and fossil evidence.

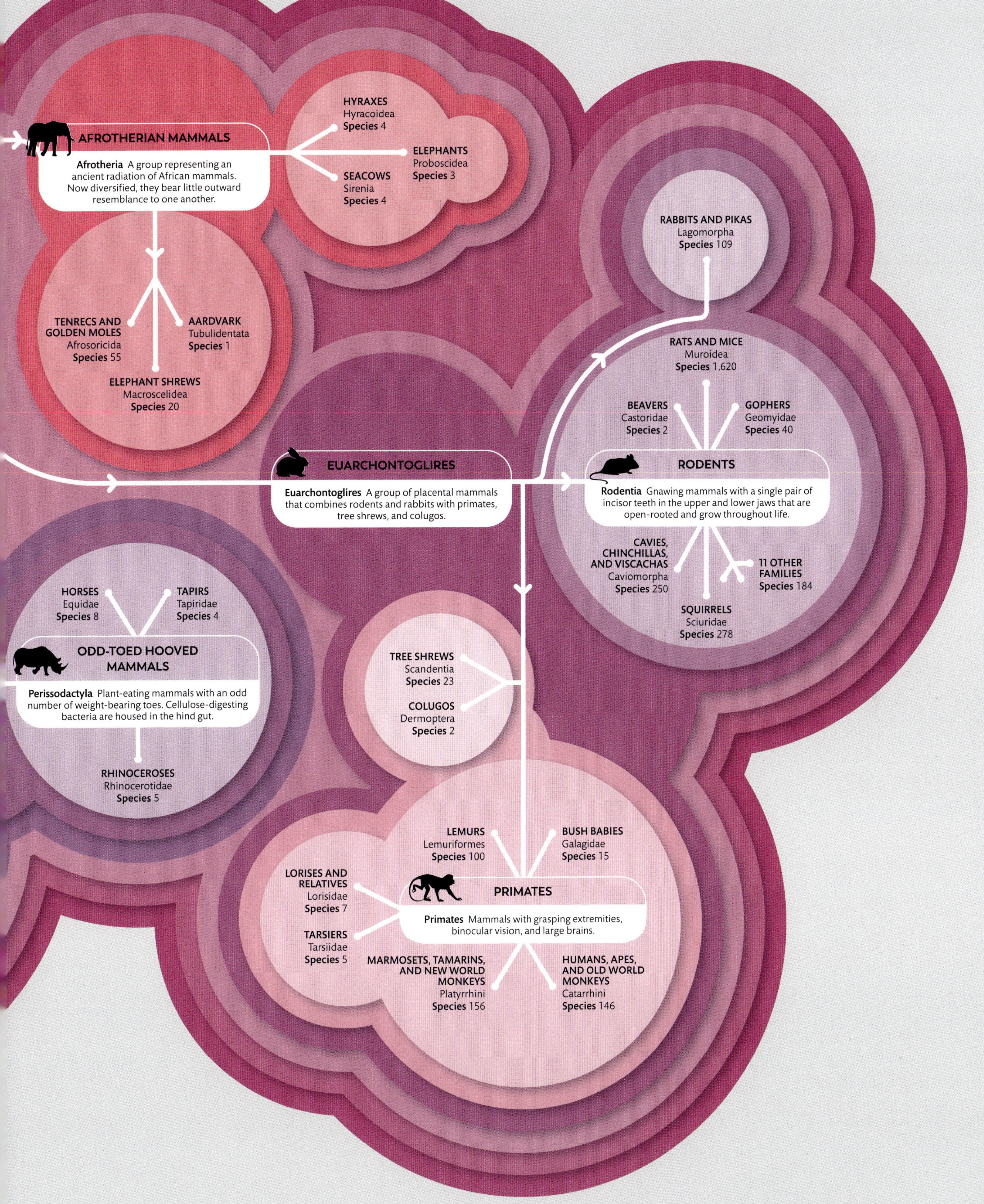

AFROTHERIAN MAMMALS

Afrotheria A group representing an ancient radiation of African mammals. Now diversified, they bear little outward resemblance to one another.

HYRAXES
Hyracoidea
Species 4

ELEPHANTS
Proboscidea
Species 3

SEACOWS
Sirenia
Species 4

TENRECS AND GOLDEN MOLES
Afrosoricida
Species 55

AARDVARK
Tubulidentata
Species 1

ELEPHANT SHREWS
Macroscelidea
Species 20

EUARCHONTOGLIRES

Euarchontoglires A group of placental mammals that combines rodents and rabbits with primates, tree shrews, and colugos.

RABBITS AND PIKAS
Lagomorpha
Species 109

RODENTS

Rodentia Gnawing mammals with a single pair of incisor teeth in the upper and lower jaws that are open-rooted and grow throughout life.

RATS AND MICE
Muroidea
Species 1,620

BEAVERS
Castoridae
Species 2

GOPHERS
Geomyidae
Species 40

CAVIES, CHINCHILLAS, AND VISCACHAS
Caviomorpha
Species 250

SQUIRRELS
Sciuridae
Species 278

11 OTHER FAMILIES
Species 184

ODD-TOED HOOVED MAMMALS

Perissodactyla Plant-eating mammals with an odd number of weight-bearing toes. Cellulose-digesting bacteria are housed in the hind gut.

HORSES
Equidae
Species 8

TAPIRS
Tapiridae
Species 4

RHINOCEROSES
Rhinocerotidae
Species 5

TREE SHREWS
Scandentia
Species 23

COLUGOS
Dermoptera
Species 2

PRIMATES

Primates Mammals with grasping extremities, binocular vision, and large brains.

LEMURS
Lemuriformes
Species 100

BUSH BABIES
Galagidae
Species 15

LORISES AND RELATIVES
Lorisidae
Species 7

TARSIERS
Tarsiidae
Species 5

MARMOSETS, TAMARINS, AND NEW WORLD MONKEYS
Platyrrhini
Species 156

HUMANS, APES, AND OLD WORLD MONKEYS
Catarrhini
Species 146

Sharing space Most African savanna animals need to visit waterholes regularly in the dry season, and sharing this space can lead to tension, especially as animals are distracted and vulnerable when drinking. Each of the larger herbivore species tends to have its preferred visiting time, and the peak time of a grazing species is more likely to overlap with that of a browsing species than it is with other grazers. Herbivores mainly come to drink by day, which helps them to avoid large predators, which mainly drink (and hunt) after dark.

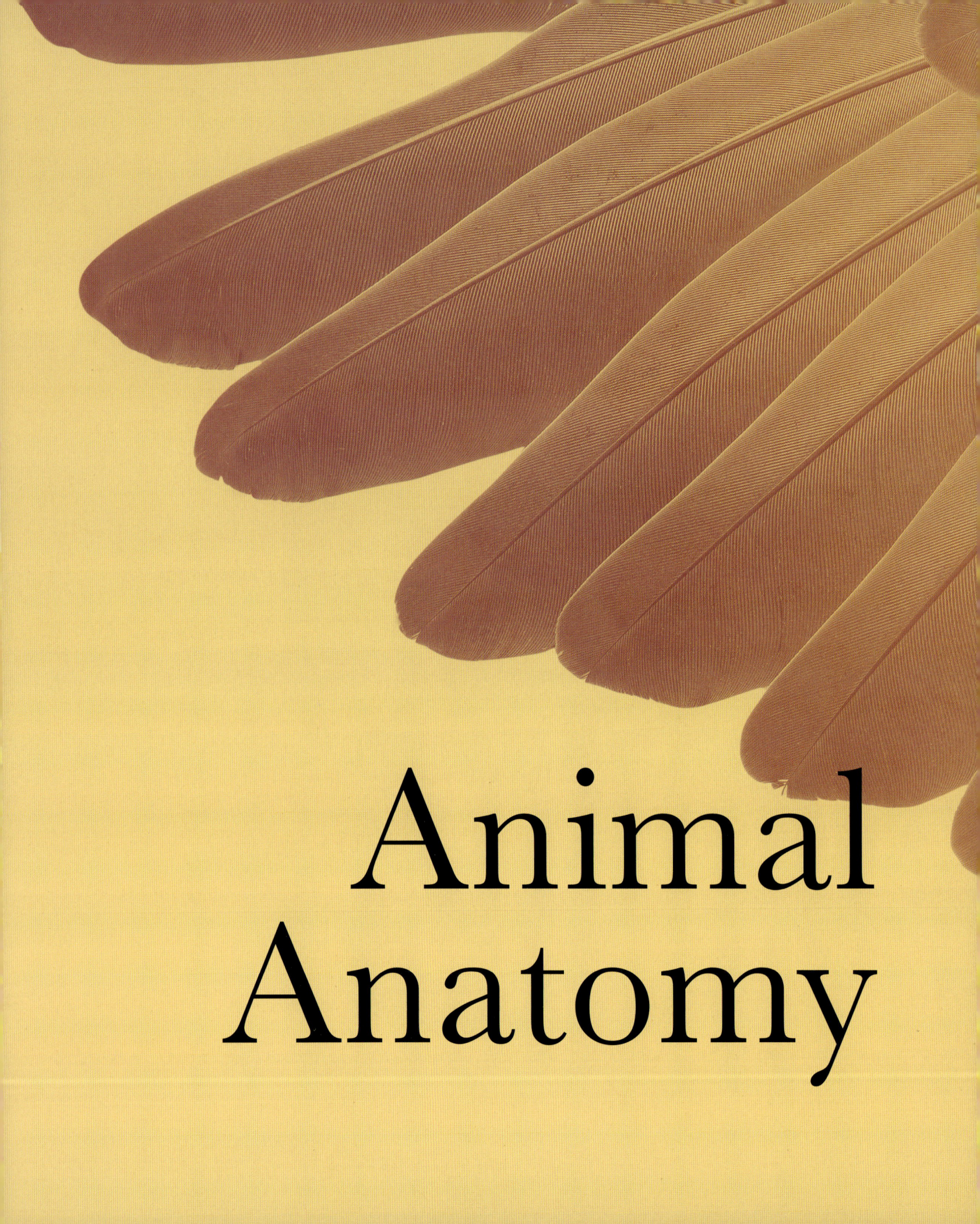
Animal Anatomy

Armoured support Up to 25 per cent of a crab's total weight may be its "shell". This is not simply an outer protective casing, it is also its skeleton – a complex set of supporting structures linked at flexible joints, enclosing and moved by intricate sets of muscles.

SKELETONS AND MUSCLES

Most members of the animal kingdom possess some kind of strong body framework, and pulling devices with which to move it. Although the principles and detailed structure of muscles are virtually constant across all major groups of animals, types of skeletons show huge variety in design and construction.

MOVEMENT AND STRUCTURE

Muscle tissue is the primary means of movement in almost all animals, except for sponges, allowing an animal to implement its behaviours and actions. Muscle is often the most plentiful tissue in the body, and it has one basic function: to shorten, or contract. As it does so, it moves parts of the skeleton or other body structures. Muscles power not only the movements visible on the outside, they are also the basis of internal activities, such as the pumping of the heart. For invertebrates with a hard outer framework, or exoskeleton, most muscles are positioned on the inside and attached to the skeleton's inner walls. In vertebrates, the situation is reversed, with the muscles attaching to the outside of the endoskeleton. In soft-bodied animals like worms, muscle tissue forms its own fluid-pressurized "water skeleton".

MUSCLE ARRANGEMENT

A typical mammal has more than 600 individual muscles, while some insects have three times that number. The inner structure of a typical muscle is based on cellular components known as muscle fibres or myofibres. In larger animals, some myofibres exceed 1 m (3¼ ft) in length, yet each is thinner than a human hair. Contraction occurs when bundles of overlapping protein filaments in the fibres slide past each other. Because muscles only contract and pull, they are arranged in opposing teams.

In the simplest arrangement, one muscle pulls a skeletal element or body part one way, while its opposing partner on the other side relaxes. To move the part the other way, the opposing muscle contracts while the first muscle relaxes. However, this two-way action is given greater range as there are usually several muscles involved, attached to the skeleton at varying places and angles, to give differing lines of pull. This allows for movement with close control in several directions. In arthropods, the muscle structure can be quite similar to that of vertebrates, but the arrangement differs in that the muscles connect to the inner walls of the exoskeleton.

JOINTS

Most animals have a skeleton or similar framework made up of numerous parts, which move in relation to each other at joints. In arthropods, the joints are relatively simple thinnings of the exoskeleton. The cuticle forms a flexible articular membrane, but the harder, rigid layers of chitin or mineralization are almost absent. In most vertebrates, the bones of the skeleton are covered in their joints by cartilage, which reduces friction and wear. The joint is enclosed in a joint capsule, inside which there is a lubricating liquid, synovial fluid, to further reduce rubbing. Strong, stretchy ligaments are attached to the bones and allow the joint to flex.

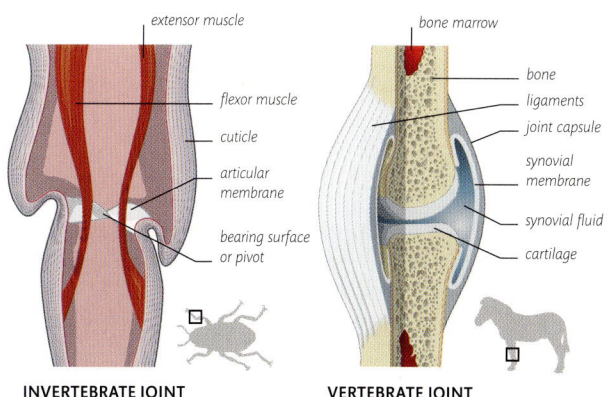

Opposite contraction
Two muscles in a vertebrate forelimb demonstrate a simple antagonistic system, where each muscle opposes the pull of the other. If both muscles exert tension, the joint can be held steady in any position through its range.

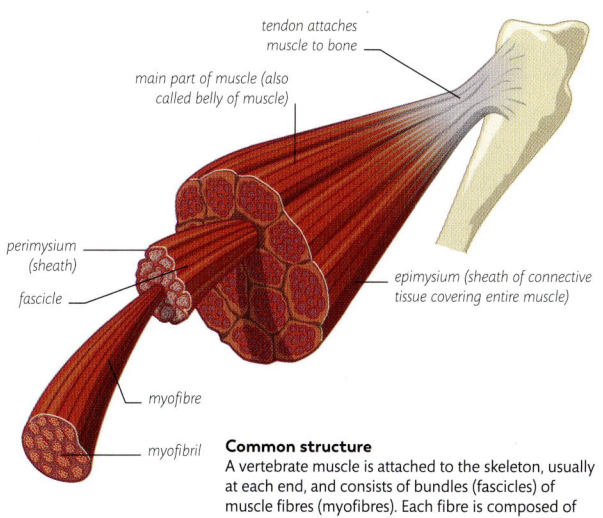

Common structure
A vertebrate muscle is attached to the skeleton, usually at each end, and consists of bundles (fascicles) of muscle fibres (myofibres). Each fibre is composed of perhaps thousands of thinner muscle fibrils (myofibrils).

Points of movement
The exoskeleton is flexible at an invertebrate joint, and the shape of the bearing surfaces usually allows movement in only one plane or direction. In a vertebrate joint, a thin layer of synovial fluid helps to prevent friction between the connecting bones.

Water skeletons

Fluid-based skeletons are found in a huge variety of invertebrates, especially worms and similar "soft-bodied" animals. Far from being soft and floppy, many of these can become rigid and resistant when muscular action compresses fluid inside an animal's body.

SUPPORT

An animal's hydrostatic skeleton, or hydroskeleton, employs similar principles to hydraulic systems in machinery. In animals, a liquid in some sort of chamber or container is pressurized by contraction of the muscular walls around it. The liquid is the internal body fluid of the animal. Its compression makes the structure become hard and rigid, forming a firm skeletal unit. The skeleton then gives support and protection to the animal's body parts. In simpler animals, the whole body covering acts as the hydroskeleton. In more complex ones, especially segmented (annelid) worms, the pressure can be limited to selected body compartments.

Limited movement Most nematode worms, such as this parasitic roundworm, have only longitudinal muscles in the body wall. As these contract on each side alternately, they produce characteristic C- or S-like thrashing movements.

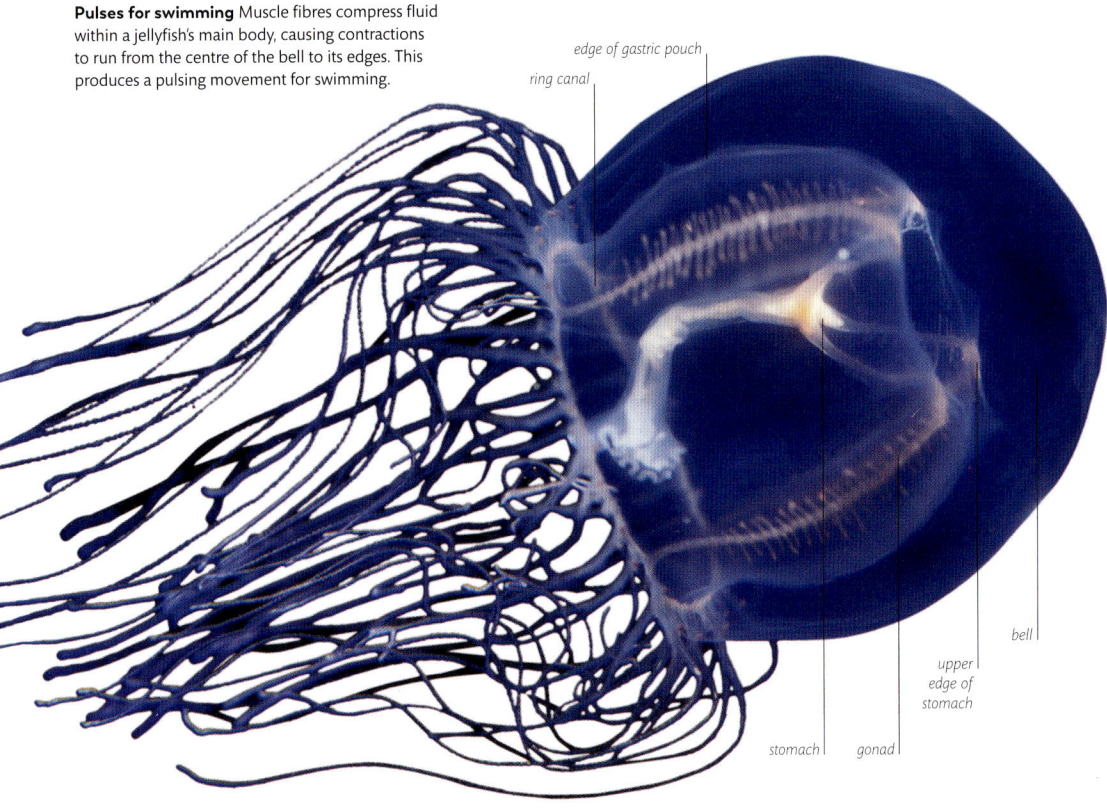

Pulses for swimming Muscle fibres compress fluid within a jellyfish's main body, causing contractions to run from the centre of the bell to its edges. This produces a pulsing movement for swimming.

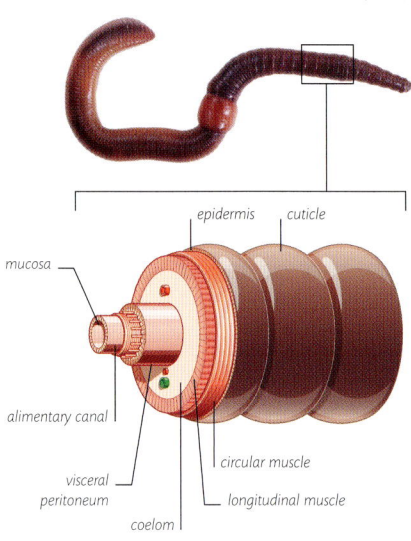

Segmented worm anatomy Each worm segment has a set of circular muscles around it. Some longitudinal muscles span a segment, while others run along many segments. This allows the worm to stretch some parts, while shortening others.

MOVEMENT

In a hydroskeleton, changes in muscle tone and the arrangement of muscles can alter the pressure within its chambers, thereby changing the skeleton's shape, and causing the structure to become rigid. This provides a stiff base against which movements can be made, and also produces the movements themselves. In many worms, for example, there are two layers of muscle in the outer body wall: ringlike circulars; and strap-shaped, longitudinal (lengthway) muscles. Contraction of circular muscles squeezes the body, making it longer and thinner; longitudinal muscle contraction makes it shorter and fatter; and when both sets contract, the body becomes tense, stiff, and rigid. Other combinations of contractions permit further movements. If the longitudinal muscles along one side shorten, the body curves to that side. Using such a system of contractions, burrowing earthworms are able to push their way between tightly packed soil particles with great force.

Bendy appendages Apart from whole body movements, hydrostatic and hydraulic principles can also be used to move smaller body parts or individual appendages. Such movements allow animals to perform tasks such as self defence and capturing prey.

Octopus suckers are able to grasp objects firmly.

Sea cucumber tentacles rely on internal pressure.

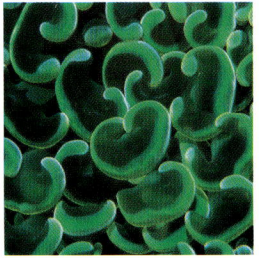

Coral polyps use muscle fibres in the stalks to "lean" in any direction.

Anemone tentacles bend to the side on which the muscle contracts.

Horny skeletons

"Horny" describes substances that are strong, tough, and resilient, yet which can also be slightly compressed and flexed. In arthropods, the main horny substance is chitin. This forms the basis of the outer body covering, or cuticle, which is the main component of the animal's exoskeleton.

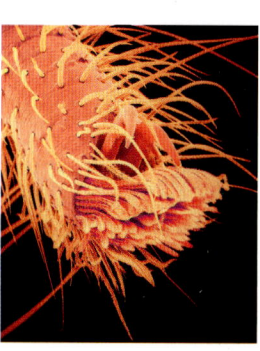

Sticky feet A jumping spider has two foot claws and a pad of tufted hairs that are formed by tiny, supple extensions of the cuticle. These can stick to a wide variety of surfaces.

TOUGH EXOSKELETON

Chitin is light, strong, translucent, and pliable, and has been compared to plastic. The substance is chemically a polysaccharide (carbohydrate), consisting of glucoselike sugar units. In most land arthropods, chitin is accompanied by various proteins, the molecules of which may take many shapes, including fibrous, sheetlike, and helical. Many hundreds of these proteins are known in the insect group alone. In some aquatic arthropods, such as crabs and other crustaceans, the chitin and protein are accompanied by minerals, especially chalky crystals of calcium carbonate. These make the exoskeleton or shell harder for protection. It also makes it heavier (which is of less hinderance to aquatic animals whose weight is supported by water) and consequently also more brittle and liable to fracture.

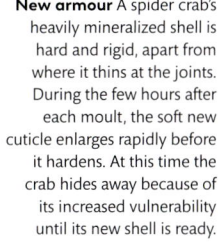

New armour A spider crab's heavily mineralized shell is hard and rigid, apart from where it thins at the joints. During the few hours after each moult, the soft new cuticle enlarges rapidly before it hardens. At this time the crab hides away because of its increased vulnerability until its new shell is ready.

STRUCTURE AND LAYERING

A typical cuticle has several main layers. The outermost layer, called the epicuticle, is the barrier to the outside world, repelling microbes, coping with physical wear, and reducing water loss. The next layer, called the procuticle, is formed from chitin fibres and mineral crystals embedded in a variable matrix of proteins. Neither of these layers contains any living cells. The epidermis, which lies beneath these two outer layers, is the layer of living cells and manufactures the top two layers. Under the epidermis, the basement membrane forms a firm support with fibres of the protein collagen. The relative proportions, compositions, and strengths of these layers vary not just between arthropod species, and also on different body parts.

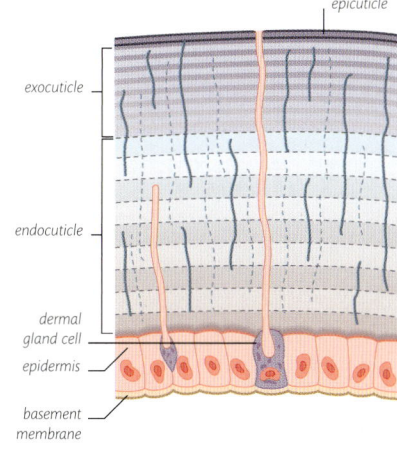

Cuticle The procuticle layer is divided into the hardened exocuticle, which has many compacted fibres, and the more flexible endocuticle. Dermal glands in the epidermis can produce chemical repellents to deter predators.

A wasp has a typical insect exoskeleton, with a head, thorax, and abdomen.

A caterpillar's thinned body cuticle allows each segment to flex and change shape.

Woodlice are terrestrial crustaceans with a shieldlike segmented exoskeleton for protection.

A rhinoceros beetle's "horn" is formed from thickened, stiff cuticle.

Chalky skeletons

The bodies of some invertebrates are supported by chalky frameworks. These can take two forms. Molluscs, such as snails, tend to have shell-like coverings, while echinoderms (including starfish and sea urchins) are more likely to have what can be termed a true skeleton. In both groups, a distinctive feature of their structure is calcium carbonate, the main constituent of rocks such as chalk and limestone.

COMPOSITION

Chalky body structures are usually laid down in the form of calcium crystals embedded in a matrix, which is usually protein-based. Calcium carbonate may be joined by allied minerals such as calcium phosphate, magnesium carbonate, and silicates. Also, calcium carbonate itself crystallizes in a variety of forms, such as angled, prismlike calcite and more rectangular aragonite. Marine molluscs tend to have calcite crystals, while aragonite is more common in terrestrial molluscs, such as land snails. The predominant material in echinoderm skeletons is calcite, whose crystals tend to lie in the same orientation within each of the small skeletal elements, called ossicles. These are almost bony in texture, being hard and stiff, and spongy rather than solid.

Calcium diet This triton trumpet is seen feeding on a crown-of-thorns starfish. The shell of this sea snail is made of calcium carbonate, which it gets from its diet and the surrounding sea water.

Brittlestars The bendy arms of the snake starfish, a type of brittlestar, writhe like worms because their ossicles are loosely bound into the pliable body wall.

CHALKY SKELETONS 49

ECHINODERMS

The standard echinoderm arrangement is a thick outer body layer containing many embedded calcium-based ossicles. These vary greatly in shape and size – from microscopic to palm-sized, depending on not only the species but also on the body part concerned. This type of skeletal structure is technically defined as an endoskeleton as it is not produced by the outermost body layers. But it functions as an exoskeleton because it encloses the main body parts. In urchins, the skeletal plates are large and locked together to form a rigid covering. In more flexible types of echinoderms, such as sea cucumbers and brittlestars, the ossicles are embedded in a matrix of proteins and other substances.

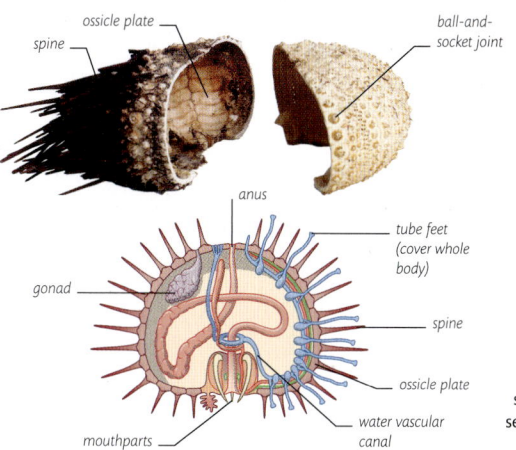

Sea urchin The inflexible, ball-shaped skeleton of a sea urchin is known as a test. Joints attach the spines to the test. The waving tube feet, part of the water vascular system, protrude through small holes in the plates.

Ossicles and spicules This microscope image shows a collection of sea cucumber ossicles (shaped like sheets, wheels, spines, buckles, and crosses) and silica-based slivers (called spicules) from a sponge's skeleton.

MOLLUSCS

A mollusc shell is secreted by a gland in the mantle, which is the animal's fleshy, cloaklike body covering. Shell form varies hugely, with segmentlike plates in chitons; two-part shells in bivalves, such as mussels and clams; a winding helix in gastropods; and a much reduced internal structure in cephalopods, such as squid, or no shell at all in octopuses. The shell includes a thick central layer, the ostracum, itself composed of two layers of calcium carbonate crystals. On the outside of the ostracum is the protein-rich periostracum that protects the calcium carbonate layers of the ostracum from dissolving or from chemical attack. The innermost shell layer is the aragonite-rich hypostracum, which in some molluscs has a lustrous sheen and is commonly known as mother-of-pearl, or nacre.

Calcium carbonate The highly magnified ostracum of an abalone shell reveals layers of overlapping, platelike aragonite crystals.

NAUTILUS SHELL   **CHITON SHELL**

MUREX SHELL

Shell shapes The nautilus adds inner walls, or septa, to its shell, and lives in the last, largest chamber. Chitons, or coat-of-mail shells, have eight sectional plates and a surrounding girdle "skirt". Murex shells are among the most complex of gastropods and of all mollusc shapes.

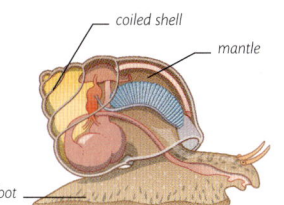

Gastropod A snail shell gradually grows in diameter as new material is added, and its size reflects the snail's age and food supply.

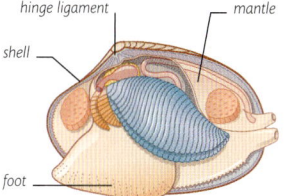

Bivalve A bivalve shell grows as the soft, fleshy mantle adds new carbonates and other substances around the edge.

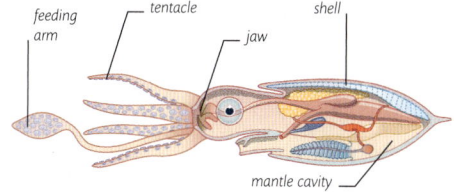

Squid A squid's shell is wholly internal and known as a pen. It is thin, lightweight, and pliable.

Internal support A squid's internal shell serves as an endoskeleton, helping the body to stay relatively stiff and giving the muscles of its water-jet propulsion system a firm base for their contractions.

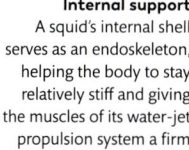

Spiny skeleton Echinoderm means "spiny skin", as exemplified by the crown-of-thorns starfish, shown here feeding at night on coral in the Red Sea.

Bony skeletons

Most vertebrate animals have an internal framework (or endoskeleton) consisting chiefly of the hard, mineralized tissue known as bone. It is divided into the axial skeleton and the appendicular skeleton. The axial skeleton runs along the middle axis of the body, from head to tail. The appendicular consists of the bones attached to the axial skeleton.

Cartilage skeleton Sharks, skates, and rays have skeletons, but these are made mainly of cartilage rather than heavier bone. The reduced weight of these animals allows them to swim more energy-efficiently.

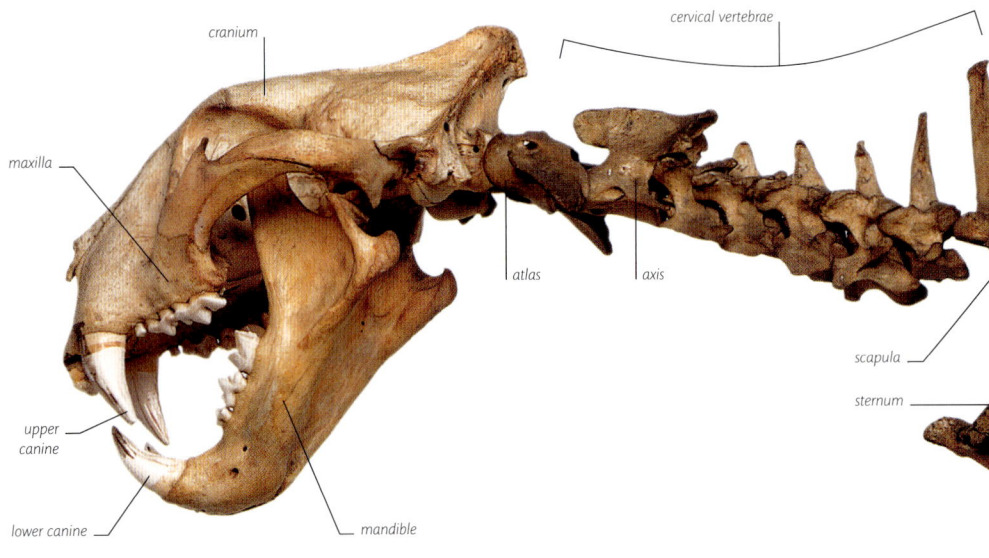

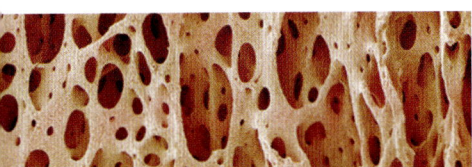

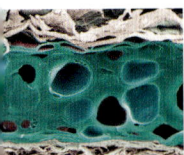

Hard and soft Under a bone's outer hard layer, cancellous bone tissue (above) has many tiny chambers. Cartilage (here coloured green) is light and pliant, forming support for body parts such as the ears.

BONE AND CARTILAGE

Bone is a complex tissue. It is composed of mineral crystals (mainly calcium phosphates), along with fibrous proteins, principally collagen, embedded in a ground tissue, or matrix, of carbohydrates, salts, and other substances. It is continually maintained by cells known as osteocytes, which can also repair damage, such as fractures. A typical bone has a dense, hard outer layer of compact bone tissue; a layer of cancellous bone tissue beneath this, which is more spongy or honeycomblike; and a central cavity of jellylike marrow, which stores fat and manufactures new blood cells. Cartilage is similar to bone, with protein fibres, carbohydrates, and other substances encased in a matrix. However, it lacks bone's hard calcifying minerals, making it somewhat lighter, softer, more pliable, and less brittle.

SKELETAL APPENDAGES

As well as an internal skeleton, some vertebrates have associated bony parts and appendages that develop in the same way as the skeleton, but elsewhere in the body. Some fishes, such as armoured catfishes, have stiff, bony plates in their skin. Their decreased mobility and increased weight are offset by improved physical protection. Reptiles such as the draco, or "flying dragon", have long, thin rods of bone that hold out flaps of skin. Among mammals, physical protection in armadillos is achieved by hard bony plates. These form crosswise bands around the body and consist of dermal bone, which has no links with the endoskeleton. It forms within the thickness of the skin and is covered by a layer of horn-coated, bone-based scales, known as scutes.

Extra bone Each of these animals possess bony parts or appendages that have developed for varying functions, such as protection and self-defence. The seahorse has developed bony plates in its skin for protection against predators. The neck frill of the frilled lizard is spread out when the lizard feels threatened, and the bony plates and scutes of an armadillo can protect its whole body.

Seahorses have an outer layer of bony plates covered by thin skin.

The frilled lizard spreads out its wide neck frill to deter enemies.

Three banded armadillos roll into balls for all-over body protection.

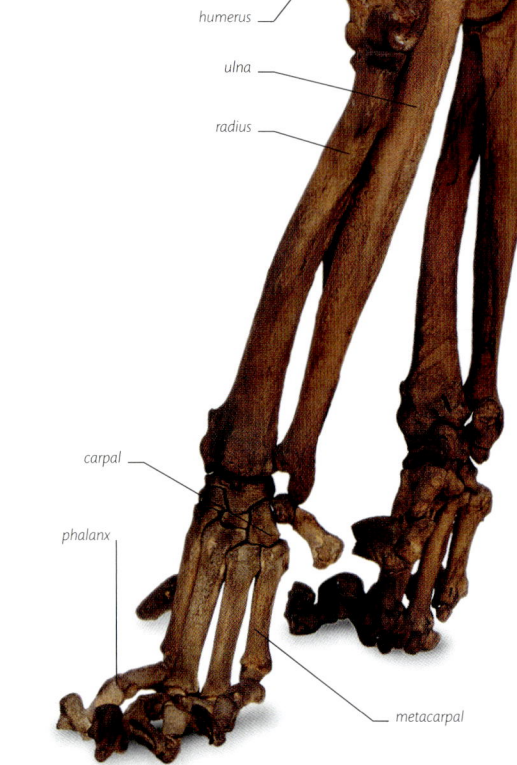

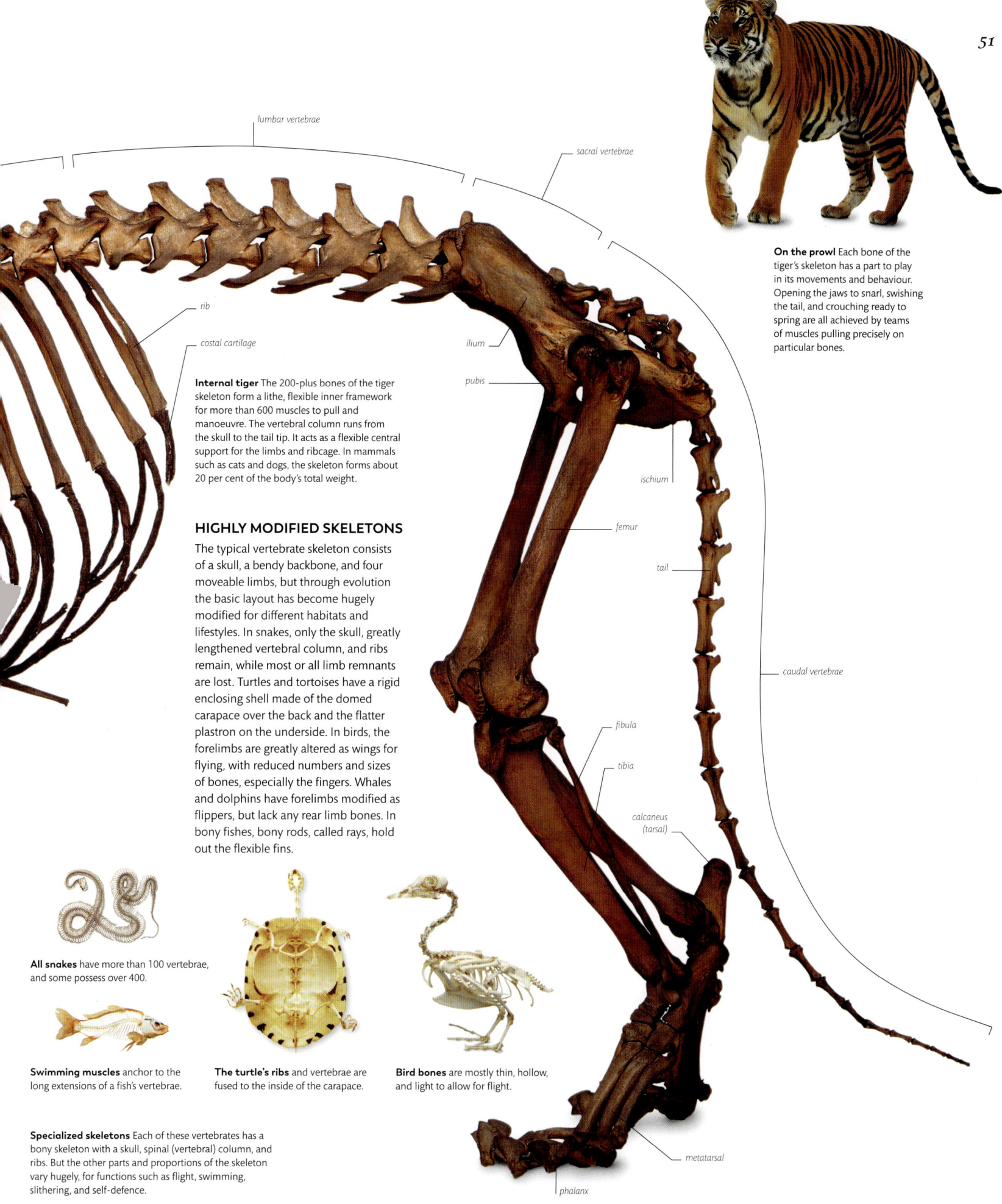

On the prowl Each bone of the tiger's skeleton has a part to play in its movements and behaviour. Opening the jaws to snarl, swishing the tail, and crouching ready to spring are all achieved by teams of muscles pulling precisely on particular bones.

Internal tiger The 200-plus bones of the tiger skeleton form a lithe, flexible inner framework for more than 600 muscles to pull and manoeuvre. The vertebral column runs from the skull to the tail tip. It acts as a flexible central support for the limbs and ribcage. In mammals such as cats and dogs, the skeleton forms about 20 per cent of the body's total weight.

HIGHLY MODIFIED SKELETONS

The typical vertebrate skeleton consists of a skull, a bendy backbone, and four moveable limbs, but through evolution the basic layout has become hugely modified for different habitats and lifestyles. In snakes, only the skull, greatly lengthened vertebral column, and ribs remain, while most or all limb remnants are lost. Turtles and tortoises have a rigid enclosing shell made of the domed carapace over the back and the flatter plastron on the underside. In birds, the forelimbs are greatly altered as wings for flying, with reduced numbers and sizes of bones, especially the fingers. Whales and dolphins have forelimbs modified as flippers, but lack any rear limb bones. In bony fishes, bony rods, called rays, hold out the flexible fins.

All snakes have more than 100 vertebrae, and some possess over 400.

Swimming muscles anchor to the long extensions of a fish's vertebrae.

The turtle's ribs and vertebrae are fused to the inside of the carapace.

Bird bones are mostly thin, hollow, and light to allow for flight.

Specialized skeletons Each of these vertebrates has a bony skeleton with a skull, spinal (vertebral) column, and ribs. But the other parts and proportions of the skeleton vary hugely, for functions such as flight, swimming, slithering, and self-defence.

Need for speed Cheetahs require fast, brief bursts of speed to catch their prey. They have an extremely flexible spine, which coils and uncoils with every movement, propelling the animal forwards. The cheetah can reach speeds of 113 kph (70 mph), but they are not built for stamina. They become breathless and overheated within 30 seconds.

MOVEMENT

Animals display an incredible variety of movements, from the hovering of hummingbirds to the slithering of snakes. Locomotion occurs when an animal's entire body moves from one place to another, as when walking, running, swimming, flying, leaping, or crawling. In addition to utilizing muscle power, animals can also harness a number of environmental features, such as the wind, water currents, and gravity, to aid movement.

LAND, AIR, WATER, AND SOIL

Methods of locomotion vary dramatically, according to the substances or "media" an animal is travelling through. Moving across the land necessitates contact with the ground, using body parts that range from legs and feet, to scales in snakes, and a slimy undersurface called a "foot" in snails. Grip against the surface provides the required forward thrust.

The huge variety of surface consistencies requires numerous specializations. For example, desert-dwellers such as kangaroo rats have enormous feet and toes as well as hairy soles to help them to jump in the soft, shifting sand. Moving through air requires large aerodynamic surfaces, such as wings in true fliers (birds, bats, and insects), or flaps of skin in gliders, such as "flying" lemurs and "flying" squirrels. Flying animals have to expend a lot of energy to provide both lift (to counteract gravity) and thrust for forward movement.

Water is a much more resistant medium than air. In general, it requires at least twice the amount of energy to attain the same speed in water as it does on land. A smoothly contoured, streamlined shape becomes extremely important in water. Aquatic creatures generally have large, flat surfaces such as tails and fins to push against the heavy, fluid medium. Locomotion in soil, sand, and mud is by far the slowest and most energy-intensive. However, as in all forms of locomotion, there are offsetting considerations. For example, burrowing animals are generally less visible to predators and are sheltered from the weather. They may also be surrounded by their common food source, such as plant roots in the case of naked mole-rats.

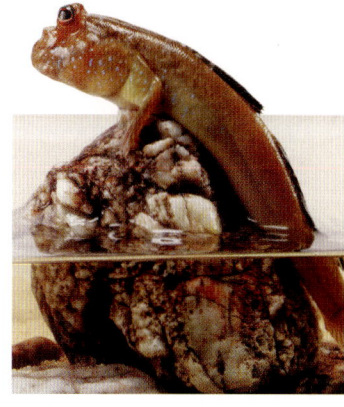

Multi-skilled fish Some appendages are a compromise between various forms of locomotion. The mudskipper's muscular pectoral fins can help this fish to burrow, swim, wriggle, waddle, and leap.

GRAVITY ASSISTED

Various animals take advantage of gravity, by tumbling or sliding down slopes, or simply falling through the air. These methods are generally used as emergency measures to escape predators. A number of animals possess the ability to curl into a ball and roll away from danger, including millipedes and woodlice. Tree-living insects, such as beetles and stick insects, simply let go and drop to the ground. Their survival is ensured by their small size, tough body casing, and soft landing site (leaf litter).

METABOLIC RATE

There is a close connection between metabolic rate (the speed of essential biochemical processes within an animal's body) and locomotive ability. Birds and mammals are homeothermic (warm-blooded) – that is, they maintain a constant high body temperature. This makes their muscles ready for action at any time. Most other animals are ectothermic (cold-blooded), so their temperatures vary according to their environment. When the temperature cools, their muscle metabolism becomes less effective, and at very low temperatures, they are actually unable to move at all.

SWALLOW

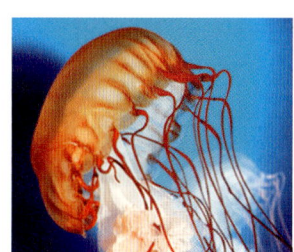

JELLYFISH

EARTHWORM

KANGAROO

Shaped to travel Swallows have scythelike wings for speedy, acrobatic pursuit of food. Earthworms are long and slim, to push between soil particles. The jellyfish's shape exploits sea currents, and the kangaroo's hops are energy-efficient on soft ground.

Walking and running

With the exception of a few extraordinary animals that are able to walk on water or along the ocean floor, walking and running are confined to land animals and require the use of legs. There are many different limb actions that animals employ to achieve locomotion on land, which are known as gaits. Individual animals often exhibit a broad variety of gaits. These methods of locomotion are most obvious in larger mammals, but they also occur in the smallest invertebrates.

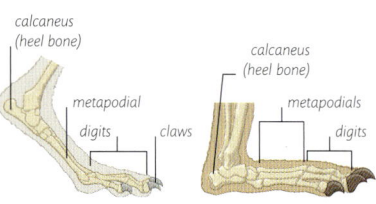

DIGITIGRADE   PLANTIGRADE

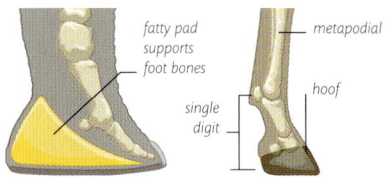

ELEPHANT   UNGULIGRADE

Mammal walking gaits Plantigrades, such as bears, walk with their heel bone, metapodials, and digits on the ground. Digitigrades, such as dogs, move with only their digits touching the ground. Unguligrades stand on one or more toe-tips. Externally, elephants appear plantigrade, but are actually digitigrades, as the heel bone is raised and only their digits touch the ground.

NUMBERS OF LEGS

The numbers of legs varies greatly through the animal kingdom, from two in birds and kangaroos, to the standard vertebrate number of four in most mammals, amphibians, and reptiles. Insects have six legs, while arachnids and some crustaceans have eight. Centipedes often possess well over 100 legs. Despite their name, millipedes do not ever have a thousand legs. Most species have between 100 and 400 legs, but one, the *Illacme plenipes*, has an incredible 750. In centipedes and millipedes, the sheer number of legs is an arthropod adaptation to a part-burrowing way of life. The many tiny limbs allow these creatures to push powerfully through loose material, leaf debris, and soil without the individual limbs needing much space for their actions. The legs move mainly to and fro rather than out to the side, which keeps their movement efficient.

Unusual walkers A crab's sideways walk is due to the direction in which its leg joints bend. A millipede's legs move in coordinated "waves" – a single wave involves lifting around a dozen legs up, lowering them, and then pushing backwards.

DIFFERENT GAITS

Many mammals use different gaits, from a slow walk to a full-speed run. These gaits are especially clear in hoofed mammals, such as horses, which alter their leg movement from walk to trot, canter, and gallop. The trot is used to cover long distances efficiently, while the gallop is used to evade predators. Unusual gaits include camel "pacing", where both legs on one side move simultaneously, to give a side-to-side swaying motion.

SPECIALIZED MOVEMENTS

In many creatures, specialized body movements aid locomotion. For example, the flexible backbone of the cheetah arches up and down to extend its stride. In salamanders, newts, and lizards (among others), "S"-shaped sideways curves pass along the body from head to tail. This gives added swinging motion to the limbs, which splay out to the sides.

S-shaped walk A tiger salamander's body curls from side to side as it walks, in a series of "S"-shaped waves. This pattern is derived from the movements of fishy ancestors of amphibians.

LEG DESIGN

In general, longer limbs allow longer strides and greater speed. With fast runners, the muscle bulk that moves the limb is near the main body, often in the shoulder or hip region. This reduces the weight of the limb towards its end, making it easier to move to and fro at speed. Many invertebrates have unjointed legs, which often utilize hydraulic pressure. Caterpillars have both jointed and unjointed legs. The latter help the caterpillar to grip, as they contain tiny hooks that act like suction cups.

Rhinoceroses have thick, sturdy limbs to carry their great bulk. In spite of this, they are able to sprint surprisingly quickly.

Ostriches contain their main musculature in their hips and thighs. They can also use their wings as rudders to help change direction. Ostriches can sustain a speed of 70 kph (45 mph) for up to 30 minutes, covering up to 5 m (16½ ft) in a single stride.

Modes of movement Rhinoceroses and ostriches rely on their muscle mass close to their main body to achieve locomotion. Starfish locomote using hydraulic pressure. They squeeze water into each of their tiny, tubed feet to extend them.

Starfish have tiny "tubes" on the underside of their five or seven arms, which lift up and move forwards.

COMPROMISE LIMBS

Animals that move both on land and in water have compromise limb designs. Inter-toe webbing is an enhanced version of the standard five-toed land vertebrate foot. It provides a broad, finlike surface for pushing against water and is found in a wide variety of semi-aquatic walker-swimmers, including otters and desmans among mammals, many kinds of seabirds and waterfowl from albatrosses to ducks, and many amphibians. The degree of webbing reflects the proportion of time spent in water – for example, tree frogs have virtually none.

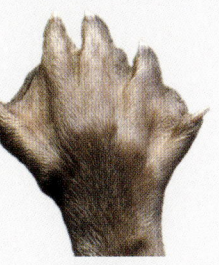

Zebra "flight" As a zebra gallops, all four hooves are off the ground for more than half of the time taken for each complete stride. Such minimal contact reduces friction with the ground and allows the zebra to "fly" in a succession of long leaps, at speeds exceeding 55 kph (35 mph).

Climbing and leaping

There is a huge diversity of climbing animals, some of which have developed extraordinary specializations, such as the acrobatic skills of gibbons or the ability of geckos to stick to almost any surface. Leaping involves progression by alternately speeding and slowing, in a series of jerky actions. Most animals use the same limbs for leaping as they do for walking and running, although some invertebrates use additional body parts specifically to leap.

GETTING A GRIP

Moving through tree branches, and up cliffs, rocks, and walls requires strong, mobile limbs and an excellent grip. Most climbers possess muscular limbs that can haul their body weight upwards. As it is necessary to hang on while the other limbs are moved to new positions, some climbing animals can support their body weight with just one or two limbs gripping. Powerful claws, fingers, toes, and tails possess various specializations to achieve grip. For example, a chameleon's five toes are grouped as two sets, of three and two, to form a "pincer" that clings onto a twig with a vicelike hold. Some animals, including a number of monkeys, possess "prehensile" tails, which are able to grasp and hold objects.

MADAGASCAN DAY GECKO

Ridges, stalks, and spoons Geckos have ridged toes (left) with thousands of minuscule stalklike bristles, dividing into billions of microscopic spoonlike hairs (right). These hairs mesh with the tiny irregularities of the surface the gecko is climbing and provides it with grip.

Spider specialization The tip of a tarantula's foot has two claws, a hook, and serrated hairs, all of which grip strongly to most surfaces.

MEXICAN RED-KNEED TARANTULA

PRIMATE HANDS AND FEET

Primates have adapted limbs not just for locomotion (chiefly in trees) but also for feeding and grooming. The chimpanzee's muscular, semi-opposable toe and thumb grip branches very well. The greatly elongated middle fingers of the aye-aye pick out grubs from under bark. The indri lemur has evolved a grooming claw on its second toe.

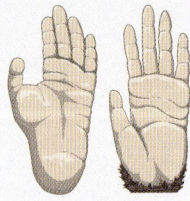

FOOT   HAND
COMMON CHIMPANZEE

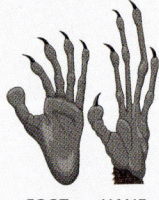

FOOT   HAND
AYE-AYE

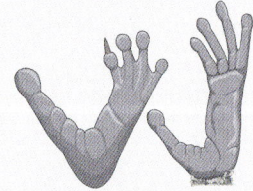

FOOT   HAND
INDRI LEMUR

Emergency exit Some species of monkey, including the proboscis monkey, make their longest leaps to escape danger. Both fingers and toes are adapted for grasping, and the tail functions as a balancing rudder.

HOW ANIMALS LEAP

Prodigious leapers, including hares, kangaroos, frogs, fleas, and grasshoppers, usually have one pair of specially adapted limbs, which are larger and stronger than the others. Each limb unfolds sequentially at its joints as a series of levers, from the hip and thigh, to the knee and shin, to the ankle and foot, and lastly, to the toes. This flings the animal up and forwards in a series of leveraged pushes, achieving a rapid gain in momentum. In addition to avoiding predators and other dangers, leaps are used in many other contexts – for example, to clear obstacles, reach a nearby branch, or as a display of fitness when courting or defending territory. Desert-dwelling animals often use short, quick leaps as an efficient way to move over soft, shifting sand.

Bounding sifaka When on the ground, some lemurs and sifakas, such as this Verreaux's sifaka, move with sideways bounds of their long, muscular legs. They raise their arms up and outwards for balance. This remarkable form of locomotion can propel the sifaka over 5 m (16¼ ft) in a single leap.

CLIMBING AND LEAPING | 57

A proboscis monkey's feet are **partially webbed, making them very effective swimmers.**

ENERGY-EFFICIENT LOCOMOTION

The energy efficiency of leaping is improved by structures in the limbs, such as ligaments around joints, and tendons, which anchor muscles to the skeleton. These structures contain rubbery, elastic substances, including the proteins elastin and resilin. As ligaments and tendons stretch or compress in preparation for the leap, they store energy like a coiled spring. The energy is then released during the leap, in a catapult action that assists the muscles. As a kangaroo lands after even a small hop, its body weight stretches its leg tendons and ligaments, storing energy for the next hop.

34cm The leap of a 2mm (1/16 in) cat flea – 170 times its own body length.

Back flip take off Before a jump, this cat flea compresses blocks of resilin at the bases of its legs.

PRONKING

Certain hoofed mammals perform stiff-limbed, springlike vertical leaps, as though bouncing along with their legs held straight. This motion is known as "pronking" and is derived from the Afrikaans word "pronk", meaning "to boast". It occurs particularly in antelopes, such as the springbok (shown here) and impala, as well as many gazelles. This behaviour is thought to be a display of fitness, showing predators that the individual is healthy, and not worth targeting.

BRACHIATION

Locomotion by brachiation (arm-over-arm swinging) occurs chiefly in tree-living primates, and most spectacularly in gibbons. There are 20 different species of gibbon, which are found in the tropical rainforests of Southeast Asia. The siamang (right) is the largest of them. It is perfectly equipped for brachiation, having long-palmed, hooklike hands with much-reduced thumbs, elongated, powerful arms, muscular shoulders, and flexible joints. This is aided by stereoscopic distance-judging vision, which helps to locate the next handhold. When swinging, the siamang's body moves forwards in a series of arcs, like a travelling pendulum. It is a highly energy-efficient way of moving, as it involves maintaining momentum.

King of the swingers >>01 At the start of each swing, the siamang's body gains speed and energy as it swings forwards. >>02 Its body swings around to allow the free hand to grab the next branch. >>03 The long, muscular arms and the momentum from the swing propel the siamang to the next branch. >>04 The grasping feet reach for a lower branch as it comes to a halt.

>>01   >>02   >>03   >>04

Burrowing, slithering, and sliding

Some forms of locomotion involve progress in tiny, often continuous stages, with a large area of body in contact with the surface. These movements include sliding and slithering, which are undertaken mainly by limbless creatures. Many animals are capable of burrowing and this occurs through many different types of terrain.

BURROWING AND TUNNELLING

There are many subterranean animal species that employ a variety of methods and body parts to push aside particles of soil, mud, sand, or similar material and force themselves forwards. This is by far the slowest and most energy-expensive method of animal locomotion. However, there are benefits of the fossorial (underground) mode of life for creatures that habitually spend their lives tunnelling or burrowing. A truly fossorial animal is relatively safe, as it is out of sight, hearing, and scent of surface predators. It is also sheltered from extreme conditions, such as droughts and blizzards. Also, many burrowing creatures exploit underground food sources such as roots, bulbs, and other subterranean plant parts.

Digging specialist The sharp claws on the European mole's enormous front feet allow each foot to work like a shovel. The mole anchors itself with its back feet and scoops soil sideways and backwards. When it nears the surface, this shovelling action pushes the soil up, forming a "molehill".

Burrowing through different substances Some animals use specialized body parts to burrow through hard surfaces, such as wood and rock. Softer substances also present challenges. Sand collapses as the burrower passes, leaving no permanent tunnel. This means that creatures like sandfish must continually expend energy as they go.

Shipworms are bivalve molluscs that possess tiny, serrated shells, which enable them to bore into wood.

Piddocks are bivalve molluscs that have shells with ridged "teeth" to rasp into soft sedimentary rock such as sandstone.

Sandfish (a species of skink) wriggle like fishes to "swim" through loose sand and soil.

Naked mole-rats use their large, constantly growing incisor teeth to bite through dry soil.

BURROWING METHODS

A typical burrower needs to push aside particles of the surrounding ground, using muscle-powered pressure from one part of its body, while at the same time anchoring another part of its body to generate sufficient burrowing force. Vertebrates, such as moles, have powerful limbs to shift soil. Many invertebrates, such as subterranean termites have saw-toothed mouthparts, which they use to cut through the soil. Some bivalve molluscs, such as the razor shell, have muscular feet, which expand and contract to enable it to burrow through mud and sand. Aided by its streamlined shape that minimizes resistance, this burrowing method allows the razor shell to dig 1 m (3¼ ft) in under 10 seconds.

SLITHERING AND SLIDING

Snakes, slugs, snails, flatworms, and similar animals move smoothly and continuously along a surface, as a result of many tiny muscular contractions. Some snakes tilt their scales to gain purchase against objects and undulations on the surface. Gastropod molluscs, such as snails, slugs, and limpets, slide on a film of mucus using rhythmic contractions of the layers of muscle in their foot. These actions move the foot along in undulating waves. The suction achieved by the sticky mucus allows them to grip onto many different surfaces, including rocks and loose soil. It even enables them to travel upside-down.

Conveyor belt A slug travels using small waves of muscle contraction, passing from head to tail along its broad, slime-coated foot, pushing it forwards like a conveyor belt.

Slow progress If this garden snail moved continuously, it would take it over a week to cover 1 km (0.6 miles).

Foot extended The razor shell burrows by pushing its valves (shell halves) slightly open and extending its long, fleshy foot into the sand with a downwards thrust.

Foot contracted The foot swells at the tip to form a lower anchor point, then the foot contracts, the valves close together, and the shell slides down.

SNAKE LOCOMOTION

In contrast to animals with legs, snakes have no concentrated point to push off from. Instead, they have a complex system of muscles, which allows them to move using four distinct methods. Often, the method used varies according to the size of the snake, the kind of surface they are travelling on, and how quickly they need to move. Most snakes can perform each of these types of locomotion as the situation arises. Sidewinding is the only exception, which is unique to the caenophidian family of snakes.

In rectilinear locomotion, the belly scales are lifted, tilted to grip the surface, then pulled forwards, in a succession of waves along the body. This method is used mainly by heavy snakes.

In concertina locomotion, the rear body folds in sideways curves, which act like a frictional anchor. The head then extends forwards, and the rear is drawn along.

In sidewinding, the snake lifts its head and extends it forwards. The rear of the snake's body lies side-on to the direction of movement, allowing for better purchase. This is employed on smooth or slippery surfaces.

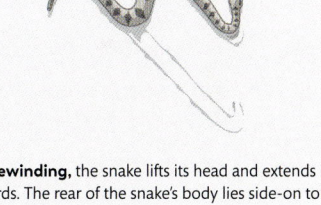

In lateral undulation, the snake exploits surface irregularities, such as rocks, tree trunks, and hillocks, by adjusting the angle of contact to gain forward thrust.

20m The length of tunnel an average European mole excavates in a single day.

Locomotive variety Most species of snake, including this Burmese python, are able to vary their style of locomotion according to the terrain they are travelling on. This python is utilizing concertina locomotion, most often used when climbing, or travelling through tunnels.

Flying and gliding

The three main animal groups to have mastered the air are insects, birds, and bats. They are considered to be "true fliers", as they are all capable of staying airborne under their own power. Some other animals are able to employ temporary airborne locomotion, but they are considered to be gliders, as they are not capable of powered flight. Gliding is also employed by some of the true fliers as an energy-efficient method of locomotion. Some birds are able to use thermals (columns of warm air) to soar for hundreds of kilometres. This means that they hardly ever need to flap their wings.

Wing protection In beetles, such as ladybirds, the forewings have become hard, protective covers, called "elytra". Before take off, these are raised and held clear as the larger, delicate, hind wings unfold for flight.

INSECT FLIGHT

Almost all the main insect groups have the power of flight. Typically they are four-winged, such as dragonflies, mayflies, butterflies, caddis flies, moths, bees, and wasps. In the true flies (more than 120,000 species of houseflies, blowflies, gnats, midges, mosquitoes, hoverflies, crane flies, and others) the hindwings have actually become tiny secondary wings. These vibrate or twirl rapidly, which adds stability and control, while the forewings actually provide lift and thrust. The flight muscles are located in the thorax (middle body section). Some insects directly contract and relax these muscles to pull the wing bases up and down. Other insects actually change the shape of their thorax in order to move their wings up and down. For both techniques, muscles at the wing bases determine the direction of flight by adjusting the angle of each stroke. Wing motion is not just up or down, but also to and fro, to generate both lift and thrust.

Aerobatic fliers Among the fastest, most aerobatic insects are dragonflies. They can rapidly accelerate to speeds of more than 56 kph (35 mph). Dragonflies are also able to beat their two sets of wings alternately, which improves manoeuvrability.

BIRD FLIGHT

Bird wings create much of their lifting force by forward movement through the air, using the aerofoil design (see panel, below). The main power for flapping comes from the pectoralis major (breast) muscles in the chest. These anchor to the sternum (breastbone) at the centre of the chest, and at the other end to the inner wing bones. As these muscles contract, they pull the whole wing down and back. Muscles within the wing, aided by long tendons running out through the leading edge, can flex or warp the whole wing, change the angle of the feathers, and alter the wing's curvature for precise control.

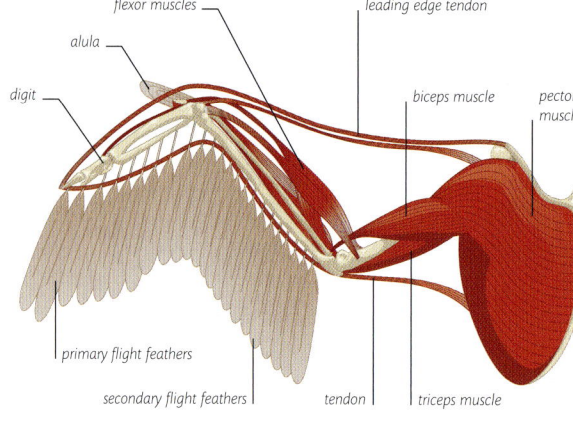

Lift, speed, and airflow The primary feathers fan or fold to control speed and direction. The secondary feathers form the main aerofoil for lift. The alula (digit covered by 3–5 feathers) disrupts smooth airflow at the leading edge to reduce speed for landing.

AERODYNAMICS

A bird's wing forms a curved shape along its upper surface, known as an aerofoil. Air passing over the upper surface has to travel slightly further at a faster pace than the air passing along the lower surface. The slow-moving air beneath the wing exerts a greater pressure, which effectively pushes up the wing from below. The faster-moving air above the upper surface of the wing produces lower air pressure and sucks the wing up from above. This creates a continuing force of lift that true fliers need to counteract the downward pull of gravity.

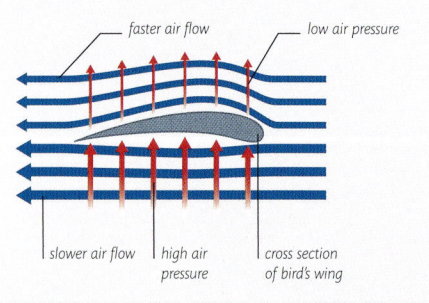

Upstroke and downstroke A barn owl raises its wings on the upstroke. It twists its feathers to allow air through and so reduce resistance. It then lowers its wings strongly on the powerful downstroke. The feathers flatten to overlap and form a continuous airproof surface. This ensures maximum lift and thrust.

GLIDING SPECIALISTS

There are a number of animals – such as flying squirrels, flying possums, flying lizards, flying frogs, and flying fishes – whose names misleadingly suggest that they can fly. They are not, in fact, true fliers, as they cannot remain airborne in a sustained way and regain height under their own power. These remarkable creatures employ winglike structures with large surface area that function as parachutes to increase air resistance. They can also generate small amounts of lift that reduce descent speed. Tilting or changing the shapes of these surfaces gives a certain amount of control over distance and direction. The most impressive mammal gliders are the flying lemurs (neither true fliers nor true lemurs) of Southeast Asia, which can travel more than 100 m (330 ft) and land with pinpoint accuracy.

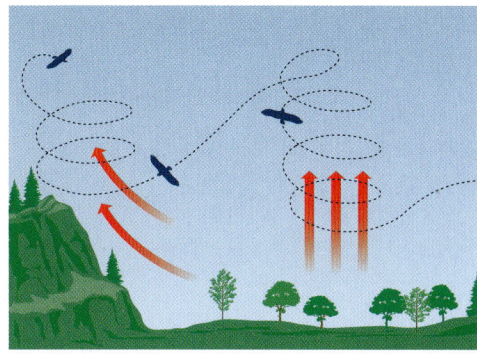

Astonishing gliders California flying fishes use their pectoral and pelvic fins as gliding surfaces. Wallace's flying frog extends its webbed toes as four mini-parachutes to slow its fall as it jumps from a tree.

Soaring When the sun warms the ground, the air above it also warms. This creates columns of warm air, known as thermals. Updraughts are formed in mountainous terrain by deflected wind. Both thermals and updraughts enable birds to soar with minimal need to flap their wings. This energy-efficient method of locomotion is used by eagles, vultures, condors, and storks among others.

CALIFORNIA FLYING FISH   **WALLACE'S FLYING FROG**

WING ASPECT RATIO

A wing's aspect ratio refers to the relative proportion of its span (length from the body to the wingtip) to its width (from leading to trailing edge). Long, narrow wings have a high-aspect-ratio and are most effective for long-distance gliding and soaring. Flapping is minimized, as the air currents provide much of the lift needed to sustain flight. Many birds feature this wing design, including albatrosses, gulls, and to a lesser extent condors and eagles. Low-aspect-ratio wings are shorter and wider. These are used for rapid acceleration, fast turns, and precise control, as in sparrowhawks. Curved, scythelike wings with tapering, drag-reducing tips are used for sustained, speedy aerobatics, as seen in swallows and swifts.

Figure-of-eight flight Hummingbirds flap their wings in a figure-of-eight pattern, providing the necessary downflow of air to allow them to hover. With slight adjustments, they can fly sideways and even backwards.

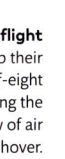

SPARKLING VIOLETEAR HUMMINGBIRD

EURASIAN SPARROWHAWK

ANDEAN CONDOR

Swimming

Swimming is remarkably similar to flying in a number of respects. Both air and water are fluid media, and many of the same principles apply to fins as to wings, such as the need to push broad surfaces backwards in order to propel an animal forwards. One significant difference is that water can be up to 1,000 times denser than air, bringing many drawbacks, but also benefits.

Shoal swimmers Juvenile blackfin barracudas often swim in large shoals. They have long, streamlined bodies with very powerful tails, which allow them to accelerate rapidly.

STAYING AFLOAT

An advantage of water over air is that it provides plenty of support, so unlike aerial animals, aquatic species do not need to generate powerful lift. However, they do need buoyancy control, as well as propulsion, in order to rise, descend, or "hover" in the water at a certain depth. Bony fishes adjust their buoyancy using an organ called the swim bladder, the gas content of which can be adjusted. Cartilaginous fishes, such as sharks and rays, lack a swim bladder. Their angled fins provide them with hydrodynamic lift as they move forwards, offsetting a tendency to sink. Sharks also have a large, oil-rich liver that adds to their buoyancy, as oil is lighter than water. In cephalopods, such as nautiluses, cuttlefish, and squid, the shell (which is internal in the latter two) contains gas-filled spaces that can be filled or emptied to adjust buoyancy. Diving and swimming birds have adaptations that enable them to sink quickly in order to catch food. Cormorants, for example, have feathers that can hold a lot of water, reducing the air trapped in their plumage.

SMALLER SWIMMERS

Some smaller animals propel themselves through water using tiny hairlike structures. Comb jellies have eight rows of tiny hairlike "cilia" that beat in coordinated action, like miniature oars. Some diving beetles (below) swim with their hind legs working simultaneously to push water backwards. Their legs are fringed with hairs, which open out to effectively form two paddles.

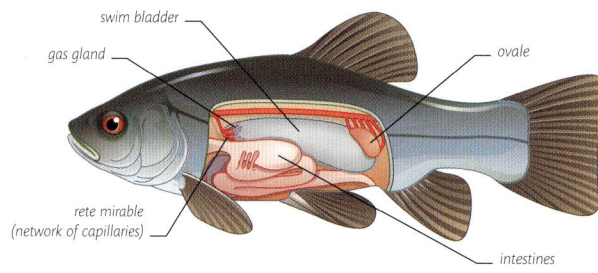

Buoyancy chambers Each chamber of a nautilus's shell is filled with fluid, which is absorbed and replaced by gas. An opening in each chamber allows the nautilus to control the volume of gas inside, and therefore regulate its buoyancy. The siphuncle removes excess water.

Swim bladder A bony fish regulates its buoyancy by exchanging gas between its bloodstream and its swim bladder. Gas is secreted into the swim bladder from the gas gland, which is supplied by the rete mirabile. The gas is removed and reabsorbed into the blood by the ovale.

SWIMMING STYLES

Most large aquatic animals, such as marine mammals and big fishes, swim using the muscles in their bodies and tails to push against the water. Some cartilaginous fishes, bony fishes such as eels, and sea snakes swim with an undulating or wriggling motion, as "S"-shaped waves travel along the entire body. Most bony fishes swim by moving their rear body and tail (caudal fin) from side to side. The other fins (dorsal on the back, anal on the underside, the paired pectorals at the front, and pelvics towards the rear) are generally used for steering and to provide stability. However, some fishes use them for their main propulsion, including seahorses, which swim by rippling the dorsal fin, and rays, which undulate their large, winglike pectoral fins. A fish's body shape usually reflects its swimming style. Powerful, fast movers have muscular, torpedo-shaped bodies that are elongated and tapered at both ends. Fishes that live in quiet waters and do not need to move at high speeds, except in short bursts, tend to be laterally compressed (narrow from side to side). Bottom-dwellers are usually vertically compressed, (narrow from top to bottom) for example flatfishes and angel sharks.

Trunk swimmers Seals like the Hawaiian monk seal move by undulating the rear body and "kicking" with their rear flippers. Eels, such as the whitemargine moray, utilize serpentine locomotion – moving in a series of muscular waves passing from head to tail. This is aided by a flattened tail, which generates more thrust.

A shark's tail fin has an uneven shape, generating both lift and thrust.

Bony fishes tend to have a symmetrical homocercal tail fin.

A tuna's tail fin lowers drag for fast cruising.

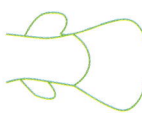

A pike's tail fin has a large surface area for fast acceleration.

Tail fins The shape of a fish's tail reveals the swimming style of its owner. Most bony fishes have a "homocercal" tail shape, with upper and lower tail lobes approximately equal.

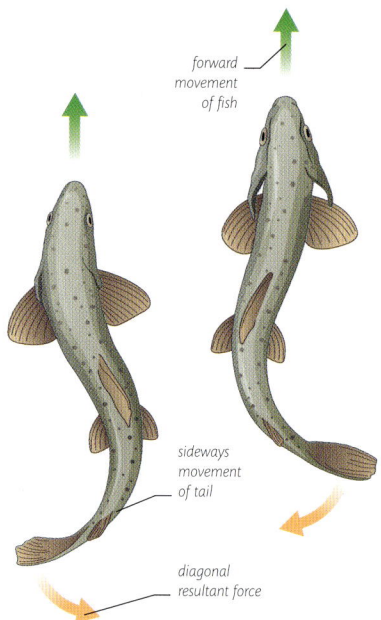

Body propulsion As a fish's tail moves laterally, it generates both sideways and backwards thrust in the water. The resultant force acts diagonally halfway between the two. As the fish moves its tail from side to side, the resultant diagonal thrusts to left and right produce a net backwards thrust, so the fish will swim in a straight line.

LEGS AND LIMBS

Many vertebrates other than fishes swim using their limbs. Seals propel themselves by wriggling the body and "clapping" their broad, well-webbed hind flippers together, while sea lions use mainly their front flippers. Birds swim by flapping or rowing with their wings or kicking with their feet, or both. Penguins, however, possess unique wings. Their bones are solid instead of hollow, increasing their density and strength. They do not row as with oars, but flap their wings and "fly" underwater. Marine turtles swim in a similar way, but they use their front limbs solely for propulsion and their hind limbs to steer. Some species of turtle can reach up to 30 kph (18 mph).

KITTIWAKE

CAIMAN

Webbed feet Aquatic animals like the kittiwake and caiman have webbing between their digits, which increases thrust due to the larger surface area.

FROG "BREASTSTROKE"

Frogs swim by pushing against the water with a synchronized motion of their hind limbs and webbed feet. The frog draws its legs up to its body by bending the hips, knees, ankles, and toes. Then is straightens its legs, with its webbed toes spread, to ensure maximum thrust. The human swimming style breaststroke may have originated as an imitation of the way a frog swims.

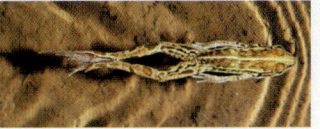

JET PROPULSION

A specialized form of aquatic locomotion known as jet propulsion is seen in various cephalopod molluscs, including octopuses, squid, cuttlefish, nautiluses, and some species of jellyfish. In a squid, the mantle muscles relax, slowly drawing the water into a chamber called the mantle cavity between the animal's main body and its fleshy, cloaklike mantle. The mantle cavity expands to accommodate the water. Muscle contraction prevents water from escaping the way that it entered. A powerful muscular action then squirts the water out very quickly through a funnel-like valve, called the siphon. The cephalopod is pushed forwards as the water jets out.

Fast escape Cephalopods like this bigfin reef squid use jet propulsion primarily to escape danger. They can also move slowly by rippling the fins along the sides of their bodies.

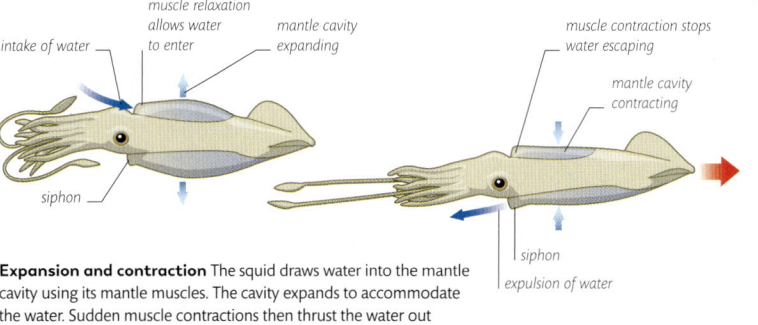

Expansion and contraction The squid draws water into the mantle cavity using its mantle muscles. The cavity expands to accommodate the water. Sudden muscle contractions then thrust the water out through the siphon and propel the squid through the water.

Intricate patterns The exquisite layout and patterning of the differently sized scales around the eyes of a reptile, in this case, a green iguana, allow sufficient flexibility for the eyes to blink, but still provide a high degree of protection.

BODY COVERINGS

Animals and their environments are endlessly varied, and so are the interfaces between them – their body coverings. The outer surfaces, casings, or skins of animals are highly adapted to their surroundings and vary from microscopically thin and fragile to thicker and more durable than a brick.

TYPES AND FUNCTIONS

An animal's outer layers are known as its integument, or integumentary system. These coverings range from basic skin and its outgrowths (scales, feathers, hairs, and bristles) to horny sheaths and rock-hard shells. Each covering is a complex compromise for a wide range of functions. Among the most important are the containment and protection of soft inner tissues, and the retention of body fluids to maintain the internal environment. The covering may also be involved in temperature regulation, nutrient uptake, waste removal, gas exchange for respiration, touch and other sensations, and features of appearance, such as camouflage, warning colours, or mating displays. The range of necessary functions of body coverings are mixed and matched for each type of animal, resulting in an extraordinary variety of appearances.

A feather star's arms are covered with side-branches, known as pinnules, which gather food particles.

The African bush viper snake, like most reptiles, has a flexible scaly covering over an inner layer of skin.

Most coverings have some degree of flexibility, apart from those on hard-shelled animals (chiefly molluscs), even if it is limited to small areas around joints, as in insects and crustaceans. Hairy, furry, or bristly coverings occur in a wide variety of animals. Such coverings are characteristic of mammals, but are also found in worms, some insects, such as caterpillars and bees, and spiders.

PROTECTION

A primary function of the body covering is defence. The external surface is the first point of impact for "insults" against a creature, which include physical damage, destructive chemicals or toxins, harmful microbes, parasites, and radiation. The covering may be extremely tough and durable and able to resist these problems long-term, as in the shells of molluscs and tortoises. These shells provide extra strong, extra rigid protection but fulfil few other functions. Some coverings are more temporary, for example, the outer casings of crustaceans and developing insects, and bird feathers. These are shed or moulted at intervals, taking any damage with them, and are replaced by new, intact coverings. Very temporary coverings, which are not part of the body itself but are bodily products, include the bubbly froth or "cuckoo spit" secreted by froghopper bugs.

TEMPERATURE REGULATION AND RESPIRATION

In some animal groups, the body covering can be adjusted to aid control of body temperature. This is especially important in homeothermic, or "warm-blooded", animals, which maintain a relatively high body temperature. In cold weather, birds fluff out their feathers and mammals plump up their fur to trap more insulating air and reduce heat loss. A body covering may also function in respiration by absorbing oxygen and giving off carbon dioxide. This function may supplement organs, such as lungs or gills, that are specialized for respiration, as in amphibians. The body covering may also be the sole means of respiration, as in some worms.

Insulating layer Walruses have a fatty blubber layer under the skin to insulate against the cold; in hot conditions, extra blood flows to the skin surface to help lose excess body heat.

Skin

Skin – as distinct from most animal shells or similar hard body coverings – generally provides all, or almost all, of the outer surface of an animal's body, forming a continuous, flexible, protective body covering. Typically, skin is made up of several layers and it may produce appendages and outgrowths, such as hairs, scales, horny or bony plates, or feathers.

TYPES OF SKIN

In everyday use, the term "skin" usually refers to the flexible outer coverings of animals, especially vertebrates (fishes, amphibians, reptiles, birds, and mammals), rather than the rigid outer casing of invertebrates such as crabs. In many animals, much of the actual skin is under a layer produced by the skin itself, such as scales in reptiles, feathers in birds, or fur in mammals. Apart from the face, large areas of exposed skin are uncommon, occurring only in a few fishes, amphibians, and certain mammals such as whales, hippopotamuses, walruses, naked mole-rats, and humans.

Caterpillars have a thin, flexible outer cuticle (an exoskeleton) that is made mainly of chitin.

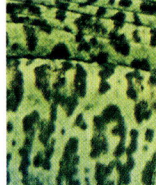
Moray eel skin is smooth and has no scales.

Whale shark skin is up to 10 cm (4 in) thick.

The fire-bellied newt has red patches on its underside which may startle predators.

Skin variations The skin of an animal is adapted to its environment and lifestyle. For example, aquatic animals tend to have smooth skin to reduce friction with the water. Terrestrial animals tend to show greater variation in skin texture, and often have specialized areas of skin on different parts of the body, such as the featherless, waxy cere on the heads of some birds.

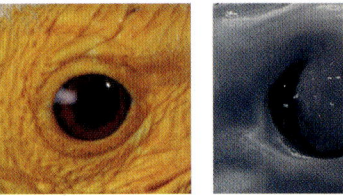
The Egyptian vulture's face is covered in yellow skin, which develops in adulthood.

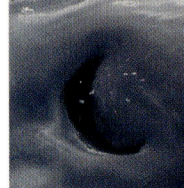
Whale skin is almost hairless, especially around the blowhole.

A gorilla's facial skin can reveal a range of complex expression.

Hippopotamus skin produces mucus to keep it moist on land.

BASIC STRUCTURE

The skin of all vertebrates has a similar basic microscopic structure, even though it may be thinner than this page or thicker than this book. There are three basic layers: the outermost epidermis, which is made up largely of keratin (a tough, fibrous protein) and continually renews itself; the dermis under this, which consists mainly of collagen and elastin fibres and contains sensory nerve endings, sweat glands, and blood vessels; and an innermost subcutaneous layer. The relative thickness and consistency of each layer varies from species to species, giving each one its unique skin features. For example, in cold-adapted birds and mammals, such as penguins, whales, and seals, the subcutaneous layer is thickened with fatty deposits that form insulating blubber to keep in body heat.

Slimy skin Hagfishes have many mucus-secreting cells in their skin. In just a few seconds, these cells produce so much slimy mucus that, when mixed with water, it would fill a bucket.

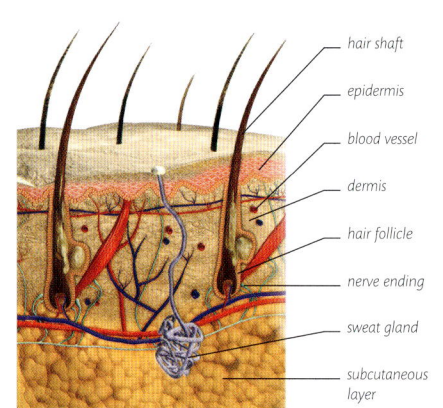
Mammalian skin The skin of all mammals is fundamentally similar. It has three main layers (epidermis, dermis, and the subcutaneous layer) and contains many specialized structures, such as blood vessels and nerve endings.

DEFENCE

One of the most important roles for skin is defence of the body and its delicate internal structures. This defence may be physical, chemical, visual, or a combination of the three. In mammals such as elephants and rhinoceroses, the main physical defensive barrier is the epidermis, which is hugely thickened and strengthened with keratin. This tough protein occurs in various forms in many vertebrates (as well as some invertebrates), and is also the main component of hairs, claws, hooves, nails, horns, bills, and feathers. Chemical defence is particularly common in amphibians; in many species, the skin has tiny glands that ooze unpleasant or poisonous secretions. Visual defence may take the form of vivid coloration, which may prevent predation, or camouflage to help an animal conceal itself by blending into the surroundings.

CANE TOAD

WOMBAT

Skin defences The cane toad's skin secretes a poisonous chemical. The wombat uses its leathery, thick-skinned rump to block its burrow against predators.

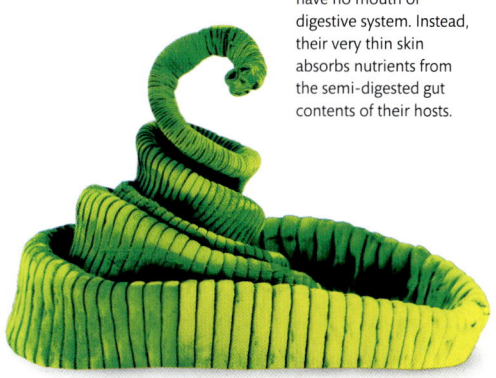

Permeable skin Parasitic tapeworms have no mouth or digestive system. Instead, their very thin skin absorbs nutrients from the semi-digested gut contents of their hosts.

NUTRIENTS AND WASTES

In some animals, especially soft-bodied invertebrates, the skin acts as a selective two-way, in-out barrier. It absorbs nutrients, oxygen, and other useful substances as part of nutrition and respiration, and removes wastes and unwanted substances as part of excretion. These dual functions are especially important in various types of worms, such as segmented worms, flatworms, flukes, and tapeworms, because many of them lack a well-developed respiratory or circulatory system. As a result, they rely on their selectively permeable skin to absorb oxygen and remove carbon dioxide and wastes in direct exchange with the environment. In the sea, arrow worms have no excretory system and expel their body wastes through the skin.

SLIPPERY SKIN

In aquatic animals a specialized function of skin, in addition to its many standard functions, is to minimize drag, turbulence, and eddying for fast, energy-efficient movement through the water. For example, dolphin skin sheds tiny particles of skin into the water flowing past, which greatly reduces drag. The sloughing skin layer replaces itself every two to four hours. In addition, the skin has microscopic ridges that hold a thin layer of water between them. So, in effect, the dolphin's outer skin layer consists partly of water as it swims, thereby reducing drag even more, as water slips past water.

A third adaptation is the dolphin's very flexible skin. As the dolphin swims, the skin distorts, bending and rippling into contours that yield least resistance to the flow of water, which again minimizes drag.

Slippery skin A dolphin's skin adapations mean that drag is reduced more than 100-fold compared to "standard" mammalian skin, which enables bottlenose dolphins to swim faster than 30 kph (19 mph).

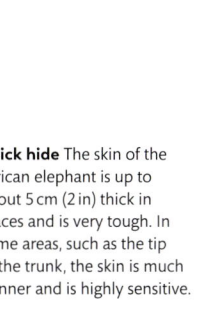

Thick hide The skin of the African elephant is up to about 5 cm (2 in) thick in places and is very tough. In some areas, such as the tip of the trunk, the skin is much thinner and is highly sensitive.

Tough squirt Sea squirts have a slippery, leathery skin that forms a tough, all-over covering. Unusually among animals, the skin is composed of a type of carbohydrate (known as tunicin) that is simlar to the cellulose found in plant cells.

Scales

Most scales are small, platelike outgrowths from an animal's skin or body covering. They provide protection while allowing flexibility, and partly determine visual appearance. Various behaviours, including parasite removal, self defence, camouflage, and courtship are linked to the structure and appearance of scales.

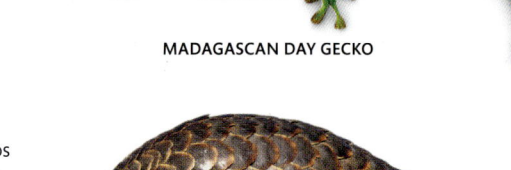

MADAGASCAN DAY GECKO

ORIGINS OF SCALES

Several groups of animals have scales or scalelike coverings, from worms and certain insects to fishes, reptiles, and birds. There are also scaly-looking mammals such as armadillos and pangolins. In most of these animal groups, scales have evolved independently. Others show an evolutionary progression; for example, the scaly legs and feet of birds may be derived from their reptile ancestors, specifically small, meat-eating dinosaurs.

INVERTEBRATE SCALES

Among invertebrates, scales are found in a group of segmented worms called scaleworms. They have 12 or more pairs of leathery scales or elytra that overlap like roof tiles. These form a protective outer covering for these stout, free-swimming, predatory worms, but also form channels for water currents that help them breathe.

Butterflies and moths form the major insect group Lepidoptera (the name means "scaly winged"). Their wing scales are flattened versions of insect hairs called setae. Numbering thousands per wing, these tiny scales are arranged in rows, and their layout and colours produce the wings' overall appearance. They also aid air flow, which improves aerodynamics and helps to maintain body temperature. The males of some species have scent scales on the forewings that release pheromones to attract females.

VERTEBRATE SCALES

Although some birds have scaled legs and feet, and mammals are represented by the unrelated armadillos and pangolins, the vast majority of scaled vertebrates are fishes and reptiles.

There are several types of fish scale. Cartilaginous fishes, such as sharks and rays, have teethlike placoid scales. Each consists of a plate of enamel embedded in the skin, a main body of dentine, and a pointed cap or spine of enamel. Ganoid scales are found in primitive ray-finned fishes such as sturgeons. These also have dentine, as well as enamel-like ganoine surface layers. In the garpike, diamond-shaped ganoid scales fit closely to form a complete covering. In sturgeons the scales are large, platelike, and thickened with bone, forming scutes. Fishes that are more advanced in evolutionary terms have thin, smooth, overlapping cycloid scales, as in cod, and rough-surfaced ctenoid scales, as in perches. The scales consist of a calcium-rich base with collagen fibres, similar to bone, covered by a thin outer layer.

Among reptiles, lizards and snakes have scales made of horny, flaplike, overlapping extensions of the outer skin, made chiefly of keratin (the tough protein that forms bird scales and feathers, and mammalian skin, horns, hoofs, claws, and nails). These contrast with the solid, fused, bone-reinforced scutes embedded in the outer skin, as seen in crocodiles and alligators, and especially in turtles and tortoises.

TEMMINCK'S PANGOLIN

RAINBOWFISHES

Varied form and function From microscopic flakes to cumbersome plates of armour, the variety of scale types in vertebrates reflects the diversity in form and behaviour of the animals that bear them.

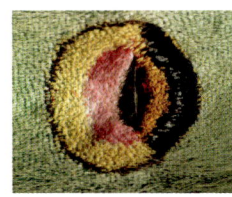

Tiny scales Flaplike scales less than 0.1 mm long cover the wings of butterflies and moths.

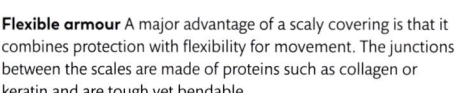

Flexible armour A major advantage of a scaly covering is that it combines protection with flexibility for movement. The junctions between the scales are made of proteins such as collagen or keratin and are tough yet bendable.

Shedding scales Most lizards and snakes shed their skin and scales several times yearly. The epidermis and scales come away to reveal newer, larger scales beneath.

— old skin and scales
— new scales revealed beneath

SCALE DEVELOPMENT

HOW FISH SCALES GROW Most fish scales originate in the dermis, the inner of the skin's two layers. Although the materials they contain differ, most scales develop in a similar way. The placoid scales of sharks (shown here) begin as small clumps of dermal cells, which form tiny mounds. As these mounds grow taller, they tilt backwards and the cells on the upper surface secrete a hard dentine layer with a cap of even harder enamel above it. This produces a tough and abrasive skin surface. These scales do not enlarge as the shark grows – it will grow more scales to cover the expanding body surface.

HOW REPTILE SCALES GROW In lizards and snakes, scales begin as pointed mounds in both the dermis (inner) and epidermis (outer) skin layers. As the dermis ages, it leaves the epidermal scale, which is hardened with a protein called keratin.

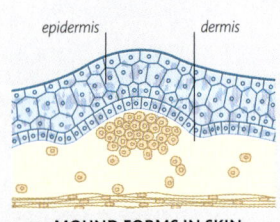

MOUND FORMS IN SKIN
epidermis — dermis

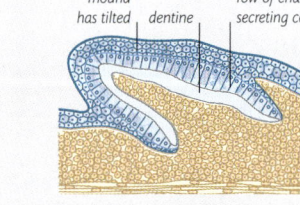

MOUND SECRETES DENTINE
mound has tilted — dentine — row of enamel-secreting cells

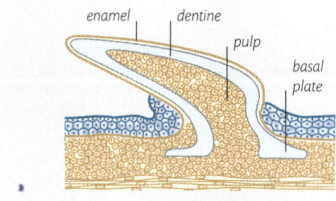

FULLY FORMED SCALE
enamel — dentine — pulp — basal plate

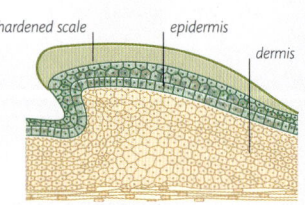

COMPLETED REPTILE SCALE
hardened scale — epidermis — dermis

SCALE VARIETY

Fish scales In more primitive fishes, scales develop as thickened areas of skin that are arranged side by side, limiting flexibility. Advanced fish have much thinner, lighter scales growing from pockets of skin. These have free edges that can be lifted or tilted, enabling flexibility and free movement.

Coelacanths have modified overlapping cosmoid scales, with tiny toothlike spines, or denticles, on each exposed portion.

In many sharks, pointed placoid scales produce a rough, abrasive surface. A shark's teeth are actually larger versions of its placoid scales.

Ctenoid scales, like those of the garibaldi, have a surface with minute ridges or toothlike projections.

The garpike's thick scales have a layer of very hard ganoine.

Cycloid scales have smooth surfaces and edges, as in the trout.

Most fish scales are transparent, allowing skin colour to show through.

Modified scales form many kinds of accessory skin structures, such as the porcupinefish's spines.

Scales thickened with bone, forming scutes, offer extra protection to the pineapple fish.

Reptile scales Most lizards and snakes have overlapping scales arranged in diagonal rows. There are also various modified scales forming flaps, spines, frills, and spikes. As well as providing protection, scales help to retain moisture. By emphasizing skin colour, they play a role in defence, courtship, and territorial displays.

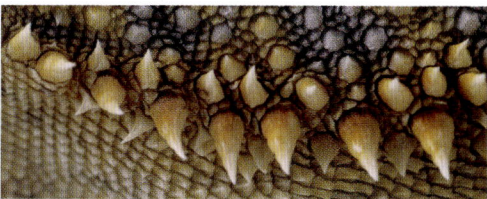

The bearded dragon has rows of spiked scales along the sides of its body, which it uses for defensive displays.

The marine iguana has differently shaped scales forming knobs, spikes, and cones, used especially in visual displays.

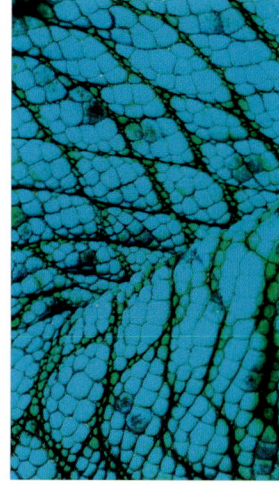

A rattlesnake's rattle is made of un-shed scales.

The Cape legless skink burrows with a strong snout scale.

Reptile scales are mostly transparent, allowing the skin pigment to be displayed.

Wide scales on a snake's underside aid in locomotion.

A snake's eye is covered by a single clear scale, the spectacle or "brille".

The horned viper's horns are scales that may work as camouflage by breaking up the outline of its head.

The skin of crocodiles and alligators is covered with non-overlapping scales embedded with bony scutes.

Feathers

Of all living animals, only birds have feathers, which are made from the tough, fibrous protein keratin. In addition to being used for flying or swimming, feathers have many other functions, including protection, insulation, waterproofing, camouflage, and display.

FEATHER TYPES

Most birds have different types of feathers on different parts of the body. The flight feathers (sometimes called the remiges) include the primary feathers; they are located towards the wing tips and can spread out like vanes of a fan. On the inner wing are the secondary flight feathers. Tail feathers, like the primaries, can also move and spread. Contour feathers form a streamlined surface over the body and where the wings join the chest. Beneath the contour feathers are fluffy down feathers, which trap air to provide insulation.

Fluffy to smooth The contour feathers form a smooth surface over the body but may have downy, flexible plumes at their bases. These plumes do not interlock and provide insulation and cushioning. The flight feathers have little or no downy base.

CONTOUR FEATHER

SECONDARY FLIGHT FEATHER

PRIMARY FLIGHT FEATHER

FEATHER STRUCTURE

Feathers grow from the epidermis of the skin and typically have a long, hollow shaft (the quill, or rachis), supporting a large flat surface, the vane. The vane is made up of small parallel strips called barbs. The barbs bear even smaller branches, called barbules, some of which have interlocking hooks. As a bird preens, it arranges the barbs into neat rows to form an airproof surface, which is essential for efficient flight and also provides insulation.

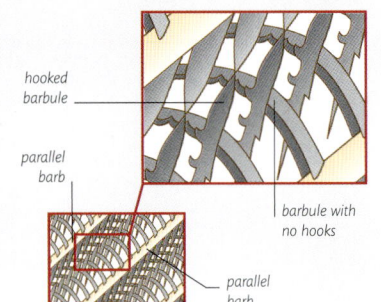

hooked barbule

parallel barb

barbule with no hooks

parallel barb

Preening As well as feeding, nest-making, and defence, a bird's bill is also used for cleaning and combing through the feathers, arranging them correctly, and waterproofing them, as this roseate spoonbill is doing.

PROTECTION AND CONDITIONING

The outer feathers give physical protection, while the down feathers beneath provide cushioning. Feathers also provide water-proofing, which is particularly important for birds that spend time in water, such as seabirds, wildfowl, and waders. As a bird preens, it cleans and tidies the feathers, removes dirt and parasites, and arranges the barbs into neat rows. The bird also spreads oils from its skin oil glands over the feathers, so that they resist water absorption and shed moisture easily. Many birds moult twice yearly and replace the shed feathers with new plumage. This gets rid of damaged feathers and also alters the bird's appearance, for example, for a spring breeding display or autumnal camouflage.

FLIGHT CONTROL

The primary feathers at the wingtip can be fanned out and twisted to adjust their resistance to airflow. This action provides the bird's main form of aerial control, allowing it to slow down, rise, descend, and bank. At slower speeds the tail is also important, used as a rudder for manoeuvring and as a fanned-out air brake for landing. The secondary feathers are less adjustable, but form an arched, aerofoil surface that generates lift as it moves through the air. A small tuft of feathers at the leading edge, the alula, or bastard wing, can be used for low-speed manoeuvring.

inner wing coverts

primary flight feathers

secondary flight feathers

Wing parts The flight feathers are long and strong. They are blended into the wing structure and body by smaller covert feathers on the inner wing, as shown on the wing of this shoveller.

Slow flier This waxwing demonstrates control at slow speed as its primary wing feathers and tail feathers fan out to increase air resistance and the tuftlike alula feathers are raised to give better lift and prevent stalling.

Fur, hair, and bristles

True fur or hair is found only in mammals. It is composed of strands of the fibrous protein alpha-keratin, which is made by specialized structures in the skin's epidermis. Fur, hair, and bristles also occur in other animals but they are made of different materials.

FUNCTIONS

Mammalian fur has a wide range of different functions: physical protection and defence; insulation of the warm-blooded body; camouflage or bright-coloured display in some species or at certain times of the year; waterproofing in semi-aquatic mammals; and various sensory functions. Each hair grows from a hair follicle, a small pocketlike pit in the dermis. Insulation is improved by "fluffing up" the hairs using the tiny arrector pili muscle attached to the base of each hair follicle. This same action is used in aggressive or defensive behaviour to make the mammal look larger, as when a dog or wolf raises its hackles.

long, coarse hairs of outer guard coat
short, dense hairs of inner undercoat

Two layers Seal fur has the two layers typical of mammalian fur. Long, coarse hairs form the protective outer guard coat and shorter, denser hairs constitute the insulating undercoat.

Woolly caterpillar The bristles of "woolly" caterpillars, like this sycamore moth larva, are made of chitin rather than keratin. In many species, the bristles break easily when touched to release noxious chemicals as a defence mechanism.

HUMAN IMPACT THE FUR TRADE

Many animals with attractively coloured or patterned fur coats have become endangered from being hunted for their pelts. Species include big and medium cats, for example, tigers, ocelots, and jungle cats, as well as foxes, minks, chinchillas, coypu (nutria), beavers, and fur seals. Captive breeding on fur farms and restriction of trade in furs and skins by the CITES agreement have reduced the need for wild kills.

Heat and cold Fur insulates against cold, as in seal pups (above), and against heat, as in bactrian camels that live in the hot desert of Central Asia (left).

TOUCH AND SENSATION

Hair or fur shafts are almost entirely dead, except at the root in the base of the follicle, where cells accumulate to increase length. The cells quickly fill with keratin, cement together, and die to form a rod or tube shape as they move up the follicle with the growing shaft. The nerve endings wrapped around the follicle are sensitive to a hair's movement when it is tilted or bent. Mammals use this sense to detect direct physical contact, and they also use the hair movements to gauge wind or water currents. Almost all mammals have whiskers, extra-large hairs with follicles that are specialized for touch. Whiskers are especially important in nocturnal animals such as cats and rats, where they extend the width of the head, thereby enabling the animal to feel its way and assess if gaps are big enough to pass through, even in darkness.

Useful whiskers Aquatic mammals, such as this beaver, and also sea lions, walruses, otters, and seals, tend to have many whiskers. They enable the animal to feel its way in murky water, especially at night, and to locate food by touch.

GROOMING

A mammal relies on its fur for survival, so it must be kept in good condition. Grooming, carried out with the teeth, claws, or nails, gets rid of dirt, mud, pests, such as lice and fleas, and tangles in the fur. It also spreads natural skin oils (sebum) from the sebaceous glands of the hair follicles, to keep the hairs smooth, pliable, and water-resistant. In some groups of mammals, mutual grooming occurs not only for hygiene but also for social reasons. It is part of the parental care of offspring and also a way of establishing a close bond between a breeding pair or rank in a hierarchy. Usually the animal groomed the most has the higher rank or is dominant and the lower-ranking or submissive animal does most of the grooming.

Grooming hierarchy Common chimpanzees show dominance and submissiveness by the relative amounts of time spent grooming each other. Grooming also serves to strengthen the alliances between individuals who regularly forage together.

Maintaining balance Jellyfish like the sea-nettle seem delicate and relatively simple, with only a few organs. But, like all animals, they need to maintain their internal conditions of dissolved nutrients, salts, minerals, and other substances, otherwise their physiological processes would grind to a halt.

BODY SYSTEMS

All animal bodies carry out similar inner processes – breaking down food for energy and nutrients, obtaining oxygen for energy release, getting rid of waste, and coordinating internal parts so they work together properly. In some animals, these processes occur in all tissues; others have complex body systems for each.

IN, BETWEEN, AND OUT

The "ins" of living involve taking in essentials such as nutrients – which provide energy and raw materials for growth, maintenance, and repair – and oxygen, which is required chiefly to release energy for useful work. The "outs" involve removing waste, leftovers, and potential toxins from the body. Between the "ins" and "outs", it is vital to maintain a suitable environment within the body, in terms of the amount and concentration of all kinds of substances, from water to complex organic chemicals. This is the concept of homeostasis – the constancy of the internal environment. It involves physiology – the functional, or biochemical, side of how living things work, usually at a molecular level. Physiology complements anatomy, which is the structure of the body and what it is made of. The collective name for all the thousands of biochemical processes in the body is metabolism. And all of these processes are under the control of chemicals known as enzymes, each of which regulates a particular reaction.

TYPES OF SYSTEM

Food is vital for all animals. This is dealt with by the digestive system, which breaks up food with enzymes. Eventually, the pieces of food are small enough for the body's tissues to absorb. In simple animals, the nutrient molecules may just drift through the cells and tissues. In more complex animals, there is a circulatory system that propels a fluid, such as blood, around all body parts to deliver the nutrients. Likewise, oxygen may simply be absorbed at the body surface and pass into the tissues, or it may be taken in through specialized parts, such as the lungs or gills of the respiratory system, and then circulated throughout the body. In a similar way, waste may diffuse outwards to the body surface, or it may be collected and disposed of by an excretory or urinary system. The immune system protects an animal from germs and disease. Coordinating all these systems are the nervous and hormonal systems.

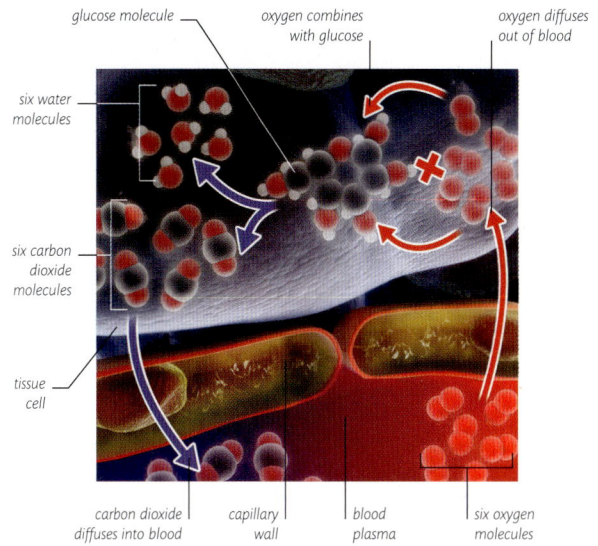

Cellular respiration Red blood cells bring continual supplies of fresh oxygen and glucose. These pass through the thin walls of the smallest blood vessels, the capillaries, into cells. The carbon dioxide produced by cellular respiration diffuses into the blood and is removed by bodily respiration.

LIFE CHEMICALS AND PROCESSES

The energy sources that power most life processes are sugars, especially glucose, which animals gain from food by digestion. Oxygen is brought into the body by the respiratory system and reacts with glucose to release chemical energy in a process known as cellular respiration. Each reaction begins with one molecule of glucose and six of oxygen, and yields six molecules each of the waste product carbon dioxide and water, plus released energy in the form of "energy carrier" molecules known as adenosine triphosphates (ATPs).

KEY TO MAJOR SYSTEMS

- Circulatory
- Digestive
- Respiratory
- Excretory
- Nervous
- Reproductive

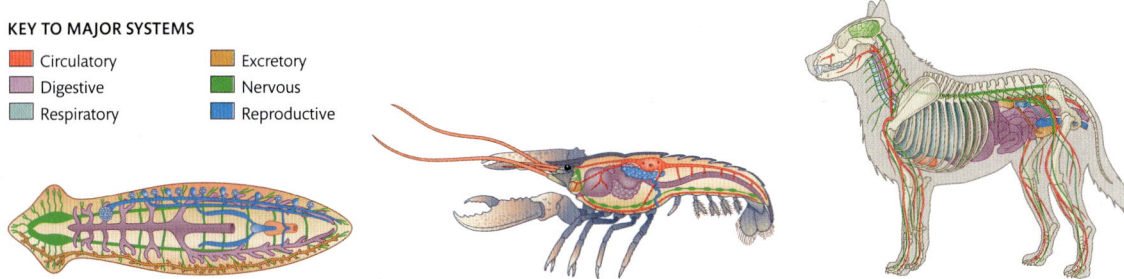

Simple invertebrate A flatworm has a nervous system for coordination, and a digestive system. It has no proper circulation with a heart and flowing fluid, and no specialized respiratory system.

Complex invertebrate Crayfish, like other arthropods, possess all the major body systems of vertebrates such as mammals, but generally in a more simplified form.

Vertebrate In mammals such as the wolf, each system is composed of several main parts, called organs, which may be close together or widely separated around the body.

Breathing

The term "breathing" is usually applied to the physical movements of inhaling and exhaling. It partly overlaps with the broader term "respiration", which can refer to the overall process of taking in oxygen or using it to release the energy from glucose and similar nutrients inside cells.

BREATHABLE SKIN

Skin can be breathable in the sense that it is a gas-exchange surface, through which oxygen is absorbed into the body from the environment as carbon dioxide passes the other way. This is known as cutaneous respiration. The skin must be thin to present a minimal barrier to the diffusion of gas. This type of respiration occurs in aquatic animals, where oxygen is dissolved in the water. The amount of dissolved oxygen rises as the water circulates or becomes colder. So cool, fast-flowing streams have abundant dissolved oxygen, while tropical swamps have much less. Swamp-dwelling fishes can absorb oxygen through their skin as well as their gills, and some, like lungfishes, gulp oxygen into their lungs.

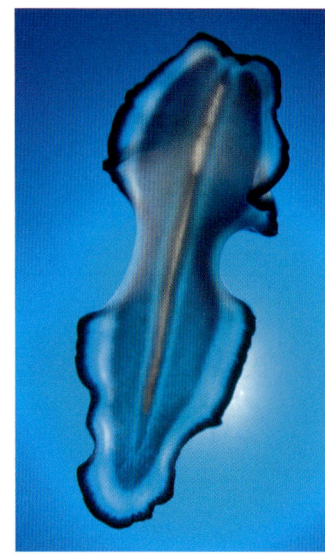

Plenty of surface Flatworms, like this marine turbellarian, lack a circulatory system to distribute oxygen. They also have no specialized respiratory parts such as gills. The leaflike body shape allows tissues to be a minimal distance from the skin surface, to receive dissolved oxygen as easily as possible.

CASE STUDY LOSING LUNG CAPACITY

Frogs respire through their skin and also have lungs to breathe air. The lungs may be very small, as is the case with the aquatic Bornean flat-headed frog, which was initially thought to be lungless. Under suitable conditions, enough oxygen can be absorbed through the skin alone – in this case, in a habitat of cool streams. Amphibians evolved true lungs more than 300 million years ago and several species of lungless salamanders have already reversed this trend.

INVERTEBRATE BREATHING SYSTEMS

Some terrestrial invertebrates, especially insects, have a respiratory network of air tubes (trachea) branching throughout the body. The tubes open at holes in the body covering called spiracles. Air movement through the spiracles, into and out of the trachea, is much more limited than the forced airflow in true lungs. It occurs mainly when the insect moves, making the trachea compress and stretch, or from air currents. However, even in still air, oxygen can diffuse to areas inside the trachea where there is less oxygen, while carbon dioxide does the reverse and is removed. Most spiders have book lungs in a chamber in the base of the abdomen. Book lungs consist of many thin, leaflike structures into which oxygen can easily diffuse.

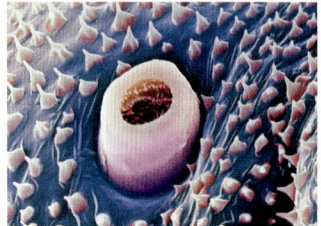

Hole in the wall Each spiracle can become smaller by contraction of the closure muscle around its opening. In dry conditions, this reduces loss of moisture from inside the body as vapour. Opening up increases the flow of oxygen to the muscles, so that the insect can move more.

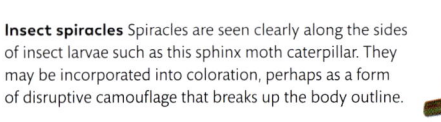

Insect spiracles Spiracles are seen clearly along the sides of insect larvae such as this sphinx moth caterpillar. They may be incorporated into coloration, perhaps as a form of disruptive camouflage that breaks up the body outline.

BREATHING WITH GILLS

Gills are body parts specialized for gas exchange in water. Their structure consists of many branching surfaces with a plentiful blood supply, to present the greatest possible area for absorbing oxygen and getting rid of carbon dioxide. Gills of various kinds are found in a wide range of aquatic animals. They form frilly tufts on the backs of sea slugs, and finlike or flaplike tail appendages on aquatic insect larvae, such as damselfly and mayfly nymphs. Fish gills are on several bony or cartilaginous arches on the sides of the head. In all cases, the gills must be exposed to flowing water, to bring continuing supplies of dissolved oxygen. The flow also takes away carbon dioxide and other unwanted substances, such as salt and ammonia. This occurs in fishes and some amphibians, where gills have become organs of excretion as well as respiration.

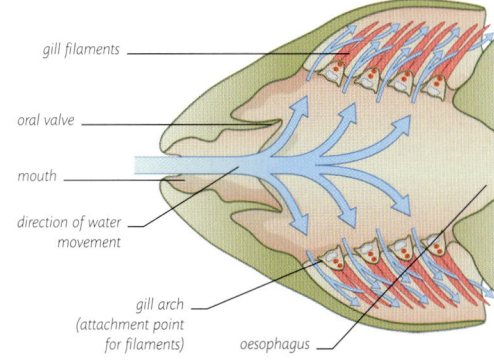

External gills Amphibian larvae, like this newt, have external gills on the sides of the head. These are delicate and easily damaged, but regrow well.

Internal gills Fish gills are composed of hairlike or feathery filaments protected within gill chambers. In most fishes, water flows in through the mouth, over the filaments – where oxygen is taken into the blood inside them – and out through the gill slits (above). The oxygenating blood gives the gills a strong red colour, as in the map pufferfish (right).

Holding breath Most seals, such as this Antarctic fur seal, and sea lions can hold their breath for several minutes, and some for over one hour. The body uses oxygen stored not only in the lungs, but in the blood and muscles, by the pigments haemoglobin and myoglobin.

BREATHING WITH LUNGS

Lungs are organs specialized to absorb oxygen from air and remove carbon dioxide into air. Most vertebrates, except most fishes, have lungs (some fishes, such as lungfishes, take in oxygen from swallowed air). Typical vertebrate lungs are paired in the chest, on either side of the heart. Their branching airways connect to the trachea (windpipe), pharynx (throat), and the nose and mouth, forming a passage along which air moves. The flow is caused by respiratory muscles in the chest and the sheetlike diaphragm between the chest and abdomen. These muscles contract to expand the lungs and suck in fresh air during inhalation, then relax so the stale air pushes out. Lungs contain millions of tiny bubblelike alveoli surrounded by blood capillaries, which absorb oxygen from the air.

CASE STUDY RECORD DIVE

Cuvier's beaked whale has been tracked to almost 1,900 m (6,200 ft) below the surface on a single dive of 85 minutes. Compared to land mammals, whale blood contains very high amounts of the oxygen-loving pigment haemoglobin. Large quantities of a similar pigment, myoglobin, are found in the muscles. These store oxygen for diving. Blood vessels to less important body parts, like the intestines, constrict on the dive, saving oxygen usage, while the vessels to the muscles, heart, and brain stay open for a plentiful flow.

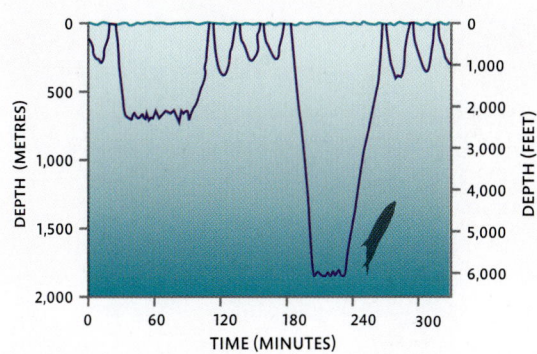

Land crab The coconut or robber crab has a combined "gill-lung" known as the branchiostegal organ in its rear abdomen. If moistened with sea water, this can take in oxygen from air for long periods, allowing the crab to move considerable distances on land.

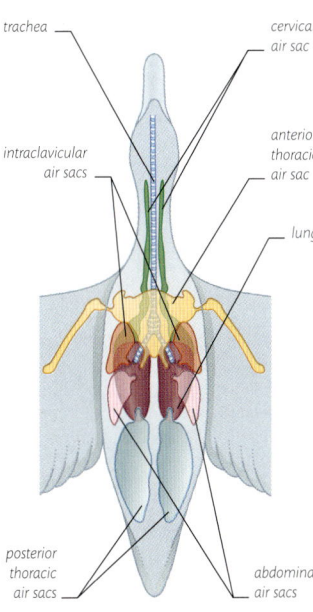

One-way lungs Mammal lungs are "dead ends"– air flows in, then back out. Birds have expandable air sacs that draw air down the windpipe and right through the lungs. This allows more oxygen to be absorbed, for the bird's energy-hungry flight muscles.

Assisted breathing As large animals, such as the pronghorn, run the continual acceleration-deceleration of each stride makes the abdominal contents move to and fro within the body. This aids normal breathing by alternately compressing and stretching the chest.

Circulation

In complex animals, the circulatory system sends blood around the body, through a network of tubes or vessels, pumped by the heart. The circulatory systems of other animals use a different fluid, or have few vessels, or no heart – and sometimes they have all these variations.

TYPES OF CIRCULATION

A dedicated circulation system is much more efficient than simple diffusion, where substances flow at random through tissues and cells. The two main types of circulation are open and closed. In the former, found in invertebrates such as insects, the circulating fluid is usually called haemolymph. For part of its journey, it permeates and oozes through the general body cavity, the haemocoel or coelom, unconstrained by vessels, before returning to the heart(s). In the closed system, as seen in most vertebrates, the circulating medium – blood – is within vessels for all of its journey. It exchanges nutrients, oxygen, waste, and other substances through their walls.

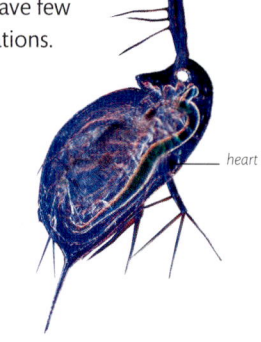

Non-stop pump The throbbing heart of a water-flea (a small crustacean) is visible through its body wall.

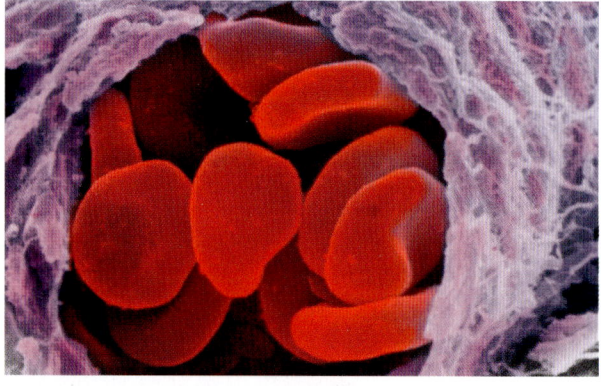

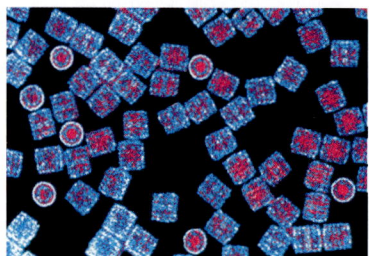

Blue blood Red blood has the iron-based pigment haemoglobin carried in red cells (above). Some crustaceans and molluscs have copper-containing pigments, like haemocyanin, so the haemolymph is green or blue, as in a whelk (left).

BLOOD, LYMPH, AND HAEMOLYMPH

The blood of vertebrates, and the haemolymph of invertebrates, carries out dozens of functions. It transports nutrients and oxygen to the cells, and gathers unwanted by-products for excretion. It carries hormones to coordinate inner processes. It goes sticky or clots to seal wounds and leaks. In "warm-blooded" animals – mainly mammals and birds – it distributes heat around the body. In a typical vertebrate, about half the blood is a pale fluid (plasma) containing hundreds of dissolved substances. Most of the rest is red blood cells (erythrocytes), which hold onto oxygen or carbon dioxide. Lymph is a circulating fluid that has important roles in the immune system. It is carried inside vessels called lymphatics. It has no pump but oozes slowly, massaged by body movements.

IMMUNE SYSTEM

The immune system has major roles in resisting disease and fighting illness. It involves various categories of white cells. Those called macrophages hunt down, engulf, and "eat" microbes such as bacteria. There are also various kinds of lymphocytes. Some are able to recognize microbes and other alien items. They instruct other types of lymphocytes to produce substances known as antibodies, which stick onto the microbes and disable or kill them. In vertebrates, all of these cells travel in the blood and the lymph.

See-through frog A glass frog reveals its heart at the front of the chest cavity. The thick muscular walls obscure the red blood inside, but blood can be seen in the main vessels leading to and from the heart.

Signs of illness Animals sometimes show signs of infection, as in the case of this elephant seal. Mucus is produced by the nasal lining as the white cells of the immune system attack invading germs there. Some seals suffer from phocine distemper, related to canine distemper which affects dogs.

Digestion

Consuming food for internal digestion and absorption marks out most members of the animal kingdom from those in other major groups of organisms, such as plants and fungi. Food provides raw materials for growth and repair, health-giving substances like vitamins, and the energy for life.

DIGESTIVE SYSTEMS

After an animal captures food it is taken in through the oral opening, or mouth, into the digestive tract. In simple animals, this is a hollow chamber or branching system with just one opening, so the undigested waste comes out the same way and the mouth functions as the anus. In complex animals, the digestive tract is a long tube or convoluted passageway with the anus or cloaca at the other end. General names are given to sections of the tract in various animals. After the mouth is the gullet or oesophagus, perhaps leading to a "crop", which is specialized for storage. The stomach is the main digestion site, the intestine is the chief area for absorbing nutrients, and the rectum, or large bowel, stores waste until it is expelled.

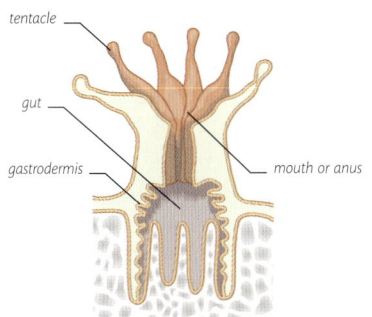

Dual purpose Cnidarians such as jellyfish, anemones, and coral polyps (above) have a single digestive opening that is the mouth when eating and the anus when expelling leftovers. Nutrients diffuse through the gastrodermis (gut lining) into the tissues.

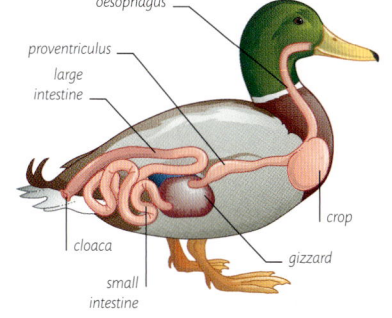

Two openings In some invertebrates and all vertebrates, the gut is a through-tube. Birds, some fishes, and some invertebrates have a gizzard - a muscular grinding chamber that follows the proventriculus (the stomach area), which secretes the digestive enzymes.

SPECIALIST DIETS

Some animals are omnivorous, with a digestive system that can cope with many kinds of foods. Others are adapted to survive on a narrow range of foods, especially those that are very low-nutrient, or distasteful, or contain chemicals that are toxic to other animals. This means the specialist feeder faces little competition for its meals, but also limits its range to the geographical distribution of its foodstuffs, and its survival to that of the food. Some specializations are physical, for example, the manipulation of bamboo shoots by the giant panda. Others are biochemical, where a unique enzyme allows an animal to cope with a particular food part or a toxin.

Unique foods The golden bamboo lemur's staple diet of giant bamboo (left) contains levels of cyanide that would kill most other mammals, while the creosote bush katydid (below) is not put off by the unpalatable taste of an acid that is found in creosote bush leaves.

Pre-digested In animals such as flies, spiders, and starfish, early digestion takes place outside the body. The mouth pours digestive juices onto the food, which turns it into a "soup" that is sucked up.

FOOD BREAKDOWN AND DISPOSAL

Digestion involves breaking food into tinier pieces, until they are small enough for absorption. Physical digestion includes crushing in the mouth and mashing in the stomach or gizzard. In chemical digestion, juices containing enzymes are secreted onto the food by the gut lining. Different enzymes attack different dietary constituents – proteases split apart proteins in meaty food, while lipases break down oils and fats in fatty food. This process may take months, as when a python digests a wild pig. In most cases, undigested material passes out through the anus as droppings or faeces, but some animals bring up or regurgitate leftovers via the mouth.

Worm casts, like that of the lugworm, consist of sand and mud particles that have passed through the gut.

Owl pellets are regurgitated and contain undigestible bits of prey such as bones, teeth, fur, and beaks.

Fluids and temperature control

The control of an animal's bodily internal environment includes regulating the concentrations of hundreds of salts, minerals, and other substances. Called osmoregulation, this involves the delicate processes of water balance. The body temperature must also be maintained within suitable limits so that biochemical reactions can take place efficiently.

WATER AND SALT BALANCE

Living on land, in fresh water, and in salt water pose different problems. Land animals tend to lose water as vapour from permeable body coverings, from moist respiratory surfaces, and in excreted urine and droppings. This must be replaced by drinking, by water contained in foods, and by water made in the body by metabolic processes. In fresh water, an animal's internal environment has a relatively high concentration of salts compared to its surroundings. Water tends to diffuse into the body and so must be removed in urine and by being actively "pumped" out. In salt water, the opposite may occur, so water must be prevented from leaving the body.

Sleeping bag The desert-dwelling water-holding frog buries itself in moist soil during drought. It forms a watertight cocoon from shed layers of skin, storing water under its skin and as dilute urine in its large bladder. The frog remains inside its fluid sleeping bag until wet weather returns.

Desert dweller Desert animals such as the banner-tailed kangaroo rat have adapted to produce very concentrated urine, which reduces water loss. This rodent is nocturnal, and it seals its burrow by day, which traps the moisture in its breath.

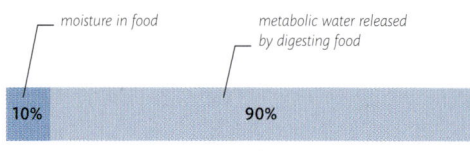

WATER IN

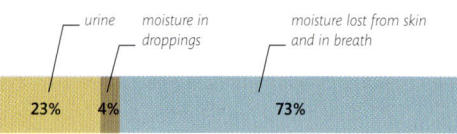

WATER OUT

Water balance in a kangaroo rat There is little moisture in the kangaroo rat's main diet of seeds. But water is actually made in the body by metabolic processes such as cellular respiration. As well as concentrated urine, the droppings are also dry, to conserve moisture.

Useful droppings A bird's urine, produced by its kidneys, is combined with digestive wastes from its intestine and leaves the cloaca as semi-liquid droppings. Thick accumulations, known as guano, from seabirds such as the blue-footed booby are collected for fertilizers and mineral extraction.

WASTE DISPOSAL

Filtering blood, haemolymph, or other body fluids is a common method of regulating water, salts, and toxins. In vertebrates, the main organs involved are the two kidneys. They remove waste products dissolved in water through microscopic filters known as nephrons. Then the required amount of water is reabsorbed into the bloodstream to maintain water balance. In mammals, the resulting fluid, urine, is stored in the bladder until it can be expelled. Urine contains various hormones and similar substances, which often have distinctive scents, so it has a secondary role as a means of communication, for example, as a sign of readiness to breed. Invertebrates have similar methods of excretion, involving filtering body fluids such as haemolymph, but the main organs have different structures. Worms or flatworms possess nephridia, while the excretory system of an insect is based on malpighian tubules.

Useful urine Behavioural aspects of waste disposal include the use of urine to scent-mark territories and warn away intruders of the same species, as seen in lions, rhinoceroses, and many other mammals.

Warming up In the early morning, a southern rock agama seeks out dark rocks to warm itself. These rocks have held the sun's heat from the previous day and are also absorbing more solar heat in the new dawn.

BEHAVIOUR AND TEMPERATURE CONTROL

Mammals and birds maintain a constant high body temperature by "burning" energy-containing nutrients to release heat. Keeping body temperature constant is termed homeothermy, popularly known as being "warm-blooded", and generating warmth in this way is termed endothermy. Such animals can stay active even in cold conditions, but the process requires energy, which must come from increased food consumption. Most other animals are ectothermic, meaning that warmth for their bodies comes from outside. A popular term for this is "cold-blooded". However, a reptile in a scorching desert may have a warmer body than a mammal next to it. Also, ectothermy does not mean having no control: by using behaviour such as resting in the shade to cool down, an ectotherm can alter its temperature.

Cool ears Elephants have large ears, not only for acute hearing, but to help control their body temperature. The ears have a plentiful blood supply, and when the body temperature rises, the ears flap to and fro to work like radiators and lose heat to the surrounding air. Animals with similar adaptations for hot climates include jack rabbits and the fennec fox.

CASE STUDY
LIZARD ACTIVITY PATTERNS

Terrestrial ectotherms, such as lizards, have an array of behaviours to help them warm up by day, and then keep their body temperature relatively constant so that they can remain active. They move from shelter to sunshine and bask on dark rocks, which soak up the sun's heat better than light-coloured ones. To cool down, they seek out shade or a breeze, gape the mouth to breathe out warm air, or enter a burrow.

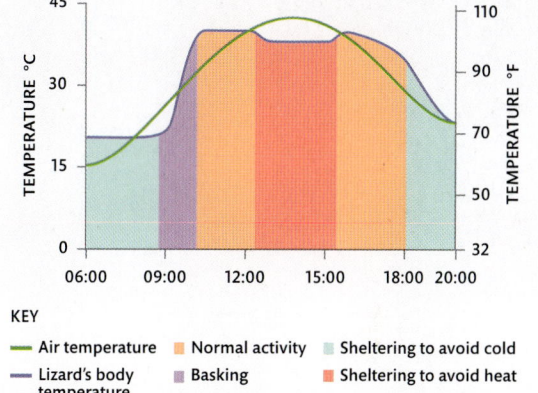

CONSERVING WARMTH

Mammals and birds in cold places, such as penguins in the Antarctic, have a specialized blood flow called the counter-current mechanism to conserve body heat. Extremities such as feet and flippers tend to cool fastest. Warm blood flowing from the body core to the extremity passes close to cool blood returning from it, and heat is transferred, leaving the outflowing blood cooler. The extremity is kept colder and so loses heat at a slower rate than if warm blood circulated through it.

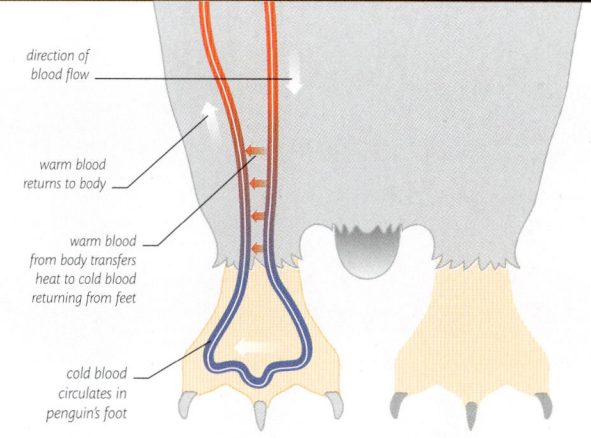

HIBERNATION AND TORPOR

True hibernation is limited to certain mammals such as bats, dormice and other rodents, insectivores including hedgehogs, and some lemurs. It is a strategy to survive adverse conditions, usually winter, by "shutting down" the body's activity and metabolic processes to save energy. Heart and breathing rates fall to a fraction of their usual levels, and body temperature drops to a few degrees above freezing. To prepare, the animal feeds well to lay down reserves of food as body fat, then finds a sheltered, safe place. Once in hibernation, it is unable to rouse quickly. Torpor is a less extreme, short-term slowing of body processes, usually just for a few hours. Some small bats and humming-birds enter torpor overnight to survive the cold.

Fat reserves The fat-tailed lemur stores food as fat in its tail to survive Madagascar's dry season, which it spends in a state of torpor in a tree hollow.

Safe cave Hibernating bats, such as the whiskered bat, choose sites that are safe from predators, and which also have constant conditions and do not freeze, for example, deep inside a cave.

Brains, nerves, and hormones

The nervous and hormonal systems of animals are vital for the control and coordination of internal body parts, ensuring they work together effectively. These systems also control the whole animal as it sees, hears, and otherwise senses its surroundings, moves about, selects a range of behaviours according to circumstances, and prepares to moult or breed.

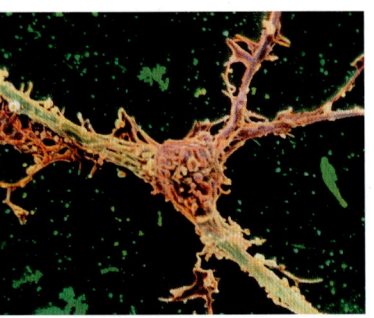
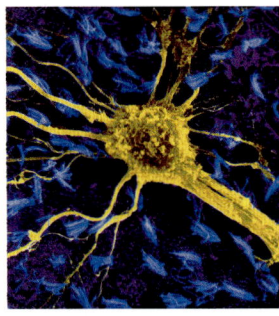

Support cells As part of the nervous system, millions of cells give physical and nutritional support to neurons, without carrying any nerve signals themselves. Astrocytes (right) are named after their starlike shape, and pass nutrients to neurons. Oligodendrocytes (left) form a type of living scaffolding to hold the neurons firmly.

NERVES

Most animals possess a system of nerves that branch into all body parts and come together at one site, known as the brain, or at several locations, where they form ganglia. The nervous system uses tiny pulses of electricity, or nerve signals, and is concerned with the whole animal sensing and reacting to the environment, instincts, memory, and learning. Its basic components are some of the most specialized of all cells – neurons, or nerve cells. Neurons have thin branches that carry nerve signals at speeds in excess of 100 m/s (330 ft/s) in some species. The branches almost touch those of other neurons, but are separated by tiny gaps known as synapses, which the nerve signals cross in the form of chemicals, called neurotransmitters, released by the neurons. Not all animals have a nervous system and brain. Sponges lack any nerves and jellyfish are "brainless", with only a simple nerve net.

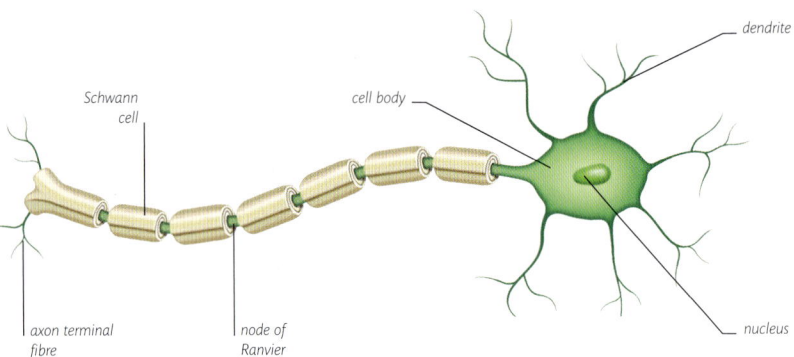

Neuron A typical neuron has a rounded cell body with short, thin branches called dendrites. These gather signals from other neurons and process them. The resulting signals travel along a thicker, longer projection, the axon (nerve fibre), to the terminal, which links to other neurons. Some axons have wrappings of fatty insulation (myelin) made by Schwann cells.

Nervous shark Many short, thick nerves run from the sense organs of smell, vision, taste, and touch to a shark's brain in its skull. In sharks and rays, thin nerves also run from the tiny electrosensing pits, ampullae of Lorenzini, scattered over the snout.

INVERTEBRATE NERVOUS SYSTEMS

Invertebrates show a range of nervous system designs, from simple nerve nets to centralized networks, which have "lumps" of neurons called ganglia or a single brain. These structures contain concentrations of neuron cell bodies, with many short, interconnected dendrites and axons. This makes the exchange and processing of information more efficient than in a diffuse network. Sensory nerves bring incoming signals from the sense organs. This information is analysed in the brain or ganglia and appropriate signals are then sent out along motor nerves to muscles, which affect movements and behaviour, and to body parts such as glands, telling them to release their chemical secretions.

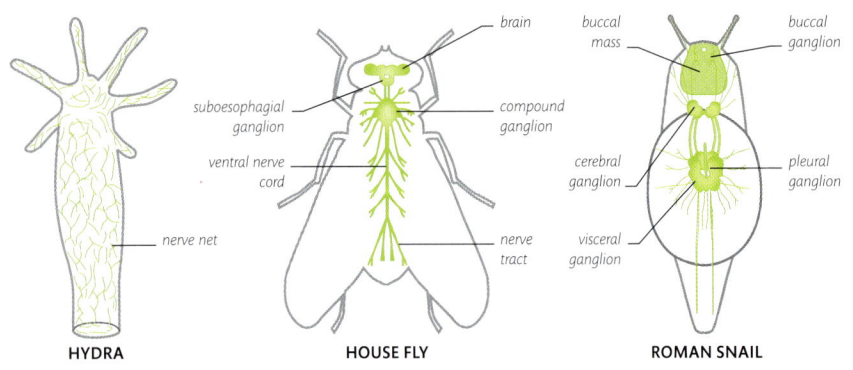

Different designs The cnidarian nerve net, as in the hydra, a tiny pond animal, consists of nerve fibres connected in a simple netlike fashion. Arthropods such as flies and other insects have a frontal brain, ganglia at various sites, and a ventral nerve cord along the base of the body. Mollusc nervous systems, shown here in the snail, have several ganglia linked by thick tracts of nerve fibres that carry signals at very high speeds.

Dog brain The vertebrate brain, coloured green in this image, is well protected inside the cranium, a bony chamber at the rear of the skull. Its wrinkled surface provides a large area for billions of neurons.

VERTEBRATE NERVOUS SYSTEM

The typical layout of a vertebrate's central nervous system consists of a brain and spinal cord, and branches from these to all body parts, forming the peripheral nervous system. The presence of a spinal column made of vertebra (backbones), which support and protect the spinal cord, is a characteristic of vertebrates. Different lobes, centres, and other parts of the brain deal with specific functions. For example, the optic lobes receive nerve signals from the eyes, while the olfactory lobes process information about smell from the nose, and the motor centres organize nerve signals going out to the muscles for movement. There is also an autonomic nervous system, partly with its own nerves, such as sympathetic ganglia chains, and partly using nerve fibres from the other systems. This system is concerned with the automatic running of essential actions inside the body, such as breathing and the passage of food through the gut. The sympathetic part of the autonomic system makes body parts more active and ready to cope with stress, while the parasympathetic part restores calm and normal working.

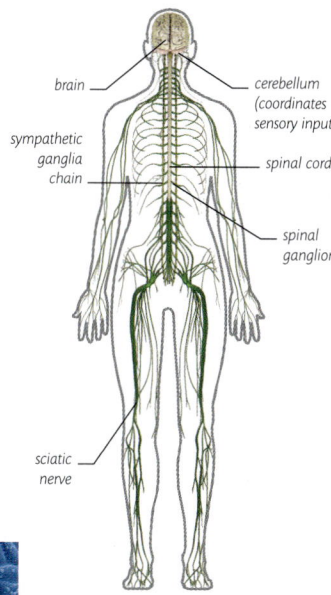

Sensory cells Many types of sensory cells have microscopic hairs that are moved by outside forces such as sound vibrations in the ear, or water currents in the neuromast organs found in a fish's lateral line (right). As the hairs move, their cells produce nerve signals that travel to the brain.

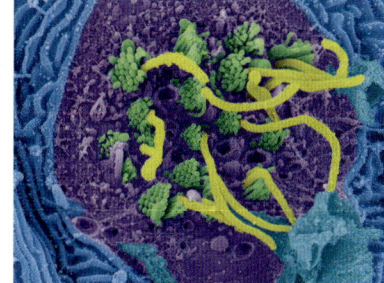

Human nervous system The spinal cord runs along a tunnel formed by aligned holes in the vertebrae, which protect it against knocks and prevent kinks. Spinal nerves, such as the sciatic nerve, branch from it into the torso and limbs. Cranial nerves branch directly from the brain to the eyes, ears, and other sense organs in the head, and to the head and face muscles.

HORMONES

In general, the hormone system works more slowly than the nervous system. Hormones are chemicals made by groups of endocrine cells scattered through various tissues or in separate endocrine glands. Each type of hormone (some animals have more than 100) spreads around the body via the blood. It works as a chemical messenger to affect certain parts known as its target organs, or tissues, usually making them work faster or release their products. Hormones maintain internal conditions, such as water balance, and control growth and development, the reproductive cycle, moulting or shedding of body coverings, and, in some animals, metamorphosis (drastic change in body shape).

Rising levels The breeding behaviour of brown hares in spring is triggered by rising levels of reproductive hormones from the sex glands – ovaries in females, testes in males. Here, an unreceptive female is boxing to fend off an unwelcome male.

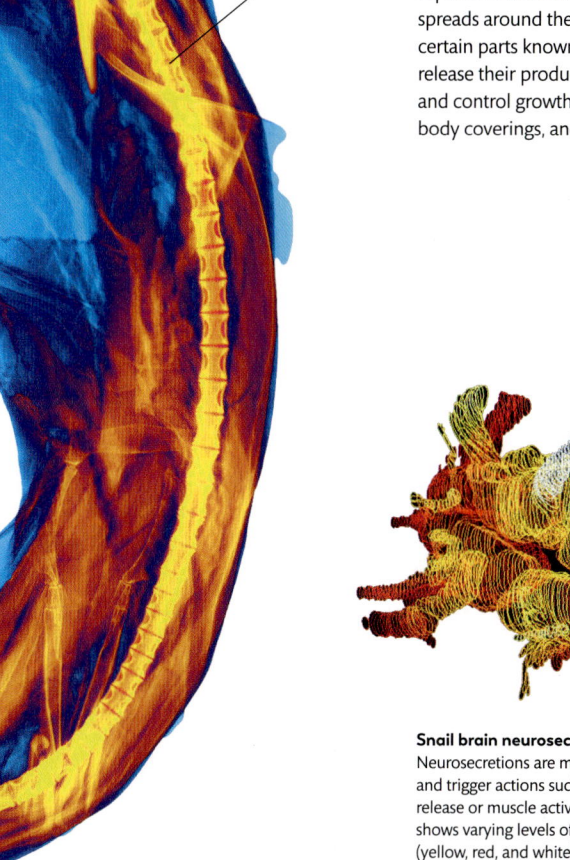

Snail brain neurosecretions Neurosecretions are made by nerve cells and trigger actions such as hormone release or muscle activity. A snail's brain shows varying levels of neurosecretion (yellow, red, and white) in response to light levels sensed by the eyes, which makes the snail active at night and restful by day.

Elephant eye Vertebrate eyes are remarkably similar in form and function. Light enters the eye through the central pupil, the size of which is controlled by muscles around the coloured iris. The light is received and processed by the retina at the back of the eyeball.

SENSES

Being able to sense what is happening around them is vital for animals' survival. Among a myriad of other things, sensory information helps them to find food and avoid predators; to know when they are too hot or too cold, or are hurt; and to improve their reproductive success by aiding the location and selection of mates.

WHAT ARE SENSES?

A sense is the reception of a stimulus that is interpreted by the brain to gain information about the external or internal environment. For example, light is gathered by the eye and interpreted by the brain into an image. The five senses most familiar to humans are hearing, sight, taste, smell, and touch. Most animals possess some or all of these senses to varying degrees, but they may also have other senses, most notably echolocation (the use of sound to locate objects), and electroreception and magnetoreception (the abilities to detect electric and magnetic fields respectively). As well as being able to sense their surroundings, animals require information about their own bodies, such as their position and movement, which is sensed by special cells. For example, thermoreceptors in the skin enable perception of temperature.

Animals may have evolved particularly acute senses, or senses in specific ranges, according to the demands of their environment and behaviour. Dogs have a well-developed sense of smell, which they use to locate prey and communicate with one another; bats can hunt at night in total darkness thanks to their ability to use ultrasound for echolocation; many insects and birds can see ultraviolet light, allowing them to detect patterns on flowers and plumage that are invisible to the human eye; and elephants can produce and hear infrasound, permitting them to communicate over many miles. The brain integrates information from all of the senses so that an animal has a mental picture of the world around it, enabling it to react accordingly. For example, a predator spotting possible prey will use sensory information to decide whether or not to launch an attack.

Tactile tasting Butterflies have taste receptors on their feet as well as in their mouthparts.

SENSORY SYSTEMS

Each sensory system comprises sensory receptors, neural pathways, and parts of the brain involved in sensory perception. Examples in vertebrates include the visual system, where receptors of colour and brightness in the retina trigger nervous impulses in the optic nerve, which travel to the primary visual cortex for processing; and the auditory system, whereby hair cells in the inner ear receive vibrations caused by sound waves, triggering nervous impulses in the auditory nerve, which travel to the primary auditory cortex. The somatosensory system detects pressure and touch; the gustatory system senses taste; and the olfactory system receives and processes information about smell. Each neuron has a threshold, above which a stimulus will cause it to fire an impulse. The nature of the nervous impulses triggered by the receptors provides the brain with information about the location of the stimulus, its intensity, and duration. For example, the longer an object touches part of the body, the more the receptor cells will trigger the nerves.

SENSES AND BEHAVIOUR

The senses play a vital role in animal behaviour. Senses are required for communication between animals – for example, to hear and see sound and visual signals, and to smell scent marks. They are needed to locate prey – for example, by sight, echolocation, or electroreception; to find mates, such as by homing in on pheromones or a mating call; and for navigation, which may be mediated by sight, smell, or magnetoreception of the Earth's magnetic field, or a combination of such cues.

Greeting ceremony Black-backed jackals greet one another by smelling scent glands located in the anal region. Smell is important in identifying members of the pack.

Nervous system In vertebrates, such as this seahorse, the central nervous system comprises the spinal cord and the brain.

Touch and vibration

Animals learn a great deal about their environment by using touch and sensing vibration. They can feel for their food and communicate without the need for sight or sound, skills that are especially helpful in the dark. The sense of touch is facilitated by structures called mechanoreceptors that respond to stimulation. Mechanoreceptors also provide feedback about an animal's movement and orientation so that it can adjust its position as necessary.

Following its nose As the star-nosed mole hunts for soil-based or aquatic prey, the 22 sensitive, fleshy tentacles around its nostrils wriggle in constant motion.

Hairy legs A spider's leg is covered in hairs that respond to touch and airborne vibrations. The base of each sensillum connects with the dendrite of a neuron, which transfers a stimulus to the brain for processing when the hair is touched.

TOUCH RECEPTORS

Most arthropods detect touch and vibration through sensory hairs called sensilla. These filaments protrude through the exoskeleton from where they are anchored in the epidermal layer below. Movement of the hair triggers a nerve impulse in an adjacent receptor cell. Vertebrate hairs work in much the same way: the base of the hair is located in a follicle with the tip of a sensory neuron wrapped around the hair shaft to receive and transmit the stimulus. In addition to hairs, the epidermal (top) and dermal (lower) layers of the skin contain a variety of different structures for detecting touch, pressure, and vibration. Mechanoreceptors may be concentrated to create a particularly sensitive area, for example on the nose of a star-nosed mole.

Multiple hairs The hairs that protrude above a mammal's skin have a variety of functions, including sensitivity to touch, insulation, camouflage, and communication.

Mammalian skin Meissner's corpuscles in the upper dermis respond to light touches, while the larger Pacinian corpuscles, located deep in the dermis, detect heavy, more sustained pressure and vibrations.

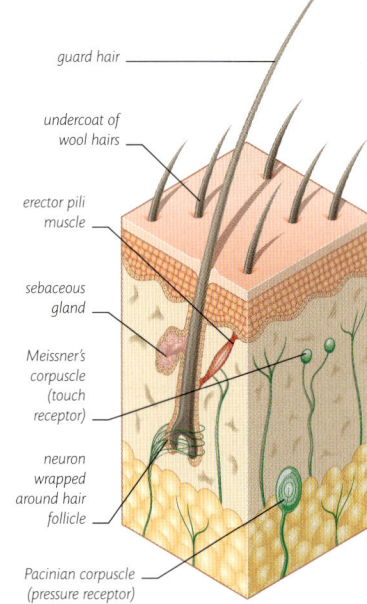

MOTION DETECTORS

Arthropod sensilla also detect movements of air or water around them, as do vertebrate whiskers (vibrissae). These stiff, long hairs are usually located around the nose and mouth or above the eyes. They are anchored in special follicles called blood sinuses, which allow even a tiny deflection of the whisker, such as might be caused by a whisper of wind, to be amplified and stimulate mechanoreceptor cells. Fishes and larval amphibians have a different system to detect movements in water. The lateral line is composed of receptors called neuromasts, each of which has several hair cells projecting into a gel-filled cap called a cupula. The cupula bends in response to water movement, allowing the animal to detect the direction of water currents.

Lateral line The lateral-line system is visible as a faint line running down each side of a fish's body. In sharks, rays, and many bony fishes, the neuromast receptor cells are located in a canal beneath the skin's surface. The canal connects with the external environment through a series of pores.

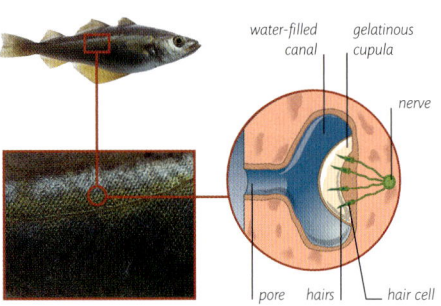

Synchronized swimming Many species of small bony fishes, such as the white salemas (grunts) seen here, form large, dense shoals as a means of protection against predators. Their lateral-line system enables the fishes to move in unison, and predators find it hard to pick out an individual target as the shoal constantly moves and makes sudden changes in direction.

GRAVITATIONAL DETECTORS

Many invertebrates possess structures called statocysts that sense changes in orientation and movement. A statocyst comprises a relatively heavy ball, the statolith, inside a hollow sphere. The statolith may be secreted by the statocyst or, as in lobsters, it may be formed of sand grains collected from the environment. The vertebrate inner ear also operates like a statocyst. Otoliths, the equivalent of statoliths, move against hair cells called cristae inside fluid-filled ducts (ampullae) to detect gravity and acceleration.

Scallops in motion Scallops propel themselves along by expelling jets of water from their shells. A statocyst provides the scallop with information on its orientation, prompting it to adjust its path accordingly.

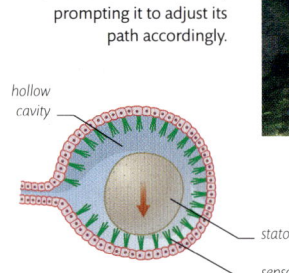

Bivalve statocyst As the animal moves, gravity acts on the statolith in the centre of the statocyst, causing it to stimulate the sensory hairs of the receptor cells against which it rests.

VIBRATION

Vibration receptors are attuned to vibrations that are transmitted through a surface, usually the ground, but also other surfaces such as tree trunks, leaves, or spiders' webs. The detection of vibrations felt through the environment is often a precursor to hearing the vibrations of sound waves transmitted through the air. In animals that lack a tympanic membrane (see p.92), such as some amphibians and reptiles, sound vibrations are transmitted through the body to the inner ear. Animals that lack ears are able to "feel" sound by detecting its vibrations, rather than hearing it. Many mechanoreceptors, including insect sensilla and Pacinian corpuscles, detect vibrations. Other vibration sensors include lyriform organs on spiders' legs, which detect the vibrations of struggling prey trapped in their webs, and Herbst corpuscles in the bills of wading birds, which detect the vibrations of prey moving in the sand. The ability to sense vibration is particularly useful underground, where sound does not travel very far and visual signals are of no use (see panel, right).

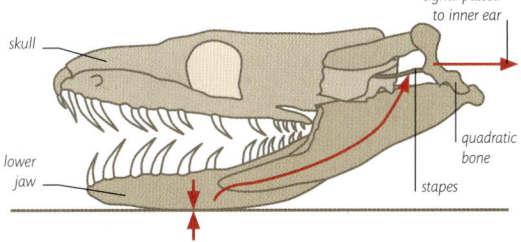

Bone conduction Snakes receive ground-borne vibrations by pressing their lower jaw to the ground. The vibrations are conducted to the stapes bone and on to the inner ear.

Sensitive feet This raft spider can detect aquatic prey by placing its front two pairs of legs on the surface of a pool of water.

CASE STUDY SEISMIC SIGNALLING

Cape mole-rats communicate by drumming their hind legs on the floor of their individual burrows to create vibrations. During a typical foot-thumping interaction, a male and a female mole-rat will drum together in synchrony. Their seismic signals travel through the ground to neighbouring burrows more efficiently than sound.

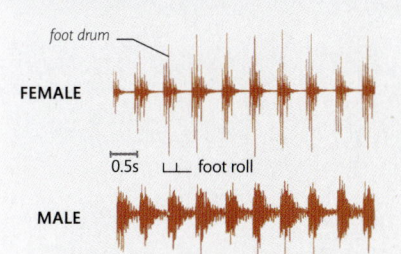

Foot-thumping session When ready to breed, Cape mole-rats signal their sex by drumming at different tempos in order to locate a mate.

The cat's whiskers Whiskers are incredibly sensitive to touch and air movement. They permit animals, such as this leopard, to feel their way and hunt in conditions of poor visibility.

Taste and smell

Taste and smell are important senses for many animals, helping them to find food and mates, communicate, and navigate. Both senses are mediated by special cells called chemoreceptors, which bind with specific chemicals then send a nervous impulse to the brain, where the taste or smell is processed.

TASTE

The sense of taste allows an animal to detect and identify molecules from objects that come into contact with its gustatory (taste) receptors. These sensory cells may be concentrated in different regions, for example, in the mouth or on mouthparts, in the skin, or on the feet, depending on the animal. They can be used to find food and check that it is good to eat. For example, flies have gustatory sensilla (hairs) on their feet with which they taste things they land on. The sensilla are sensitive to different substances, such as sugars, salts, or water. Taste is also used by some animals as a means of chemical communication.

Catfish whiskers The whiskerlike barbels around the mouths and noses of catfishes are covered with taste buds. The barbels are used to locate food in the murky waters at the bottoms of streams and rivers.

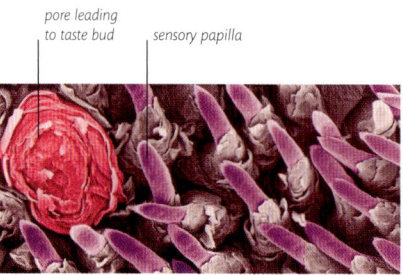

pore leading to taste bud   sensory papilla

Tasting with care The surface of a mammal's tongue (above) is covered with sensory papillae, which surround small pores that lead to barrel-shaped taste buds beneath. Mammals detect flavours with their tongues and some, such as the brown hyena (left), will taste scent marks to gain information about another individual.

Forked tongue Snakes flick their tongues in and out to transfer odour-bearing molecules from the air, water, or ground to the Jacobson's organ. Elephants do the same thing, but instead use the fleshy "finger" at the tip of their trunks.

SMELL

The sense of smell is governed by olfactory receptors, which detect odour molecules from objects at a distance. The molecules may be carried on the air or in water. On reaching an animal, the molecules bind to the membrane of olfactory hairs (cilia). In arthropods, these are usually located in pits within the exoskeleton or on bristly extensions of the exoskeleton. In vertebrates, the cilia are usually located on the surface of the olfactory tissue (epithelium) in the nasal cavity of the nose. Glands within the epithelium secrete mucus that keeps the surface moist, helping to trap the odour molecules. Mammals, particularly rodents and carnivores, have a good sense of smell. They use it to find food, and many use scent as a means of communication – to mark their territory, for example.

Mouse olfactory system The main olfactory epithelium is rich in neurons that are receptive to odour. They join to form the olfactory nerve, which connects to the olfactory bulb in the forebrain. The vomeronasal organ detects pheromones and connects to the accessory olfactory bulb.

Eurasian water shrews have poor eyesight, but this is compensated for by their acute sense of smell.

Southern giant petrels have long tubular nostrils with which they can locate food by day or night.

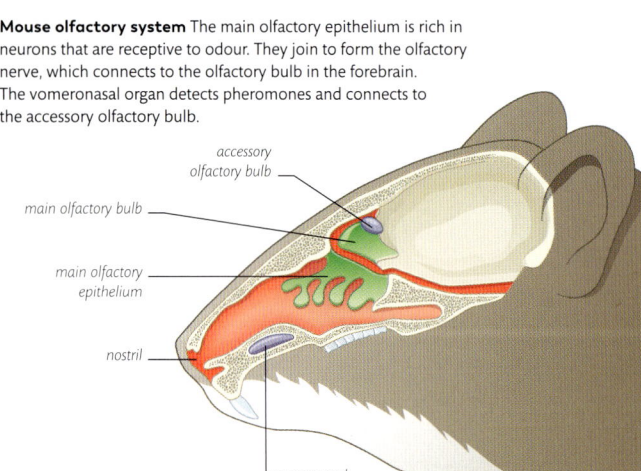

accessory olfactory bulb
main olfactory bulb
main olfactory epithelium
nostril
vomeronasal organ

Emperor moth males can detect the scent of a female 11 km (6 miles) away using their antennae.

CASE STUDY
SNIFFING OUT CANCER

Dogs are renowned for having a good sense of smell. Their sensitive noses have been employed by humans to assist in various tasks, such as tracking missing people and detecting illegal substances. Research shows that dogs can sense whether or not a person has breast or lung cancer according to the smell of their breath. Cancerous cells produce different metabolic waste products to normal cells, and it is these products that dogs identify. The advantage of canine help is that cancers may be diagnosed earlier, leading to more effective treatment.

TASTING THE AIR

Many vertebrates have a Jacobson's or vomeronasal organ, a patch of specialized olfactory epithelium, situated in the roof of the mouth at the base of the nasal cavity. This organ is particularly sensitive to airborne molecules contained in scents such as pheromones, which are used for chemical communication between animals of the same species. Some mammals, including most ungulates and felids, such as lions and tigers, raise their heads and grimace when testing the sexual receptivity of a female, a behaviour known as the flehmen response. Lizards and snakes use the Jacobson's organ to detect chemicals such as those produced by potential prey or a possible predator, transferring the molecules from the air with their tongues. This is why they constantly flick their tongues when exploring their surroundings or when they have been disturbed.

Flehmen response Ungulates such as zebras (top) and giraffes (bottom), show a characteristic behaviour when tasting the air for pheromones. They pull the upper lip back and draw air across the vomeronasal organ. Through its use, a male is able to tell whether a female is ready to mate.

Jacobson's organ In snakes, the Jacobson's organ has two small openings in the roof of the mouth into which the tips of the snake's forked tongue are inserted when it is withdrawn.

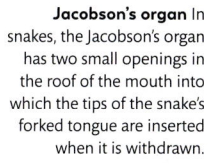
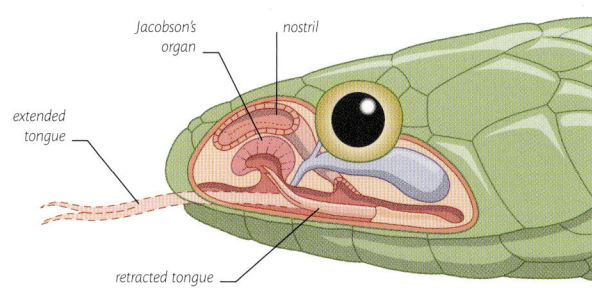

Vision

Vision, or visual perception, is the way in which animals interpret information about their environment using visible light. Some animals are sensitive only to the presence or absence of light, while others can determine differences in the wavelength of light, an ability known as colour vision. The visual ability of an animal influences many aspects of its behaviour, including feeding, defence, and courtship.

WHAT IS AN EYE?

Light is effectively parcels of energy called photons, which travel in a wave, the frequency (or wavelength) of which is proportional to the energy they contain. An eye is an organ that detects this light and translates it via nervous impulses to the brain, where the information is processed further. There is a wide variety of eye designs across the animal kingdom, relating to the different types of environments that animals inhabit and the different behavioural tasks they undertake.

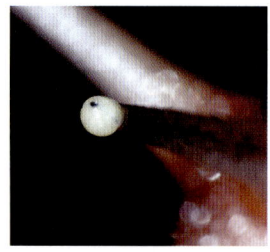

African land snail eyes can only distinguish between light and dark.

COMPOUND EYES

Most arthropods have eyes formed from multiple units called ommatidia. Each of these consists of a lens to focus light into a cell, a transparent crystalline cone to funnel the light, and visual cells that absorb the light and trigger a nervous impulse. The more ommatidia an eye has, the more refined the resulting image. Each cell is angled in a slightly different way, collecting light from a slightly different area of the visual scene. This makes compound eyes excellent at detecting motion, as the ommatidia are consecutively turned on and off as an object passes across the field of vision.

Hoverfly eyes The multi-faceted compound eyes of the hoverfly are composed of many thousands of tightly packed ommatidia. Different ommatidia have different visual pigments, allowing the fly to see different colours of light.

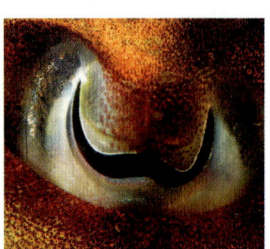

Cuttlefish have excellent eyesight and distinctive w-shaped pupils.

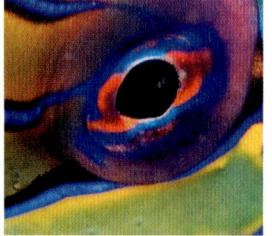

Mandarin fishes, like most tropical fishes, have good colour vision.

Red-eyed treefrogs have a third eyelid that helps keep the eye clean.

Chameleons can move their eyes independently of each other.

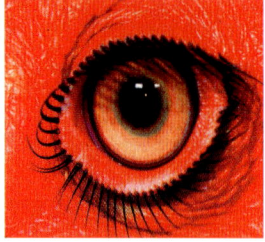

Southern ground hornbill eyes have long eyelashes that act as sunshades.

Tigers can see well at night because of a mirrorlike layer in their eyes.

MONOCULAR AND BINOCULAR VISION

There are many benefits to having two eyes, both as a backup system should one become damaged, and as a way to increase the field of view. But perhaps the greatest benefit is that they can be used together to gather information about distance. Eye position relates to an animal's behavioural need. Many animals have eyes positioned on the sides of their head, offering a very wide field of view, of up to 360°, from which to watch for predators. Most of this field is monocular, with little sense of depth. Predators, however, typically have forward-facing eyes, with a comparatively wide overlap of the visual fields. This binocular vision enables predators to judge distances with great accuracy.

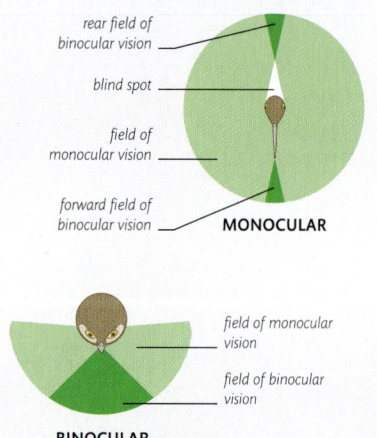

VERTEBRATE EYES

Light enters a vertebrate's eye through the transparent cornea, which bends the rays. The light rays pass through a fluid-filled space to the iris, a pigmented, muscular layer that can alter the diameter of its central hole, the pupil, and so control light entering the eye. The light rays reach the crystalline lens, which can be squeezed or relaxed to bend and focus the light rays onto the retina at the rear of the eye, where an upside-down image is formed. The retina is a layer of light-sensitive cells, which convert the information from the light rays into nerve signals. The optic nerve carries the signals to the brain, where an upright image is formed.

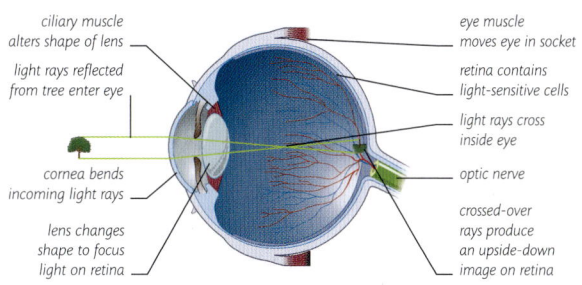

Camera eye The eyes of all vertebrates share a common design, which works like a camera, using a lens to focus light and form an image.

Rods and cones There are two types of photoreceptor in the retina. Rods (stained yellow) are sensitive in low light while cone cells (stained blue) are involved in colour vision.

Ommatidia Each ommatidium sees a single image, which the animal's brain puts together, forming a mosaic.

Most complex eye Mantis shrimps have 12 different spectral receptor types in their compound eyes, sensitive to wavelengths ranging from ultraviolet to infrared.

COLOUR VISION

Colour vision is the ability of an animal to differentiate between objects based upon the wavelength of light they emit or reflect. Cone cells contain pigments that are "tuned" to absorb light from different regions of the visible spectrum (see below), which the brain detects and translates as colour. The more cone pigments an animal has, the more colours it can tell apart. Old World monkeys and primates (including humans) have three types of cone cell, while many fishes and birds have four. Most mammals have just two cones and see in a similar way to a "colour-blind" human.

ABSORPTION RANGES OF THREE CONE PIGMENTS

Cone pigments are classified by the wavelength of light they are most sensitive to, for example short-wave (or "blue" light), medium-wave ("green" light), or long-wave ("red" light).

Mandrill In the animal kingdom, colour is widely used for sexual signalling. The red colour of a male mandrill's face conveys information about his age, rank, and testosterone levels.

BEYOND THE VISIBLE SPECTRUM

Humans are sensitive to wavelengths of light in the range 400–700 nanometres (nm), but many animals, including birds, insects, reptiles, and fishes, can detect short-wavelength light in the near-ultraviolet (UV) range (320–400 nm). UV sensitivity is used in many behaviours, including courtship (see p.301) and predation. An unrelated ability is that of many animals, including insects, birds, and cephalopods, to perceive polarized light. Polarization occurs when, for example, sunlight is scattered by atmospheric particles to vibrate in a specific plane. The way in which sunlight is polarized is related to the sun's position, so animals can use it to navigate.

Nectar guides To human eyes, this flower is yellow, but a UV-sensitive camera reveals the patterns that guide insects to the nectar at its centre.

Extra eyes A number of flying insects, such as the greater banded hornet (*Vespa tropica*), have additional light-sensing eyes, or ocelli. The three single-lens ocelli can be seen in this image near the top of the head, between the two compound eyes. An ocellus does not build up an image, but can rapidly detect changes in light intensity, which helps the insect to avoid danger.

Hearing

The ability to hear allows animals to sense the rustles of approaching prey or respond to a mating call. In order to hear, an animal must have a mechanism for detecting the vibration of sound waves; sound receptor cells have tiny hairs that are deflected by sound waves, triggering nervous impulses that are processed in the brain.

SOUND

Sound is produced by pressure waves that create disturbance in a medium (usually air or water) detectable by hearing apparatus. Pressure waves that are transmitted through a solid medium, such as the ground, are usually referred to as vibrations. The number of oscillations or vibrations per second is called the frequency of the sound and is measured in hertz (Hz). The frequency of the sound wave determines its pitch: a high-pitched sound, such as a bird whistling, makes the air molecules vibrate backwards and forwards more times each second than a low-pitched sound, such as the croak of a bullfrog.

SOUND DETECTION

Movement-sensitive sensilla (hairs) in insects detect the vibrations of sound waves. Some insects, including grasshoppers and some moth species, have tympanic ears, which are more similar in structure to those of frogs, some reptiles, birds, and mammals (although grasshoppers have eardrums in their abdomen rather than their head). Tympanic ears have a thin membrane that transmits sound vibrations. In many frogs, the membrane is visible on the sides of the head, while in other animals it is obscured by elaborate ear structures that improve sound reception. Some fish use their swim bladder as a hydrophone to transmit sound waves through small bones that connect it to the inner ear. To communicate over long distances, elephants make infrasonic rumbles that they can detect through their feet and trunks as well as with their ears (see p.434).

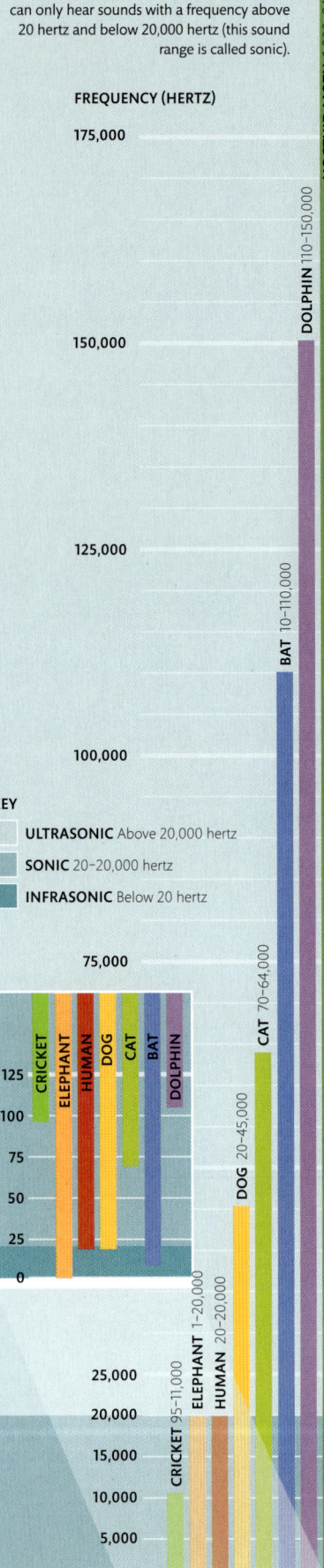

Hearing ranges There is a vast array of hearing ranges across the animal kingdom. Humans can only hear sounds with a frequency above 20 hertz and below 20,000 hertz (this sound range is called sonic).

ULTRASONIC ABOVE 20,000 HERTZ

SONIC 20–20,000 HERTZ

INFRASONIC BELOW 20 HERTZ

Sound waves Sounds emitted and perceived by animals can be broadly separated according to frequency into infrasonic (very low frequency), sonic, and ultrasonic (very high frequency).

Large eardrum For each species of frog, the size of the tympanic membrane (behind the eye), and the sensitivity of the female's ear, is related to the frequency of the male's call.

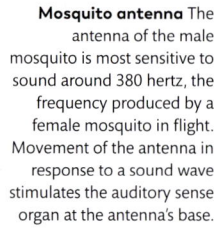

Mosquito antenna The antenna of the male mosquito is most sensitive to sound around 380 hertz, the frequency produced by a female mosquito in flight. Movement of the antenna in response to a sound wave stimulates the auditory sense organ at the antenna's base.

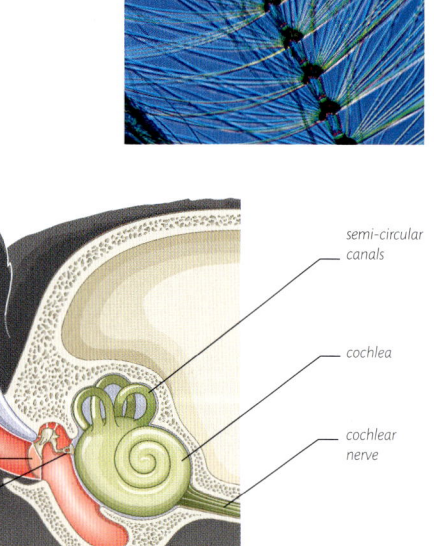

Mammalian ear structure A typical mammalian ear comprises the external ear (pinna or auricle), which leads to the tympanic membrane; the middle ear, an air-filled cavity across which sound is transferred by the auditory ossicles; and the inner ear, where the sound receptor cells are located.

SOUND LOCALIZATION

The presence of two ears allows an animal to determine the origin of a sound through localization. Unless the animal is facing directly towards the sound source there is a delay between the sound arriving at the ear nearest to and furthest from the source. The brain uses this split-second delay to calculate the direction from which the sound came. To gain information about the height of a sound, the two ears must be asymmetrically placed, as in the barn owl. Its heart-shaped facial disk of feathers acts like a radar dish, collecting sound and guiding it to the ear drums within the skull.

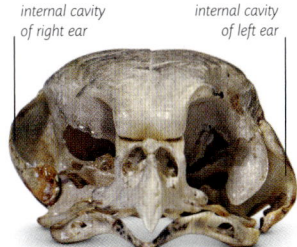

Asymmetric ears In some species of owl, the right ear cavity is usually higher (and larger) than the left, so a sound coming from below the owl's line of sight will arrive sooner at the left ear.

SOUND RECEPTION TIME LAG

A Western barn owl can detect a time lag of 30 milliseconds (ms) between sound reaching each of its ears. This information is processed by 10,000 space-specific neurons. To pinpoint its prey, the owl moves its head until the sound reaches both ears at the same time.

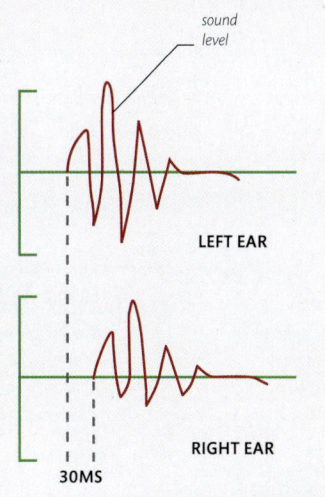

Pinpointing prey A barn owl localizes sound so well that it can hunt in total darkness by listening for the movement of its prey, usually small rodents, rustling through the undergrowth.

Collecting sound The huge ears of the bat-eared fox gather and amplify the sounds of its insect prey moving beneath the surface of the soil.

Wrens are tiny, but their songs can be heard from hundreds of metres.

Rattlesnakes shake the modified scales at the tip of their tails.

SOUND GENERATION

Animals produce sounds in many different ways. Perhaps the simplest form of sound production is hitting something, often the ground, with a body part. For example, ants stamp their feet, fiddler crabs bang their claws, and mole-rats thump with their heads or feet. Many insects and some other arthropods generate sound by rubbing parts of their body together, a method called stridulation (see p.425). Terrestrial vertebrates make vocalizations by using the movement of air in the respiratory system. For example, vibrations of the vocal cords of the larynx produce a wolf's howl, while bird calls and songs are produced by the syrinx (see right).

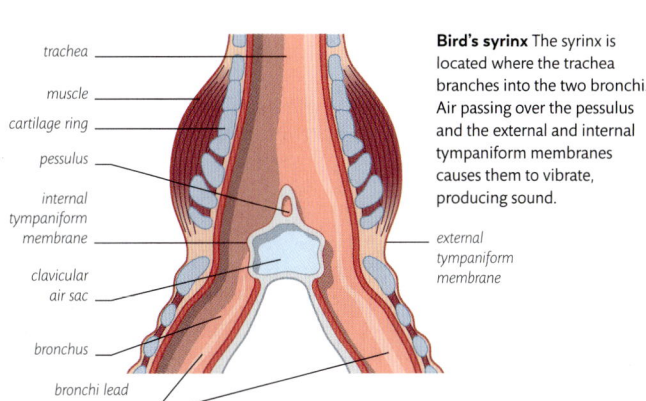

Bird's syrinx The syrinx is located where the trachea branches into the two bronchi. Air passing over the pessulus and the external and internal tympaniform membranes causes them to vibrate, producing sound.

Wolves howl to signal ownership of their territory to other wolf packs.

Echolocation

Echolocation, also called biosonar, is the ability to locate objects through the use of sound. Animals that echolocate form an image of their surroundings from returning echoes, allowing them to pick a path through vegetation or a cave system, or to home in on their prey in the dark. The majority of bats use very high-frequency (ultrasonic) calls to echolocate, whereas dolphins and most other echolocators use clicks.

Ghost bat False vampire bats such as the ghost bat of northern Australia have pointed, leaf-shaped nose-leaves through which they direct their calls at both invertebrate and vertebrate prey. Their large ears meet in the middle and each has a prominent tragus.

ECHOLOCATION CALLS

Echolocation calls can be sonic – that is within the range of human hearing – but most echolocators use very high-frequency, or ultrasonic, calls, which are measured in kilohertz (kHz). The types of call are incredibly diverse. Different bat species produce different calls according to the habitats in which they forage. A fast-flying species that hunts in the open air uses relatively low-frequency calls that travel further ahead of the bat, while a slower-flying species feeding in a cluttered habitat, such as among trees, requires detailed resolution gained from higher-frequency calls. Bat echolocation calls typically range from 20–100 kHz, whereas some species of toothed whales use even higher-frequency clicks, with those of bottlenose dolphins reaching 220 kHz. Sperm whale clicks range from 40 Hz–15 kHz.

BAT SONOGRAMS

Sonograms depict the frequency range, duration, repetition rate, and shape of the echolocation call. Calls from common pipistrelle, Daubenton's, and Leisler's bats differ in all of these attributes.

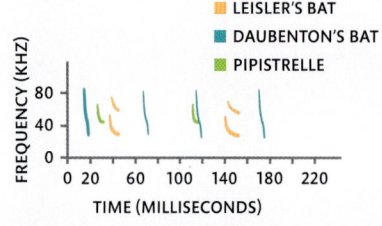

BATS

The majority of bat species are sophisticated echolocators, producing their ultrasonic calls in the larynx. Most of these bats emit the call through their mouth, but some send it out through their nose, which has lead to the evolution of elaborate nose ornamentation. Many bats have large, forward-facing ears with a projecting lobe called the tragus that helps to receive returning echoes. Bats usually emit one call for each wingbeat when flying. Their calls are so loud that bats risk deafening themselves. To avoid this, muscles in the middle ear contract when the bat calls and then relax to allow the returning echo to be heard before the bat calls again. When potential prey has been located, the rate of calling increases as the bat homes in on its target.

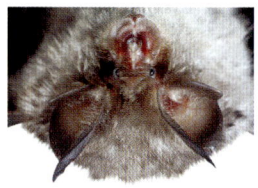

Lesser horseshoe bat This bat is named for its small size and horseshoe-shaped nose-leaf. Furrows in the nose-leaf help to shape and focus the beam of sound as it is emitted through the nose.

Egyptian fruit bat This species belongs to a genus of fruit bats that echolocate by producing pairs of sharp clicks with their tongue. They have good eyesight and use this relatively crude form of echolocation to find their way in dark caves.

Sperm whale At up to 20 m (66 ft) in length, the sperm whale is the largest toothed whale. Its huge, square-ended head contains a spermaceti organ, a large mass of waxy oil, which focuses echolocation clicks into a beam.

SPERM WHALE SONOGRAM

This sonogram of a single sperm whale echolocating shows it emitting a steady series of clicks while searching for prey. Sperm whales eat mainly octopuses and squid, even giant squid.

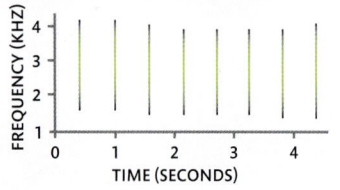

Bottlenose dolphins vocalizing Dolphins produce rapid bursts of ultrasonic clicks to locate prey. They also make an array of other, lower-frequency sounds to communicate with each other, including whistles and squeaks.

TOOTHED WHALES

Echolocation allows toothed whales to pursue agile prey, even in dark or turbid waters. Porpoises and dolphins produce ultrasonic clicks by forcing air between phonic lips in their nasal passages. The lips open and close, causing the surrounding tissue to vibrate and form sound waves. These bounce off the bony cribriform plate at the front of the skull and are focused into a beam by the melon, which the hunter aims at its prey. Sperm whales have a different anatomy for producing echolocation clicks. The left nasal passage is used for breathing, while the right is used for sound production. Sound waves pass through an oil-filled spermaceti organ, rebound off an air sac at the rear of the head, and are focused into a beam of sound through several fatty lenses. Experiments with bottlenose dolphins have shown them to be extremely sophisticated echolocators, capable of identifying submerged objects by size, shape, or composition. This enables them to learn the echo signatures of their preferred prey species.

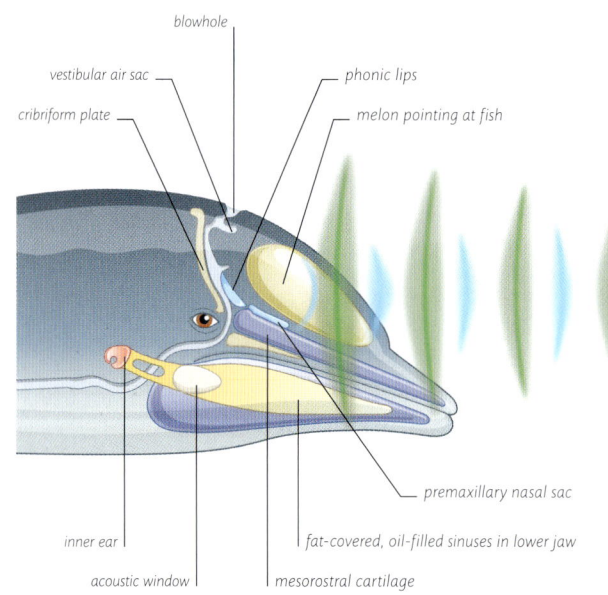

BIRDS

Only two families of birds are known to echolocate: the cave swiftlets of Southeast Asia and Australia and the oilbirds of South America. Both roost deep inside caves, where the ability to see is not of much use, so instead they use sound to avoid bumping into the rock walls and each other, and to find their nests. They produce low-frequency clicks of less than 15 kHz by contracting muscles around the vocal organ, or syrinx (see p.93), which cause the tympaniform membranes to vibrate. Their echolocation is low resolution and both groups feed by sight; swiftlets on insects during the day and oilbirds on oil palm and laurel fruits at night.

AUSTRALIAN SWIFTLET ECHOGRAMS

The swiftlet's clicks are emitted in pairs around 18 milliseconds apart. The first click has a frequency of most energy between 3.3 and 5.5 kHz and the second, louder, click has a frequency of between 4.1 and 5.5 kHz.

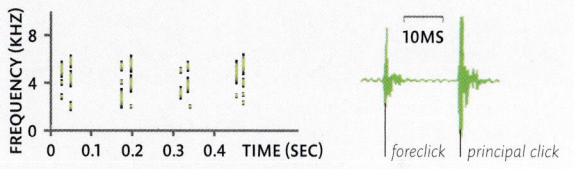

Cave bird As the Australian swiftlet flies deeper into the darkness of its cave, it lessens the interval between the pairs of clicks it emits to gain more information from faster-returning echoes.

OTHER MAMMALS

Bats and toothed whales have by far the most sophisticated echolocation among mammals, although some nocturnal insectivores also use primitive echolocation to explore their habitats and catch their insect prey. Shrews produce ultrasonic calls from the larynx, whereas the tenrecs of Madagascar use less-specialized tongue clicks. In addition, both may communicate with other individuals at ultrasonic frequencies. The aye-aye, also from Madagascar, uses sound to locate its prey too, but in a very different manner. It taps a tree trunk with its long, bony middle finger and listens for the larvae of wood-boring beetles moving underneath (see p.215).

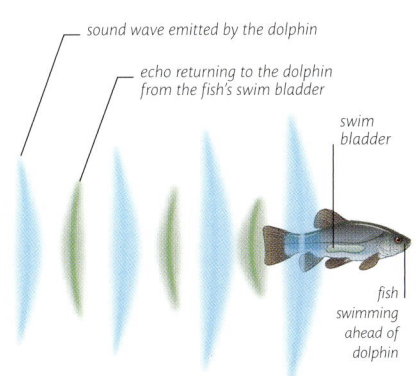

Detecting prey Dolphins use the melon, an oily lump of tissue behind the forehead, to focus their outgoing sound waves into a beam. Echoes returning from a fish in the dolphin's path are transferred through oil-filled sinuses in the lower jaw to the inner ear.

Tongue-clicking tenrec The streaked tenrec searches for worms and grubs in the Madagascan rainforest floor, making a series of low-frequency tongue clicks to locate its prey.

Electricity and magnetism

Many animals possess the ability to sense electric and magnetic fields. Some detect the electrical signals generated by the muscles of other animals, while others produce their own electricity, either to use in prey location, navigation, or communication, or as a means of defence or prey capture. Animals with a magnetic sense use the Earth's magnetic field for navigation or orientation.

Sensitive bill The duck-billed platypus has around 40,000 electroreceptors in its bill, which sense the electric fields of prey concealed in muddy river bottoms.

ELECTRORECEPTION

Animals that are capable of detecting electrical impulses but do not generate them are said to show "passive" electroreception. Those that both receive and generate electrical signals are capable of "active" electroreception. Electroreception is more common among animals living in water than on land because of the capacity of water to conduct electricity. The majority of electroreceptive animals are fishes, but monotreme mammals also possess the ability. For example, the long-beaked echidna, which lives in wet tropical forest, has around 2,000 electroreceptors in its beak, which it uses to track down earthworms and other soil-dwelling prey. This use of electric fields to find food is known as electrolocation. The structures responsible for electroreception are called ampullary receptors. The electroreceptive sense organs found in sharks and rays are known as ampullae of Lorenzini after the Italian anatomist Stefano Lorenzini, who described their structure in 1678; their function remained a mystery until the 20th century.

Elephantnose fish Weakly electric fishes, like this elephantnose fish, generate small electrical pulses of less than 1 volt. They then detect distortions in the electrical fields they produce and use these for navigation, location of prey, and communication.

Short-beaked echidna The short-beaked echidna inhabits drier habitats than the long-beaked echidna and has only around 400 electroreceptors at the tip of its beak. It uses them to locate prey when conditions are wet, for example, when it rains.

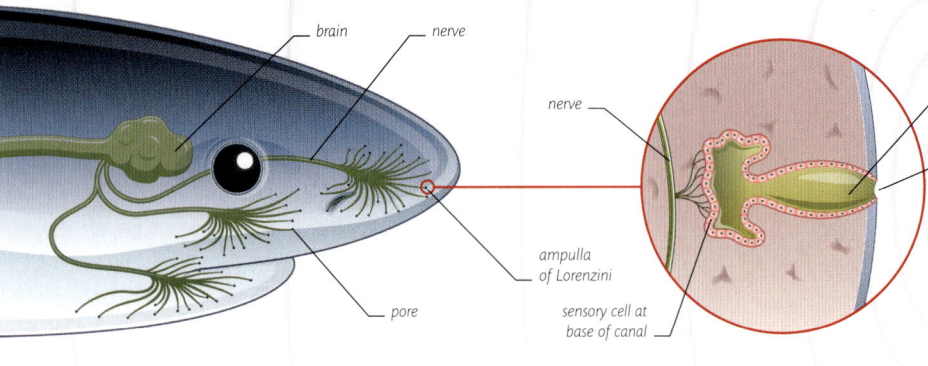

Sensing electric fields An ampulla of Lorenzini consists of a pore in the skin opening to a gel-filled canal. It works by detecting the difference in voltage between the pore and the base of the canal, allowing the shark to sense electric fields such as those generated by the muscles of a fish.

ELECTROGENESIS

Electrogenesis is the production of an electrical discharge by an animal. Strongly electric fishes, such as the electric eel, electric catfishes, and electric rays, produce much higher voltage pulses than weakly electric fishes. The organs of electrogenesis, called electrocytes or electroplaques, are usually modified muscle cells or occasionally nerve cells. The electric eel has between 5,000 and 6,000 electroplaques stacked in series in its abdomen, enabling it to generate huge shocks of up to 600 volts to stun prey when hunting. The electric eel also uses lower-voltage pulses of around 10 volts for navigating and detecting prey. Electric rays use the electric organs in their heads to electrocute prey or stun a potential predator. The size of the electric discharge varies from 8 to 200 volts, depending on the species. The electric catfish produces its electrical discharge in its skin.

Stunning predator Despite its name and appearance, the electric eel is not a true eel but a type of freshwater fish known as a knifefish.

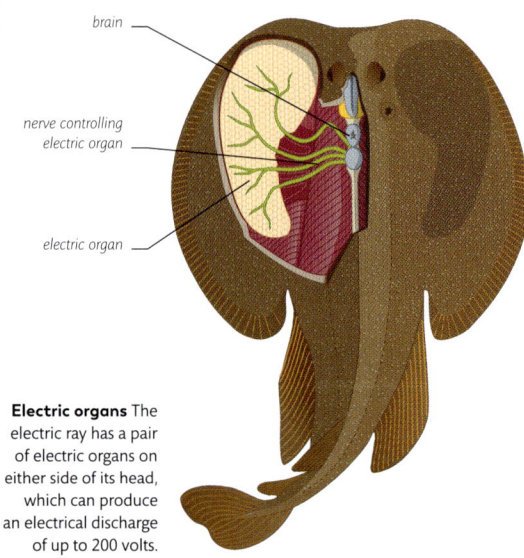

Electric organs The electric ray has a pair of electric organs on either side of its head, which can produce an electrical discharge of up to 200 volts.

Mako shark Sharks' snouts are covered with electroreceptors called ampullae of Lorenzini, which appear as dark spots. Sharks may also orient themselves relative to the Earth's magnetic field by using their own electric field and those generated by ocean currents.

MAGNETORECEPTION

Some animals are able to perceive the Earth's magnetic field and use it for navigation. This ability to detect changes in the magnetic field is called magnetoreception. At least two different mechanisms may be involved. The first involves crystals of magnetite, a magnetic form of iron oxide, which has been found in many species – for example in the upper bill of pigeons, in the abdomen of honey bees, and in the head of trout. Clusters of the mineral are thought to be sensitive to changes in magnetic intensity. The second mechanism is known as the "radical pair model". It is thought that a magnetic field alters the spin of electrons in a specialized photopigment called cryptochrome, allowing the direction of the field to be determined. It is possible that birds might use both mechanisms simultaneously: magnetite in the beak to sense the intensity of the magnetic field and so locate magnetic north; and cryptochrome in the right eye to sense the direction in which they are flying.

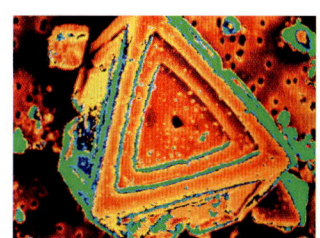

Magnetic mineral This scanning electron micrograph of a particle of magnetite reveals the mineral's classic octahedral shape. It is the most magnetic of all the naturally occurring minerals on Earth.

North and south Magnetic termite mounds are aligned north-south so that their broad, flat sides face east and west, helping to keep the mound at a stable 30°C (86°F). Experiments have shown that termites use the Earth's magnetic field to orient their mounds.

Heading for home Experimental alteration of the magnetic field around the lofts of homing pigeons has been shown to disrupt their homing ability, lending weight to the theory that they use magnetic fields when navigating their way home.

Animal Behaviour

Living space

104
Home ranges and territories

116
Migration

130
Animal architects

At home on the ice The Antarctic ice floes are among the most extreme habitats on the planet. Temperatures regularly plunge below freezing, yet chinstrap penguins make their home in this spectacular landscape with few predators and access to plenty of food in the sea.

LIVING SPACE

An animal's living space should contain all an animal needs to survive. The living space might be very small if the animal is fixed in position, such as an adult barnacle, or very broad if the animal moves about a lot in the course of feeding or if it is a species that migrates.

HABITAT CHOICE
Put simply, an animal's habitat is its living space. Animals choose to live in a habitat that enables them to maximize their fitness by providing all they need to produce offspring and increase their own survival. Animals show adaptations, both physical and behavioural, to their preferred habitats. For example, coal tits prefer to live in pine forests while blue tits like oak woods. Young coal tits are better adapted to foraging among pine needles, whereas blue tits are more adept at searching for food among oak leaves.

HOME RANGE, TERRITORY, AND MIGRATION
An animal's home range contains places for it to sleep, breed, and feed. It may spend the majority of its time in one or more core areas of the range and venture to the periphery only occasionally. Animals may disperse from their home range into another or migrate periodically between different home ranges, which can be separated by vast distances. Many animals defend all or part of their home range as a territory, either year round or just at certain times. For example, they may guard a mating site during the breeding season, or a particular seasonal food source, or a shelter such as a den or nest. Territories are often marked to warn neighbouring animals of the territory owner's presence. These behaviours – dispersal, migration, and territoriality – have costs in terms of predation risk, energy, and time. In order to be worthwhile, the benefits must outweigh the costs.

SURVIVING EXTREMES
Around the world, animals cope with an astounding variety of environmental conditions, and they have evolved a wide range of physiological and behavioural adaptations to enable them to survive. Some animals possess a natural antifreeze and can survive being frozen; others have thick insulating blubber, fur, or feathers to avoid becoming chilled. Many animals hibernate during cold periods or aestivate during warm ones, reducing their metabolic, heart, and breathing rates to the bare minimum until conditions change and they can be active again. And some species can survive on very little water by storing it or obtaining it only from their food.

EXTREME PLACES TO LIVE

Coldest Emperor penguins live in Antarctica, where temperatures reach -40°C (-40°F). Arctic beetles also withstand -40°C in the wild, but have been chilled to -87°C (-125°F) in a laboratory.

Hottest Pompeii worms live around deep-sea hydrothermal vents in the Pacific Ocean, where water is heated to 300°C (570°F). The worms hold their heads in cooler water than their tails.

Driest Péringuey's desert adder lives in the Namib Desert in Namibia, which receives less than 1cm (3/8 in) of rain each year. The snake obtains most of its water requirements from the lizards it eats.

Highest altitude Yaks roam up to 6,000m (19,700ft) and red-billed choughs up to 8,000m (26,000ft) above sea level in the Himalayas. Cranes have been recorded at 10,000m (33,000ft).

Highest pressure The fangtooth fish is found at depths of 5,000m (16,400ft). In addition to high pressures, deep-sea fishes must cope with cold water temperatures, reduced oxygen, and little to no ambient light.

Highest salinity Brine shrimps live in hypersaline lakes where salinity may be 25 per cent (normal sea water is around 3.5 per cent). The shrimps and algal blooms colour the water red and green.

Home ranges and territories

A home range is the place where an animal lives. Whether an animal defends all or part of its home range as a territory or coexists peacefully with others on an undefended home range depends on whether the benefits of being territorial outweigh the costs of territory defence. Some species become territorial for part of the annual cycle and are non-territorial occupants of a home range for the rest of the year.

HOME RANGES

A home range comprises all areas used by an animal during its everyday movements. It should be large enough to contain food for the animal and its young, and other resources, such as shelter and water. Home ranges consequently vary in size according to resource availability. Polar bears, for example, have huge ranges of up to 125,000 square km (48,250 square miles) because their prey is sparsely distributed. An animal's home range might overlap with those of others, or it may travel beyond its own home range to find a mate. Home ranges can be three-dimensional; plankton and fishes move up and down within the water column, while bats and vultures soar into the sky.

CASE STUDY SPATIAL LEARNING

In 1958, Dutch ethologist Niko Tinbergen showed that digger wasps find their nest entrance by remembering the configuration of objects around it. After emerging from her burrow, the female wasp flies around the landmarks, in this case a circle of pine cones. If the circle is moved once the wasp has left to hunt she will search for her nest in the location indicated by the cones when she returns.

TERRITORIES

Many animals defend territories against intruders. Territorial boundaries are often marked to announce the owner's presence, and so avoid potentially harmful confrontations between neighbours. Marking may involve visual displays, scent, or audible signals. An incursion into another animal's territory can escalate to combat if the intruder persists. In social species, larger groups often win territorial disputes. The advantage of territoriality is that the territory holder can monopolize resources such as food or a good breeding site within the territory.

Aggressive defence A northern gannet's territory comprises its nest and a small space around it. It viciously attacks any bird other than its partner that ventures within reach.

DISPERSAL

Dispersal occurs when an animal leaves one home range or territory to establish its own elsewhere. It may be forced to depart because changing environmental conditions have rendered its current habitat unsuitable. Alternatively, an animal may leave an area to avoid competition with rivals for food or other resources. Dispersal is also a mechanism whereby animals avoid breeding with near relatives. In many species, the males disperse while the females stay at, or close to, their birth territory. In some cases, once young animals become independent, they are chased away by their parents. These behaviours ensure that the species does not become inbred.

Scent-marking Adult black bears rub their backs, shoulders, and the backs of their heads on trees to scent-mark their territorial boundaries and to advertise their presence to prospective mates.

Spiderlings dispersing Newly hatched garden spiders cluster for defence, then disperse in different directions by walking or using a strand of silk to catch the wind.

Common limpet
Home scar
SPECIES *Patella vulgata* **SIZE** Up to 6 cm (2¼ in) (shell diameter) **DISTRIBUTION** Temperate rocky shores throughout Europe, from Norway southwards to Portugal

The common limpet grinds circular scars with the edge of its shell into the rocks it lives on. When submerged at high tide, it moves 1 m (3¼ ft) or more away from its home scar to forage on algae. It returns before the water recedes by following chemical cues in its mucus trail (but can navigate home via a different route if needed). Settling in the scar helps it create a strong seal to avoid both predation and desiccation when left exposed on the rocks at low tide. Limpets play an important role on rocky shores, keeping the substrate clear of algae, allowing other organisms to colonize.

Dancing white lady spider
Keeping a distance
SPECIES *Leucorchestris arenicola* **SIZE** 1.5–3.5 cm (½–1½ in) **DISTRIBUTION** Namib Desert, Namibia

The dancing white lady spider inhabits a long, silk-lined burrow covered by a trap door made from an interwoven sheet of sand and silk. She rests deep underground during the day, becoming active at night, ready to ambush prey. Each spider's territory has a radius of 1–3 m (3¼–9¾ ft) around its burrow, depending on its age and sex. Females stay put at night while an adult male may wander some 300 m (985 ft) across the dunes in search of a mate. This perilous journey may take him into the territories of several males that readily resort to cannibalism to protect their patch. When he encounters a female's burrow, he must tap out a satisfactory seismic signal with his foremost legs to encourage her to mate or she, too, may try to eat him. If he survives, he needs to find his way back to his burrow. Miraculously, males appear to travel in an almost-straight line back home.

Confrontation dance Male dancing white lady spiders drum their feet on the sand when they are close to other males, causing rivals to withdraw or keep out of the way of the signalling spider.

Common whitetail
Perch patrol
SPECIES *Libellula lydia* **SIZE** Up to 5 cm (2 in) **DISTRIBUTION** Wetland habitats throughout North America

Mature male common whitetail dragonflies develop a whitish bloom known as pruinescence on their blue abdomens. In territorial displays, dominant males raise up their abdomens to intruders as a threat, while less dominant males lower theirs as a sign of submission. Common whitetails guard perches from where they patrol their territory, a 10–30 m (33–98 ft) stretch of water's edge, for several hours a day. Males with larger territories have greater success in mating with females that visit the water to breed. They also defend their territories against other species such as the cardinal meadowhawk, as pictured below.

Poplar petiole gall aphid
Fighting for position
SPECIES *Pemphigus populitransversus* **SIZE** 1.5–3 mm (1/16–1/8 in) **DISTRIBUTION** Eastern cottonwood trees in Illinois, Missouri, and Utah, USA

In spring, female poplar petiole gall aphids hatch from eggs that have overwintered on cottonwood trees. Each aphid selects a leaf and starts feeding at the base, causing a hollow ball of tissue called a gall to form. The female moves into the gall, where she gives birth to a brood of winged females, the result of asexual reproduction. These females disperse and continue to reproduce. The last generation of the year contains both male and female aphids, which reproduce sexually and lay eggs on cottonwood trees to overwinter. The females are extremely territorial and may spend several hours, or even days, fighting with one another over a leaf. Large leaves are preferred, presumably because they contain more sap on which to feed. Defeated and small females must accept smaller leaves or less favourable positions closer to the centre of large leaves.

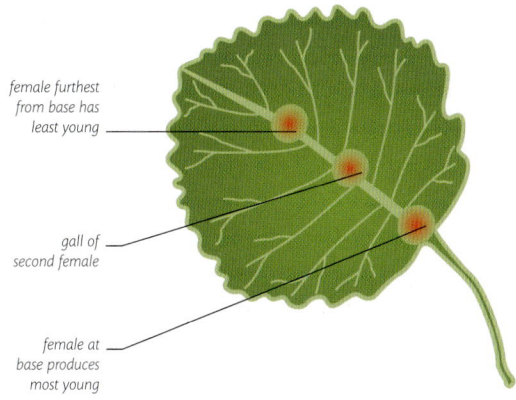

female furthest from base has least young
gall of second female
female at base produces most young

Aphids and galls Aphid galls are typically located at the base of the leaf where it joins the petiole (stalk). Each gall contains new aphids, which are produced parthenogenetically by the female that created the gall. They eventually emerge to establish their own galls elsewhere.

Position and reproductive success Where three females occupy the same leaf, the reproductive success of the female closest to the base is always greater than that of the female furthest away. On average, the female at the base produces 138 young, the middle female 75, and the most distant female 29.

Malaysian giant ant
Border guards

SPECIES *Dinomyrmex gigas* **SIZE** 2 cm (¾ in); 3 cm (1¼ in) (soldier) **DISTRIBUTION** Rainforest from lowland peat swamps and mangroves to mountain forests of Southeast Asia, from Sumatra north to Thailand

Territorial behaviour is well developed in the Malaysian giant ant. Colonies defend their borders against ants of the same species and also enter into violent combat with ants of different species. Colonies may contain around 7,000 workers divided among 8–14 underground nests. A colony's territory extends up into the tree canopy and may cover an area of 8,000 square metres (86,100 square feet). Barrack nests near the territory borders contain a high proportion of major workers – large soldier ants that take part in ritual combat with other Malaysian giant ants during boundary disputes. These fights can take place over a number of days, or even weeks, with majors squaring up to one another repeatedly each night. The majors also patrol trunk trails through the colony's territory, attacking impostors of their own and different species, and serve as sentinels at points known as bridgeheads. These are usually at the base of tree trunks that give access to the canopy.

Ritual combat Malaysian giant ant majors engage in ritual fights at tournament sites on their territorial boundaries. Two ants stand on their hind legs and box one another with their forelegs. The ant that holds its legs up longest and throws its opponent off balance wins the bout.

HUMAN IMPACT **NASTY BITE**

The titan triggerfish is notorious for charging at divers and snorkellers that enter its territory while it is guarding eggs and may even ram into them. These fish have strong front teeth, used for crushing shellfish, and can inflict a nasty bite if the intruder does not swim out of its territory, which includes a cone-shaped body of water above the nest. A swift exit to the side is therefore the best option, from where the fish can be watched from a safe distance, as it gently blows currents of water through the eggs to oxygenate them.

Titan triggerfish
Aggressive defence

SPECIES *Balistoides viridescens* **SIZE** Up to 75 cm (30 in) **DISTRIBUTION** Coral reefs of the Indo-Pacific Ocean

The titan triggerfish is a large, colourful rhomboid-shaped tropical reef fish that defends its territory aggressively during the breeding season. If approached, it will repeatedly swim at both human and fish intruders. At other times when out feeding on the reef, a triggerfish may hide between rocks and erect the spines on its back, bracing itself in position and thus rendering it immovable. As the largest triggerfish in its range, the titan is usually dominant to other species in competitive encounters.

Nest site Titan triggerfish typically build their nests in sandy patches of coral rubble on the sea bed. They use jets of water to clear debris from a patch of sand on which the female lays her eggs.

HOME RANGES AND TERRITORIES 107

Territorial boundaries Distinct territorial boundaries are maintained between different Malaysian giant ant colonies, and between them and colonies of other large, nocturnal ants with which they compete.

KEY

- DINOMYRMEX GIGAS NESTS
- CAMPONOTUS FESTINUS NESTS
- OTHER CAMPONOTUS SPECIES' NESTS
- OECOPHYLLA SMARAGDINA NESTS
- DINOMYRMEX GIGAS SENTRIES
- CAMPONOTUS FESTINUS SENTRIES

Harlequin poison dart frog
Watery crib

SPECIES *Oophaga histrionica* **SIZE** 2.5–4 cm (1–1½ in)
DISTRIBUTION Tropical rainforest of western Ecuador and parts of Colombia

The female harlequin poison frog gives each of her tadpoles its own pool in the base of an aerial plant. Water collects where the leaves join, and the female drops one tadpole into each reservoir. The tadpoles are kept apart because they tend to be cannibalistic. The adult frog returns every other day to deposit an unfertilized egg into the pool as food for her developing offspring. The young frog emerges from its aquatic nursery after three months.

Eater of eggs The generic name *Oophaga* means "egg-eater" and refers to the tadpoles' diet of unfertilized eggs.

Common side-blotched lizard
Fighting colours

SPECIES *Uta stansburiana* **SIZE** 4–6.5 cm (1½–2½ in) **DISTRIBUTION** Desert and semi-arid areas of Pacific North America and north-central Mexico

Male side-blotched lizards occur in three genetically determined forms, or morphs. These employ different strategies when it comes to mating. Orange-throated males are territorial and aggressive. They are dominant over both blue- and yellow-throated males, and consequently mate with the most females. Blue-throated males are also territorial and guard their mates carefully. They are able to chase yellow-throated males away, but often lose out to orange-throated males unless they co-operate to protect their mates. Yellow-throated males do not defend territories at all; instead, they attempt to sneak past the territorial males to mate. Early in the breeding season, before the males' coloration has developed, competitions for the best territories are decided on the basis of size rather than colour.

CASE STUDY **ROCKS COUNT**

Researchers tested the theory that male common side-blotched lizards in a high-quality habitat maintain a smaller territory than those in a poor habitat. They altered territories so that some males had valuable, sun-warmed rocks taken away and others were given more. Males in areas with fewer rocks expanded their territories to compensate for the poorer-quality resource, while those with more rocks contracted the size of their territory, but still managed to attract a higher density of females.

BEFORE ALTERATION | **ROCKS ADDED**

Soaking up the sun Male (right) and female (left) common side-blotched lizards bask on a rock that has been warmed by the sun, to absorb the heat contained in the rock.

Andean condor
Canyon soaring

SPECIES *Vultur gryphus* **SIZE** 1.2–1.3 m (4–4¼ ft)
DISTRIBUTION open grassland and rocky areas of the Andes and Pacific coast of South America

The Andean condor soars at altitudes of up to 5,500 m (18,000 ft) while scanning the ground for carcasses to scavenge. It has a large home range and may travel up to 200 km (125 miles) in a day. This bird's excellent eyesight enables it to spot food from several kilometres away, and it occasionally uses the presence of other vultures (which forage by scent more than sight) to reveal the location of livestock or deer carcass, or even a beached whale. Condors rarely flap their wings when flying; instead, they ride on updrafts of warm air, circling with their wing tips bent upwards. Andean condors nest at 3,000–5,000 m (9,850–16,400 ft) above sea level on rocky ledges. Like their relative, the California condor, they have in the past been subjected to persecution, which has caused their numbers to fall. Captive breeding and rearing programmes aim to improve their breeding success to secure the bird's future.

Flying high These Andean condors are soaring on an updraft in the Colca Canyon in Peru. They typically hunt in the early morning and late afternoon.

Koala
Fixed range

SPECIES *Phascolarctos cinereus* **SIZE** Up to 78 cm (31 in) **DISTRIBUTION** Native to eucalyptus forests of eastern Australia; introduced to western Australia and nearby islands

Koalas are mainly solitary animals that occupy distinct home ranges. In wetter forests in the south of their distribution, koalas require only small home ranges of 0.5–3 hectares (1.2–7.4 acres) to meet their needs, while in drier, less productive areas in the west their home ranges can be as large as 100 hectares (250 acres). A dominant male's range may overlap with those of up to nine females. Adult males travel widely at night during the breeding season (October to February), fighting with rival males and mating with receptive females. They also call to advertise their presence and scent-mark tree trunks using a gland on their sternum.

Up a gum tree Koalas feed on the leaves of around 30 species of eucalyptus. Their opposable digits and curved claws help them grip branches.

CASE STUDY SELECTIVE LOGGING

A study in New South Wales has shown that carefully managed logging can minimize the effect on koala's home ranges. About a quarter of white cypress pines, a tree that is used as a daytime shelter by the koala, were removed from a forest during the study, but the koala's main food trees, three species of eucalyptus, were deliberately left untouched. The koalas' population density was unaffected by the loss of the pine trees.

HOME RANGES AND TERRITORIES 109

European robin
Seasonal variation

SPECIES *Erithacus rubecula* **SIZE** 12–14 cm (4½–5½ in) **DISTRIBUTION** Woodland, parks, gardens, and farm hedgerows across Europe

The European robin maintains territories in both the breeding and non-breeding seasons. Spring and summer breeding territories average 0.55 hectares (1.3 acres), while winter territories may be only half that size. The first territories to become colonized in an area are the most resource-rich, wooded habitats, which are favoured for breeding. During winter, migrant birds may arrive and colonize territories in less valuable shrub habitats. During the breeding season, males sing and patrol their territories more often; they are also quicker to attack neighbouring males, which are more likely to trespass.

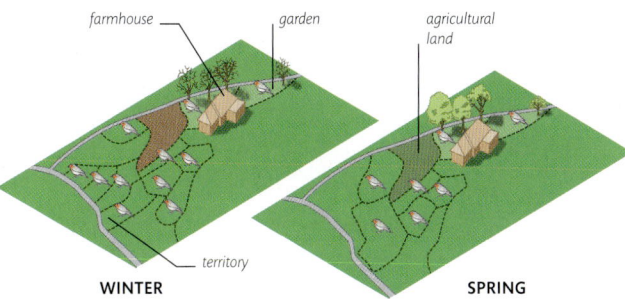

Changing territories Male and female robins hold separate territories in winter and defend them with song. By spring, some birds will have died, enabling survivors to increase the size of their territories.

Seeing red An intruder's red breast triggers territorial defence behaviour in a resident robin. A warning song can quickly escalate into a vicious fight in which one or other of the opponents might lose not only their territory but also their life.

Black-browed albatross
Pecking distance

SPECIES *Thalassarche melanophris* **SIZE** 80–95 cm (31–37 in)
DISTRIBUTION Islands and open waters of the Southern Ocean

Like many seabirds, black-browed albatrosses are colonial, coming together in huge nesting colonies during the breeding season. They nest together because of the limited availability of islands suitable for breeding in the Southern Ocean, and also because communal living decreases the risk of predation of eggs and chicks. Because they find all their food out at sea, they have no need to defend a territory for resources, beyond the immediate area of the actual nest. The optimal nesting density leaves them just out of pecking reach of the bird next door. The colony therefore appears to be evenly spaced across the tussock-grass plateau, each bird the ruler of its own small territory. When away from their nests, black-browed albatrosses range over hundreds of kilometres of ocean, feeding on fishes, squid, and octopuses. Many albatross species are classed as endangered because of the high number of deaths caused by long-line fishing (see p.123).

On the nest The world's largest breeding colony of black-browed albatrosses is on Steeple Jason Island in the Falklands. A pair raises just one chick each year, so their population is slow to recover from decline.

VARIATION IN TERRITORY SIZE AND PREY DENSITY

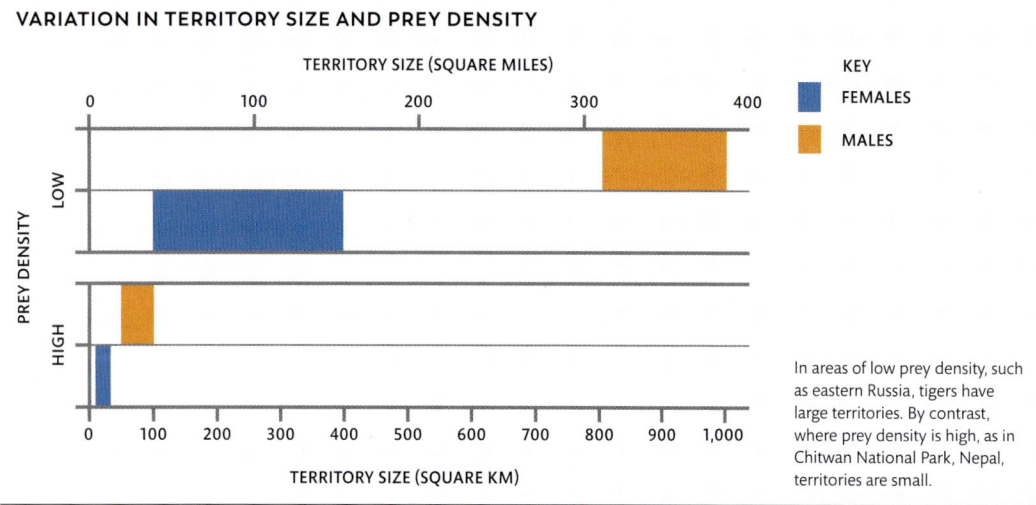

In areas of low prey density, such as eastern Russia, tigers have large territories. By contrast, where prey density is high, as in Chitwan National Park, Nepal, territories are small.

HOME RANGES AND TERRITORIES

Tooth and claw Tigers are generally solitary, so when a stranger is encountered on another's territory a fight usually ensues. They are powerful animals with an impressive weaponry of sharp teeth and claws.

Tiger
Cat fight

SPECIES Panthera tigris **SIZE** 2–3.7 m (6½–12¼ ft) **DISTRIBUTION** Forest, shrubland, and grassland in northeast China, Korea, Russia, northern India, Bangladesh, Nepal, Laos, Myanmar, Thailand, and Malaysia

Both male and female tigers maintain territories. These need to have dense vegetation for cover, a source of water, and plenty of prey. Also, a territory usually contains several dens where the tiger can rest and where females give birth to and rear their cubs. Territories of male tigers are up to three times larger than females' territories, and male and female ranges overlap. A male tends to retain exclusive breeding rights to the females in his territory so long as he can defend them from invaders. To minimize the risk of conflict, tigers leave signs that an area is occupied by scent-marking their territories with urine and faeces or leaving scratch marks on trees, with males marking more frequently when females are in oestrus. They are also quick to colonize ranges that have been vacated by another tiger dying. If a male takes over another's territory, he may kill any offspring he finds before mating with the resident females. Humans threaten tiger populations by poaching, fragmenting their habitats, and reducing the density of their prey.

Male Amur Tiger hunting Tigers hunt by stealth, approaching potential prey (which includes deer, buffaloes, and wild pigs) silently in a crouching position, before launching an ambush. They kill by breaking the animals' necks or by suffocation.

Female bengal tiger scent-marking Tigers spray urine mixed with a musky scent from an anal gland onto trees and rocks to mark their territories. Females increase their rate of spraying just before they are ready to mate.

Brown-throated three-toed sloth

Treetop territory

SPECIES *Bradypus variegatus* **SIZE** 42–80 cm (16½–31 in) **DISTRIBUTION** Lowland rainforest in Central and South America

Brown-throated three-toed sloths live in the rainforest canopy, typically 20–30 m (66–98 ft) high, feeding on leaves, sleeping, and resting. They transfer from tree to tree using overlapping branches and climbing plants. Sloths move slowly, hanging upside-down by the three hooklike claws on each limb. They also metabolize their food slowly and have relatively small muscle mass, so cannot generate much body heat and seek or avoid sunshine during the day to adjust their body temperature as required. Usually solitary, sloths occupy a range of less than 2 hectares (5 acres). To mate, the female attracts males with a screaming call. She has one baby a year, which she carries around on her chests until her offspring is able to be independent, when it either disperses to another territory or inherits its mother's, which she then vacates.

Risky descent Three-toed sloths make an energetically expensive descent weekly to defecate. This allows the *Cryptoses* moths that live on their fur to lay eggs in the dung. The larvae then recolonize the sloths once mature. The moths encourage the growth of algae on the sloths' fur. This provides the sloths with camouflage and also a fat-rich additional source of food.

European badger

Making a mark

SPECIES *Meles meles* **SIZE** 25–30 cm (9⅘–35½ in) **DISTRIBUTION** Found in woodland and scrub throughout most Europe, as far east as the Volga River in Russia

European badgers live in clans of six to twenty animals, comprising adults and their cubs living together in a sett (a den) or series of setts. Clans have well-defined territories that range from about 20–180 hectares (50–445 acres), depending on clan size and the quality of the area. Territories are principally marked and maintained by scent. Urine as well as hormonal secretions from specialized glands are used on prominent objects, such as trees and tufts of grass, while significant territorial boundaries are regularly marked by defecating into a series of open latrines (dung pits).

Scientists can use the latrines to study the boundaries of badger territories. A mixture of food (usually peanuts and syrup) containing harmless indigestible coloured pellets is placed near badger setts to be consumed by the resident badgers. Using different-coloured markers for each sett, the scientists are able to survey latrines, noting the colour of markers in each to determine the boundaries of adjacent groups of badgers.

A sett is situated roughly in the middle of a clan's territory. These elaborate networks of tunnels, sleeping chambers, and openings can extend for 300 m (1,000 ft) and take many years to complete. One sett in northeastern Germany has been in use for more than 10,000 years.

Badgers forage closest to the sett first, moving further away as they exhaust food resources. When it comes to defending their territories, core areas of the territory are vehemently defended against intruders, while boundaries are maintained passively. This means that it is not worthwhile for badgers of other clans to venture deep into neighbours' territories and, at boundaries, there may be some overlap, especially when food supplies are low.

Woodland wanderers Badgers that live in densely wooded habitats roam further and faster, and follow more convoluted paths, than those living in more open areas.

Red fox
Town and country

SPECIES *Vulpes vulpes* **SIZE** 46–90 cm (18–35 in) **DISTRIBUTION** Wide variety of habitats in the northern hemisphere, including forest, tundra, desert, farmland, and towns

The red fox is a very adaptable carnivore that lives in many different habitats across its extensive range. In recent decades, it has become an increasingly common fixture in urban areas, where it exists in close proximity to humans. Foxes often form small social groups consisting of a male (known as a dog fox), several females (vixens), and their dependent young (cubs). Each group's territory contains a den, or earth, where the females give birth to and rear their cubs. Well-trodden pathways connect the earth to other dens, hunting grounds, and food caches. Fox home ranges vary in size from 10–5,000 hectares (25–12,350 acres) depending on habitat quality. Territories are smaller and less stable in urban than in rural areas, probably because the urban environment changes more rapidly than the countryside.

Easy pickings Foxes frequently scavenge from rubbish bins in urban areas. They may also be fed by humans putting food out in their gardens, which makes fox territories smaller. In some areas, 50 per cent of a fox's diet may be from human sources.

Coming to blows Foxes mark their territories with urine and scent. When a male ignores these warnings and enters a rival's area, a fight may ensue, during which the foxes rear up and attempt to push one another over.

African forest elephant
Trunk roads

SPECIES *Loxodonta cyclotis* **SIZE** 2.5 m (8¼ ft) (male); 2.1 m (7 ft) (female) **DISTRIBUTION** Equatorial forests of Central and West Africa, in particular the Congo Basin

African forest elephants live in small family groups of between five and eight individuals deep in the forests of the Congo Basin. The dense vegetation makes these animals difficult to study, but satellite radio tracking indicates their home ranges could cover approximately 2,000 square km (1,243 square miles). An elephant may travel 1–15 km (⅔–9¼ miles) a day, feeding on grasses and leaves in the dry season and fruit in the wet season. Forest elephants visit watering holes daily, not only

> **Generations** of forest elephants have created a **network of trails** throughout the forest, linking fruit trees.

for water, but also for soil containing minerals, such as calcium, potassium, and magnesium, which they need to stay healthy. In 2001, genetic analysis of the DNA of poached elephant ivory revealed that the African forest elephant is a separate species from the larger and more widespread African bush elephant, rather than a subspecies of it.

Following the trail Forest elephants move along three main types of "highway": boulevards, which allow them to travel rapidly between distant, favoured areas such as forest clearings; foraging paths through medium-density forests with plenty of food; and alleys around the clearings.

Taking the waters Each day between 40 and 100 forest elephants visit the Dzanga Bai in the Central African Republic. Forest elephant herds gather at bais (swampy forest clearings) to dig for and eat mineral salts contained in the soil and to drink the mineral-rich water.

Auditory boundaries Wolves use howling to maintain territory and to avoid dangerous physical confrontations with other packs. Howls can tell neighbours a lot about their opponents – not only the size of the pack but also the sex, rank, physical condition, and intentions of those howling. In a confrontation, the relative size of a pack is crucial to the outcome and when howling to maintain territory, all individuals, even pups, join in both to show solidarity and to create the impression of a large number of individuals. Both howling and scent marking are important for maintaining space but play complimentary roles, with scent marking being long-term and site specific, while howling is immediate and long range.

Migration

Migration is the periodic movement of animals to and from different areas, usually along well-defined routes. In long-lived species, individuals make repeated annual migrations throughout their lives once they are sexually mature. In short-lived species, such as the monarch butterfly, which produce several generations within a season, the migration is undertaken by a succession of different individuals as the butterflies breed along the route.

WHY MIGRATE?

Many animals migrate to find the best location in which to lay eggs or rear young. This is often related to the need to avoid the lack of food in one area and exploit an abundance of food elsewhere. Such movements are usually in response to predictable changes in the environment, for example the different seasons in temperate latitudes, where weather conditions vary from harsh to favourable, and the wet and dry seasons in the tropics.

RECORD MIGRATIONS

RECORD	ANIMAL	DISTANCE
Longest round trip	Sooty shearwater	65,000 km (40,400 miles)
Longest non-stop flight	Bar-tailed godwit	13,560 km (8,435 miles)
Highest journey	Bar-headed goose	10,175 m (33,380 ft)
Longest aquatic journey	Gray whale	22,511 km (13,990 miles)
Largest land migration	Blue wildebeest	1.3 million
Largest air migration	Desert locust	69 billion

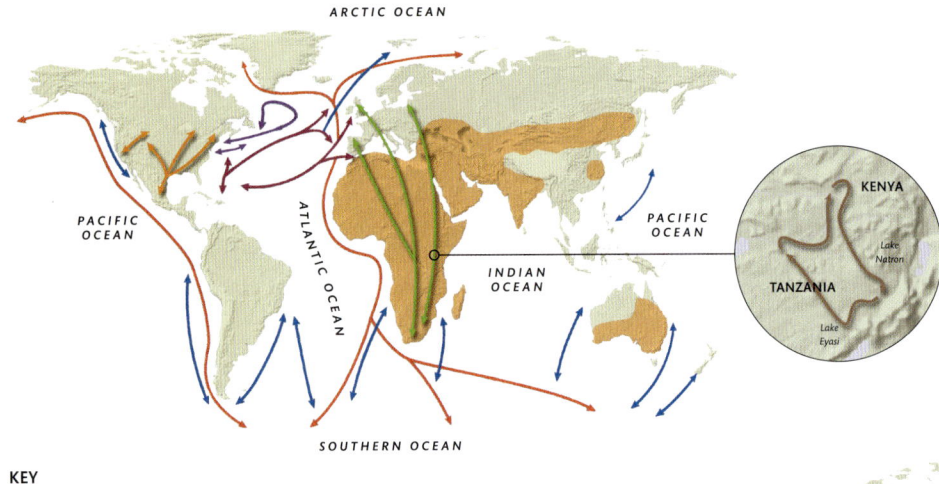

KEY
- BLUE WILDEBEEST (INSET)
- ARCTIC TERN
- ATLANTIC SALMON
- RORQUAL WHALES
- EUROPEAN EEL
- MONARCH BUTTERFLY
- BARN SWALLOW
- LOCUSTS

PARTIAL AND FULL MIGRANTS

In some species all individuals migrate (full migrants), while in others some remain resident in parts of the range (partial migrants). Whether or not an animal migrates can depend on local climate. For example, in Finland most European robins migrate south to escape the harsh winter, whereas in the British Isles, where winters are milder, most robins remain all year round. Migration can also depend on the stage an animal has reached in its life cycle. An immature American or European eel, for example, has no need to migrate to breeding grounds; it will make the journey from inland waterways to the Sargasso Sea when it is ready to reproduce (see p.120). Migration may also depend on an animal's circumstances. Older, more experienced common blackbirds in possession of a territory remain resident while younger, less experienced birds migrate.

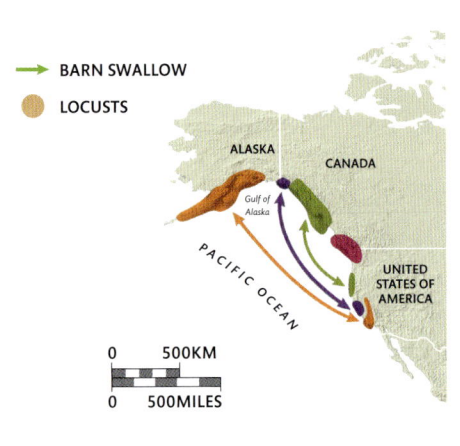

Leapfrog migrations Fox sparrows migrate along the western seaboard of North America. Populations that breed in Alaska and Canada migrate south in autumn to overwinter in the USA, leapfrogging populations with shorter migrations and those that do not migrate at all.

KEY
- POPULATION A
- POPULATION B
- POPULATION C
- POPULATION D

HAZARDS

Migrations are often long and hazardous journeys. Some birds choose to travel over land even though it is a longer journey, while others go over the sea by the shortest route, where there are fewer predators and they can often benefit from tailwinds. But birds migrating over open sea risk winds blowing them off course (resulting in birds stopping in places they are not normally seen) or storms forcing them to land on water. There may be increased risk of predation at journey's end: in autumn, the Eleonora's falcon preys on exhausted songbirds that have flown over the Mediterranean to North Africa. Migrating over land can have its hazards, too, such as crossing inhospitable places, such as deserts.

Zebra crossing During their annual migration, Burchell's zebras must risk crossing the crocodile-infested waters of the Mara River in Kenya's Masai Mara nature reserve.

MIGRATION 117

TRIGGERS AND PREPARATION

Triggers to migrate include lengthening days as spring approaches, increased reproductive hormones and fat deposits, and growing restlessness. Many animals have an innate, near-annual rhythm that tells them when to migrate. Once in good condition, favourable weather may be the final trigger to move. Physiological changes are often necessary before migration. Birds' heart, flight, and skeletal muscles enlarge, while other organs may diminish in size. Fishes moving between fresh and salt water display changes in their levels of salt tolerance, whereas amphibians that move between terrestrial and aquatic habitats alter the permeability of their skin.

NORMAL BODY FAT · READY TO MIGRATE

Laying down body fat Birds that cross deserts or open oceans cannot guarantee regular food during migration. They deposit fat in their bodies as fuel for their flight. Small birds can double their weight before leaving.

NAVIGATION

Animals that migrate use various cues to help them navigate. Compass cues indicate direction and might include the sun, stars, or the Earth's magnetic field (see p.97). Visual cues or landmarks, such as coastlines and mountain ranges, are used by animals to pilot their way towards their goal. Distinctive odours are also used to home in on breeding or roosting sites. True navigation relies on a mental map to determine position relative to a destination. In some species, young birds migrating for the first time travel with adults in flocks, but in many the adults leave first and the young follow on later. They are born with the information for the distance and direction of their journey.

Finding the way Birds use a combination of cues during migration and may switch from one to another depending on conditions. If the sky is cloudy, they may rely more heavily on the magnetic field.

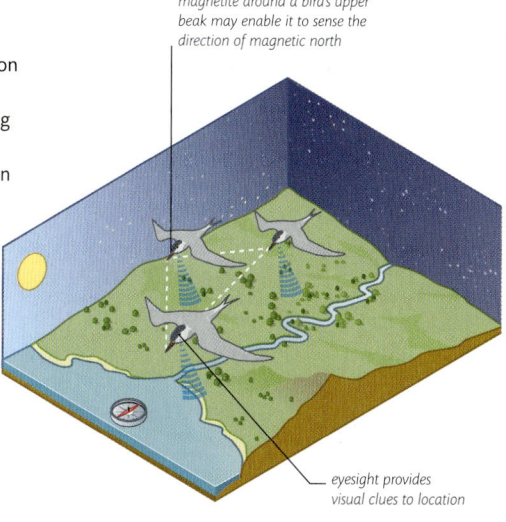

magnetite around a bird's upper beak may enable it to sense the direction of magnetic north

eyesight provides visual clues to location

Formation flying Flying in a V-shaped formation allows migrating geese to save energy and communicate about orientation cues. Barnacle geese migrate seasonally between the high Arctic and more southerly latitudes.

HUMAN IMPACT
LESSEPSIAN MIGRATION

The opening of the Suez Canal in 1869 connected the Red Sea to the Mediterranean Sea. For a long time, part of the canal was so salty that few animals could survive in it. However, over time the salinity gradually decreased and Red Sea species have been able to travel northwards into the eastern Mediterranean. This movement is known as Lessepsian migration after the engineer of the Suez Canal, Ferdinand de Lesseps. At least 300 species are known to have made this human-assisted migration.

HUMAN-ASSISTED MOVEMENT

Throughout history, humans have moved animals around the world for various purposes, sometimes with disastrous consequences. Goats were introduced to many oceanic islands to provide food for passing ships. In many cases, they have since caused significant environmental damage by stripping the land bare of vegetation. People have also taken animals, such as cats, to new places as pets, where they then kill the local fauna. And many species have been introduced in an effort to control others. For example, cane toads were imported to Australia to eat pests of sugar cane, but instead they eat almost anything else (see p.252).

Illegal immigrant The black rat has colonized much of the world by "stowing away" onboard ships. Other invasive species have been transported in the water in ships' ballast tanks or attached to the hulls.

Christmas Island red crab
Ocean bound

SPECIES *Gecarcoidea natalis* **SIZE** 12 cm (4½ in)
DISTRIBUTION Forests of Christmas Island and the Cocos Islands in the Indian Ocean

For most of the year, the red crabs on Christmas Island live in burrows in the rainforest floor, feeding on leaf and fruit litter, but as the monsoon rains begin around October/November, tens of millions of these vibrant crustaceans start marching together towards the coast. Their journey takes about a week and, after a dip in the sea, males dig burrows in the beach terraces where they mate with females (the burrows protect the crabs and their eggs from heat, desiccation, and predators). The male crabs leave soon after to trek back inland, but the females stay in their burrows for two weeks while their eggs develop. Then, at the turn of the high tide during the last quarter of the moon, the females each release up to 100,000 eggs into the sea, where they hatch immediately.

At the shore Once they reach the beach, all the crabs head straight into the ocean for a cooling dip after their arduous journey.

47 million

The number of red crabs that migrate from the forests of Christmas Island down to the sea to spawn each year.

HUMAN IMPACT **ROAD CLOSURES**

Each year, thousands of red crabs are killed while crossing roads to reach the sea. To reduce this number, Christmas Islanders close roads at peak times on the main migration paths. Other roads have tunnels beneath and bridges over them. Clearing their forest habitat for settlement and phosphate mining also threatens crabs, forcing them to travel further in the open. Fortunately, two-thirds of the island is now protected by a national park.

Green darner
North and south

SPECIES *Anax junius* **SIZE** 7–8 cm (2¾–3¼ in)
DISTRIBUTION Still and slow-moving fresh water in North and South America, the Caribbean Islands, and Asia

Each spring, a new generation of green darner dragonflies migrates from the southern USA to the north and to Canada, where they spend the summer breeding and feeding on mosquitoes. Approaching cold fronts in autumn trigger the next generation of dragonflies to return south, sometimes covering as much as 140 km (87 miles) in a day. On arrival, the dragonflies breed and their offspring overwinter as nymphs, then metamorphose into adults in spring to start the cycle again. In this way, successive generations of offspring migrate first north then south, then north again. The migrating dragonflies are a temporary food source for kestrels.

Caribbean spiny lobster
Across the sea floor

SPECIES *Panulirus argus* **SIZE** 60 cm (23½ in)
DISTRIBUTION Coral reefs and seagrass beds in the west Atlantic Ocean, Caribbean Sea, and Gulf of Mexico

In late October and early November, regimented lines of spiny lobsters make their way across the sandy bottom of the Caribbean Sea. The migrations are thought to be triggered by autumnal storms that make the shallow waters cooler and more turbulent. The lobsters walk mainly at night and shelter in crevices or in stationary groups in the open during the day. They take several days to travel 30–50 km (18–31 miles) to reach the edge of the deep ocean channels, where they spread out along the less disturbed reefs on the ocean fringe. Females spawn in this deeper water in spring and early summer, before returning to the shallows. Once the eggs have hatched, the larval lobsters drift on the ocean currents, eventually being brought back to the Caribbean Sea, where they mature.

Defence position The spiny lobster is protected from most predators by the sharp spines on its exoskeleton, but if attacked it tucks its tail under its body.

Single file Each lobster uses its antennae and front legs to keep in touch with the abdomen and tail fan of the lobster in front. This "queuing" behaviour may be a defence against predators and also reduces drag.

MIGRATION

Monarch butterfly
Mass migration

SPECIES *Danaus plexippus* **SIZE** Wingspan 8.5–12 cm (3¼–4½ in)
DISTRIBUTION Native to open habitats and forests in North America; also found in Australasia and parts of Europe

One of the most conspicuous of all insect migrations is that of monarch butterflies in North America. In autumn, they move south to avoid the cold temperatures of more northerly parts of the continent. They overwinter in milder climates in a state of reproductive diapause, meaning they do not breed

A flutter of butterflies Millions of monarch butterflies undertake the epic journey south to the highlands of Mexico every autumn. Stored fat fuels their flight, and they may glide on air currents to save energy.

during this time. In spring, these striking butterflies move north in search of their food plant, milkweed (plants of the genus *Asclepias*, which produce milky sap). As they move, females lay eggs and die, and the new generations continue the journey. By the time they have reached the most northerly parts of their range, the butterflies will be second-, third-, or even fourth-generation descendants of those that left the south. Monarch butterfly migration appears to be triggered by changes in day length and temperature, and there must be a genetic component to the species that allows flight routes to be inherited by offspring, as no individual butterfly ever makes the journey twice. The overwintering populations of monarch butterflies in Mexico are threatened by destruction of their forest refuges for timber; intact forest is vital to maintain the microclimate needed for the butterflies' survival. Gaps in the forest cover can leave the butterflies susceptible to cold and rain. Several sanctuaries have been established for the protection of monarch butterflies.

Monarchs in Mexico Suitable conditions for overwintering monarch butterflies in Mexico occur only in a relatively small area in the state of Michoacán. The fir trees are festooned with the orange-and-black butterflies from November to March.

KEY
- SUMMER RANGE
- WINTER RANGE
- SPRING RANGE
- → NORTHERLY MIGRATION ROUTES

Migration routes Monarch butterflies that overwinter in coastal California spend the summer inland, to the west of the Rocky Mountains. Those that winter in the highlands of Mexico travel via Texas to northern US states lying east of the Rockies, though some butterflies have been tracked flying to states to the west. The distance between summer and winter ranges can be as much as 4,800 km (3,000 miles).

Boree moth
Moving in convoy
SPECIES *Ochrogaster lunifer* **SIZE** 4 cm (1½ in) (mature caterpillar); 4 cm (1½ in) (moth wingspan) **DISTRIBUTION** Acacia and eucalyptus trees in Australia

Caterpillars of the boree moth have voracious appetites, which compel them to keep moving. Having stripped bare the tree they were living on, they have no choice but to venture forth in search of a new food source. As each caterpillar walks, it extrudes a trail of silk, which is faithfully followed by its siblings, creating the illusion of one incredibly long, hairy caterpillar snaking across the ground. The caterpillars nest communally in their food tree in a ball, surrounded by silk and shed hairs, which has given rise to their alternative name of the bag-shelter moth.

Blue shark
Riding currents
SPECIES *Prionace glauca* **SIZE** Up to 4 m (13 ft) **DISTRIBUTION** Tropical, subtropical, and temperate waters worldwide

After mating off the coast of northeastern USA in spring, female blue sharks in the North Atlantic Ocean set off on an epic journey across to Europe. Here they give birth to their pups in sheltered, coastal waters off Spain and Portugal. The pregnant females swim with the prevailing current, helped along by the Gulf Stream and the North Atlantic Current, part of a clockwise circular system called the North Atlantic Gyre. After giving birth, some at least complete the circle, with the whole journey taking up to two years. Travelling west, the sharks may use the Canary and North Equatorial Currents, though their route remains unclear. The longest distance so far recorded from a recaptured tagged shark is 6,840 km (4,250 miles) from Ireland to Venezuela, but journeys of around 3,000 km (1,900 miles) are common.

On the move The migrations of the Atlantic population of blue sharks have been the most extensively studied, but the Pacific population has been found to migrate long distances too. There is also a population in the Indian Ocean.

CASE STUDY
TRACKING SHARKS
Since the early 1960s, blue sharks have been tagged to provide information on their movements. Anglers and commercial fishermen are encouraged to take part in the programme, applying identification tags to sharks they have caught either intentionally or accidentally, before they are released. The tags are attached to the shark's dorsal fin or implanted in the muscle of its back. If the shark is recaptured, scientists can start to draw a map of its migratory journeys. More recently, satellite tags have meant the sharks' travels can be mapped without the need for their recapture.

European eel
Return journey
SPECIES *Anguilla anguilla* **SIZE** Up to 1.3 m (4¼ ft) **DISTRIBUTION** Coasts, estuaries, and rivers of northern Europe

The European eel spends most of its life in fresh water but returns to salt water to breed, a behaviour known as catadromy. Having started life in the ocean, young eels (elvers) arrive at estuaries and travel inland along rivers. The eels remain upstream for anything between 5 and 20 years or more, feeding and maturing. In late autumn each year, mature eels return to the sea, sometimes crossing wet grass to reach a different watercourse. These eels develop larger eyes to see in the ocean depths and a silver coloration below that helps to conceal them from predators.

Young and old The European eel progresses through various stages. The first-stage larva is called a leptocephalus (right). It then becomes a glass eel, an elver, and a yellow eel, before becoming a fully mature adult (silver eel, far right).

CASE STUDY
FINDING THE SPAWNING GROUNDS
From 1904 to 1922, Danish biologist Johannes Schmidt led expeditions in the Mediterranean Sea and the North Atlantic to find the spawning grounds of the European eel. He recorded the length of larval eels caught in various locations, eventually catching the smallest, 1 cm (⅜ in) long, in the Sargasso Sea. In the western Sargasso, Schmidt also found the breeding grounds of the American eel (*Anguilla rostrata*), a related species that matures in the rivers of the eastern USA. The first direct evidence of European eels arriving in the Sargasso Sea was obtained in 2018–19, using pop up satellite tags.

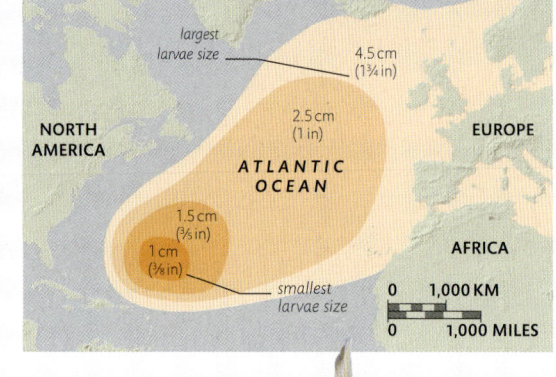

MIGRATION **121**

Leaping falls It is hard work returning to the spawning grounds. Salmon must jump up waterfalls and rapids, propelling themselves forwards against the flow of water with their strong muscles and flicking tails.

Chum salmon
Heading upstream

SPECIES Oncorhynchus keta **SIZE** Up to 1 m (3¼ ft)
DISTRIBUTION Temperate and cold waters of North Pacific and adjacent rivers

Salmon are anadromous, meaning that they live mostly in the sea but return to fresh water to breed. Chum are one of five species of salmon that frequent the North Pacific Ocean and the rivers that border it in countries including Canada, Japan, Korea, and the USA. After spending between one and three years at sea, chum salmon travel inland up river; in the case of the Yukon River, as far as 3,200 km (2,000 miles) through Alaska into Canada. The annual "salmon run" occurs during autumn, with spawning taking place between November and January. Around two weeks later, the adults die, contributing valuable nutrients to the ecosystem. Their eggs remain protected in the gravel riverbed over winter and hatch in early spring. The fry stay in the river for a year or more before travelling downstream to the sea between March and July.

HUMAN IMPACT PARASITIC LICE

Salmon is a popular food fish, which has prompted a boom in commercial salmon-farming. However, the industry is threatening wild salmon populations by exposing them to parasites. Sea lice are crustaceans that occur naturally on the salmon's skin, but the rearing of thousands of adult fish in close proximity in pens causes parasite numbers to rise far beyond normal levels found in the wild, lowering the fitness of the fish. Young wild salmon migrating downstream from their spawning grounds pass the salmon farms on their way to the ocean and become infested with parasites as they go.

Spawning grounds By the time they reach the spawning grounds, these sockeye salmon (*Oncorhynchus nerka*) have developed distinctive coloration, with red upper bodies and green heads. The males have hooked snouts.

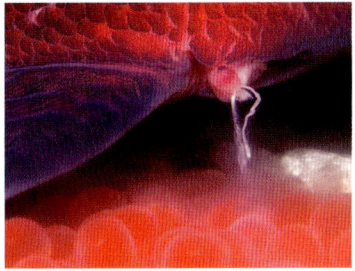

Fertilizing eggs Female salmon lay between 2,000 and 6,000 eggs in shallow depressions called redds. Males then release sperm over the eggs before the females cover them with gravel for protection.

Next generation Recently hatched salmon are known as alevins. They remain in the redd for around 12 weeks, until the yolk sacs attached to their bellies are used up and they have to emerge to feed themselves.

European common toad
Perilous journey

SPECIES *Bufo bufo* **SIZE** Up to 18 cm (7 in)
DISTRIBUTION Terrestrial and wetland habitats throughout most of Europe

Like salamanders, European common toads attempt to migrate back to the pond in which they were born in order to breed. The migration begins in autumn but is interrupted by a period of hibernation in midwinter, when the toads hole up underground to wait until the cold weather has passed. They resume their journey in spring, and it is then that large numbers of toads are frequently killed while crossing roads built on their traditional migration routes. Those toads lucky enough to reach the breeding ponds mate in a frenzy between March and June, before returning to their home range, which may be anything between 55 and 1,600 m (180 and 5,250 ft) away from the pond.

Avoiding traffic Tunnels or underpasses built beneath roads close to breeding ponds can help to reduce toad mortality caused by collisions with cars. Other measures include warning signs and people carrying the toads across in buckets.

Leatherback turtle
Long-distance swim

SPECIES *Dermochelys coriacea* **SIZE** 1.6–2.1 m (5¼–7 ft) **DISTRIBUTION** Temperate, subtropical, and tropical waters worldwide

This giant of the ocean makes lengthy annual migrations. Using ocean currents to help it on its way, the leatherback turtle feeds in the rich, temperate waters of the northern and southern Atlantic and Pacific oceans in spring and summer, but it returns to more tropical climates to find beaches on which to lay its eggs. Although only females venture onto land, males also migrate, coming close inshore to mate with the females. Satellite tagging has revealed extensive migrations: one record-setting leatherback was tracked swimming 20,557 km (12,774 miles), from a beach in Indonesia across the Pacific to the west coast of the USA and part of the way back again. Leatherbacks are prone to eating plastic refuse, mistaking it for jellyfish, and can choke to death as a result. They are also sometimes caught in fishing nets.

Landfall The females pull themselves onto gently sloping, sandy, tropical beaches to lay their eggs above the high-tide line. Most species of turtle return to the beach of their birth and the leatherback is no exception, although they may visit another beach in the same general vicinity.

Mission accomplished Female leatherback turtles lay an average of 110 eggs per clutch in a hole in soft sand that they dig with their flippers. The young hatch after 60–70 days and rush headlong to the sea.

Open ocean With a span of up to 2.7 m (8¾ ft), leatherback turtles have the longest front flippers relative to their size of any turtle. They usually cruise at around 2 km (1¼ miles) per hour.

CASE STUDY
SATELLITE TRACKING

Scientists increasingly use satellite tags to track the movements of leatherback turtles in the world's oceans. The tags are mounted directly onto the carapace of a turtle. The tages are usually fixed to the females once they have finished nesting and to males that are accidentally caught at sea by fishermen. The tag can relay information about a turtle's whereabouts via satellite to a computer. In addition to location information, the tag transmits data such as dive depth and duration, which give clues about behaviour such as foraging.

Bar-headed goose
Peak performance

SPECIES Anser indicus **SIZE** 70–82 cm (28–32 in)
DISTRIBUTION Mountain lakes and wetlands in Central Asia

Bar-headed geese reach extreme high altitudes during their migration over the peaks of the Himalayas. The birds are supremely adapted to the demands of their journey: their wings have a large surface area relative to the bird's weight to provide extra lift; their blood haemoglobin absorbs oxygen faster than that of other birds; and they have larger hearts and lungs and more capillaries in their flight muscles for rapid oxygen take-up. Bar-headed geese are capable of travelling more than 1,600 km (1,000 miles) each day and can fly at speeds of 80 kph (50 mph). Annual migration allows the geese to avoid severe winter storms on the high plateaus of Central Asia, where they breed in the summer, and summer monsoon rains in the Indian subcontinent.

Breeding grounds In summer, bar-headed geese live at high altitudes, on the Qing Zang Gao Yuan (Tibetan Plateau) and Qinghai in China, and Ladakh in Kashmir. The geese, such as the ones on the water in this photograph, congregate at mountain lakes to breed and feed on short grass.

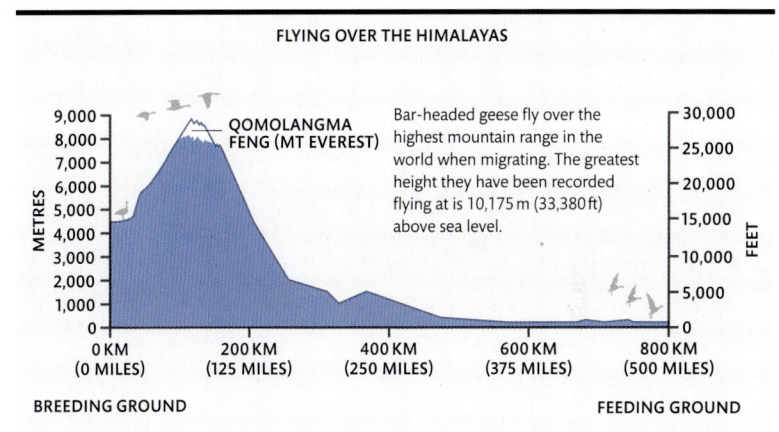

FLYING OVER THE HIMALAYAS

Bar-headed geese fly over the highest mountain range in the world when migrating. The greatest height they have been recorded flying at is 10,175 m (33,380 ft) above sea level.

Snowy albatross
Roaming the ocean

SPECIES Diomedea exulans **SIZE** 1.1–1.4 m (3½–4½ ft) **DISTRIBUTION** Open ocean and remote oceanic islands of the Southern Ocean

This albatross spends most of its life at sea, soaring above the waves or resting on the surface. It ventures thousands of kilometres across the southern hemisphere from its breeding islands close to the Antarctic Circle, occasionally crossing the Equator or circumnavigating Antarctica. One bird was tracked travelling a staggering 6,000 km (3,700 miles) in just 12 days. Snowy albatrosses nest on a few islands covered in tussock grass between November and July. Males and females take turns to incubate the egg and then guard their single chick while the other hunts at sea for food for the chick.

Flying solo Young albatrosses take up to 10 years to reach maturity and, during that time, may hardly ever make landfall. They often accompany fishing vessels, feeding on discarded fish.

3 m The wingspan of the snowy albatross, which is greater than that of any other flying bird.

HUMAN IMPACT
LONG-LINE FISHING

It is estimated that 100,000 albatrosses drown each year on long lines baited for bluefin tuna. The lines, which are pulled behind fishing boats, can be up to 130 km (80 miles) long and carry as many as 10,000 hooks. The birds try to catch the bait while it is close to the surface, become hooked, and are dragged underwater as the lines sink. International conservation efforts advocate the use of measures by fishermen to help prevent these deaths.

CASE STUDY RECORD SETTERS

Since 2007, biologists have been fitting satellite transmitters to bar-tailed godwits to record flight distances between Alaska and Australasia, and have found that some individuals undertake incredibly long non-stop flights. The map below shows the full migratory route taken by godwit "E7", whose 11,570-km (7,189-mile) non-stop southbound flight was the longest of the original group tracked in 2007. The current record holder is a juvenile bird ringed in 2022. This bird (ring number 234684) began its first migration on 13 October and travelled from Alaska to Tasmania, a distance of 13,560 km (8,425 miles), in just over 11 days. On their return flight to their Alaskan breeding grounds, bar-tailed godwits take a longer, coastal route, which allows them to stop and refuel as necessary, as the prevailing winds would not assist an oversea return flight.

Bar-tailed godwit
Longest non-stop flight

SPECIES *Limosa lapponica* **SIZE** 37–41 cm (14½–16 in)
DISTRIBUTION Arctic coastal tundra and sandy intertidal areas in South Africa, Australia, and New Zealand

This large wading bird is a long-distance globetrotter, capable of flying non-stop from breeding ranges in the Arctic regions of Europe, Asia, and western Alaska across the Equator to feeding grounds in South Africa, Australia, and New Zealand. During the northern-hemisphere summer, bar-tailed godwits are resident on the coastal tundra of the far north, where they lay between two and four eggs in cup-shaped nests in the grass. After rearing their young, the birds fly to "refuelling stations", such as estuaries, to feed and bulk up their bodies before flying south to the southern hemisphere. As the southern-hemisphere winter approaches, the birds moult into their russet-coloured breeding plumage and put on weight in advance of their northward migration. Some bar-tailed godwits overwinter in Europe, so are closer to their breeding grounds and require less energy to get there. Although their feeding rate is the same as birds that migrate from Africa, they spend less time feeding before they begin their journey.

Communal feeding grounds Bar-tailed godwits (seen here in a mixed flock with other shorebirds) frequent estuaries in the winter. They use their long, sensitive bills to probe for crustaceans, molluscs, and worms in the mud.

Fattened up for flying The bar-tailed godwit lays down huge fat stores (up to 55 per cent of its body mass) before embarking on its epic non-stop journeys. Its digestive tract shrinks in size to make room for the extra fuel, and its heart and pectoral muscles expand to improve sustained flight ability.

Whooping crane
Learning the route
SPECIES *Grus americana* **SIZE** 1.3 m (4¼ ft)
DISTRIBUTION Open, grassy plains and marshland in northern Canada and Texas, Florida, and Wisconsin, USA

The young of many water birds follow their parents on their first migration in order to learn the route. Naturally occurring whooping cranes migrate 4,000 km (2,500 miles) between a single summer breeding area in Wood Buffalo National Park, Canada, and a single wintering site in Aransas National Wildlife Refuge, Texas, USA. The birds' reliance on just two sites prompted conservationists to establish other populations in Florida and Wisconsin, USA, and to assist birds in their migration (see panel, right).

Rare birds In 1941, the migratory flock of whooping cranes numbered just 15 birds. In 2023, this had grown to 506 birds, and the total population (including whooping cranes involved in reintroduction projects) was 802.

HUMAN IMPACT
OPERATION MIGRATION
In 2001, conservationists hatched a plan to reintroduce whooping cranes to Wisconsin, USA. To teach the hand-reared birds the migration route from Wisconsin to Florida the cranes were "imprinted" on an ultra-light aircraft. The birds were played the noise of the aircraft's engine while still inside the egg and soon after hatching were introduced to the plane. Their first flights were taken following the aircraft down the runway and they eventually followed it 2,010 km (1,250 miles) across seven states to Florida.

Taking a break Barn swallows migrate in large flocks and frequently stop to rest on structures such as telegraph wires. Flocks gather in pre-migratory roosts in late summer and early autumn, often alongside other closely related species (here they are seen with house martins), before embarking on their southerly journey.

Barn swallow
Following the sun
SPECIES *Hirundo rustica* **SIZE** 18 cm (7 in) **DISTRIBUTION** Open grassland, meadows, and farmland habitats worldwide except Australia and Antarctica

Barn swallows breed throughout the northern hemisphere in summer but travel south to sunnier climes in South America, Africa, southern Asia, and north Australia for the northern winter. They migrate during the day, feeding on insects caught on the wing. In contrast to some migratory birds, they do not put on much weight before the journey. This makes them vulnerable to starvation when crossing large areas with little food such as the Sahara Desert. They are also at risk from storms and exhaustion. Barn swallows can cover up to 320 km (200 miles) per day when migrating. If they manage to survive the journey, barn swallows usually return to the same nest site and often reuse the same nest for years. Given that gathering materials for nest construction takes an average of 1,300 trips, it is unsurprising that birds that have just made a journey of some 10,000 km avoid using up their precious energy reserves building new nests from scratch.

Prolific breeders A female Norway lemming can begin breeding at four weeks of age, and can produce a new litter every six weeks. However, the survival rate of young is usually very low.

Norway lemming
Population pressure
SPECIES *Lemmus lemmus* **SIZE** 10–13 cm (4–5 in)
DISTRIBUTION Tundra, mountain heaths, and alpine and boreal forests of Scandinavia and Russia

Norway lemmings migrate sporadically every few years when their populations explode. In a typical year, the rodents live in tunnels beneath the snow in winter, moving to higher or lower ground in spring. There they live on mountain heaths or in forests, continuing to breed before returning in autumn to the alpine zone. Lemmings breed in both summer and winter, and population migrations are linked to high levels of breeding during the winter months.

Lemmings are often wrongly said to commit mass suicide by jumping from cliffs. Population pressure can trigger mass migration, usually away from the heaths and towards the forests. These population dispersals during boom years will result in plenty of death, but much of this is due to predation.

River crossing Caribou frequently cross lakes and rivers while migrating. They are strong swimmers, and their thick, air-filled coats help them to stay buoyant and warm in the icy water. These caribou are crossing the Kobuk River in Alaska, USA.

Caribou
Endurance test

SPECIES *Rangifer tarandus* **SIZE** 1.5–2.3 m (5–7½ ft) **DISTRIBUTION** Arctic tundra and boreal forest of USA, Canada, Asia, and northern Europe

Some populations of caribou undertake one of the most arduous annual migrations of any terrestrial mammal. Herds may number thousands of animals and complete a 5,000-km (3,100-mile) round trip, visiting spring calving areas and summer and winter feeding grounds. They are forced to move on by the seasonal availability of the tundra plants on which they feed. In summer, the herds take refuge from flies and mosquitoes in windy coastal areas; in winter, they move into subarctic boreal forests, where snow cover is less than on the open tundra. Caribou herds have been recorded running as fast as 80 kph (50 mph) while migrating. Groups are largest during the spring migration and smaller during autumn, when mating occurs. Some other populations are non-migratory, surviving winter food scarcity by building up fat stores. Caribou are also called reindeer, particularly in Europe and Asia, where many are partially domesticated.

Wolf kill Although young caribou are able to run soon after birth, large numbers of calves succumb to predators such as grey wolves, which track migrating herds. In British Columbia, a controversial wolf cull to help struggling caribou populations was initiated in the 2020s.

New life A female caribou tends to her minutes-old twin calves in Canada's Northwest Territories. Twins are a rare occurrence and most females have only one calf each year. Births take place in May or June on inland calving grounds.

HUMAN IMPACT
LIVING WITH REINDEER

Indigenous peoples of the Arctic and subarctic have a close association with reindeer, relying on them for food, skins, and transport. They live a nomadic life, moving with the semi-domesticated herds as they make their way between the coast and inland areas. Reindeer are rarely bred in captivity, but they have been tamed for milk production and to pull sleighs. Here, a Nenet herder leads her reindeer across snow-covered pastures in Siberia, Russia. Reindeer-herding is also an important part of Sami culture in northern Scandinavia (Lapland). Indigenous peoples in North America and Greenland have a long history of hunting wild caribou for their meat and hides.

Straw-coloured fruit bat

African odyssey

SPECIES *Eidolon helvum* **SIZE** 14–22 cm (5½–8½ in)
DISTRIBUTION Forest and savanna in sub-Saharan Africa, the southern Arabian Peninsula, and Madagascar

These African bats feed on fruit and undertake quite a journey to find enough of it. Bats from northern sub-Saharan Africa follow the annual rains north into savanna before returning south at the end of the rainy season. Their extensive migration takes them hundreds of kilometres. One bat was recorded travelling a cumulative distance of 2,518 km (1,565 miles) in 149 days. Along the way, they spend the day in large, noisy colonies in tree roosts. At night, they venture forth to find fruit, spreading out to feed. The vast population of straw-coloured fruit bats plays a vital role in pollinating and dispersing the seeds of many economically important plants, including timber trees such as iroko, a valuable hardwood, and cash crops such as bananas, plantains, mangoes, and figs.

Timely arrival Every November, between 5 and 10 million fruit bats descend on Kansaka National Park in Zambia. Their arrival coincides with a boom of fruit in the park. It is estimated that the bats eat 5,000 tonnes of fruit each night.

Humpback whale

Ocean voyagers

SPECIES *Megaptera novaeangliae* **SIZE** 14–18 m (46–59 ft)
DISTRIBUTION Open oceans worldwide, except extreme north and south

Many of the great whales make extraordinary journeys through the world's oceans in search of food and safe places to give birth, and humpback whales are no exception. The high-latitude oceans provide rich feeding grounds during each hemisphere's summer, and here the whales gorge themselves to store up energy for their long migration and the months that follow. In the northern hemisphere, humpback whales feed more often on fish than those in the southern hemisphere, where they eat mainly krill. As winter approaches, humpback whales move towards the equator on a journey of 5,000 km (3,100 miles) across the open ocean in search of warm, sheltered waters, where the females give birth and mating takes place. During this time, adults survive by metabolizing layers of fatty blubber beneath the skin, and the calves drink their mothers' rich milk. Eventually, they must return to polar waters to feed. Humpbacks have been recorded travelling 8,300 km (5,150 miles) from Costa Rica to Antarctica. The population in the northern Indian Ocean may be resident all year (see panel, below).

Mother and calf on the move
A female humpback whale makes the return journey to polar waters with her young calf. The calf is weaned at around 11 months but may stay with its mother for more than a year.

Looking for landmarks? When spy-hopping, a whale lifts its head vertically out of the water while rotating to look around. It may be checking for landmarks while migrating.

CASE STUDY MIGRATION ROUTES

Northern-hemisphere humpbacks spend the summer in feeding grounds in the northern Atlantic and Pacific oceans. In winter, they migrate south to breed in warmer waters around the Caribbean, West Africa, Japan, Hawaii, and Mexico. Southern-hemisphere humpbacks spend the summer feeding in the rich, cold waters of the Southern Ocean off Antarctica and migrating north to overwinter in the warm waters of Australia, the Pacific islands, southern Africa, or South America.

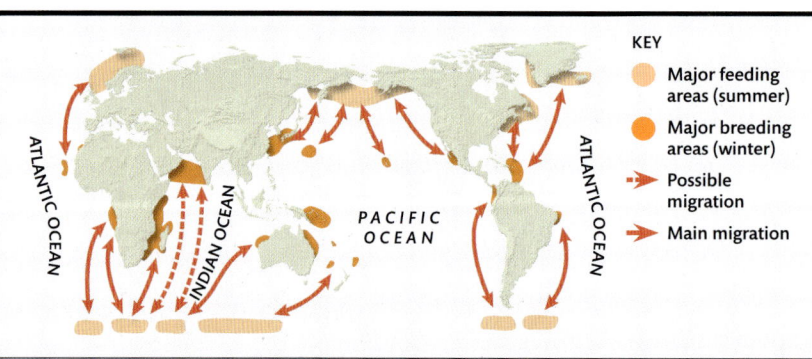

Blue wildebeest

Mass movement

SPECIES *Connochaetes taurinus*
SIZE 1.9–2.1 m (6¼–7 ft) **DISTRIBUTION** Plains and savanna grasslands in East Africa, from the Equator south to the tip of South Africa

Each year, around 1.3 million white-bearded wildebeest (one of five subspecies of the blue wildebeest) undertake a spectacular migration on the plains and savanna grasslands of East Africa. Their herds are further swelled by hundreds of thousands of other ungulate species, including Thomson's gazelles, zebras, and elands. The animals are compelled to move on in search of fresh food, water, and minerals such as phosphorus and potentially, calcium and nitrogen, that are important to their health. Mineral deficiency is thought to spur the herds to leave their dry-season ranges just before the onset of the rainy season and head south to the short-grass plains. Along the way, the wildebeest have to contend with predators, including lions and hyenas on the plains and crocodiles in the rivers.

Keeping up with mother
Wildebeest calves are born in the middle of the herd and within days can keep up with the adults when running. This helps them avoid becoming prey during the migration.

Trekking across the plains
As they cross the Serengeti Plain in Tanzania, white-bearded wildebeest throw up clouds of red dust from their hooves. Not all wildebeest are migratory; smaller herds may remain resident throughout the year.

Animal architects

Animals produce some of the most impressive architecture on Earth. Their building methods vary from simply fetching and dropping materials to more advanced construction techniques, including interlocking, weaving, or gluing materials together to ensure they stay in place. Some animals model their nests out of pliable substances such as mud, while others spin structures from silk, or dig burrows in the ground. Social animals build large structures relative to their body size by working as a team.

WHY BUILD?

Animals build structures for a variety of functions. Many live in their constructions for only a short time; for example, caddis fly larvae build themselves a protective case from grains of sand or other materials, and some frogs excavate shelters to help them stay moist during drought. Animals often build structures for raising young, as in the case of birds' nests and mammals' burrows. Social insects, such as ants, termites, bees, and wasps, construct elaborate nests to house entire colonies. Some animals build structures to capture prey or store food, while others communicate using architecture – for example, bowerbirds build courtship "stages".

Winter den Female polar bears dig dens under the snow to provide a safe, warm environment during the winter, when they give birth to their cubs. They suckle them for several months before emerging into the spring sunshine.

BUILDING BEHAVIOUR

Animals may be genetically programmed to build in a certain way without an image of the end goal and its function, or they may display a degree of ingenuity and flexibility. For example, a beaver can adapt the shape of its dam according to local conditions. Building usually involves relatively simple, repetitive behaviours, and most animals select or make standardized materials for their constructions. For example, caddis fly larvae reject sand grains that are either too small or too large for their cases, and martins choose just the right consistency of mud for their nests. Most animals use their feet or mouthparts to manipulate their building materials; their level of specialization depends on whether they are used for other functions as well, such as feeding.

Convergent evolution Both weaver ants (left) and tailorbirds (right) use silk to stitch leaves together to make their nests. Weaver ants use silk extruded from their own larvae, while tailorbirds make use of the silk from spiders' webs. They may also use plant fibre or even stolen household thread. These similar sewing behaviours have evolved independently of one another in unrelated species.

CASE STUDY LEARNING BUILDING SKILLS

To find out how the ability of adult male village weavers to build nests was affected by their experience when young, researchers gave some fledgling males fresh green building materials to handle (control group), but other fledglings received none (experimental group). When a year old, the experimental males were unable to weave a single strip in the first week that they were given reed grass. After three weeks of practice, their success rate at weaving was still only 26 per cent, whereas the experienced control group achieved a rate of 62 per cent.

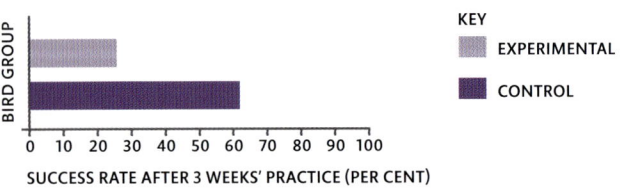

BUILDING MATERIALS

The natural world provides numerous organic and mineral building materials, such as grasses for weaver nests and trees for beaver lodges, sand and pebbles for many fish nests, and the earth itself for burrows. Some materials require little in the way of processing, but others need to be manipulated or mixed with other substances, such as saliva or water, before being used for building. Many animals secrete building materials, such as silk, mucus, or wax, from glands in their bodies. Some use materials derived from others in their constructions; for example, many birds collect soft feathers or fur to line their nests, whereas others find spider silk with which to build them. Animals can be very choosy about the materials they use in their architecture, selecting particular colours, for example.

Cavity nester A pair of northern flickers takes between one and two weeks to excavate a cavity in a tree, where they lay their eggs and rear their chicks. Abandoned flicker nests create homes for other cavity nesters.

MATERIALS AND STRUCTURES

PROVIDED BY THE ENVIRONMENT
Paper wasps chew fibres from dead wood to make a paper pulp with which they construct their intricate chambered nest, which is resistant to water. Male featherfin cichlids pile sand into a nest that also serves as an arena for displaying to prospective mates. Mute swans collect reeds and other bankside vegetation to build their nests.

PAPER WASP

FEATHERFIN CICHLID

MUTE SWAN

PROVIDED BY THE ANIMAL
Silkmoth caterpillars spin a cocoon of silk around themselves for pupation. Spiders also use silk, but for building webs. Termites mix saliva with mud to construct the walls of their termite mounds. Cave swiftlets also use spittle to build their nests. Other animal-derived materials include beeswax and mucus, which is used by some frogs for foam nests.

TERMITE

CALLETA SILKMOTH

PROVIDED BY ANOTHER ANIMAL
Hermit crabs take over the empty shells of marine molluscs, including the edible periwinkle. As the crab grows, it moves into progressively larger shells. Many animals live in cavities that were created by another species; for example, the elf owl nests in old woodpecker holes in the stems of cacti. Increasingly, humans provide homes for wildlife, such as a birdhouse for a colony of purple martins.

HERMIT CRAB

ELF OWL

PURPLE MARTIN

Hard corals
Stone walls

The world's most impressive underwater constructions are built by colonies of coral polyps, each joined individual resembling a tiny anemone. A colony starts when a coral larva settles from the plankton and develops into a polyp. This divides or buds asexually (see p.296), and each new polyp secretes its own skeleton cup (a corallite) of aragonite (a form of calcium carbonate), building up the colony. Over time, many different coral species growing close together build up into coral reefs. Mature coral colonies reproduce sexually (see p.301) to produce larvae.

Coral reefs are typically found in shallow, clear water around tropical coasts and islands. This is because corals need plenty of sunlight for their symbiotic algae, zooxanthellae, to photosynthesize and provide them with the nutrients needed to build their massive skeletons. When water temperatures rise, stressed corals eject these food providers, and turn white – a process known as coral bleaching (see p.301).

2,000 km
The total length of the Great Barrier Reef, the world's largest reef system.

Coral reef Corals come in many different shapes depending on how the polyps grow and secrete their skeleton. Over time, reefs erode and lower layers are compacted to form limestone.

Paper nautilus
Delicate case

SPECIES *Argonauta nodosus* **SIZE** 10–30 cm (4–12 in) (female); 3–4 cm (1¼–1½ in) (male) **DISTRIBUTION** Surface waters of southern-hemisphere oceans, from the Indo-Pacific to the east coast of South America

The paper nautilus (or knobby argonaut) is actually a type of octopus. The female paper nautilus secretes a delicate calcareous shell that serves as a mobile home for the animal as it drifts in the oceans. It also acts as a brood chamber, a shelter in which to lay and protect her eggs. The paper nautilus's egg case is usually around 12–15 cm (4½–6 in) long, and the empty shells can occasionally be found washed up on the shore.

Secreted shelter The paper nautilus's shell is secreted by the web between a pair of the animal's eight arms and is added to along the outer edge as the paper nautilus grows.

Water spider
Diving bell

SPECIES *Argyroneta aquatica* **SIZE** 0.7–1.5 cm (¼–½ in) **DISTRIBUTION** Ponds, streams, ditches, and shallow lakes in northern and central Europe and northern Asia

The water spider is able to spend its whole life beneath the water's surface, thanks to its own supply of air. It spins a web that is anchored to underwater vegetation, and then fills it by returning repeatedly from the surface with air bubbles. This "diving bell" serves as a place to breathe, hide from predators, consume prey, and breed. Male water spiders build their diving bells adjacent to those of females and break through to the adjacent bell when ready to mate. The female creates a silken cocoon around 30–70 eggs at the top of her diving bell. Water spiders may seal their bell when hibernating and build a separate bell elsewhere in which to shed their skin.

Silken retreat The water spider rarely needs to replenish the air supply in its diving bell, because oxygen diffuses in and carbon dioxide diffuses out.

Black and yellow garden spider
Complex web

SPECIES *Argiope aurantia* **SIZE** 9–28 mm (⅜–1¼ in) (female); 5–9 mm (³⁄₁₆–⅜ in) (male)
DISTRIBUTION Sunny habitats, from southern Canada, through USA, Mexico, and Central America as far as Costa Rica

The black and yellow garden spider is one of several species of orb-web spiders, which weave relatively large, circular webs that are suspended vertically to catch prey. The black and yellow garden spider spins a web that is up to 0.6 m (2 ft) in diameter and positioned 0.6–2.4 m (2–8 ft) above the ground. Orb-web spiders have three claws on each foot, to help them handle the threads while spinning. Silk is extruded from several spinnerets on the underside of the spider's abdomen. The spinnerets are served by different glands that produce silk of different types and thicknesses. For example, sticky thread is used for prey-catching parts of the web. Orb-web spiders typically consume much of their web each evening and rebuild it anew for the next day.

30 The number of minutes it takes most orb-web spiders to build an entire web.

Orb web The spider sits and waits on its web for an insect to become trapped. The central part of the web is called the stabilimentum.

Constructing an orb web First, the spider connects two structures with a strand of silk forming a bridge line or primary thread. Then it begins the web by constructing scaffolding lines, which connect the structure to its support. Next, the spider makes a frame of threads radiating from a central hub. Then it attaches a temporary spiral to the radial threads. Finally, the web is completed by the spider spinning close spirals of sticky thread.

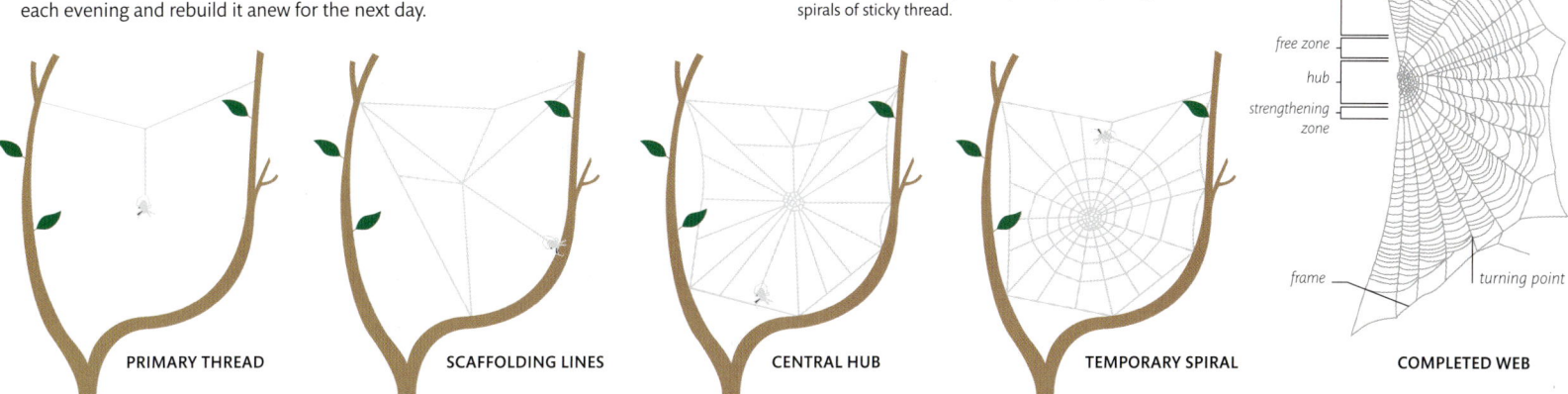

PRIMARY THREAD | SCAFFOLDING LINES | CENTRAL HUB | TEMPORARY SPIRAL | COMPLETED WEB

African mound-building termites
Multi-purpose structure

GENUS Macrotermes **SIZE** Up to 3 cm (1¼ in)
DISTRIBUTION Savanna in Africa and Southeast Asia

For such small insects, termites construct incredibly large and elaborate structures in which to live. A mature termite mound may be home to 3–5 million individual termites. Inside, there is a complex network of chambers, passageways, and ventilation channels that extend above and below ground level. The mound has specific areas designated for waste, for storing and growing food, and for egg-laying and larval development. The queen termite resides in a royal chamber, built to surround her pulsating, egg-producing abdomen. Worker termites tend her, removing the eggs, as she lays them, to nursery chambers, where they develop. The queen termite secretes a pheromone from her body, which stimulates the workers to build pillars, arches, and eventually walls around her to create the royal chamber. Pheromone deposits may also help to direct the construction of walls and passageways within the termite mound.

Fungus garden Many termites cultivate fungal fruiting bodies on which they and their nymphs feed. The fungi thrive on the cellulose contained in chewed plant matter supplied by the termites.

Air-conditioning system Termite mounds have an ingenious, in-built ventilation system: variations in pressure or temperature cause air to circulate, cooling and freshening the colony. Wind, passing over openings on top of the mound, decreases the air pressure, drawing clean air into openings at the mound's base and through its passageways.

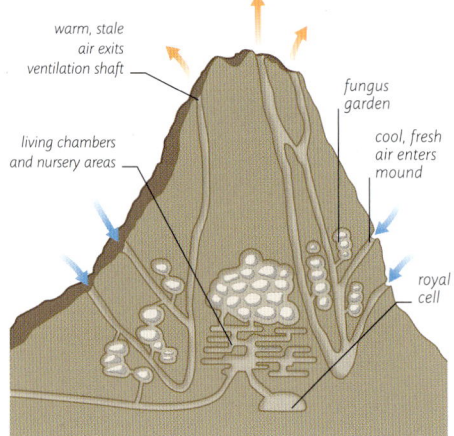

Tower block *Macrotermes* termite mounds can reach heights of 6–7 m (20–23 ft). In dry areas, vertical shafts are excavated to reach the water table, which can be as much as 45 m (150 ft) below the ground.

CASE STUDY
4,000-YEAR-OLD TERMITE NETWORK

An enormous area of roughly 200 million ancient termite mounds, covering 230,000 square km (88,800 square miles) – roughly the size of Great Britain – was discovered in Northeast Brazil. The conical mounds, believed to be 4,000 years old, had been obscured by the dry, deciduous shrubby (or Caatinga) forests of the region. Joined by an extensive network of interconnecting tunnels, each mound, measuring up to 4 m (13 ft) tall and 9 m (30 ft) in diameter, has no obvious internal structure. The mounds are thought to have formed as termites excavated tunnels to reach and store fresh vegetation during rainy seasons. The termites, *Syntermes dirus* (which are still present in the area), forage after dark using narrow, vertical tunnels to reach the surface, which are sealed after use.

ANIMAL ARCHITECTS **135**

Common wasp
Paper house

SPECIES *Vespula vulgaris* **SIZE** 1–1.5 cm (⅜–½ in) (worker); 1.5–2 cm (½–¾ in) (queen) **DISTRIBUTION** Nests underground or in buildings near gardens, woodland, and meadows in Europe, Asia, North Africa, and North America

Common wasps are social insects that build nests out of paper to house their colonies. Only the queen wasps (the sole egg layers) survive the winter to found a new colony in spring. They select a suitable site for the nest, either underground in an abandoned animal burrow or in a sheltered location, such as a garden shed. There they begin to construct a nest from chewed wood sourced from nearby trees or timber. The wood pulp dries into paper, a remarkably strong yet light building material. Once complete, the nest typically has a number of horizontal layers of cells that open downwards. These house the eggs and developing larvae of the colony. Surrounding these brood cells are a series of spiral chambers, which provide strength to the nest as well as trapping air for insulation.

Early stages A single queen starts by constructing a stalk from which the nest is suspended. She then begins to add cells, laying a single egg into each one. When fully grown, the workers complete the nest.

Curved walls As the colony grows, the workers gradually demolish the innermost walls of the nest and build new ones around the outside. A completed nest can house 5,000–10,000 wasps.

Honey bee
Wax comb

SPECIES *Apis mellifera* **SIZE** 1.5–2.5 cm (½–1 in) **DISTRIBUTION** Worldwide. Some subspecies native to Europe, Africa, Middle East, and Asia. Introduced to North and South America

Honey bee colonies live in beehives formed from several layers of honeycomb. The honeycomb's cells are used to house the colony's developing brood and to store food in the form of pollen and honey. Worker bees build the comb out of wax, which is secreted from glands in their abdomen and manipulated with their mouthparts. Workers produce different cells according to their intended purpose. Cells for the larvae of drones (whose only duty is to mate with the queen) are larger than those for worker larvae; and those that will contain future queens are even bigger, oval in shape, and are arranged vertically rather than horizontally.

Honeycomb Honeycomb consists of sheets of regular, six-sided cells. When a cell is filled with mature honey, or when a larva is ready to pupate, each individual cell is capped with a wax lid. Wild bee colonies (right) live in hollow trees or rock cavities.

Weaver ants
Leaf nest

GENUS *Oecophylla* **SIZE** About 6 mm (¼ in) **DISTRIBUTION** Trees in tropical forest in Africa, Asia, and Australia

Weaver ants, also called green or tree ants, use living leaves to construct their nests in the tops of trees. The nests provide shelter for the workers and developing young. A single colony of weaver ants can consist of 100,000–500,000 individuals and may have up to 150 different nests in 12 or more trees. One of the colony's nests will contain several egg-producing queen ants. This nest is characterized by having more ant trails connecting with it than any other. Workers travel along these trails to distribute eggs to other nests. At the edge of the colony's territory there are barrack nests, where older worker ants live and defend the boundary. Weaver ants are voracious predators of pests that damage fruit crops, such as citrus fruits, mangoes, and cashews. Fruit-growers therefore introduce weaver ant colonies into their plantations and install bamboo bridges between trees to help the ants move around. The ants reduce the need for chemical insecticides.

sticky silk

150
The number of nests that may be found in a mature colony of weaver ants.

Green house Once several leaves have been glued into place, the nest is complete. Worker ants move in with some of the colony's eggs, which they tend through the larval and pupa stages to adulthood.

Living shuttles Adult weaver ants use sticky silk extruded by the larvae to join leaves together when nest-building. Unlike other ant species, the larvae do not use their silk to create cocoons.

Shell-brooding cichlid
Second-hand home

SPECIES *Lamprologus callipterus* **SIZE** 12 cm (4½ in) (male); 4.5 cm (1¾ in) (female) **DISTRIBUTION** Fresh water of Lake Tanganyika, central East Africa

This shell-brooding cichlid uses empty snail shells as nurseries for brooding its eggs. Female cichlids are attracted to nests of shells collected by the much larger males. The larger the males are, the more likely they are to win territorial disputes and wrangles over shells. Conversely, it is an advantage for females to be small, so they can fit deep inside the snail shells, where they lay their eggs and remain for up to a fortnight to brood them until the hatchlings are ready to leave. Some medium-sized males will sneak into a resident male's territory, where as many as 14 females may be nesting in different shells, in an attempt to mate with the females. Another tactic is employed by dwarf males, which are small enough to enter a shell to fertilize the female's eggs.

Shell collectors Male cichlids collect empty snail shells and carry them back to a nesting area, which they attempt to defend from intruders. The largest males tend to have more shells and consequently attract more females than smaller males.

Grey foam-nest frog
Foam nursery

SPECIES *Chiromantis xerampelina* **SIZE** 4.5–7.5 cm (1¾–3 in) (male); 6–9 cm (2¼–3½ in) (female) **DISTRIBUTION** Subtropical and tropical forest, savanna, scrubland, and grassland in central and southern East Africa

The grey foam-nest frog breeds during a brief window of time in the rainy season when seasonal pools are available. The females build communal nests on branches overhanging pools by producing a fluid that they whip up with their long legs and webbed feet. These communal nests involve numerous males in amplexus (mating position) with females, as well as unpaired or "satellite" males who also release sperm into the foam. On average, the nests contain approximately 1,200 eggs, which take around four to six days to hatch into tadpoles at a temperature of 25°C (77°F). The tadpoles live in the foam for another two days before emerging simultaneously and dropping into the pool below.

Whipping up a nest The female lays her eggs into the foam she has whipped up (main). The outer layer of the foam hardens around a moist interior, preventing the eggs from drying out. Oxygen diffuses through the foam, enabling the tadpoles to breathe until they begin to drop into the pool of water below (inset).

Carmine bee-eater
Sandbank burrows

SPECIES *Merops nubicoides* **SIZE** 27 cm (10½ in) **DISTRIBUTION** Lowland river valleys, floodplains, and riverine forests in sub-equatorial Africa

Carmine bee-eaters excavate horizontal burrows in vertical sandbanks along rivers. Their colonies may contain thousands of individuals, often divided into smaller groups known as clans. When starting to excavate a nest burrow, a bird flies repeatedly at the bank beak first, until it makes a slight depression onto which it can cling. It then uses its beak and feet to dig a narrow tunnel measuring 1–2 m (3¼–6½ ft) in length. Two of the carmine bee-eater's toes are fused at the base, making them perfect for using as a shovel. Immature birds without a mate may help their parents to dig a new tunnel.

Hamerkop
Solid structure

SPECIES *Scopus umbretta* **SIZE** 47–56 cm (18½–22 in) **DISTRIBUTION** Freshwater wetland habitats in sub-Saharan Africa, Madagascar, and southwest Arabian Peninsula

Also known as the hammerhead, the hamerkop builds the largest roofed nest that is used by a mating pair of any bird. It is built in a fork between tree branches. First, a platform is made out of sticks, then the sides are built up into a deep basin. Next, a domed roof of sticks and mud is added. The small entrance is usually located at the side near the base, as a precaution against predators. Both the entrance tunnel and the nest chamber are lined with mud. The nest can reach 2 m (6½ ft) high by 2 m (6½ ft) wide and may take up to six weeks to build. When complete, it can support the weight of a aadult person on its roof. The whole structure is decorated with unusual objects such as feathers, snakeskin, bones, and even human-made items. A pair of hamerkops may build several nests within their territory, but use only one. Other birds, such as owls and Egyptian geese, often move into the spare nests.

Team work Hamerkops mate for life, and a pair labours for about four hours a day to build its massive nest. When it is finished, the female lays between three and nine brown eggs in the nest chamber.

Safe from predators
At Los Berruecos in Spain's Extremadura region, white storks nest out of harm's way on the top of dramatic granite boulders.

White stork
High-rise living

SPECIES *Ciconia ciconia* **SIZE** 1–1.2 m (3¼–4 ft)
DISTRIBUTION Breeds in Europe, northwest Africa, and southwest Asia; winters in tropical to southern Africa and the Indian subcontinent. Inhabits open farmland close to marshy wetland feeding areas

The white stork builds one of the largest nests of all bird species. A pair mates for life and tends to return to the same nest site every year, providing they bred successfully there in the previous year, adding a new layer of sticks and earth to the huge nesting platform that was used the year before. Both males and females take part in building the nest, although the male collects most of the materials. In addition to sticks, he may select rags and paper discarded by humans. White storks also help to boost the survival of their eggs and chicks by bringing fresh cattle dung to the nest to help keep it warm.

Pileated woodpecker
Tree house

SPECIES *Dryocopus pileatus* **SIZE** 42 cm (16½ in)
DISTRIBUTION Coniferous and deciduous forest of North America, particularly southern Canada and eastern USA

The pileated woodpecker uses its strong bill to excavate large nest cavities in trees, typically 4.5–24 m (14¾–79 ft) above the ground. It will normally excavate a new nest each year although, occasionally, it will reuse an existing hole. The trees used for nests are often dead and already hollow, making them easier to drill into. The nests frequently face east or south, to benefit from the warmth of the sun. Other birds, such as American kestrels, wood ducks, and screech owls, may use old pileated woodpecker holes for nesting once they have been vacated. Pileated woodpeckers also chip away at trees to uncover food in the form of carpenter ants and beetle larvae that live in the wood. They pick these up with their sticky, barbed tongues. Woodpeckers' feet are adapted for walking up vertical tree trunks by having two toes that point backwards.

Spitting sawdust Both sexes assist with building the nest cavity, which is lined with wood chippings. The female lays between three and five eggs, which are incubated alternately by each parent.

ANATOMY SHOCK ABSORBERS

A woodpecker hammers trees 20 times a second at a speed of 24 kph (15 mph). It has several adaptations to allow its body to cope with the shock of hitting such a hard substance so fast and furiously: the chisel-shaped bill is anchored to the skull by a thick bone to prevent jarring; the skull is relatively thick and formed of spongy bone that acts as a cushion for the brain; the muscles behind the bill and in the neck contract just prior to the impact to help absorb the pounding and transmit the shock through the whole body to protect the head; and its third inner eyelid closes to secure the eyeball, cushion the retina to prevent it tearing under the vibration of drumming and chiselling, and shield the eye from flying splinters.

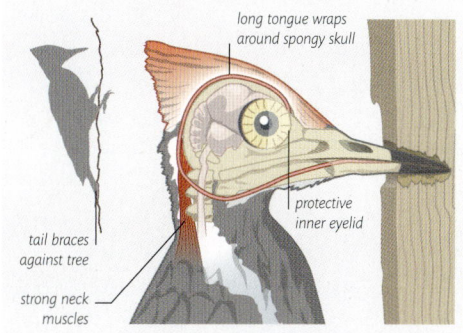

138 LIVING SPACE

ANIMAL ARCHITECTS 139

Competing for females A male southern masked weaver displays by flapping his wings beneath his finished nest (bottom left). A rival male has only just started his nest (centre), but he may yet be successful, as females prefer fresh green nests to older brown ones.

Southern masked weaver
Woven globes

SPECIES *Ploceus velatus* **SIZE** 11–14 cm (4½–5½ in)
DISTRIBUTION Southern African scrubland, savanna, grassland, open woodland, inland wetland, and semi-desert

The southern masked weaver bends, knots, and stitches pliable grasses into a globe-shaped nest suspended from a tree branch. Groups of male southern masked weavers build their nests in the same tree, selecting positions at the ends of twigs as protection from tree-climbing predators, such as snakes. Once the initial hoop of woven grass is in place, the weaver starts to construct the nesting chamber. The length of the bird's reach determines the size of the spherical chamber, and a porch-like entrance is added once the nesting chamber is complete. When a female moves in, she lines the nest with soft grasses and feathers before laying a clutch of about five eggs.

Male weavers prefer to select fresh green vegetation for their nests. Young leaves are more flexible than older ones and can be woven more easily. Also, the females prefer nests made from newer materials. Weavers use a complex array of fastenings, including spiral binding and knots such as the half hitch, overhand, and slipknot. Birds that are experienced in handling fresh green building materials are better able to construct their woven nests than those without similar experience. Male southern masked weavers can fly a total distance of 370 km (230 miles) to collect materials when building their nests.

Each male southern masked weaver builds 20 or more new nests during a single breeding season in order to attract multiple female weavers. Several nest may be used by different females, but he also regularly destroys his own nests, sometimes even when they are in use, as their materials dry out and degrade over time.

Similar species There are around 60 species of weavers in the genus *Ploceus* and all share similar traits. To collect nest material, male weavers, for instance the village weaver (*P. cucullatus*, above), land near the base of a leaf, cut into it, and fly off with a long, thin strip. Female weavers, such as the little weaver (*P. luteolus*, right), inspect a potential mate's nest before deciding whether to stay and breed.

370 km

The total distance travelled by male weavers to collect fresh plant material when nest-building.

Vogelkop bowerbird
Decorated stage
SPECIES *Amblyornis inornata* **SIZE** 25 cm (10 in)
DISTRIBUTION Mountain habitats of the Vogelkop Peninsula of Irian Jaya, Indonesia

Male Vogelkop bowerbirds build elaborate display stages out of sticks in order to attract mates, and even steal unusual items from neighbours for their own bowers. Their large, impressive constructions are built on the ground, measuring up to 1.8 m (6 ft) across and 1.2 m (4 ft) high. Populations of Vogelkop bowerbirds differ in their bower design and taste for decoration. For example, in the Arfak mountains they build huts with arched entrances, adorned with colourful fruits and flowers; while in the Fakfak mountains they build tall spires and decorate them with comparatively dull decorations, such as snail shells, nuts, and fungi.

Different cultures Although there is little genetic difference between bowerbird populations, they are unlikely to hybridize as the styles of their bower displays differ so dramatically, females would be unimpressed by the "wrong" bower type.

Long-tailed tit
Expandable home
SPECIES *Aegithalos caudatus* **SIZE** 13–15 cm (5–6 in)
DISTRIBUTION Deciduous woodland, hedgerows, and scrub in Europe and Asia

The long-tailed tit builds a globe-shaped nest out of spiders' webs, mosses, lichens, and feathers. Usually situated in shrubs, such as gorse, bramble, blackthorn, or hawthorn, the nest is held together by the small, rough leaves of the mosses, which hook onto the loops of the stretchy spider silk. As the brood grows, the nest expands to accommodate them. The outside of the nest is covered with silvery lichens and white spider cocoons, both of which provide camouflage by reflecting light off the exterior. The nest is lined with a soft, warm layer of 2,000 or more feathers, which can comprise about 40 per cent of the nest's mass. Long-tailed tits adjust the thickness of the insulating feather layer in their nest according to prevailing environmental conditions, the most important being ambient temperature.

Growing family Between 6 and 12 eggs are laid in the cosy nest. Once the chicks have hatched, both parents work hard to provide their growing brood with insects. Relatives, whose own breeding attempts have failed, sometimes help.

Sociable weaver
Thatched roof
SPECIES *Philetairus socius* **SIZE** 14 cm (5½ in)
DISTRIBUTION Open savanna grassland and thorn scrubland in northern South Africa and southern Namibia

Sociable weavers live communally in groups of over 100 birds and their young in the avian equivalent of an apartment block. The huge nests, built in acacia trees, resemble haystacks. The birds maintain their nests all year round: this is vital, as the thick thatched roofs provide protection from the cold winter nights and hot summer days that are typical of the desert. There may be up to 300 openings in the underside of a nest, each leading to a tunnel that terminates in a chamber. Sociable weavers' nesting chambers may be taken over by other birds such as the African pygmy falcon, as well as lizards and wasps. The weavers are ecological engineers: a supersized nest creates a stable micro-climate that can support a distinct ecosystem.

Building material Weavers use various materials when building their nests. The initial structure consists of large twigs and stems, into which grasses are poked; sharp spikes of straw deter predators from the entrances, and the chambers are lined with soft fur and cotton.

North American beaver
Hydro-engineering

SPECIES *Castor canadensis* **SIZE** 90–117 cm (35–46 in)
DISTRIBUTION Wetland, streams, and rivers in North America, except far north of Canada and parts of southern USA and Mexico

North American beavers are masters at controlling water through construction. In order to have sufficiently deep ponds in which to build their homes, known as lodges, they first build dams to control the flow of water and raise its level. The longest beaver dam discovered so far, in Wood Buffalo National Park, Canada, measures roughly 775 m (2,540 ft). One dam found at Three Forks in Montana, USA, measured 650 m (2,130 ft) long, 4 m (13 ft) high, and was 7 m (23 ft) thick at the base. In addition to dams, beavers construct canals from favoured feeding areas, along which they float food back to the lodge.

Beaver activity is known to have many beneficial effects, including improving water quality and flow, which reduces the likelihood of flooding. It also dramatically boosts biodiversity by creating new and structurally varied wetland habitats for other wildlife.

The ponds and lodges beavers create help to protect them against predators such as wolves, lynxes, and bears. They also provide shelter from the cold in winter. When the ponds freeze over, the beavers remain in their lodges or move freely under the ice.

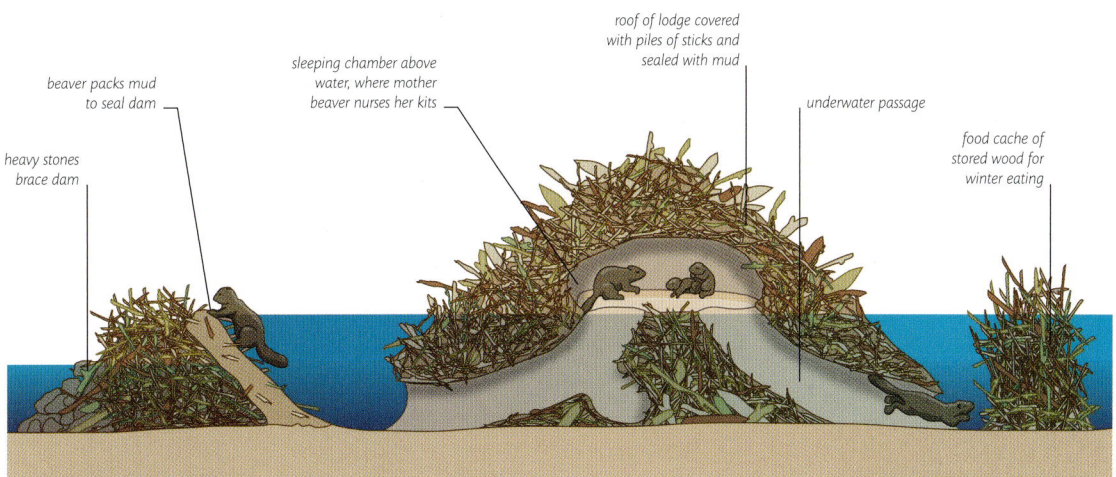

Beaver lodge A beaver lodge may be located on an island behind the dam, on the edge of the pond, or on the shore of a lake. Some beavers excavate burrows rather than build a lodge.

Maintenance work Beavers are quick to rebuild their dams if they become damaged. They drag tree trunks by their teeth and carry mud and stones in their forepaws.

Black-tailed prairie dog
Underground town

SPECIES *Cynomys ludovicianus* **SIZE** 35–43 cm (14–17 in)
DISTRIBUTION Dry, open, short- to mid-grass prairies from central Texas, USA, to southern Canada

Colonies of black-tailed prairie dogs live in extensive underground burrow systems called towns. Towns are divided into wards, and the wards into coteries. Each coterie is home to several closely related females, an unrelated adult male, and their offspring. A coterie may have as many as 70 entrances into the burrow system. The burrows are on average 5–10 m (16½–33 ft) long and 2–3 m (6½–9¾ ft) beneath the ground. Some entrances are surrounded by a mound of earth up to 1 m (3¼ ft) high, resembling the rim of a volcanic crater. The mound helps to ventilate the burrow system by altering the air flow over it, causing fresh air to be drawn through the tunnels. Its steep sides also help to protect the animals from predators and flash flooding. Other entrances have a shallower, domed mound, and some have no mound at all.

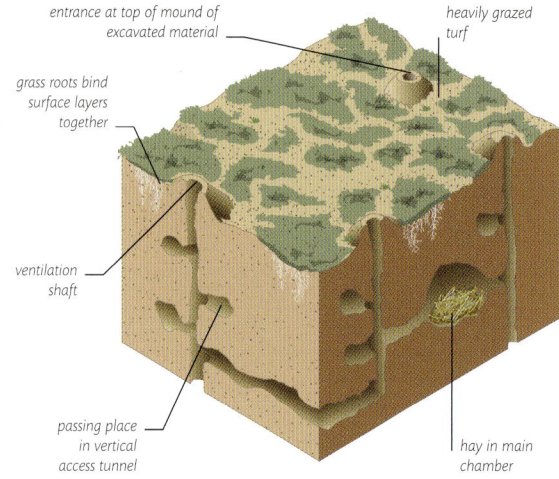

400 million
The largest number of animals ever estimated in a single prairie dog town, in Texas, USA.

Staying alert Their mounds afford the prairie dogs a good view of the surrounding prairie. They maintain a lookout for potential predators, which may include coyotes, bobcats, eagles, and hawks. If they spot a predator approaching, they give an alarm call and dive underground.

Burrow system Black-tailed prairie dogs spend time underground in their burrow systems at night, in the heat of the day in summer, and during inclement weather in winter.

Making the bed First, the chimpanzee pulls several thick branches together and presses them down to make a stable platform. It then weaves thinner branches and twigs around the edge and uses broken twigs and leaves to provide padding for the centre of the bed.

Lazing around The daytime nests of chimpanzees may be old rather than freshly built and are frequently in the same tree in which the animals have been feeding. They are likely to be located lower down in the tree than night-time nests.

Common chimpanzee
Night nest

SPECIES *Pan troglodytes* **SIZE** 73–95 cm (29–37 in)
DISTRIBUTION Gallery forest, rainforest, and woodland savanna across equatorial Africa

Most nights, chimpanzees build a new nest in which to sleep. Their beds are usually high up in trees, 10–20 m (33–66 ft) off the ground, safely out of the reach of predators, with females nesting higher than males. They use tree branches and leaves to construct a round platform measuring about 90 cm (35 in) in diameter. Nest-building can take as little as one to seven minutes, depending on the experience of the builder. Chimpanzees generally sleep for around 12 hours each night and also rest in nests during the day, between bouts of foraging. In addition, they may retreat to bed if they are ill or injured. Infants sleep with their mothers until a new sibling arrives, at which point they start to build their own nests, and it is likely they practise their technique on the ground. Biologists can use the number of fresh nests in trees to estimate the number of chimpanzees in an area, while the noise of construction can also reveal their location. Gorillas and orangutans construct arboreal nests similar to those of chimpanzees, although gorillas also nest on the ground.

ANIMAL ARCHITECTS 143

Honduran white bat
Leaf tent

SPECIES *Ectophylla alba* **SIZE** 4–5 cm (1½–2 in)
DISTRIBUTION Rainforest in lowland Central America, including parts of Honduras, Nicaragua, Costa Rica, and Panama

The Honduran white bat lives in rainforests containing plenty of *Heliconia* plants, and it uses their long, broad leaves to make tents under which it roosts. The bat nibbles through the veins on either side of the leaf midrib, causing the leaf to fold down to form an inverted V-shape. Each tent may be inhabited by four to eight bats, although group size is limited by the maximum weight capacity of the leaves of different species of *Heliconia* plants. A group usually consists of a single male and his harem of females. A colony of bats may have several tents scattered throughout its area of forest. The bats use the tents during the day when sleeping to provide protection from the elements, such as the sun and rain, and from predators, which include monkeys and snakes. The green light filtering through the leaf onto the white fur of the bat makes them almost indistinguishable from their shelter. They are so confident in their camouflage that the bats will take flight only if they detect movement on the main stem of their *Heliconia* plant.

Temporary shelter The building process requires several nights' work for the Honduran white bat, and is performed by both males and females. Tents last for just over seven weeks on average, after which new ones are constructed elsewhere.

European mole
Earthworks

SPECIES *Talpa europaea* **SIZE** 11–16 cm (4½–6½ in)
DISTRIBUTION Rich, deep soil beneath arable fields, deciduous woodland, and permanent pasture in temperate Europe

European moles spend most of their lives underground. They are able to dig about 20 m (66 ft) of tunnels each day, throwing up characteristic mounds of discarded soil as they excavate, much to the chagrin of gardeners attempting to achieve the "perfect lawn". A single mole's tunnel system may cover an area up to 70 m (230 ft) across, although some estimates are greater. They are solitary and territorial, behaving aggressively to their neighbours and taking over their tunnels if they leave or die. They breed during spring, when male moles may extend their burrows in search of mates. Females give birth to between two and seven young underground, where they remain for about five weeks before striking out overland to establish their own territories.

Under the hill A fresh molehill is a sure sign that moles are present in an area. Beneath, a network of shallow and deeper tunnels leads to one or more nest chambers filled with dry plant matter. This is where moles sleep and where females raise their young.

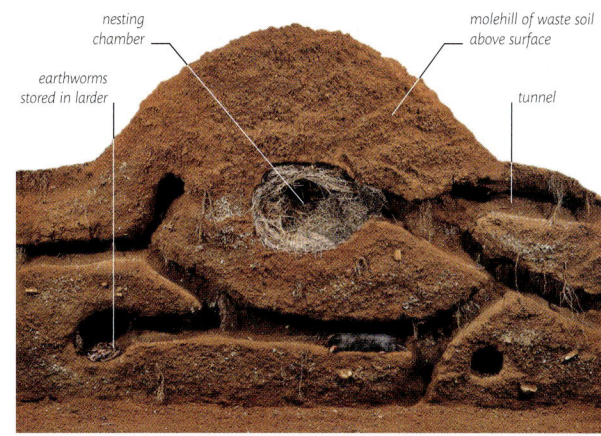

nesting chamber · molehill of waste soil above surface · earthworms stored in larder · tunnel

Worm trap Moles immobilize earthworms that drop into their tunnel systems by delivering a bite to the head. Earthworms can sense the vibrations of a digging mole and will endeavour to get out of the way.

ANATOMY **DIGGING TOOL**

The mole's front paws are shaped like shovels, with five strong claws. They are permanently turned out in a perfect position for pushing earth aside. Moles also have other features that help them in their burrowing lifestyle – their tiny eyes are almost completely covered by fur, their nostrils open to the side rather than the front, and they have no external ears that might otherwise get filled with earth.

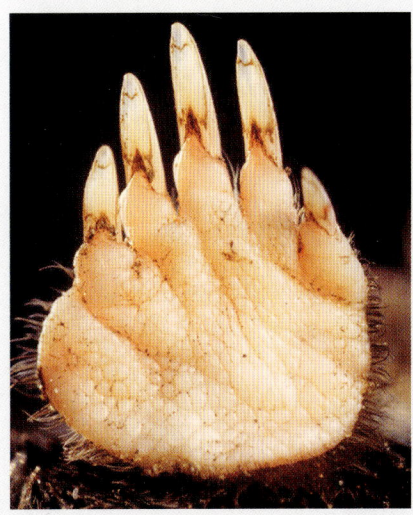

Hunting and feeding

150
Feeding on plants

162
Omnivores

170
Predation

218
Scavenging

228
Feeding relationships

Meal manipulation Grey herons typically smack large fishes against a rock to kill them. They then flip them so that they can be swallowed head first. This enables the heron to eat the fish easily, without its fins, spines, and scales sticking in the heron's throat.

HUNTING AND FEEDING

Feeding is a fundamental need of almost all animals because they require food to provide energy for the various internal chemical processes essential for life. Even though the details of how food is obtained and what food is eaten may vary between animals, the basic processes involved are common to all of them. They must locate food, capture or gather it, process it (by chewing, for example), ingest it, and digest it. To achieve this, a range of feeding behaviours have evolved.

HUNGER

The physiological motivation to eat – to replenish spent reserves, maintain a positive energy balance, or fatten-up for an event such as migration or hibernation – is controlled by a part of the brain called the hypothalamus and by fluctuating levels of hormones. But there are also other motivations that drive animals to feed. Some may become conditioned to feed at a particular time of day or in response to a particular sight, smell, or taste. In some cases, simply coming across food is sufficient motivation to feed, particularly if food is scarce. For many social species, seeing group mates feeding is enough to stimulate feeding. In such situations, an animal may eat more food than it would if were it alone, and it is more likely to eat a novel food if others are eating it.

CARNIVORES, HERBIVORES, AND OMNIVORES

Animals can be classified according to their diet. Carnivores feed on other animals. To do so they must be able to locate, kill, and eat their prey, and so many have specialized prey-detection mechanisms, well-developed weapons, and exhibit specialized feeding behaviours, such as stalking and ambushing. Some carnivores feed on species far larger than themselves and so must cooperate with one another to bring down prey. Herbivores feed on plants, and many specialize in a particular part of the plant, such as fruits or leaves. Like carnivores, herbivores require special feeding adaptations, such as grinding teeth to chew tough plant material. Omnivores, scavengers, and detritivores (which feed on decaying organic matter) are usually generalists; they eat a wide variety of foodstuffs and therefore often (but not always) lack the kind of highly specialized feeding adaptations seen in carnivores and herbivores. Instead, they require behavioural and anatomical flexibility to locate, process, and utilize a wide variety of foods.

FOOD CHAINS AND WEBS

Feeding is essentially the transfer of energy from one organism, the prey, to another, the predator. The energy in an ecosystem originates from organisms that harness energy from the sun (plants) or from chemical reactions (deep-sea bacteria). These primary producers are eaten by primary consumers, which may in turn be eaten by other consumers. In this way energy is transferred through "chains" of organisms. Each step in the chain is called a trophic level. Typically, the bottom of a chain (primary producers) consists of a large number of organisms, whereas the top (apex predators) consists of fewer, often larger, individuals. Chains are components of more complex food webs involving many species and many levels.

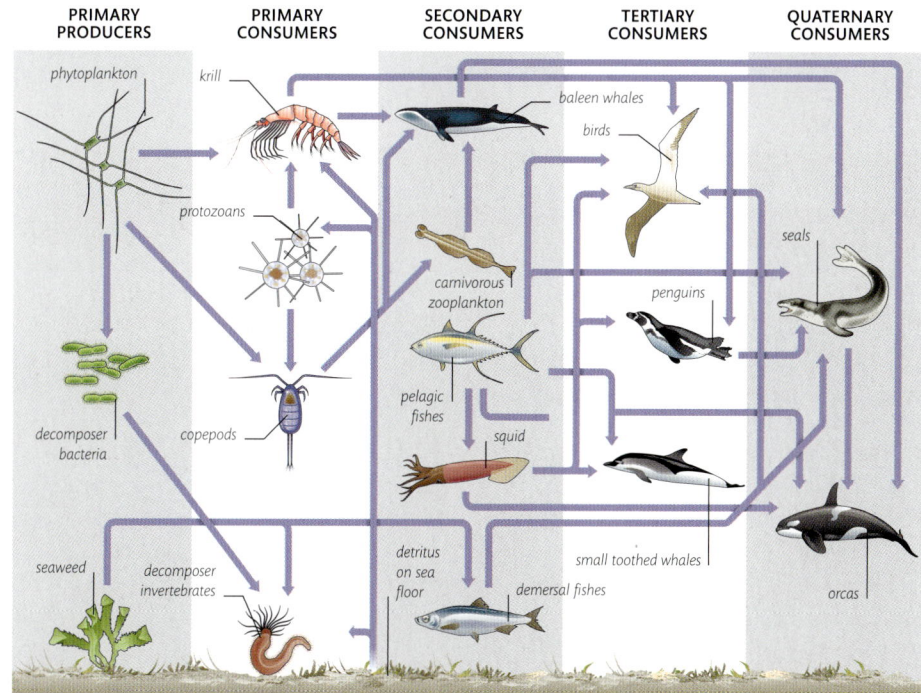

Food web The Antarctic Ocean food web may seem complex, but it is actually less complicated than the food webs of many other ecosystems. Like all food webs, it is delicately balanced and is vulnerable to disruption, from climate change or over exploitation, for example. Disruption of one link in the web might affect the entire web and could even lead to ecosystem collapse.

COMPETITION AND COOPERATION

Food resources are not infinite, and so individuals and populations have to compete to secure their share. In some situations, one animal will be dominant with respect to another and may be able to monopolize a food source because of this heightened status. Or by defending a feeding territory, an individual or group may be able to secure for itself all that it needs. But when food is distributed across too large an area or numbers of competitors are very high, territoriality may not be an effective strategy. Species can coexist and minimize competition by each occupying a particular niche in the environment. For example, they might feed on slightly different foods or feed at different times or in different places. On the other hand, individuals may need the help of others of their species to be successful. Cooperation may increase the chance that a territory can be defended and also that food will be found, either because a group can search a larger area or through direct communication about the location of food. Cooperation may also allow animals to catch prey that they cannot catch alone or allow a group to manage a resource for mutual benefit.

Caching food When a kill is too large to eat in a single meal, or if it is to dangerous to eat it where it fell, solitary hunting carnivores like this leopard will often store the carcass and return to it later.

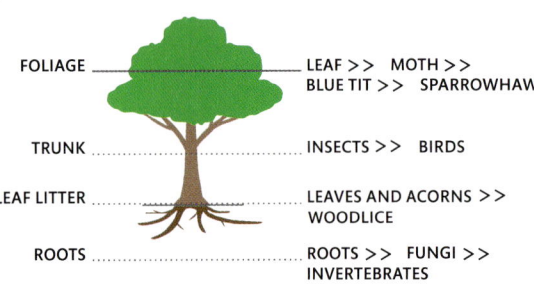

Oak tree niches An oak tree is a complex habitat that provides various niches for specialist decomposers, herbivores, omnivores, and carnivores. These, in turn, are linked in several food chains.

Detritus feeders Detritivores, like woodlice, feed on detritus such as decaying wood, leaves, and other plant material. In this way they assist in the recycling of plant material back into the soil.

Hunting partners Coyotes catch small mammals startled by digging badgers and are more successful when hunting with badgers than when hunting alone.

FORAGING STRATEGIES

Carnivores and herbivores eat different foods, but the basic principles of feeding are common to all species. They need to find food, process it, and eat it. They need to make sure that they get the particular food they need when they need it, and to do so they need to maximize the efficiency of their foraging. So just as a bear usually selects only the most nutritious salmon, a goose usually grazes only the best-quality grass. Another herbivore, the surgeon fish, is restricted to a low-quality diet of algae and so simply eats a lot to obtain enough energy. Foraging strategies also need to be flexible, and animals need to learn what foods they can and cannot eat.

OPTIMAL FORAGERS

Animals are not indiscriminate in their feeding behaviour. Instead, they optimize efficiency through a trade-off between the costs of finding and processing food, and the benefit of the energy gained from the food. For example, small marine iguanas restrict themselves to low-quality food found between the high- and low-water lines because the extra energy they would get if they fed on better-quality food from beyond the low-water line is less than the energy costs involved in diving to reach it. Shore crabs show a similar behaviour when feeding on mussels (see below). Even sessile fan worms feed optimally, balancing the energy spent opening and closing their fans against the amount of food in a current of water.

Breaking shells Ravens drop shells to open them. They fly only as high as necessary for the drop to break the shell.

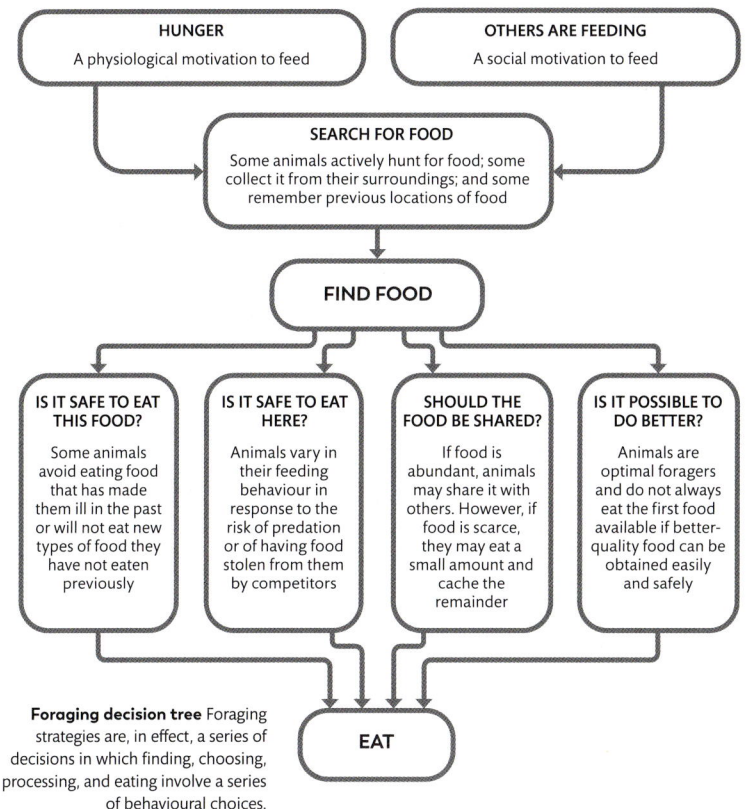

Foraging decision tree Foraging strategies are, in effect, a series of decisions in which finding, choosing, processing, and eating involve a series of behavioural choices.

Mussel energy When feeding on mussels, shore crabs preferentially select mussels 2–2.5 cm (¾–1 in) long because they give the highest energy profit, taking into account their calorific value (E) and the time spent opening them (T).

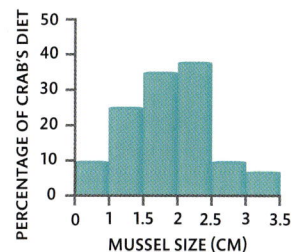
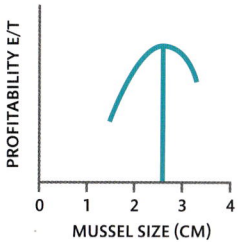

Feeding on plants

Plant material is available as a potential food source in nearly all of the environments of the world. Plants turn the energy of the sun into food (a process know as autotrophy) that is usable by animals and underpins almost all food chains. Therefore, the eating of plants is fundamentally important to ecosystems.

PLANTS AS FOOD

Some animals specialize in eating one kind of plant, or even one part of one kind of plant, while others generalize, consuming a range of plants. Grazers eat grasses, and are often anatomically specialized for this, while browsers consume plants selectively. Granivores and frugivores eat seeds and fruits respectively, and ultra-specialists like hummingbirds drink nectar from flowers. Nectar is energy-rich, as are fruits, while seeds are rich in proteins and oils. Leaves and grasses are not very nutritious, meaning animals often have to consume large amounts of them. Plants are not passive in this relationship: some deter predators with toxins or spines, while others encourage them for the purposes of seeds pollination or dispersal.

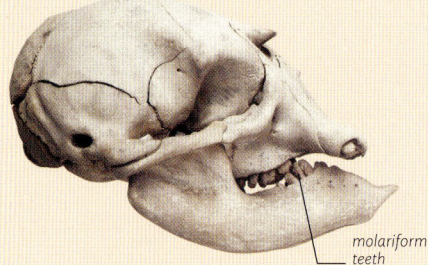

Elephant skeleton Elephants have large, ridged molariform teeth, arranged on a conveyor; as the front teeth wear out, those behind them slide forwards, taking their place.

Hummingbirds are hovering nectivores, with long beaks and tongues for drinking nectar from flowers.

Koalas are leaf-eaters with a diet composed almost entirely of eucalyptus leaves.

Types of plant food When thinking of plants as food, there is a tendency to picture animals grazing grasses. Plants, however, are more than just green matter, and animals have adapted to prey upon almost every part of the plant. Insects, birds, and mammals consume nectar and pollen, and a wide variety of animals eat flowers, fruits, and seeds. Species such as pigs dig up plant roots and tubers, and in desperation browsers will chew twigs and bark. Termites and the larvae of wood-boring beetles have evolved the ability to digest cellulose, which allows them to eat wood.

Furniture beetles are domestic pests. They burrow into damp timbers, where their larvae eat the wood.

Wild mustangs are grazers, using their incisor teeth to clip the short grasses that make up 80–90 per cent of their diet.

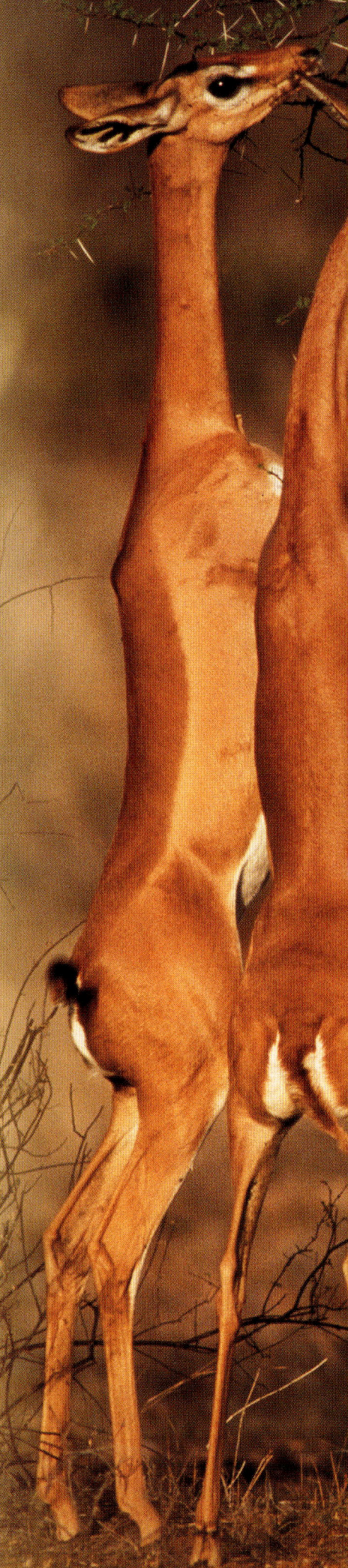

Gerenuks feeding on acacia Gerenuks are unique among browsing antelopes, as they stand fully erect on their hind legs when leaning against a tree with their front legs while feeding. They can reach heights of more than 2.5 m (8¼ ft).

ANATOMY TOXIC LEAVES

As a defence against being eaten, the leaves of many plant species are laced with toxic chemicals. Some caterpillars that feed on these toxic leaves disable the plant's defences by severing leaf veins to slow the flow of the poison. Others excrete the toxins they eat and some, like the monarch butterfly caterpillar (left), use them for their own defence.

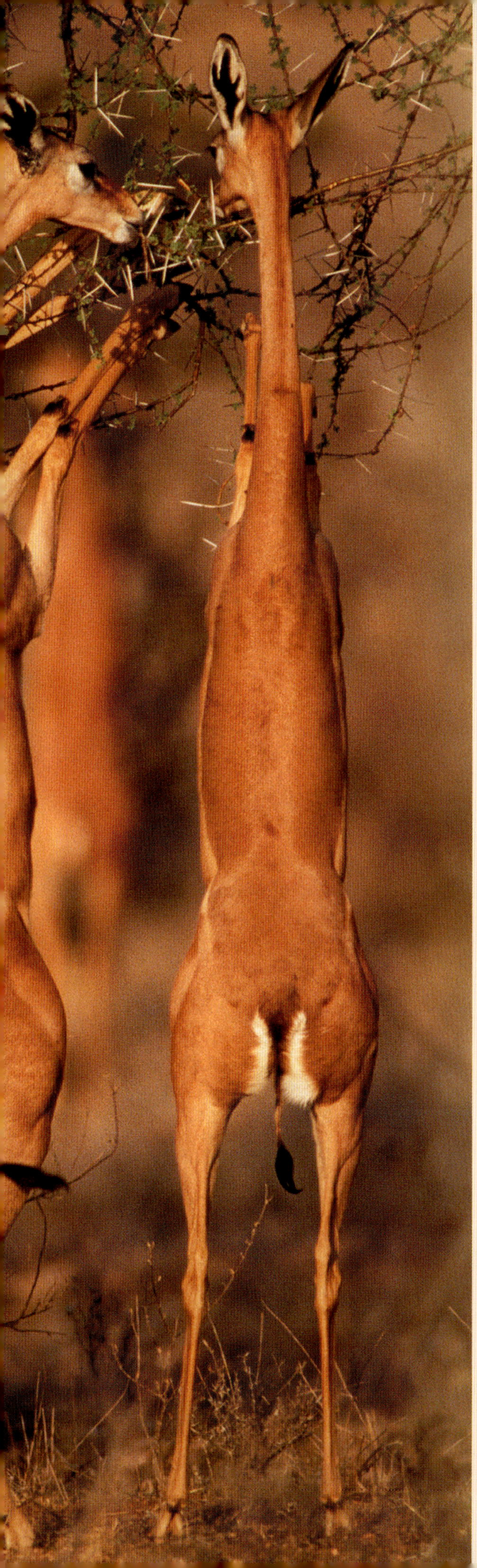

FEEDING ON PLANTS

MANAGING CROPS

Some foods become available in a glut, with availability far outstripping demand. When the food is perishable, animals recruit others to share the supply. If the food can be stored, animals may benefit from managing it. Some birds, for example, store seeds and nuts in autumn to prevent winter food shortages. Other animals manage quality rather than quantity. Some grazers struggle to digest grasses, but new grass is slightly more digestible, so some species crop and rotate patches of grass, ensuring a fresh supply.

Brent geese wait for a period of 4 days before they return to heavily grazed land to feed.

Scattered larder During the autumn months, a jay will store 4,500–11,000 acorns, each in a different site. Remarkably, it will retrieve them many months later as food for its nestlings.

Rotating harvest In winter, Brent geese move as a flock from one feeding field to the next. They coordinate their movements to ensure that they do not return to individual fields too soon.

MUTUAL BENEFIT

Some plants benefit from being food. Many flowers are pollinated by animals moving between blooms as they eat nectar and pollen. Some seeds have a tough coating that requires them to be digested before they will germinate, and many seeds have far higher germination rates if they have passed through the gut of an animal. Also, animals can carry the seeds a long distance from the parent plant.

African elephant dung Large seeds pass through an elephant's gut and are deposited to germinate in a pile of dung. Elephants disperse the seeds of many tree species, including some with no other known dispersal mechanism.

PLANT DEFENCES

While some plants do benefit from their relationships with herbivores, most attempt to resist predatory animals. They defend themselves with toxins and spines, or have a growth form that makes feeding difficult. Animals can adapt to plant defences: some eat an antidote to plant toxins; some develop immunity to them; and others utilize the poisons for defence. Some herbivores have evolved to reach past spines, some have harder teeth to grind tough plants, and some, like the chimpanzee, use tools to crack open tough nuts.

Giraffe The 50 cm (20 in) long tongue of the giraffe snakes between thorns to pick small clumps of leaves. Giraffe saliva is thick, coating spines eaten accidentally so that they can be safely swallowed.

Antarctic sea urchin

Seabed scrapers

SPECIES *Sterechinus neumayeri* **SIZE** Up to 7 cm (2¾ in) **DISTRIBUTION** Shallow waters of the Southern Ocean

Sea urchins are inveterate grazers and possess powerful jaws that consist of five downward-pointing, chalky, bladelike teeth. Whether on a coral reef, rocky shore, or, as here, on the seabed under the Southern Ocean, their feeding activities can scrape surfaces clean of algae and fixed animals such as bryozoans. The Antarctic sea urchin mostly clears its way through films of diatoms, which it collects from the sediment surface, but is opportunistic and will even consume seal faeces if it encounters any. Large numbers of sea urchins can have a significant effect on seabed growths.

Group grazing Groups of Antarctic sea urchins congregate at diatom mats, where they graze on these microscopic algae.

ANATOMY ARISTOTLE'S LANTERN

Sea urchins are the only echinoderms to have an elaborate apparatus for feeding called Aristotle's Lantern. Shaped like an old-fashioned lantern, and named after the philosopher Aristotle, who first described it, this complex system of muscles and hard skeletal elements supports and operates five strong teeth arranged in a downward-pointing cone. The urchin moves slowly along the seabed, opening and closing the teeth and scraping up its food.

Desert locust

Voracious swarming

SPECIES *Schistocerca gregaria* **SIZE** Up to 8 cm (3¼ in)
DISTRIBUTION Northern Africa, Middle East, and southwest Asia

During times of drought, the desert locust is a solitary, drab, well-camouflaged insect. When the desert rains finally fall and the desert blooms, numbers of locusts rise, but they remain solitary among the abundant vegetation. Once the rains stop and the vegetation dies back, the insects become concentrated on the remaining patches of food. This crowding triggers a radical transformation in appearance and behaviour. Previously shy and camouflaged, juveniles (hoppers) become both gregarious and brightly coloured. They form larger and larger marching bands that flow through the landscape eating everything green in their path. After five or six nymphal moults, they fledge as adults, taking to the air in vast flying swarms numbering billions of individuals. Swarms travel hundreds of kilometres per day in search of fresh habitats in which to continue to feed and breed. Desert locusts are indiscriminate feeders, eating leaves, stems, shoots, fruits, and seeds of both non-crop and crop plants, and they can cause devastation to the rural economies of the countries they afflict. Eventually the swarms peter out due to lack of food, predation, and disease and the residual populations revert to the solitary form.

Plague proportions A swarm of locusts can cover up to 1,200 square km (463 square miles) and will consume any vegetation in their path.

69 billion

The estimated number of locusts in a swarm that devastated parts of northwest Africa in 2004.

Crowding together When adult desert locusts crowd, physical contact on their hind legs triggers biochemical changes that result in the production of gregarious juveniles.

Cabbage white butterfly

Probing proboscis

SPECIES *Pieris brassicae* **SIZE** 5–6.5 cm (2–2½ in) (wingspan)
DISTRIBUTION Farmland, meadows, and parkland throughout Europe, North Africa, and Asia to the Himalayas

Caterpillars of the cabbage white butterfly are typical folivores (leaf-feeders). The female usually lays its eggs on the leaves of cabbages, cauliflowers, or other similar plants. Once the eggs hatch, the green caterpillars feed on the flowers and leaves of their host plant. As a free-flying butterfly, the diet of the cabbage white changes, and it then becomes a nectivore (nectar-feeder).

Capable of powerful flight, the butterfly searches for food plants across a wide area and locates them by their scent. Having landed on a suitable flower, it applies hydrostatic pressure to two joined and specially elongated mouthparts that are usually held coiled beneath the head. Once straightened, these mouthparts form a drinking tube, the proboscis, which can be guided into the flower to extract the sweet nectar.

Precision drinking The proboscis of this butterfly dips repeatedly into the multiple nectaries of the flower, sipping sweet nectar from each of them.

Honey bee
Processing pollen

SPECIES *Apis mellifera* **SIZE** 1.5–2.5 cm (½–1 in) **DISTRIBUTION** Thought to have originated in India, now one of the world's most widespread domesticated insects

This social insect uses sophisticated communication to find sources of food and builds elaborate structures to process it. Foraging worker bees visit up to 40 flowers per minute, collecting pollen and sucking up nectar to be stored in the honey sack, a specialized gut structure. Bees find food by sight and smell, but when a successful bee returns to the hive it communicates to other workers the location of nectar-rich flowers by means of the waggle dance (see p.431). The way in which the dancing bee moves communicates both the direction and distance of the flowers from the hive.

The colony is made up of sterile female workers, male drones, and a queen. In the hive, flower nectar is repeatedly swallowed and regurgitated by the workers until it becomes honey. Stored pollen and honey are then fed by workers to the developing larvae in their care. Some of the larvae are put into separate chambers, and fed royal jelly, a secretion from the feeding glands of the workers themselves. These individuals will develop to become future queens.

Bee keeping Commercial bee keepers collect honey and take it away from their hives. Hives may also be moved between farms to maximize the pollination of crops.

Honey comb The hexagonal cells of a honeycomb serve as both a larder in which to store honey and pollen, and a nursery in which the young bees are reared.

Pollen gathering Bees collect pollen from the flowers they visit. This is stored in the pollen basket, easily visible as a yellow-orange ball on the hind legs. While nectar is gathered as an energy source, pollen is collected primarily for its protein and other nutrients, and is used as food for larvae.

Living larders Some honeypot ant workers (called repletes) have enlarged abdomens filled with nectar, which they regurgitate on demand for other members of the colony. The repletes are fed by other workers, which obtain food by gathering nectar from flowers, as well as "milking" aphids and scale insects for honeydew and preying on other invertebrates, such as termites.

Powderblue surgeonfish
Reef grazing

SPECIES *Acanthurus leucosternon* **SIZE** Up to 51 cm (20 in) **DISTRIBUTION** Coral reefs of the Indian Ocean and Indonesia

Surgeonfishes or tangs are supreme grazers, feeding on the fine turfs and mats of seaweed and other algae that grow over dead corals and coral rock. They have an unusually long intestine (for a fish) and a wide range of gut symbionts (beneficial organisms) that help digest the large volumes that they consume. Their small mouths are equipped with tiny, close-set teeth for precision feeding between corals and they can scrape and clear away algae down to bare rock.

Along with parrotfishes, they perform an important ecological function in keeping vegetation that might overgrow corals in check and exposing surfaces for settlement of coral larvae and other invertebrates. Large groups of powderblue surgeonfishes can be seen searching shallow reefs and flats, streaming down to feed once the leaders discover a new patch of algae. Many surgeonfishes will defend their grazing grounds from other herbivores, especially when food is scarce but will tolerate species such as the sapphire devil (*Chrysiptera cyanea*), a small 8 cm (3 in) long damselfish that takes a relatively small share of the food, but is an aggressive defender of the communal patch.

Precision grazing The small mouth and teeth of the surgeonfish allows for such a precise bite that they can pick algae from coral without damaging it.

Marine iguana
Diving for seaweed

SPECIES *Amblyrhynchus cristatus* **SIZE** 50–100 cm (19½–39 in)
DISTRIBUTION Galapagos Islands off the coast of South America

Marine iguanas are traditionally portrayed as strong swimmers that dive to feed on beds of offshore seaweeds. In fact, only larger animals – those above 1.8 kg (4 lb) – habitually dive to feed. Smaller animals – those up to 1.2 kg (2¾ lb) – feed exclusively on the less lush seaweeds of the intertidal areas, restricting their feeding to the period of the day when the tide is out and the sea is relatively calm.

The constraints of the tide present difficulties to small iguanas, who have to limit their exposure to sea water so that their body temperatures do not fall too far: the sea around the Galapagos Islands is often cold, with a 14–25°C (57–77°F) annual range. These animals must feed whenever the tide is out, but if this is shortly after dawn they risk being too cool and sluggish to feed. Similarly, if the tide falls shortly before dark, they may be chilled by splashing waves and not have sufficient daylight to reheat before nightfall. Small iguanas huddle together at night to conserve heat.

Underwater foragers do not face such problems and typically bask each morning before concentrating their foraging time during the late morning and around noon. This allows plenty of time to bask and reheat during the early afternoon when the sun still heats the island rocks.

Smaller iguanas do not feed underwater because iguanas are actually relatively poor swimmers, and smaller animals are the poorest swimmers of all. They would therefore take a long time to reach the beds of seaweed or algae, risk being dashed on the rocks by waves, and use up a lot of their energy. Smaller bodies cool faster than larger ones and therefore small iguanas would be restricted to short dives. So the limitations of their small size seems to restrict their feeding opportunities to the shore.

Underwater feeding Using their claws and powerful legs, large iguanas are able to resist the swell of the sea to tear at submerged algal mats and seaweed.

30 The number of minutes that marine iguanas can spend underwater while diving for food.

Intertidal feeder Younger and smaller iguanas are unable to swim to underwater seaweed mats and so must graze in the intertidal area between the low- and high-water marks.

Heating up By day, marine iguanas bask on sun-warmed rocks to raise their body temperatures. By night, they crowd together in groups to conserve heat.

FEEDING ON PLANTS 157

Galapagos tortoise
Grazing giant
SPECIES *Chelonoidis niger* **SIZE** Up to 1.4 m (4½ ft)
DISTRIBUTION Galapagos Islands off the coast of Ecuador, South America

Galapagos tortoises graze on the leaves and fruits of more than 50 species of plant. They prefer lush grass, but their toothless jaws are well adapted to cut and tear at all types of vegetable matter, including tough bromeliads, fallen fruits, and the fleshy but prickly pads of cacti. On the wetter islands, the tortoises drink water when it is available, but on the drier islands they obtain much of the liquid they need from their food and can also store fat within their large shells.

A favoured food On the wetter islands, tortoises migrate across the islands to take advantage of fresh, lush grass. They can also obtain most of the moisture they need from the dew on such vegetation.

Stretching to eat On the drier Galapagos Islands cacti tend to be taller and the tortoises have to rear up and stretch their necks to feed. The saddleback shape of the shell allows greater neck movement than the domed shells found in tortoises that live on wetter islands.

Monkey-tailed skink
Arboreal browser
SPECIES *Corucia zebrata* **SIZE** Up to 75 cm (30 in) **DISTRIBUTION** Tropical rainforests on the Solomon Islands

The monkey-tailed skink is herbivorous and uses chemical cues to identify edible leaves and flowers. It spends the daylight hours sheltering in the trunk of a hollow tree and emerges at night to feed, using its prehensile tail to climb through vegetation. The tail is so crucial to the skinks' arboreal lifestyle that, unlike most lizards, it is unable to shed it when attacked. Their young are live born rather than hatched from an egg, and ride on the back of their parent until they are able to climb themselves.

Built to climb Monkey-tailed skinks use their long, grasping tails and razor-sharp, hooked claws to climb through the tropical rainforest in search of the leaves and flowers on which they feed.

Acorn woodpecker
Larder tree

SPECIES *Melanerpes formicivorus* **SIZE** 19–23 cm (7½–9 in)
DISTRIBUTION Oak woodland in southwest USA and Central America

As its name suggests, the acorn woodpecker often eats acorns, although it primarily feeds on insects, which are its most important food source, and the fruits of other plants. In common with other woodpeckers, it has a stiffened tail and two forwards- and two backwards-pointing toes on each foot to enable it to climb the trunks of trees, and a specially adapted bill and skull to allow it to drill into wood.

In many parts of their range, extended family groups drill huge numbers of holes into the trunks of trees, which they stuff full of acorns to serve as a winter food store. In other areas, they make use of natural crevices or even suitable cracks and holes in human-made structures. A group of woodpeckers will defend its tree larder and use it as a common resource, and may even breed communally, with one or more pairs of birds in a group breeding and being assisted by a number of non-breeding birds. Although they are often sedentary birds, using the same larder for a number of years, acorn woodpeckers will move great distances should a failure of the local acorn crop occur.

50,000
The number of acorns often stored by acorn woodpeckers in a single tree.

Arranging acorns Each acorn woodpecker in a flock works to defend the larder and to maintain the quality of the storage holes. It will regularly rearrange the acorns into smaller and smaller holes as they dry and shrink.

Toco toucan
Plucking fruits

SPECIES *Ramphastos toco* **SIZE** 53–60 cm (21–23½ in)
DISTRIBUTION Lowland rainforest (below 1,700 m/5,500 ft) in northeast and central South America

Although massive in appearance, the prodigious bill of the toucan is surprisingly fragile and lightweight. It is composed of a hollow horny sheath over criss-crossing supporting rods of bone, and can break easily. Toucans will forage for food on the forest floor, but are primarily birds of the forest canopy, where their long bill enables them to reach out and pluck fruits from hard-to-reach branches. A fruit held firmly in the tip of the bill can be manoeuvred towards the throat by the bird's very long tongue, or it may be flicked back with a toss of the head and swallowed. This toucan's diet consists almost entirely of fruit taken from more than 100 species of plant. They do eat insects for protein during the breeding season.

Thermoregulation The toucan's bill is full of blood vessels that can be contracted and rapidly radiate heat. It is the largest bill in a bird of this size, making up as much as 50 per cent of the bird's total surface area.

Blue-chested hummingbird
Hovering for nectar

SPECIES *Polyerata amabilis* **SIZE** 9 cm (3½ in)
DISTRIBUTION Forest in Central America and northern South America

Like all hummingbirds, the blue-chested hummingbird is specially adapted to its nectar-feeding lifestyle. The unique arrangement of the wing bones and joints enables these birds to hover almost motionless, and their long bills and even longer tongues enable them to reach deep into flowers to collect nectar. Although nectar forms 90 per cent of the hummingbird's diet, it lacks many essential nutrients, so they supplement their diets with insects. As spending all of their time on the wing would be too energy-costly, 85–90 per cent of their time is spent sitting still.

FEEDING ON PLANTS 159

Marsh tit
Secret store
SPECIES *Parus palustris* **SIZE** Up to 12 cm (4½ in)
DISTRIBUTION Woodland in Europe and Asia

These avid food hoarders may hide up to 100 seeds in a single morning, and thousands across a winter. Each seed is stored in a different place, often some metres apart. Impressively, marsh tits have the ability to relocate and retrieve stored seeds days or weeks after burial. Another hoarder, Clark's nutcracker, uses triangulation of landscape features to "mark the spot" of its caches (which are often buried under snow by the time they are needed). Comparisons of the brains of storing and non-storing bird species reveal that hoarders have a well developed hippocampal region, the area associated with spatial memory.

Hoarding acrobat Because it is able to retrieve food it stores even weeks after hiding it, the marsh tit can take advantage of food from sources that cannot be consumed in a single sitting, such as a sunflower head or a garden birdfeeder. It is an accomplished acrobat and is able to hang upside down to collect seeds.

HUMAN IMPACT **BIRDFEEDERS**
Garden birdfeeders save the lives of millions of birds worldwide each year when there is a shortage of wild food. Feeding in this way can bring birds and humans closer together than ever before. Provision of food all year round has even changed the behaviour of some species, and the list of regular garden birds continues to grow. However, by increasing the densities of birds in a relatively small area, birdfeeders therefore may increase the risk of disease transmission, so good feeder hygiene is essential.

Red crossbill
Cone feeder
SPECIES *Loxia curvirostra* **SIZE** 14–20 cm (5½–8 in)
DISTRIBUTION Coniferous forest in the northern hemisphere, particularly Scandinavia and northern Britain

Also known as the common crossbill, this bird feeds almost exclusively on the seeds of coniferous trees. The distinctive crossed bill enables it to prise open the tough cones of conifers before they ripen and open naturally. This gives these birds an advantage over other finches that share their forest habitat but which do not have an adapted bill. Their resinous diet means that crossbills must often visit water to drink and clean their bills. By specializing in this way, crossbills are able to breed whenever the cone crop ripens, even in the middle of winter.

CASE STUDY **ADAPTED BILL**
Although crossed mandibles are a common feature of the bills of all crossbills, the particular size and shape of the bill varies between species and even between populations within a species. Each distinct bill form is an evolutionary adaptation to enable the birds to specialize in prising apart the scales of their preferred type of cone, whether it is spruce, pine, or larch.

longer upper bill

Closing and opening A crossbill feeds by poking its closed bill into a cone and then opening the bill's crossed tips. This prises open the scale of the cone and enables the bird to extract the seed.

Weaning baby After emerging from her pouch, a young koala eats small amounts of its mother's "pap", a specialized form of faeces that is soft and runny. This introduces into the young's digestive system the bacteria it will need to digest eucalyptus leaves. The pap is also a rich source of protein for the growing young koala.

Koala
Exclusive diet
SPECIES *Phascolarctos cinereus* **SIZE** 72–78 cm (28–31 in)
DISTRIBUTION Eucalyptus forest and woodland in eastern Australia

Although they occasionally browse other tree species, koalas feed almost exclusively on the fibrous leaves of eucalyptus trees. Powerful forelimbs, opposable digits, and strong claws enable koalas to move with ease through trees to reach their food, which they nip off with sharp incisors. Their modified cheek teeth, a single premolar, and four molars with high crowns on each jaw, enable them to grind the leaves to a smooth paste. Eucalyptus leaves are low in protein, high in toxins, and difficult to digest, but the digestive system of the koala is specially adapted to meet this challenge. The toxins are deactivated and the paste is digested by bacterial fermentation in a greatly enlarged caecum, which, at about 2 m (6½ ft) long, is the longest of any mammal relative to their overall size.

Great fruit-eating bat

Flying frugivore

SPECIES *Artibeus lituratus* **SIZE** 9–11 cm (3½–4½ in)
DISTRIBUTION Caves or large trees in forested areas of southern Mexico through Central America, to southern Brazil, and northern Argentina

Around one-third of the world's bat species are herbivores, feeding on fruits, leaves, pollen, and nectar. The great fruit-eating bat is an important pollinator and seed disperser for a wide range of plant species, some of which are economically important crops, for example mango and wild banana. Flowers and fruits are often locally super-abundant, and vast flocks of bats may descend upon a fruiting tree attracted by one another's calls and by the smell of the ripe fruit. These flocks increase competition between bats and attract predators, so many bats use their teeth to tear off a fruit, which they carry away to consume in solitary safety.

A taste for fruit Great fruit-eating bats are considered pests in some areas because of the devastating impact they can have on crops.

Bamboo bear The giant panda is so closely associated with bamboo forests, and so reliant on bamboo, that it is known to local people as the bamboo bear.

Giant panda

Bamboo specialist

SPECIES *Ailuropoda melanoleuca* **SIZE** Up to 1.9 m (6¼ ft) **DISTRIBUTION** Temperate forest with a dense bamboo under-storey in southwest China

Classified as a bear, the panda may be presumed to be a carnivore or an omnivore rather than a herbivore, particularly given that its diet is known to include meat, fishes, eggs, tubers, and plant material. It also has bear-like teeth and a digestive system more typical of a carnivore.

However, 99 per cent of a panda's diet is vegetarian and is composed of just bamboo. Having a carnivore's gut, the panda is not efficient at digesting cellulose and digests just 17 per cent of the food it eats. Pandas need a diverse diet of various parts of different bamboo species. The shoots are preferred when available, after which pandas eat leaves until winter, when they opt for stems. The bamboo is crushed and ground by powerfull muscled jaws equipped with large flat molars, but even this processing does not make bamboo a high-quality foodstuff, and pandas need to eat a lot of it. An adult panda can consume up to 12.5 kg (28 lbs) of bamboo per day and take 12–14 hours doing it.

Strands of bamboo are synchronous in their flowering, death, and regeneration, which means that pandas need to range across relatively large areas of forest supporting a range of bamboo species to ensure a sufficient supply of food. They feed mainly on the ground, but they are also excellent climbers and able to swim.

ANATOMY EXTRA DIGIT

At first glance, the giant panda paw appears to have an extra digit: five fingers and one thumb. This thumb, however, is actually an elongated wrist bone, the radial sesamoid, which is used by the panda as a pseudo-thumb. With it the panda is able to handle food with considerable dexterity, gripping bamboo shoots firmly in one hand, while biting leaves from them.

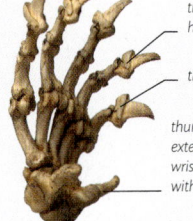

true digits have claws
thumb
thumb-like extension of wrist bone without claw

Hippopotamus

Night grazer

SPECIES *Hippopotamus amphibius* **SIZE** 3.3–3.5 m (10¾–11¼ ft) **DISTRIBUTION** Rivers and lakes in West, Central, East, and South Africa

Given their bulk, hippopotamuses eat surprisingly little each day. Most of their time is spent wallowing in warm water, but they do not feed on aquatic plants. Each night they leave the water and venture out to feed almost exclusively on grasses, which are digested in their multi-chambered alimentary canal by the fermenting action of micro-organisms. Remarkably, hippopotamuses consume just 3 per cent of their enormous body mass each day, which would indicate that their daytime wallowing and nocturnal grazing is particularly energy efficient.

Getting a mouthful Hippopotamuses have formidable teeth, but they use their thick lips to nip at vegetation. They have occasionally been recorded supplementing their diet by scavenging on the carcasses of dead animals.

African buffalo
Chewing the cud

SPECIES *Syncerus caffer* **SIZE** 2.4–3.4 m (7¾–11¼ ft)
DISTRIBUTION Grassland and woodland in sub-Saharan Africa

This buffalo has been described as one of the most successful grazers in Africa. It can be found in as diverse a range of habitats as swamp, forest, and grassland. It prefers taller grasses, using its long, almost prehensile tongue to pull at clumps of grasses that are then clipped by its wide incisors and grazed to a pulp by its broad molars. Through their grazing, herds of buffaloes modify their habitat in a way that makes it more suitable for other more selective grazers, and this promotes the growth of fresh food. As a result, herds of buffaloes may be quite mobile. They are able to avoid overheating by remaining inactive by day and feeding at night.

Super grazer One of the most successful of the grazing vertebrates, the African buffalo prefers lush grass but will graze coarse grass and herbs when this is scarce.

ANATOMY FOUR STOMACHS

The stomachs of ruminants (mammals that chew the cud) have four chambers. Food passes into the rumen and reticulum, where digestion begins, fermentation takes place, and solids are combined into a bolus. This bolus is regurgitated and re-chewed. This is then re-swallowed and passes into the third stomach, the omasum, where liquid and essential minerals are absorbed into the bloodstream. Remaining solids pass into the final stomach, the abomasum, to be digested further.

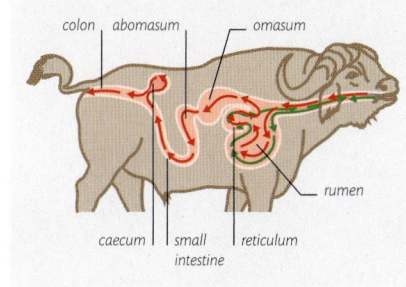

→ PASSAGE OF FOOD (FIRST TIME)
→ PASSAGE OF FOOD (SECOND TIME)

Giraffe
Reaching the heights

SPECIES *Giraffa camelopardalis* **SIZE** 3.8–4.7 m (12½–15½ ft) **DISTRIBUTION** Savanna, grassland, and open woodland in sub-Saharan Africa

The extraordinarily long neck of the giraffe is an evolutionary adaptation that enables it to compete with the many smaller herbivores of the crowded savanna ecosystem. Giraffes' extreme height enables them to reach above their competitors and to selectively browse the best parts of the tallest trees. They feed on the fruits, flowers, and fresh shoots of 40–60 different tree species, including *Vachellia* (acacias), *Commiphora* (myrrhs) and mimosa.

Giraffes are able to nip leaves from between the long thorns of acacia because their long muzzles, flexible lips, and long, dextrous, tongues can reach deep within clumps of tree branches and because their lips and tongue are protected from the thorns by thick, horny bumps called papillae.

An adult giraffe consumes up to 35 kg (77 lbs) of food each day, and to ensure access to a sufficient quantity and quality, roams widely. In lean times, giraffes eat dried leaves, twigs, and even tree spines. In common with other ruminants (see panel, left), they first chew and swallow their food, then regurgitate and re-chew it several times prior to complete digestion. Uniquely, they are able to ruminate while walking, an adaptation which perfectly suits their nomadic lifestyle.

Overcoming a prickly problem Thick, leathery lips and a very long tongue enable the giraffe to selectively browse tender leaves from around the sharp spines of acacia trees.

Dugong
Grazing the ocean floor

SPECIES *Dugong dugon* **SIZE** 2.5–4 m (8¼–13 ft)
DISTRIBUTION Shallow tropical waters of the Indo-Pacific region

The only strictly marine mammalian herbivore, the dugong, or sea cow, slowly meanders through the seagrass beds that are common in shallow, sandy bottomed waters. As they rip out clumps of seagrass, they leave behind trails of bare sand and uprooted plants. This encourages regeneration of the seagrass, promoting the nutritious new growth that they favour. By repeatedly re-cropping the seagrass, they maintain the quality of their food.

Digging deeper Dugongs graze sandy bottomed waters and dig for rhizomes using their flexible, thick upper lip.

Omnivores

Omnivores eat a wide variety of foodstuffs, often mixing vegetable and animal material. They respond quickly to changes in the availability of food and take advantage of new food sources. Their breadth of diet enables them to survive in situations where specialists would struggle.

FEEDING PATTERNS

Generalist feeders may seem to be indiscriminate in their food selection, but most do discriminate, choosing to eat less tough leaves, for example. Filter-feeding molluscs ingest all small solids in their feeding current, but have an internal mechanism to separate food from non-food. Many omnivores appear to specialize at a particular point in their annual cycle so variations can be seen in their diets over the year. Some species, such as starlings (see below), undergo physical changes to coincide with this cycle.

FEEDING BEHAVIOUR

As generalists, omnivores tend to lack physical adaptations for feeding, and their anatomy often combines that of carnivores and herbivores. Omnivore teeth, a mixture of carnivore and herbivore teeth, are a good example of this. Omnivores do exhibit behavioural adaptations, such as an ability to manipulate and process a variety of foods, and they are often good problem solvers: several omnivores have learned to open rubbish bins. There are drawbacks to having a relatively indiscriminate diet. Animals feeding on seasonal foods often suffer nutritional imbalances, but they are physiologically adapted to withstand them.

Fear of the new Rats are highly neophobic, showing a strong reluctance to eat unknown foods. This behaviour may have evolved to protect them against accidental poisoning.

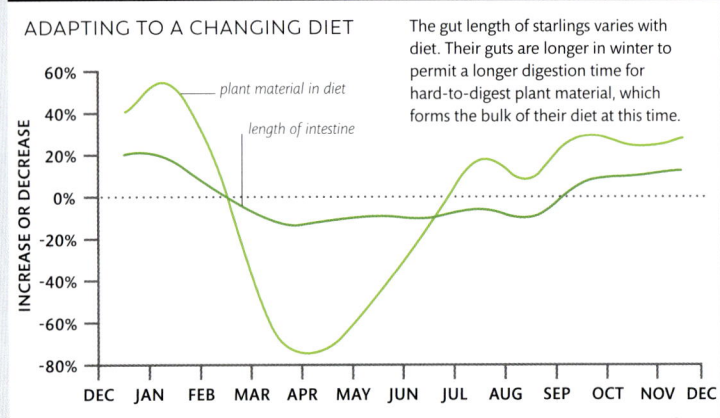

ADAPTING TO A CHANGING DIET

The gut length of starlings varies with diet. Their guts are longer in winter to permit a longer digestion time for hard-to-digest plant material, which forms the bulk of their diet at this time.

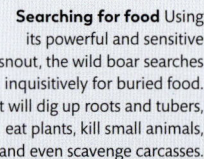

Searching for food Using its powerful and sensitive snout, the wild boar searches inquisitively for buried food. It will dig up roots and tubers, eat plants, kill small animals, and even scavenge carcasses.

All day feeding Chimpanzees feed all day, starting early and eating almost everything in reach. As the day goes on, they become more selective, choosing the ripest fruits and most succulent leaves. Presumably, when satisfied, they can afford to be more discerning.

Opportunism and adaptability Despite the fact that the polar bear is the most carnivorous of the bears, and is dependant upon the fat of marine mammals for much of its energy, it is a highly adaptable opportunist omnivore, and in times of need will eat berries, kelp, and rubbish.

Filter feeding Baleen whales, such as this Southern right whale, feed by swimming open-mouthed through water containing zooplankton and other small pelagic animals. Water enters the front of the mouth and then passes out of the sides, through baleen sieves.

OMNIVORES 163

Soldier beetles
Predatory pollen lover

FAMILY Cantharidae **SIZE** Up to 3 cm (1¼ in) **DISTRIBUTION** Herbaceous vegetation in sunny positions worldwide

Both the grey-brown larvae and vividly coloured adult soldier beetles are mixed feeders, feeding on pollen, nectar, and insect prey. Adult females lay eggs in soil. As they develop, the wormlike larvae spend most of their time among leaf litter or soil, where they feed on a range of soft prey such as ground-dwelling invertebrates, including snails and slugs.

Soldier beetles feed on aphids and other insects. Adult soldier beetles congregate on the flowers of herbaceous plants, particularly pollen and nectar-rich species such as golden-rod and umbillifers, where they mate and prey on other visiting insects. While inhabiting the flowers, the beetles supplement their diet with pollen and nectar.

Soldier beetles are named for their coloration, which resembles a military uniform. Bright colours warn predators that the beetles taste unpleasant. They may secrete defensive chemicals from paired thoracic and abdominal glands. Their flexible wing covers inspired their alternate name of leatherwings, and their long bodies are soft, unlike those of other beetles.

Rising up By adding material to their tubes as they filter the sea water around them, peacock worms are able to increase the length of their tube.

Conspicuous crown This peacock worm has extended its feathery, banded tentacles into the water to feed.

Peacock worm
Fan feeder

SPECIES *Sabella pavonina* **SIZE** Up to 30 cm (12 in)
DISTRIBUTION Mud, sand, and silt-covered rock in shallow water around the shores of Europe

The peacock worm lives in a muddy tube that extends from the seabed. It constructs the tube itself, secreting mucus and binding it with sand and mud. To feed, the worm comes to the mouth of its tube, extending a double fan of finely divided featherlike tentacles into the water. The tentacle net acts as a filter, trapping plankton, detritus, and sediment particles carried in the water. The worm sorts its catch using the tiny hairlike structures (cilia) that cover its tentacles. Edible particles are transported towards the mouth to be eaten, while larger, inedible particles are discarded or added to the tube that surrounds the worm. If threatened, the worm will instantly disappear into the safety of its tube.

Welcome arrival Colourful soldier beetles are welcomed by gardeners, as they are predators of aphids and caterpillars, which are perceived as pests.

American lobster
Picking up a scent

SPECIES *Homarus americanus* **SIZE** 20–60 cm (8–23½ in)
DISTRIBUTION In rocky habitats along the North Atlantic coasts of Canada and USA

During its planktonic larval stage, the American lobster is an opportunist, feeding on other plankton. Once it settles on the seabed, this crustacean becomes a generalist omnivore. It will scavenge and eat detritus and seaweed, but prefers to hunt for crabs, molluscs, bristleworms, echinoderms, and sometimes other lobsters. Usually a nocturnal hunter, it mostly locates its prey by smell using a pair of shorter antennules that are located between the lobster's long antennae. These antennules are incredibly sensitive and allow it to discriminate between the odours of different prey. The lobster has many mouthparts, with various functions, which include holding food or passing it

Tools for the job The American lobster has two massive front claws. One is used for crushing and breaking the shells of its prey, while the other has a sharp cutting edge for tearing at flesh.

to the its jaws, where food is crushed and ingested. Thriving in cold, shallow waters, the American lobster is fiercely territorial, occupying holes and crevices in and under rocks.

Piranhas
Lethal teeth

GENUS Serrasalmus **SIZE** Up to 33 cm (13 in)
DISTRIBUTION Rivers of South America, east of the Andes

Piranhas have a reputation for being fearsome predators. Their typically sharp, slicing teeth, which interlock when their mouths are closed, and their protruding lower jaws make them efficient biters. Piranhas also have a keen sense of smell, which is used to locate food even in the murky waters of flooded rivers. They usually prey on fishes and invertebrates that are smaller than themselves, but they occasionally feed in a frenzied pack, and sometimes kill and eat larger animals, such as capybaras, horses, and even humans. However, there is a less fierce side to these fishes. During flooding, piranhas move out into inundated areas and feed on decaying vegetation and the seeds and fruits of forest plants. The pacus, close relatives of the piranha species, specialize to a greater extent on fruits and seeds, and tend to have flatter, thicker teeth more suited to crushing seeds than to biting flesh. Pacus are important seed dispersers in the Pantanal wetland region of South America.

Stripping fruit The sharp biting teeth of piranhas are perfect for stripping the flesh from forest fruits. Some species have thicker crushing teeth to break up the seeds inside.

Razor sharp A large mouth and interlocking, razor-sharp teeth enable this piranha to tear chunks of flesh from larger animals and even humans.

OMNIVORES **165**

Possible meal The huge, gaping mouth of a whale shark may be about to scoop up this shoal of small fishes. However, sometimes small schools of pilot fish will hang around the shark's head but avoid being eaten.

Similar species Whale sharks are not the only filter-feeding sharks. Basking sharks (left) and megamouth sharks (above) also have huge mouths and enormous gill arches. Such adaptations enable them to be efficient filter feeders.

Whale shark
Filter feeding

SPECIES *Rhincodon typus* **SIZE** 12–20 m (39–66 ft) **DISTRIBUTION** Worldwide, in tropical and warm, temperate waters

This giant fish, the largest in the world, feeds on plankton and tiny fish, shrimp, and squid. Whale sharks migrate long distances through the oceans to areas of rich feeding, such as the Australian Ningaloo Reef. There, they congregate to feast on the plankton explosion associated with the mass spawning of corals, other invertebrates, and fishes.

Whale sharks are thought to be able to determine the best feeding areas by the use of olfactory cues. They usually feed by cruising slowly through food-rich waters, passing huge volumes of water in through their mouths and out through their gills, where food particles are trapped for swallowing. Whale sharks have also been seen using their mouths like a giant bucket, swimming upwards through a dense patch of food to engulf it.

ANATOMY GILL FILTERS

Whale and basking sharks are two of only three filter-feeding sharks that extract plankton from the water as it passes through their mouths and out through their gills. Food is trapped on tightly packed gill rakers, tough projections arranged like a comb on the tops of the gill supports. The much finer gill filaments, which extract oxygen from the water, hang below. Basking sharks mostly ramfeed, simply swimming along with their mouths wide open. Whale sharks may also actively suck in water by expanding their buccal cavity (throat) as may the third filter-feeder, the little known megamouth shark. White tissue inside the mouth may attract shrimp, a major food item.

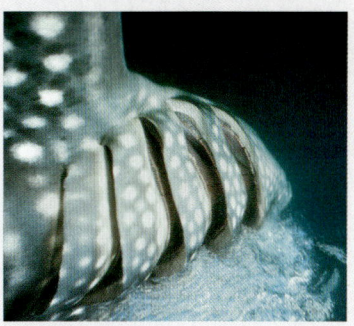

Izecksohn's Brazilian tree frog
Mixed diet

SPECIES *Xenohyla truncata* **SIZE** Up to 4 cm (1½ in)
DISTRIBUTION Subtropical and tropical marshes of Brazil

While the tadpoles of many species of frogs are omnivorous, feeding on vegetable material, carrion, invertebrates, and even cannibalizing one another, adult frogs are almost entirely carnivorous. However, Izecksohn's Brazilian tree frog is the exception. It rests in the pools of water that form within bromeliads during the day and forages by night, when it eats invertebrates, but its diet also includes the brightly coloured fruits and seeds of a range of plants. The seeds of one of its preferred plants, *Anthurium harrisii* (an arum), are known to germinate when they have been defecated by the frog, so it is thought that this might be an important method of dispersal for this particular plant.

Birdlike beak The hawksbill turtle gets its name from its narrow, horny beak. In the past, the turtles were hunted for their scutes, known as "tortoiseshell", which were used in various artefacts. They are now protected.

Berries not bugs Fruit-eating frogs, although only 4 cm (1½ in) long, are able to eat berries that are up to 1 cm (½ in) in diameter.

Hawksbill turtle
Toxin tolerance

SPECIES *Eretmochelys imbricata* **SIZE** 0.6–1 m (2–3 ft 3 in) **DISTRIBUTION** Shallow reefs and inshore areas of subtropical and tropical waters worldwide

Hawksbill turtles feed among the shallow algal beds of inshore waters or around coral reefs. They consume a wide variety of foods, including seaweed, molluscs, crustaceans, and small fishes. Their strong, sharp beaks are used to bite off chunks of both soft and hard coral colonies. When feeding on jellyfish, such as the deadly Portuguese man-of-war, turtles close their eyes as a defence against stinging. The bulk of their diet, however, consists of sponges, many of which are highly toxic and packed with siliceous structures, called spicules, that are as sharp as shards of glass. Neither defence appears to deter the turtle.

African harrier-hawk
Flexible feeder

SPECIES *Polyboroides typus* **SIZE** 60–66 cm (23½–26 in)
DISTRIBUTION Forest, woodland, and grassland in sub-Saharan Africa

The African harrier-hawk, or gymnogene, often eats palm nuts and other fruits but it is also an accomplished hunter, and includes insects, small mammals such as rabbits, birds and their eggs, bats, and reptiles in its varied diet. A harrier-hawk will walk on the ground to search out food, or undertake low foraging flights over patches of short vegetation, pouncing on its prey. However, most often this species is observed clambering through trees and shrubs to forage using its wings, feet, and bill to steady itself as it climbs. The hawk's slender bill is used to probe beneath bark and in crevices to find insect larvae and small reptiles. There are also observations of the bird hanging upside down from a grey-headed social weaver's nest, and grabbing an adult bird in its bill as it exited the nest hole.

The most remarkable thing about the African harrier-hawk is its double-jointed ankles; the joints bend both forwards and backwards. The bird uses its long, flexible legs to reach at seemingly impossible angles in search of hidden prey. Using this technique, African harrier-hawks have been seen hanging from the nests of weaver birds and reaching deep inside them to find the eggs and young.

Cavity explorer The combination of small head, long neck, slender bill, and long, flexible legs makes the African harrier-hawk skilled at finding food in small holes and crevices.

Eastern bearded dragon
Changing tastes

SPECIES *Pogona barbata* **SIZE** 25–30 cm (10–12 in)
DISTRIBUTION Desert, scrubland, and forest in eastern Australia

These lizards alter their feeding habits during their lives. Juvenile bearded dragons are largely insectivorous and so are considered to be carnivores. They hunt small insects on the ground and in trees, constantly turning their heads as they look for prey and, when they have spotted an insect, bursting into activity to chase and catch it. Between periods of hunting, the young lizards rest and bask, often in trees. As the lizards grow, their diet changes and they begin to consume more and more vegetable material, including leaves, fruits, and flowers. These plant parts are bitten off by powerful jaws. Bearded dragons have rounded rather than pointed snouts, a typical shape among herbivorous lizards. The tongue also plays an important part in their feeding: it can be flicked out to taste a food to check if it is edible and it can also be used to pick up fallen fruits and flowers.

Winged snack Adult bearded dragons still consume animal prey, and their larger size allows them to diversify, feeding on larger insects, like this one, smaller reptiles, and small mammals.

Kea
Fruit and meat

SPECIES *Nestor notabilis* **SIZE** 46 cm (18 in) **DISTRIBUTION** Wooded and alpine areas of New Zealand's South Island

Like all parrots, the kea eats fruits, nuts, and seeds, but unlike other parrots, it has a taste for meat. Some dig into the nesting burrows of sooty shearwaters to kill and eat their chicks. Others, living in the hills and mountains (sometimes above the snowline) scavenge the carcasses of dead sheep. In the past, keas were seen eating the fat from the backs of live sheep, as a result of which they were hunted almost to extinction.

Roadside vandal The kea's elongated bill is perfect for biting, tearing, and lifting a variety of objects, even prising rubber fittings from cars. "Roadside gyms" have been built at popular tourist parking places, to divert these clever parrots' attention from cars.

OMNIVORES

Self-medication Macaws regularly travel considerable distances to gather at favoured clay licks and eat the soil. The soil may detoxify toxins from some of the plants in the macaws' diet, and soil-eating may therefore be viewed as a form of self-medication.

Red-and-green macaw
Soil supplements
SPECIES *Ara chloropterus* **SIZE** Up to 1 m (3¼ ft)
DISTRIBUTION Tropical forest in eastern Central America and north-eastern South America

In common with some other herbivores, red-and-green macaws exhibit geophagy, literally, soil-eating. Large flocks of red-and-green macaws (and other parrot species) congregate on the eroded faces of river banks and mud-cliffs to socialize and sometimes to nest in crevices, but most commonly in order to eat the soil.

The macaw diet is composed largely of fruits, seeds, berries, and nuts. Using their keen eyesight to forage in the forest canopy, groups of red-and-green macaws locate food and dextrously pluck fruits from the trees. Using their feet and sharp, hooked bill they tear open the flesh so that they can get at the hard seed or nut within. The macaw's bill can generate an enormous biting force of 2,000 psi, making it able to crack even the hardest nuts.

In order to avoid competition with other forest herbivores, for example monkeys like the saki, macaws eat under-ripe fruits and plants that are chemically defended and generally unpalatable, or even toxic to other animals. It is possible that macaws eat soil to supplement the mineral content of their diet, but it has also been shown that, by electing to eat the particular soil type found at clay licks, the birds are able to neutralize the toxins in their gut.

Great bustard
Seasonal food
SPECIES *Otis tarda* **SIZE** Up to 1.1 m (3½ ft) **DISTRIBUTION** Scattered populations are found across the grasslands of Europe and Asia

Historically a bird of open grassland, the great bustard is well adapted to survive in the modern agricultural landscape, particularly in areas of cereal growing. However, its persecution by humans has reduced its population considerably. Young bustards are almost entirely insectivorous, but as they age, the birds include increasing amounts of vegetable material in their diet. They forage in open areas, meandering in loose flocks and picking at selected food items. The birds adapt their diets in response to fluctuations in food availability associated with seasonal agricultural practices and a habitat dominated by annual plants. In summer they consume more insects (particularly beetles and their larvae) and also take small vertebrates, such as frogs and mice; in spring, autumn, and winter they are almost exclusively vegetarian, with a very varied plant diet, including cereal crops.

Heavyweight competition One of the world's heaviest flying birds, male great bustards congregate at leks (communal display sites) and compete for the attention of females.

HUMAN IMPACT
RE-INTRODUCTION IN BRITAIN

After an absence of almost 200 years, the great bustard has once again become a familiar bird in parts of Britain. A programme of re-introduction using birds of Russian origin (genetically the most similar to historical UK populations) was started and, in 2007, a released bird laid eggs, although unfortunately they did not hatch. The first successful nest followed in 2009, and by 2022 more than 20 nests were found, with the wild population of about 100 now considered self-sustaining. Extensive surveys determined that in the release areas, insect numbers in the summer would feed the growing chicks.

Wild boar
Tireless forager

SPECIES Sus scrofa **SIZE** 0.9–1.1 m (3–3½ ft)
DISTRIBUTION Woodland in Europe, North Africa, and Asia

To obtain the high levels of protein they need to survive, wild boars are generalist omnivores, using their snouts to locate and then dig out buried food. Their ability to find food in a wide range of habitats explains their global success. Ranging widely, and foraging from dawn to dusk, wild boars rest during the middle of the day and at night. Plants, especially fruits and nuts, constitute 90 per cent of their diet. The remaining 10 per cent has been known to include insects, eggs, small vertebrates, carrion, and even refuse, their exact diet varying with the seasons.

An adventurous palate Young wild boars are even less particular about what they eat than their parents, which increases their chance of survival in an environment where food availability fluctuates.

HUMAN IMPACT
ACCIDENTAL REINTRODUCTION

Three hundred years ago, wild boars in Britain had been hunted to extinction. In the 1990s they were again found in the wild, having escaped or been released from the wild boar farms that were popular ventures at the time. Significant numbers survive in many rural areas throughout southern and western England. While some do not welcome their return, wild boars and their rooting, earth-turning behaviour have many beneficial effects on their habitat.

White-nosed coati
Shovel snout

SPECIES Nasua narica **SIZE** 0.8–1.3 m (2½–4¼ ft) **DISTRIBUTION** Wooded areas of southeast Arizona, USA, and Mexico, through Central America to Panama and northeast Colombia

A member of the raccoon family, the white-nosed coati spends its days in a bustle of gregarious activity as it searches, often in groups, for food. It forages for its food mostly on the ground, digging and snuffling through the leaf litter, although it is also a skilled climber. Coatis eat nuts, fruit, carrion, eggs, and small animals, such as insects and other invertebrates and small reptiles, which they sniff out with their excellent sense of smell and highly developed snout. The snout is shovel shaped and long, protruding beyond the lower jaw. It is muscular and flexible and can be pushed into crevices or under bark in the search for food. Coati teeth differ from those of most other mammalian carnivores in that the molars are flattened, for crushing and grinding rather than for shearing flesh. These omnivores even feed on nectar, thus pollinating certain tree flowers.

Fond of fruit The white-nosed coati can climb to reach fruits and other arboreal foods, using its long tail to help it balance; however, this species is primarily a ground forager.

Getting a mouthful Krill undertake a daily migration between deep water and the ocean surface. To reach them, blue whales feed at depths of 100 m (330 ft) by day and close to the surface at night.

Blue whale
Huge appetite

SPECIES Balaenoptera musculus **SIZE** 24–27 m (79–89 ft)
DISTRIBUTION May be found in all of the oceans of the world, although absolute numbers are small

Believed to be the largest animal ever to have lived, the blue whale is a filter feeder that migrates to the southern oceans each summer to feed mainly on krill (small shrimps), and also consume other crustaceans, squids, and small fishes associated with krill swarms. During the summer feeding season, a blue whale can consume up to 4 tonnes (3.9 tons) of krill every day. This allows the whale to lay down reserves of fat and oil, which will provide energy during the rest of the year when food is less abundant. A feeding whale opens its mouth, relaxes its throat, and takes in a vast volume of water and associated food. It then closes its mouth, tightens its throat, and uses its massive tongue to force the water out through huge baleen sieves that hang from its upper jaws. The krill are trapped against the inner surface of the baleen sieves and are then swallowed by the whale.

Blue whales can be found in oceans all over the world, although the three primary populations are in the North Atlantic, North Pacific, and the southern hemisphere. Typically living in groups of two or three animals, they mate and calve in tropical to temperate waters in the winter months and feed in polar waters in the summer.

1,000 kg
The amount of food needed to fill up a blue whale's stomach.

Brown bear
Occasional carnivore

SPECIES *Ursus arctos* **SIZE** 1.7–2.8 m (5½–9¼ ft)
DISTRIBUTION Upland forests and tundra regions in North America, northern Europe, and Asia

Although they are often perceived as fearsome carnivores, brown bears are actually dietary omnivores, consuming much plant material. Their diet varies with the season and geographical location, but tends to include green vegetation, berries and fruits, roots and tubers, insects, and carrion. When they are available, bears will catch fishes, and they occasionally hunt mammalian prey, particularly newborn deer in spring. They have the well-developed canines of a typical carnivore, combined with extremely powerful jaws with which to kill prey and crush food. Their paws and strong forelimbs enable them to dig, and their sheer bulk means that they are able to defend carrion against predators such as wolves.

Berry time Brown bears on the Alaskan tundra like to eat bright red, carbohydrate-rich bearberries (hence their name) when they appear in autumn.

Gone fishing Brown bears exhibit a range of fishing techniques, from waiting and watching the water before pinning down a passing fish, to simply diving in and chasing their prey. When fishes are plentiful, a bear will choose the younger, more nutrient-rich fishes, sometimes only eating the most energy-rich parts, and discarding the remainder.

CASE STUDY PLANT-EATERS AND MEAT-EATERS

A study of brown bears in North America revealed that those that feed predominantly on meat and fish (mainly salmon), which are comparatively rich in nutrients, are significantly heavier than those whose diet consists mainly of plant material, which is relatively poor in nutrients: female plant-eating bears had an average weight of 95 kg (209 lb) compared to 215 kg (474 lb) for female meat-eaters. In addition, female meat-eating brown bears had larger litters, on average, than plant-eaters, and the population density of meat-eating bears tended to be higher. However, factors other than diet may also affect population density in bears – for example, human activities, such as logging and recreational pursuits.

PLANT-EATING BEAR, 95 KG (209 LB)

MEAT-EATING BEAR, 215 KG (474 LB)

Predation

All organisms need energy to survive, and in order to obtain energy, most animals have to feed on living organisms, such as plants or other animals. Predators are animals that have evolved to hunt, capture, and feed on other living creatures. As their prey animals have developed ways to avoid being caught, predators have had to develop skills and behaviours that allow them to successfully find, catch, and kill their chosen food.

FEEDING STRATEGIES

Many predators specialize on one species of prey or a few closely related species, the numbers of predators and prey being an important factor in regulating both populations. When prey is abundant, the population of predators tends to increase. This may continue until there is a shortage of prey, causing the numbers of predators to fall. Large fluctuations in predator and prey populations can occur due to factors such as disease and weather conditions. Some predators may feed on a number of species within the same size range, while others attack anything suitable they encounter in a particular type of habitat.

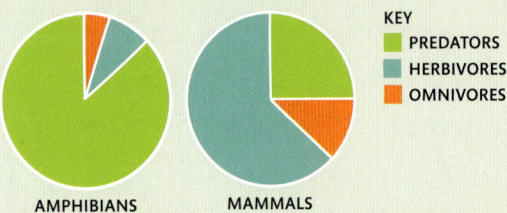

KEY
- PREDATORS
- HERBIVORES
- OMNIVORES

AMPHIBIANS   MAMMALS

Ratio Within an animal group there may be a range of feeding strategies. Amphibians are mostly predatory, while most mammal species are herbivores. Although many species are entirely carnivorous or herbivorous, there are some that are omnivorous (use both feeding strategies).

CANNIBALISM

Cannibalism is widespread, with many animals eating members of their own species due to factors such as overcrowding or food shortage. Female tiger sharks have two wombs and, in each, the largest of the developing embryos will eat any smaller embryos. Sexual cannibalism, observed in praying mantids and some spiders, is a special case where males are eaten during copulation. By eating young cubs, male lions taking over a pride bring the females into heat so that they can mate and produce their own litter. Sometimes cannibalism occurs when individuals are injured or die, as with the scavenging tadpoles shown here.

SPEED

To avoid being eaten, an animal has a limited number of options. It can avoid detection by being camouflaged and still; it can protect itself mechanically with spines or armour, or chemically with a noxious odour or taste; or it can try to outrun a predator. In this case, the need for speed has generated an "arms race" over time, where hunting animals and their quarry evolve increasingly better morphological, physiological, and behavioural traits. Often predator and prey become very evenly matched, and so success or failure is down to luck, surprise, or health.

HIGH-SPEED PREDATORS

KPH	Speed
PEREGRINE FALCON	185 KPH
CHEETAH	112 KPH
LION	80 KPH
COYOTE	69 KPH
BLACK MAMBA	20 KPH
SAILFISH	109 KPH
SHORTFIN MAKO SHARK	74 KPH

- AIR
- LAND
- WATER

The top speed attainable by predators depends to a large degree on the medium in which they operate. Stooping peregrines, the fastest of all predators, minimize wind resistance by being streamlined and are helped in acceleration by gravity. The high density of water restricts the speeds that can be achieved by aquatic predators.

Cheetah The cheetah is well adapted to hunting. Its lightweight skeleton, large muscle mass, and non-retractable claws give it good acceleration and a top speed of up to 113 kph (70 mph) over short distances.

DETECTING PREY

Predators have evolved a range of senses appropriate to their prey, the environment in which they live, and their hunting strategy. In aquatic habitats, some predatory species may simply wait for the water currents to bring food to them. Active predators need to look for food and can increase their chances of success by concentrating on areas where their prey is likely to congregate. For diurnal (day) predators, vision is likely to be the most important sense, and their eyes need to be forward facing to allow them to judge distance accurately. Nocturnal predators, such as owls, may have good hearing and eyesight. Subterranean predators may rely exclusively on touch – cave-dwelling whip-spiders feel for their prey in total darkness using their long, slender front legs. Chemosensory organs that detect airborne odours or waterborne chemicals enable some predators to locate their prey at a distance.

> **Sharks have an incredible sense of smell and can detect certain molecules in the water at concentrations of only 1 part per 25 million.**

PREDATORY SENSES

SIGHT
Eye structure differs between animal groups. Most arthropods have compound eyes made up of multiple light-gathering units, while vertebrates and cephalopods have cameralike eyes that use a single lense to focus light and form an image.

HEARING
Hearing is the ability to detect sound vibrations transmitted though air, water, or a solid medium. Hearing organs vary in complexity, from simple structures to the highly complex ears of mammals. A barn owl can locate prey through hearing alone.

SMELL
Smell is a chemoreceptive sense for detecting odours in air. Most mammals, especially carnivores, such as foxes, have a well-developed sense of smell for detecting prey. Animals give off odours for communication purposes.

TOUCH
Mechanoreception is found in a wide range of animals. It is highly developed in spiders (such as this tarantula), which use sensitive vibration receptors on their legs to detect the presence and movements of prey.

TEMPERATURE SENSING
The ability to visualize infrared radiation has evolved in snakes such as boas, pit vipers (shown here), and pythons. Temperature-sensing organs on the head allow these species to find warm-blooded prey in complete darkness.

ECHOLOCATION
Echolocation (biological sonar) has evolved in most bats, dolphins, porpoises, and other toothed whales. Echoes received from high-frequency calls are used to locate and identify prey.

Stalking jaguar Hunting in the dense rainforest of Central and South America, the jaguar takes a wide range of prey, including caimans, anaconda, peccaries, and capybaras. It has a very powerful bite, enabling it to crush skulls and shatter turtle shells.

STEALTH

Many predators, whether they are active chasers or ambushers that lie in wait, rely heavily on stealth to be successful. Hunting of any kind expends huge amounts of energy, and failure may not only result in hunger, but also seriously reduce the survival chances of the predator's young. As it is likely that its prey has also evolved good vision, often with eyes located on the sides of the head to give a wide, non-overlapping field of view, a predator needs to be able to approach its target without being detected itself. Prey species may feed in groups, and large numbers of eyes mean that some can always keep watch, making life difficult for a predator. One adaptation that helps both predators and prey conceal themselves is camouflage. Colouring can allow an animal to blend in with its background and disruptive markings can help break up its body outline. This makes prey difficult to see, but also helps predators get close enough to make a kill. To increase their chances, predators often make use of vegetation cover and move as noiselessly as possible, keeping low to the ground as they stalk.

Silk traps Spiders have developed the ability to produce silk and use it to trap insects. In many species, the snare takes the form of a characteristic web, spun across a gap in vegetation.

Lures Several snakes have evolved lures to entice prey closer. Often the lure is wiggled about, its colour contrasting strongly with the rest of the predator's body.

OPPORTUNISM

Many predators are opportunists. Rather than targeting any particular species or type of prey, they simply move about their preferred habitat looking for suitable food. Hedgehogs forage on the ground and among leaf litter, where they find earthworms, insects and their larvae, slugs, and even small vertebrates.

Lying in wait A pack of wolves attacks a group of muskoxen. The oxen will attempt to form a defensive circle with their horns facing outwards.

COOPERATIVE HUNTING

In some species, cooperation enables members of a group to obtain more food than they would be able to by hunting alone. Cooperative hunting is more likely to arise if individuals are related to each other, and is an important element in the evolution of social groups. There are many benefits associated with cooperative hunting: it increases foraging success, affords better protection from rivals or enemies, allows larger, better-defended prey to be targeted, and reduces the risk of injury to individuals. In African hunting dogs, the size of the pack determines the size of the prey. Small packs will select impalas and small antelopes, while larger packs are able to kill species such as wildebeests. Cooperative hunting has been studied in vertebrates such as chimpanzees, dogs, lions, hyenas, orcas, porpoises, sharks, fishes, and birds. Among invertebrates, social insects, such as army and driver ants, are well-known for this feeding strategy.

WEAPONS

Predators have evolved an array of weapons to seize and kill prey. The most common weapons among vertebrates are teeth and claws. Mammalian carnivores have enlarged canine teeth for killing, and their carnassial teeth mesh together to tear through flesh. The claws of carnivores are large and curved for catching and holding prey. Fish-eating species typically have a large number of sharp, pointed teeth for securing slippery prey. Birds that dive for fishes have sharp, pointed bills with backward-facing serrations for gripping. Birds of prey have large talons for holding prey and strong, hooked bills for tearing it apart. Invertebrates have a great variety of weapons, including venomous stingers.

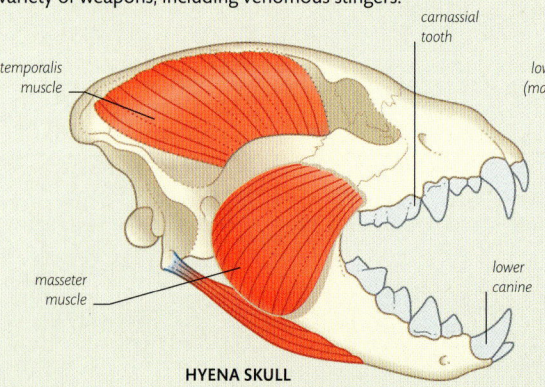

HYENA SKULL

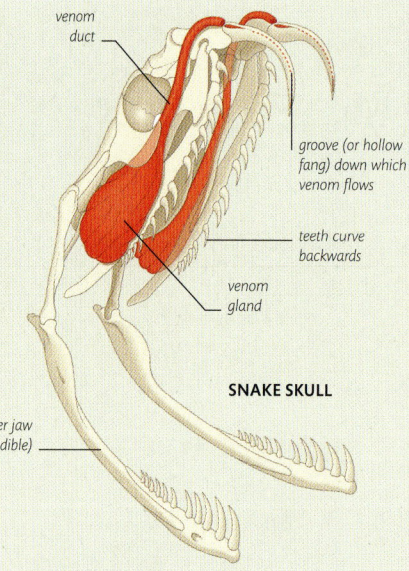

SNAKE SKULL

Contrasting skulls The hyena has a massive skull with relatively short jaws, giving it a powerful grip. In most mammalian carnivores, the carnassial teeth are sharp, shearing flesh before it is swallowed. In contrast, a snake's skull is delicate, and the loosely articulated, flexible jaws open very wide. Vipers kill by injecting toxic venom into their prey using two fangs.

Talons Three forward-pointing talons and one backward-pointing talon ensure that this red-backed hawk gets a firm grip on its prey.

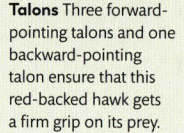

Claws Scorpions combine claw strength and venom to subdue and kill prey. Although this fat-tailed scorpion has relatively slender claws, its potent venom allows it to easily overcome a small reptile.

PREDATION 173

EATING PREY
Prey may be eaten in a number of ways depending on the predator. With very large predators consuming large numbers of small prey, such as baleen whales feeding on krill, there is no need for pre-processing and the food is simply swallowed. In contrast, snakes are adapted to eating prey as large as themselves. Since they cannot chew it, it is swallowed whole and digested. Most predators cut their food into pieces in order to eat the most nutritious parts. In other animals, such as starfish, digestion takes place outside the body.

Digesting first The mouthparts of many flies are adapted for sponging and licking. The house fly cannot eat solid food, so has to liquefy it before it can be consumed. To do this, it regurgitates part of its previous meal, as well as salivary enzymes, before feeding.

Before death An assassin bug picks a weak spot in its prey's exoskeleton, such as the soft, flexible membranes between plates of cuticle. Its sharp mouthparts stab through the surface, injecting toxic, protein-dissolving enzymes. Once liquefied, the body is sucked up by the bug.

KILLING TECHNIQUES
Predators kill in various ways, depending on the size and nature of each species. Dismemberment, strangulation, drowning, impaling, and poisoning are the main methods. Large carnivores, such as tigers, kill their prey as quickly as possible, avoiding either personal injury or prey escape. Small prey is bitten on the back of the neck, breaking the spinal cord and severing the blood vessels. Death is often instantaneous. Larger animals are seized by the throat and held until they die of asphyxiation. Toxic salivary secretions have evolved in many animals, including snakes, spiders, jellyfish, and even some molluscs.

Clam eaters Some species are not just eaten by one predator, but by a whole range of predators, each using a different technique. Although they have tough, hinged shells and strong muscles to keep them shut, bivalve molluscs are a favourite food of many animals, including small sharks, walruses, squid, and many shore birds.

Eating whole Like all snakes, the eyelash viper cannot chew its food and swallows it whole. Once caught on the viper's back-curved teeth, the prey is propelled slowly down the throat in a ratchetlike fashion.

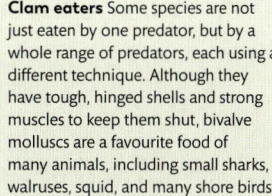

The shore crab uses its strong claws to crack and prise open bivalves.

A moon snail drills a hole in the prey's shell before injecting enzymes to dissolve the contents.

BIVALVE

American oystercatchers probe into mud and either prise or hammer shells open.

This common starfish pulls the shell open and everts its stomach inside.

Sea otters eat floating on their backs and often use rocks to bash open the shells.

Playing with food Young predators, such as cats, that play with their prey before killing it are thought to be practising their hunting and prey-handling techniques. This polar bear is tossing a piece of meat into the air before consumption.

Save for later The red-backed shrike stores food it cannot eat immediately. It makes a larder by impaling items on thorns or wedging them in forked twigs. This behaviour allows the bird to hoard prey when it is abundant, and to handle larger items such as small lizards.

Box jellyfish
Lethal sting

SPECIES *Chironex fleckeri* **SIZE** 0.25–3 m (10 in–9¾ ft) including tentacles
DISTRIBUTION Ocean waters off northern Australia and Papua New Guinea, and also wider Indo-Pacific to at least the Philippines and Malaysia

The box jellyfish uses the venom in its stinging tentacles not just for defensive purposes but also for killing prey. It belongs to the class Cubozoa, and although cubozoans are not true jellyfish, they are closely related. The box jellyfish's transparent body makes it all but invisible to prey as it floats in the water. Capable of moving at speeds of up to 7.2 kph (4 knots) using a form of jet propulsion, it is a formidable predator. It has 24 small eyes arranged in four groups of six on each side of its body. Most of these eyes simply respond to dark and light, but one pair of eyes in each cluster has the capacity to form images and guide the animal through mangroves as well as towards its victims. Its usual quarry, small fishes and prawns, are stunned and paralysed instantaneously when they come into contact with the long tentacles. As many as 15 tentacles, each armed with thousands of stinging cells, trail from the four corners of the body. The box jellyfish is among the world's most venomous species and poses a significant threat to human swimmers and divers. Its stings are excruciatingly painful and can quickly cause heart failure. Shock, leading to drowning, accounts for many of the deaths in human victims. Wetsuits and special stinger suits can provide protection and specific antivenin treatment can save lives.

bell has cubelike shape

tentacles may reach 3 m (10 ft) in length

each tentacle has about 5,000 stinging cells

venom has quickly killed prey before it damages box jellyfish's tentacles

Speared shrimp Speared and held fast by hundreds of stinging cells, this shrimp was unable to escape before the box jellyfish's venom took effect. The tentacle will draw the shrimp to the underside of the body where the mouth will engulf it whole.

ANATOMY STINGING CELLS

About 5,000 specialized stinging cells, or nematocysts, are ranged along each tentacle. Each cell contains a filament armed with barbs. When triggered by contact or chemical stimuli from its prey, the filaments are released explosively. One of the fastest cellular processes ever recorded in nature, this turns the filament and barbs inside out with the same energy as that of a small-calibre bullet.

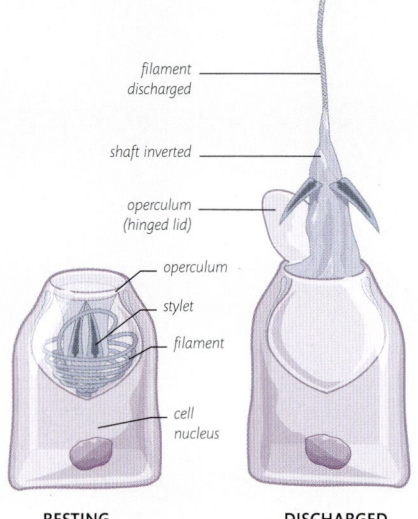

filament discharged
shaft inverted
operculum (hinged lid)
operculum
stylet
filament
cell nucleus

RESTING   **DISCHARGED**

Giant cuttlefish
Camouflaged hunter

SPECIES *Sepia apama* **SIZE** Up to 1.5 m (5 ft)
DISTRIBUTION Rocky reef areas and amongst kelp and sea grass in coastal waters around southern half of Australia, including Tasmania

The giant cuttlefish, the world's largest, stalks or ambushes its prey. Like other cuttlefishes, it can change the colour and texture of its skin (see pp.268–69) and so remain hidden until it pounces. Two of its ten arms are specialized long, prehensile tentacles covered in suction pads and, after careful positioning using its excellent binocular vision to judge distance, these are shot out at great speed to snare its prey, which is then pulled back into the arms. This technique is used for fast-moving prey such as fishes. For slow movers like crabs, the cuttlefish simply pounces and wraps its arms around its victim. Once brought to the mouth, the prey is bitten by a sharp parrotlike beak and toxic saliva is injected to subdue it before it is ripped apart.

> Giant cuttlefish **raise and wiggle their arms** to lure prey.

Deadly strike When prey is spotted, a giant cuttlefish turns towards it and, holding its arms together, launches its two specialized feeding tentacles with deadly speed and accuracy.

PREDATION 175

Horned helmet shell
Pinned down
SPECIES *Cassis cornuta* **SIZE** Up to 40 cm (15½ in)
DISTRIBUTION Indian Ocean from East Africa to Australia and Pacific Ocean east to Hawaii

Also called the giant horned helmet shell or conch, this marine snail hunts and eats sea urchins, including burrowing species, as well as other echinoderms. It is one of the few species that can destroy the notorious coral-killing crown-of-thorns starfish. The front of the shell has an upturned groove along which a siphon lies and projects into the water. It is through this siphon that the snail "tastes" the water for the chemical scent trails left by wandering sea urchins and other types of echinoderms, its principal food. During the day, the horned helmet shell lies partly buried in shallow water with just the tips of its horns exposed, but when darkness falls it moves out of its hiding place to hunt for food. Once it has closed in on its prey, it raises its body and pins down its victim using its large muscular foot. The size and weight of its shell help protect it from the urchin's sharp spines.

Stalking a sea urchin >>01 The snail locates its prey by detecting its scent trail. **>>02** It raises its body by flexing its foot. **>>03** The snail moves over the urchin before pinning it down. **>>04** It then secretes mucus to dissolve a hole in the urchin's shell. Using a toothed "tongue" it enlarges the hole through which it can extract the urchin's internal organs.

Rufous net-casting spider
Casting a net
SPECIES *Deinopis subrufa* **SIZE** Legspan up to 13 cm (5 in) **DISTRIBUTION** Wooded and garden habitats in southeast Australia and Tasmania

The way in which net-casting spiders catch their prey is unique. The spider hides during the day and comes out after dark to catch nocturnal prey such as ants, crickets, beetles, and other spiders. It first spins a framework of silk attached to vegetation. Then it combs out a special pale blue, fuzzy silk to create a rectangular capture net. This cribellate silk has a 400–600 per cent stretch capacity. When the capture net is ready, the spider holds each corner with its first two pairs of legs and waits motionless. As soon as prey is detected beneath the net, the spider propels itself forwards, stretching out the net then, releases the tension – all in a split second – to cast the net and ensnare the prey in the woolly loops of silk. Deinopids can also intercept flying prey with their nets, using a ballistically fast, overhead back-twist.

Large eyes The spider holds its capture net, ready to trap prey. Not visible here are two huge forward-facing eyes on its top side that collect light more efficiently than those of a cat or owl. The spider relies entirely on sight to detect prey.

Cone shells
Poison dart
FAMILY Conidae **SIZE** Up to 25 cm (10 in)
DISTRIBUTION Warm tropical seas worldwide

These sea snails hunt marine worms, other molluscs, and even fishes, paralysing them with the venom from a poison gland that is injected by a harpoon-shaped dart. The venom (known as conotoxin) is very fast-acting, causing almost instant paralysis. Conotoxins interfere with nerve impulses and are so powerful, they have been developed as specialist pain blockers.

Alerted by the smell of prey nearby, the snail extends its proboscis, and when within reach, it fires a harpoon with explosive speed into the body of the prey. With some of these fish hunters, the victim remains attached so it can be drawn back into the proboscis, which expands to engulf it. Indigestible parts of the prey and the used harpoon are later expelled.

Proboscis and harpoon The snail's proboscis emerges from the opening at the end of its shell. Just behind its tip lies a hollow, barbed harpoon that it uses to impale its prey or ward off potential predators.

Fishing spider With its fangs sunk deep into its victim's flesh, a fishing spider begins to feed. As an adult, the leg span of this species can reach 12 cm (4½ in). It is widespread in northern South America, where it sits by rainforest pools waiting for passing prey, which it seizes with its front legs before injecting a fast-acting toxin.

Jumping spiders

Leaping for prey

FAMILY Salticidae   **SIZE** Legspan up to 1.8 cm (⅝ in)
DISTRIBUTION A wide range of habitats worldwide

Jumping spiders do not make a web to catch their food but stalk prey during the day and move within range before leaping to seize it. They have excellent binocular vision, with the middle pair of front-facing eyes greatly enlarged. Not only is their eyesight extremely acute but, uniquely, jumping spiders can move the back of their main eyes inside their head so that they can look from side to side without moving. When hunting, these spiders attach a safety thread to a fixed point.

Seizing prey Jumping spiders can jump 50–60 times their own body length. Their legs extend not by muscular action but by having fluid forced rapidly into them.

Decoy spider

Decorated trap

SPECIES *Cyclosa insulana*   **SIZE** Legspan up to 2 cm (¾ in)
DISTRIBUTION Forests and gardens from the Mediterranean to Southeast Asia and northern Australia

This decoy spider decorates its vertical orb web with conspicuous patterns of silk, called stabilimenta, which incorporate the remains of its prey, its own shed skins, and even plant and fungal material. Studies have shown that by decorating their webs decoy spiders may attract or intercept more prey, although the decorations may have other functions. It has been suggested that these obvious patterns may prevent birds and large insects from flying through the webs by accident, or that sitting at the centre of its web, legs folded, the decoy spider is camouflaged from predators. It is also possible that the web debris advertises the success of a female spider to potential mates.

Common praying mantis

Sudden ambush

SPECIES *Mantis religiosa*   **SIZE** Up to 9 cm (3½ in)   **DISTRIBUTION** In all kinds of vegetation in Europe; introduced to North America

Like all other mantids, the common praying mantis has a highly specialized predatory lifestyle. A skilled ambusher, it remains motionless and relies on its cryptic green or brown coloration to avoid being seen. It has a distinctive triangular head that is very mobile and has a pair of large compound eyes, which face forwards to provide it with true binocular vision. It gauges distance to its prey by moving its head to measure the prey's apparent movement relative to its background. Known as binocular triangulation, this technique is widespread among vertebrates but much less common among invertebrates.

There are many modifications of the mantis's body that make it a superb hunter. The first segment of the thorax, which carries the specialized front legs, is very long. Together with the elongated upper segment of the front legs, this gives the mantis a very broad reach. The front femur is greatly enlarged to house the muscles that operate the tibia, and has rows of sharp spines on its inner surface. The front tibia is also spined and folds back like a jack-knife to mesh with the spines on the femur, making a formidable trap. The middle and hind pair of legs are used for walking and holding onto vegetation. Between the hind legs on the metathorax, the mantis has a hearing organ that is regarded as a "true ear" – it can detect a range of frequencies, including ultrasound.

The common praying mantis is mainly active during the day and eats a wide range of insects, spiders, and other arthropods. When prey is caught and subdued, the mantis uses its tough jaws to slice through tissue and chitin with equal ease.

>>01

>>02

Rapid strike >>01 Using its acute vision and a specialized location technique, the mantis calculates the exact distance, speed, and direction required to snatch its prey.   >>02 The front legs are fully extended before the tibiae are flexed around the prey in a vicelike grip.   >>03 The mantis retracts its legs and brings its prey towards its mouth. The strike has lasted less than 100 milliseconds, and can be as fast as 30 milliseconds.

PREDATION 179

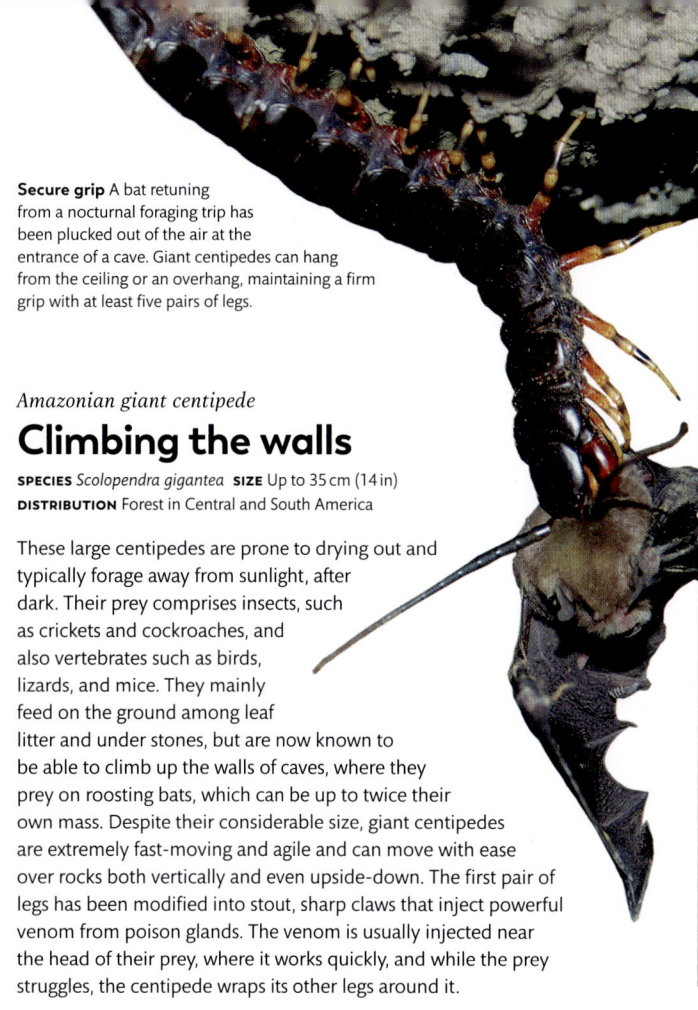

Secure grip A bat returning from a nocturnal foraging trip has been plucked out of the air at the entrance of a cave. Giant centipedes can hang from the ceiling or an overhang, maintaining a firm grip with at least five pairs of legs.

Amazonian giant centipede
Climbing the walls
SPECIES *Scolopendra gigantea* **SIZE** Up to 35 cm (14 in)
DISTRIBUTION Forest in Central and South America

These large centipedes are prone to drying out and typically forage away from sunlight, after dark. Their prey comprises insects, such as crickets and cockroaches, and also vertebrates such as birds, lizards, and mice. They mainly feed on the ground among leaf litter and under stones, but are now known to be able to climb up the walls of caves, where they prey on roosting bats, which can be up to twice their own mass. Despite their considerable size, giant centipedes are extremely fast-moving and agile and can move with ease over rocks both vertically and even upside-down. The first pair of legs has been modified into stout, sharp claws that inject powerful venom from poison glands. The venom is usually injected near the head of their prey, where it works quickly, and while the prey struggles, the centipede wraps its other legs around it.

Lesser emperor dragonfly nymph
Extending mouth
SPECIES *Anax parthenope* **SIZE** 7 cm (2¾ in)
DISTRIBUTION Lakes and ponds in Europe and Asia

As with all dragonflies, the nymphs of the lesser emperor dragonfly live in lakes and ponds among vegetation and bottom debris, where they hunt for prey, which they catch using a concertinalike lower mouthparts (see panel, right). Their gills are located within the rectal chamber and, if required, water can be forced out at high speed for a jet-propelled escape from potential enemies.

Calculated strike >>01 A passing fish has alerted this dragonfly nymph to its presence. The nymph watches it for a short distance. >>02 When ready, the nymph launches itself upwards and extends the lower mouthpart forwards from underneath the head. >>03 Impaled on either side by the sharp hooks on the palps, the fish is brought to the mandibles.

ANATOMY
SPECIALIZED MOUTHPARTS

The aquatic nymphs (or naiads) of dragonflies are highly predatory and have specialized mouthparts for catching prey. The mouth is long, hinged, and prehensile, with a pair of hooked palps, and folds back on itself. It can be shot forwards using muscular action and hydraulic pressure in 25 milliseconds or less.

>>01   >>02   >>03

>>03

Giant water bug nymphs

Aquatic assassin

FAMILY Belostomatidae **SIZE** Up to 15 cm (6 in)
DISTRIBUTION Freshwater streams and ponds worldwide, especially the Americas, southern Africa, and Southeast Asia

Giant water bugs are fierce predators, both as adults and as nymphs. Nymphs have large, bulging eyes and either lie in wait for prey to pass close enough to lunge forwards and grab it with their specially modified front legs, or hunt actively using their middle and hind legs to swim. Once the prey is caught, the bug uses its sharp mouthparts to stab it, usually in the neck, and inject its highly toxic saliva, which paralyses the victim. Similar in composition to some snake venom, the toxin dissolves the prey's flesh so that the liquefied meal can then be sucked up by the bug. Although the larvae of aquatic insects form a large part of the diet of giant water bugs, surprisingly, they will also readily attack crayfish, tadpoles, frogs, fishes, and even small water birds: all prey that are much larger than themselves.

Throat wound This giant water bug nymph has successfully ambushed a frog by attacking it from below, injecting its toxic venom, and keeping clear of the amphibian's powerful hind legs.

Easy glider The long limbs of the common pondskater repel water, allowing it to move on still water without effort. Its shorter front limbs are held in the air and used to grab prey.

Common pondskater

Surface predator

SPECIES *Gerris lacustris* **SIZE** 1.5 cm (½ in) **DISTRIBUTION** On still or slow-moving water in Europe

Pond skaters have exploited a unique world between water and air; they catch small insects trapped in the film of water tension at the surface of fresh water. They are well adapted to the task. Their front legs are short and used to grasp prey as the pondskater eats, while the middle and hind legs are very long, and splay out to support the insect on the water and propel it across the surface at great speed. Pondskaters are covered in dense, water-repellent hairs, and the front legs have long ripple-sensitive hairs that enable them to detect and locate the movement of their prey.

Giant antlion larva

Open jaws

SPECIES *Palpares immensus* **SIZE** 5 cm (2 in) **DISTRIBUTION** Sandy areas and arid shrublands among long grass in southern Africa

Giant antlion larvae bury themselves in coarse sand, with just the top of their heads and open jaws showing above the surface, while they wait for insects and other prey to ambush. Sensitive hairs and relatively good eyesight tell the antlion when to strike. Anchored deep in the sand, it can subdue large prey. The toothed, sickle-shaped jaws are formed by a deeply grooved mandible and the maxilla, which fits over the top, forming two hollow tubes through which salivary enzymes can be injected into the prey to paralyse it and dissolve its internal organs. The resulting soup is then sucked back up and eaten. Some antlion larvae build special conical pits in loose sand. They then flick sand grains at passing insects to knock them into the bottom of the pit where they are seized and eaten.

Sand trap The toothed jaws of this antlion larva are visible in the coarse sand. Once the jaws have snapped shut on prey, the antlion will quickly drag the prey under the surface and consume it.

PREDATION 181

Glowing trap The gnat larvae have to live in very sheltered locations as the slightest gust of wind would tangle the sticky beadlets on the threads, making the trap useless.

Fungus gnat larva
Sticky snare
SPECIES *Arachnocampa tasmaniensis* **SIZE** Up to 3–5 mm (1/8–3/16 in) **DISTRIBUTION** Caves, overhangs, and deep gullies in Tasmania

Often called glow-worms, the larvae of this gnat live in a mucus tube supported by a loose scaffolding of silken threads. From this structure hang as many as 50 vertical threads coated in small beadlets of a sticky, gluelike substance. To attract flying insects such as mosquitoes, midges, mayflies, caddisflies, and even beetles to their sticky snares, the larvae produce a soft, blue-green glow from the rear half of their bodies. When an insect becomes trapped in the glue, the larva moves slowly along one of the horizontal parts of the web to the end of the thread and begins to reel the victim in.

Cooperative pseudoscorpion
Pack arachnids
SPECIES *Paratemnoides nidificator* **SIZE** Up to 5 mm (3/16 in) **DISTRIBUTION** Mexico and South America

Pseudoscorpions are tiny, antlike arachnids only few millimetres long but they are ferocious predators. Most are solitary hunters, but *Paratemnoides nidificator* hunt in packs to bring down prey many times their size, such as beetles and spiders. They take on different roles during a hunt, with some "profiteers" not helping at all. They then share the meal fairly. Attackers are the first to eat, followed by the nymphs, with profiteers feeding last. Profiteers are allowed to feed because they perform other useful roles, in reproduction, care of nymphs, and building reproductive silk chambers. Waiting for one's turn to eat and looking out for the next generation appears to be the secret of this tight-knit community. Indeed, mothers show an extreme form of parental care by making the ultimate sacrifice for their young during food shortages. A mother will go out of the nest and wait passively for the nymphs to attack and feed on her.

No stinger The pseudoscorpions are a group of arachnids that get their common name from the resemblance their front pedipalps have to the pincers of scorpions.

Asian giant hornet
Bee killer
SPECIES *Vespa mandarina* **SIZE** Up to 5 cm (2 in) **DISTRIBUTION** Mostly upland areas in Japan, China, Korea, India, and Nepal

Asian giant hornets hunt and kill a wide range of insect prey, including other hornets. Able to cover relatively long distances, the hornet carries its prey back to its nest, where it uses its strong jaws to butcher the victim. It is then fed to the developing hornet larvae. However, the adults do not feed on what they catch, but are instead fed by their own larvae, which regurgitate a rich mixture of amino acids for them to drink. When Asian giant hornets attack bee colonies, it is not the adult worker bees they carry off, but the soft-bodied bee larvae. Just a handful of hornets can decimate a bee colony in a short time, an attack for which the introduced commercial honey bee has no defence.

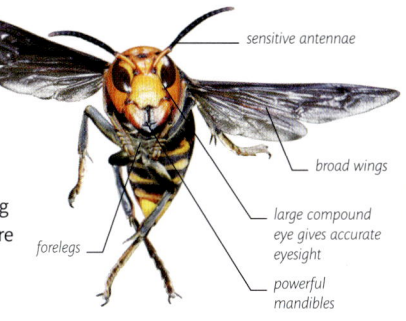

Winged raider This species can fly at more than 20 kph (12 mph). Besides powerful venom, it also has strong jaws.

Labels: sensitive antennae, broad wings, large compound eye gives accurate eyesight, powerful mandibles, forelegs

However it has been discovered that Japanese populations of the Asian honey bee (*Apis cerana*) have evolved a unique thermal-execution technique to deal with such an attack. Hundreds of worker bees form a tight ball around the invaders, and the intense heat generated by their wing muscles kills the hornets (see p.281).

On the move Bigger soldier ants, which are armed with large, curved, and toothed jaws, patrol the outside edges of the perpetually moving column and are constantly on guard for potential attackers.

Driver ants
Path of destruction
SPECIES *Dorylus* species **SIZE** Up to 2.5 cm (1 in) **DISTRIBUTION** Savanna and woodland in Africa and East Asia

Also known as safari ants, these ants form colonies that can comprise many millions of individuals. They may stay in one place for anything from a week to several months. When local food supplies start to diminish, the ants move off in a large column, consuming anything they encounter. During this nomadic phase, the workers carry their developing brood in their jaws. Although insects and other invertebrates are their main prey, larger animals such as vertebrates can be overwhelmed and, if unable to escape, will be hacked to pieces and eaten.

Allomerus ant
Hairy trap
SPECIES *Allomerus decemarticulatus* **SIZE** 2 mm (1/16 in) **DISTRIBUTION** Rainforest in South America

These ants have evolved a unique mechanism for capturing prey that might otherwise escape them by jumping or flying away. They create a giant trap to ambush prey, constructing a false surface over the hairy stems of *Hirtella physophora* beneath which they hide. First, they trim away some of the hairs of the host plant, leaving pillars of hairs. These are used to support a spongy platform made from woven hairs and regurgitated material. This is then reinforced by the mycelium of a sooty fungus controlled by the ants. The ants puncture holes in the platform just big enough to poke their heads through and hide below with their jaws open, ready to grab the legs or antennae of any unwary prey that passes along the stem. Once they have got hold of the prey, scores of workers stream out to sting and immobilize it and then carry it off to their nest to be dismembered.

False floor The stem of the ant plant *Hirtella physophora* (left) is covered by a secondary surface built entirely by the hiding ants. Large prey, such as this grasshopper (above) are fooled by the false surface and walk across the ants' trap, where they are immobilized and stung.

White shark
Attack from beneath

SPECIES *Carcharodon carcharias* **SIZE** Commonly up to 6 m (20 ft), but may be longer **DISTRIBUTION** Found mainly in coastal waters where prey is abundant. Worldwide in temperate waters

The white shark, a formidable predator also known as the great white, typically employs a lightning-fast strike from below to disable large prey. The blow can seriously incapacitate or even kill prey in an instant.

Despite its size, the white shark is effectively camouflaged by countershading. Its body is grey or bluish-brown on top so that prey swimming near the surface find it hard to see the shark when looking down into the water beneath them. Similarly, the shark's underside is pale so that, when its prey is below, the shark's silhouette against the sky is minimized.

White sharks are able to maintain their body temperature, especially that of their brain and eyes, which increases their hunting efficiency in cold water. They use electroreception, scent, hearing, and vision to locate prey. They will often have an exploratory bite to test if an item of prey is suitable. Juveniles eat small fish and squid, but adults hunt seals, sea lions, dolphins, and large fishes, such as tuna. Although this shark is a top predator, it will also scavenge carrion, such as whale carcasses.

Full breach The sheer force of its attack has carried this female white shark clear of the water. Having spiralled through the air, she re-enters the water with her prey still gripped in her mouth.

HUMAN IMPACT **ATTACKS ON PEOPLE**

The decline in white shark populations reflects the fact that the losers in most shark–human encounters are the sharks. As humans spend more time in the sea, they inevitably encroach on the habitats of sharks, so this enforced interaction has resulted in increased numbers of shark attacks. However, the perception that sharks, especially the white shark, eat people is contradicted by the fact that a decreasing proportion of shark attacks has resulted in fatalities.

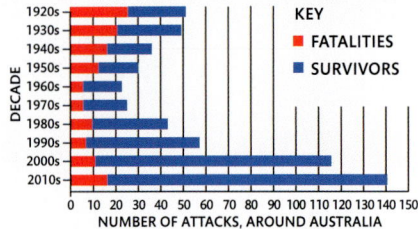

Survival rates While the number of white shark attacks on humans increased during the 20th century, the proportion of fatalities dropped considerably, probably due to improved medical help.

Impact from below >>01 This shark has stalked and attacked a seal from below, launching it out of the water. **>>02** Although the seal has avoided the shark's grasp, its body has taken the full force of the strike. **>>03** The injured seal falls back into the sea. The shark may attack the seal repeatedly until it is weak enough to be eaten.

PREDATION 183

Scalloped hammerhead shark
Electrical sensing
SPECIES *Sphyrna lewini* **SIZE** Up to 4.2 m (13¾ ft) **DISTRIBUTION** Warm temperate to tropical coastal waters worldwide

Like other hammerheads, the scalloped hammerhead shark's most distinctive feature is its broad, flat head. The most likely explanation for this bizarre shape concerns the capture of its prey. All sharks have special sense organs, called the ampullae of Lorenzini, capable of detecting weak electrical fields emitted by other animals. These organs form a system of jelly-filled canals in the head and snout connected to the outside via small pores. In hammerhead sharks, the underside of the hammer is particularly well endowed with these organs, and the increase in area due to the shape of the head may help them detect bottom-living prey more effectively.

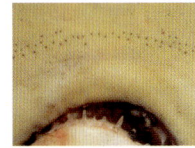

Sense organs It is thought that sharks can detect electrical signals as low as 15-billionths of a volt from the movement of prey. Their sense organs appear as black dots on the underside of the head (below).

Banded archerfish
Water cannon
SPECIES *Toxotes jaculatrix* **SIZE** Up to 40 cm (15½ in)
DISTRIBUTION Mainly in mangrove swamps of Southeast Asia, India, Australia, and the western Pacific

Although the banded archerfish catches aquatic prey such as shrimps and worms, it is best known for the unique way it catches prey out of water. The fish uses its mouth to squirt a narrow, powerful jet of water to knock insects from the vegetation above it. The head is narrow, with the eyes close to the snout, giving it binocular vision. When the fish spots potential prey, it sticks its snout out of the water and presses its tongue onto a groove that runs along the roof of its mouth. By rapidly closing its gill covers, a stream of water is forced along the groove and out through the small aperture at the end. Adults are very accurate and can shoot a number of times in quick succession to dislodge prey, which is then swallowed, sometimes before it reaches the water. If prey is close to the water, the archerfish may jump out of the water to catch it.

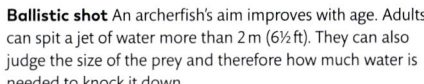

Ballistic shot An archerfish's aim improves with age. Adults can spit a jet of water more than 2 m (6½ ft). They can also judge the size of the prey and therefore how much water is needed to knock it down.

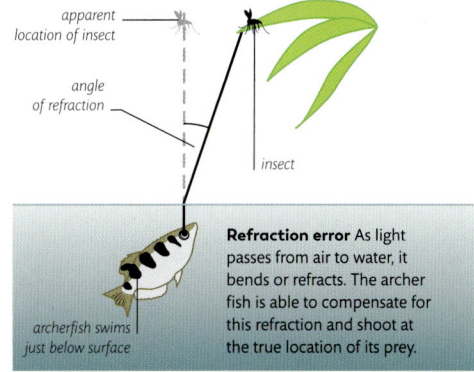

Refraction error As light passes from air to water, it bends or refracts. The archer fish is able to compensate for this refraction and shoot at the true location of its prey.

apparent location of insect
angle of refraction
insect
archerfish swims just below surface

Hairy frogfish
Hidden angler
SPECIES *Antennarius striatus* **SIZE** Up to 25 cm (10 in) **DISTRIBUTION** All subtropical oceans, to depths of 10–200 m (33–656 ft)

Also known as the striated or striped frogfish, the hairy frogfish is a stealth predator that lives on the sea floor, hidden among rocks, weed, and coral. Concealed by highly effective camouflage, it draws prey towards it with a lure. Its coloration is variable, and its body is covered with long and branching skin tufts that completely obscure the outline of the fish. The unusual small, round openings of the gills are hidden just below the pectoral fins, and to make their disguise even more effective, these fishes will hide among urchins and sponges, and in coral crevices.

The hairy frogfish's stalked lure is a modified dorsal spine that can be bent backwards along the head when not being used to attract prey. The lure can even regrow if it gets damaged or bitten off. Frogfishes do not always need to use their lure, as they are so well camouflaged against the substrate that small fishes will sometimes even mistake them for a place to shelter.

Swift snatch The speed of the frogfish's gape-and-snatch movement has been measured at an extraordinary $1/6{,}000^{th}$ second, making it among the fastest known predatory movements of any vertebrate.

enlarged dorsal spine has appearance of weed

"bait" at end of stalk

Angling for prey Frogfishes sit absolutely motionless on the sea bed, camouflaged against the substrate. This keeps them hidden from predators but also accentuates the movement of the lure, which they twitch to attract prey.

Easy meal Also known as the copper shark due to its colour in sunlight, the bronze whaler shark can grow to over 3 m (9¾ ft) in length. It feeds on other sharks, squid, and bottom-living fishes but is often attracted by large shoals of fishes, such as sardines on an annual run that takes place off the east coast of South Africa between May and July.

Mosaic moray eel
Concealed weapon
SPECIES *Enchelycore ramosa* **SIZE** Up to 1.5 m (5 ft)
DISTRIBUTION On reefs off southeast Australia, northern New Zealand, and islands of the southwest Pacific

Hiding in crevices and under rocky ledges, these thick-skinned, mucus-covered eels typically lie in wait for something to pass close enough to be seized. They mainly feed at night on fishes, crustaceans, and molluscs and move with a snakelike, sinuous motion powered by their long dorsal and anal fins. They sometimes feed during the day and have been observed to stalk their prey over short distances. The eel's head has a characteristic long snout with curved jaws, armed with many razor-sharp, needlelike teeth. A second set of jaws (see panel, below) ensures that the eel can secure its prey even if it only gets a partial grip on it. This mechanism is unique to moray eels. Other bony fishes typically use suction to swallow prey; sudden expansion of the mouth cavity causes water to rush in, taking the prey along with it. In moray eels, the head is relatively narrow so it would be difficult to ingest anything but small prey using this feeding technique.

Scenting prey Although their eyes are prominent, moray eels have relatively poor eyesight and rely instead on a good sense of smell and sensory pores on the head to detect their prey.

ANATOMY **EXTRA JAWS**
Moray eels have a second set of jaws halfway down their throat called pharyngeal jaws. These bear large, back-curved teeth. Prey is caught and held by the sharp teeth on the primary jaws. Next, the contraction of special muscles rapidly pulls the secondary jaws forwards from well behind the skull into the mouth. Once they secure the prey, other muscles contract, pulling the pharyngeal jaws backwards and dragging the prey down into the oesophagus.

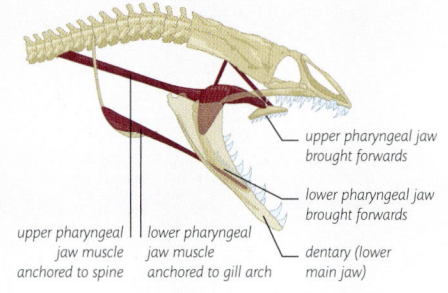

Deep-sea devil The stoplight loosejaw's striking appearance remains hidden from the crustaceans and fishes that it feeds on.

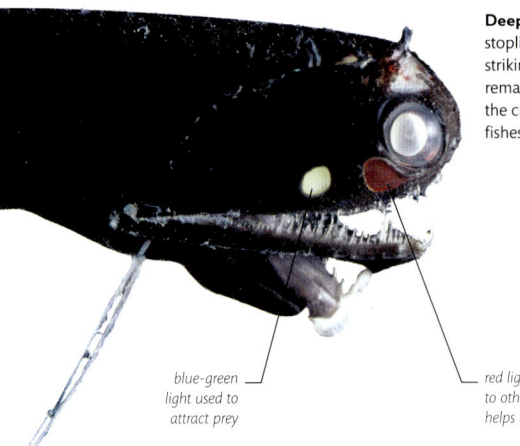

blue-green light used to attract prey

red light is invisible to other fishes and helps to detect prey

Stoplight loosejaw
Secret flashlight
SPECIES *Malacosteus niger* **SIZE** Up to 25 cm (10 in) **DISTRIBUTION** Deep areas of the Atlantic, Indian, and Pacific oceans

The "stoplight" part of this fish's common name comes from the presence of red and green photophores (light-producing organs) on the sides of its head, which it uses to find prey. Most deep-sea species can see blue-green bioluminescence (light generated by living organisms) but are not very sensitive to red light. The stoplight loosejaw's flashing red photophore allows it to pinpoint its prey while remaining invisible.

This fish is also named after its lower jaw, which is very long and armed with slender, back-curved fangs. To seize prey, the jaw can be pushed forwards in front of the head. Once prey is snagged on the teeth, the jaw is retracted. There is no skin between the bones of the lower jaw, and the species can swallow prey almost as big as itself.

Elephantnose fish
Electric organs
SPECIES *Gnathonemus petersii* **SIZE** Up to 35 cm (14 in)
DISTRIBUTION In muddy, slow-moving rivers in West and Central Africa

These fishes live in muddy and murky water and need a system other than eyesight to locate and determine the nature of nearby objects. They use a kind of radar by producing electrical discharges from a special organ near the tail, which is made up of modified muscle cells. The discharges then generate a weak electrical field around the mucus-covered body of the fish. Obstacles, prey, or other fishes that come into range of the electric field alter its shape according to their own conductivity, and these changes are picked up by electroreceptors sited over most of the body. These receptor cells are particularly abundant on the head and the strange-looking, downward-curved snout, or schnauzenorgan, which the fish also uses to probe the bottom. The brain of these fishes is enlarged to process the complex information coming from the electrolocating system, the ratio of brain to body mass being close to that of primates.

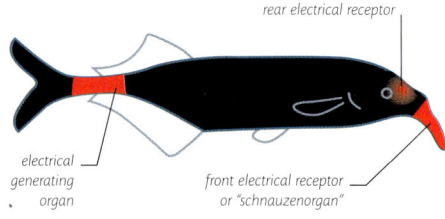

Electric organs The scientific name, meaning "thread jaw", refers to the fingerlike sensory organ on the bottom jaw, which the elephantnose fish uses to feel for worms, insects and crustaceans in the bottom sediment.

Nocturnal feeder These nocturnal fishes hide during the day in dark crevices and under submerged wood. They have poor eyesight but have a special electrolocating system to move around in the darkness and find food.

Brown trout
Fly catcher
SPECIES *Salmo trutta* **SIZE** Up to 1.4 m (4½ ft)
DISTRIBUTION Rivers and streams of Europe and Asia, and the northeast Atlantic, but widely introduced elsewhere

Wild brown trout return from the sea to spawn in fresh water and, while there, eat a wide range of insects, worms, molluscs, crustaceans, and even smaller fishes and frogs. They feed from the bed of the stream, and when certain insect species are hatching and rising to the surface, the trout gorge themselves. They often rise out of the water to reach flying insects. Because of their varied feeding habits, anglers use lifelike models of a wide range of insects for fly-fishing, where they try to mimic the appearance and behaviour of the trout's natural food. Trout can be very selective in their feeding, and fishermen have to try to imitate what the trout are currently eating.

Powerful leap Using its powerful tail to jump clear of the water, a brown trout will sometimes try to catch fast-flying, agile prey such as damselflies.

Garden eels
Plankton pickers
SPECIES *Gorgasia maculata* **SIZE** Up to 70 cm (28 in)
DISTRIBUTION Sandy shallows of the western Pacific Ocean, from the Maldives to the Solomon Islands and the Philippines

Garden eels have good eyesight and rely mainly on this sense to catch zooplankton, other invertebrates, and even small fishes that drift past in the current. They live in colonies and typically remain in their burrows in the sand. Even when feeding, they only emerge partially, and always leave one-third of their body length buried below

Deceptive appearance Garden eels live gregariously in colonies known as eel gardens (hence their name), where they sway about like stalks of sea grass.

the surface. The burrow is coated on the inside by mucus secreted by a special gland in the eel's tail. This substance binds the sand grains together and prevents the burrow from collapsing. Also known as the Indian spaghetti eel, the garden eel is extremely wary of predators, and will retreat in an instant, sealing the entrance of the burrow with a plug of mucus until the danger has passed.

Perez's frog
Unfolding tongue
SPECIES *Pelophylax perezi* **SIZE** Up to 10 cm (4 in)
DISTRIBUTION Rivers and ponds in France and the Iberian Peninsula

These frogs never venture very far from permanent bodies of water and typically sit at the water's edge on muddy banks or rocks to sunbathe and feed. The males have a pair of vocal sacs and call to attract mates.

Perez's frogs can be active by day and night, and their diet consists primarily of insects, spiders, and other small invertebrates, which they catch using their sticky extendable tongues. When not in use, the tongue is folded backwards towards the throat. A row of very small teeth in the upper jaw, as well as some small teeth in the roof of the mouth, hold prey in place before it is swallowed. The frogs in turn are eaten by owls and several species of aquatic birds. They are always ready to dive into the water and hide at the slightest sign of danger.

ANATOMY SWALLOWING WITH THE EYES
Frogs' large, bulging eyes have an extra job besides watching prey. When a frog swallows its prey, the eye muscles contract, pulling the eyes shut and moving them down through small openings in the skull. The eyes take up a space near the back of the mouth and this action helps to push the food down.

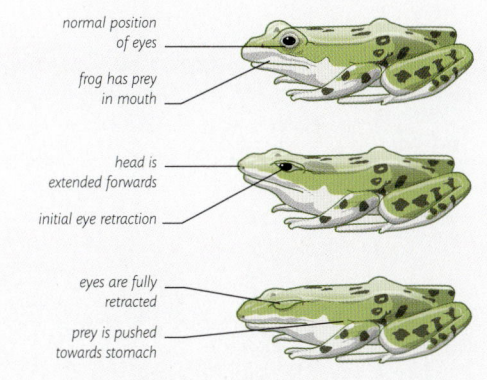

Long reach The tongue of the Perez's frog has a sticky upper surface, and is attached towards the front of the mouth rather than at the rear. This, together with their ability to jump, gives the frogs a longer reach for capturing prey.

Komodo dragon
Lethal bite

SPECIES *Varanus komodoensis* **SIZE** 2–3 m (6½–9¾ ft)
DISTRIBUTION Grassland and lowland forest on the Indonesian islands of Komodo and Flores and others in between

Although Komodo dragons also eat carrion, they will ambush other reptiles and small mammals, as well as goats and deer, usually administering a lethal bite (see panel, right). Swallowing can be a slow process, and so that the lizards do not asphyxiate while eating, a breathing tube under their tongue connects to the lungs. A loosely hinged lower jaw and an elastic stomach cope with meals that may be up to 75 per cent of the Komodo dragon's own bodyweight.

Aiding digestion The Komodo dragon's powerful legs and strong claws hold down prey as they tear off large chunks of flesh. To accelerate its digestive process a lizard will then bask in the sun.

ANATOMY **DEADLY SALIVA**

The mouth and teeth of Komodo dragons are home to more than 50 species of pathogenic bacteria. Animals that are bitten and manage to escape will usually die from the effects of blood poisoning. This may work to the lizard's advantage as it is able to detect the smell of a dead animal up to 10 km (6 miles) away. The bite of other monitor lizards is also slightly venomous, causing swelling and pain for many hours.

Nile crocodile
River ambush

SPECIES *Crocodylus niloticus* **SIZE** Up to 6 m (20 ft)
DISTRIBUTION Waterways throughout Africa and western Madagascar

Young Nile crocodiles eat insects and other invertebrates, and as they grow, will take larger prey such as reptiles, amphibians, and birds. Their ability to rest motionless in the water with just the eyes and the tip of the nostrils showing allows them to get very close to unwary prey before they launch an attack. On land, they are rather slow-moving, but can swing their legs underneath their body for a faster gait. In the water, they are incredibly swift, using their powerful body and tail to propel themselves forward at bursts of up to 30 kph (18 mph). Adults usually eat fishes, but will lie in wait for animals to come down to the water's edge to drink. Sometimes they gather in numbers at river crossings where groups of migrating species such as wildebeest have to run a deadly gauntlet.

As they cannot use their teeth to cut through meat, crocodiles spin themselves around in the water to tear meat from the carcass – although this is known as the death roll, the prey is usually dead already. Nile crocodiles can go for long periods without eating, but when food is available they can consume up to half their own body weight at a single meal.

Powerful jaws With a huge gape and formidable bite, a Nile crocodile can hold on to large prey, such as zebras, buffaloes, or wildebeest, and drag them into the water to drown.

Green tree python
Sensing heat
SPECIES *Morelia viridis* **SIZE** Up to 2 m (6½ ft)
DISTRIBUTION Rainforest in New Guinea, Queensland, Australia, and some islands in Indonesia

This snake is a non-venomous constrictor that lives mainly in the tree canopy and eats small mammals, such as rodents and bats, as well as reptiles and birds. It rests curled in loops over horizontal branches, looking out from the middle of the draped coils. Prey is usually caught by the snake holding on to a branch with the rear part of its body while it strikes with its head. The snake has special temperature-sensing pits along the margins of the lower jaw that enable it to detect the presence of warm-blooded prey. The pits detect radiant heat and allow the snake to track and catch prey even in total darkness. Once prey is caught, the snake wraps several coils of its body around it and tightens its grip every time its victim exhales, suffocating it in the process.

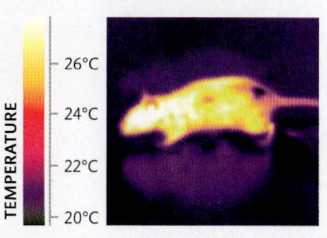

IMAGING PREY IN INFRARED
Seen through a thermal imaging camera, a rodent stands out clearly from the cool background. Prey may seem just as obvious to the green tree python.

Ready to strike Vivid green colouring, with blue, yellow, and white flecks provide superb camouflage, while enlarged front teeth enable the snake to grasp its prey securely.

Alligator snapping turtle
Tongue lure
SPECIES *Macrochelys temminckii* **SIZE** Up to 65 cm (26 in)
DISTRIBUTION Lakes and rivers in southern North America

This turtle lies in the water with its hooked jaws held wide open. The inside of its mouth, like the rest of the head, is drably coloured and patterned to blend in with its background, apart from the tip of its tongue, which is long and reddish. The turtle wiggles its tongue about, imitating the movement of a worm to lure fishes close enough so that it can snap its jaws shut on top of them. As well as eating fishes, snakes, amphibians, and even other turtles, this species will also readily eat carrion if given the opportunity.

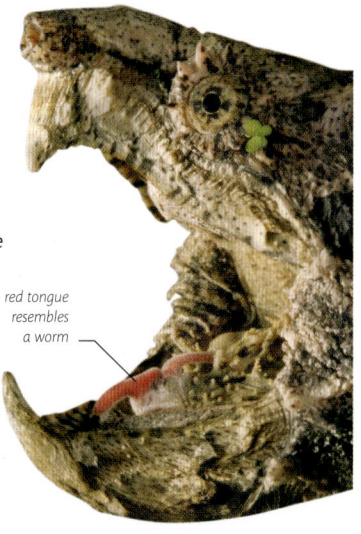

red tongue resembles a worm

Well camouflaged Even the outline of the turtle's eyes is broken up by radiating lines, so the only conspicuous thing is its red tongue.

Inland taipan
Most toxic
SPECIES *Oxyuranus microlepidotus* **SIZE** Up to 2 m (6½ ft)
DISTRIBUTION Arid scrub and grassland in central Australia

Small mammals such as mice and rats form this snake's prey, and it will also takes over their burrows. It gives several bites in quick succession, and the venom is so fast acting that the prey is limp and paralysed almost the instant it is bitten. The inland taipan is the most toxic land snake in the world. The venom is hundreds of times more toxic than that of a diamondback rattlesnake and 50 times more toxic than that of the Indian cobra. A bite can prove fatal to a human unless antivenin is available.

Black head Having a dark head allows the snake to warm up rapidly in the morning sunshine by simply poking its head out of its burrow.

Central American boa
Death grip
SPECIES *Boa imperator* **SIZE** Up to 4.5 m (14¾ ft)
DISTRIBUTION Forest, savanna, cultivated areas, and mangrove swamps in Central America

The general background colour and patterning of these solitary snakes serve as good camouflage against the forest floor and among trees. Boa constrictors eat rodents, bats, and other mammals as well as birds and lizards, and when fully grown can tackle capybaras, monkeys, and even wild pigs. To help them locate prey, there are some simple heat-sensitive scales on the head, and they have a good sense of smell. When catching bats, they hang from trees or cave entrances where the bats roost and snatch them out of the air as they fly past. The mouth has curved teeth to hold the prey as the body coils around it. Once the prey has been killed and swallowed whole, it may take several weeks for the snake to digest it completely.

Deadly coils Boa constrictors are non-venomous and kill by asphyxiating their prey, squeezing them slowly to death in their powerful coils.

Telescopic tongue The tongue of a panther chameleon is extended by a unique system that catapults it towards prey at speeds in excess of 5 m (16½ ft) per second. The sticky end wraps around the prey, and the tongue is retracted into the mouth.

White-tailed eagle
Snatching fish

SPECIES *Haliaeetus albicilla* **SIZE** Up to 90 cm (35 in)
DISTRIBUTION Coastal areas, but also inland wetlands, rivers, and lakes, in Europe and Asia

One of the most distinctive features of birds of prey is the way they often kill with their feet. The white-tailed eagle feeds mostly on fishes, small mammals, and other birds, such as ducks. When hunting for fishes, it sits in a good perch and scans the water using its excellent eyesight before swooping down to seize fishes swimming near the surface with its large, hooked talons. The bottoms of its feet have sharp outgrowths to help keep a firm hold of the slippery prey. The eagle takes food back to its nest or perch, where it holds it down and rips it apart using its large vulturelike bill. It prefers open coastal locations over inland sites and the territory of a white-tailed eagle may be more than 80 km (50 miles) across if prey is not abundant.

Each adult bird needs to consume around half a kilogram (18 oz) of prey each day, but can survive short lean periods. Although they are superb hunters, these eagles will sometimes take carrion, searching the shore for dead fishes, or stealing prey from other predators such as otters and ospreys. In some areas, these eagles may compete with golden eagles for rabbits and hares.

After a spectacular aerial courtship, which involves the birds cartwheeling through the air with their claws locked together, pairs of eagles bond for life and build a large nest, or eyrie, of twigs and sticks in a tree or on a sheltered rocky cliff. Females usually lay one or two eggs, and the young are fed for three months. The mortality rate is high, with 60–70 per cent of the young birds failing to survive their first winter.

Peregrine falcon
Dive bombing

SPECIES *Falco peregrinus* **SIZE** Up to 55 cm (21½ in)
DISTRIBUTION Worldwide, but absent from New Zealand, high mountains, deserts, and polar regions

Peregrine falcons have extremely acute vision and power-dive at high speed from above their prey. Typically a peregrine will come out of its dive just behind the prey, aiming to hit the wings of the victim with a "punch" from its curled feet rather than risk injury with a direct body hit. If the impact does not kill the bird, it will break the bird's neck with its sharp, notched bill. Its diet mainly comprises pigeons, doves, waterfowl, and gamebirds.

Helpful marking The dark marking below the eye reduces glare from the sun as the falcon searches for prey while on the wing.

Osprey
Feet first

SPECIES *Pandion haliaetus* **SIZE** 65 cm (26 in)
DISTRIBUTION Anywhere there is open water and plenty of fishes, worldwide except Antarctica

Ospreys are exclusively fish-catchers, and have several special adaptations for catching fishes up to 2 kg (4½ lb) in weight. Their toes are of equal length, and the outer toe is reversible, allowing the bird to have two toes hooked into either side of a fish's body. Not only do the feet have sharp talons to hold slippery fishes, they also have barbed foot pads to increase grip. The osprey's hunting technique consists of flying high above the water to spot fishes then, after hovering for a second or two, diving to enter the water talons-first with outstretched legs. They enter water to a depth of nearly 1 m (3¼ ft) to catch fishes, and escape with their prey using powerful wingbeats against the water.

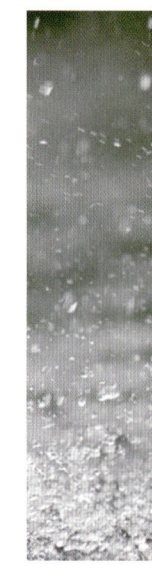

PREDATION 193

This large eagle occupies a similar ecological niche to the bald eagle in North America.

Surface swoop Swooping low over the water on its powerful broad wings, a white-tailed eagle can pluck a fish from the surface without getting itself wet.

Secretarybird
Stamping for prey

SPECIES *Sagittarius serpentarius*
SIZE Up to 1.4 m (4½ ft)
DISTRIBUTION Open grassland in sub-Saharan Africa

This large bird feeds on snakes such as puff adders and even cobras, but will also consume lizards, amphibians, rodents, young birds, bird eggs, and insects. Small animals are eaten directly, but larger prey is stamped to death before being consumed. Dangerous prey, such as snakes, are first stamped on to stun them and then pecked behind the neck to kill them. Small creatures are eaten whole, while larger prey are pinned to the ground and pulled apart.

long, powerful legs used for striking and pursuing prey

Looking for movement A secretarybird stamps on the ground with its large, stout-toed feet to flush prey out of hiding.

Stewart Island brown kiwi
Flightless forager

SPECIES *Apteryx australis lawryi* **SIZE** Up to 40 cm (15½ in)
DISTRIBUTION In forest and coastal scrub, only on Stewart Island off southern New Zealand

This bird is a subspecies of the tokoeka or southern brown kiwi. Like other kiwis, the Stewart Island brown kiwi is flightless and well adapted to terrestrial living. It has large, powerful legs with claws to scrape and dig, and, unusually for a bird, foot pads that enable it to move about silently on the forest floor as it probes for food. Kiwis are the only birds to have nostrils at the end of their bills, and they use these to smell for prey among vegetation and below the ground. Away from mammal-free New Zealand, this ecological niche is occupied by species such as hedgehogs, opossums, and badgers.

Probing bill After sunset the kiwi hunts for snails, spiders, and insects. It uses its keen sense of smell and hearing to locate prey underground.

Ospreys can close their nostrils to keep water out of their nasal passages when diving.

Difficult take-off Sometimes ospreys have difficulty getting airborne from the water. Once in flight, they carry the fish head-first to reduce wind resistance.

HUNTING AND FEEDING

Setting a trap The Péringuey desert adder employs a hunting technique called caudal luring, using the black tip of its tail to entice prey.

Péringuey's desert adder
Tail lure

SPECIES *Bitis peringuey* **SIZE** 25–30 cm (10–12 in)
DISTRIBUTION Coastal sands in Angola and Namibia

This species, also known as the Namib desert sidewinding or sand adder, hunts by burying itself in the sand with just its eyes (which are located on the top of its head) and tail showing, making good use of its excellent camouflage colouring. The end of the tail is exposed and this, especially in very dark-tailed examples of the species, is used as a lure. The prey, attracted by the movement and grub-like appearance of the tail, is grabbed and injected with venom. This subdues the prey, which the adder then swallows whole. Favourite prey of this snake include desert lizards and geckoes. As an adaptation to living on shifting desert dunes, and even to climbing steep inclines, Péringuey's desert adder moves by a process known as sidewinding. The body is moved in a series of lateral movements, leaving sinuous marks that are characteristic of the species. Living in very dry conditions, such as the almost rain-free Namib desert, the snake gets most of the water it needs to survive from its prey, particularly lizards, which have a high water content. However, it also draws a supply of fluid from the condensation that settles on its body.

Snakes have **rectangular scales** on the undersides of their bodies, the edges of which **provide traction** like tread on a tyre.

Keeping cool Péringuey's desert adder buries itself in sand (far right and above) to keep cool and conserve moisture as well as to conceal itself from prey.

Taking the bait A desert lizard has fallen for the snake's appetizing-looking tail lure and is in the process of being swallowed whole.

ANATOMY SIDEWINDER MOVEMENT

Sidewinding is a variation of the more typical undulating motion that snakes use to move around, and is seen especially in species that live on loose sand in deserts or slippery mudflats where there are no firm objects such as rocks against which the snake can push. By throwing its body into a series of lateral loops, the snake moves sideways with most of its body clear of the surface at any time. This allows it to move over very hot sand, leaving behind a series of J- or S-shaped tracks.

Harris's hawk
Group hunting

SPECIES *Parabuteo unicinctus* **SIZE** Up to 75 cm (30 in) **DISTRIBUTION** Semi-desert, open woodland, and scrubland in Central and South America, and southern North America

This hawk's prey comprises small mammals such as ground squirrels and wood rats, birds, and reptiles, but by hunting together in groups of up to six individuals, it is able to take prey as large as jack rabbits, hares, or large gamebirds. They spread out to find and watch prey, then use varied techniques, including a relay chase whereby one bird flushes the prey, the next one blocks off its nearest escape route, with two or more making the final kill together. Group hunting, which is very unusual among raptors, may be an adaptation to the scrubby terrain in which they live. These social groupings are formed with a breeding alpha female and male, subordinate beta adults, and gamma birds of either sex, usually juveniles.

Raptor pair Group members co-operate when catching and sharing food and defending their breeding territory from predators such as ravens, great horned owls, and coyotes. Harris's hawks are not fast fliers but have excellent vision and hearing.

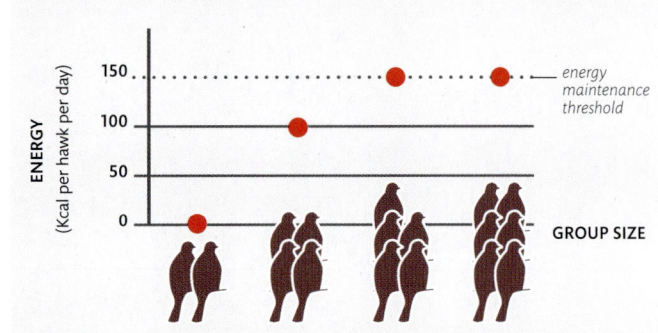

ENERGY MAINTENANCE

For Harris's hawk, the benefits of group hunting are considerable. It has been observed that, by hunting in groups, each individual bird can obtain a much larger amount of food energy per day compared to hunting alone or as one of a pair. Groups of five or more were able to maintain a sufficient energy level for survival.

Great white pelican
Mob rule

SPECIES *Pelecanus onocrotalus* **SIZE** Up to 1.8 m (6 ft) **DISTRIBUTION** Lakes and wetlands in southern Europe and Asia, Africa

These large birds catch fishes in their bill pouches while swimming on the surface of water. They often fish co-operatively in groups, attracted by large numbers of fishes. Several pelicans form a line or a semicircle and drive the fishes into shallower water, where they can be collected easily. The pouch below the lower jaw of the bird extends back to the throat and is very elastic, being able to hold more than 10 litres (20 pints) of water. Fishes are swallowed whole by the bird holding its head upright. After squeezing out the excess water, it lets the entire catch slip down its throat.

Feeding frenzy A group of great white pelicans have corralled a number of small fishes into shallow water and have begun to scoop them up, filling their pouches.

Cape gannet
Plunge diving

SPECIES *Morus capensis* **SIZE** Up to 95 cm (3 ft 1 in) **DISTRIBUTION** Coastal islands off southern Africa

These birds use a plunge-diving technique from as high as 30 m (98 ft) above the surface to catch shoaling fishes such as sardines and anchovies. When suitable fishes are spotted, the gannets start a dive from a height determined by the depth of the shoal. Just before they hit the water, the gannets pull their wings back and close to the body to form a streamlined arrowhead shape. Having entered the water, they can chase prey through it by using their large webbed feet and wings for propulsion. The sharp bill has fine, toothlike, backward-pointing serrations for holding on to slippery fishes. After a dive, they then return to the surface using their natural buoyancy, and typically swallow their prey before they take to the air again. These foraging trips may last many hours, with the birds feeding first, and resting on the surface to digest food for themselves before catching more fishes and returning to their nesting site to feed their chicks.

6 m The distance below the ocean surface that Cape gannets may reach when diving for fishes.

On the sardine run Cape gannets are attracted to a spectacular annual migration event that takes place between May and July off the east coast of South Africa, in which shoals of sardines many kilometres long pass through the waters.

PREDATION 197

Eurasian oystercatcher
Mud probing

SPECIES *Haematopus ostralegus* **SIZE** Up to 45 cm (17½ in) **DISTRIBUTION** Estuaries, sandbanks, and mudflats in Europe and Asia

These distinctive waders hunt for shellfish such as cockles and mussels, though not oysters, and will also feed on limpets, marine worms, and crabs. They use one of two techniques (prising or hammering) to open shellfish, and those that prefer to prise have slimmer, more pointed bills. However, they can switch technique if necessary, and over time this can cause the bill to change shape.

Buried prey Oystercathers have a strong bill for stabbing and probing into sand or silt for shellfish.

ANATOMY FEEDING STRATEGIES

The competitive exclusion principle states that no two species sharing a habitat will use exactly the same feeding niche. Wading birds have different sizes and shapes of bills to deal with the great variety of prey living buried in sand and silt. Long-billed species can reach deeply buried prey such as lugworms, whereas shorter-billed species can only penetrate to a depth of a few centimetres (but can pick at the surface more quickly and efficiently). In this way, several species can coexist, feeding in the same area, as they do not compete for the same foodstuff.

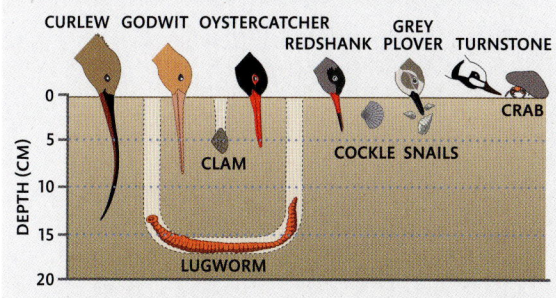

Black heron
Parasol technique

SPECIES *Egretta ardesiaca* **SIZE** Up to 65 cm (26 in) **DISTRIBUTION** Wetlands, lagoons, and lake margins in sub-Saharan Africa and Madagascar

Sometimes called the black egret, the black heron is also known as the umbrella bird for its unique fishing technique, variously called shading, mantling, or canopy feeding. When hunting, the bird stands in the water, flicks its wings open, and holds them both in front of its body to form an elegant parasol-like shelter over the surface of the water. Small fishes are then attracted to the shade cast by the feathery shelter, as this is where they might expect to find some protection from predators. By creating shade, the bird also greatly reduces the glare from the sun so that it can bend its neck to see the fishes in the water below more easily. Black herons will often feed near spoonbills, which stir up the mud with their long bills. Disturbed fishes will then generally flee to the nearest available shelter, which might be provided by a submerged log, or more unfortunately for them, a heron's spread wings. Black herons also stalk aquatic insects and amphibians, and follow seasonal rains to find food.

Creating a canopy When the heron is using its shading technique, the front of its wings meet and the tips of the wing feathers dip into the water all around the bird.

Great grey owl
Stealth attack

SPECIES *Strix nebulosa* **SIZE** Up to 85 cm (33 in) **DISTRIBUTION** Boreal forest and taiga in North America, Canada, northern Europe, and Asia

The great grey owl is a stealthy predator, hunting in silence, mostly after dark. In open areas such as forest clearings, it generally adopts a sit-and-wait strategy, listening for the movement of prey from a perch, but it also flies close to the ground in search of food. Small mammals form most of its diet with voles being the most important food in many regions. Other prey includes mice, squirrels, rabbits, moles, and weasels.

ANATOMY **DISH FACE**
The large, concave facial disc of the great grey owl acts like a flexible radar dish to focus the sounds of moving prey onto its asymmetrically placed ears. It has very acute hearing and can even detect small mammals moving through tunnels under more than 30 cm (12 in) of snow. The owl will then crash through the snow layer to seize the prey in its talons. Indigestible parts are later regurgitated as a pellet.

Striking bird Long, broad wings and distinctive markings distinguish this impressive bird. It is the tallest owl species, but weighs less than the great horned owl and the snowy owl.

European bee-eater
Sting extraction

SPECIES *Merops apiaster* **SIZE** Up to 30 cm (12 in)
DISTRIBUTION Open countryside and near rivers in southern Europe, north Africa, and parts of Asia

These colourful birds eat large insects such as dragonflies, large flies, and butterflies, but are best known for eating stinging insects such as bees, wasps, and hornets, which they catch in mid-air. Several bee-eaters perch together where prey is plentiful and keep watch. When an insect is spotted, they fly to intercept it and return to the perch. If the prey is a bee or wasp, a bee-eater strikes it against a hard surface again and again to disable it or remove the sting and also squeezes it in its bill to try to empty the venom sac. After this, it eats the prey or feeds it to its young. In a single day, a bee-eater may consume more than 200 bees.

bill used to squeeze out venom

Squeezing venom The bee-eater hunts for prey in open arid or semi-arid habitats and catches insects in mid-air before returning to a perch.

Red-backed shrike
Butcher bird

SPECIES *Lanius collurio* **SIZE** Up to 18 cm (7 in) **DISTRIBUTION** Heathland and scrub in Europe and western Asia

Red-backed shrikes choose prominent perches, including human-made objects such as posts and telephone wires, that give them a good view of the surrounding habitat. They then wait for passing prey, which can be caught in flight or on the ground. When there is an excess of food, the birds store their victims by impaling them on plant thorns for a short period of time. These "larders" are typically located in bushes or trees, but sometimes the birds use artificial structures such as barbed wire. Prey includes insects, reptiles, and small mammals such as shrews. Smaller items are eaten whole, but larger prey are impaled or wedged securely before being pulled apart by the shrike's stout, hook-tipped bill.

Butcher's hooks Impaling their victims allows red-backed shrikes to feed on larger prey, such as mammals or lizards, over time.

>>01

PREDATION 199

Swift catch Having caught a fish by the middle of its body, a kingfisher begins its return to the surface, carried partly by its natural buoyancy and partly propelled by wing action.

Common kingfisher
Lightning strike

SPECIES *Alcedo atthis* **SIZE** Up to 18 cm (7 in)
DISTRIBUTION Near clear ponds, lakes, streams, and rivers in Europe, Africa, and Asia

Also known as the Eurasian kingfisher, this species feeds entirely on aquatic animals. Individual birds have a number of perches along a riverbank. From these vantage points, which may be up to 2 m (2½ ft) above the surface, the bird will look for movements in the water below. When it spots prey, it either dives into the water or hovers momentarily, with its bill pointing downwards, as it gathers a final accurate fix on its victim. The problem of refraction (the change in the direction of light as it travels from water to air) is minimized by the bird's keen eyesight and vertical dive. As it enters the water, the kingfisher's bill opens slightly; its eyes are protected from damage by a membrane. As it makes contact with the prey, the bird shuts its bill around it. Once at the surface, insects, crustaceans, and small fishes are swallowed immediately, but large fishes are beaten against the kingfisher's perch before being swallowed head first. It is important that large fishes are killed before being swallowed to avoid the bird being damaged internally by moving fins or scales.

Plunge-diving for prey >>01 With pinpoint accuracy and lightning speed, a common kingfisher dives towards its prey. >>02 Just before it hits the water it spreads its tail feathers and opens its wings to slow it down. >>03 The bird opens its bill slightly as it enters the water, and its momentum carries it just far enough to catch the fish. >>04 The kingfisher lifts its catch clear of the water before returning to its perch.

Kingfishers' eyes have filters that reduce glare and reflection from the water's surface.

ANATOMY **RIPPING AND SIEVING**

The leopard seal has pointed front teeth and long canines that curve backwards, features that are well adapted for holding firmly onto prey. The molars, which are also sharp, can mesh together, allowing them to act as sieves to strain krill from the seawater. Unlike its terrestrial namesake, the leopard seal does not have carnassial teeth – that is, the teeth do not fit very closely against each other in a way that could slice and cut cleanly through meat. Instead, to break up its prey into manageable pieces, a leopard seal thrashes its victim around violently in the water and beats it against the surface of the sea.

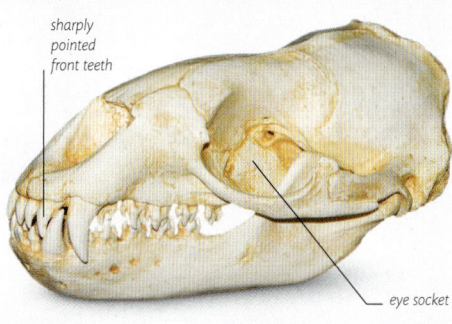

sharply pointed front teeth

eye socket

Huge jaw The skull of a leopard seal is long and almost reptilian in shape. The loosely hinged lower jaw, which can open very wide, is powered by muscles attached over a large area of the skull.

PREDATION 201

A penguin's last moments This fleeting glimpse of a leopard seal's head may be the last thing a penguin sees, although in many cases the bird will never know what hit it. By being such fast, agile swimmers, leopard seals can take their prey totally by surprise.

Leopard seal
Underwater ambush

SPECIES *Hydrurga leptonyx* **SIZE** 3–3.5 m (9¾–11½ ft) **DISTRIBUTION** Primarily ocean water in Antarctica, also found in subantarctic waters and as far north as New Zealand, Australia, and South America

Leopard seals are keystone predators in the Antarctic marine ecosystem. This means that their presence is essential to the stability of the food chain. Orcas are their only natural predators. Leopard seals are cumbersome on land and, as a result, hunt only in the water, feeding on a wide variety of prey. When young, the seals eat krill, squid, and fishes, but when they become adult they tackle larger prey, such as penguins, and smaller seals, such as crabeater seals and fur seals. These very agile hunters have excellent eyesight and a good sense of smell.

In summer, they hunt around pack ice, keeping close to the shoreline. They lie in wait, partially submerged, to look out for penguins on the ice floes and ambush them when they dive into the water. Their dark back and pale underside makes them hard to detect from above or below, and as they can swim faster than the fastest penguin they do not need to dive deeply to find prey. Their powerful hind flippers are used in a side-to-side motion to propel them, and their long front flippers allow them to change direction very quickly. In a typical ambush attack, a leopard seal seizes a penguin by its hind legs from behind and thrashes it around until it dies. Seabirds resting on the surface are not safe either, as leopard seals sometimes take them too.

Torn apart The leopard seal's torpedo-shaped body enables it to propel itself through the water at great speed and so surprise its prey. Once it has caught a penguin in its jaws, the seal shakes it vigorously to tear off chunks of flesh.

Duck-billed platypus
Electric bill

SPECIES Ornithorhynchus anatinus **SIZE** 40–50 cm (15½–19½ in) **DISTRIBUTION** Streams and rivers in eastern Australia and Tasmania

Also known simply as the platypus, this semi-aquatic mammal is more at home in water than on land and has adaptations to be an efficient aquatic hunter. It feeds mainly in the evening and after dark, diving to catch crustaceans as well and worms and insect larvae. When hunting, it shuts its eyes and relies on its sensory snout to locate prey by sensing both the disturbance in the water and tiny electrical signals released by shrimps and other prey. While evidence suggests dolphins may also use electric signals for short-range prey detection, the platypus is the only mammal with which we know this to be the case. Once caught, food is stored in cheek pouches behind the broad, flat bill and eaten when the platypus returns to the surface. The egg-laying platypus is the survivor of an ancient group of mammals and has several primitive features, of which the most obvious is the reptilian way it walks with its legs at the sides of its body.

Swift swimmer The platypus is an agile water predator. It uses its strong, webbed front feet for propulsion and its semi-webbed back feet for steering.

- fully webbed front feet
- waterproof fur makes platypus buoyant
- nostrils on top of snout

Giant anteater
Sharp claws

SPECIES Myrmecophaga tridactyla **SIZE** Up to 2 m (6½ ft) **DISTRIBUTION** Savanna and forest in Central and South America

Giant anteaters are specialist predators of termites and ants and may consume tens of thousands of these small but nutritious insects every day. They are solitary animals, and although their eyesight and hearing are not well developed they have a superb sense of smell. The feet have five digits, but the middle three digits on the front legs are equipped with huge, curved claws for breaking open termite nests. This strength is necessary as the nests, which are made of soil mixed with termite saliva, are baked in the sun and become extremely hard.

Having long, curved claws means that the anteater has to walk on its knuckles. As well as breaking open termite nests, it also searches for insects under tree bark. It uses its long tongue to scoop out the insects, and although it has no teeth it crushes the prey against padlike growths inside its mouth before swallowing. Typically, an anteater will eat as many worker ants or termites as it can before the bites or stings of the soldiers become too irritating and it has to move on.

Probing for termites The anteater's skull lacks teeth but accommodates an extraordinarily long tongue to probe deep inside ant or termite colonies. Coated in sticky saliva to trap insects, it can be flicked in and out twice per second.

Grant's golden mole
Underground detection

SPECIES Eremitalpa granti **SIZE** Up to 9 cm (3½ in) **DISTRIBUTION** Coastal dunes and desert in southern Africa

Grant's golden mole travels at night on the surface of the sand dune or just below, "swimming" under the sand in search of prey. Although completely blind, these moles have extremely sensitive hearing and can detect the slightest vibration in the sand. This ability to detect tiny seismic waves allows them to locate termites, burrowing beetles, ants, grasshoppers, and spiders.

Well adapted to digging, Grant's golden mole has a small leathery nose and stout, and strong shoulders and front legs. The front claws are curved and concave and used as tiny shovels when digging, while the hind feet are webbed for scooping and shifting sand or soil backwards.

Sand burrower A Grant's golden mole has made a conspicuous ridge by burrowing just under the surface of the sand. At night it may forage for food on the surface but, during the hottest part of the day, will burrow up to 35 cm (14 in) down.

Cheetah
Swift pursuit

SPECIES *Acinonyx jubatus* **SIZE** Up to 1.5 m (5 ft)
DISTRIBUTION Open grassland in North, East, Central, and southwest Africa

The cheetah has many adaptations that allow it to reach speeds of 113 kph (70 mph) and accelerate to 64 kph (40 mph) in just three strides. Its spine is very flexible, and when the animal is galloping it is alternately flexed and straightened, allowing the powerful hind legs to achieve an even longer effective stride. The cheetah's face is short and flat, with the eyes positioned to give good binocular vision. The eyes also have an image-stabilization system to keep the prey in sharp focus when running. A black line down the face under each eye acts like an anti-glare device.

The cheetah's nasal passages are large, as are the lungs, and the body has a low skeleton-to-muscle-mass ratio, with lighter bones and longer legs than other cats. The long tail acts as a rudder and allows the cheetah to achieve extremely tight turns when pursuing agile prey. Its shortish, relatively blunt claws are non-retractable, giving it permanent grip on the soil at high speeds much like spiked running shoes. Closing in on prey such as a fleeing impala, a cheetah can put on an extra burst of speed over a couple of hundred metres.

Closing in A perfectly timed swipe to the rear quarters will bring this gazelle down. Before it can recover, the cheetah will bite its throat to finish it off.

59
The longest time recorded, in seconds, of a cheetah – the word's fastest land animal – closing in on its prey.

>>01   >>02   >>03

Pouncing on prey >>01 To locate prey hidden under the snow, the Arctic fox listens intently for the sounds of burrowing or movement. It rears up in the air with its eyes focused on a spot on the snow above its victim. **>>02** At the peak of its leap, the fox extends its front legs and rotates its body forwards. **>>03** The fox plunges head-first towards the ground and thrusts its front paws through the snow into its victim's tunnel or lair beneath.

Arctic fox
Adaptable hunter

SPECIES *Alopex lagopus* **SIZE** Up to 55 cm (21½ in)
DISTRIBUTION Arctic tundra in North America, Europe, and Asia

Arctic foxes hunt and eat animals such as lemmings and Arctic hares in the warmer months. In the winter, when prey is scarce, not only will they attack young seals in their dens and find fishes, but they will also scavenge carrion left by larger predators such as polar bears.

The key to the success of these hardy animals is that they are very adaptable and can survive by eating birds' eggs and even plant material such as berries if they are available. On the shoreline, they will feed on dead fishes or seals that have been washed ashore and may also eat shellfish and sea urchins from time to time. In winter blizzards, Arctic foxes dig dens in deep snow and can survive in extremely cold conditions of -50°C (-58°F), protected by their thick fur and, if the feeding has been good, a layer of body fat. They maintain a foot temperature of about 0°C (32°F), but a counter-current heat-exchange system in the legs ensures that blood returning to the body from the feet is warmed up. This means that, although the feet must survive at a lower temperature than the rest of the body, heat is not lost from the core of the body.

The Arctic fox has fur on the bottom of its feet to enable it to walk on ice.

ANATOMY **SEASONAL COATS**

The coat of the Arctic fox changes from its brownish grey in summer, to blend well with the colour of rocks and low-growing plants, to pure white in winter, providing very effective camouflage against the bright, snowy background. In addition, the fur grows much thicker in winter, to insulate the fox against the bitter cold of the Arctic tundra. When resting, the fox will use its bushy tail to cover its face.

Ambush at a water hole >>01 After a short chase, a lioness has caught up with a fleeing greater kudu. Sometimes lions will lash out with a front paw to trip the prey, but usually use a burst of speed to jump at the prey's hindquarters. >>02 The lioness leaps onto the kudu's back, using her sharp claws to dig into its hide. >>03 As the kudu stumbles under the weight, the lioness is able to manoeuvre herself up towards the neck of the stricken beast, where she opens her huge jaws to more than 25 cm (10 in) wide and delivers the fatal bite. >>04 The animal is dead within a few seconds, and soon after, the other members of the pride gather to share the meal.

Lion
Family hunting

SPECIES Panthera leo **SIZE** 1.7–2.2 m (5½–7¼ ft)
DISTRIBUTION Parkland and open savanna in sub-Saharan Africa. A few hundred Asiatic lions (subspecies *Panthera leo persica*) live in the Gir Forest in Gujarat, northwest India

When it comes to hunting prey, lions are adept at teamwork. Lionesses are lighter and quicker than males and do the vast majority of the hunting, although recent studies suggest that males might be as capable as females at hunting, despite hunting less cooperatively. Pride members hunt cooperatively and, by doing so, can take much larger prey than they would be able to tackle on their own. Although males may be large enough to attack buffaloes, single lions are seldom able to take on really large species, such as elephants or male giraffes. Cooperation means that kills are easier and carry less risk of injury, and also that enough food will be available for every member of the pride to eat.

Hunting techniques vary. Typically one lioness will spook a prey animal, or chase it at speeds of up to 70 kph (40 mph) towards other members of the pride lying in wait. Sometimes, the pride will surround a herd of prey and try to pick off a lone, young, or weak individual. Once the pride has made a kill, cooperation ensures that it keeps possession of its prize: a single lion would really struggle against a pack of hyenas intent on taking over the kill.

Cooperative hunting is made possible because lions form close social groupings that last for many years. A pride of lions comprises a number of related adult females and their young. The young are raised by the pride and may suckle from other females as well as their own mother. Adult males tend to live alone or in small groups called coalitions. When they take over a pride, the males, one of which will be dominant, are responsible for marking the boundaries of the pride's territory or area, which may be anything from a few tens to a few hundreds of square kilometres, defending it against threats, and mating with the females.

Apart from their large size and formidable teeth, lions have other attributes that make them efficient predators. They have excellent binocular vision, which allows them to judge distance very accurately, and their eyes are capable of working at low light levels, making night hunting possible. They use their strong, sharp, retractable claws for grasping and grounding prey, before killing it with a neck-breaking bite or by asphyxiation. Although lions are top predators, they also scavenge from carcasses when the need arises, and steal prey from hyenas.

HUNTING SUCCESS

Research has shown that, apart from the number of lions cooperating and the type of prey, other factors can greatly affect hunting success. The brightness of the moon has a marked effect, success being much higher on moonless nights, especially in open habitats. The moon has less of an effect when lions are hunting in wooded areas. Habitat features are also important, with long grass cover bringing significantly greater success than short grass.

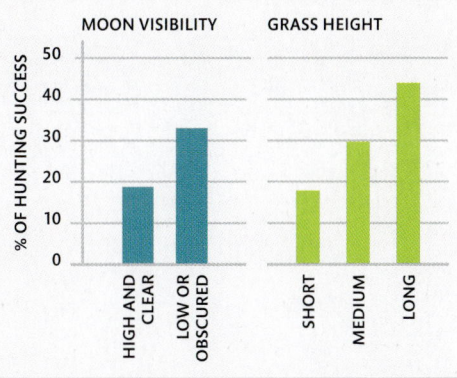

Night hunters Although lions will hunt at other times, they prefer the cover of darkness. Moonlight reflected by the back of their eyes gives away the presence of a large pride of lions waiting to start a foray.

Pack hunting An attack by a pack of African wild dogs reaches a climax: surrounded by the snarling pack and already injured, this lone warthog is going to need a lot of luck if it is going to escape. The dogs have to be careful as the warthog's sharp tusks could inflict a potentially lethal wound but, as always, there is safety in numbers.

African wild dog
Cooperative hunting

SPECIES *Lycaon pictus* **SIZE** Up to 1.5 m (5 ft)
DISTRIBUTION Savanna and lightly wooded parkland in sub-Saharan Africa

Like most members of the dog family, African wild dogs, or painted hunting dogs, live in groups tied together by intense social bonds. These bonds are an advantage in the hunt, as the dogs cooperate as a pack, running down and overpowering their prey in a long-distance chase. Strategically, their hunting methods are not cunning or stealthy. Relying on their excellent vision during the cool of early morning or late afternoon, they approach prey such as wildebeests, impalas, or zebras in full view. Surprise is unnecessary as they have the stamina to chase their prey until it is exhausted. The quarry is often able to gallop faster than the wild dogs' top speed of 60 kph (37 mph), but will eventually be chased down over distances of up to 6 km (3½ miles). The hunting pack keeps in touch constantly with high-pitched, yapping contact calls. During the chase, the dogs spread out to head off any sideways escape attempts. Zigzagging evasion movements of the prey, which would confound a lone hunter such as a cheetah, are ineffective against a pack of wild dogs. As the exhausted prey slows down, the dogs surround it, often targeting its soft underbelly and disembowelling it. On average, about 30 per cent of hunts result in a kill. Hunting dogs have a very powerful bite and their large molars and premolars allow them to crush bone. When they have eaten, food is regurgitated to older dogs, pups, and other members of the pack that did not take part in the hunt.

Scouring the savanna A typical African wild dog hunt is an endurance chase. While a whole impala herd might be targeted, the eventual victim will be the impala that falls behind, due to age or sickness. Evasive manoeuvres are usually useless, as sideways escape is prevented by the flanking dogs, and the impala's erratic flightpath can be predicted and headed off by dogs bringing up the rear.

Hunting grounds The home range of African wild dogs varies with the size of the pack and the availability of prey, but can often be more than 1,000 square km (620 square miles).

The Hunt A canyon bat closes in on a small moth. The bat can consume prey equal to 20 per cent of its body weight in a single night.

Canyon bat
Winged assault
SPECIES *Parastrellus hesperus* **SIZE** Up to 7 cm (2¾ in)
DISTRIBUTION Desert and scrubby grassland in North America and Mexico

This common species of bat starts to forage in the early evening, well before dusk, and may also be seen flying after dawn. Using echolocation (see panel, below) to source its prey, the canyon bat feeds on a wide range of soft-bodied insects such as moths, flies, caddis flies, and small beetles. The exact nature of its diet changes over the course of a year, and the bat will feed on any species that is locally abundant or swarming nearby. It flies in a characteristically slow, fluttery fashion, 3–15 m (9¾–49 ft) above the ground. The smallest bat species in the USA, the canyon bat is sometimes mistaken for a large moth. Being a weak flier, it usually hunts in calm conditions. By day, it roosts singly or in small groups in caves and crevices. Although it lives in arid habitats, roosting sites tend to be near any available water as this usually provides a good source of hatching aquatic insects.

large, widely spaced ears

sound emitted via nose as well as mouth

ATTACK SEQUENCE

As well as making calls for communication and other reasons, bats emit ultrasound for hunting prey. This species produces its echolocation calls in the frequency range 45–75 kHz, with the highest energy being produced at around 45 kHz. Each frequency modulated note has a duration of between 4 and 5 milliseconds.

1 SEARCH PHASE To conserve energy, calls are produced, in the form of a series of "notes", at a rate of less than 20 per second.

2 APPROACH PHASE When prey is detected, the bat increases the rate of calls to get a more accurate location.

3 TERMINAL PHASE Call rate may increase to 200 times per second.

Greater horseshoe bat
Sound detection
SPECIES *Rhinolophus ferrumequinum* **SIZE** Up to 7.5 cm (3 in)
DISTRIBUTION Open woodland, farmland, and parkland in Europe and parts of Asia

This species of bat has a number of different hunting techniques and catches medium- to large-sized insects such as cockchafers, dung beetles, and large moths. Sometimes they will perch and fly out in pursuit of passing insects, while at other times they will attack prey from above or glean insects from the surface of foliage. When hunting, the greater horseshoe bat flies low and slowly, using an echolocation call with a constant frequency of 79–84 kHz. Leaving its roost at sunset, it typically forages while flying over open pasture, farmland, and in parkland, often next to water where prey can be abundant. When large prey has been captured, it is taken back to a convenient perch to be consumed. Along with some other bats, this species may make use of doppler-detection calls. To do this, a bat must emit a long note with a constant frequency. If the bat and the prey are moving relative to each other at the same distance, there will be no change in the frequency of the perceived echo. If the prey is flying towards the bat, the frequency will appear to increase; but if the prey is moving away from the bat, the frequency of the reflected sound will appear to drop. This is exactly the same as when a vehicle with a loud siren passes a stationary listener – the pitch of the siren appears to increase as the vehicle approaches and decrease as it passes.

CASE STUDY **RECOGNIZING ECHOES**

Bats emit a series of ultrasound squeaks, which are reflected by prey in different ways according to the size, shape, texture, and frequency of wing beats. From this a bat can determine the location, speed, and nature of its prey. The motion pattern of flying insects provides a hunting bat with additional information. As the insect's wings move up and down, at one point they will be perpendicular to the direction of the sound transmitted by the bat, causing a brief increase in the level of the sound energy reflected, known as a "glint".

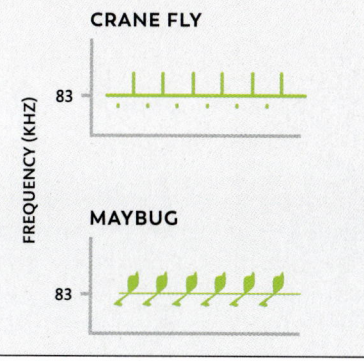

Flying prey A greater horseshoe bat makes a final turn towards its prey, which it will seize in its jaws. From the reflected sound waves received, the bat already has a good idea of what it is about to eat.

Night fishing The fishing bat uses ultrasonic calls to detect activity on the surface of the water. It has long hind legs with large talonlike claws that act as fishing gaffs. The bat rakes its claws through the water to snatch fishes from beneath the surface. Its catch is transferred to its mouth, chewed, and stored in extendable cheek pouches as it continues to hunt.

HUNTING AND FEEDING

Feeding circle These common dolphins have taken control of a fish shoal. While some of them dart in to feed, others will keep circling to contain the shoal.

Common dolphin
Rounding up
SPECIES *Delphinus delphis* **SIZE** Up to 2.5 m (8¼ ft)
DISTRIBUTION Coastal waters of the Atlantic, Pacific, and Indian oceans

The main prey of these fast-swimming marine mammals are fishes and squids, and in some parts of the world pods of common dolphins hunt shoaling fishes cooperatively. Members of a pod swim around schooling fishes, herding them into a tight ball before individuals take turns plowing through the fishes, attacking and eating them as they go.

Common dolphins are very sociable, communicating with each other by sonar clicks and travelling in pods numbering anything from less than a dozen to many hundreds of individuals.

The jaws of a common dolphin can have more than 200 teeth for gripping slippery fishes and squid.

Corralling a shoal Here a fish-eating orca is corralling a shoal of fishes. It flashes its white underside at them then slaps the fish ball with its tail flukes.

Beach attack This orca has almost beached itself by rushing into the shallows to catch seals. Mother orcas teach their young how to carry out this risky manoeuvre.

Sure grip Although the Amazon river dolphin swims quite slowly, its neck is also extremely flexible, allowing it to turn its head at almost right angles to its body as it looks for food. It has a thick, long, and low dorsal fin, and large flippers and tail flukes, which are an adaptation for swimming in shallow water or flooded forest. It is also capable of swimming backwards.

Amazon river dolphin
River hunter
SPECIES *Inia geoffrensis* **SIZE** Up to 2.5 m (8¼ ft)
DISTRIBUTION Slow-moving waters in the Amazon and Orinoco river basins of South America

The largest of the freshwater dolphins, the Amazon river dolphin, or boto, is a generalist feeder that has a number of adaptations for finding food in murky, slow-moving waters. Although it has good eyesight and hearing, it is able to echolocate prey and has stiff, sensory hairs along the front of its beak that help it to feel among the sediment on the riverbed. The beak has peglike teeth at the front to seize prey, such as crustaceans and fishes, and flatter molar teeth further back to crush and grind the food. It can even eat small turtles, armoured fishes, and catfish.

Orca

Versatile predator

SPECIES *Orcinus orca* **SIZE** Up to 8 m (26 ft) **DISTRIBUTION** Coastal and offshore waters in oceans worldwide from polar regions to the tropics

The orca, or killer whale, is the largest dolphin species in the world. Intelligent and social animals, orcas often travel in large, maternally based family groups called pods and communicate with each other with a range of whistling and clicking calls. There are physical, behavioural, and genetic differences between populations or "ecotypes" of orcas, and it is not certain exactly how many subspecies or even species there are. Three – potentially five – distinct ecotypes have been identified, some of which feed on a range of fishes, sharks, cephalopods, and turtles, while others attack seals, sea lions, and even whales. Feeding behaviour depends on the ecotype of orca and its prey. Orcas that follow migrating herring shoals may feed singly or work in a group to corral fishes into a tight ball, slapping it with their powerful tail flukes to stun or kill as many as they can. Orcas that hunt marine mammals may kill their prey by ramming it, hitting it with their tails, or tossing it into the air. When hunting whales, members of a pod usually select a calf or a weak adult. By chasing and tiring it out, they separate it from the rest of the group and drown it by not allowing it to resurface for air. In shallow water, orcas may almost beach themselves to feed on seals, elephant seals, and sea lions.

CASE STUDY WAVE HUNTING

Orcas have a unique cooperative hunting technique for capturing seals resting on small ice floes. "Wave-hunting" or "wave-washing" begins with a number of orcas looking for likely targets by holding their heads out of the water, a behaviour known as spy-hopping. Several orcas will then swim together towards and under the floe to create a large wave to wash over the ice and carry the seal into the sea. To ensure that the seal is dislodged, some orcas may deliberately nudge the floe from the side. At the other side of the floe, another orca waits to eat the seal when it is finally knocked off. While wave-hunting, adult orcas can be accompanied by juvenile individuals, which learn how to perform this technique by example. When fully trained, the juveniles will take part in the hunt themselves. This complex behaviour relies upon communication and coordination to make it effective.

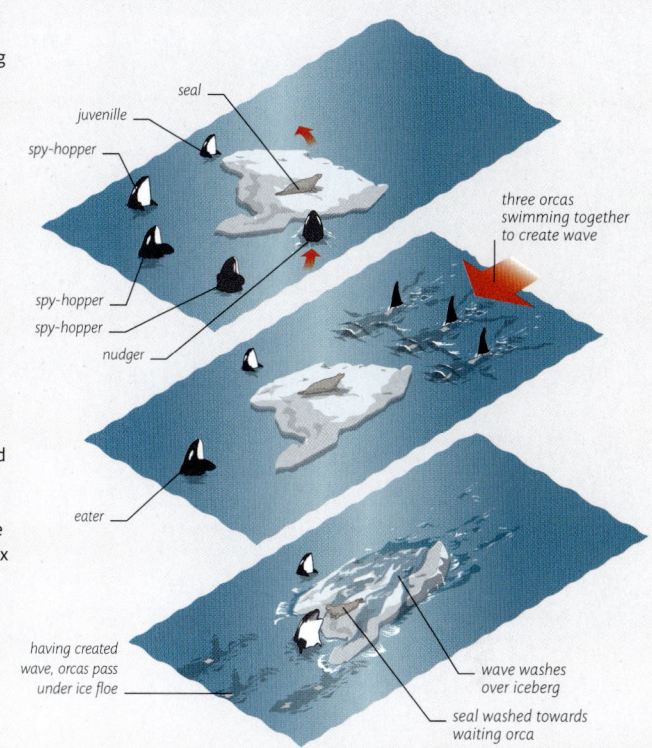

Humpback whale
Bubble-netting

SPECIES *Megaptera novaeangliae* **SIZE** 5–20 m (49–66 ft), females larger than males **DISTRIBUTION** Oceans and seas worldwide. Whales migrate thousands of kilometres, from summer feeding grounds in polar waters, to equatorial waters in winter to breed

Humpback whales sieve food from surface water using up to 400 bristly baleen plates located on either side of the mouth. When the mouth is closed, water is squeezed out through the baleen plates, trapping food. Different populations have different feeding habits. North Atlantic pods feed mainly on fishes, such as herring, sand lance, salmon, and mackerel, but those in southern oceans also feed on krill. Humpback whales use a number of feeding techniques, ranging from hitting fishes with the pectoral fins or tail flukes and "pectoral herding" (in which they may use their long flippers to direct food into their mouths), to swimming through shoals or schools, swallowing fishes as they go. A more complicated approach, referred to as surface-level bubble-netting, involves the whale slapping the surface of the water with its tail as it swims in a circle around a shoal of fishes to create a circle of foam. It then dives down and swims up through the ring of foam, swallowing fishes that have gathered in the centre. A vertical extension of this technique, and the most impressive feeding method practised by humpback whales, is known as bubble-netting. Here a single whale, or several acting cooperatively, dives down and then swims up towards the surface while exhaling continuously. The rising air forms a curtain, or if the whales swim in a wide circle, a complete cylinder of bubbles, inside which the fishes become trapped. The whales then swim up through the concentrated shoal, swallowing thousands of fishes. Besides confusing and herding the fishes, bubble-netting may also make the whales less visible to their prey.

Throat pleats Deep throat pleats, running from the front of the head to halfway down the underside of the body, allow humpback whales to accommodate large volumes of water containing food.

Rising bubbles Bubble nets are formed when a whale swims in a set pattern underwater while slowly exhaling. When cooperating with other whales, there is a division of labour. Some whales make the bubbles, others herd the fishes from below.

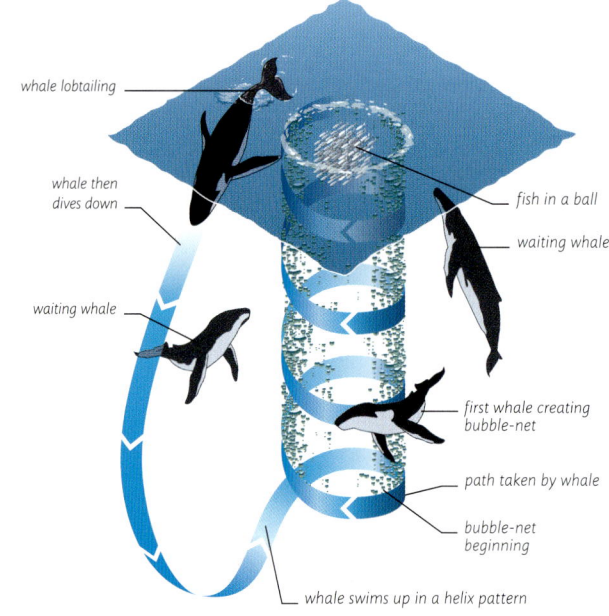

Whale group A group of humpback whales has surfaced inside a ring of bubbles to swallow trapped fishes. Bubble nets created by groups of whales may have diameters of up to 30 m (98 ft).

CASE STUDY
LEARNING TO LOBTAIL-FEED

Humpback whales may produce variations of existing feeding techniques, which are then learned by other whales. In one such case, an Atlantic population of humpbacks initiated the bubble net technique using a lobtailing behaviour in which one whale slaps the surface of the water with its tail. This tail slap may act as a marker for the whales as they rise from below or may temporarily stun the prey.

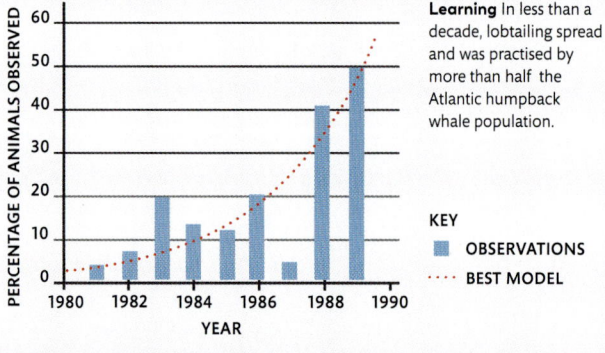

Learning In less than a decade, lobtailing spread and was practised by more than half the Atlantic humpback whale population.

PREDATION 215

Aye-aye
Probing bark

SPECIES *Daubentonia madagascariensis* **SIZE** Up to 40 cm (16 in) **DISTRIBUTION** Rainforest in Madagascar, seasonally dry forest, and cultivated plantation

Aye-ayes sleep during the day and forage in the forest canopy at night. Although they eat nuts, fruits, seeds, and fungi, they are best known for finding insect grubs buried deep in wood. Aye-ayes have excellent hearing and tap on the surface of wood to locate hollow cavities beneath bark. They then chew a hole in the wood using long incisor teeth before using their bony, elongated, double-jointed middle fingers to pry insect larvae from inside. They also use their middle fingers to tear at fruits, extracting the nutritious pulp. One has been recorded using this long finger to pick its nose.

Larvae seeker These elusive primates are the ecological equivalent of a woodpecker. Larvae of woodboring insects, such as the longhorn beetle, make up an important component of their diet.

Star-nosed mole
Sensitive nose

SPECIES *Condylura cristata* **SIZE** 18–19 cm (7–7½ in) **DISTRIBUTION** Eastern North America, in a wide variety of habitats with wet soil, including forest, meadow, marshland, and the margins of streams, lakes, and ponds

This mole's most distinguishing characteristic is a circle of 22 pink, fleshy tentacles at the end of a hairless snout. These tentacles are in constant rapid motion and are covered with thousands of sensory receptors. They are used to identify food solely by touch, and a large portion of the mole's brain deals with processing this detailed tactile information. The star organ is vertically symmetrical with 11 tentacles varying from 1–4 mm (1/16–3/16 in) in length on each side. On contact, the lower tentacles, which are the shortest and most sensitive, assess the nature of the food. The diet consists mainly of invertebrates, such as earthworms, encountered when tunnelling, but also freshwater leeches, the larvae of aquatic insects, crustaceans, snails, and small fishes encountered while swimming.

Sensory compensation Although the star-nosed mole is virtually blind, only able to detect light and dark, the incredibly sensitive nasal organ allows it to detect, identify, and consume small prey in a fraction of a second.

Common chimpanzee
Planned assault

SPECIES *Pan troglodytes* **SIZE** Up to 1.6 m tall (5¼ ft) (standing height) **DISTRIBUTION** Tropical forests and wet savanna in west and central Africa

Chimpanzees are largely omnivorous, their diet consisting mainly of fruits, leaves, nuts, and roots, as well as insects and bird eggs. They may also hunt larger vertebrates, such as bush pigs and colobus monkeys, usually targeting young individuals. These hunts require forward planning, learning from the observation of others, and trial and error. Cannibalism between chimpanzee groups is known to take place. Chimpanzees are intelligent, highly social primates. They move on the ground using a form of quadrupedal locomotion called knuckle-walking, while their long front limbs and strong hands also allow them to swing from branches in the forest canopy. Their thumbs are short but opposable, permitting a precision grip and delicate manipulation of food and other objects.

The chimpanzee makes tools specifically for hunting. They have been seen breaking branches from trees, which they strip of bark and sharpen to spear bushbabies as they sleep. Sticks are also used as hammers, thrown as weapons, or used to probe termite and ant colonies.

Successful hunting A successful hunt means that there is enough meat to go around. Males tend to eat more meat than females, who usually get their protein from insects.

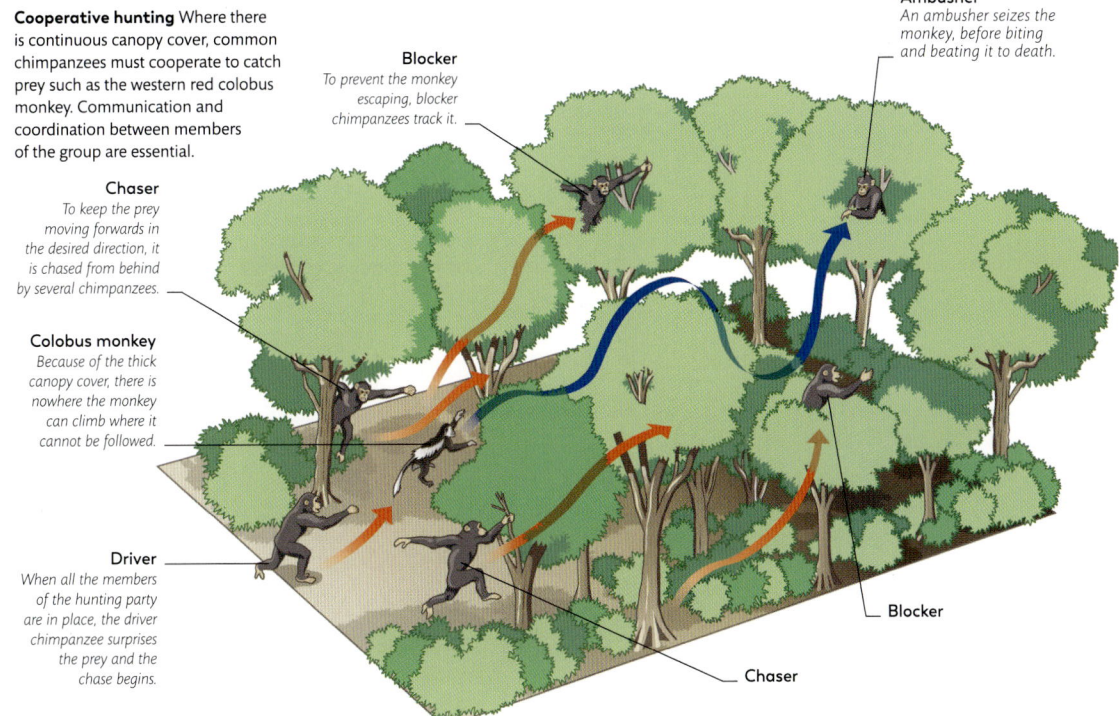

Cooperative hunting Where there is continuous canopy cover, common chimpanzees must cooperate to catch prey such as the western red colobus monkey. Communication and coordination between members of the group are essential.

Chaser To keep the prey moving forwards in the desired direction, it is chased from behind by several chimpanzees.

Colobus monkey Because of the thick canopy cover, there is nowhere the monkey can climb where it cannot be followed.

Driver When all the members of the hunting party are in place, the driver chimpanzee surprises the prey and the chase begins.

Blocker To prevent the monkey escaping, blocker chimpanzees track it.

Ambusher An ambusher seizes the monkey, before biting and beating it to death.

Blocker

Chaser

Rooting in sediment A walrus disturbs the sediment as it roots around the sea bed searching for food. Walruses feed almost exclusively on bivalve molluscs, which they locate in the sediment using their stiff, moustachelike whiskers. When they have found prey, they usually eat it using their mouth and tongue to suck out the soft, inner parts.

Scavenging

Scavengers are animals that feed on the decaying remains of other living things. While some animals feed exclusively this way, others turn to scavenging if their food is in short supply when conditions are harsh.

RECYCLING NUTRIENTS AND ENERGY

When plants and animals die, large amounts of nutrients are locked in their bodies. These valuable energy-producing resources become available to scavengers, who do not waste them. Human activity has greatly increased the opportunities for some scavengers. The growth of cities, the extensive rearing of livestock, and the availability of roadkill provide scavenging species with rich pickings.

Evolved for scavenging The black-and-white plumage of Marabou storks has inspired the name "undertaker bird". These scavengers have featherless heads and necks – special adaptations for reaching inside carcasses to feed.

Feeding on small carrion The carcasses of small mammals and birds attract larger scavengers, such as foxes and crows, as well as burying beetles, which conceal carrion underground in order to feed their young.

Vital soil conditioners Earthworms primarily consume decaying plant material. Their feeding activities maintain soil structure and fertility.

DECOMPOSERS

Once scavengers have consumed the accessible portions of the carrion, the rest, including indigestible parts (such as bones, hair, and feathers, as well as excrement) is broken down by decomposing organisms such as fungi and bacteria. Decomposers are vital in the food chain. Their activities convert leftover organic matter into carbon dioxide and essential nutrients such as nitrogen and phosphorus, in forms that can be easily taken up by photosynthesizing algae and plants – the primary producers in the food chain. In this way, nutrients are returned to the system. Ecosystems depend on the maintenance of such biochemical cycles.

BENEFITS OF SCAVENGING

Scavengers consume the leftovers of predators or the bodies of animals that have died by accident, from disease, or from other natural causes. Freshly dead animals are just as nutritious as live ones, and one advantage of being a scavenger is that it is easier and safer than being a predator. A scavenger doesn't have to tackle the defences against predation that the dead animal may have had, such as biting, kicking, jumping, or running, or chemical defences such as repugnant odours, unpalatable secretions, or poisons.

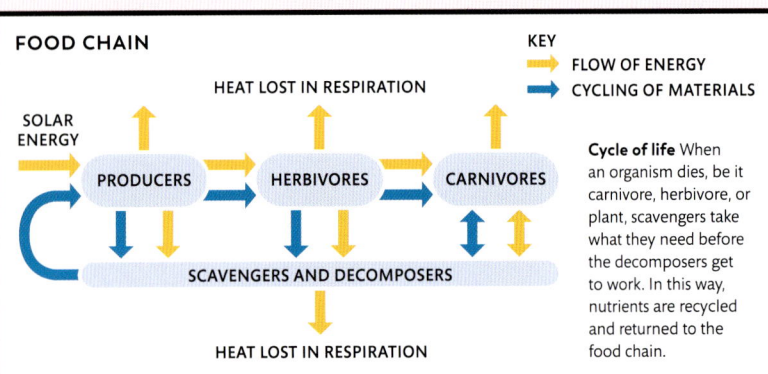

Cycle of life When an organism dies, be it carnivore, herbivore, or plant, scavengers take what they need before the decomposers get to work. In this way, nutrients are recycled and returned to the food chain.

Woodland recycler Woodlice eat dead plant, fungal, and animal matter. Their feeding activities and faeces return nutrients to the soil, especially in woodland.

Maggots Blow flies lay their eggs on dead animals. Their larvae feed by producing enzymes that liquefy the tissues of the carrion into a rich soup.

Common earthworm
Soil conditioning
SPECIES *Lumbricus terrestris* **SIZE** Up to 25 cm (10 in) (extended body) **DISTRIBUTION** In soil, especially in grassland, in Europe, but widely introduced elsewhere

Earthworms play an important ecological role in conditioning soil. Charles Darwin famously drew attention to their importance, writing "It may be doubted if there are any other animals which have played such an important part in the history of the world as these lowly organized creatures". Worms pull leaf litter and other decaying matter from the surface of the soil down into their burrows, where it breaks down and is then eaten. Worm casts (their excrement) are rich in nutrients essential for micro-organisms and plants. They are five times richer in nitrogen, seven times richer in phosphates, and eleven times richer in potassium than the surrounding topsoil.

Made for burrowing Each body segment bears eight short, bristlelike hairs that grip the sides of burrows as the earthworm moves. The tail can be flattened to anchor the worm as it retracts the front of its body.

25 tonnes
The combined weight of common earthworms that can be present in just 1 hectare (2.5 acres) of land.

Distinctive shell The horseshoe crab is actually more closely related to spiders and scorpions than to true crabs. The front part of its body, the prosoma, is covered by a tough, horseshoe-shaped shell, or carapace.

Horseshoe crab
Grasping food
SPECIES *Limulus polyphemus* **SIZE** Up to 60 cm (23½ in) **DISTRIBUTION** Muddy or sandy bays and estuaries along eastern coast of North America

Horseshoe crabs are generalist scavengers that move along the sea bed and dig across its surface to find food. Their broad diet consists mainly of snails, marine worms, decaying seaweed, and algae. Horseshoe crabs have five pairs of legs, the first four of which have pincers. These are used to feel for and grasp food as the animal lumbers over the sediment, and pass it to the mouth, which is situated between the legs. The feeding activities of these scavengers aerate the surface of the sea bed.

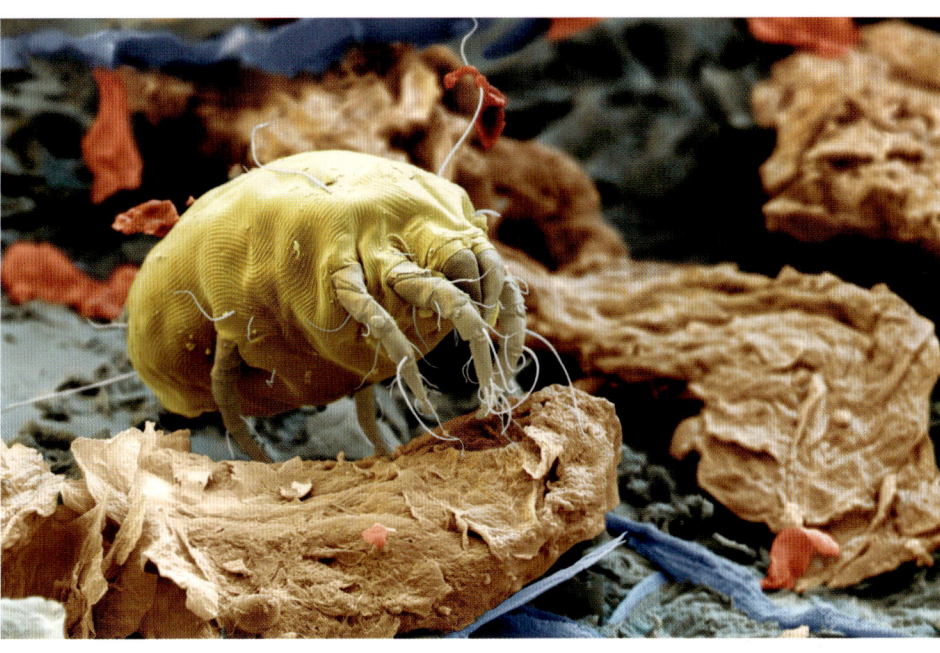

Miniature muncher The tiny dust mite, with its pale, translucent appearance, is barely visible to the unaided eye. A scanning electron microscope is needed to reveal details of its morphology and its striated surface.

European house dust mite
Skin scavenger
SPECIES *Dermatophagoides pteronyssinus* **SIZE** 0.2–0.3 mm (less than ¹⁄₆₄ in) **DISTRIBUTION** Humid microhabitats such as nests and human dwellings, nearly worldwide

Humans shed up to 2 g (¹⁄₁₆ oz) of skin flakes each day. Dust mites feed on these as well as hair fragments and fibres that accumulate in homes. They cannot tolerate dry conditions or sunlight, but can be abundant in sheltered, humid areas such as mattresses, pillows, or other bedding. They secrete digestive enzymes onto a particle of organic matter to break it down before ingesting it into a very basic gut, and eat the same food particles several times over to extract the full food value. Dust mites produce as many as 25 minute particles of faecal matter per day.

HUMAN IMPACT **ALLERGIC REACTIONS**
The dust mite is a common trigger of allergic symptoms in humans. It reproduces rapidly, given the right conditions, and many thousands of mites can be found in just 1 g (¹⁄₃₂ oz) of house dust. Shed bodies of dead mites, as well as the many thousands of faecal pellets they produce when alive, contain allergens that can trigger and exacerbate conditions such as eczema and dermatitis. Inhaled dust-mite allergens cause asthma and hay feverlike symptoms in millions of people worldwide.

Sand bubbler crab
Sifting sand
SPECIES *Scopimera inflata* **SIZE** Up to 1.5 cm (½ in) **DISTRIBUTION** Sheltered sandy beaches along eastern and northern coasts of Australia

These small crabs live in vertical burrows in the sand between high water and mid-tide level. They emerge when the tide is out, clearing sand from the burrow on the way, then begin to feed. The crab first uses its front claws to scrape an escape trench in the surface of the moist sand, moving in a straight line away from its burrow. Then, using a claw, it scoops sand into its mouthparts where it is sifted to collect organic matter, which is eaten. During this process, the waste sand is manipulated into a small ball, which is left to one side. Hundreds of individuals feeding near to each other, each producing many such balls, can convert what was a smooth sand surface into a sea of minute spheres.

Making sand balls Sand bubbler crabs leave intricate patterns of balls of compressed sand around their burrows as they feed. The number of balls is an indication of how long the tide has been out.

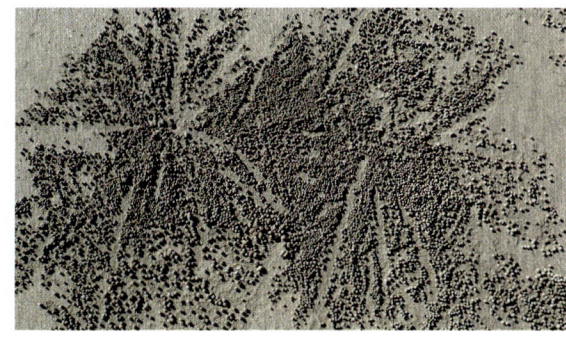

Dung beetles
Faeces foraging

SPECIES *Scarabaeus* species **SIZE** Up to 4 cm (1½ in)
DISTRIBUTION Savanna in southern and East Africa

These beetles feed and rear their young on animal faeces. Competition for dung is intense – one pat of elephant dung can attract 4,000 beetles in 30 minutes. The female constructs a large ball, and the male rolls it away to bury it. Underground, the female smears the dung ball with soil and her own excrement. Once it has aged for a while, she divides it into smaller balls, lays an egg in each, and stays to care for her brood.

The big push Dung beetles can roll balls of dung as large as 5 cm (2 in) across, and are able to move dung balls that weigh 50 times or more their own body weight.

HUMAN IMPACT
HELPING FARMERS

Dung beetles are important recyclers in natural and agricultural habitats. Their activities can clear vast quantities of dung in a relatively short time, return valuable nutrients to the soil, and maintain good soil structure and aeration. If beetles are not present, the recycling process is less effective and nitrogen, essential for plant growth, is lost to the system. Pastures and arable land can become seriously degraded, and uncleared dung provides a breeding ground for disease-carrying and nuisance flies that can have an adverse effect on humans and livestock.

American cockroach
World traveller

SPECIES *Periplaneta americana* **SIZE** Up to 4 cm (1½ in)
DISTRIBUTION Widespread in tropical and subtropical regions; indoors in warm temperate regions

American cockroaches originated in Africa but have travelled on the ships of traders to become widely established in much of the world. They feed on a broad range of plant and animal material and tend to forage for food after dark using long, sensitive antennae to feel their way around. Fast-moving and very agile, they are able to move about 50 body lengths in a second, and their flattened bodies allow them to squeeze through small cracks. Although they have wings, they do not fly readily except in very hot conditions. These natural scavengers are serious pests when they invade food-processing factories, kitchens, and other places where they can find warmth, shelter, and food. Around houses they are found in cellars, drainage systems, and sewers.

downward-pointing head

leathery wings *spiny leg*

Laboratory testing Because of its large size and ease of culturing, the cockroach has been used extensively by scientists for research, including insecticide testing.

Burying beetles
Grave diggers

SPECIES *Nicrophorus* species **SIZE** Up to 3 cm (1¼ in)
DISTRIBUTION Widespread in a range of habitats

These beetles seek the carcasses of small birds and mammals as a food source for their larvae. When a dead animal is found, a mating pair excavate the soil beneath the carcass so it caves in, burying the body. The beetles then remove the fur or feathers, using these to line the burial chamber. The female lays her eggs in the soil close to the chamber, and the hatched larvae move in to feed. Competition for a found carcass can be intense, with several pairs of beetles fighting over it for control. Females will lay more eggs if the carcass is large.

Inside the burial chamber >>01 Burying beetles have large antennae that detect the presence of a dead animal from some distance. >>02 When a carcass is located, it is buried to safeguard it from other scavengers and flies. >>03 The brood develops inside the burial chamber, eating the carcass. >>04 The parents also eat the flesh and regurgitate liquids for their young to eat.

>>01   >>02   >>03   >>04

Striped red mullet
Detritus digger

SPECIES *Mullus surmuletus* **SIZE** Up to 40 cm (15½ in)
DISTRIBUTION Muddy and sandy-bottomed inshore waters of Mediterranean Sea, eastern North Atlantic, Black Sea

This bottom-dwelling marine fish is adept at locating small invertebrates such as worms and crustaceans, along with edible debris, by using a pair of long sensory barbels that is located under its chin. It then uses its mouth to dig out its meal. The barbels are constantly moved back and forth, but when the fish is resting they can be folded back under the head.

Clouds of silt As the striped red mullet searches for food it disturbs silt from the sea bed, which rises in clouds. Other small fish, such as gobies, may be attracted in by this sign of hunting to share the meal.

Japanese hagfish
Tied in knots

SPECIES *Eptatretus burgeri* **SIZE** Up to 60 cm (24 in) **DISTRIBUTION** Inshore temperate waters of northwestern Pacific

Like other hagfishes, this species feeds on small, bottom-living invertebrates, but is also an expert scavenger of fish and whale carcasses. It rasps off pieces of rotting flesh and can gain a purchase by tying its body in a knot, which it moves along the length of the body until it is up against the carcass. This gives it more leverage for the mouthparts to tear off mouthfuls.

Slippery customer Any predator trying to eat this tasty looking hagfish will end up with its mouth clogged with mucus that the Japanese hagfish secretes. This secretion forms a thick, strong slime on contact with water.

Tiger shark
Ocean dustbin

SPECIES *Galeocerdo cuvier* **SIZE** Up to 5.5 m (18 ft) **DISTRIBUTION** Inshore or open ocean in tropical, subtropical, and warm temperate waters worldwide

Most large sharks, including tiger sharks, are active predators and hunt live prey, but the tiger shark is also one of the few shark species that is a true scavenger. It will investigate anything that looks and smells vaguely edible and will feast on the carcasses of dead fishes, whales, and seals. However, it is not very discerning and stomachs of tiger sharks have been found to contain many indigestible human-made and waste items, such as bits of tyre, bottles and tin cans. Its apparent disregard for the food value of the items it eats has earned it the name of "the garbage can with fins". Tiger sharks also live up to their name and hunt a wide range of live food, from fishes, turtles, sea snakes, porpoises, seabirds, and other vertebrates to invertebrate squid, shellfish, lobsters, and crabs – in fact, practically anything.

When hunting it uses its excellent eyesight, electrosensory pits called ampullae of Lorenzini (which enable all sharks to detect small muscle movements of prey, even in darkness), and an excellent sense of smell to track down its prey. Its size, curiosity, and indiscriminate feeding behaviour make the tiger shark, potentially, a very dangerous animal, but unprovoked attacks on humans are rare.

ANATOMY **UNIQUE TEETH**

The teeth of tiger sharks have a distinctive cockscomblike outline. They are notched and finely serrated on both sides. The shape may have evolved to allow the shark to cut through the shells of large molluscs and turtles as well as flesh and bone. When biting, the snout rises and the lower jaw opens to give a large gape. The lower jaw then lifts and the upper jaw moves forwards as the mouth closes. The upper jaw then retracts – this action helps the shark to cut chunks out of its prey. In its lifetime, a shark may replace many thousands of teeth as new ones grow forwards constantly, displacing the teeth at the front of the jaws.

Impromptu meals A tiger shark bites voraciously into the carcass of a marlin found in Australian waters.

Fork-tailed drongo
Manipulative mimic

SPECIES *Dicrurus adsimilis* **SIZE** 23–26 cm (9–10 in) **DISTRIBUTION** Africa south of the Sahara

These birds trick other animals into handing over their food by imitating their alarm calls. Some drongos have a repertoire of about 30 different alarm calls, such as those of meerkats, pied babblers, crowned plovers, and glossy starlings. When they spot an animal with a tasty morsel, they mimic the alarm call of that species, causing it to drop its food and flee. Other animals do not get wise to this ploy as drongos mix it up, changing the mimicked alarm calls of different animals to keep their victims guessing. Moreover, drongos do give alarm calls in response to actual predators too, and because they monitor a wide area from high treetops, it is risky to ignore their warnings.

Prank caller A fork-tailed drongo calls from a perch in a tree. It is known to steal food using its ability to mimic a wide range of animal alarm calls, but this insect-eater also hunts for its own food.

Black-browed albatross
Fatal attraction

SPECIES *Thalassarche melanophris* **SIZE** 80–95 cm (31–37 in) **DISTRIBUTION** Islands and open waters of the Southern Ocean

Long-line fishing and trawling are responsible for killing many of these impressive birds. Many albatross species are now endangered. They feed on fishes as well as octopuses and squid. But it is the attraction to floating carrion that has led them to fall victim to modern fishing practices. Albatrosses dive to catch baited hooks and become caught themselves. By using bird-scaring devices and setting lines only after dark, fishermen are able to reduce the slaughter. After feeding at sea for months, ranging over vast distances, albatrosses return to land to breed.

A free lunch Fishing boats that are at sea for long periods throw large quantities of fish offal and bycatch overboard. Here, a large number of black-browed albatrosses gather behind a trawler to feast.

Remains of the day Using its claws to hold its food, a griffon vulture stands over what is left of a dismembered carcass. This species eats only carrion, and it is thought that it softens any tough meat with blows of its large, strong bill.

Eurasian griffon vulture

Carrion feeder

SPECIES *Gyps fulvus* **SIZE** Up to 1.1 m (3½ ft) **DISTRIBUTION** Southern Europe, North Africa, and Asia. Mountainous and open regions, grassland, and shrubland

As soon as temperatures rise in the morning, griffon vultures take to the skies in the mountainous regions in which they live and, using rising air currents, soar high above the ground. They remain on the wing, often in groups, for many hours and can cover great distances as they scan the terrain below for promising objects to investigate. Their diet consists almost entirely of fresh carrion, although they will resort to rotting meat if no other food is available.

Griffon vultures have a weak sense of smell and rely on the highly visible activities of other animals feeding at a carcass. When something attracts them, they descend rapidly and, depending on the number and nature of the other scavengers present, may either wait their turn or take over the situation. As they have relatively small heads and bills, they generally need another (usually mammal) scavenger to have ripped open the skin of a freshly killed animal before they can feed. After eating, griffon vultures like to wash their feathers in fresh water before resting in the sun.

A nose for carrion Old World vultures, like the Eurasian griffon vulture and African white-backed vulture (right), locate food by sight. Many New World vultures primarily use smell, like the turkey vulture (above), which has an enlarged olfactory bulb in the brain.

Lounging together These sociable vultures share nest sites and also feed and rest together in small colonies of up to 20 pairs of birds.

Competitive scavengers Hyenas are the most abundant large carnivores in Africa and obtain food by both hunting and scavenging. They are often one of many different scavengers to find a carcass. Sometimes, ferocious fighting breaks out when competing scavengers congregate around potential food. This spotted hyena is trying to hold off a pack of African wild dogs.

Tasmanian devil
No waste

SPECIES *Sarcophilus harrisii* **SIZE** 0.75–1.1 m (2½–3½ ft)
DISTRIBUTION Variety of habitats, especially forest and heath, in Tasmania, Australia

This nocturnal animal is the largest carnivorous marsupial in the world. It eats a wide range of dead and live foods including small mammals, birds, reptiles, insects, and amphibians. It has excellent hearing, sensitive whiskers, and a good sense of smell, enabling it to find carrion in the dark. This efficient scavenger spends less time hunting, but does hunt prey up to the size of wallabies. Its large head, powerful jaws, and sharp teeth allow it to tear through flesh and splinter bone, leaving nothing behind.

Carcass competition The Tasmanian devil is a solitary scavenger. The smell of a large carcass may attract several devils, and loud screeching and aggressive displays are used to establish dominance without risking injury.

Common raccoon
Urban opportunist

SPECIES *Procyon lotor* **SIZE** 65–100 cm (26–39 in)
DISTRIBUTION Grassland, woodland, and suburban habitats in North and Central America, from southern Canada to Panama

Mainly nocturnal, common raccoons (or northern racoons) lead an omnivorous lifestyle and have good hearing and night vision. As well as live food, they will also eat fresh roadkill and other carrion. In suburban areas, they have become able scavengers. Their front paws are very sensitive, allowing them to select, manipulate, and examine small items of food before eating them. Their varied diet includes insects, eggs (including turtle eggs), crustaceans, molluscs, fishes, small mammals, and birds as well as fruits, seeds, and other plant material.

Nimble foragers Common raccoons can be pests in suburban areas because they are scavengers, often found around waste dumps. They are agile climbers and use their slender front paws to open simple fastenings and remove dustbin lids as they forage for food.

Spotted hyena
Bone crusher

SPECIES *Crocuta crocuta* **SIZE** Up to 1.9 m (6¼ ft)
DISTRIBUTION Sub-Saharan Africa, mostly in savanna

Also known as the laughing hyena after its characteristic vocalizations that sound like human laughter, this species is often thought of as a scavenger but it is, in fact, also the most common predator in sub-Saharan Africa. Mostly solitary hunters, hyenas increase their success rate and tackle much larger species (such as wildebeests and kudus) if they hunt in groups. They often chase prey for long distances without tiring until eventually, their quarry becomes exhausted and is pulled to the ground. Hyenas and lions compete for food and often fight over it. Sometimes hyenas steal the remains of kills from lions, but in some cases, the reverse happens.

Super-efficient digestion Hyenas can consume up to a third of their own body weight in one meal. They can crush and eat bones, even those of elephants, and can digest just about every part of their prey.

SCAVENGING 227

The intestines of polar bears are adapted to digest the fats of marine mammals. Growing bears eat the meat while adults consume mainly seal blubber.

Polar bear
Natural scavengers

SPECIES *Ursus maritimus* **SIZE** Up to 2.5 m (8¼ ft)
DISTRIBUTION Sea ice and coastal areas throughout Arctic (circumpolar)

The main prey of polar bears are ringed seals and sometimes bearded seals, but they will eat anything they can kill, such as young walruses and whales, fishes, seabirds, and caribous. To hunt, mostly they sit very still by a hole in the ice where seals surface to breathe. When a seal appears, the bear strikes the seal with a front paw and then drags it out onto the ice before biting its head. On the surface of the ice, polar bears rely on their superb camouflage to stalk resting seals. They creep up as close as they can and, when they get within range, can run at about 45 kph (30 mph). Even so, only a few hunts are successful, so scavenging is important. Carcasses of whales or walruses on the seashore, or caribous or muskoxen on land, provide an important source of food. Polar bears have an excellent sense of smell and can detect a carcass from great distances. As natural scavengers, they will investigate novel items, which can lead to problems near human settlements in the Arctic where some have suffered serious internal injury due to eating human-made materials.

A lucky find A gray whale carcass on the coast of northern Alaska attracts a number of polar bears. The retreat of sea ice in the summer can leave bears stranded on land and unable to reach seals, their preferred prey. If this occurs, hunting caribou or scavenging remain the only options.

Feeding relationships

Not all feeding relationships involve one animal killing and eating another. In some cases, animals of different species form a partnership from which they derive mutual benefit. However, in many cases the benefits are all one-sided and, while the recipient does well, the other party either gains nothing or actively suffers.

SYMBIOSIS

Symbiotic relationships are long-lasting associations between members of two species. In obligate symbioses, one of the species involved cannot survive without the other. For example, the ant *Acropyga sauteri* and the mealy bug *Pseudociccidae rhizoecinae* are entirely dependant upon one another. The bug needs the ants' nest as a place to live, and the ants rely upon the bugs for food. Other forms of symbiosis are facultative, meaning that although both parties can survive alone, at least one of them would suffer from independence. Some symbioses, such as that of the bug and the ant, clearly benefit both of the animals involved, but others are more exploitative and one animal suffers at the other's expense. Infestations of parasites are a good example of this. Parasitic relationships also show the intimate nature of some symbioses, with one animal living inside, or on the other. In other cases, the two animals share a common home. Some partners come together for a short period, when one needs the other to clean it of ticks and dead skin, for example.

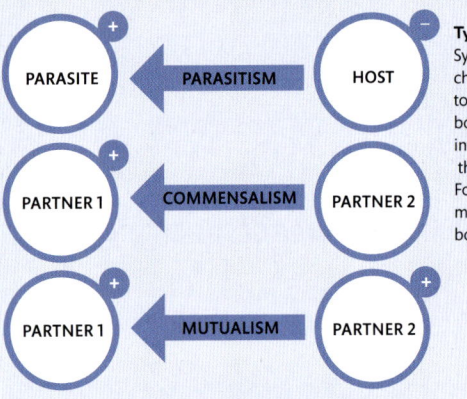

Types of symbiosis Symbiosis is usually characterized according to whether one or both of the animals involved gains from the relationship. For example, in a mutualistic partnership, both parties benefit.

COMMENSALISM

It is easy to show that an organism benefits or suffers as a result of its relationship with a member of another species, but it can be surprisingly difficult to prove that a relationship has no effect at all. Many relationships defined as commensalisms involve phoresy – the transportation of one animal as the passenger of another. The larvae of some midge species, for example, attach themselves to the scales of Amazonian catfishes. They are transported by these fishes to better feeding areas than they would be able to reach on their own, and hosts are unaffected by their presence. White-fronted terns follow hunting pods of Hector's dolphins to quickly find fishes during the birds' breeding season, an example of facultative commensalism.

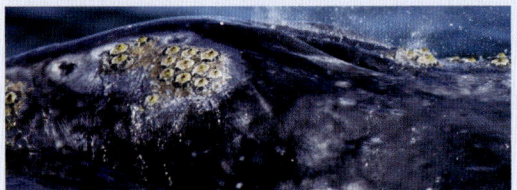

Barnacles and whale lice In an example of phoretic commensalism (left), whales carry barnacles through food-rich water. Whales suffer, however, from carrying parasitic whale lice (above). These in turn are the food of several species of fishes, with whom the whales enjoy a mutualism.

Feeding and fertilizing Honey bees visit flowers to collect pollen and nectar to take back to their hives. As they move between flowers, they transfer pollen from one plant to another, thereby ensuring fertilization.

MUTUALISM

Mutualism is a symbiotic relationship that benefits both of the animals involved. In many cases, one animal cleans another, eating parasites and cleaning wounds. In other cases, such as the pollination of flowering plants, the reproduction of one organism relies on the feeding behaviour of another. Ants feed off the honeydew of aphids, but offer them protection in return. Termites and their gut bacteria could be said to be a further example of mutualism; without the bacteria, the termites would not be able to digest wood.

Dental hygiene Some partnerships appear risky but may be mutualism. These cleaner shrimps are literally in the jaws of death, but the coral grouper they are cleaning suppresses its motivation to feed while cleaning is in progress.

Eating the insides Pearl fishes live inside sea cucumbers, feasting upon their gonads. The fish enters by reversing into the host's anus. It can twist round to defecate through this without leaving home.

PARASITISM

Parasites live at the expense of their hosts. They feed directly from them and, in some cases, live out part or all of their life cycle in or on them. A host animal may die as an indirect result of a parasitic infection, but it is unusual for a parasite to kill its host directly. They are usually far smaller than their hosts and reproduce at a far faster rate. In many cases, parasites and their hosts have coevolved to the extent that some parasites have only one host. Parasites may live their entire life associated with a single host, or have a complex life cycle involving a number of host species. The feeding apparatus and behaviour of parasites is usually highly specialized.

ANATOMY **REPLACEMENT TONGUE**

Cymothoa exigua is a crustacean parasite of the spotted rose-snapper. This 3–4 cm (1¼–1½ in) long parasite sneaks into the snapper's mouth via the gills and attaches itself to the tongue. It feeds on the fish's blood, diverting it from the tongue into its own mouth via six claws on its first three pairs of legs. Eventually, starved of blood, the tongue withers away. The crustacean attaches itself to the tongue stump and, incredibly, becomes a functioning tongue substitute. At this stage, the parasite reduces the amount of blood it takes from the host and switches its diet to include food particles in the mouth of the fish. The fish is able to carry on feeding as usual, suffering only in that it is forced to share its meals with this unusual parasite.

Infestations Ticks, like those on this hedgehog, are blood-sucking parasites that are very hard to remove. Severe infestations can reduce a host's vigour.

Blood sucking The piercing mouthparts of a female mosquito act like a serrated syringe, and her saliva promotes blood flow from her host.

Protecting the flock Ants effectively farm their aphid charges for their honeydew (which is a waste product of the aphids) by herding them and offering protection.

90 m The approximate distance worker carpenter ants are willing to travel from a nest in search of food.

Carpenter ants and aphids
Farming aphids

Many species of ant, including carpenter ants, have a mutualistic relationship with aphids. Rather than eating the aphids, ants tend small groups of them, stroking the aphids' bodies with their legs and antennae to stimulate them to produce a drop of sugar-rich honeydew. After taking honeydew from a number of aphids, and storing it in its abdomen, an ant returns to its nest, where it regurgitates the honeydew to feed to its siblings. The aphids also benefit from this relationship because the ants protect them from potential predators, such as ladybird beetles, aphidlions, and lacewings, and transfer them from wilted to healthy plants. Carpenter ants are omnivores, eating insects, fruits, and other plant material. They use their powerful biting jaws to hollow out nests in wood. If the wood is part of a building these insects can become serious pests, although contrary to popular perception the ants don't actually eat the wood, because they are unable to digest cellulose. Scout ants locate food by day and lay down pheromone trails that are followed by foraging parties under the cover of darkness.

Boxer crab and anemone
Stinging gloves

Crabs and anemones often associate with each other for mutual benefit. Small crabs make a good meal for fishes and octopuses, so some species live under or within the tentacles of anemones for protection, in the same way that anemonefishes do (see p.251). Hermit crabs are well known for placing certain stinging anemones on the mollusc shells in which they live and carrying them around. In both cases, the anemone also benefits from the messy eating habits of its mobile crab home. Boxer crabs are unusual in that they collect and hold a small anemone in each of their two modified front claws. If the crab is disturbed, it waves its anemone "boxing gloves" at any intruder. It is therefore probable that the boxer crab is using the stinging anemones as defensive weapons. The anemones, though, are small, so this could be a signalling bluff. Since its claws are busy holding its anemones, this scavenging crab has adapted to use its mouthparts and small claws on its first pair of walking legs to collect its food. It will also "steal" bits of food that the anemones have trapped or picked up.

Mopping up food Boxer crabs use their anemone "gloves" as mops to wipe up scattered food particles. They pick and eat some of the food off the anemone, then they leave the rest for the anemone to finish off.

FEEDING RELATIONSHIPS

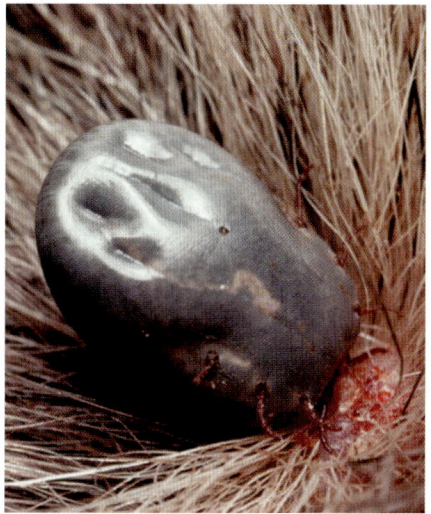

Sheep tick
Spreading disease
SPECIES *Ixodes ricinus* **SIZE** 2–4 mm (1/16–3/16 in)
DISTRIBUTION Scrubby vegetation in woods and heaths in temperate regions worldwide, mainly Europe

The sheep tick feeds directly on the blood of its host and, in the process, may be the vector of a number of diseases, including louping-ill in sheep and Lyme disease in humans. It attaches itself to its host by means of the backward-pointing spikes of its harpoonlike mouthparts (known as a hypostome). Ticks can feed on blood for up to two weeks before falling from the host. Mature females can lay thousands of eggs, after which they die.

long mouthparts

Full of food Engorged ticks swell as they fill with the blood of the host; females can increase in size by 200 per cent. When they have had enough blood they will drop off.

Heat seekers Unable to jump or fly, hungry ticks wait in the vegetation for a host to pass by, then drop onto the animal as it passes. The ticks are attracted to both the body heat and respired carbon dioxide of their hosts.

Tarantula hawk wasp
Buried alive
SPECIES *Pepsis heros* **SIZE** Up to 11 cm (4½ in)
DISTRIBUTION Arid areas of southern USA and Central and South America

The male tarantula hawk is a wasp that feeds on the flowers of milkweed and other plants, while the female drinks nectar and eats rotting fruits, which often intoxicates them to the point of being unable to fly. But when it comes to raising their young, these wasps are fearsome parasites of tarantula spiders. Female hawk wasps track down spiders using scent and tend to attack spiders resident in a burrow, which usually means females during the breeding season or both sexes at other times. Breeding male spiders are often ignored by tarantula hawk wasps because they do not feed themselves while searching for mates and therefore become emaciated. When a tarantula hawk wasp locates its prey, an intense fight often takes place, until eventually it manages to penetrate the spider's guard and sting it. The wasp's powerful venom does not kill its victim, it only paralyses it. Once subdued, the spider is then dragged either into its own burrow or into a burrow prepared by the wasp as a nest-chamber. In the burrow, the female lays a single egg on the spider and leaves, sealing the burrow behind it. If the egg fails to hatch, the spider may recover. However, if the egg hatches, the spider's fate is sealed: the larval wasp feeds on the still-living spider, sucking its juices until it eventually dies, then the larva consumes the remains of its host, leaving the vital organs until last as a means of keeping the meal fresh.

Asian tiger leech
Blood sucker
SPECIES *Haemadipsa picta* **SIZE** Up to 2–3 cm (¾–1¼ in)
DISTRIBUTION Tropical forests in Borneo, Taiwan, and Indochina

Leeches are segmented worms found in marine, freshwater, and wetter terrestrial habitats. Some of them are predators, feeding on a range of small invertebrates, such as snails, insect larvae, and worms. The most familiar leeches, however, are haemophagic parasites, which suck blood directly from living hosts. Leeches in the genus *Haemadipsa*, including the Asian tiger leech, are all bloodsuckers. Leeches attach to their host by means of biting jaws or a sucking proboscis. They maintain the flow of blood by secreting a long-lasting anticoagulant called hirudin into the wound. Once full, they simply fall away and digest their meal.

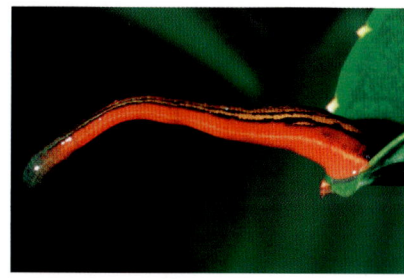

Waiting for dinner This Asian tiger leech waits on a leaf for a passing animal on which to feed. It detects its host by sensing movement with its 10 eyespots as well as the carbon dioxide its host breathes out.

Final journey Having subdued its prey, the tarantula hawk drags the unfortunate spider into a burrow that will soon become a sealed tomb.

Subduing the meal Having found a victim, the giant tarantula hawk wasp thrusts with its stinger to inject a powerful venom that paralyses its prey.

HUMAN IMPACT MEDICINAL USES

Leeches have been used in medicine since the time of the ancient Egyptians. Historically, they were prized as a means of blood-letting, a practice thought to rid the body of the noxious humours that were considered to be responsible for illness. Contemporary medicine has proved the futility of such blood-letting as a treatment and so one might assume that the medicinal leech has no place in a modern surgery. Yet leeches can be very useful for restoring venous blood flow to patients following skin grafts and some reconstructive surgeries, and in the repair of small blood vessels, where clotting would be bad.

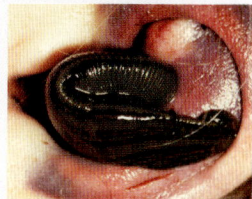

Opportunistic scavengers Sally lightfoot crabs are scavengers that feed primarily on algae uncovered by the retreating tide, but they are happy to eat almost anything, including dead animals. They have been observed picking over the bodies of basking marine iguanas. The lizards presumably tolerate this behaviour because the crabs are picking off dead skin and ectoparasites.

Sea lamprey
Boring fish

SPECIES *Petromyzon marinus* **SIZE** Up to 1.2 m (4 ft)
DISTRIBUTION Coastal seas of North Atlantic and rivers draining into it

The sea lamprey attaches itself firmly to larger marine fishes by its suckerlike mouth. It cuts a hole in their flesh to feed on blood, aided by an anticoagulant it secretes into the wound to promote blood flow. It detaches once sated, leaving its victim with a wound that is slow to heal and susceptible to infection. Host fishes are weakened and can die as a result of this form of parasitism. Sea lampreys hatch in rivers where, as wormlike larvae, they remain for a number of years in a muddy burrow, feeding by filtering plankton from the water. After they gradually assume a free-swimming form, these jawless parasitic fishes migrate to the sea. Specialized cells in their gills control the passage of ions such as sodium into the body, helping the fishes adapt to salt-water life. Adult fishes eventually return to rivers to breed.

Suction power Once attached to a host, a sea lamprey is almost impossible to detach. Here, a lamprey is being carried upstream by a migrating salmon. Incredibly, the host fish is still able to leap despite the extra drag caused by the parasite.

ANATOMY **RINGS OF TEETH**

Lampreys attach to their prey by suction, clamping themselves to the skin of their host with the sucking lips of their oral disc. The disc is filled with concentric rings of horny teeth, which become progressively larger the closer to the centre of the disc they are. These teeth hold the fish firmly in place while the tooth plates on the tongue rasp a hole in the victim's flesh.

Cookiecutter shark
Flesh eater

SPECIES *Isistius brasiliensis* **SIZE** Up to 56 cm (22 in) **DISTRIBUTION** Tropical waters worldwide, from the surface to 3,500 m (11,480 ft) deep

This small, cigar-shaped shark has a macabre habit of biting lumps of flesh from much larger fishes, whales, dolphins, and even seals. The cookiecutter shark migrates towards the surface from deep water at night and sneaks up on slow-moving targets, then uses its strong lips to latch onto its prey like a suction pad. It sinks the large, razor-sharp, triangular teeth of its bottom jaw into its hapless victim, then twists around to cut out a neat plug of flesh. Keeping hold of the plug with its small, hooklike upper teeth, it pulls free to consume its prize. The cookie-shaped wounds inflicted by the cookiecutter shark give it its name. Some faster-moving, predatory fish or dolphins in search of a meal may be lured towards the shark by the green-glowing bioluminescent organs that cover its belly, but this can only be surmised. It is also known to eat squid, small fishes, and crustaceans.

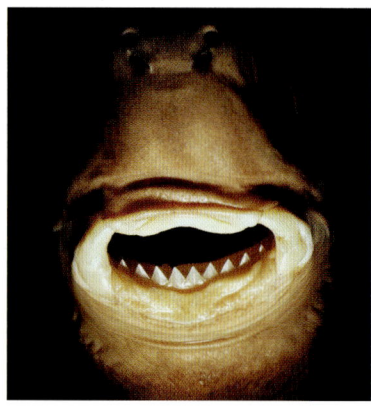

Lethal grin The lips of the cookiecutter shark form a suction seal around the mouth. The teeth are small in the upper jaw and large and triangular in the lower jaw.

Live sharksucker
Hitching a ride

SPECIES *Echeneis naucrates* **SIZE** Exceeds 1 m (3¼ ft)
DISTRIBUTION Tropical and subtropical waters worldwide

The live sharksucker, a species of remora, can and does swim and hunt freely, but prefers to hitch a ride on larger species of fishes (including sharks), whales, dolphins, manatees, and even turtles. The sharksucker benefits from being carried because it saves energy. Respiration is also easier, because a sharksucker at rest uses energy to pump water across its gills, whereas one being carried is held in a current and does not need to expend the extra energy. Meanwhile, the host may have to expend extra swimming energy when carrying a sharksucker. Some sharksucker species feed on the scraps of food left by their feeding hosts, while those that attach to manatees and dolphins can be cophragic – they sometimes eat the faeces of their hosts. The relationship between sharksucker and host may be one-sided, but some sharksucker species do enjoy a more mutually beneficial relationship with their hosts, cleaning their skin and gills and picking off parasitic copepods.

Suction disc Unlike other fishes, which use their mouths for attachment, the dorsal fin of the live sharksucker has evolved to become a serrated cartilaginous suction plate on the top of the head and neck. Disc muscles raise and lower the serrations to create suction. In some communities, a traditional fishing technique involves attaching a line to a sharksucker, then releasing it to attach to a host. The fisher can then haul in both sharksucker and host.

Holding on A large host, such as this whale shark, is able to support a large number of sharksuckers, each imposing a drag cost upon their host, potentially slowing it down. The energetic leaps and splashes of the spinner dolphin may in part be a behaviour developed to dislodge sharksuckers.

FEEDING RELATIONSHIPS 235

Candiru
Chemical trails
SPECIES *Vandellia cirrhosa* **SIZE** Exceeds 15 cm (6 in)
DISTRIBUTION In sediment burrows in river beds of the Amazon and Orinoco basins

This tiny parasitic catfish is haemophagic, feeding on the blood of other fishes. When hungry, candirus emerge from their burrows in the river bed and follow chemical cues in the water that have been expelled from the gills of their victims. When a candiru locates prey, the slimline fish wriggles under the victim's gill cover and inserts its front end into the gill chamber. Here, it bites into an artery with needlelike teeth, releasing blood that pumps out into its mouth under pressure. It takes just 30 seconds to 2 minutes for the candiru to feed. After taking its fill, it leaves the way it came in. Some fishes resist attack by closing their gill covers.

Transparently hungry This candiru has not fed recently. If it had, its gut would be visible through its translucent skin as a greatly distended sac.

HUMAN IMPACT FEARED FISH
Candirus are infamous for their ability to parasitize humans by entering the urethra of unfortunate bathers. However, this appears to be a stubborn myth that has been perpetuated for many years. There are no scientifically confirmed reports of this happening, and what documentation there is does not stand up well to scrutiny.

Bluestreak cleaner wrasse
Cleaning stations
SPECIES *Labroides dimidiatus* **SIZE** Up to 14 cm (5½ in) **DISTRIBUTION** Reefs of the Indo-Pacific, Red Sea, and East Africa

Coral reef fishes are subject to blood-sucking external crustacean parasites, but they have help at hand in the form of the bluestreak cleaner wrasse. These boldly marked fishes maintain "cleaning stations" at prominent reef landmarks, where they pick over the bodies of their clients, nipping off parasites and consuming dead skin and mucus. The cleaners may perform a dance to advertise their services to new "clients", which often wait patiently, even forming queues. To indicate its desire to be cleaned, a fish will hold is fins outspread and mouth open. Cleaner fish that nip their clients risk losing future custom. This liberty taking is less likely to occur in areas with many cleaning stations, as competition for clients forces them to offer a better service. Cleaners are essential to the health of the reef and its fishes.

Dangerous game Bluestreak cleaner wrasse react to predatory "clients", such as this tiger grouper, more quickly than they do to non-dangerous fishes, and spend longer cleaning their potential predators, presumably in order to pacify them.

Galapagos penguin
Stealing the catch
SPECIES *Spheniscus mendiculus* **SIZE** 35 cm (14 in)
DISTRIBUTION Endemic to the Galapagos Islands

In common with its close relatives, the Galapagos penguin is a carnivore, preferring to feed on small fishes, including the sardines, anchovies, and pilchards that abound in the cold waters around the Galapagos Islands. These penguins often feed alongside pelicans, which retain bigger prey in their throat pouches, allowing smaller fishes to escape, which are subsequently snapped up by the waiting penguins. Recently, however, penguins have been seen to abuse this harmonious relationship by stealing larger fishes directly from pelicans' pouches.

The Galapagos penguin also actively hunts its prey: propelled by stout, flipperlike wings, it pursues its victims through the water at great speed. Because of the position of their eyes in relation to their bills, penguins usually attack their prey from below, grabbing fishes and then holding them in their short, stout bills. Flocks of penguins often feed together, driving shoals of confused fishes towards one another and breaking up larger shoals so as to more easily target their catch. Pelicans may move in to take a share of the herded fishes for themselves, but in doing so they leave themselves open to theft of their catches by enterprising penguins.

Smash and grab Galapagos penguins nip greedily at the bulging pouch of a pelican, hoping to steal a fish rather than hunting for their own.

Robbing from the flock Herons are ruthless flock mates, stealing from one another with a brutality that is as shocking as it is effective. Here, an adult overpowers a juvenile. Kleptoparasitic attacks on young herons have a 44.4 per cent success rate, which falls to 17.6 per cent if the victim is an adult.

Grey heron
Mugging for a meal

SPECIES *Ardea cinerea* **SIZE** 90–98 cm (35 in–3¼ ft)
DISTRIBUTION Wetlands in Europe, Asia, and sub-Saharan Africa

The grey heron is an opportunistic carnivore that eats whatever prey it comes across. Its cosmopolitan diet commonly includes fishes, amphibians, crustaceans, reptiles, insects, mammals, and small birds. It stalks its prey with deliberate strides or stands motionless in ambush and jabs at it with its strong, sharp bill and long, powerful neck. Small prey is swallowed immediately with a toss of the head, while larger items are clubbed, shaken, or stabbed to death and swallowed whole, usually head first to smooth their passage.

Often feeding in the company of others, herons are accomplished kleptoparasites: individuals and groups will attack and steal from other birds, usually other herons. Observations suggest that adult birds are more successful as both hunters and robbers than younger individuals.

FEEDING RELATIONSHIPS 237

Great skua
In-flight piracy

SPECIES *Stercorarius skua* **SIZE** Up to 60 cm (23½ in) **DISTRIBUTION** Breeds in colonies in Iceland, Norway, Faroe Islands, and Scotland; winters throughout northeast Atlantic

Skuas are carnivores and scavengers that feed on a wide range of foodstuffs, including invertebrates, fishes, birds, and carrion. Great skuas will catch their own prey if they have to, and have been known to kill and eat smaller seabirds, such as puffins and guillemots, but as skilled kleptoparasites they prefer to steal from other birds. These pirates of the sky patrol seabird colonies and harass birds returning to their nests with food. The skuas pull at the wings and tails of the other birds, causing them to stall in flight, and they peck at their heads and bodies. When the persecution becomes unbearable, the other birds drop their catch, which is snapped up by the skuas. Of course, the skuas will steal from one another too, and a prize may change hands several times.

Attack! Breeding skuas defend their nests vigorously and will attack all comers, including humans. They repeatedly dive at their target, pecking with their hook-tipped bill.

Defending the nest Skuas that patrol breeding colonies will eat eggs and kill unattended chicks. By breeding in colonies, birds like this gentoo penguin (right) may be able to work together to fend off attacks by south polar skuas.

Yellow-billed oxpecker
A taste for blood

SPECIES *Buphagus africanus* **SIZE** Up to 20 cm (7⅞ in) **DISTRIBUTION** Savanna of sub-Saharan Africa, from Senegal to Sudan, and south as far as South Africa

Like a number of species of insectivorous birds, the yellow-billed oxpecker feeds in association with herds of grazing and browsing mammals, possibly because the herds disturb insects as they move and their dung attracts swarms of flies. But the oxpecker–herbivore relationship is an intimate one. Oxpeckers spend most of their day perching on a mammal host – for example, a buffalo, rhinoceros, giraffe, or elephant – and spend almost 70 per cent of their time feeding there, either alone or in the company of flock mates. This relationship is often described as a mutualism, which means both parties benefit. The benefit to the bird is that it has a moving larder, and the host benefits because the bird cleans it. Oxpeckers will eat ticks and other irritating parasites that their host cannot scratch off, feeding particularly around the eyes, ears, and anus.

However, it has been discovered that there is a more sinister side to this relationship. The birds do eat huge numbers of ticks, but it seems that their taste is for the blood that is inside the engorged tick rather than for the actual tick itself. Oxpeckers have been observed using their bills to scissor open their host's wounds and drink their blood. By keeping wounds open, the birds expose their hosts to the risk of infection and parasite infestation.

There is one way that oxpeckers can benefit large herbivores that is unquestionably helpful: they can provide an early warning system, thanks to their keen eyes and loud alarm calls. Studies show that black rhinos are nearly 50 per cent more likely to avoid approaching humans without being seen if they have oxpeckers feeding on them at the time.

Open wound Oxpeckers use a particular scissoring beak action to maintain the flow of blood from open wounds in the skin of their host.

Pest control An oxpecker can remove between 600 and 1,200 ticks from a host, in this case a buffalo, in a single day. However, they prefer ticks that have already fed from the host, making their value to the host somewhat questionable.

Common raven and grey wolf
Exploiting the pack

Ravens depend on carrion as a food source and have even learned to fly towards gunshots to scavenge the carrion left by a hunter. However, a main source of carrion in some areas is the prey of wolves. Ravens follow wolf packs and scavenge at their kills. Such is the competition between them that the size of wolf packs may have evolved in response to it: a small pack of wolves will lose on average 75 per cent of a kill to the ravens attracted to it, but a medium-sized pack will lose just 34 per cent because they are more able to chase the ravens away. A large pack loses almost nothing. The relationship between ravens and wolves is not entirely one-sided, however. Ravens often find carrion that has died of other causes – if this is the carcass of a large animal, such as a deer or moose, their bills cannot tear into it and so the ravens call to attract other ravens for assistance. When this occurs, wolves in the vicinity also hear the calls, follow the sight of gathering birds, and so are led to the carcass. The wolves are able to open the body with their sharp teeth, and so by working with the ravens they are able to share the spoils.

Competition for the kill As many as 135 ravens may be attracted to a kill. This grey wolf in Minnesota, USA, is unlikely to be able to chase the birds away from its deer kill without some help.

FEEDING RELATIONSHIPS 239

Cape gannet and dolphins
Following the leaders

Cape gannets feed primarily in flocks on anchovies and sardines, which they catch with spectacular plunge-dives, plunging from mid-air to seize individual fishes with their daggerlike beaks. They are strong fliers and will travel great distances to find shoals of fishes, often with dolphins swimming below. The dolphins are the leaders in this partnership. They guide the gannets to their prey and then force the fishes to the surface in dense "bait balls" several metres in diameter. As both dolphins and birds plunge repeatedly into the ball, air bubbles produced by the plunging birds probably help to concentrate the fishes within the killing zone, making it easier to catch them.

The race is on Cape gannets follow a pod of long-beaked common dolphins as they pursue a shoal of sardines off the coast of South Africa. Both species follow the annual migration of the sardines.

Feeding frenzy Cape gannets leave trails of bubbles as they dive to feast on a sardine bait ball that has been formed by a pod of long-beaked common dolphins.

Banded mongoose and warthog
Feeding the troop

Parasites such as ticks are a real problem for mammals that move through the densely vegetated savanna and forests of Africa. Tick levels and transmission rates may be higher still among species, such as the warthog, that make use of burrows. To rid themselves of parasites, warthogs roll in mud or on baked earth, but they can dislodge only some of the parasites in this way, and their stocky bodies make it difficult to reach all of the affected parts of their skin. However, the banded mongoose can be very useful in removing the warthogs' remaining ticks. Mongooses are largely insectivorous, but they will consume a wide range of foods, including ticks. Warthogs may allow troops of mongooses to pick the ticks from their bodies, providing the whole troop with a meal, but it can be risky for the mongooses, who can die from warthog aggression or accidental squashing.

Common vampire bat
Blood letting

SPECIES *Desmodus rotundus* **SIZE** Up to 9 cm (3½ in)
DISTRIBUTION Widespread in Mexico, Central America, and South America

Common vampire bats locate their prey (usually horses and cattle) by listening for the sounds of their breathing. The wounds that a bat inflicts on its prey when biting into its flesh cause the victim to bleed freely for more than the 20 minutes that it takes the bat to drink its fill. In that time, a bat may consume 50 per cent of its body mass. Flying animals are at risk if they gain too much weight, but these bats are able to process their meal quickly, successfully avoiding weight gain by converting nutrient-poor blood plasma to a stream of dilute urine within minutes of starting a meal.

Lapping up Vampire bats do not suck blood from the necks of their victims. Instead, they use their cheek teeth to shear hair away before using razor-sharp incisors to cut into the skin. They then lick the flowing blood from the wound with a rapid flicking of their tongue.

ANATOMY STOPPING CLOTTING

The saliva of a vampire bat is considered a venom, as it contains two important classes of chemical compounds that assist it in feeding. The first are anaesthetics, numbing the pain receptors of their prey so that they do not feel the bite. The second are anticoagulants that maintain the flow of blood from a wound by preventing blood clotting. One of the anticoagulants, draculin, is being tested for use in human medicine.

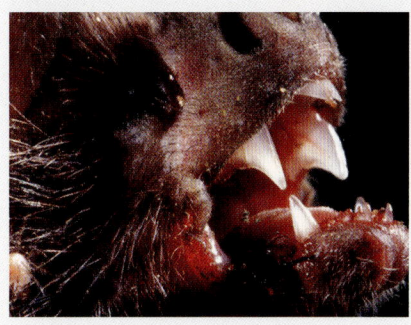

A good scratch This large group of banded mongooses will quickly pick the blood-filled ticks from the skin of this warthog, reaching places it cannot reach itself.

Defence

244
Weapons and threats

264
Camouflage and deception

280
Group defence

Defensive armour Slow-moving animals often rely on physical defences for protection when out in the open. Thorns, spines, and bristles are a common defence in reptiles, such as this thorny devil, echinoderms, and insects, which all have naturally hard skins.

DEFENCE

Most animals need to defend themselves from attack by predators, making defence an everyday necessity, especially for those lower down in the food chain. All animals must eat, and to do so often means coming out into the open to forage or hunt. The pressure to survive has resulted in a wide array of defence mechanisms, involving both behaviour and body design.

EVADING PREDATORS

The easiest method of defence is to avoid contact with predators. Hiding in a nest, burrow, or dense vegetation is a good way to achieve this. Small, nocturnal mammals emerge under cover of darkness, when predators that hunt by sight are at a disadvantage. Using smell, they can easily forage for food. In the ocean, sediment plains are dotted with numerous burrows where fishes, crabs, and prawns live in safety, rarely leaving their shelters. Running, swimming, or flying away is another device for evading attack. Many animals living out in the open can outmanoeuvre their predators if they see them soon enough. Poisonous animals can stay put, their colour often warning predators not to touch them.

Shock tactic False eye spots are part of the camouflage of butterflies, butterflyfishes, and even frogs. In order to startle or confuse a predator, the animal must behave in a certain way, normally by suddenly revealing the eye spots.

false eye spot

Hiding Many ground-nesting seabirds, like this puffin, rear their young in deep burrows, where they are safe from aerial predators such as gulls.

CONFUSING PREDATORS

If a predator does not recognize an animal as prey, it will ignore it. The ability to look and behave like something else, either animate or inanimate, helps some animals survive. A huge range of techniques has evolved throughout the animal kingdom, all of them aimed at preventing predators from spying their prey. If the prey is spotted, then confusion becomes the aim. Camouflage enables animals to merge into the background, so that they are difficult for a predator to spot. The physical shape and colour imposed on an animal by its camouflage is only part of the story. If an animal does not behave in the right way, its disguise will be ineffective. Keeping still is often important. The animal must rest in a place where it matches its surroundings, or be able to change its camouflage to suit. Some parasites exploit this by altering the behaviour of their host, so that it moves to a conspicuous position where it will be eaten by the animal that forms the next host for the parasite. Other animals confuse predators by pretending to be larger than they really are, or by imitating something dangerous or unpleasant. Some insects and amphibians use various strategies at different stages of their life cycle. A caterpillar may resemble a bird dropping, whereas the butterfly adult has false eyes on its wings.

STAND AND FIGHT

Animals with good physical defences in the form of weapons can fight their enemies. Predators cannot afford to use too much energy or be injured when capturing their prey and will often give up on a difficult target. Small animals with no obvious weapons may still be successful in deflecting a predator away from their nests or young. Birds are especially good at this, because they can fly up and escape if the predator gets too close. Similarly, small fishes, such as clownfishes, will try to drive larger fishes (and even divers) away from their home, as long as they have somewhere safe to take refuge if necessary.

Standing firm The ability to move quickly out of harm's way allows small animals to stand up to larger ones in order to defend their nest site or territory. This water dikkop can move much faster than a crocodile.

Weapons and threats

Predators have evolved a fearsome array of teeth, claws, and venom to help them catch and eat their prey, and for their own defence. In response, prey animals have evolved defence weapons, physical and chemical armour, and complex behavioural strategies for evading their enemies. Many animals try to avoid an attack in the first place by warning off would-be predators.

Defensive weapon Although potentially deadly, rhinoceroses, such as this black rhinoceros, only use their horns to protect themselves and their young from predators, and their territories from rivals. Many herbivores live and graze in the open, and so need to be able to defend themselves, or run fast and escape their predators.

WEAPONS

Carnivorous and scavenging animals are naturally equipped with weapons, such as teeth and claws, that can also be used for defence. Peaceful herbivores need extra protection, and many have armoured heads equipped with horns, antlers, or spikes. In mammals, these are usually specialized teeth, such as the tusks of elephants, or are made from the horny material that comprises nails and hooves. Dolphins simply use their tough snout as a battering ram to defend themselves against sharks. In contrast, hoofed mammals often lash out with their hind legs, and tropical surgeonfishes protect themselves with knifelike spines on either side of the tail. Some fishes even employ electric weapons to stun and deter their predators.

TYPES OF WEAPON

Hooves and limbs Hard hooves and feet, adaptations for running quickly, also make excellent blunt weapons with which to kick a predator, or even a rival in the case of zebras. Ostriches have powerful leg muscles and feet that can dismember a lion. Mantis shrimps use their claws to punch with a force that can break bones and are so fast that the victim does not have time to react.

Claws Strong claws are used to dig burrows or root out food, but are just as effective when used to protect young, such as bear cubs, against predators. Large predators, such as tigers, use their claws primarily to bring down prey, but may need to defend their territories and young from rivals of their own species. When not in use, most cats can sheath their claws.

Projectiles Apart from humans, only a few primates are known to pick up and throw objects at their enemies. However, many animals, such as the fireworm (right), have irritant hairs or loose spines that break off in the mouths or limbs of predators that try to attack them. These can then be re-grown. Some tarantulas can spray irritant hairs like a rain of miniature arrows.

Venomous spines Many marine animals live sedentary lives on the sea bed and are protected by venomous spines. These are generally used for defence and are only brought into play if the animal is attacked or trodden on. Venomous fishes such as weever fishes (right) and stonefishes have sharp spines in their dorsal and pectoral fins that act like hypodermic needles.

Teeth and fangs While most animals capable of biting will do so in self-defence, some have modified teeth or jaws that make formidable weapons. Some snakes use hollow fangs to inject venom, and blue-ringed octopuses do the same using a beaklike structure in the mouth. Working together, even small ants can drive a predator away from their nest by repeatedly biting it.

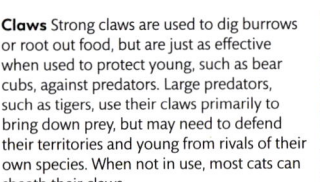

WEAPONS AND THREATS 245

protective carapace

Protective box A heavy suit of armour is an effective defence, but severely limits movement. This tortoise would be helpless against fire or flood.

External skeleton Many crustaceans are well protected by their hard external armour, but become vulnerable whenever they shed their shell to allow for growth. The animal must hide during these periods.

ARMOUR

Armour is widely used by slow-moving animals, such as tortoises, that are unable to escape from fast predators. In the oceans, many animals are completely immobile and physical protection is essential for their survival. Reptiles and bony fishes already have protective scales, and many species from these groups have developed their scales into body armour. However, this is often at the expense of mobility. Boxfishes, for example, are well-protected but are clumsy swimmers. Crustaceans and molluscs have external shells, which can be reinforced to make protective boxes. The oceans provide them with minerals to build up their shells, but this is less easy in mineral-deficient fresh water.

limpet shell

Mobile homes Limpets and other marine snails can rapidly retreat inside their shells, clamping down or shutting the door when danger threatens.

Amphibians that are toxic or distasteful often exhibit striking colorations. Predators soon learn to avoid these warning signs.

SURVIVAL STRATEGIES

Animals with no armour or weapons need either an effective means of escape or a way of intimidating and deterring their predators. Poison, stings, or bristles are good defences, and have been adopted by many otherwise defenceless amphibians and insects. This only works for individual animals if their predators learn to avoid eating them. Bright warning colours (usually yellow, red, or orange against a contrasting dark background) can be seen easily by vertebrates with colour vision, and are used by animals as diverse as shield bugs, poison frogs, and sea snakes. Unusual behaviour is also an effective survival strategy. Pretending to be dead, for example, will put off predators that are used to hunting live prey.

Feigning death is a tactic used by the Virginia opossum when it is threatened by a predator.

With nowhere else to hide, open-water fishes often leap above the surface to escape aquatic predators.

Against all odds, small animals will sometimes stand up to larger ones, especially when they are protecting their young.

Starfish
Limb regeneration
GENUS *Fromia* **SIZE** About 8–10 cm (3¼–4 in) in diameter **DISTRIBUTION** Coral reefs in Indo-Pacific

If a starfish loses one or more arms to a predator, the missing appendages simply grow back. Most species of starfish have this amazing ability. A few starfish go a stage further: if their body is torn apart, a single arm can regenerate the entire central disc as well as the other arms. Usually the arm needs to include part of the disc to do this. During the initial stage of this process, the starfish is called a "comet form".

original arm

Comet form This regenerating starfish has grown five new arms instead of four. They will eventually grow to the same size as the surviving arm.

Leopard sea cucumber
Sticky tentacles
SPECIES *Bohadschia argus* **SIZE** Up to 30 cm (12 in) **DISTRIBUTION** Shallow water reefs and rubble areas in Indo-Pacific

A predator grasping this apparently succulent animal is in for a surprise. Sea cucumbers are sluggish relatives of sea urchins. They lack urchins' sharp spines but are far from defenceless. If threatened, a sea cucumber ejects a mass of sticky tentacles, called Cuvierian tubules, out of its anus. Once in the water the tubules, part of the respiratory apparatus, lengthen, writhe around, and deter the attacker, or even entangle it completely.

Rear assault These ejected tubules will eventually break down and disintegrate. The cucumber grows new ones internally and repairs its ruptured rectum.

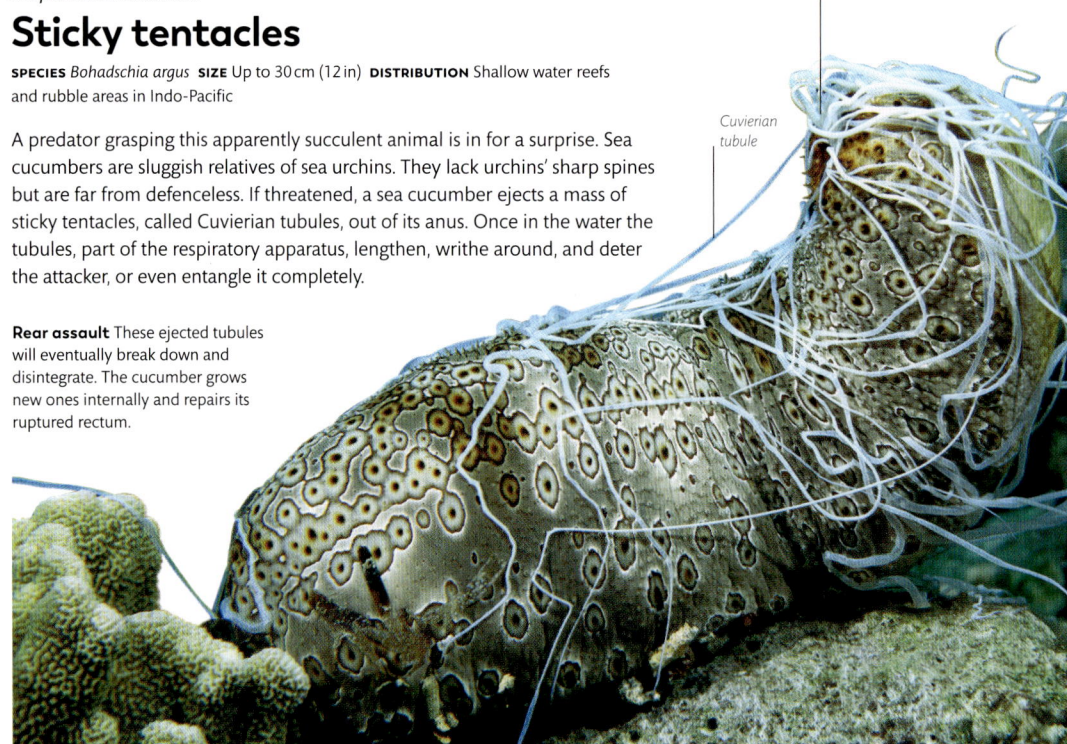

anus

Cuvierian tubule

Christmas tree worm
Swift retreat
SPECIES *Spirobranchus giganteus* **SIZE** About 2 cm (¾ in) (visible part) **DISTRIBUTION** Inside corals in shallow tropical waters worldwide

The combination of lightning-fast reactions and a stonelike outer case enable this marine worm to survive attack by predators. Only its twin spirals of feeding tentacles, resembling miniature Christmas trees, are visible to the outside world. The rest of the worm is hidden inside a tough tube made of calcium carbonate, which the animal secretes around its body. For extra protection, it embeds itself in the head of a large coral. The Christmas tree worm is extremely sensitive to water vibrations and shadows, and if approached, withdraws almost instantaneously into its tube. When the danger has passed, the worm slowly extends its tentacles once more and resumes feeding. The colour of the tentacles is highly variable. A single coral head may be peppered with yellow, blue, purple, red, orange, and brown individuals. Related fan worms and feather duster worms also build their parchment tubes in coral and rock crevices for protection.

Open tube With its tentacles extended, the worm can collect plankton and organic matter from the water. The tentacles are also used to extract oxygen from the water.

Closed tube When the worm retreats into its tube, the entrance is neatly plugged by its operculum (a lidlike structure). This one is not quite closed.

Venus comb murex
Spiny deterrent
SPECIES *Murex pecten* **SIZE** Up to 13 cm (5 in) **DISTRIBUTION** Muddy sea beds in the Indo-Pacific

A starfish or any other predator that wants to eat a Venus comb murex will have great difficulty getting anywhere near the shell entrance. Similarly, even fishes with strong jaws have trouble crushing the shell of this marine snail, and after its death the ferociously spiny shell remains a hazard to unwary bare-footed bathers. However, some scientists speculate that the real function of the spines is not defence, but to support the animal when it is moving over soft sediment.

Spiky procession The muscular foot and head tentacles of this murex are visible through its shell spines as it creeps forwards (from left to right).

Blue-ringed octopus
Flashing blue

GENUS *Hapalochlaena* **SIZE** 10–24 cm (4–9½ in)
DISTRIBUTION Shallow reefs, rocky areas, and coasts in tropical west Pacific and Indian Ocean

The blue rings on this small octopus warn of its venomous nature. When it is agitated, these markings pulse a vivid and iridescent blue, but when it is resting the blue is more subdued. The animal's saliva contains a dangerous venom, made by stored bacteria, that is uses to subdue or kill its prey, but it is equally effective against potential predators. Those that survive soon learn to leave the octopus alone. There are three or four similar species in the same genus, all called blue-ringed octopus, and all are venomous.

Potent venom Blue-ringed octopuses are not aggressive and only bite if touched or cornered. Most people survive a bite, especially if given prompt medical treatment.

1 The number of milligrams of blue-ringed octopus venom needed to kill a human.

Day octopus
Cloud of ink

SPECIES *Octopus cyanea* **SIZE** Body 16 cm (6½ in); arms about 80 cm (31 in) **DISTRIBUTION** Shallow reefs in Indo-Pacific, from eastern Africa to Hawaiian Islands

The day octopus is most unusual among octopuses in that, as its name suggests, it is active during the day. When it comes out of its hiding places to hunt, it usually sidles along with precise movements, using its arms. If frightened, it uses a very different method. An individual attacked by a predator discharges a jet of water and shoots off backwards with its arms trailing. At the same time, it releases a cloud of dark ink and changes colour. The predator is either distracted by the ink cloud or enveloped in it, and the octopus can swim away behind it. Squid have a similar escape response but also use jet propulsion for normal swimming. In both octopuses and squid, water is sucked into the mantle cavity and squirted out of a tubelike funnel when the mantle contracts. This is normally a rather gentle movement linked with the animal's respiration.

Octopus ink, made in a special sac and released into the funnel, is a concentrated form of melanin, the pigment that colours and protects human skin. Other chemicals in the ink temporarily dull a predator's sense of smell and irritate its eyes. Some deep-sea squid release a burst of luminous material to dazzle their predators in the dark ocean depths.

Vanishing act This day octopus is seen leaving a trail of black ink as it jets away over a shallow reef in Hawaii. Day octopuses often excavate their own lairs in reefs or the rubble around them.

Similar species The giant Pacific octopus, shown here moving rapidly away from the camera, has few predators but may still release a cloud of ink if threatened.

1,000 The number of times one day octopus was seen to change its skin patterns during a seven-hour period.

European hornet
Venom injection
SPECIES *Vespa crabro* **SIZE** 2–3.5 cm (¾–1½ in)
DISTRIBUTION Woodland in Europe and temperate Asia, from Britain eastwards to Japan; introduced to North America

Like other wasps, the European hornet is protected by a powerful sting. It is the largest European social wasp, with a sting big enough to deter predatory lizards and birds. The sting is also used as a weapon to kill other insects for food. For humans, a single sting is usually painful but not harmful. However, a hornet killed near its nest releases alarm pheromones to summon other hornets, which can result in multiple stings. Multiple stings of the Asian giant hornet can be lethal to humans.

Smooth sting This hornet is being held so that its sting is visible. The sting has no barbs, so it can be withdrawn and used again many times.

Tarantula spiders
Hair spray
FAMILY Theraphosidae **SIZE** Legspan up to 28 cm (11 in)
DISTRIBUTION In trees and ground burrows worldwide, especially in subtropical and tropical regions

Although these large spiders deliver a venomous bite, it is used to subdue prey and seldom to defend themselves. The primary defence for many tarantulas is the ability to release a spray of irritant hairs known as urticating hairs. These grow on the spider's abdomen, which is known as the opisthosoma. The hairs come off easily and a spider releases them by rubbing its legs over the opisthosoma. The hairs have barbs and can be mildly to intensely irritating, depending on where they land. If inhaled by small mammals they can even be fatal. Some species of tarantula also incorporate urticating hairs into and around their burrow entrance. This acts as a territorial signal and may deter animals trying to dig them out. Even the egg cocoon, guarded by the female, may have hairs woven into it. Tarantulas in parts of the world other than the Americas do not have urticating hairs.

Defensive spray A large bird-eating spider in the genus *Pamphobeteus* uses its legs to flick a hail of tiny barbed hairs at an attacker. The irritant hairs are extremely unpleasant.

Protective partnership Pictured here are the shrimp *Alpheus randalli* and the shrimp goby *Amblyeleotris yanoi*, in Indonesia.

Snapping shrimps and shrimp gobies
Keeping watch
The relationship between snapping shrimps and shrimp gobies provides a rare example of cooperative defence. These species must work together to survive. The shrimp digs a burrow as a shelter, working like a tiny bulldozer. It has poor eyesight and, engrossed in its work, relies on the shrimp goby to keep watch. The shrimp communicates with the goby using its long tentacles, and can tell from the fish's tail movements when danger threatens.

Leach's hermit crab
Mutual defence
SPECIES *Pagurus prideaux* **SIZE** About 7 cm (2¾ in)
DISTRIBUTION Shallow sediment in northeast Atlantic, from Norway to Mediterranean and Cape Verde Islands

Hermit crabs live in empty mollusc shells, which they use to protect their soft abdomen. Leach's hermit crab gains extra protection by living in association with the cloak anemone, *Calliactis palliata*. The anemone wraps its wide base around the crab's shell and body, hanging its own body and tentacles downwards. If a predator attacks, the anemone discharges stinging threads called acontia. In return for this protective role, the anemone can eat the remains of the crab's meals. As the crab grows so does the anemone, which means it never has to perform the risky manoeuvre of finding a larger shell home.

At ease The anemone's red-spotted base envelops the hermit crab's body and its shell home. The anemone grows at the same rate as the crab, so the pair never need to part.

Under attack The anemone has fired its stinging threads in defence. Its soft body is tucked safely under the hermit crab's legs.

Arabian fat-tailed scorpion
Sting in the tail
SPECIES *Androctonus crassicauda* **SIZE** Up to 10 cm (4 in)
DISTRIBUTION Under stones and debris and in walls in arid areas of Turkey and Middle East

A scorpion's sting is effectively its second line of defence, the first being to run away and hide. If cornered, a fat-tailed scorpion will raise its tail up into the classic curved posture ready to strike with its pointed sting. This species and others in its genus are among the most venomous, injecting a neurotoxin that is sometimes fatal in humans, although an antivenin is available. It catches its prey with its strong claws, and may also use the sting to subdue larger prey.

metasoma (tail)

sting

chela (claw)

Superpowered sting The thickness of the tail and the relatively small claws indicate that this scorpion has a very potent sting.

WEAPONS AND THREATS **249**

African foam grasshopper
Toxic foam
SPECIES *Dictyophorus cuisinieri* **SIZE** 5–7 cm (2–2 ¾ in)
DISTRIBUTION Sub-Saharan Africa

This small African grasshopper defends itself against predators by secreting foul-tasting yellow foam. The secretion, derived from the insect's blood, is turned to foam by mixing it with air taken in through the spiracles (breathing holes) on the thorax. The foam's unpleasant active ingredient comes from plants eaten by the grasshopper. The yellow colour of the foam probably acts as a warning that this species is not good to eat. It belongs to a family called gaudy grasshoppers, because many species are very brightly coloured.

African bombardier beetle
Chemical cocktail
SPECIES *Stenaptinus insignis* **SIZE** 1–2 cm (⅜–¾ in) **DISTRIBUTION** On the ground in tropical areas of Africa

When under attack, this beetle gains time by spraying a potent cocktail of boiling chemicals from its rear end. Ants, one of the beetle's chief enemies, are small and mobile and can bite it almost anywhere. However, the beetle can aim its potentially lethal spray like the nozzle of an aerosol can. The chemicals react and heat up as they are mixed, just before spraying, and released oxygen acts as a propellant. The beetle gets drenched in the process, but scientists have not yet established how it is able to survive.

Aiming the spray The beetle aims its spray with great accuracy, directing it with movable reflectors. It can hit targets all around its body. The temperature of the spray is close to 100°C (212°F).

ANATOMY **CHEMICAL REACTION**

This scanning electron micrograph shows the slit through which the beetle sprays its deterrent. The spray is made from two sets of chemicals stored in separate glands. Hydroquinones and hydrogen peroxide from one gland are mixed with enzymes from the other. The enzymes release oxygen from the hydrogen peroxide and this in turn oxidizes the hydroquinones, making them active.

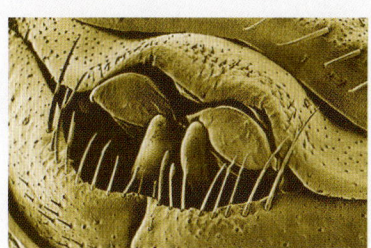

Plunging to safety Curled up into a ball, this catshark nearly dropped straight down onto the photographer below. The species is sometimes called the shy shark because of this behaviour. Its leopardlike spots are not visible from the underside.

Leopard catshark
Sinking escape
SPECIES *Poroderma pantherinum* **SIZE** Up to 85 cm (33 in)
DISTRIBUTION Rocky reefs and kelp forests on and near to the sea bed off coast of South Africa

When danger threatens, leopard catsharks have an unusual response – they bury their heads in their fins. If a catshark feels threatened when swimming in the open, it curls round, covers its eyes and snout with its tail, and sinks rapidly down to the sea bed. This behaviour not only protects the catshark's vulnerable head but is also confusing to a predator. With its eyes hidden and its shape changed, it no longer looks like a fish and is effectively pretending to be dead. Unlike many sharks, catsharks are very flexible and, when lying on the sea bed, will readily whip round and bite if grabbed by the tail. Their escape strategy may have evolved from this ability. Catsharks are slow swimmers, and are vulnerable to faster-swimming predators such as larger sharks and seals. The patterning on their back helps to camouflage them when they are resting but is of less help when hunting.

Atlantic flying fish
Airborne escape
SPECIES *Cheilopogon melanurus* **SIZE** Up to 32 cm (12½ in) **DISTRIBUTION** Warm coastal surface waters in Atlantic Ocean

In warmer parts of the Atlantic, sailors are often treated to the sight of flying fishes skimming the waves in front of their boat. Vibrations from boats and ships scare the fishes into thinking that they are being chased by a large predator, such as a dolphin or tuna, and this triggers their defensive manoeuvre. With powerful beats of its tail, a flying fish launches itself into the air, spreads its large pectoral fins wide, and glides for many metres before dropping back into the sea. It will sometimes perform a series of leaps and glides to ensure that the predator is left confused as to where its prey has gone. During its "flight", the fish maintains momentum by vibrating the long lower half of its tail from side to side in the water below, leaving ripples on the surface.

Similar species While the Atlantic flying fish has both pectoral and pelvic fins expanded for flight, two-wing flying fishes (left) use only their pectoral fins. The so-called flying gurnard (above) cannot fly but, instead, may use its greatly enlarged, colourful pectoral fins to startle predators when lying on the sea bed.

Adaptations for flight The pectoral fins of the Atlantic flying fish are almost as long as its body, and expand and stiffen while in the air. The fish's powerful tail fin may sweep from side to side in the water up to 50 times a second.

Mobile spines The venomous fin spines of the common lionfish are individually mobile, so can be directed at a predator to avert attack.

Common lionfish
Warning spines
SPECIES *Pterois volitans* **SIZE** Up to 38 cm (15 in) **DISTRIBUTION** Tropical waters of eastern Indian Ocean and western Pacific

In contrast to the reef stonefish (see p.272), to which it is closely related, the common lionfish is protected not by camouflage, but by vivid warning colours. Its fins and body are boldy striped in contrasting shades of red and white to indicate that it is best left alone. Its pectoral and dorsal fins are highly modified, consisting of long, venomous spines. These can inflict a very painful sting, though this is generally not life-threatening to humans. Emerging at dusk, the lionfish will often stand its ground in the face of large predators and divers alike. The fish swims slowly, confident of its spiny protection. Its pectoral fins have the secondary function of helping to corral fish against the reef to be snapped up.

Black-spotted porcupinefish
Rapid inflation

SPECIES *Diodon hystrix* **SIZE** Up to 90 cm (35 in) **DISTRIBUTION** Coral reefs in tropical and subtropical Atlantic, Pacific, and Indian oceans

When a black-spotted porcupinefish is attacked, it sucks water into its expandable stomach, erects its spines, and turns itself into a prickly ball several times its original size. Few predators will tackle it in this state. As soon as the danger has passed, the water is regurgitated and the fish deflates back down to its normal size and shape. Although this is a very effective defence, these fishes prefer to hide during the day and are often found in holes and under rocky overhangs. Inflation uses up energy and it is better to avoid confrontation. When caught, they will often inflate at the surface, gulping in air instead of water. There are about 20 species of porcupinefishes, variously called porcupinefishes, balloonfishes, and burrfishes, which share the same defence mechanisms. The closely related pufferfishes have a further deterrent – a lethal poison in their internal organs, called tetrodotoxin. Porcupinefish eggs float in the plankton, and the young fishes develop their spines 10 days after hatching. When small, they fall prey to many pelagic fish.

ANATOMY **EXPANDING STOMACH**
The stomach of porcupinefishes has evolved into a water reservoir, and is no longer used for digestion. Instead, food is absorbed in the intestine. The lining of the porcupinefish stomach is highly folded, but as the fish sucks in water, the folds stretch out like the pleats in a skirt until the stomach expands to nearly 100 times its original size to accommodate its huge load. The rest of the fish's organs are pushed upwards against the vertebral column, which itself curves dramatically into a bow shape. The two-layered skin has a thin, elastic outer layer and a thicker, pleated inner layer. When the pleats are stretched out, the skin is stiff enough to hold the spines rigid, and the fish takes on its unpalatable bristling appearance.

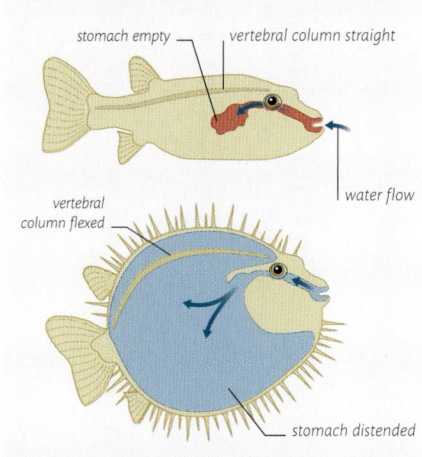

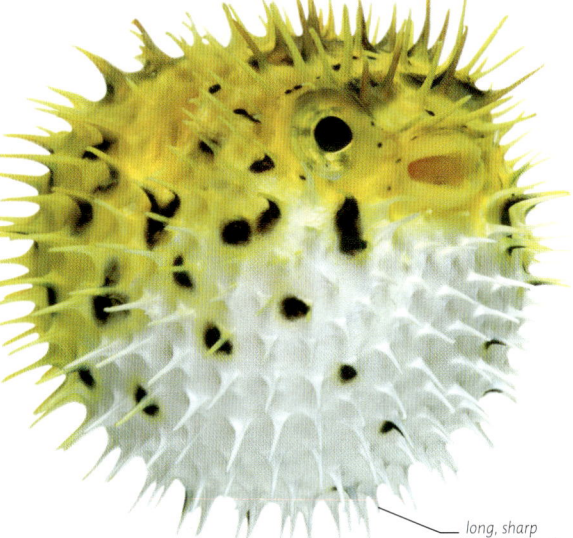

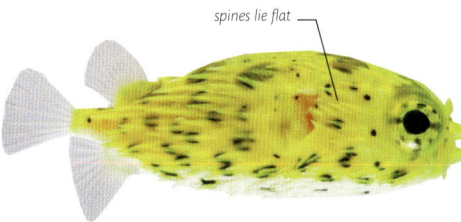

Before and after expansion When a possible threat presents itself, a black-spotted porcupinefish will hover quietly with its spines laid flat (below). It will inflate (right) only as a last resort. With its stomach full of water and all its spines erect, the fish now resembles a spiky football and can hardly move.

Bleeker's parrotfish
Mucus tent

SPECIES *Chlorurus bleekeri* **SIZE** Up to 50 cm (19½ in) **DISTRIBUTION** Coral reefs in eastern Indian Ocean and western Pacific

Many coral-reef fishes, including Bleeker's parrotfish, sleep tucked away in coral and rock crevices to avoid nocturnal predators. But this species greatly improves its chances of escaping detection by making itself a sleeping bag of slime. At night the parrotfish finds a suitable crevice and envelops itself in a cocoon of mucus. It can take half an hour to secrete the mucus from special glands in its opercular cavity, the protective chamber containing the gills. On contact with the water, the mucus swells and becomes gelatinous. Many night predators hunt by smell, and the cocoon stops them from detecting the parrotfish's scent. Parasitic isopods and other blood-sucking crustaceans are also prevented from latching on whilst the parrotfish sleeps.

Slimy covering Safe in its mucus cocoon at night, this Bleeker's parrotfish seems to be unaware of the grey-faced moray eel next to it, although the one seen here is too small to harm the parrotfish.

Safe quarters An anemonefish keeps watch from the safety of its tentacled home, ready to wriggle further in if danger threatens

False clown anemonefish
Protective partnership

SPECIES *Amphiprion ocellaris* **SIZE** 9–11 cm (3½–4½ in) **DISTRIBUTION** In giant anemones in eastern Indian Ocean and western Pacific

A false clown anemonefish will spend its entire life in or near to a giant stinging anemone, even sleeping on it at night. Few predators risk reaching into the anemone's tentacles to attack the fish. Other fishes of a similar size would be stung and devoured by the anemone, but the anemonefish is protected by an invisible cloak of slime. The anemonefish must aquire its immunity by gently touching a new host, and so gaining anemone proteins in its mucus. The anemone then no longer notices the fish. In return, the anemonefish is thought to deter tentacle-nibbling butterflyfish, and clean up debris.

252 DEFENCE

Anderson's spiny crocodile newt
Hard to handle

SPECIES *Echinotriton andersoni* **SIZE** 13–16 cm (5–6½ in)
DISTRIBUTION Damp forest, grassland, and marshes in Japan; believed extinct elsewhere

Anderson's spiny crocodile newt's defence is to be very difficult to handle. Except during the breeding season, it is secretive and spends most of its time hidden under leaf litter or in vegetation. If it does encounter a predator, it flattens its body, curls up, and raises its head and tail to deter its attacker. If this does not work and the crocodile newt is picked up, it is likely to be dropped again because it has sharp spines along both flanks. These are the tips of its long ribs, which stick out of its skin at the end of lumpy warts. Unfortunately, this does not deter humans – the species is endangered by collection for the pet trade.

Spiky character This is one of several newts or salamanders that use the protruding ends of their sharp ribs to deter attackers.

>>01

>>02

>>03

>>04

Stop, drop, arch, and roll **>>01** On realizing that it has been seen by a potential predator, the yellow-bellied toad's first reaction is to stop still. **>>02** Next, it drops down and flattens its body as much as possible against the ground. **>>03** The toad quickly raises its head and arches its back to expose its bright underbelly, while lifting up its legs, which are also patterned on the undersides. **>>04** As the toad remains under threat, it now rolls over onto its back with its legs tucked in, exposing the whole of its brightly coloured belly.

Yellow-bellied toad
Flipping over

SPECIES *Bombina variegata* **SIZE** 3.5–5.5 cm (1½–2¼ in)
DISTRIBUTION Well-vegetated habitats in hills and mountains of central and southern Europe

The small size of this toad means that it is especially vulnerable to predators such as birds and snakes. Often it manages to avoid being seen by simply squatting down and keeping still. Its brown, warty back helps it to blend in, particularly in muddy areas. But if this does not work and a predator sees through its camouflage, the toad has another line of defence. Like many other toads, it secretes toxic, foul-tasting chemicals through its skin. The fiery coloration on its belly is an advertisement that it tastes unpleasant, and when threatened the toad shows it off through a series of defensive postures called the unken reflex, an example of stereotyped behaviour. First the toad flattens its body, then it arches up into a bent-back position and raises its legs to reveal as much colour as possible. If necessary, it rolls right over onto its back to display the full splendour of its bright orange belly. In this position a predator might not even recognize the toad as a food item and will clearly see the warning coloration.

Cane toad
Deadly secretion

SPECIES *Rhinella marina* **SIZE** Up to 23 cm (9 in)
DISTRIBUTION Native to terrestrial habitats in Central and South America; introduced to Australia and USA

This huge amphibian, one of the largest toads in the world, protects itself by exuding a highly toxic secretion onto its skin from parotoid glands behind its eyes. When threatened, the toad turns so that the glands face the attacker, as the toxin can be sprayed a short distance. In its native countries, predators have adapted to tolerate the toxin to some extent, but in Australia and Hawaii many pet dogs have died after picking toads up and humans have become ill.

HUMAN IMPACT **INTRODUCED PEST**
The cane toad was introduced into Australia in 1935 in order to control beetle pests in sugar-cane plantations. It ignored the pests but was happy to eat almost anything else. The toad is itself now a serious pest, has spread widely in Queensland and further afield, and occurs in enormous numbers in some areas. It has a significant adverse effect on endemic wildlife.

Slimy poison The white secretion on the shoulders of this toad is a heart poison that can kill its predators.

Defensive stand-off Confronted by a grass snake, one of its main predators, this common toad has inflated its body to make itself look bigger and has taken up a typical defensive posture.

European common toad
Inflated posture

SPECIES *Bufo bufo* **SIZE** Up to 15 cm (6 in) **DISTRIBUTION** Wide variety of habitats in Europe, but absent from Ireland

A rapid getaway is not an option for this toad, which is rather a sluggish amphibian, although it can run for short distances and will sometimes jump. So if it encounters a fast-moving predator, it tries to intimidate its enemy by pretending to be much larger than it really is. When confronted, the toad raises itself up as high as possible on its legs and gulps in air to puff itself up.

Poisonous touch The vivid orange-red skin on the back of this splash-backed poison frog (*Adelphobates galactonotus*) is a clear indication of its toxicity. Most predators will keep well away.

Poison frogs
Toxic skin
FAMILY Dendrobatidae **SIZE** 1–5 cm (⅜–2 in)
DISTRIBUTION Rainforest in Central America and northern South America

Almost all poison frogs (also known as poison dart frogs) are vividly coloured to advertise their extreme toxicity and unpleasant taste. They have evolved their highly poisonous skin secretions because many of their predators, especially snakes and spiders, are resistant to mild toxins. Different types of toxins are produced by different groups of poison frogs. The most toxic species will hunt for their insect prey out in the open during the day, confident that predators will heed their warning coloration. Some of the least toxic poison frogs have become mimics, with similar colours to the most poisonous species, and tend to be left alone too. All poison frogs are very agile, so their final line of defence is to leap out of harm's way.

Rainbow colours Poison frogs exhibit an astonishing variety of aposematic (warning) colours and patterns, even within the same species. Pictured are *Dendrobates tinctorius* (below) and a black-spotted red form of *Oophaga pumilio* (left).

HUMAN IMPACT **DIET-DEPENDENT POISON**

Indigenous people in Colombia use the deadly secretions from poison frogs to tip their blowpipe darts. One species, the golden poison frog (below), is preferred because it has the most potent poison of all. A single frog contains enough poison to kill 10 people, and simply rubbing a blowpipe dart over the frog's back will tip the weapon with sufficient poison to kill a monkey. The frogs obtain their poison, batrachtoxin, from eating certain species of beetle. In New Guinea, batrachtoxin has been found in the feathers of birds that eat beetles, and this behaviour may yet be discovered in other species too.

254 DEFENCE

False glare As well as exposing its huge false eyes, this frog has puffed itself up to reinforce the illusion that it is a formidable animal.

Four-eyed frog
Backwards glance
SPECIES *Physalaemus nattereri* **SIZE** 3–4 cm (1¼–1½ in)
DISTRIBUTION Grassland and wetland in Brazil, Paraguay, and Bolivia

Turning your back on your enemy may seem a foolish thing to do but this is how the four-eyed frog scares off would-be predators. On the rear of its body there are two large, round black markings. When the frog is squatting down, these are hidden by its thighs, but if it raises itself up on its hind legs, a predator is faced with what looks like a pair of staring eyes. Defensive eyespots are also found in a heronlike bird called the sunbittern (see p.259), but are more common in insects than among vertebrates.

Eastern box turtle
Trap door
SPECIES *Terrapene carolina* **SIZE** 10–21 cm (4–8½ in)
DISTRIBUTION In moist forest and wet grassland in eastern half of USA

The slow-moving box turtle spends most of its life out in the open, searching for slugs, earthworms, and mushrooms, so is highly visible to predators. It has evolved a suit of armour for protection. Its tough, heavy shell has a domed upper part called the carapace and a flattened underside known as the plastron. When danger threatens, the turtle quickly pulls its head, neck, and feet back inside its shell. The plastron has a movable hinge, which enables it to close tightly against the carapace to hide the head and limbs.

Active foraging A box turtle is a sitting target when in the open, but extends its head out of its shell to check for danger.

Tight seal When the turtle retreats in its shell, its plastron shuts like a trap door.

Decoy tail The shed tail thrashes around for some time to distract the predator from the skink.

African blue-tailed skink
Tail shedding
SPECIES *Trachylepis quinquetaeniata* **SIZE** Up to 25 cm (10 in)
DISTRIBUTION Widespread in moist, shaded habitats in Africa

If a predator finds an African blue-tailed skink, it will probably try to grab the lizard by its tail, attracted by the bright blue colour. A few seconds later, the predator will be left with just a writhing tail, while the skink has scuttled away to safety. The skink purposely sheds its tail by a process called autotomy, as a distraction strategy to help it escape. The tail regrows but will be shorter and, in most cases, the same colour as the rest of the body. This means that tail shedding is a last-ditch resort for the skink. Similar species of skink occur in the Americas and Oceania, and tail shedding is also found in other lizards.

Texas horned lizard
Shooting blood
SPECIES *Phrynosoma cornutum* **SIZE** 6–18 cm (2¼–7 in)
DISTRIBUTION Open, dry areas and grassland throughout central parts of southern USA

The unappetizing, toadlike appearance and sharp spines of this American lizard will themselves deter more timid predators. However, if it is approached by a sufficiently determined attacker, this lizard can squirt a stream of blood at its enemy from a pore near the corner of each eye. The blood contains a foul-tasting chemical that is guaranteed to repel most wolves, coyotes, and domestic dogs and can be squirted for up to 1.5 m (5 ft). Due to pressure from human collectors, this unique lizard is now a threatened species.

Horny head The horned lizard's mottled camouflage is its first line of defence, while the large "crown of thorns" on its head make it a tricky meal for most predators.

Bloody defence The Texas horned lizard can squirt up to one-third of the blood in its body without suffering any adverse effects. However, it has a limited ability to aim the stream of blood at its tormentor.

Armadillo lizard
Nose to tail
SPECIES *Ouroborus cataphractus* **SIZE** 16–25 cm (6½–10 in)
DISTRIBUTION Dry scrub and rocky desert areas in southern Africa

Like its mammalian namesake, the armadillo lizard rolls up into a ball when it feels threatened. It holds on to its tail with its strong jaws and is almost impossible to unravel. Its body, legs, and tail are covered in rows of tough, square scales with spiny edges that spring up as it curls round. When in this position, it does not look like a living animal and is usually left alone. The lizard's elaborate defence mechanism allows it to lead a sluggish lifestyle in open terrain.

erect spines

Ring of spines By rolling into a spiny ball, the armadillo lizard is able to protect its soft underparts and deter predators such as birds of prey.

WEAPONS AND THREATS 255

Flying lizard
Sudden launch
SPECIES *Draco volans* **SIZE** 20–30 cm (8–12 in)
DISTRIBUTION Tropical forest in southern India and Southeast Asia, including Borneo and Philippines

Like many of their relatives, these forest-dwelling lizards spend much of their time clinging to tree trunks and keeping perfectly still. Their cryptic coloration makes them difficult to spot, and they rely on this camouflage and their agility in climbing trees for protection. However, the lizards can also turn head down, launch themselves into the air, and glide to another tree. Large, loose flaps of skin on each side of the body extend out as temporary wings, supported by the animals' long ribs. The ribs are movable and can be stretched out sideways. Strong claws help the lizards to land safely up to 8 m (26 ft) away. Gliding is frequently used to move from tree to tree and is not just an escape system.

long tail

Winglike skin extension, known as a patagia

Bright wings The beautiful scarlet coloration of the flying lizard's "wings" normally remains hidden to avoid attracting the attention of predators. It is only revealed in flight and when the male is displaying to one of his females.

Deadly aim A Mozambique spitting cobra can rear up to at least one-third of its length and so can easily spit into the eyes of most predators. The venom can cause severe damage and may even result in blindness.

Mozambique spitting cobra
Venomous spray
SPECIES *Naja mossambica* **SIZE** 0.9–1.4 m (35–54 in)
DISTRIBUTION Savanna, woodland, and clearings in southeast Africa

Cobras are highly venomous snakes, and the Mozambique spitting cobra is especially threatening because of its ability to discharge venom over a distance of up to 3 m (9¾ ft). The snake raises itself off the ground and flattens its neck to appear larger, then takes careful aim at a predator's head, especially the eyes. The venom is highly toxic but the cobra rarely bites, most predators being warned off by its aggressive posture and spitting prowess. It is, however, very nervous and, because of its volatile temperament, is considered one of the most dangerous snakes in Africa. Its bite is potentially fatal but effective first-aid treatment is usually successful. If the cobra is continually molested it will often play dead, in the hope that its tormentor will lose interest.

Western diamondback rattlesnake
Warning sound
SPECIES *Crotalus atrox* **SIZE** 0.8–2.1 m (2½–7 ft)
DISTRIBUTION Dry rocky and desert habitats in southwestern USA and Mexico

The loud, rattling noise made by a rattlesnake when under threat is one of the most famous warning sounds in nature. Usually a western diamondback rattlesnake will stand its ground rather than slither away. Expending energy on an unnecessary strike is counter-productive, and so the snake warns of its presence by rattling the specially adapted tip of its tail. It will also lift its head up and stare at the intruder to look as intimidating as possible. If the warning is heeded and the snake is left alone, it normally then retreats to a safer hiding place. A rattlesnake bite is potentially fatal to humans but the snake attacks people only in self-defence. It uses its venom to kill birds and rodents for food.

Double warning Both the posture and the erect, shaking rattle of this western diamondback rattlesnake warn that the snake will strike if approached too closely.

ANATOMY **RATTLE RINGS**

A rattlesnake's rattle consists of a series of hollow, interlocking rings made from modified scales, each one overlapping the next. When the tail is shaken, the rings rattle against each other, making the characteristic noise. The size and sound of the rattle increase with the age of the snake because a new rattle segment is added at each moult.

youngest scales are at base of tail

DEFENCE

Sailfin lizards
Walking on water

SPECIES *Hydrosaurus* species **SIZE** Up to 90 cm (35 in) **DISTRIBUTION** Forests of Indonesia, Borneo, Philippines, and Papua New Guinea

The sailfin lizards of Southeast Asia live along rainforest riverbanks and are almost as much at home in water as out of it. They settle on branches overhanging water, both at night and during the day when basking. When disturbed, for example by a predator such as a snake, they instantly drop off their perches and run or swim away over the water.

Small insects, such as pond skaters, are well known for their ability to glide across water, using the surface tension to support themselves, but it would seem impossible for a relatively bulky vertebrate to do the same. This is, of course, true, but although sailfin lizards cannot truly be said to walk on water, they can nevertheless sprint over the surface for a short distance to escape from predators. They must run fast and slap their feet down hard to create an upward force. Rather like a person riding a bicycle, they will fall unless they maintain their forward momentum. They are good swimmers, too, aided by their flattened tails. Male sailfin lizards have a high crest of skin along the base of the tail; the crest is kept flat while the animal is running but erected during territorial displays. The "sail" may also be used to help catch the sun, so the lizard can warm up in the early morning and after swimming.

The sailfin lizards are the largest members of the Agamidae family. They share their remarkable ability to run on water with several other lizards, including the basilisks of the genus *Basiliscus*, which live in Central and South America. Basilisk lizards never stray far from water (like sailfin lizards, they settle on branches overhanging water). Young ones can run further over the water than adults, but often they simply swim away. They can stay underwater for several minutes – unconfirmed reports say two hours – sufficient time for a predator to lose interest. Their predators are numerous and include raptors, snakes, larger lizards, and even fishes.

Similar species Basilisk lizards, sometimes known as Jesus lizards, are well adapted for escaping from their predators over water. They have unusually large hind feet, and each toe is edged with skin flaps. These are kept folded when the lizard runs on land but are unfurled when it runs over water. Pictured here are the striped basilisk (below, left) and plumed basilisk (below, right).

CASE STUDY THE MECHANICS OF WALKING ON WATER

High-speed photography of the plumed basilisk lizard in laboratory tanks has shown that each stride over the water has three phases. During the "slap", the lizard's foot goes straight down, displacing water and creating a pocket of air around the foot; the upward force generated by the slap is enough to keep the lizard's body above the surface while it kicks its leg backwards. This is the "stroke", which gives forward momentum. Finally comes the "recovery" phase, when the foot is pulled up and out of the water ready for the next step. As long as it runs fast enough, the lizard stays upright by pushing sideways with its feet when necessary. This basilisk is able to reach speeds of up to 10 kph (6 mph) when running on water; juvenile lizards can cover greater distances before sinking.

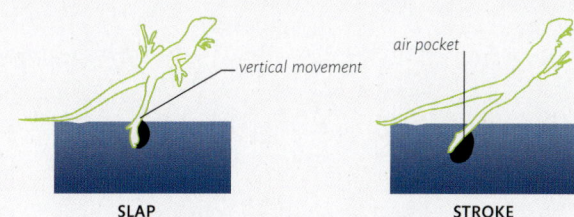

SLAP — vertical movement

STROKE — air pocket

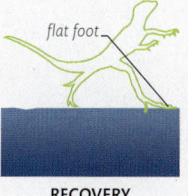

RECOVERY — flat foot

Sprint to safety Looking like an Olympic sprinter, this sailfin lizard leaves a trail of water droplets as it races over the water surface. Here, the action has been captured in a studio, but in the wild a lizard fleeing from a predator would eventually run out of momentum, drop into the water, and swim the rest of the way.

limp tongue

Feigning death This grass snake has turned on its back, opened its mouth, and allowed its tongue to hang out in an effort to convince its tormentor that it is dead.

Grass snake
Playing dead

SPECIES *Natrix helvetica* **SIZE** Up to 1.2 m (4 ft); rarely up to 2 m (6½ ft)
DISTRIBUTION Damp places, woods, fields, and gardens throughout Europe

A grass snake will sometimes play dead if it feels threatened or is cornered by an enemy. Predators such as birds of prey, used to catching live victims, may then ignore the snake entirely or be startled if it suddenly comes to life again. If an animal does pick up the snake, it releases a foul-smelling liquid from its cloacal gland. The grass snake is shy and non-venomous, and rarely bites, but under pressure it may hiss and feign a strike with its mouth closed.

Red-cockaded woodpecker
Sticky defence

SPECIES *Leuconotopicus borealis* **SIZE** 20–23 cm (8–9 in) **DISTRIBUTION** Mature, open pine forest in southeast USA; often in fire-burned clearings

Most woodpeckers nest in holes in trees, where their eggs and young are safe from many predators. However, their nest holes remain vulnerable to attacks by snakes, which can easily slither inside. To defeat marauding rat snakes, the red-cockaded woodpecker has developed a form of defensive behaviour that puts its nest out of bounds. It drills small holes beside the entrance to its nest so that treacly sap exudes from the bark and congeals around the hole. It re-drills the holes regularly to ensure sap continues to flow. Sometimes the woodpecker also strips away bark, leaving a smooth surface that is difficult for snakes to grip.

The red-cockaded woodpecker nests only in living pine trees. The resin clings to a snake's scales and inhibits its climb.

Nest protection Mounds of adhesive paste formed by exuded tree resin can be seen caked around the nest hole of this red-cockaded woodpecker.

Water dikkop
Living dangerously

SPECIES *Burhinus vermiculatus* **SIZE** 40 cm (15½ in)
DISTRIBUTION Lakes, rivers, and wetland, especially with sandy banks, throughout southern Africa

Choosing a nest site on a riverbank near to that of a Nile crocodile might seem unwise, but this is exactly what a wading bird called the water dikkop is suspected of doing. The usual explanation for this behaviour is that the bird gains added protection for its nest, because the female crocodile will aggressively chase away any potential nest thieves, such as lizards, that get too close to her stretch of bank. The water dikkop is a nocturnal bird. It keeps quiet and hides during the day but at night it calls loudly and its alarm calls are believed to alert its crocodile companion to the approach of predators. When threatened, the bird also lowers its head, opens its wings, and runs towards the attacker. Scientists have questioned whether the water dikkop's choice of nest site is a deliberate defensive strategy or simply the result of chance, as dikkops and crocodiles both need sandy banks to nest and might end up as neighbours anyway. However, there are other cases of birds nesting near dangerous animals – for example, in Central and South America oropendolas hang their stockinglike nests from branches beside wasp or bee nests for protection. In the Arctic, geese whose chicks may be prey for the snowy owl will nonetheless choose to nest close to owl nests, and benefit from the predators' vigilance (although the tactic is riskier in years when the owls' preferred prey, lemmings, are scarce).

Lizard intruder This monitor lizard is distracted by the threat display of a water dikkop, a mainly nocturnal bird that has been stirred into action to save its nest on the riverbank. Monitor lizards prefer to steal eggs from unattended nests, and this means the dikkop has a good chance of repelling its larger enemy.

WEAPONS AND THREATS 259

Deadly kick The massive leg muscles that give ostriches such a powerful kick are clearly visible in this photograph of two rival males running at speed. In contrast to hoofed animals, ostriches can kick only forwards.

Common ostrich
Leg power
SPECIES *Struthio camelus* **SIZE** 1.7–2.8 m (5½–9¼ ft) high
DISTRIBUTION Savanna, scub, grassland, and semi-desert in Africa; introduced to Australia

Ostrich legs and feet are designed for speed, and this bird comfortably outruns most predators. When alarmed, it can sprint at 30 kph (19 mph) and even produce brief spurts of up to 70 kph (45 mph). Its top speed is only just short of the cheetah's, the fastest land animal of all (see p.203). If an ostrich is caught, it kicks out with its legs and can deliver a blow powerful enough to kill or badly injure its pursuer. The ostrich will also use posture to intimidate a rival or a predator. Its wings, useless for flying, are spread out and the feathers fluffed up, and the bird hisses loudly.

Sunbittern
Shock tactics
SPECIES *Eurypyga helias* **SIZE** 45 cm (17½ in)
DISTRIBUTION Well-vegetated riverbanks, ponds, and wooded streams in Central and South America

This normally secretive bird of swampy forests and wetlands uses visual shock tactics to startle would-be predators. The sunbittern is difficult to spot when quietly hunting fish and frogs with its wings folded. It creeps slowly along the water's edge, where its camouflaged plumage helps it to blend in with the shadows. But the bird has a surprise hidden on the flight feathers of its wings. If it is challenged by a predator, especially when nesting, the sunbittern opens its wings to reveal a pair of false eyes. The eyespots are red and black on a yellow background, so create a dramatic impact. Confronted by an apparently huge animal with glaring eyes, most predators retreat. Eyespots are uncommon in birds, but many small owls have false eye markings on the backs of their heads, discouraging predators from attacking them from behind.

Alarming plumage
A sunbittern displays the colourful false eyes on its fully spread wings in an attempt to protect its nesting site. This stunning display is also used in courtship.

Temminck's pangolin
Armour plating

SPECIES *Smutsia temminckii* **SIZE** 40–70 cm (15½–28 in)
DISTRIBUTION Open forest and grassland in central and southern Africa

While most mammals are covered in fur or hair, the Cape pangolin is sheathed in a protective layer of close-fitting overlapping scales, although its soft belly has hairs. Its scales extend over its head almost to the end of its snout and the entire length of its tail and legs. The pangolin lives on the ground and digs a burrow where it can rest and give birth. If threatened, it runs for its burrow, but if it cannot get there in time, it curls up into a large, scaly ball that is virtually impossible to unroll. Hyenas are among the very few predators able to penetrate these defences. They have bone-crunching jaws, and full-grown adults can bite through the scales, especially of a young pangolin. As a last resort, a cornered pangolin may rear up and squirt a foul liquid at its attacker using special glands at the rear of its body.

Tough scales In close-up, pangolin scales look rather like the surface of a mature pine cone. The scales can be raised so that their sharp edges point outwards, making it more difficult for a predator to penetrate the armour.

Brazilian three-banded armadillo
Ball of scales

SPECIES *Tolypeutes tricinctus* **SIZE** 30–37 cm (12–14½ in)
DISTRIBUTION Wooded savanna and dry, open country in central and northeast Brazil

Armadillos are famous for being able to roll their heavily armoured body into a tight, impenetrable ball – a highly effective form of defence. In fact, only two of the world's species of armadillo, the Brazilian and southern three-banded armadillos, can do this. The other species have defensive armour as a deterrent, but if attacked they still prefer to flee to cover or quickly dig a burrow to get out of danger. Three-banded armadillos are different: by rolling into a ball and completely encasing themselves in their own shell, they can safely stay out in the open to confront the threat. Armadillo armour consists of bony, interlocking plates that form a rigid case over the shoulders and hips. In between are rows of plates alternating with thick skin, which open out like an accordion so that the animal has some flexibility. Armadillos belong to the order Cingulata, meaning "belted animals".

Rolling into a ball >>01 A captive Brazilian three-banded armadillo walks across the ground, showing its distinctive shuffling gait, low to the ground with few soft parts of its body exposed. >>02 As the animal starts to roll up, its tough skin stretches out between three bands of bony plates in the middle of its back. >>03 The armadillo tucks in its head and limbs, and its hip and shoulder plates meet. >>04 Finally the armadillo's armoured head and tail join, completing its transformation into a scaly ball.

Cape porcupine
Flesh-piercing quills

SPECIES *Hystrix africaeaustralis* **SIZE** 50 cm (19½ in)
DISTRIBUTION Variety of vegetated habitats in Africa, especially south of Sahara in rocky hills

Porcupines normally carry their quills lying flat along the back, but if danger threatens they erect a prickly defence of sharp, stout quills and longer spines. With their defences up, they look much larger and more threatening. If a predator, such as a hyena, lion, or leopard, is brave or inexperienced enough to corner one, the porcupine shakes its hollow tail spines to produce a snakelike rattle as a warning signal. In extreme cases, the opponent receives a face full of spines as the porcupine runs backwards into it. The nasty wounds may get infected, so a porcupine strike can prove fatal.

Spiny rodent Porcupines have a spiny defence that is unique among rodents. The quills are shed easily, but contrary to the widely held belief, porcupines cannot flick them in the face of their enemies.

Dangerous game The defence put up by these Cape porcupines may not be sufficient against this young Kalahari lion. He will eventually learn to flip a porcupine over to expose its soft underside and kill it.

WEAPONS AND THREATS **261**

Powerful display Standing up on his hind legs, and beating his chest, this silverback is showing his opponent how large and powerful he is. If the intruder does not leave, he may charge and knock the intruder over.

Mountain gorilla
Chest beating
SPECIES *Gorilla beringei beringei* **SIZE** 1.3–1.9 m (4¼–6¼ ft) **DISTRIBUTION** Montane forest on borders of Rwanda, Uganda, and Democratic Republic of the Congo

The dominant male of each gorilla group, known as a silverback for his silvery grey mantle, has to protect his family from the threat of wandering male rivals or humans, the only predator of adult gorillas. He mainly deals with such threats by intimidating his opponents with an aggressive display, tearing wildly at the surrounding vegetation and beating his chest. This is combined with a terrifying series of loud hoots ending in a roar, and usually averts a violent encounter.

California ground squirrel
Hot tail
SPECIES *Otospermophilus beecheyi* **SIZE** Body 30–50 cm (12–19½ in); tail 13–23 cm (5–9 in) **DISTRIBUTION** On ground and in burrows in most habitats in western USA

If caught out in the open by a rattlesnake, one of its main predators, the California ground squirrel raises its bushy tail and shakes it like a flag. But first the squirrel pumps more blood into its 15 cm (6 in) long tail to warm it up by several degrees. Rattlesnakes hunt by detecting infrared radiation (heat), using special pits in their face. The sudden rush of extra heat and tail wagging may make the squirrel seem much larger and more intimidating to the snake.

Warning in the tail The California ground squirrel tries to ward off snakes by throwing earth and tail-waving. If all else fails, it uses a rush of blood to warm its tail – an unusual form of thermal defence that seems to be effective against rattlesnakes.

Serval
Hostile posture

SPECIES *Felis serval* **SIZE** 70–100 cm (28–40 in) **DISTRIBUTION** Widespread but uncommon in open habitats of sub-Saharan Africa

Only a little larger than a pet cat, the serval does not have the advantage of impressive strength or size, and so, it must rely on posture to dissuade potential predators from attacking. If cornered, this small, slim cat raises its hackles, arches its back, flattens its ears, raises and fluffs its tail, and spits and snarls. If this does not work, the serval may make slashing movements with its forepaws to encourage its aggressor to back off. The serval lives alone, marking out a hunting territory of several square kilometres by spraying urine, leaving piles of faeces in prominent locations, and rubbing its scent glands against bushes and rocks. Other servals read these signs and stay away, with the result that individuals rarely meet outside the breeding season. In this way dangerous fights between servals are avoided.

Spitting rage This serval has adopted a defensive posture and is hissing and snarling. The small size of this hunter means that it could itself easily be attacked by a larger cat or hyena.

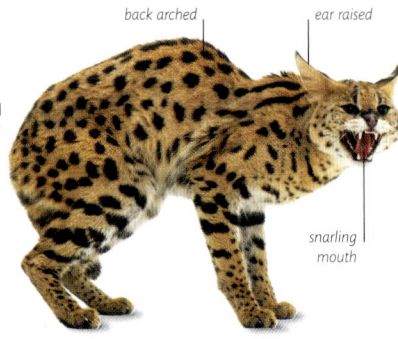

back arched *ear raised* *snarling mouth*

Striped skunk
Offensive odour

SPECIES *Mephitis mephitis* **SIZE** Body 33–45 cm (13–17½ in); tail 18–25 cm (7–10 in)
DISTRIBUTION Widespread throughout much of Canada and USA

Being relatively small, a skunk might seem a straightforward target to a young and inexperienced predator. However, the bold black-and-white stripes of this solitary animal warn that it is extremely unpleasant to deal with. If approached too closely, it squirts a noxious-smelling fluid from glands on either side of the anus, with great accuracy, for a distance of up to 4 m (13 ft). The skunk gives advance warning of its intent by pattering its front feet and lifting up its conspicuous white tail, but if these gestures are ignored it will quickly spray its attacker.

Stink bomb One spray from a skunk's anal glands is usually sufficient to teach a predator to leave well alone next time. Here, an inquisitive red fox cub advances closer than its more experienced parents.

Indian rhinoceros
Tough hide

SPECIES *Rhinoceros unicornis* **SIZE** Up to 4 m (13 ft)
DISTRIBUTION Tall, swampy grass and forest areas close to rivers in northern India, Nepal, and Pakistan

With its huge size, tough, layered skin, and curved horn, the Indian rhinoceros has few natural predators. Tigers will attack young rhinoceroses, but heavy folds of skin at the shoulder joints, flanks, and neck give armour-plated protection from smaller predators. The thick skin also helps to protect individuals during occasional aggressive interactions between males. In spite of its ungainly bulk, an Indian rhinoceros can charge fast and furiously, and rival males will clash horns. Large adults are quite capable of killing an unwary tiger or a person. They have poor eyesight and may not notice a predator approaching upwind, but their hearing is excellent. Keeping their protective skin in good condition is essential, and these rhinoceroses spend the hottest parts of the day wallowing in shallow pools. This keeps the skin supple and offers relief from biting insects, as well as preventing sunburn. In deeper water, these animals are excellent swimmers. Mostly, Indian rhinoceroses lead solitary lives, but loose groups form at favourite wallows. Unless numbers are high, newcomers to the wallow are usually tolerated after an exchange of grunts.

Unfortunately, neither its hide, nor its horn, are any protection against guns, and people are the Indian rhinoceros's main enemy. In Nepal, rhinoceros populations are protected by armed rangers, but the high price fetched for the animal's horn means that poaching and illegal trading still go on. The rhinoceroses are also disliked by farmers as they trample and feed on crops. Habitat loss has driven them to search for food in cultivated areas.

Rare breeding The Indian rhinoceros is critically endangered in the wild. This baby, closely following its mother, was born in San Diego Zoo in 2006 as part of an endangered species breeding programme. Females have only one baby about every three years.

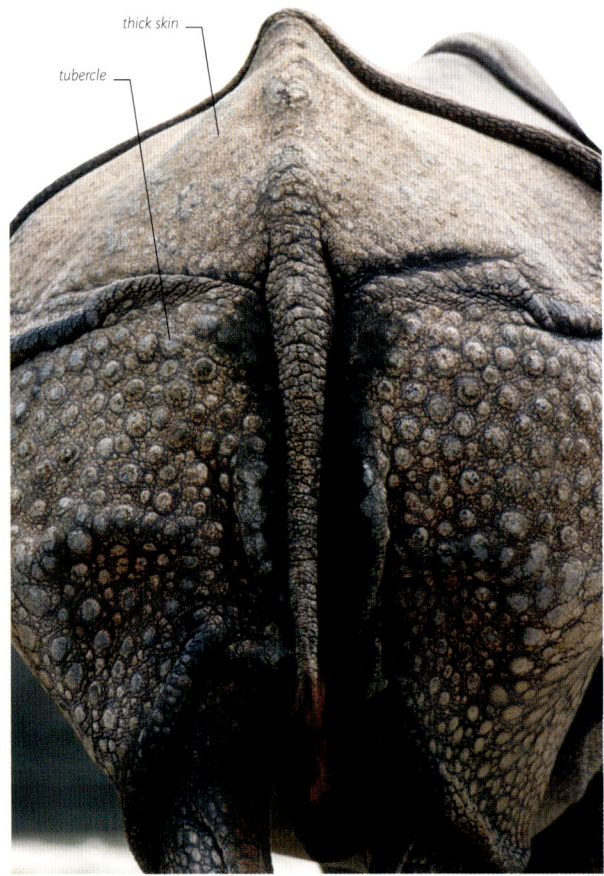

thick skin *tubercle*

Thick skin The legs and buttocks of this Indian rhinoceros are protected by thick skin, which is covered in large, hard tubercles. Heavy folds of skin hang down like a protective skirt, and even the tail is armoured.

African bush elephant
Angry charge

SPECIES *Loxodonta africana* **SIZE** 5.5–7.5 m (18–24½ ft)
DISTRIBUTION Open grassland, scrub, woodland, and occasionally desert, in Africa south of the Sahara

The sight of a charging African elephant moving at full speed is terrifying, though in healthy elephant societies (see panel, right) it is a rare spectacle. Elephants are by nature peaceable, living and travelling in family groups led by a mature female. Their size alone deters most predators, and young elephants are closely guarded by the extended family. However, a close approach by a pack of lions, or even unwary tourists, may not be tolerated, especially by a mother protecting her baby. When enraged, an elephant will face its tormentor, raise its head and tusks, and bring its huge ears forward and out. If this threat display does not work, the elephant may charge, holding its trunk high and trumpeting loudly. Usually, the elephant stops or turns aside, but if very distressed it will gore and trample anything in its path. Bull elephants live on their own or in young bachelor groups and can be dangerous when in musth. A bull in musth has high levels of reproductive hormones, especially testosterone, in his blood, which makes him aggressive and more likely to charge.

Charging bull Disturbed while cooling off in a water hole, this bull elephant has brought his ears forward and is swinging his trunk to appear as large and intimidating as possible.

HUMAN **FRACTURED FAMILIES**

Decades of poaching for the ivory trade, culling, and habitat loss seem to be having a destabilizing effect on elephant society in some areas. Unprovoked attacks by elephants on crops, people, and even other wildlife such as rhinoceroses, were once rare but appear to be on the increase. This "elephant rage" may result from long-term stress. The death of a matriarch often leaves her group floundering, while orphaned elephants (right) have no mother from which to learn. Careful management is required if elephants and growing human populations are to coexist.

Camouflage and deception

Camouflage and deception are mainly used by animals whose predators employ good eyesight to spot their prey. This survival strategy is especially common in insects, small mammals, and reptiles preyed on by sharp-eyed birds, and in sea bed fishes that are hunted by larger fishes. Predators may also use camouflage when stalking prey. Camouflage is ineffective against predators that use smell or echolocation to track down their prey.

TYPES OF CAMOUFLAGE

Camouflage is achieved through the colour, pattern, and texture of the outer covering of an animal. At its simplest, the animal matches the background colour of its habitat, and so can remain completely still. Disruptive patterning (for example, stripes) breaks up the shape of the animal, so the predator sees patches of colour that do not appear to relate to its prey. In open water, fishes and aquatic mammals use countershading. Their dark backs and pale bellies merge with their surroundings, whether viewed from above or below.

Disruptive pattern Zebra stripes help to hide individuals in tall grasses on Africa's plains. A herd of zebras will appear to an approaching lion as a mass of moving lines.

Stalking aid Dappled with sunlight, a Bengal tiger hunting in long grass is so well disguised by its stripes that it can stalk unsuspecting prey to within a few metres.

Home from home This allied cowrie closely resembles its sea-fan home in shape, colour, and texture. It remains well hidden as it feeds on its host.

Well hidden This green crested lizard is coloured to match its leafy home in the canopy of a Southeast Asian rainforest, hiding it from predatory arboreal snakes. Its camouflage also allows the lizard to stalk unsuspecting grasshoppers, its favourite prey.

PERMANENT CAMOUFLAGE

Permanent camouflage is most effective in animals that remain in the same habitat most or all of the time. Extreme examples of this are animals that use other animals as a living home, often feeding on their hosts as well. In tropical oceans, sea fans and sea whips are host to a wide variety of small molluscs, shrimps, and fishes that live on their branches and are coloured, patterned, and even shaped like their hosts. Pygmy seahorses (see p.273) and spindle cowries are just two sea-fan inhabitants that are covered in tubercles resembling the polyps, or feeding heads, of their living home. Their disguise is so good that many of these creatures have only been discovered after scientists have collected the sea fans on which they were living. Many leaf-eating insects adopt a similar strategy.

brown colour matches that of a dead leaf

closed wings are leaf-shaped

Disappearing trick With closed wings, this Indian leafwing butterfly resembles a brown leaf. The upper surfaces of its wings are bright orange.

CAMOUFLAGE ON DEMAND

Animals that move frequently need a flexible system of camouflage. This is often provided by an ability to change colour and sometimes texture to suit the animal's surroundings and is best developed in cephalopods, such as the common octopus, crustaceans, lizards, and fishes. The animal's skin contains layers of cells called chromatophores, which are filled with coloured pigment. The pigment can be dispersed or concentrated to vary the skin tone. Cuttlefish, for example, display almost-instantaneous colour changes, which are controlled by the nervous system. In contrast, the slow colour change seen in isopods, such as the isopod *Idotea*, is controlled by hormones.

>>01   >>02

Coming out of hiding >>01 This Parson's chameleon is mostly green in colour and blends in well against its background. >>02 The chameleon now has a reddish hue. Changes in colour and pattern are often used to attract mates and to intimidate territorial rivals.

MIMICRY

An edible species living alongside a similar-looking poisonous or distasteful species can gain protection by mimicry. Animals as diverse as insects, snakes, and coral reef fishes have evolved this type of behaviour, which is known as Batesian mimicry. For the harmless species to benefit, it must live in the same habitat and have the same predators as the poisonous species. Predators that have learned to avoid the poisonous species will also avoid the edible mimic. Many insects make full use of this type of mimicry. Palatable caterpillars and butterflies mimic poisonous species, while many harmless fly species resemble stinging wasps and bees. In most cases of Batesian mimicry, the model is far more common than the mimic. Too many mimics might result in predators learning by trial and error that the mimic is not poisonous after all. Another form of mimicry is Müllerian mimicry, in which several inedible species evolve to resemble each other. Over time, predators learn to avoid the patterns these animals exhibit.

Imitated The large tiger is a poisonous butterfly that lives in rainforests in Central and South America. Birds rarely make the mistake of eating it as they quickly learn that it tastes nasty. This protects the butterfly when it is feeding out in the open.

Imitator The pattern of the butterfly *Papilio zagreus* is sufficiently similar to the large tiger butterfly for birds to avoid it, even though it is perfectly edible. This mimicry allows the harmless butterfly to feed in safety.

imitation markings

COMMUNITY CAMOUFLAGE

Sometimes, different species adopt the same camouflage to suit a specific environment. For example, floating rafts of Sargassum seaweed support a whole community of animals that drift along with the weed in the Atlantic Ocean. Within the confines of their seaweed home, kept afloat by numerous gas-filled bladders, the animal residents must live, mate, feed, and avoid being eaten. There are no holes to hide in and no rocks to slip underneath, so most of the inhabitants are camouflaged to resemble the seaweed in colour and shape. As a result, animals as varied as prawns, crabs, and fishes all wear the same colours, and are mostly yellow and brown. The speckled colour and slow movements of a filefish, for instance, help it blend in as it hunts for worms. Irregular seaweedlike skin flaps on the body and fins of the Sargassum fish make an excellent disguise.

A golden seahorse sways in the water with the seaweed, clinging on with its prehensile tail.

A swimming crab scavenges for scraps. Even its eyes look like small Sargassum seaweed bladders.

CASE STUDY **SLEEPING SAFELY**

The mottled coloration of this great grey owl renders it virtually invisible against the rough grey and brown bark of the coniferous tree on which it is perching. When hunting, this owl will often use a tree branch to sit and wait, scanning the ground for small rodent prey. It hunts through forests across northern North America, Europe, and Asia, usually early in the morning and in the late afternoon, but also at night. The great grey owl is one of the largest owls in the world and it has few enemies. Even so, its camouflage allows it to doze in safety during the day, hidden from predators such as martens and wolverines, which will readily snatch inexperienced and clumsy juveniles.

Spider crabs
Masters of disguise
FAMILY Majidae **SIZE** 0.8–50 cm (⁵⁄₁₆–19½ in)
DISTRIBUTION Worldwide, except in polar oceans and seas

Spider crabs are slow-moving and have weak pincers and so make easy pickings for predatory fishes. To protect themselves, many of the smaller species gather tiny anemones or pieces of seaweed, sponge, or other living material and attach these to their shell as camouflage. The material is hooked onto spines and hairs like Velcro, and in some cases it may grow and flourish on the shell, providing a highly effective living disguise. This defensive behaviour is found in spider crab species worldwide, but is especially prevalent on coral reefs where predatory fishes abound. Crab species that exhibit this behaviour are often called decorator crabs.

Sea fan cover This delicate spider crab from the Red Sea is using a piece of broken sea fan to conceal its tell-tale outline. Some species of spider crab attach noxious organisms such as stinging sea anemones or bad-tasting sponges to deter predators.

Katydids
Tree imitators
FAMILY Tettigoniidae **SIZE** Up to 13 cm (5 in)
DISTRIBUTION Most species tropical, but family occurs in lush vegetation worldwide

Katydids are also known as bush crickets. Like the true crickets (to which they are related), katydids sing to establish their territories and attract mates. Male katydids sing by stridulation (rubbing special areas of their forewings over one another). Females recognize the unique song made by males of their own species. However, the katydids' courtship system carries a risk because the sound can also attract the attention of predators, including birds, snakes, and small mammals. As a defence, most katydids are therefore coloured green or brown to match the vegetation on which they live. Many have also evolved specialist camouflage. Depending on where they live and feed, different species imitate lichen, bark, twigs, or leaves. They are not adept fliers, so if a predator approaches they prefer to stop singing, remain still, and rely on their camouflage for protection. Some return to the same branch or twig after foraging and chew out depressions to help mould themselves to their background.

Lichen mimic As long as it remains still, this lichen-mimic katydid can remain hidden. It lives in the humid cloud forests of Ecuador's mountains, where lichens abound.

Invisible cloak Even at close range this lichen-mimic katydid from Sabah, Borneo, is very difficult to spot. The colour and texture of its body and wing covers exactly match the lichen-covered tree trunk.

Forest stick A stick insect hangs motionless under a branch in a Madagascan forest. Its hook-like feet help it to cling on tightly. If attacked, the insect may drop limply to the ground like a broken twig.

Giant stick insect
Twig impersonation
SPECIES Phasma gigas **SIZE** Up to 19 cm (7½ in)
DISTRIBUTION Trees and bushes in Papua New Guinea

Also known as walking sticks, these huge insects bear a remarkable resemblance to twigs and are extremely hard to spot, even from close up. They depend on good camouflage as they move awkwardly and cannot easily fly away from danger – the females in particular have very small wings. Some related species have no wings at all. Giant stick insects are expert at keeping still and position themselves to look like just another twig of the plant on which they are feeding. By swaying from side to side, they give the illusion of plant stems moving in a gentle breeze. Like most stick insects, the female of this species lays fertile eggs without mating (parthenogenesis) and so does not even have to move to find a mate.

CAMOUFLAGE AND DECEPTION 267

Leaf insects
Leaf mimics
FAMILY Phyllidae **SIZE** 3–11 cm (1¼–4½ in)
DISTRIBUTION Well-vegetated areas in Mauritius, Seychelles, Southeast Asia, and Australasia

These insects belong to the same group as stick insects, but have flattened bodies that look like leaves and are much rarer. Their flattened lateral extensions make them look like a small leaf or leaf segment and the abdomen is expanded. The disguise may be completed by false midribs, veins, or disease spots and holes. The phyllids also have small eyes and short antennae to avoid giving themselves away. They can rock gently back and forth, to mimic the wind blowing on a leaf. If their disguise fails, some phyllids can produce sounds by rubbing thickened segments of their antennae together to scare their attacker.

Wingless female A female phyllid leaf insect crawls over a leaf. Her body is massively flattened but she lacks wings and cannot fly away from predators. By contrast, male phyllids have fully functional wings.

Thorn bugs
False thorns
SPECIES *Umbonia crassicornis* **SIZE** 0.5–1.5 cm (³⁄₁₆–½ in)
DISTRIBUTION Forest, orchards, and gardens worldwide, mainly in warmer regions

Female thorn bugs have a greatly enlarged, unusually shaped thorax that make them perfect plant mimics. They spend their lives sucking sap from trees, especially fruit trees and ornamental varieties. Such a lifestyle might be expected to leave them vulnerable to attack, but thorn bugs in fact have few predators because of their thorny camouflage and unpleasant taste. The nymphs hatch from eggs laid under tree bark, stay in a group, and are guarded by the mother. Their disguise is not as effective as the adults', and so protection is vital. If a predatory insect approaches, the nymphs vibrate in unison, and this warning signal soon passes to the mother. Safe in her armour, she fans her wings and kicks out with her hind legs to deter the attacker.

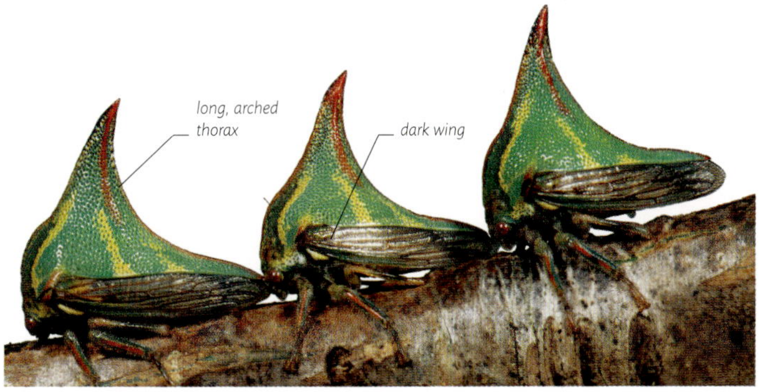

Line of thorns Neatly lined up along a twig, these three female thorn bugs in Costa Rica closely resemble sharp thorns. Male thorn bugs have a quite different disguise and resemble flat-topped twigs.

long, arched thorax
dark wing

Spicebush swallowtail
Fake snake
SPECIES *Papilio troilus* **SIZE** About 6 cm (2¼ in) (caterpillar)
DISTRIBUTION On spicebush and similar aromatic plants in eastern North America (from southern Canada south to Florida and Texas)

To avoid being eaten by birds, the caterpillar of this swallowtail butterfly has several lines of defence. It uses silk to fold a leaf in half to make a daytime shelter, emerging only at night to feed and moult. But if its shelter is pulled apart, the larva turns to shock tactics to frighten away its attacker. Raising its swollen front end and tucking its head down suddenly gives it the appearance of a green snake or tree frog, confusing its potential predator.

Mature larva This head-on view shows the caterpillar's false eyespots, which have two smaller white spots that give the illusion of reflections in rounded eyes.

Disappearing trick By rapidly modifying its appearance, this cuttlefish is able to blend in with its surroundings and escape the gaze of potential predators.

Broadclub cuttlefish
Rapid transformation

SPECIES *Sepia latimanus* **SIZE** Up to 50 cm (19½ in)
DISTRIBUTION Shallow reefs and rocky areas throughout Indian Ocean and tropical western Pacific

This large cuttlefish is well known for its amazing ability to change colour instantaneously. It can also modify the texture of its skin, which may start completely smooth but quickly becomes covered in little bumps and tall projections known as papillae. This double ability provides the cuttlefish with excellent camouflage in a wide range of marine habitats. When the cuttlefish is among seaweed it will also hold its tentacles up and crinkle the edges to resemble the algae's waving fronds.

The broadclub cuttlefish can perform sudden, unexpected alterations in colour to confuse and startle a potential predator. Different colour patterns are also used to communicate intentions during courtship and territorial defence – for example, a striped zebra pattern is commonly worn when males challenge each other. When hunting, broadclub cuttlefish put on a light show of rapidly changing colours that may mesmerize shrimps and other prey while keeping their own predators at bay. These kaleidoscopic visual displays are controlled by layers of specialized pigment cells, known as chromatophores (see panel, opposite), in the cuttlefish's skin. Those nearest the surface contain yellow pigments, those in the middle layer are orange and red, and the deepest ones appear brown to black. By rapidly expanding and contracting the chromatophores under nervous control, the cuttlefish can produce a huge variety of skin patterns. The deep skin layers also contain iridophores, special cells that reflect light and modify the colour.

Background match Chromatophores are also found in cuttlefish's close relatives, octopuses and squid. This day octopus has changed colour to blend in with the background coral. It can achieve a good match in an instant due to the complex layers of chromatophores in its skin.

Iridescence The intense luminous coloration of this tiny bobtail squid is caused by cells in the lower layer of the squid's skin, called iridophores, which reflect polarized light.

ANATOMY HOW SKIN COLOUR CHANGES

Each chromatophore cell is like a stretchy bag of pigment to which a ring of muscle fibres is attached. When these muscles are relaxed, the chromatophore remains as a tiny sphere with its surface in folds like a deflated balloon. When they contract, the muscles pull the sphere and flatten it into a plate shape, allowing coloured pigment granules to spread out. The contracted chromatophore cell in the diagram shows the pigment densely packed. Nerves control the muscle fibres, which can alter the pigment dispersal in a flash.

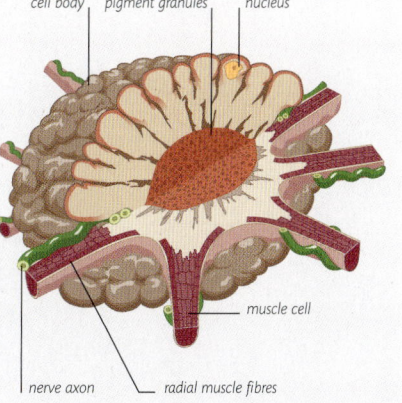

Chromatophore movement Viewed with polarizing filters, this squid skin shows chromatophores contracted (far right) and expanded (right) over underlying iridophores.

CONTRACTED

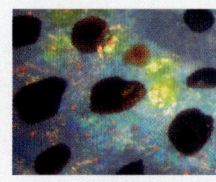

EXPANDED

Leafy disguise Resting on a forest floor, this large moth is almost invisible, thanks to its very effective camouflage. Its brown colour matches that of the dead leaves, while dark patches on its wings mimic holes chewed out of the leaves by other insects. By remaining completely still during the daytime, the moth avoids detection by predators.

Razorfish
Spine mimic
SPECIES *Aeoliscus strigatus* **SIZE** Up to 15 cm (6 in)
DISTRIBUTION Reefs in tropical Indian Ocean and western Pacific

This relative of seahorses and pipefishes is hidden from predators by a combination of its body shape and swimming style. It swims in synchronized groups in a vertical position, the fish seeming to glide sideways through the water. Each fish is enclosed in transparent bony plates that form a sharp ridge along the belly. As the fishes cannot flex their bodies, they swim using precise fin movements. This behaviour helps to disguise the fact that they are edible fishes, especially when they group tightly together. A favourite hiding place is among the long spines of sea urchins, where they hang vertically. Here, the dark stripe along their body helps foster the illusion. Their prickly urchin shelter also helps to deter predators. Other hiding places include the branches of corals and sea whips.

Facing the sea bed A compact group of razorfishes hovers over the sea floor. The fishes swim head-down while searching for minute planktonic crustaceans with their long, tubular snouts.

Transparent fish A glass catfish is remarkably difficult to see – even when these fishes gather in large shoals, they are almost invisible. After death the fish loses much of its transparency, becoming milky white in colour.

Glass catfish
Almost invisible
SPECIES *Kryptopterus bicirrhis* **SIZE** 7–15 cm (2¾–6 in)
DISTRIBUTION Rivers, streams, and floodplains in Southeast Asia

The glass catfish, or ghost fish, looks like a swimming skeleton as it is almost entirely transparent. This provides excellent camouflage, even in crystal-clear water, and seen from head-on the flattened fish merges into the background so effectively that it is virtually impossible to spot. Its transparency is a result of thin skin, oily flesh, and a lack of pigmentation. The glass catfish clusters in groups, with the fishes lining up at an oblique angle to the water surface so that they are less visible. Like all catfishes, they have sensory barbels around the mouth to help detect prey, mainly aquatic insects and smaller fishes.

Reef stonefish
Blending in
SPECIES *Synanceia verrucosa* **SIZE** Up to 40 cm (15½ in)
DISTRIBUTION Tropical waters of Red Sea, Indian Ocean, and western Pacific

This sea-bed resident has perhaps the best camouflage of any marine fish, enabling it to be an expert at ambushing prey. Its squat shape and knobbly skin help it to merge into its surroundings as it lies in wait for prey. To enhance its disguise, the reef stonefish can remain motionless for hours or days at a time. Small tufts of seaweed may grow on its skin, and sediment settles on its back. A row of 12–14 venomous spines on the back of this fish gives it a defence of last-resort against its own predators.

Similar species Whilst stonefish venom can be deadly to people, closely related scorpionfish have a less potent but nevertheless painful sting. If spotted, some species display brightly coloured pectoral fins as a warning.

venomous spine

colour of warty skin varies with background

Living rock Due to its thickset head and rough, mottled skin the reef stonefish looks more like a rock on the sea bed than a live fish.

Clearwing moths
False flag
GENUS *Synanthedon* **SIZE** 1–3 cm (⅜–1¼ in)
DISTRIBUTION Trees and bushes in Europe and North America

Camouflage is not effective for active insects such as clearwing moths, which feed on nectar, juice, and other plant liquids, and need to move around constantly between food sources, making them highly visible. Instead, many species gain protection by a resemblance to stinging or unpalatable insects, especially hornets, wasps, and bees. This is an example of Batesian mimicry and is found in many different groups of animals. Predators that recognize these insects by their contrasting black and yellow stripes will avoid them.

False stripes Clearwing moths that mimic wasps and bees have no need to hide and so can be active during daytime. They often rest in the open, confident in the protection afforded by their coloration.

Coral lookalike This pygmy seahorse was spotted by a sharp-eyed photographer off Mabul Island, East Sabah, Malaysia. The species also comes in yellow with orange tubercles to match its particular sea fan home species.

Similar species An Australian relative of seahorses, the leafy seadragon scarcely looks like a fish. Its slow movements and loose, elaborate body tassels have evolved to mimic seaweeds and seagrass.

Pygmy seahorse
Disappearing act

SPECIES *Hippocampus bargibanti* **SIZE** 2.5 cm (1 in)
DISTRIBUTION Tropical waters of southwest Pacific

Together with stonefishes (see opposite), pygmy seahorses are serious contenders for the best-camouflaged fishes in the ocean. These minuscule fishes spend most of their life clinging on to the stems of *Muricella* sea fans with their prehensile (gripping) tail. A single large sea fan can be home to many seahorse pairs, and the fishes have no need to leave their home at all. It therefore makes sense for them to be effectively invisible to the outside world.

The fishes' blunt snouts and tubercles mimic the closed feeding polyps of the sea fan and their bodies match the hosts' stem. In fact, the camouflage is so good that this species was discovered only after divers had collected a sea fan and placed it in a tank to study. The seahorses have little need to move because they have tubular mouths for sucking up minute planktonic animals – the same food being caught by the polyps of their sea fan host.

Plaice
Toning down

SPECIES *Pleuronectes platessa* **SIZE** Up to 1 m (3 ft 3 in)
DISTRIBUTION On sediment in northeast Atlantic Ocean, Arctic Ocean, Mediterranean, and Black Sea

Plaice live out in the open on sand, mud, and gravel sea beds, where camouflage is essential to their survival. They half-bury themselves in the sediment to disguise their shape, and can lighten or darken their brownish skin colour according to the type of surface on which they are lying. Their bright orange spots are a constant feature, but if the fishes move into an area of the sea bed with many pale shell fragments, for example, they can fade their spots to a much paler yellow.

Related species of flatfishes that range over a wide variety of sediments have developed this ability further. In the laboratory, Mediterranean flounders can make a good attempt to match the chequered squares or spots of an artificial background. Their colour changes are, however, limited to the colours of their natural environment. Young flatfishes slowly develop chromatophores (pigment cells) in their skin after settling on the sea bed, but only in the skin of the side facing upwards. The result is that only the upper side of these fishes is coloured.

Imitation spine This partially buried plaice is well camouflaged but is also holding its pectoral fin vertically, presumably in an attempt to mimic the venomous spiny dorsal fin of a weever fish.

Bicoloured Pigmentation is restricted to the upper side of the plaice. Its underside is plain white and seldom, if ever, revealed.

Longnose butterflyfish
Hidden head

SPECIES *Forcipiger flavissimus* **SIZE** Up to 22 cm (8½ in)
DISTRIBUTION Coral reefs in Indo-Pacific

Colourful butterflyfishes are one of the most obvious fish residents of coral reefs and so might attract the attention of predators, but their coloration also has the ability to confuse attackers. Many species, such as the longnose butterflyfish, have a patch of dark pigment hiding their real eye and a contrasting false eyespot near their tail end. A predator, such as a grouper, thinks that the tail is the head and attacks the wrong end, allowing the fish to dart away in the opposite direction.

Red salamander
Red for danger
SPECIES *Pseudotriton ruber* **SIZE** 10–18 cm (4–7 in)
DISTRIBUTION Wooded areas near clean, cool streams in eastern USA

The woodland habitat of this salamander is shared by birds of prey, raccoons, and skunks, all of which might be expected to prey on it. However, the salamander is similar in colour to the young stage of the eastern newt, which is protected from predators by distasteful skin secretions. Any animal that has learned to leave eastern newts alone is likely to avoid eating red salamanders too.

Toxic mimic The harmless red salamander (left) is a mimic of the juvenile eastern newt (above), which is protected by toxic skin secretions.

Borneo horned frog
Hard to spot
SPECIES *Pelobatrachus nasuta* **SIZE** Up to 12 cm (4½ in) **DISTRIBUTION** Rainforest floors in Malay Peninsula, Borneo, and Sumatra

During the day, the Borneo horned frog stays motionless on the rainforest floor and relies on its camouflage to avoid detection. The "horns" and sharp ridges on its body break up its outline and look like the edges of leaves. The frog keeps still in the face of danger, only leaping away at the last second if spotted. Rainforests are home to many other species of frog, most of which, like the Borneo horned frog, rest during the day and are protected by skin colours that closely match their habitat. Some frogs can alter their colour to match their background. The main exceptions are poison frogs (see p.253), which have toxic skin and brilliant warning colours instead of camouflage.

Borneo horned frog Thick creases on this frog's body mimic leaf edges, and the "horns" on its head cover its large eyes from above and behind. The eyes reflect light and so can easily give the frog's position away.

Darwin's frog This frog is highly variable in colour and closely matches its surroundings.

Eyelash viper
Shielding the eyes

SPECIES *Bothriechis nigroadspersus* **SIZE** Up to 75 cm (30 in); usually much less **DISTRIBUTION** Rainforest in Central and northern South America

Often it is the eyes of an animal that reveal it to be a predator. To avoid this problem, the eyelash viper has evolved modified scales above its eyes. These scales look rather like large eyelashes and are thought to break up the outline of the eyes so that a potential predator will not be able to tell which end of the snake is which. As the viper is venomous, this is likely to be an efficient deterrent in most cases. The eyelash viper is a relatively small snake that occurs in a wide range of colours, from orange and red through to mossy green and mottled combinations of brown, green, and grey. It lives in trees, where its prehensile (gripping) tail helps it to hold on to branches. An ambush predator, the viper is active at night and hunts small birds, rodents, tree frogs, and lizards, which it locates using a pair of heat-sensitive pits on its head.

modified, hornlike scales protrude over each eye

Mottled form This eyelash viper from Costa Rica is beautifully camouflaged in the dappled light of the forest.

Orange form The golden colour form of the eyelash viper, known as the orapel, is relatively easy to spot. It is uncommon in the wild but a popular snake in captivity.

Keeping still Having pressed itself tightly against a tree trunk, this gecko will not flinch unless prodded or grasped.

Mossy leaf-tailed gecko
Bark blending

SPECIES *Uroplatus sikorae* **SIZE** Up to 30 cm (12 in) **DISTRIBUTION** Rainforest in eastern Madagascar

Geckos are well known for their ability to cling to vertical surfaces and even hang upside-down, but the mossy leaf-tailed gecko is a camouflage expert as well. It lives in the rainforests of eastern Madagascar, and spends the day resting head-down on tree trunks, venturing out in search of insect prey under the cover of darkness. Its camouflage, which mimics tree bark perfectly, is in subtle shades of grey and greenish brown. The texture of this gecko's skin is the secret of its disappearing trick. The skin is covered with small knobbles, fissures, and flaps that help to break up the animal's outline. Even the surface of its eye, complete with a faint, indistinct pupil, resembles bark. The gecko also has an extra fold of loose skin around its head, body, and legs that forms a frilly "curtain". When threatened, the gecko flattens itself against a branch or tree trunk so that this skin splays out against the bark, thereby removing the tell-tale dark shadow that would otherwise catch a predator's attention.

Similar species The flat tail for which leaf-tailed geckos are named is obvious in this image of a giant leaf-tailed gecko. The lizard's gaping mouth and erect tail are a response to being touched and are its final attempt to intimidate a potential predator.

White out The Arctic fox's thick white winter coat makes it almost invisible against the snow and ice of its northern home. Even its dark nose and eyes seem to match the scattered rocks. This disguise helps the fox when hunting and protects it from predators such as polar bears and wolves. In spring, as the snow melts, the fox will grow a lighter coat of grey or brown to match its changed surroundings.

Willow ptarmigan
Seasonal plumage

SPECIES Lagopus lagopus **SIZE** 40–43 cm (15½–17 in)
DISTRIBUTION Tundra, moorland, and open woodland with dwarf willow scrub in Alaska, Canada, northern Europe, and northern Asia

Like many gamebirds, the willow ptarmigan, or willow grouse, lives and nests on the ground in open habitats, and so camouflage is essential for its survival. The feathers on its upperparts are barred with chestnut, black, and white, giving it a speckled appearance well matched to the willow scrub and moors that are its preferred home. Most willow ptarmigans stay in the same range all year, which means coping with deep snow for several months in winter. In their mottled brownish summer plumage, the birds would be very conspicuous against the blanket of white snow and so, as winter approaches, they gradually moult into a pure white plumage. The populations in the British Isles, where the bird is known as the red grouse, do not change their plumage in this way because this far south the winters are milder and snow is less common than in more northerly regions.

Autumn colours Willow ptarmigans, such as this female photographed in Alaska in autumn, blend in perfectly with tundra vegetation. Male willow ptarmigans are unique within the grouse family because they help with parental duties and defend their young.

Winter colours Because their colour change is controlled by day length rather than weather (see panel, far right), these birds and other species that turn white in winter are at risk of having the "wrong" (non-camouflaged) plumage as climate change affects weather patterns.

CASE STUDY LIGHT AND HORMONE LEVELS

The main factor controlling colour change in the willow ptarmigan is day length, not temperature. To test this, captive birds were exposed to artificially long springlike days but kept at cold winter temperatures; they began moulting into their coloured plumage. An increase in daylight hours stimulates production of hormones that control moulting. The white plumage develops when hormone levels are at their lowest.

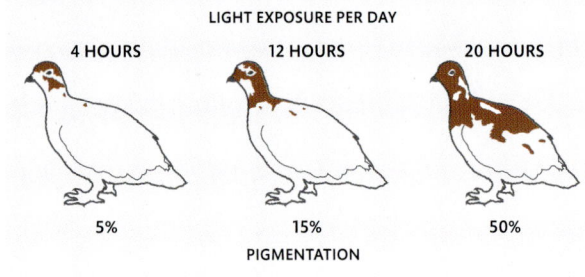

LIGHT EXPOSURE PER DAY
4 HOURS — 5% | 12 HOURS — 15% | 20 HOURS — 50%
PIGMENTATION

Distraction display Humans walking too close to a plover's nesting area on a pebbly beach are often treated to its broken-wing display. The "injured" bird makes itself as obvious as possible, while its mate stays out of sight nearby.

Semipalmated plover
Feigning injury

SPECIES Charadrius semipalmatus **SIZE** 15–19 cm (6–7½ in)
DISTRIBUTION Breeds on stony beaches and flats in Canada and Alaska; winter range extends from USA to South America

Many ground-nesting birds, including several members of the plover family, use a distraction display to draw predators away from their eggs. This behaviour is well known in the American semipalmated plover. During the nesting season, if a predator such as a fox comes dangerously close to the hidden nest of a pair of these plovers, the parent bird sitting on the eggs crouches down and stays perfectly still, while its mate moves away from the area and feigns a broken wing. This bird acts as a lure by walking away with one wing drooping and the other flapping furiously. The predator, seeing that the bird is in distress and would make an easy kill, starts to follow it. When the predator has been led far enough from the nest, the plover suddenly picks itself up and flies off, confusing the would-be attacker, which is left empty-handed.

Similar species All plovers nest on the ground. Their eggs, such as these belonging to the double-banded plover of New Zealand, are extremely well camouflaged.

CAMOUFLAGE AND DECEPTION

Wood perch A common potoo clings motionless to its daytime roost in the cerrado (savanna woodland) of northeast Brazil. It is able to hold the stance for hours at a stretch.

Plumage pattern mimics fissures found in tree bark and bare wood

Common potoo
Branch impostor
SPECIES *Nyctibius griseus* **SIZE** 33–38 cm (13–15 in)
DISTRIBUTION Tropical forest and grassland in Central and South America

During the day, the common potoo perches upright on a broken branch or tree stump, wings clasped firmly to its side, head held up, and its bright orange eyes shut. In this position, helped by its ability to stay statue-still, the bird looks just like an extension of the tree on which it is resting. Its subdued greyish-brown plumage, speckled with shades of black and tan, helps the illusion. At night, the potoo becomes active and may choose another perch from which to dart out and catch large flying insects in its wide, net-shaped mouth. The common potoo also uses tree stumps for nesting, and lays its single egg in a hollow where it can be safely incubated by both parents.

Fallow deer
Dappled disguise
SPECIES *Dama dama* **SIZE** 1.4–1.9 m (4½–6¼ ft)
DISTRIBUTION Woodland and farmland in Europe; introduced to North America and Australasia

Female fallow deer give birth in woodland among dense undergrowth, such as bracken. The single fawn is left alone while the mother grazes some distance off so as not to attract predators to her baby. The fawn instinctively curls up in the thick vegetation, where its speckled coat provides good camouflage in dappled sunlight. So strong is this instinct that a young fawn will not move if approached. Adult fallow deer also have a spotted coat in summer, which helps to conceal them as they wander through forest glades. However, adult deer are less dependent on camouflage because they can run quickly.

Unscented As well as being hard to see, newborn fawns are hard to smell, as their scent glands are yet to develop. They have only a faint odour, which predators are likely to overlook.

Coat moths Sloth fur harbours resident moths, whose presence encourages the growth of the algae that camouflages sloths. The moths lay their eggs in the dung the sloth deposits on the ground once per week.

Brown-throated three-toed sloth
Green cloak
SPECIES *Bradypus variegatus* **SIZE** 42–80 cm (16½–31 in)
DISTRIBUTION Lowland rainforest in Central and South America

A sloth spends virtually its entire life in tall rainforest trees and moves through the forest canopy extremely slowly, spending up to 20 hours per day hanging upside-down or propped in the fork of a branch. Most tree-living mammals are acrobatic climbers that can escape predators quickly. By contrast, the sloth's slow metabolism and sluggish lifestyle mean it cannot leap away to safety, so it relies on being invisible instead. It has coarse, greyish brown fur that blends in with surrounding foliage, and its slow, deliberate movements usually go unnoticed. During the rainy season, the sloth is even harder to spot because the high humidity causes green algae to spread across its back. If attacked, the sloth adopts an upright posture to lash out fiercely with its sharp claws.

Beluga
Ice white
SPECIES *Delphinapterus leucas* **SIZE** 4–5 m (13–16½ ft)
DISTRIBUTION Polar seas off coasts of Arctic Russia, Alaska, Canada, and Greenland

Adult belugas are completely white except for a dark edge along the tail and flukes (tail fins). This camouflage gives the whales reasonable protection against their main predators, orcas and polar bears, when travelling along the edge of pack ice and among shifting ice. However, when the pack ice is continuous, they must rely on surfacing at breathing holes. Here, they may be easy prey for polar bears in particular, which swipe out with their claws until the whales are too weak to dive again. Young belugas are dark grey or bluish grey, gradually becoming lighter as they grow, and fully white by 7–9 years old.

Breathing party Three belugas breathe at a hole in the ice. Surfacing is risky because polar bears wait by these holes, and the noisy expulsion of air might give the belugas away.

Reflected light Dancing light reflections help this beluga to blend in with the sea ice behind it. The species is a slow swimmer compared to other whales, making cryptic coloration a useful defence underwater.

Group defence

Living in a group is advantageous for animals with little individual defence against predators in the open. Migrating birds, fishes, mammals, and some invertebrates frequently travel in large groups for protection. Animals also live in groups for reasons other than defence, such as reproduction, warmth, and foraging efficiently.

Alarm call Group-living pikas use loud calls to alert others in their colony to danger, before scurrying to the safety of their burrows.

SAFETY IN NUMBERS

In many instances of group defence each individual is concerned only with its own survival. By living and travelling in a large group, an otherwise defenceless small migrating bird, fish, or wildebeest, reduces its chances of being attacked by predators. The bigger the group, the less risk a particular individual faces of being picked out by a predator. For highly intelligent social animals, such as dolphins and whales, living in an extended family provides active protection. Group members protect young or ailing family members from shark attacks by surrounding them, before leaping and slapping the water to intimidate their tormentor. If the size of their group is not sufficient for protection, they may summon nearby dolphin groups using special calls. In these instances, individuals are protecting their family group, not just themselves as individuals.

Silvery retreat A shoal of silversides divides as a predator (a tarpon) tries to single out individuals. The split shoal may reform behind the predator. Shoals under attack often crowd closer together as individuals try to remain in the centre.

Rockhopper group Rockhopper penguins in the Falkland Islands run and dive into the sea en masse to avoid being picked off by hunting leopard seals.

Individual survival Wildebeests and zebras crossing a river during their annual migration pack close together, jostling for space in the centre. Those on the edges of the group are more likely to be attacked by crocodiles or disturbed hippopotamuses.

GROUP COMMUNICATION

Flying, swimming, or running in huge groups requires instant responses between the individuals if the movement is to be coordinated and collisions avoided. Various senses are employed to achieve this. Group coordination is highly developed in fishes, which use both vision and the lateral-line system (which detects vibrations) to maintain a nearest-neighbour distance by following rules of attraction and repulsion that keep the group together but individuals apart. Only those on the periphery can see a predator approach. As these fishes change direction and speed, their neighbours detect this and follow suit, so the whole shoal reacts quickly and almost in unison. Sound is widely used among social animals, especially mammals, to warn others in their group of approaching danger.

GROUP DEFENCE

Spiny spider crab
Protective mound
SPECIES Maja brachydactyla **SIZE** Up to 20 cm (8 in); claws up to 45 cm (17½ in) **DISTRIBUTION** Eastern Atlantic from UK south to at least Morocco

Like all crustaceans, spiny spider crabs must moult their hard outer shell at regular intervals to enable growth, and after moulting they are soft and vulnerable to predators. During this dangerous time, these crabs gather together for protection, forming mounds on the sea floor. In summer, the crabs migrate to shallow water to breed, walking many miles from their deep-water winter feeding grounds. They form heaps on the sea bed that contain up to 50,000 individuals. In most crabs, the only time a male can mate with a female is immediately after she has moulted, when she is still soft, but this crab has a final moult as it becomes sexually mature and can mate without moulting.

spiny shell

Temporary armour Sharp spines on this spider crab's shell make it a difficult mouthful for most predators much of the time, but the crab is briefly vulnerable to attack when moulting.

Asiatic honey bee
Deadly heat ball
SPECIES Apis cerana **SIZE** 0.7–1.5 cm (¼–½ in) **DISTRIBUTION** Flower-rich habitats in south and Southeast Asia, from sea level to 3,500 m (11,500 ft)

Japanese populations of this small honey bee have a very unusual way of dealing with one of their enemies: the asian giant hornet (see p.181). This fearsome 5 cm- (2 in-) long aerial predator is fond of both honey and bee larvae and has huge jaws, so only a concerted mass defence by the honey bees has any chance of success. They swarm all over the hornet and vibrate their wings to generate heat, raising the temperature inside the ball to a lethal 44°C (111°F), which cooks the predatory hornet.

In the wild, Asiatic honey bees nest in holes and crevices in trees and logs, and between rocks. Himalayan hill farmers keep colonies of the bees for their honeycombs.

Chemical alarm signal If a worker honey bee spots a giant hornet near the nest it releases pheromones to alert the other bees. A number of them will probably be killed before the invader succumbs to their heat ball.

Cooked alive Somewhere beneath this pile of bees is a giant hornet fighting for its life. The bees can survive a higher temperature than the hornet, so are able to cook it to death. They must kill the predator before it has time to release a pheromone to attract reinforcements from the hornet nest.

CASE STUDY THERMAL EXECUTION

This photograph, taken with a thermal imaging camera, shows the temperature inside a scrum of honey bees at its peak of 40–44°C (104–111°F), with multiple bees vibrating the flight muscles in their wings to produce heat. High-temperature areas appear white, yellow, or red; cooler zones are blue, green, or purple.

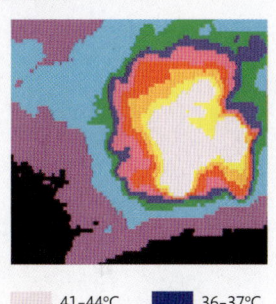

Temperature tolerances The body temperature of Asiatic honey bees, like most other invertebrates, is closely linked to air temperature. However, this species is adapted to survive extremes of weather, and can survive a maximum heat of 48–50°C (118–122°F), several degrees above that needed to kill a giant hornet.

41–44°C	36–37°C
40–41°C	35–36°C
39–40°C	34–35°C
38–39°C	33–34°C
37–38°C	32–33°C

ANATOMY FORMIC ACID STORE

Inside a wood ant's abdomen is a gland lined with cells that synthesize a watery solution of formic acid. This is passed along a duct into a reservoir, where it is stored until needed. The acid is strong – at a concentration of up to 60 per cent – so the reservoir is protected by a special lining. The ant fires the acid from an opening near the tip of its abdomen, which it can aim at an enemy. Alarm pheromones are released to alert other workers.

opening at tip of abdomen

legs braced

Red wood ant
Acid spray
SPECIES Formica rufa **SIZE** Worker from 6 mm (¼ in); queen and male 1 cm (⅜ in) **DISTRIBUTION** Sunny areas of open woodland, parkland, and heath in Europe, and Asia, possibly North Africa

These ants protect their nest from predators by swarming to its surface to squirt a jet of formic acid from their anal glands. A single ant's acid spray is unpleasant enough, but many ants firing together is a formidable defence. If a piece of fabric is dropped on top of the nest, it will soon be damp with spray and smell strongly of formic acid. Such a fierce attack is usually enough to deter a predator. Other glands in the ants' abdomens release alarm pheromones, summoning other workers. If this coordinated onslaught still does not deter a predator, the ants can also bite. Each colony may contain up to 300,000 workers, which build a huge mound of pine needles, twigs, and leaves over an extensive system of underground tunnels and chambers. The mound protects the nest and helps to keep the temperature constant. At night, the nest entrances are sealed and guarded.

Mass spray By squirting their defensive acid simultaneously, the wood ants in this colony produce a toxic mist several centimetres above the nest.

Striped catfish

Crowd confusion

SPECIES *Plotosus lineatus* **SIZE** Up to 32 cm (12½ in)
DISTRIBUTION Coastal reefs in Indian Ocean and western Pacific

Divers exploring coral reefs in the Indo-Pacific region frequently encounter strange ball-shaped objects hanging suspended in the water. These are compact shoals of juvenile striped catfishes, each containing about 100 individuals or more. The young catfishes pack together for protection during the day, and the unrecognizable form of their shoals may deter potential predators. At night the catfishes hunt for crustaceans, molluscs, and worms on the sea bed, each using the four pairs of sensitive barbels around its mouth to locate prey hidden in the sand. They remain in a loose group, with those at the bottom of the shoal feeding while those at the top guard the shoal and wait their turn. Adult striped catfishes live on their own or in small groups of up to about 20 fishes, but are well protected by highly venomous spines located just in front of the first dorsal fin and in each of the pectoral fins. During the day, they often hide in crevices or under ledges on the reef.

Daytime retreat Flashlightfishes conceal themselves by day (this shoal is hiding inside a shipwreck). At night they swim out into the open to feed, using bioluminescence to confuse their enemies.

Defensive ball A dense, writhing ball of striped catfishes moves like a single large organism, making it difficult for would-be attackers to isolate individuals. The array of body stripes adds to the confusion.

Splitfin flashlightfish

Dazzling escape

SPECIES *Anomalops katoptron* **SIZE** About 35 cm (14 in)
DISTRIBUTION Near caves and along steep outer walls of coral reefs in tropical Indo-Pacific. Large form found in deep water

Shoals of these small fishes use bewildering displays of pulsing light to outwit predatory fishes that might be tempted to eat them. The splitfin flashlightfishes hide in caves and under overhangs of coral during the day, emerging at night to feed. Each fish has a glowing, light-producing organ under its eye, which it switches on and off as it swims along, hunting for small floating zooplankton. The constantly blinking lights produced by a shoal confuse predators, which cannot pick out individuals from the crowd, and by turning all their lights off and changing direction, the fishes can escape. On bright moonlit nights, this defence is less successful, so the flashlightfishes may not emerge from their hiding places.

ANATOMY **BIOLUMINESCENCE**

A flashlightfish employs bacterial symbionts to produce light. Its light-producing organs contain bioluminescent bacteria – that is, bacteria that glow continuously. They make this bluish light by oxidizing a compound called luciferin. The fish covers each organ with a flap of skin to control the flash frequency, at up to 50 flashes a minute.

On and off These photographs of a small flashlightfish show it with its light-emitting organ covered (left) and uncovered (right).

Carrion crow

Mob mentality

SPECIES *Corvus corone* **SIZE** 47–52 cm (18½–20½ in)
DISTRIBUTION Open country and urban areas; Europe and Asia

Carrion crows frequently harass birds of prey and other potential predators, even humans. This behaviour, known as mobbing, is a form of calculated pre-emptive attack in which several crows gang up to chase away the intruder. When a crow spots a bird of prey, it flies up and swoops down on it from above and behind, while making loud alarm calls to attract other crows. Soon the raptor finds itself being bullied by a crowd of hostile birds, some of which may even strike it with their bill or feet. This is often too much for the victim, which flies away to find somewhere quieter to hunt.

Group mobbing is a safe and effective method of removing a threat from an area, especially if there are vulnerable nestlings nearby. Young crows appear to learn, or refine, the mobbing habit by watching their parents. Many species of passerines (perching birds) also use mobbing to defend themselves – harassing a roosting owl at its daytime perch, for example, and using loud alarm calls to attract other small birds to assist.

Mobbing response Although this pair of crows is under no threat from the common buzzard, which preys mainly on rabbits and rodents, they respond similarly to all larger raptors. Common buzzards can certainly take crow chicks from the nest, so they are unwelcome in the crows' breeding territory.

GROUP DEFENCE

Common starling
Mass distraction

SPECIES *Sturnus vulgaris* **SIZE** 19–22 cm (7½–8½ in)
DISTRIBUTION Wide variety of habitats throughout Europe, especially farmland and urban areas; introduced to North America, South Africa, Australia, and New Zealand

Having many eyes means that predators are quickly spotted, which is why common or European starlings are usually found in flocks, especially in winter. These highly gregarious birds feed together in fields, parks, and other areas of open ground, where they probe the soil for prey, such as earthworms. Each bird in the flock can feed for longer and be less vigilant than when foraging on its own. At dusk, the flock streams back to a roosting site, usually in a wood or reedbed or on a building. Flocks may have a number of favourite roosts within an area. Often several different feeding flocks converge on the roost and merge into a single flock that may contain several hundred thousand birds, though such large flocks are increasingly rare. As the birds circle around the area, they form amazing shapes in the darkening sky. Flying in a flock protects the starlings from aerial hunters such as falcons and hawks, which cannot pick out an individual to strike and may be confused by the ever-changing shape of the flock. As the predator approaches, the flock may split, which confuses the predator further. The aerial gyrations of a starling flock coming in to roost may last for half an hour or more. Once at the roost, the birds can huddle together for warmth. As dawn approaches, the starlings leave the roost in waves, forming new feeding flocks that move off to begin the day's foraging.

CASE STUDY FLOCKING TECHNIQUES

When a lone hunter, such as a falcon, flies towards a starling flock, the birds pack together tightly, sometimes forming a ball. This makes it hard for the predator to pick out a particular bird, and also more dangerous for it to attack, because it risks injury by diving through the massed birds. How the starlings achieve such synchrony is not fully understood, but each bird must react to what its immediate neighbours in the flock are doing, then adjust its speed and course accordingly. The effect of many such adjustments is that the flock moves as one. Falling darkness may increase the desire of each bird to head for the roost site, and to spot known landmarks, so that the flock eventually finds its way to the roost.

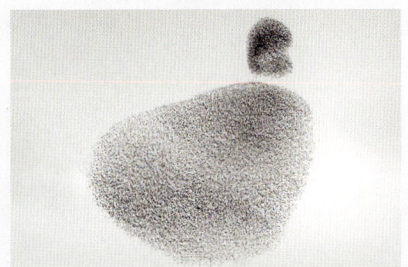
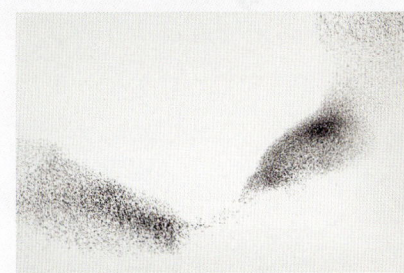

Predator evasion This sequence of photographs shows how a flock of starlings responds to an attack by a peregrine falcon. When the falcon approaches, the flock bunches together, then splits into smaller flocks that move in different directions. This gives the falcon little time to mount an effective strike.

Twilight display As they fly in to roost, wave after wave of common starlings create complex, rapidly changing patterns in the evening sky in a phenomenon that is known as a murmuration. The flock protects individuals from predators. Starlings are sociable birds, and often coexist with humans in urban areas.

Protecting each other A shoal of round scad, or cigarfishes, swirls around a goliath grouper off the coast of Florida, USA. By surrounding the larger fish when it is swimming, the round scad gain protection from predators, such as trevally. Although the goliath grouper can grow to 2.5 m (8¼ ft) long, it also benefits from the cover provided by its smaller companions.

ANATOMY **POWERFUL CLAWS**

A meerkat has strong feet and claws suited to its burrowing lifestyle, and can shift its own weight in sand in a few seconds. Each foot has four toes equipped with 2 cm- (¾in-) long, non-retractable, curved claws, which act like shovels. The claws are slightly longer on the front feet. Meerkats can also close their small ears when digging to keep out flying sand. These characteristics enable meerkats to dig multiple holes quickly when foraging.

Creating a dust cloud Meerkats dig fast and furiously in search of buried invertebrates and may even disappear from sight during their frantic hunt for food. Throwing up a sand cloud is also a good way of distracting predators.

40°C

The temperature a meerkat sentry may have to endure out in the open during its guard duty.

GROUP DEFENCE 287

Solar gain To get a better view, sentries stand bolt upright, using their long tail to prop them up. In the early morning and evening, they prefer to face the sun, orienting their darker chest skin to absorb heat. A mask of black fur around their eyes cuts down glare so that they can look into the sun.

Meerkat
Sentry duty

SPECIES *Suricata suricatta* **SIZE** 25–35 cm (10–14 in)
DISTRIBUTION Dry sandy plains and scrub in southern Africa

Meerkats are second to none in their ability to use group living as a collective defence against predators. Close-knit colonies of 20–40 individuals share a large system of burrows in which they sleep and raise young. Each morning as the adults emerge, sentries are posted on mounds or bushes to watch for danger. The sentries stand up on their long hind legs, using their tails for balance, and scan their surroundings intently. They bark a shrill warning if they spot anything suspicious.

Usually only the colony's matriarch, or dominant female, is allowed to give birth, yet she must continue to lead foraging expeditions, so the subordinate females in the group play the role of helpful "aunts". They baby-sit the new pups and the older juveniles from the matriarch's previous litter and guard the colony throughout the day. Meanwhile, all of the other adults go out to hunt for food. Each individual in the foraging party takes it in turn to be the lookout. If the alarm is given and the burrow is too far away, the meerkats dash for temporary bolt holes or stand nervously scanning the skies until the coast is clear.

Fear of big objects in the sky is probably instinctive in young meerkats, because they scatter if an aircraft passes overhead. They are also taught essential survival skills by their elder siblings, such as how to deal with scorpions and other dangerous prey.

Close to home With several sentries on guard, the other meerkats in this group can afford to indulge in grooming and play. They will all vanish underground within just a couple of seconds if one of the sentries sounds the alarm.

Group offensive Meerkat clans are highly territorial and will make concerted mock attacks on any rival clan members that stray into their territory, a behaviour that is known as mobbing.

Mexican free-tailed bat
Explosive exit

SPECIES *Tadarida brasiliensis* **SIZE** About 9 cm (3½ in)
DISTRIBUTION Caves of western and southern USA, Mexico, Central America, Chile, and Argentina

At nightfall, millions of these bats stream out of their daytime roosts in Texas, USA, and Mexico in one of the world's great natural spectacles. The largest roosts in caves contain up to 20 million bats, but even small colonies are home to thousands of individuals. From a distance, the massed bats resemble a smoke trail across the sky. The purpose of this dramatic, coordinated exit is to make it difficult for predators, such as owls, to pick off individual bats. Inside their roost, the bats are relatively safe from danger, although snakes sometimes take young and sick animals. Living in such enormous colonies has disadvantages, though: the bats must forage further from their roost to find enough insects for all of them to eat; and disease can spread quickly, which means the bats must invest more bodily resources into mounting a strong immune response.

HUMAN IMPACT PERSECUTION

Colonies of free-tailed bats are vulnerable to human interference. These bats can carry rabies and, although the threat is small, numerous colonies have been destroyed as a result. Free-tails are sometimes demonized as "vampires", but in fact they eat only insects. The species is beneficial because it controls agricultural pests such as the cotton bollworm moth; a single colony of 20 million bats can consume 250 tonnes of insects every night.

Dusk exodus On summer evenings, millions of free-tailed bats pour out of this cave in Texas. The swirling torrent of bats can take over an hour to pass and the sheer number of animals involved is sufficient to swamp potential predators. The entire Texan breeding population migrates to Mexico for the winter.

Mass attack Four dwarf mongooses surround a venomous African puff adder. If the dominant female has young nearby and the snake does not retreat, they will kill it to protect the group. Dwarf mongooses form strong social bonds and, when one raises the alarm, its closest friends are first to respond.

Dwarf mongoose
Gang warfare

SPECIES *Helogale parvula* **SIZE** 20–30 cm (8–12 in)
DISTRIBUTION Dry savanna, scrub, and semi-desert in central and southern Africa; often makes dens in termite mounds

Mongooses are renowned for killing and eating snakes, but it is usually only large, solitary species, such as the Indian grey mongoose, that do this. Dwarf mongooses are among the smallest members of the mongoose family and never attack snakes alone. What they lack in size they make up for in numbers, however. These mongooses live in groups of 12–15 family members led by a dominant female, and if a snake strays into their territory it is repelled by a concerted group effort. A few mongooses hold the snake's attention with carefully timed rushes, staying just out of striking range, while the others try to edge into a position where one of them is able to dart in and nip the snake behind its head. The mongooses have sharp teeth, so can deliver a fatal bite.

Each dwarf mongoose group contains a single breeding pair and young of varying ages. The mongooses form a close-knit extended family unit, hunting together and taking turns to baby-sit their younger relatives. They roam through a territory that they defend from neighbouring groups.

Thomson's gazelle
Leaps and bounds

SPECIES *Gazella thomsoni* **SIZE** 70–90 cm (28–35 in) **DISTRIBUTION** Dry, grassy plains of East Africa, mainly in Kenya and Tanzania

Not only are these gazelles impressive sprinters, they also run in a special way to communicate with the rest of their herd and confuse their pursuer. As the gazelles race along, they perform sudden bounding high leaps, a behaviour known as pronking or stotting. The leaps alert other gazelles to the danger and startle the predator, usually a cheetah or lioness, which finds it harder to follow its prey. Another possibility is that the gazelles leap to demonstrate their fitness, in the hope that their enemy will give up the chase.

I say jump In some gazelles, stotting is most common in adult females, suggesting it may be a way for mothers to teach their young how to avoid predators.

African buffalo
Teamwork

SPECIES *Syncerus caffer* **SIZE** 2–3.5 m (6½–11½ ft)
DISTRIBUTION Grassy plains and open woodland within reach of water, in Africa south of the Sahara; a smaller subspecies occurs in equatorial forest in West and Central Africa

Due to their massive bulk, African buffaloes make intimidating opponents and are quite capable of goring a lion to death. However, they are vulnerable to attack by a pride of lions hunting together. They are also at risk from crocodiles, as they need to drink at least once a day. By living in large herds, sometimes several hundred strong, the buffaloes greatly reduce their chances of being attacked.

Repelling an attack >>01 Confronted by a group of lions, this buffalo herd has packed together to form a defensive blockade. >>02 The buffaloes stand their ground, keeping their calves behind a bristling wall of horns and hooves as the lions manoeuvre to locate a point of weakness. >>03 One of the lions rushes in to break the buffaloes' formation, but is immediately chased and harried by the lead animals in the herd. Most encounters like this end in stalemate, although the lions may try again later.

United front A lioness turns to run as a buffalo herd squares up to her. If provoked, large buffaloes can toss lions aside with their horns, inflicting slashing wounds, so the cats are usually forced to retreat.

A herd will often run from its enemies initially, moving at a surprising pace for such large animals, but the buffaloes soon bunch together and turn to face the predators, with their calves safely behind them. The lions' strategy is to force the herd onto the run again, and then to single out young or sick animals that lag behind. In order to catch a buffalo, the lions must leap onto its back to bring it down. Even then, the herd will respond to distressed bellows from the victim and large adults might come running to its aid.

The largest buffalo herds, comprising mainly females and their young, are able to roam open savanna, travelling constantly in search of fresh grazing. In contrast, the males form smaller "bachelor" herds and keep to safer terrain with plenty of trees and scrub to provide cover. Older, mature males are frequently driven away from the female herds and must fend for themselves. They wander alone, only joining the females during the breeding season from March to May. The bulls rely on their enormous size to deter lions, but as they get older are likely to be brought down if attacked. Nevertheless, the success rate of lions hunting buffalo is often lower than 15 per cent.

57 kph The top speed reached by a buffalo bull weighing three-quarters of a tonne during a headlong charge.

>>01   >>02   >>03

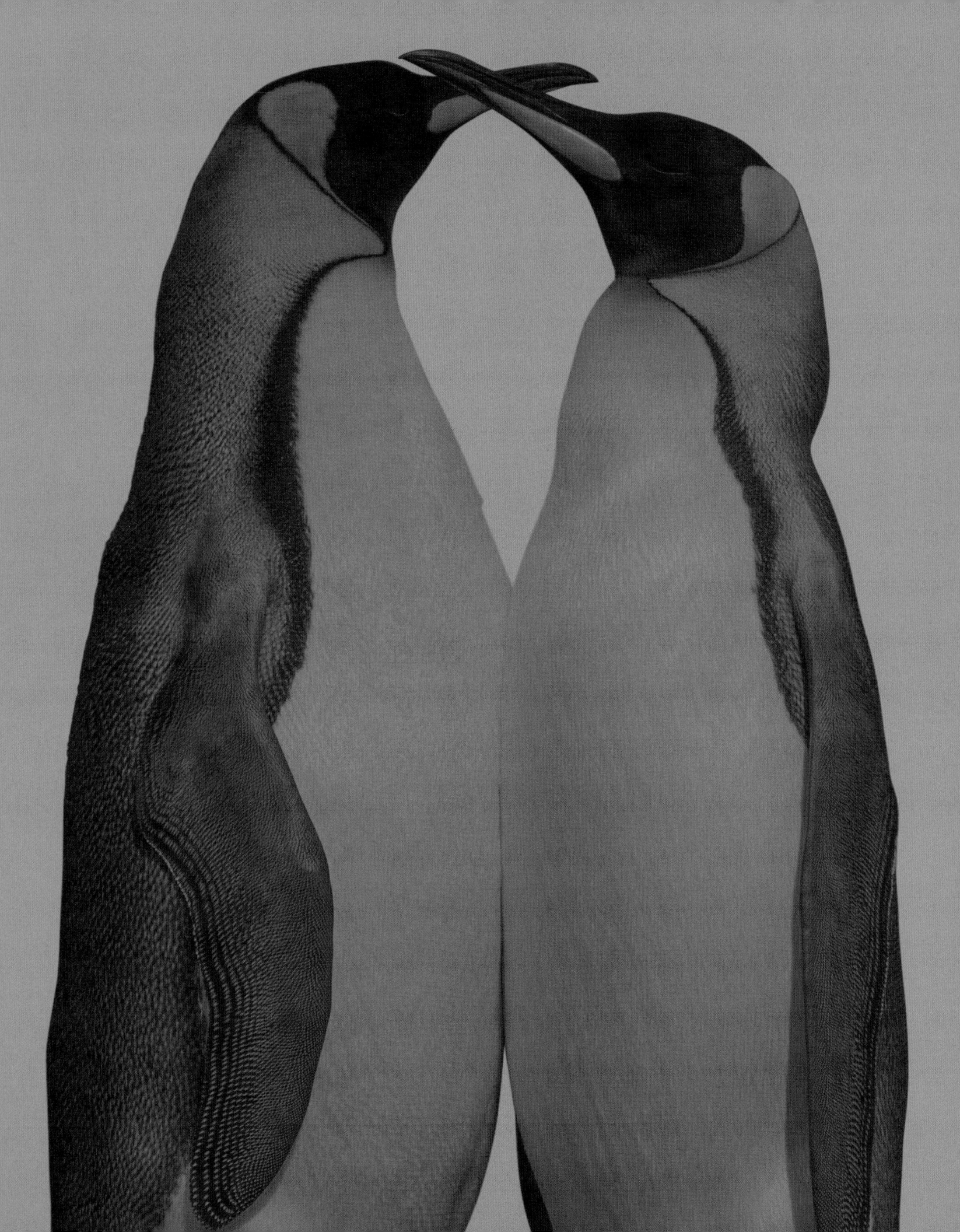

Sex and Reproduction

296
Reproducing without a mate

300
Finding a mate

308
Sexual rivalry

320
Courtship

334
Mating

Clasped together A male damselfly uses special pincers at the tip of his abdomen to clasp a female around the neck while he holds onto the stalk of a plant. She curves her abdomen forward to receive his sperm.

SEX AND REPRODUCTION

Reproduction is a fundamental feature of all living things. All mammals, including humans use sexual reproduction, in which offspring are produced by the fusion of special cells from two parents. Across the animal kingdom, however, there are many other ways of reproducing.

WAYS OF REPRODUCING

There is great diversity in animal reproduction. At one extreme is asexual reproduction, in which parents use methods such as budding, to produce offspring that are genetically identical to themselves. At the opposite extreme, true sexual reproduction involves two genetically different parents, a male and a female, producing offspring that are genetically distinct from one another, and from their parents. In between these extremes, there is a variety of reproductive methods that produce varying amounts of genetic diversity among offspring. For example, hermaphrodites function as both males and females. Some hermaphrodites mate with themselves, producing offspring that are less genetically diverse.

Asexual and sexual reproduction
Asexual reproduction produces offspring that are exact copies of their parents, carrying the same genes (A, B) as their parents. Sexual reproduction, involving gametes (see middle row) that each contain half the parent's genotype, produces genetically varied offspring carrying different combinations of their parents' genes.

SEXUAL REPRODUCTION

Sexual reproduction involves two essential features. First, special cells called gametes (eggs and sperm) are produced by a form of cell division called meiosis (see below), which results in each gamete being haploid – containing half the genetic complement of its parent. In meiosis, parental genes are "shuffled" so that each gamete contains a unique subset of parental genes. Second, each egg is fertilized by a sperm from a parent different from its mother, to form a zygote. The zygote is diploid, containing two alleles (copies) of each gene – one copy from its mother and one from its father. Eggs and sperm differ markedly in form and size; eggs tend to be large and immobile, containing the cellular material necessary to form the zygote, while sperm are much smaller, are very mobile, and are produced in much larger numbers.

Meiosis
Meiosis is the form of cell division by which gametes are made. Before parental cells divide, exchange of genetic material among chromosomes occurs, so each gamete has half of its parents' genes.

1 PREPARATION Before meiosis starts to occur, chromosomes replicate in the cell nucleus to produce double chromosomes. *double chromosome / nucleus*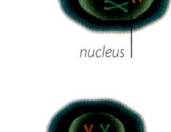

2 PAIRING Chromosomes align in matching pairs and genetic material can now be exchanged between the pairs through crossing over. 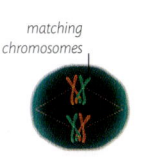 *matching chromosomes*

3 SEPARATION The pairs of chromosomes separate, and a spindle pulls one of each pair to the ends of the cell as it splits. *spindle / cell splits / pair separates*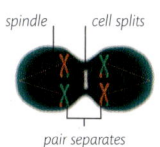

4 TWO OFFSPRING The separated cells each have one set of double chromosomes, of maternal and paternal pairs. *duplicated chromosomes*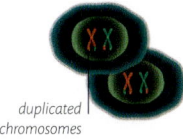

5 SECOND SEPARATION As the cells separate again, the double chromosome splits, each half moving to one end of the dividing cell. 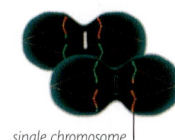 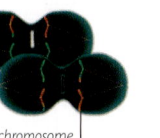 *single chromosome*

6 FOUR OFFSPRING Four sex cells – with different genetic make-up from the parent cell and each other – are created. *nucleus / chromosome*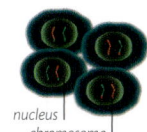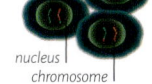

REPRODUCTIVE DIVERSITY

Parthenogenesis This is a form of reproduction in which a female's eggs develop into offspring without being fertilized. In one form, eggs are produced by meiosis (see above), and develop into offspring that differ slightly from their mother, and one another.

Sequential hermaphroditism This involves animals that produce both eggs and sperm, but not at the same time. In protandrous hermaphrodites, sperm are produced when the animal is young, and eggs when it is older. In protogynous hermaphrodites, the reverse is true.

Hermaphroditism Animals that exhibit this behaviour have male and female sex organs, and can produce eggs and sperm. Most do not fertilize their own eggs, but exchange sperm with a partner; exceptions include some parasites that are unlikely to meet a partner.

Asexual and sexual combination Some animals can reproduce asexually at certain times, and sexually at others. Typically, they reproduce asexually when their environment is stable, but switch to sexual reproduction when conditions deteriorate and become unpredictable.

Fishing spider A female raft spider carries her eggs wrapped in a silk cocoon. Raft spiders are aquatic predators, feeding on tadpoles, insects, and small fishes; they are able to stay underwater for up to an hour.

SEXUAL EVOLUTION

Animals live in environments that are constantly changing, presenting each generation with fresh challenges. This means that, in order to maximize the chance that at least some of their young will survive, animals need to produce as many offspring as possible that differ both from themselves and from one another. Although genetic mutation can produce some variation in species that reproduce asexually, this is not enough in most circumstances, and many animals need the capacity of sex to produce sufficient genetic diversity among their young.

EXPLAINING REPRODUCTIVE DIVERSITY

The existence of diverse reproductive mechanisms is related to the fact that the environments in which animals live are variable, in both space and time. In a uniform or stable environment, animals that have survived to breed will thrive best if they reproduce themselves exactly, by asexual reproduction. In variable and unpredictable habitats, however, producing offspring that are genetically diverse, by sexual reproduction, increases the chances that some will survive. Reproduction is like a lottery; asexual reproduction produces tickets that all have the same number, but, in sexual reproduction, each ticket has a different number.

THE CONSEQUENCES OF SEX

A fundamental feature of sexual reproduction is that a very large number of tiny sperm compete to fertilize a limited number of large eggs. In many species, this is reflected in intense competition among males to mate with females. Males may compete violently, fighting one another, or they may compete to be attractive to females. The result is sexual dimorphism, in which males are commonly larger, and more brightly coloured than females, or are equipped with weapons. In many animals, the female alone cares for the young, but there are a number of species in which the male also has a parental role, and a few where the male is the sole caregiver. In some species with male care, sex roles are reversed, and females compete for the opportunity to mate with males.

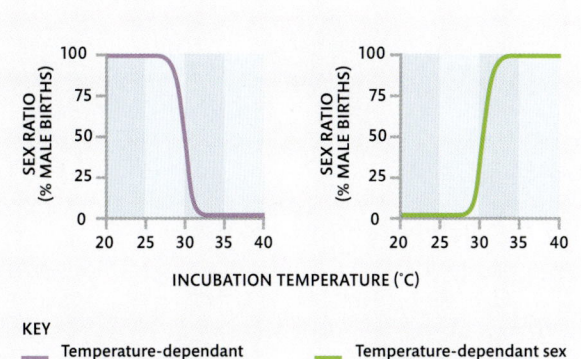

Sex and violence These two peaceful Caribbean cnemidophorus lizards (right) reproduce by parthenogenesis and exist only as females. Two male rival black grouse (above) fight for the possession of a small territory, on which they can display to females.

TEMPERATURE AND SEX

In many reptiles, the sex of the offspring is influenced by the temperature at which the eggs develop. Turtle eggs reared at low temperatures of less than about 30°C (84°F) are mostly male; eggs reared at higher temperatures are mostly female (right). The reverse is true in lizards (far right). In crocodilians, males develop from eggs reared temperatures of 23–32°C (73–90°F). Climate change could have serious consequences for these reptiles.

KEY
— Temperature-dependant sex determination in turtles
— Temperature-dependant sex determination in lizards

Reproducing without a mate

There are a number of animals that reproduce without mating with another individual. In some species, all members are female and reproduce asexually through methods such as budding or division, while others are hermaphrodites and fertilize themselves.

ASEXUAL REPRODUCTION

Asexual reproduction is common in plants, but it is relatively rare among animals. It involves the production of anatomic and genetic replicas – these offspring are called clones. Some animals, such as flatworms, can divide into two. Others, such as hydra (small freshwater predators), reproduce by budding – growing as a part of their mother's body, before detaching. Very few animals, however, rely solely on asexual reproduction. Cloning is only effective when conditions allow, but it does enable animals to build up very large populations in a short time. Most asexually reproducing animals switch to sexual reproduction when conditions are harsh or unpredictable.

VIRGIN BIRTH

Some animals reproduce by a process called parthenogenesis, in which eggs develop without being fertilized by sperm. This tiny Komodo dragon was produced by a female who had not been kept with a male at Britain's Chester Zoo. This is the first time that parthenogenesis has been reported in this species, which is native to several islands in Indonesia. The capacity to reproduce in this way may have evolved to enable females to reproduce in isolation from males. However, it produces young with low genetic diversity that are less able to cope with disease and adverse conditions.

Two-headed worm Flatworms can reproduce by splitting in two, starting at the head. They separate, and form two new flatworms.

Cloning aphids Under good conditions in spring and early summer, aphids reproduce asexually, producing very large numbers of offspring that cause huge damage to crops and plants.

Anemone budding Sea anemones reproduce by budding from an adult's body, or by "basal laceration", when pieces of tissue from the base of an anemone break off. Eventually, these break-aways become independent individuals.

HERMAPHRODITES

Hermaphrodites are animals that produce both eggs and sperm. For these animals, every member of their species is a potential sexual partner. Being hermaphrodite is often an adaptation for life where mating opportunities are rare. It is common among animals that live in isolation, such as parasites, and in sedentary or slow-moving animals. Most hermaphrodites use sexual reproduction when they can, exchanging sperm with a partner, but some fertilize their eggs with their own sperm if no partner is available. Animals such as snails mate with themselves only as a last resort, producing fewer young than when they reproduce sexually.

Scale insect Cottony cushion scale insects are serious pests of citrus trees. In most cases they are self-fertilizing hermaphrodites, but some males do occur.

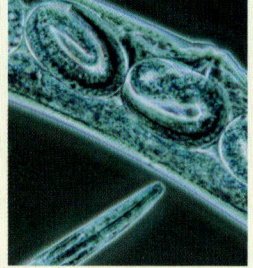

Nematode eggs This nematode worm, *Caenorhabditis elegans*, contains larvae developed from self-fertilized eggs. While a few members of the species are males, most are hermaphrodites. Those fertilized by a male produce up to 1,000 eggs, three times more than those that self-fertilize.

Hydra
Budding potential

SPECIES *Hydra vulgaris* **SIZE** 1–20 mm (1/16–3/4 in)
DISTRIBUTION Attaches to vegetation in unpolluted freshwater ponds and rivers in the northern hemisphere

This species (like other hydras) is a tiny animal that, in reproductive terms, enjoys the best of both worlds. When conditions are good and food is abundant, it reproduces asexually, by developing buds that grow into new individuals that detach from their parents and become independent individuals when fully formed. If conditions deteriorate in its pond (for example, if the pond starts to dry out or winter approaches) it grows ovaries and testes, which eject eggs and sperm into the water. These fuse to form a zygote (a fertilized cell) with a resistant covering that can survive until conditions improve.

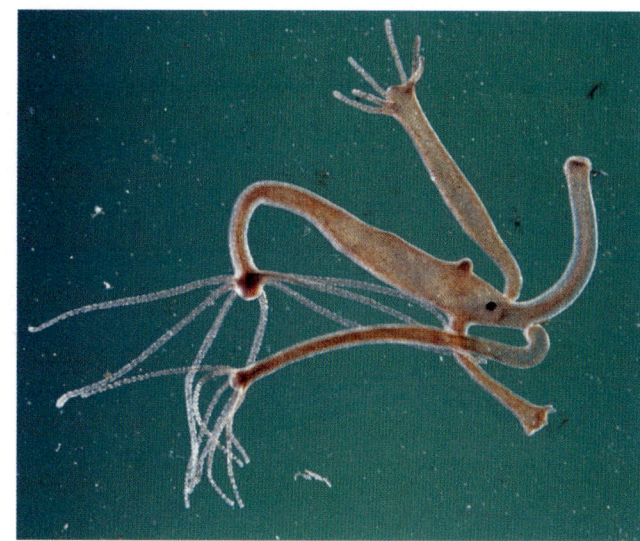

Break away To the right, a hydra produces three offspring by budding. When fully formed, they will detach and become independent. Hydras are green (above) or brown, depending on the kind of symbiotic algae living in their cells.

Jewel anenome
Colourful colonies

SPECIES *Corynactis viridis* **SIZE** Diameter 10 mm (3/8 in); height 1.5 cm (1/2 in). Colonies can be several metres across **DISTRIBUTION** Attached to rocks mainly below the low tide mark in the British Isles, southwestern Europe, and the Mediterranean Sea

Jewel anemones reproduce asexually by simply dividing into two, resulting in a pair of genetically identical animals. The two small anemones can then go on to split again once they have grown. If conditions are good, anemones can reproduce very quickly, building up vast numbers. Such dense colonies cover rocky surfaces below the shore, especially on vertical surfaces.

Jewel anemones are amazingly variable in colour, ranging from pinks and greens, to reds and whites. Within this technicolour spectrum, each individual anemone itself has contrasting coloration – the tentacles tend to differ in hue to the body column, and the dozens of knobbled tentacle tips are often white. As individual anemones split and replicate themselves, distinct patches of colour become visible within large colonies. The specatular displays that result are often described as resembling a "multicoloured quilt".

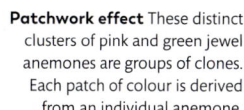

Patchwork effect These distinct clusters of pink and green jewel anemones are groups of clones. Each patch of colour is derived from an individual anemone.

In the pink A large colony of pink jewel anemones covering the face of a rock. Asexual reproduction enables anemones to colonize areas of good habitat quickly.

ANATOMY SPLITTING UP

Jewel anemones divide in half vertically, in a process known as longitudinal fission. Division begins at the head, so that an individual has two mouths and two sets of tentacles. The body then splits in half downwards, leaving two independent but genetically identical individuals. The splitting process can take from just five minutes to several hours.

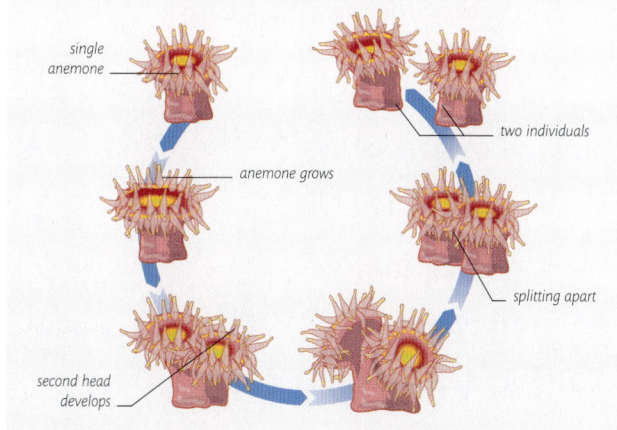

Giant clam

From a distance

SPECIES Tridacna gigas **SIZE** Up to 1.5 m (5 ft)
DISTRIBUTION Coral reefs within 35 m (115 ft) of surface in Indian and southwest Pacific oceans

Giant clams are immobile creatures and cannot go in search of a mate. They are hermaphrodites, possessing both male and female sex organs, and release both eggs and sperm into the water. However, they try to avoid fertilizing their own eggs by discharging each at separate times; usually the sperm is released first. Also, they begin their sexually mature lives as males, developing female organs as they age, so younger clams can only release sperm. It has been estimated that they reach full sexual maturity at between three and seven years of age.

After the eggs have been fertilized in the water, each develops into a trochophore, then a veliger larva that drifts in the open sea for some time before settling on a reef and developing into a clam. Genetic studies of giant clams on Australia's Great Barrier Reef show that clams living close together are no more closely related to one another than those living 1,000 km (620 miles) away, suggesting that larvae disperse widely on ocean currents. While the giant clam usually fertilizes others of its own species, it is also thought capable of cross-fertilization with at least one other clam species.

100 The number of years a giant clam is thought to live, though some may live as long as 200 years.

Egg release This giant clam ejects a cloud of gametes from its siphon directly into the water. Spawning of eggs and sperm can last up to 30 minutes with millions of eggs, and billions of sperm, being released and carried away on the current.

ANATOMY **CLAM SIPHONS**

Two siphons circulate water around a clam's body, allowing it to breathe, obtain food, and eliminate waste products. Inflowing water is sucked in through the inhalant siphon, passed over the gills, and strained to remove food – microscopic algae (phytoplankton) and animals (zooplankton). Waste water is expelled through the exhalant siphon, which is also used to release sperm and eggs. Circulation is maintained by microscopic hairs called cilia, which are located on cells inside the clam.

Bdelloid rotifers
Surviving without sex
ORDER Bdelloida **SIZE** Microscopic **DISTRIBUTION** Fresh water (common in ponds) and on mosses

Rotifers are microscopic aquatic animals, many of which reproduce asexually when conditions are good, and resort to sexual reproduction when conditions deteriorate. One group, however, consisting of about 380 species, is entirely female and there is no evidence that they ever exist as males. These are the bdelloid rotifers, which first evolved about 80 million years ago. They produce eggs that require no fertilization but, crucially, they are still able to produce genetically different offspring. Researchers have found two copies of a gene in the bdelloid rotifer helps them adapt and survive. The gene prompts the manufacture of proteins that protect the rotifer when its aquatic habitat dries out. One copy stops protein molecules clumping together, while the other supports delicate cell membranes. This remarkable adaptation allows the bdelloid rotifer to stay alive even if it desiccates.

Colourful loner The mangrove killifish's colour varies according to its habitat. In muddy environments it is dark brown or green, in sandy places, pale yellow.

Mangrove killifish
Hermaphrodite fish
SPECIES *Kryptolebias marmoratus* **SIZE** Up to 7.5 cm (3 in)
DISTRIBUTION Tropical regions with coastal mangrove swamps such as Brazil, Central America, Caribbean islands, and Florida

This fish and at least one other in the same genus are thought to be unique among vertebrates in being hermaphrodites that can fertilize themselves. The mangrove killifish lives in mangrove swamps that frequently become so toxic that it has to escape to terrestrial refuges, which is partly why it spends much of its life alone. Creating offspring without a partner is therefore a necessity. The killifish's self-fertilized eggs are deposited out of the water, attached to plants and debris, to be dispersed by water movements.

CASE STUDY **FISH OUT OF WATER**
The habitat of mangrove killifishes frequently dries out due to weather changes or can become toxic due to the formation of hydrogen sulphide. When this happens, the fishes escape by flipping and jumping over land. Remarkably, the structure of their gills and skin changes to allow them to absorb oxygen from the air, and they can survive in damp places for weeks. Some ride out the hostile spells by hiding in the burrows of blue land crabs; others wriggle into termite galleries.

Bonnethead shark
Adaptable female
SPECIES *Sphyrna tiburo* **SIZE** Up to 1.5 m (5 ft)
DISTRIBUTION Deep, warm water in the western Atlantic and eastern Pacific oceans

Also known as shovelheads, bonnethead sharks usually reproduce sexually, the female mating with a male and giving birth to between 8 and 12 young, called pups. In 2001, however, a female that had been kept on her own at a zoo in Nebraska, USA, gave birth to a single pup. DNA analysis showed that it was genetically identical to its mother, confirming that this was indeed a "virgin birth", the pup having developed by parthenogenesis from an unfertilized egg. This had not previously been observed in cartilaginous fishes. Bonnetheads are often found in large shoals but, should a female not be able to find a male, it appears that she has a mechanism for producing young on her own.

A head for scents The wide, flat head of the bonnethead shark allows for a greater concentration of electrical sensory cells, hence its enhanced sense of smell.

Mourning gecko
Whole eggs
SPECIES *Lepidodactylus lugubris* **SIZE** 7–9.5 cm (2¾–3¾ in) **DISTRIBUTION** Wide variety of habitats, including buildings, in tropical Asia and Pacific islands, Central America, and Australia

Although some male mourning geckos have been reported, most populations consist entirely of females capable of producing eggs that will develop into young without being fertilized by sperm. The eggs contain the same number of chromosomes – 44 – as their mother. Mourning geckos are communal breeders, with several females laying two eggs each in a nest in a tree cavity, a leaf axil, or under bark. Because every individual can reproduce, their numbers increase very rapidly, and they have successfully colonized many parts of the world, including northern Australia, where they have been introduced.

Prolific immigrants Like many other geckos, mourning geckos have successfully colonized oceanic islands, such as Hawaii. One reason for this may be that their eggs can survive immersion in sea water.

five toes   *satiny brown skin*   *dark spot on "W" or chevron markings on tail*

Finding a mate

For animals that live in long-term social groups, finding a mate is not difficult. Many animals, however, live solitary lives and have evolved ways to find mates, often over a great distance. In many insects and frogs, for example, males produce loud sounds that attract females.

ADVERTISING FOR A MATE

When attracting a mate, it is usually the male that has to produce sounds, visual signals, or odours that draw the attention of females, and some species expend a huge amount of energy doing so. Typically, they advertise in competition with other males of the same species, and the males that put most energy into their display are the most successful in attracting females. Advertising is dangerous, because a male's conspicuous signals may also be noticed by his enemies, such as predators or parasites. Some calling frogs, for example, are eaten by bats that home in on their calls. When the frog-eating bat *Trachops cirrhosus* is hunting, the risk to frogs may force them to stay quiet and miss out on the chance to mate.

Male mole crickets "sing" for females by rubbing their wings together in a burrow that amplifies the sound.

Male water lily frogs call to attract females to join them at breeding ponds.

STAYING TOGETHER

Animals with long life spans can breed several times in their lives, and it is often advantageous to form long-term pair bonds. In a number of birds, pairs that breed together over several years improve their breeding success from year to year. Parrots and pigeons, for example, are renowned for their long-term monogamy, which can last many years. This is because, as well as developing individual breeding skills, stable pairs learn to complement one another. Australian sleepy lizards live solitary lives but, for up to 20 years, they seek out their regular partner in the breeding season. Pairs of animals that fail to breed successfully in their first year together often separate and find new partners the following year.

Staying close Like many bird species, ring-necked doves are monogamous, forming pair bonds that may last several years.

Baboon troop Olive baboons live in troops of 15–150, consisting of a few males, several females, and their young. Males fight to establish dominance, and the more dominant males enjoy greater mating success.

PARASITE MATING STRATEGIES

Mass egg-laying
Parasites that live inside their hosts have great difficulty finding a mate, as their host must become infected more than once by the same species of parasite before mating can occur.

Hermaphroditism
If no mate is available, a simultaneous hermaphrodite parasite (one that is capable of producing both eggs and sperm) can simply mate with itself. This is a solution sometimes used by tapeworms.

Manipulation
Some parasites can manipulate the behaviour of their host, making them more conspicuous to predators. This increases the chance of the parasite being passed to a new host.

Permanent copulation
Some protists, such as the species that causes the disease bilharzia, have another solution to the difficulty of finding a mate – male and female live attached to one another, in a state of permanent copulation.

TIME AND PLACE

One way of finding a mate is for males and females to gather at a regular breeding site. Many amphibians, for example, return to the pond where they were born and continue to return there throughout their lives in order to breed. In some birds and mammals, mating occurs at traditional sites called "leks", where males fight over small display areas, and females choose which male to mate with; they base their choice on each male's appearance and the quality of his display.

Heading to a lek
Gemsboks of southern Africa live most of their lives in herds. When it is time to breed, they head for traditional mating sites, or leks.

Hard corals
Mass spawning
GENUS Lobophyllia **SIZE** 0.1–2 m (⅓–6½ ft) **DISTRIBUTION** Shallow, tropical regions of the Atlantic, Pacific, and Indian oceans

Hard corals are colonial organisms, consisting of many tiny individuals, called polyps, each of which lays down a calcareous "shell" to sit in. All individuals on the same reef synchronize their reproductive activity, shedding their sex cells into the water on the same day to produce large numbers of fertilized eggs; this precise timing is related to the lunar cycle. Eggs and sperm fuse in the water to form microscopic larvae, or planulae, that swim towards the surface of the sea, where they drift away from the parent colony. After a few days they sink to the sea bed and, if they land on a suitable surface, start a new colony.

Egg and sperm release Sperm is shed into the sea by large numbers of individual polyps. This is coordinated, so that the sperm emerges in clouds, as shown here. The eggs, which are released on the same day, mingle with the sperm and external fertilization takes place.

CASE STUDY CORAL BLEACHING
New research shows that, after a bleaching event (which is caused by raised water termperature), the reproductive output of some coral species, such as branching stony coral (*Acropora millepora*), is down by 21 per cent, despite low mortality at the time. This has significant consequences for the ability of reefs to recover.

Purple sea urchin
Close relationship
SPECIES Strongylocentrotus purpuratus **SIZE** 5–10 cm (2–4 in) **DISTRIBUTION** Low intertidal zones, with strong wave action, in association with kelp forest, on Pacific coast of North America, from Alaska to Mexico

Purple sea urchins have no need to go in search of a mate, as they typically live close to one another in large colonies. Individuals mature at two years of age and breed between January and March. Males release sperm and females release eggs into the water, where they fuse to form tiny embryos; these fall back to the sea floor, where they settle and begin to grow. In general, adult urchins are sedentary but are able to move slowly to new places in search of food. They feed on fragments of algae that fall out of the kelp forest with which they are associated. They have the ability to scrape a depression in the rock, making themselves better protected against being displaced by waves.

Cicadas
Chirping call
FAMILY Cicadidae **SIZE** 2–15 cm (¾–6 in) **DISTRIBUTION** Restricted to areas with trees or bushes; mainly tropical, but some species inhabit temperate regions

Male cicadas attract females from far away by producing one of the loudest noises in the natural world. Unlike crickets and grasshoppers, which rub their wings, or wings and legs together to make a chirping sound, cicadas create a clicking noise using a pair of organs, called tymbals, on their abdomens. Tymbals are flat, circular structures that, like a metal tin lid, can be clicked in and out by the action of powerful muscles. The sound is amplified by air sacs that lie just beneath the tymbals. Close to the tymbals, the sound reaches an intensity of 120 decibels, which is painful to the human ear. Cicadas have a strange life history, living as nymphs under the ground for years and as adults for only a few weeks.

Out in the open Cicadas are more often heard than seen. Most species are well camouflaged and sing from within vegetation.

Ornate jumping spider
Fluorescent attraction
SPECIES Cosmophasis umbratica **SIZE** 7 mm (¼ in) **DISTRIBUTION** Vegetation in sunny open woodland in Southeast Asia from India to Sumatra

Male ornate jumping spiders have special scales on certain parts of their bodies that reflect ultraviolet light, enabling females to recognize males of their own species. Both sexes have cells in the retinas of their many eyes that are sensitive to ultraviolet light, but only the males have the light-reflecting scales. Males are very active in sunlight, displaying to both females and rival males with elaborate dances that involve waving their forelimbs and drumming their legs on a leaf: these provide both visual and vibrational cues to potential mates and rivals. Males engage in frequent, often violent, interactions with other males, in order to defend their leaf. When a male detects a female, which is attracted to the male by its distinctive markings, it performs a courtship dance that leads to mating.

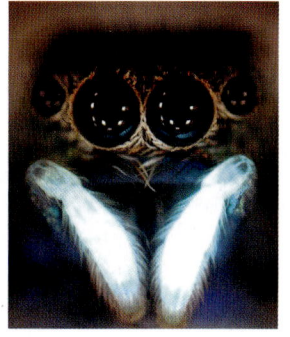

Ultraviolet glow Males reflect ultraviolet light in order to attract females; the light-reflecting scales are especially prominent on their forelegs.

Midday activity Ornate jumping spiders are most active during late morning and early afternoon on plants that are exposed to sunlight.

Tree dweller This Douglas fir glow worm (*Pterotus obscuripennis*) is one of several species of glow worm found in North America, where they are more commonly known as fireflies. Glow worms are, in fact, neither worms nor flies, but beetles.

Night lights Two female common glow worms (*Lampyris noctiluca*) give out a soft glow.

Glow worms
Blinking lights

FAMILY Lampyridae **SIZE** Up to 3.5 cm (1½ in), female much larger than male **DISTRIBUTION** Vegetation throughout temperate and tropical regions

Female glow worms attract males by producing bright green light at night. Glow worms are beetles but, while the male has a normal beetle life cycle and transforms from a larva into an adult capable of flight, the much larger female remains in the larval form and is unable to fly. The hindmost three segments of the female's body contain light-producing organs. These contain a layer of a protein called luciferin, which reacts chemically with the enzyme luciferase, water, and oxygen to produce light, but very little heat. The luciferin layer is backed by light-reflecting crystals and is covered by a transparent cuticle. A female is able to turn her light organs on and off by changing the flow of oxygen into them. She glows at night while sitting on a leaf or twig, and the male flies down to mate with her. Glow worm larvae and adult females are predators of arthropods, including millipedes, whose formidable chemical defences they are somehow able to overcome. Adult males have much larger eyes than females and live for a shorter period of time. In some species, both females and adult males have no mouths and so are unable to feed. Instead, they conserve as much energy as possible while searching for a mate and then die shortly after reproducing.

Mirror image Two male zebra longwing butterflies hang upside-down from a female chrysalis, each trying to stake their claim on the female.

Life's a beach The California grunion spawns at the water's edge at high spring tide, leaving its eggs to develop in the sand out of reach of marine predators.

Zebra longwing butterfly
Standing guard

SPECIES *Heliconius charithonia* **SIZE** 7–10 cm (2¾–4 in) **DISTRIBUTION** Forests, among dense clumps of trees, and at forest edges in Southern USA, northern Mexico, and Caribbean islands

Male zebra longwing butterflies seek out females to mate with before the females have even emerged from the chrysalis. They locate pupae using visual cues and volatile chemicals produced by host plants in response to leaf damage caused by the caterpillars. When a male has identified a female, which has a unique pheromone known as linalool oxide (male pupae emit a variant – linlool), they then try to guard it, typically visiting it for about a week and fighting off other males that may come to perch on it. Fights can last for hours and consist of males opening their wings or trying to throw off an intruder with the pressure of their heads or antennae. As the female begins to emerge, the winner inserts his abdomen into the pupa to mate with her, then anoints her abdomen with a secretion that repels other males. Despite their efforts, experiments have shown that males get it wrong sometimes – about a third of the time will avidly guard a pupa that turns out to be another male.

California grunion
Perfect timing

SPECIES *Leuresthes tenuis* **SIZE** Up to 15 cm (6 in) **DISTRIBUTION** Southern California, south to Baja California, Mexico

Precise timing is the key to reproductive success for California grunions. Mass spawnings, called grunion runs, occur mostly in April and May, always one to three days after the two highest tides (spring tides) in the monthly tidal cycle. At this time males and females gather and ride the waves in to form a writhing mass at the water's edge. A female uses her tail to wriggle vertically into the sand and, when she is ready to deposit her eggs in it, a male wraps himself around her and sheds his sperm onto the eggs. The eggs develop in the sand and, when the water reaches them at the next monthly high tide, they wash out and hatch, and the young disperse into the ocean.

FINDING A MATE

Before and after An initial phase male (top) swims above a terminal phase male on a reef. Only the terminal phase males have the blue head that gives this species its name.

Plainfin midshipman
Humming for a mate

SPECIES *Porichthys notatus* **SIZE** Up to 38 cm (15 in) **DISTRIBUTION** Intertidal zones of the Pacific coast of North America, from Alaska to Mexico

Male plainfin midshipman fishes invite females to visit their nests by producing a loud humming sound, interspersed with whistles, grunts, and growls. Courtship happens at night, and when a female is close, the male uses the luminescent spots on the underside of his chin to display to her, lifting his head back to expose them. During the summer breeding season this normally deep-sea fish migrates up into the intertidal zone. Each male excavates a cavity nest beneath a rock where visiting females lay their eggs attached to the roof. A successful male continues to court different females and guards all egg batches until they hatch after about two months, and the young are large enough to fend for themselves. During this time he eats nothing until he finally returns, emaciated, to deep water.

Bluehead wrasse
Changing sex

SPECIES *Thalassoma bifasciatum* **SIZE** Up to 25 cm (10 in) **DISTRIBUTION** Coral and offshore reefs, seagrass beds, and coastal bays in western Atlantic, Bermuda, Florida, Gulf of Mexico, northern South America, and the Caribbean

Many species of wrasse, including the bluehead, go through a series of different colour phases as they grow, and some also change sex as part of their life history. Small, mature male and female blueheads look similar, and have an "initial phase" colour pattern. These may spawn in shoals, gathering together and then rushing upwards before simultaneously releasing clouds of sperm and eggs. A small proportion of larger males change colour and become "terminal phase" or "supermales". Within a reef area, one or two of these can dominate a shoal, and one supermale will spawn individually with as many as 50–100 females in a day. In the absence of a dominant male, the largest female present can change sex and function as a male.

ANATOMY BECOMING A SUPERMALE

Juvenile bluehead wrasse are yellow with a dark stripe along the sides, which breaks up into blotches in initial phase fishes. Terminal phase males develop a bright blue head, ending in a black-and-white and green body. The aggressive presence of a terminal phase male in a female shoal prevents any of the latter from changing sex but, if the male dies, at least one of the larger females will change sex to take his place.

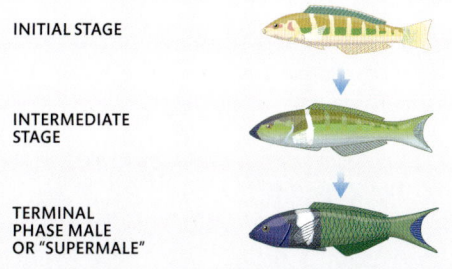

INITIAL STAGE

INTERMEDIATE STAGE

TERMINAL PHASE MALE OR "SUPERMALE"

Noisy neighbour As with the toadfish (see p.425), the sounds made by the male plainfin midshipman are so loud they can be heard above water. They can even keep humans awake at night.

Short-tail stingray
Summer gathering

SPECIES *Dasyatis brevicaudata* **SIZE** Up to 4.3 m (14 ft) **DISTRIBUTION** Coastal and offshore waters and estuaries around Australia, New Zealand, South Africa, and Japan

Short-tailed stingrays, as with some other wide-ranging stingrays, find their mates by gathering in large numbers at certain traditional sites in the summer breeding season. After mating, the female retains the fertilized eggs in her body and gives birth to fully formed young rays. While they are still inside their mother, these gain nourishment first from yolk, then by absorbing a milklike fluid that contains mucus, fat, and proteins, which is secreted into the mother's uterus. At birth they measure some 36 cm (14 in) across.

The short-tail is the world's largest stingray, weighing up to 350 kg (772 lb). Like most rays, it spends the majority of its time on or near the sea bed, feeding on molluscs and crustaceans by crushing them with the hard, flattened teeth in its jaws. The spine on the tail can be up to 40 cm (15½ in) long, contains poison, and is used in defence. A wound from any stingray is very painful, but fatalities are exceedingly rare.

Drawn together A large group of short-tail stingrays gathers off New Zealand's Poor Knight's Island to find a mate and breed. Outside the breeding season this species is usually solitary.

Coqui frog
Two-part call

SPECIES *Eleutherodactylus coqui* **SIZE** 3.5–6 cm (1½–2¼ in)
DISTRIBUTION Woodland; native to Puerto Rico and introduced to several other places, including Florida and Hawaii

Male coqui frogs produce a two-part advertisement call, which is made up of a low-pitched "co" and a high-pitched "qui" – hence the name "coqui". The ears of males are particularly sensitive to the low-frequency sound in the "co"; for them, it is a threat signal and it warns them to keep their distance. The ears of females are tuned to the higher frequency "qui", which is a mating call; females respond by approaching a calling male. Males call from leaves 1–2 m (3¼–6½ ft) above the ground. After mating, the fertilized eggs are deposited on the ground under leaves, and unlike most frog species, develop into tiny frogs without experiencing a tadpole stage.

True calling Males have very large, sausage-shaped vocal sacs, representing a third of their overall size when fully inflated.

Great Plains toad
Pneumatic trill

SPECIES *Anaxyrus cognatus* **SIZE** 4.5–12 cm (1¾–4½ in)
DISTRIBUTION Deserts and prairies in central USA, northern Mexico, and southern Canada

The Great Plains toad spends much of its life in an underground burrow, emerging only at night and after rain to feed. Heavy rainfall in spring and summer triggers mass migrations of toads to temporary pools, where large, noisy choruses can form. Breeding occurs over a few days. Larger males call from the edge of the pond, producing a prolonged, loud, metallic trill. Smaller males tend not to call but gather as "satellite" males (see panel, right) around the callers. Females are attracted to males that call most often.

CASE STUDY **SILENT SNEAKERS**

Calling male Great Plains toads both attract females and alert other males to their presence. By staying quiet, smaller males avoid conflict but also improve their chances of mating. They loiter near larger males, out of sight but within earshot. When females approach, drawn by the larger toad's calls, they intercept them and mate with them.

Adder
Following a trail

SPECIES *Vipera berus* **SIZE** Up to 65 cm (26 in) **DISTRIBUTION** Widespread in northern and western Europe, Russia, and UK (absent from Ireland)

A few weeks after emerging from hibernation in the spring, male adders shed their skin and begin to move around their home range, looking for the odour trails left by females. When a male finds a trail, he follows it to locate the female. The male guards the female for several days, wrestling with rival males and seeing off any smaller individuals (larger males tend to be more successful). The "winner" then mates with the female several times, with each mating episode lasting around two hours. Because female adders only breed in alternate years, producing between three and 18 young in each litter, there are fewer of them, so there is fierce competition among males for females.

Tasting the air A male adder uses its tongue to pick up airborne scent particles (including odour trails left by females) and transfer them to a gland in its mouth. In this way it is able to "taste" its surroundings.

Tiger salamander
Favoured location

SPECIES *Ambystoma tigrinum* **SIZE** 7.5–16 cm (3–6½ in)
DISTRIBUTION Grassland and wooded areas near water in North America

The tiger salamander migrates at night to "traditional" breeding ponds after heavy rain. Males arrive a few days before females. Breeding populations can be very dense, making mating a competitive and sometimes chaotic business. The male courts a female by nudging her tail with his snout. When she responds, he deposits a spermatophore, which she walks over and picks up. Males interfere with one another's mating attempts by depositing their spermatophores on top of those of their rivals. In some subspecies, eggs are laid in clumps; in others they are laid singly. The timing of breeding varies across their range; in northern areas, for example, the salamanders migrate in early spring as soon as the ice on their breeding ponds begins to melt.

On the move Tiger salamanders are found over a vast range and include a number of local variants, mostly classified as subspecies. This is the eastern tiger salamander, which is found in northern Minnesota, USA.

Green turtle
Round trip

SPECIES Chelonia mydas **SIZE** Up to 1.5 m (5 ft)
DISTRIBUTION Tropical and subtropical seagrass beds and open water in Atlantic and Indo-Pacific oceans

For green turtles, mating is just part of a huge journey across the ocean that they must undertake in order to breed. They live in one part of the ocean, but breed in another, sometimes making a round trip of 4,800 km (3,000 miles). Females breed at intervals of two or six years, so there are always more males than females in mating groups and males must compete to mate.

The female comes ashore at night, to the same beach where she was born, and lays up to 200 eggs in a deep burrow in the sand. The eggs hatch after two months, when the young make a hazardous journey down to the sea. Along the route, many are eaten by birds and other predators. The young feed on plankton and, being soft-shelled, are prey for fishes. The few that survive mature at 10–24 years of age and they may live to be 100 years old. Green turtles are endangered, largely as a result of hunting by humans. From the 17th century, there was a steady trade of turtles from the Caribbean to London, to provide turtle soup. Even today, sea turtles continue to be captured for food and many are accidentally caught and killed in fishing nets. The most effective means of conserving green turtles in the wild is to protect the beaches where they lay their eggs so they can continue to breed.

Meeting up Female green turtles gather in the shallows near a traditional nesting beach. Green turtles nest on sandy beaches in large numbers. By laying their eggs together over the same few nights, they maximize the chances of their young surviving, as the sheer number of hatchlings emerging at once overwhelms predators.

The big swim Green turtles are powerful swimmers and can travel continuously for several weeks at a time. It is not known how they manage to navigate their way back to the same breeding site each season, but it is thought to include an ability to sense the Earth's magnetic fields.

CASE STUDY TRACKING TURTLES

Green turtles can be tracked by fitting them with radio transmitters. Experiments have been done in which radio-tagged turtles approaching Ascension Island were displaced off course. Those displaced downwind easily found Ascension, but those displaced upwind took much longer to find it. This suggests that green turtles use wind-borne cues, possibly odours, to find their way back to the beach where they were born.

Snowy lek Male capercaillies pose and strut while females observe and assess each male's condition. Capercaillies are large birds, similar in size to a turkey.

Fighting spirit A male capercaillie (right) looks formidable, but the smaller, drabber females are also aggressive to each other and may destroy the nests of other nearby females.

Western capercaillie

Mating ground

SPECIES *Tetrao urogallus* **SIZE** 0.6–1 m (2–3¼ ft)
DISTRIBUTION Coniferous forest in Asia and northern Europe, including Scotland

Capercaillies find their mates at a traditional communal mating site called a lek during a long breeding season lasting through spring and summer. At the beginning of the season, males display from positions high up in trees, but later they move to the ground, each male defending a very small territory in which he displays. Male displays involve fanning the tail, jumping in the air, and producing a loud, complex call incorporating a variety of rattling, popping, and grinding sounds. Males defend their territories fiercely, not only against rival males, but also against dogs and humans.

Southern royal albatross

Mate for life

SPECIES *Diomedea epomophora* **SIZE** 1.1–1.2 m (3½–4 ft)
DISTRIBUTION Open ocean in the southern hemisphere

The southern royal albatross may live for up to 80 years and normally pairs for life. It reaches sexual maturity at 9–11 years of age, when it goes to one of a small number of breeding sites on offshore islands to find a mate. Pair formation involves an elaborate display in which the wings extend and the bill points skywards. A pair produces only one egg every two years and the chick takes months to reach adult size. Spending the non-breeding season apart, at sea, they reunite and renew their bond with displays at the start of each breeding season.

Equality of the sexes Males and females look alike and are equally involved as parents, taking turns to spend days foraging at sea to bring home a meal for the chick.

White-winged fairywren

Changing plumage

SPECIES *Malurus leucopterus* **SIZE** 12 cm (4½ in)
DISTRIBUTION Sparse, stunted vegetation in western Australia

White-winged fairywrens have a complex mating system, in which only a few males have bright blue plumage. They are cooperative breeders, with small territorial groups, in which a female feeds the young, assisted by helpers. In most of these groups, the males are brown, like the females, but some are bright blue (or black in some subspecies); this "nuptial" plumage is not developed until a male is three years old. The nuptial male is usually the dominant male. Courtship may involve presenting the female with a petal as a gift. He nests with only one female and contributes to rearing the resulting young. Cooperative breeding helps these birds to raise larger broods than individual pairs could alone.

Black and blue This sexuallly mature male white-winged fairywren (above left) has developed bright blue nuptial plumage. Females and non-breeding males, in contrast, are brown.

European rabbit

Prolific breeders

SPECIES *Oryctolagus cuniculus* **SIZE** 35–50 cm (14–19½ in)
DISTRIBUTION Now found in heathland, farmland, and woodland throughout the world, but originally from Europe

European rabbits are renowned for their breeding capabilities. Their living and breeding patterns vary with the nature of the soil. On soft, easily diggable ground, they tend to spread over a large area, but if the soil is hard they use the same burrows for a long time and live in small colonies, called warrens. Males have larger home ranges than females and compete to mate with females as they become receptive, while females compete for optimal nesting sites. Females can produce several litters, of five or six kittens, in a year. Both sexes form separate dominance hierarchies, with the most dominant male closely following and guarding a receptive female, seeing off rival males, until she is ready to mate. Both males and females have more than one mate, but the dominant male tends to attract the dominant female. While he fathers most of the young born in a group, other males may father around 16 per cent.

Ready to mate When seeking out a mate, male rabbits use their powerful sense of smell to assess the reproductive condition of several females at a time. If a female is ready to breed the male rabbit will track her.

Moose
Scent and sound

SPECIES Alces alces **SIZE** 2.5–3.2 m (8¼–10½ ft)
DISTRIBUTION Deciduous forest around the world at northern latitudes: eastern Eurasia and northern North America

Male moose produce long, moaning calls that can attract females from as far as 3.2 km (2 miles) away. They also produce a powerful smell and urinate around their wallow holes. Males compete for females and may fight, but often they avoid injury by assessing their relative size, the smaller male giving way to the larger. However, a bull often loses his harem to a rival after a few days. Mating occurs in September or October; a single calf, occasionally twins, is born eight months later. The young stay with the mother for a year. Otherwise moose live solitary lives, coming together only for mating. Adult moose live for 8–12 years, with the longevity of males sometimes shortened by injuries sustained in fights. Unable to sweat to keep cool, moose are confined to areas where the temperature does not exceed 27°C (81°F).

Heavyweight contender The male moose is a formidable animal. An adult male can be up to 2.1 m (7 ft) high at the shoulder and weigh over 500 kg (1,100 lb). The moose is the largest species of deer in the world.

Dugong
Group attraction

SPECIES Dugong dugon **SIZE** 2.5–4 m (8¼–13 ft)
DISTRIBUTION Shallow coastal waters of Indian Ocean, East Africa, Red Sea, northern Australia, and Pacific islands

Highly sociable animals, dugongs used to occur in large herds. Their populations have been seriously depleted by humans and they are now seen either alone or in small groups. Most dugongs display relatively simple breeding behaviour. Both sexes reach sexual maturity at around nine years of age. When a female becomes sexually receptive, she attracts a group of three to ten males, who jostle and fight to gain access to her. Mature males have small tusks, which may be used in these battles, although serious injuries are rare. Females also often bear scars on their heads and backs from male tusks, suggesting males may use sexual coercion. A lekking breeding system (see panel, right) may have been much more widespread in the years before numbers of this species declined.

Close relatives of manatees, dugongs are mammals and must breathe air. They dive for up to three minutes at a time to feed, using their muscular snouts to dislodge seagrass plants, which they then eat whole.

Travelling together A small group of dugongs swim over coral in search of seagrass beds. Dugongs and their relatives the manatees are commonly known as sea cows, due to their plant-eating habits. They are the world's only herbivorous marine mammals. Their preferred food ties them to coastal habitats.

CASE STUDY **DUGONG GROUPS LEKKING**

In Shark Bay, off Western Australia, male dugongs hold small territories and display to attract females. The territories are temporary and defended against other males. When a female enters a male's territory, he performs various manoeuvres to encourage her to mate. These include short swims across the sea bed and turning belly up towards her.

Sexual rivalry

Like most other aspects of animal life, reproduction is a highly competitive business. Individuals have to compete for access to mates, as well as for the resources, such as food and space, that are needed in order to procreate successfully. The fundamental differences between the sexes that result in sexual "dimorphism", or two distinct body shapes, also mean that, in most instances, it is males that vie with each other for females – but there are also several species in which females compete for males.

MALE SEXUAL RIVALRY

A female maximizes her reproductive success by producing, protecting, and feeding a limited number of young, as well as by ensuring that they are fathered by a high-quality male. Unless they help care for young, males maximize their success simply by mating with as many females as possible; as a result, they compete with one another for partners. Evolution thus favours greater male strength, large body size, and weapons, such as horns, claws, and teeth for use in fighting. This explains why many males are larger and more heavily armed than females.

Fighting it out Two Madagascan short-horned chameleons grapple on a branch. Males have a short horn on the snout that is used when fighting over females.

RITUALIZED COMPETITION

Fighting takes its toll in terms of energy and time. It can also be fatal, especially when males possess dangerous weapons. Fortunately, natural selection has developed less costly and life-threatening methods of settling disputes in some species, usually based on signals or poses that indicate strength. Before resorting to violence, rival males often engage in postures and displays that reveal their true size to their opponent, providing an opportunity for the smaller animal to back down. With some animals, disputes are settled using entirely arbitrary criteria: for example, an individual claiming a preferred rock or sunny spot is recognized as the "owner" and is not attacked. This occurs when the benefits gained from the resource are low and the costs of fighting for it are high.

A place in the sun Male speckled wood butterflies claim spots of sunlight, to which females are attracted. Sunspots are short-lived, so males do not waste time and energy contesting them.

Blue for a girl An Australian satin bowerbird decorates a mating bower with blue objects that attract females. Blue items are rare, and so are often stolen from rivals' bowers.

CONFLICT AND COOPERATION

It is an evolutionary irony that, in some species, males can often attract females more effectively if they act together. The combined flashing displays of these male fireflies, for example, create an unmissable beacon for any females who happen to be in the vicinity. Of course, the presence of so many rival males in one place also means that, when the females do arrive, competition for the right to mate with them will be all the more intense. There is an additional risk: studies have shown that longer and brighter flashes among males, which are exactly what attract females, also attract potential predators, so the line between sex and death is fine indeed.

FEMALE SEXUAL RIVALRY

In a few animal species, the usual pattern of sex differences, or dimorphism, is reversed: females are noticeably larger and more powerful than males, and are therefore the ones who compete for mates. Large size in females usually evolves when larger females can produce more or bigger young than smaller females. Female competition for males is also associated with a situation in which males play a major role in feeding, rearing, and protecting the young; male care then becomes a limited resource over which females will fight for possession. In some species, this results in polyandry (literally, "several husbands") in which a female has more than one mate. In moorhens, for example, females are like large, egg-laying machines: their clutches are often flooded or taken by predators and so must be replaced. They fight over the smaller males, who carry out all the duties of incubating the eggs and protecting the chicks once they have hatched. Some female moorhens even have two nests, each with its own male custodian.

Fighting moorhens Two female moorhens lash out at one another in a battle over a male (right). Moorhens often produce two broods of offspring in a year, and the chicks from the first brood help to feed the chicks in the second brood (below).

SEXUAL TENSION

The reproductive interests of male and female animals sometimes conflict, resulting in patterns of behaviour in which one partner acts in its own interests at the expense of those of its mate. One example of this is infanticide, when a male kills a female's young so that she can produce his own offspring more quickly. When a male lion takes over a pride of females, he kills any cubs still suckling from their mothers. Females do not come into heat until they have finished suckling their cubs, so killing these cubs means the females quickly come into season, ready to conceive young from the new male. Infanticide also occurs among primate species, including chimpanzees and baboons.

Mountain-top duel Two male Spanish ibexes battle for the possession of a group of females. Much larger than females, male ibexes have massive shoulders, thickened skulls, and huge horns. Fights are frequently very violent and can lead to serious injury or, occasionally, death.

Infanticide A male lion (above) attacks a cub while its mother tries unsuccessfully to protect it. A female chimpanzee (left) threatens a male that is trying to kill her infant.

Giant cuttlefish
Battling broadside
SPECIES *Sepia apama* **SIZE** 0.8–1.5 m (2½–5 ft)
DISTRIBUTION Rocky reefs and seagrass beds in coastal waters around southern Australia

Giant cuttlefish die at the end of just one breeding season, after an orgy of communal breeding. They migrate in large numbers to reefs off southern Australia, where males fight for the right to mate with females. They align themselves side by side, signalling their aggressiveness by changing colour and fanning out their highly patterned arms in order to make themselves appear as large as possible. A smaller male will generally back down, but if two males of equal size meet they may attack each other with their arms and sharp beaks. Many cuttlefish bear scars from fierce battles, and some males may even lose tentacles.

Side stripes Two rival male cuttlefish swim alongside each other in a threat display. They pulsate, creating a flashing effect with the stripes along their sides.

Grappling crabs Two sally lightfoot crabs interact on lava rocks in the Galapagos. The crab's distinctive blue underside is clearly visible on the crab furthest from the camera.

Sally lightfoot crab
Pincer moves
SPECIES *Grapsus grapsus* **SIZE** 28 cm (3¼ in)
DISTRIBUTION West coast of South America, Central America, and Mexico; Galapagos Islands. Rocky shores, just above the water line

Sally lightfoot crabs use their chelipeds, or large pincers, in aggressive interactions with their rivals. Male sally lightfoot crabs have an enlarged right front pincer, which is held out from the body like a shield and brandished at an opponent. Disputes are usually resolved by a bout of mutual pincer waving, and only rarely does this escalate into a fight. These crabs feed on algae and the carcasses of dead animals on the seashore. Young crabs are dark brown, which camouflages them among the rocks; adults are brightly coloured and rely on their agility to avoid predators.

Colourful characters A peacock mantis shrimp uses its large swivelling eyes to pinpoint prey, then will strike with lightening speed, unfolding its claws from under its head.

Peacock mantis shrimp
Lashing out
SPECIES *Odontodactylus scyllarus* **SIZE** 15–18 cm (6–7 in)
DISTRIBUTION Coral reef environs in shallow water in Indian and Pacific oceans

Mantis shrimps have special appendages with which they can deliver one of the most powerful blows in the animal kingdom. Generally, this is used to break open the shells of their prey (snails, crustaceans, and bivalves) but they have been known to smash the glass of aquariums when held in captivity. In the wild, they live in a variety of excavated or borrowed burrows and crevices. A female enters a male's burrow to breed where he guards her, lashing out at rivals with his powerful appendages.

Kerengga ant-like jumper
Claw display
SPECIES *Myrmarachne plataleoides* **SIZE** 6–12 mm (¼–½ in)
DISTRIBUTION Trees and bushes where there are weaver ant colonies in India, Sri Lanka, China, and southeast Asia

This jumping spider gains protection from its enemies by resembling a kerengga, or red weaver ant, both in appearance and the way it moves. The female resembles a single ant, the adult male an ant carrying a small ant. The "small ant" is in fact a pair of long chelicerae (claws) that make up a third of his total length. Males use their claws as swords when fighting over females and open them to reveal fangs. The claws are too clumsy to be of any use for feeding so males no longer eat once they are sexually mature.

Head-to-head When fighting, rival males face each other with their giant claws open, showing off their fangs. The victor is usually the male with the widest claw span.

Hercules beetle
Body slam

SPECIES *Dynastes hercules* **SIZE** 0.5–0.9 cm (³⁄₁₆–³⁄₈ in) excluding horn, males with horn can reach 17.5 cm (7 in) **DISTRIBUTION** Tropical rainforest in Central and South America and some Caribbean islands

Male hercules beetles have two long horns, which can be longer than the rest of body. The upper (thoracic) horn is fixed and has a hairy lower edge; the lower (cephalic) horn can be moved up and down so that the two horns act as pincers. Females differ in appearance to males, having a layer of reddish hairs on their wing cases and no horns. Hercules beetles are solitary, but if males meet in the presence of a female they may fight, engaging first in head-bobbing that produces a chirping sound. This sometimes progresses to a battle in which each male tries to grasp his rival between his horns and slam him to the ground.

Similar species *Chalcosoma mollenkampi* (far left), from Borneo and other parts of Indonesia, has three horns – two above and one below. The European rhinoceros beetle, *Oryctes nasicornis* (left), has a single, backward curving horn.

Power move When a confrontation becomes physical, the male Hercules beetle uses its powerful horns to try and grip a rival.

A hercules beetle can lift an object many times its own body weight, and is proportionally one of the strongest animals on Earth.

Diopsid fly
Wide-eyed winners

SPECIES *Teleopsis dalmanni* **SIZE** 6–9 mm (¼–³⁄₈ in) **DISTRIBUTION** Low-lying vegetation in humid places, such as on banks of streams or rivers, and in wetlands in Malaysia

These flies are also called stalk-eyed flies, because their eyes are on long stalks that protrude outwards from the sides of their heads. Males with the longest eye-stalks are preferred by females and they usually win contests with shorter rivals that tend to have shorter eye-stalks. Males compete for prime positions at leks (mating grounds) and meet each other face-to-face in contests so that they can compare the distance between their own eyes with their rival's. The male with the shorter span generally backs down, avoiding what could be a costly fight that he is likely to lose.

Stalk span A diopsid fly rests on vegetation near a river. Groups of flies meet in the morning at lekking sites near water to mate. Females cluster around males with the longest stalks. Males defend their positions in frequent displaying contests and the wide span between the fly's eyes is key to determining his success.

Fig wasps
Fruit fight

FAMILY Agaonidae **SIZE** 1–3 mm (¹⁄₁₆–⅛ in) **DISTRIBUTION** Develops in fruit of fig trees, which are found throughout the tropics, and in warmer temperate regions of southern Europe and Asia

Fig wasps, of which there are around 650 species worldwide, live in a symbiotic relationship with fig trees. The wasps nest inside figs, their larvae feeding on the fleshy interior, and female wasps, which have wings, carry pollen from one fig to another. In some species, males occur in two forms: winged and wingless. Wingless males never leave their home fig, but dig a tunnel that enables winged males and females to reach the outside world. The wingless male fig wasps use their large, slicing jaws to engage in vicious fights with rivals for the right to breed with females that they encounter inside the fruit. In contrast, winged males lack jaws, do not fight, and mate with flying females outside the fig.

Leaving home These fig wasps are emerging from the fruit that provides them with shelter and sustenance. All fig wasps hatch inside the fruit, and males fight each other for the chance to mate with females. Males compete with wasps from other broods that may have hatched in the same fig.

Locking horns Two male stag flies grapple with one another for the right to claim a site where females will come to mate. Raising themselves up as high as they can on their long legs, they lock horns and seek to push one another over. Eventually, one is pushed back and gives way to the victor.

Stag fly
Fighting flies

SPECIES *Phytalmia cervicornis* **SIZE** 1 cm (⅜ in)
DISTRIBUTION Forests in Papua New Guinea and Indonesia

Male stag flies fight for the possession of sites where females will come to lay their eggs so that, when a female fly arrives, the winner is able to mate with her. Males have pronged, antler-like projections on their heads, and they use these to grapple with one another when fighting, locking their antlers together in a similar way to red deer stags (see p.318). At the same time, they extend their long legs, stretching them out as far as they can in order to make themselves appear as tall and threatening as possible to their rivals. Larger males have larger antlers and generally defeat smaller males, which tend to have small antlers (see panel, right). Contests between males over a female are usually resolved before mating begins, but rival males sometimes try to knock a mating male off the back of the female. Egg-laying sites are typically located on recently felled tree trunks that contain the rotting wood on which the stag fly larvae will feed. Once a male holds such a site, he releases a pheromone from a gland on his abdomen, which attracts females that are in a breeding condition and ready to lay their eggs. After mating, the male stays with the female, guarding her while she lays her eggs, and preventing other males from mating with her until she has finished.

ANATOMY **SIZE MATTERS**

The relative size of two males' antlers determines which one will win a fight and thus earn the right to mate. Males vary in size, reflecting differences in their growth as larvae. The antlers of the smallest males are little more than stumps, as seen in the stag fly below, and these males have low mating success. In many animals that have specialized weapons, males try to avoid physical fights, so as to reduce costs in terms of time, energy, and possible injury. Instead, they assess the size of each other's weapons and the male with the smaller weapons backs down.

small antler

Similar species A male moose fly (*Phytalmia alcicornis*) from New Guinea (above) has broad, flat antlers, which can be so large and cumbersome that they become a hindrance. Two male goat flies (*Phytalmia mouldsi*) from Northern Australia (right) use their long legs as stilts and grapple with one another, their short, stout horns locked together.

Ideal mate The nest-building "parental" male bluegill sunfish has sperm of a superior quality to the males that don't build nests, which is why female fish favour parental males with their eggs.

Bluegill sunfish
Breaking and entering
SPECIES *Lepomis macrochirus* **SIZE** 10–15 cm (4–6 in), occasionally up to 41 cm (16 in) **DISTRIBUTION** Lakes and slow-moving rocky streams in USA and Canada

When it comes to fertilization, male bluegill sunfishes take one of three roles: "parental" males, "sneaker" males, or "satellite" males, each with a different reproductive strategy. The parental male builds a nest. It finds a depression on the bed of a lake or stream and clears it of debris. It then grunts to attract a passing female. After courtship, in which they swim in circles and touch bellies, the female deposits eggs in the parental male's nest and he fertilizes them. The male then guards these eggs against predators and fans them to keep them well oxygenated. A female can lay up to 50,000 eggs, allocating batches of them to several different parental males, each of whom guards eggs from several females. Sneaker males dart into undefended nests, while satellite males mimic female appearance and behaviour in order to gain access to nests. Both will shed their sperm once inside the nest, in an attempt to fertilize any unfertilized eggs.

Aggressive lip-lock Also known as "red terrors", red cichlids are extremely aggressive fishes. Here, two equally matched male rival cichlids have locked their mouths together in a trial of strength.

Red or *Guayas cichlid*
Mouth to mouth
SPECIES *Mesoheros festae* **SIZE** Up to 25 cm (10 in); female smaller than male **DISTRIBUTION** Lakes and slow-moving rivers in South America.

The female red cichlid looks after up to 3,000 eggs in a nest hidden in a cave or crevice, while the male keeps guard outside. If there are confrontational interactions between the defending male and an interloper, they are normally resolved by means of a temporary display of bright colours, after which the smaller fish backs down. However, well-matched fishes of similar size and colour engage in bouts of mouth-wrestling.

Galapagos giant tortoise
Butting in
SPECIES *Chelonoidis niger* **SIZE** Up to 1.4 m (4½ ft) **DISTRIBUTION** Moves between open, dry grassland and vegetated areas with pools on Galapagos Islands (six subspecies – one on each of six islands)

Now highly endangered, these impressive creatures can live for over 100 years and reach maturity at 20–30 years. They spend their days moving between open areas during the cool part of the day and shady wooded areas when it is hot.

Galapagos giant tortoises mate during the rainy season, between January and June. Males use a variety of techniques to establish their dominance and protect their mating rights, including raising their heads at rivals (see below) and shell butting, in which one male butts the shell of another in a show of aggression until one tortoise backs down. Mating itself is a lengthy process, and the underside of a male's shell is concave, which enables him to maintain a precarious grip on the back of the female during the slow task of mating. Once mating has taken place, females retire to dry areas of the island between June and December in order to nest.

Higher status Male Galapagos giant tortoises have an interesting method of establishing power. In a dispute, each tortoise raises its head as high as possible. The one that raises its head the highest gains dominance.

Strawberry poison frog
Wrestling match

SPECIES *Oophaga pumilio* **SIZE** 1.5–2.5cm (½–1in)
DISTRIBUTION Rainforest, from sea level up to 960m (3,165ft) in Costa Rica, Nicaragua, Panama

Male strawberry poison frogs live only about 3m (9¾ft) apart from one another, and engage in prolonged bouts of wrestling in defence of their small mating territories. Active by day, they produce territorial calls in the morning and then, later in the day, change the nature of their call to one that attracts females. If a rival male enters another's territory, the resident male increases its call rate as a warning to the intruder. If this fails to deter the rival, the two then grapple with each other, trying to force their opponent to the ground, until a winner emerges. The loser then vacates the territory, leaving the winner in possession. The bright coloration of poison frogs warns predators that they are toxic.

Powerful leg push Strawberry poison frogs do battle chest-to-chest, each pushing down hard with their strong back legs, and trying to shove its opponent over. A victor emerges when one male manages to force the other to the ground, the victor gains dominance over the loser and wins the contested territory.

Ground anole
Hidden warning

SPECIES *Norops humilis* **SIZE** Up to 11.5 cm (4½ in); female slightly larger than male **DISTRIBUTION** Lowland forest, especially common in abandoned cacao plantations in Costa Rica, Panama, and Nicaragua

This South American lizard feeds among leaf litter on the forest floor and is frequently found perched on tree trunks with its head pointing downwards. Its pale and dull brownish green coloration affords it excellent camouflage in the gloom of the forest. However, when necessary, the male ground anole is able to produce a brilliant flash of colour that makes it highly visible, both to potential mates and to rivals.

The dewlap is a flap of skin positioned under the ground anole's chin. It is the only brightly coloured part of the lizard's body. Normally, it is folded away, but it can be unfolded and revealed to create a brilliant display. A special bone that is hinged at the base of the tongue is flicked outwards and downwards. This bone pushes out the dewlap to expose it. When defending its territory, the ground anole makes use of this colourful part of its body, displaying it to warn off other males that want to encroach on its territory. If the display fails to deter the rival, a fight ensues. The defender bobs his head, then rears up and proceeds to chase his rival. They then bite one another and use their long, muscular tails to lash each other, until in the end the weaker of the two males submits.

The colourful dewlap also serves another important function. Female ground anoles are attracted to the bright displays made by the territorial male. Different species of ground anole, otherwise very similar in appearance, have dewlaps of different colours, and the colour helps the female identify males of her own species to mate with.

Warning signal The brightly coloured flap of loose skin hanging from the ground anole's neck acts as a flag of aggression, warning off rivals who challenge the male for its territory.

Speckled rattlesnake
Writhing around
SPECIES Crotalus mitchellii **SIZE** 62–77 cm (24–30 in)
DISTRIBUTION Arid scrub and desert in southwest USA and Mexico

Rattlesnakes have lethal weapons but avoid using them when fighting among themselves. They reserve their venom to kill prey and to defend against enemies. However, males fight over access to females and engage in prolonged wrestling bouts lasting for over an hour, in which each attempts to pin his opponent's head against the ground. Mating occurs in spring, and females give birth to 3–11 young in late summer.

Male-to-male combat Males from most rattlesnake species fight during the breeding season, with the dominant male winning the right to mate with any nearby females.

Love bite A male slow-worm has a female, identifiable by her darker flanks, in his jaws prior to mating. Fully mature males are identified by their blue dots.

Slow-worm
Neck lock
SPECIES Anguis fragilis **SIZE** 30–50 cm (12–19½ in)
DISTRIBUTION Well-vegetated, slightly damp habitats, including gardens, in Europe

Male slow-worms are not territorial but frequently fight with rival males for the possession of females. They wrestle and bite each other around the head and neck, and older males often have many scars from previous fights. Females may also be scarred, as males grasp them firmly round the neck during mating, which can last for 10 hours. Fighting and mating occur in April, and in September or October females give birth to 6–12 live young. The exact timing of the birth depends on the average temperature during the summer. Young slow-worms are born later if the summer has been cold and, like their parents, go into hibernation during the winter months. Though they are often mistaken for snakes, slow-worms are in fact legless lizards.

Ruffled feathers Two independent male ruffs with darker colouring (left and right) display their breeding plumage along with a paler satellite male (centre).

Ruff
Dressing the part
SPECIES Calidris pugnax **SIZE** 29–32 cm (11½–12½ in) **DISTRIBUTION** Marshes, lake shores, and estuaries in northern Europe, Scandinavia, and Russia; migrates to Africa, Asia, and western Europe in winter

In the spring, ruffs gather at hereditary mating sites, called leks. The males display silently, jumping up and down and erecting the spectacular ruff and ear tufts around their heads. Males have three different mating strategies, each associated with a particular, genetically determined plumage pattern. Independent males have black or brown plumage and many defend small mating territories within the lek. Paler-plumaged satellite males gather in groups around the independent males. A third group of males, known as faeders, whose plumage is like that of females, mimic female behaviour and wander about the lek. A female, called a reeve, enters a lek and inspects the displaying males, before selecting one to mate with.

Mute swan
Pecking contest
SPECIES Cygnus olor **SIZE** 1.2–1.7 m (4–5½ ft) **DISTRIBUTION** Rivers, lakes, and reservoirs in Europe and Asia, naturalized in North America

Among the heaviest of flying birds, a male mute swan can weigh as much as 12 kg (26 lb) and is a formidable opponent, both to rival males and to other animals, including humans, that approach his nest. Mute swans are monogamous, forming pairs in March or April. Males, known as cobs, and females, called pens, share in nest building, incubation of the eggs, and protection of the young. The cob, which is slightly larger, is particularly aggressive in defending the territory, assuming a posture, called "busking", in which the neck is curved and the wings are arched over the back. If a rival is not deterred by this, a fight ensues in which they peck at each other and strike out with their wings. The nest, a large mound of vegetation built at the water's edge, is often used for several years. A pair normally produces five to seven young, called cygnets, but may produce up to 12. Pairs that breed successfully generally stay together for several years.

Getting in a flap Fights between mute swans can be violent and occasionally end in death. As soon as a rival swan enters a male's territory he charges across to confront it. By raising their bodies out of the water, each is able to judge the other's size, giving the smaller male a chance to back down and escape.

Cleaning up A female dunnock (right) presents herself, ready to mate with a male. The male will attempt to remove a rival's sperm before mating with her himself.

Dunnock
Three's company
SPECIES Prunella modularis **SIZE** 14 cm (5½ in)
DISTRIBUTION Woodland in Europe and Asia

Both male and female dunnocks may pair with more than partner through the breeding season (a type of mating pattern known as polygynandry). A female's two (or more) mates compete to father as many of her young as possible by mating with her frequently. Before mating, a male pecks at the female's cloaca, or reproductive opening, causing her to eject sperm left from previous matings. This increases the chance that his own sperm will fertilize her eggs. Both males provide paternal care for the young (perhaps of two or more nests at once), and the amount of help each provides to each nest is related to the proportion of the young in the clutch he "believes" he has fathered, based on the number of successful matings.

SEXUAL RIVALRY 317

CASE STUDY FEMALE CHOICE

The different strategies of male ruffs have evolved as a result of female choice. Females prefer to mate with males in busy parts of the lek. Therefore, independent males encourage satellite males to come close by bowing. This increases the chances of a satellite male mating with a female attracted to an independent male's spot on the lek, but also increases the independent male's chances.

SATELLITE WELCOMED

INDEPENDENT MALE ATTRACTS FEMALE

SATELLITE CONCEDES DEFEAT

Andean cock-of-the-rock
Holding court

SPECIES *Rupicola peruvianus* **SIZE** 20 cm (8 in)
DISTRIBUTION Cliffs and rocky outcrops in tropical and sub-tropical rainforest in French Guiana, Guyana, and Surinam

Male Andean cocks-of-the-rock display communally, competing with each other for the attention of females by performing elaborate displays at leks. Fifteen, or more, males assemble in the branches, each in his own area. They raise their fan-shaped crests and perform a complex range of bowing, bobbing, and hopping movements while showing off their plumage and making a variety of sounds. Even in the absence of females, the males spend hours perfecting their displays, often pairing up to compete or to practise together by performing "confrontation displays" in a strange kind of competitive alliance. When a female arrives, all the males erupt into even more frenzied activity. She moves among the males before choosing one, mating with him, and then leaving the lek to go to a rocky area where she makes a nest. Once the mated female has left, the males wait for the next female to arrive and then display again. She often selects the same male as the female before her.

Bright and beautiful The male Andean cock-of-the-rock stands out like a jewel in the shade near the rainforest floor. His crest, raised here in display, is normally held flat against the top of his head.

Choosing a mate The female Andean cock-of-the-rock (on the right in this image) is less brightly coloured than the males. As with many birds that do not form pair bonds, it is she, rather than the male, who decides who to mate with.

Red deer
Locking horns

SPECIES *Cervus elaphus* **SIZE** 1.5–2 m (5–6½ ft)
DISTRIBUTION Open woodland, plains, mountains, moorland in Western Europe, Asia, northwest USA, northwest Africa

During the autumnal rut, red deer stags compete to attract a harem of hinds (female deer) with whom they mate exclusively. Older males are heavier with larger antlers; they proclaim the ownership of a territory, into which they herd their harem, by roaring. Harem holders are challenged by rivals in a vocal contest. If this does not settle the dispute, the two stags go into a parallel walk, in which they walk side-by-side to assess each other's size. A closely matched pair will fight by charging at each other and locking antlers. The stresses of the rut, during which males abstain from eating, take a tremendous toll on body condition. After the rut, the deer live in single-sex groups, the males forgetting their hostilities until hormones stir again the following autumn.

Assertive call With head thrown back and nostrils flared, the roaring red deer stag signals his presence. The call is used to advertise his status, pronounce his territory, ward off rival males, and attract breeding females.

Parallel clash Two bucks size each other up as they begin to fight, clashing their huge antlers. Some stags are injured or killed in such contests.

Northern elephant seal
Winner takes all

SPECIES *Mirounga angustirostris* **SIZE** 3–5 m (9¾–16½ ft)
DISTRIBUTION Coastal waters of the Pacific; breeds on offshore islands between Alaska and Mexico

Only a minority of male elephant seal males mate with females, and for those that do, success is short-lived. Between December and March, large breeding groups of seals gather on offshore islands. Males are much larger than females and fight violently to become "harem masters", giving them exclusive access to 10 or 12 females.

Males vying for dominance will initially use visual and vocal displays to fend off any rivals, inflating their distinctive proboscises to emit incredibly loud roars. Should these displays fail to settle matters then physical combat ensues. Competing males rush at each other, rear their necks, slap, butt, and bite in fierce clashes. The males' necks and shoulders develop thick, corrugated skin and a layer of protective fat to help minimize injury during these encounters. Despite this, severe injuries among males are common and may be fatal.

Only one in 10 males becomes a harem master and none holds the status for more than three years, whereas females may breed for 10 years. Older females are more likely to mate with the highest-quality males and successfully rear pups. Younger, less dominant females in crowded colonies often fare better if they leave their natal colony and establish new ones.

Clash of the titans When two bull elephant seals fight, they roar loudly through their inflated noses, slam each other with bodies raised, and tear at the thick fat on their opponent's neck with their teeth. The resulting bloody wounds are usually superficial but can be fatal.

Bottlenose dolphin
Biting and butting

SPECIES *Tursiops truncatus* **SIZE** 1.9–4 m (6¼–13 ft)
DISTRIBUTION In tropical and warm temperate open sea and coastal waters worldwide

Male bottlenose dolphins often have deep scars on their skin, suggesting that they fight one another for access to females. Dominant males bite, head-butt, and scratch younger males with their teeth to establish sexual dominance. Acrobatic swimming displays are generally aimed at impressing females but they can also be used as a form of attack (see right). Despite this rivalry, groups of males may cooperate in coercing females to breed. Coalitions of male bottlenose dolphins are known to have forced a female dolphin away from her pod by butting and body slamming her before taking it in turns to mate with her. They cooperate to fend off other male alliances who attempt to join in.

>>01 >>02

Dive bombing >>01 A male bottlenose dolphin leaps high out of the water, off the coast of Hawaii in the Pacific Ocean, and strikes another dolphin in the head with his fluke. A dolphin's tail is incredibly powerful, as it is needed to propel the animal through the water. >>02 The lower dolphin retaliates by rising up to strike the jumping dolphin with his rostrum, or beak.

The roar of the male elephant seal can be heard several kilometres away.

Giraffe
Neck and neck

SPECIES *Giraffa camelopardalis* **SIZE** 4.7–5.7 m (15½–19 ft) tall
DISTRIBUTION Open woodland and wooded grassland in Northern Kenya, and Somalia

Young male giraffes establish dominance among themselves with neck-wrestling contests that can last up to 30 minutes. These look friendly, but occasionally a male's neck may be broken. Giraffes live in loose social groups of up to 20 animals. Mature bulls roam among groups looking for females ready to mate. If challenged by another male, they fight by kicking and head-butting.

Ritual combat These young male giraffes are engaged in a neck-wrestling contest. These are generally more of a ritual than violent clash. The winner may mount his opponent in a display of dominance.

ANATOMY ARMOURED SKULL

As they age, bull giraffes develop thickened deposits of bone on their foreheads. This layer gives vital protection to the brain, which could otherwise be damaged by the violent swinging and clubbing actions employed by competing bulls. A giraffe bull's brain can survive a swing of 3.5 m (11½ ft) and the impact of a blow that could knock a 1,500 kg (1.6 ton) rival off his feet. The bone is deposited at a rate of 1 kg (2½ lb) per year.

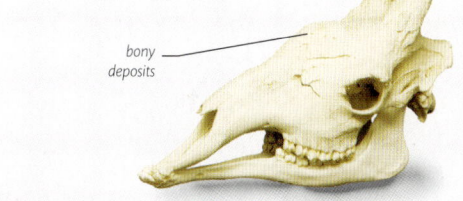

bony deposits

CASE STUDY PUP MORTALITY

Elephant seals spend most of their time at sea, but must come ashore to give birth, to mate, and to moult. Mating takes place soon after the female has given birth, and the tiny pups are often crushed beneath the clumsy, lumbering adults, especially when they are fighting. As the population rises and breeding beaches become more crowded, mortality among pups becomes more common.

Courtship

Courtship involves interaction between males and females that culminates in mating. Ranging from the superficial to the very elaborate, successful courtship is about "getting it right" – mating with the right species and right sex, at the right time, and being in the right "mood", which means suppressing behaviour incompatible with mating. It also means persuading a potential mate of your beneficial traits or abilities. In most species, females invest much more energy in producing offspring than males, so need to be more choosy about who they mate with.

THE RIGHT SPECIES

Mating with a member of another species is a serious mistake – it can mean that an individual's reproductive potential is wasted. In order to avoid this, males and females have evolved methods to send out signals that enable potential partners to distinguish them from members of other species. For example, male birds have species-specific colour patterns and songs; male frogs have distinctive calls (see below); and male and female mammals produce chemical scents called pheromones. Females have more to lose by making a mistake when choosing a partner; because they may have only one chance to reproduce, they need to be more discerning.

Calling male Male Verreaux's tree frogs call to attract females from perches on the banks of ponds. Their call differs to those of other nearby male frogs.

Dominant frequencies In some Australian ponds, male frogs of several species call for mates on the same nights. Species recognition is made easier for the female as males each have distinctive calls and call from particular places. The calls of species that are adjacent differ more than those that hold widely separated sites.

RECOGNIZING THE OPPOSITE SEX

Recognizing a member of the opposite sex is easy in species with sexual dimorphism, where one sex is markedly larger or more brightly coloured than the other. Many species also have special signals, which can be visual, olfactory, or auditory, and signal which sex they are. Some male frogs are not good at sex recognition and clasp males as readily as females. A clasped male gives a "release call" that makes the other male let go. When sexual dimorphism is extreme, as in spiders, the male is in danger of becoming prey.

Little and large This tiny male black widow spider approaches a female with caution, signalling that he is a potential mate and not a meal.

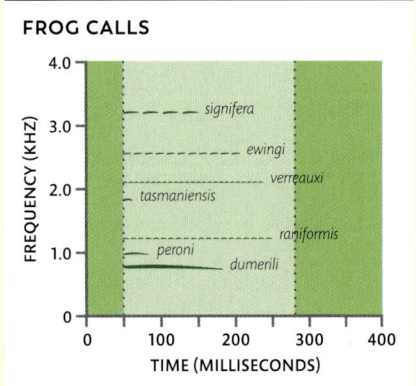

Life and death >>01 A male praying mantis has to persuade a female to mate with him, but not to eat him. However, this female bites off the male's head, taking it as a nuptial gift. >>02 The male has paid a high price for his chance to reproduce; a more cautious male might have survived.

COURTSHIP

CHOOSING A MATE

Animals can improve their reproductive success by favouring certain partners over others. Many male fishes and amphibians select larger females as they produce more eggs. In species where males help to care for the young, females prefer males that are better at building a nest, at defending it, or at feeding young. In species where males provide only sperm, a female's choice of mate is often based on male appearance and behaviour, which show that he has "good genes".

Size matters Female three-spine sticklebacks prefer males that are very aggressive in defending nests; males prefer fatter females.

Scent of a stranger Mice discriminate among potential mates on the basis of their smell, preferring those that are not genetically closely related to them.

THE RIGHT TIME

In many species, courtship behaviour serves to synchronize the activities of males and females so that mating occurs at the best moment. Female mammals typically have a brief period when their eggs can be fertilized; courtship behaviour both signals this and determines when it occurs by stimulating egg production. In colonial species, it is beneficial for individuals to lay eggs or produce young at the same time, as this lessens the risk of predation. The combined effect of many pairs displaying to their partners is to prompt such synchronization. In species with external fertilization (see p.334), precise coordination is needed to ensure that eggs or sperm are not lost before they can meet.

Smooth newt Female smooth newts must signal to a male that they are ready to gather up his spermatophore (sperm packet) by touching his tail; if they do not, his sperm may be lost.

Gift wrapped A male European bee-eater presents a dragonfly that he has caught to a female. Courtship gifts like this serve two functions: they provide extra nourishment for the female as she develops her eggs, and they provide her with information about his potential as a provider for her young.

PERSUASION

A function of some aspects of courtship behaviour is to raise the sexual motivation of the partner and, at the same time, to suppress behaviour that is incompatible with mating, such as aggression. This is especially true of animals, such as polar bears, that are solitary, and for whom any other animal is normally an enemy. In social animals, such as baboons, all group members compete frequently for food and their natural aggression must be overcome if mating is to occur. Being hard to persuade acts as a mechanism of mate choice for a female, as it ensures that she will mate only with males that can sustain a high level of courtship activity; such males are likely to have better genes.

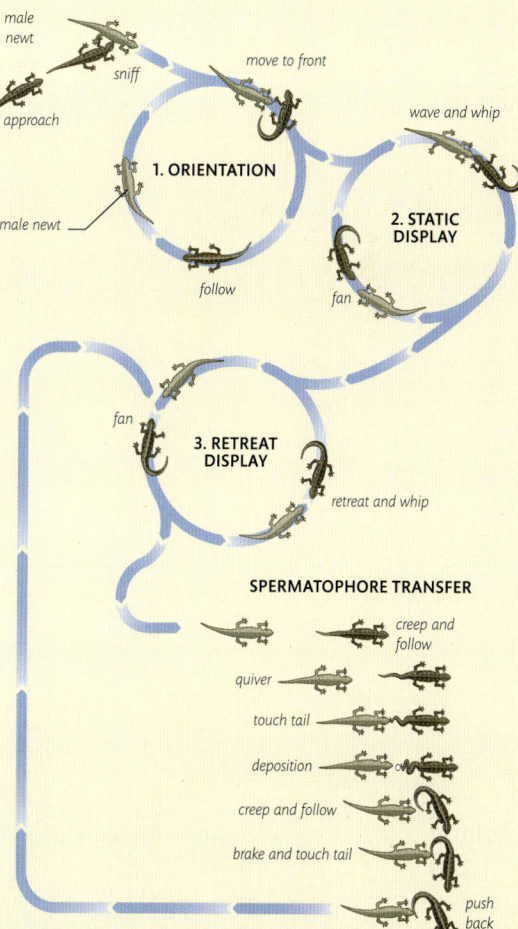

Courtship dance The courtship behaviour of newts consists of a number of distinct phases. The male does not proceed from one phase to the next until the female has responded positively to the current phase by approaching him. Despite this, some spermatophores are missed by the female, and so the later parts of the sequence are repeated.

Dance flies

Dance routine

FAMILY Empididae **SIZE** 1–11 mm (1/16–3/8 in)
DISTRIBUTION On vegetation in lowland and damp habitats worldwide but mainly in northern hemisphere

These slender flies are named for their dancing courtship displays. Some species perform these while perched, the males using a ritual series of wing-flicks followed by a pedalling action of their front legs. If a male gets the dance right, the female responds in kind, and they mate. But if he is the wrong species of fly, with the wrong dance routine, the female may treat him as prey and eat him.

Among most species of dance flies, the males "dance" in the air to draw attention to the nuptial gifts that they carry in their long legs. These are usually freshly killed insects such as other flies – including rival male dance flies of the same species. The gift-carrying males form dancing, airborne swarms to attract females, and when a male is approached by a female, he passes her the insect in mid-air and seizes her as she takes it. The linked pair then fly to a nearby perch, where the male supports the feeding female while he mates with her.

After mating, the male often retrieves his "gift" and flies back to the swarm to attract another female. He may use it several times, so it begins to look battered. Females can be picky and reject a male with a substandard nuptial gift.

CASE STUDY **EMPTY PROMISES**

Some male dance flies seduce females by presenting them with inedible gifts, saving them the trouble of catching other insects. This female *Empis opaca* dance fly has been tempted by a ball of willow seed fluff that resembles an insect cocoon, and the male mates with her while she probes the fake offering. But careful observation has shown that many females see through the deception, and reject anything that is not clearly edible.

Nuptial gift A male *Empis tessellata* dance fly mates with a female while she is sampling the plant bug that he has offered her. The male is supporting the weight of all three with his front legs.

Yellow scorpion

Holding hands

SPECIES Buthus occitanus **SIZE** 10 cm (4 in)
DISTRIBUTION Desert and arid semi-desert regions of North Africa, the Middle East, and Southern Europe

Courtship can be hazardous for a male scorpion. The female is larger, and although he is immune to her venom, she could easily overpower and eat him. After identifying himself with vibrating calls and distinctive scents, the male grasps the female's pincers with his own – partly to immobilize them, but also to guide her in a "dance" over the ground that ends with her taking up the spermatophore (sperm packet) he has deposited.

Deadly dance A pair of yellow scorpions dances with their tails entwined. As soon as the female picks up his sperm packet the male will beat a rapid retreat.

Marmalade hoverfly

Aerial acrobatics

SPECIES Episyrphus balteatus **SIZE** 8–12 mm (5/16–1/2 in)
DISTRIBUTION Forest, grassland, and gardens in Europe and northern Asia

Marmalade hoverflies are accomplished flyers, a skill that the males exploit by hovering on the spot to display their fitness to females. True flies, such as this species of hoverfly, have just one pair of functional wings, instead of two like most flying insects. The second pair of wings are reduced to clublike structures that act as balancing organs, giving them superb control in flight. Each male hoverfly claims an aerial territory and hovers there for many minutes at a time, leaving his chosen point in space only to drive off airborne intruders, or dart after interested females and begin the mating process.

Fragrant fuel Male hoverflies claim aerial territories close to flowers where females may perch. The flowers also supply sugary nectar to fuel their flights.

COURTSHIP 323

Pot-belly seahorse
Elaborate ritual
SPECIES *Hippocampus abdominalis* **SIZE** 18–30 cm (7–12 in)
DISTRIBUTION Rocky reefs and seagrass beds in coastal waters around southeast Australia and New Zealand

Seahorses are bony fishes with armoured bodies and prehensile tails, which they use to cling to seaweed or other material as they feed. Almost uniquely, a female seahorse places her eggs in a pouch on the male's belly, where they develop until they are ready to hatch. One of the largest species, the pot-belly seahorse has an elaborate courtship ritual in which the male becomes more vividly coloured and inflates his brood pouch with water. He swims towards a female with head tucked down and fins fluttering. If she is receptive, her own colours intensify and she adopts the same posture. The two then swim together, sometimes with their long tails entwined. Eventually, after bouts of dancing, the male urges the female to swim vertically upwards by tilting his snout in that direction. Once in position, often near the surface, the female transfers 300 or more eggs to the male's pouch, injecting them through an opening at the front. He retains them for about four weeks until they hatch as tiny seahorses.

Dancing partners As pot-belly seahorses dance together, their patterns intensify, with paler colours becoming brighter to contrast with the dark spots on their bodies. Here the male is on the left, tilting his long snout to encourage the female to swim towards the surface.

Swollen pouch When a male is ready to court a female, the brood pouch on his belly swells with water and changes colour, turning white or pale yellow. If she is unreceptive, he deflates his belly and may search for another female.

Pinned down Once the sharks have dropped to the sea floor, the male keeps a tight grip on the larger female's pectoral fin as he manoeuvres his clasper into position.

Horn shark
Chase and drop
SPECIES *Heterodontus francisci* **SIZE** 1.2 m (4 ft)
DISTRIBUTION Warm waters of the eastern Pacific, off California and Central America

Most bony fishes release large numbers of small eggs into the water, where they are fertilized by sperm released by the males – a process known as spawning. Sharks, by contrast, mate like land animals, with the male placing sperm in the female's body to fertilize her eggs internally. To achieve this, he must court the female to ensure her cooperation in the mating process. The male horn shark, for example, chases the female through the water until she is ready to accept his advances. They then sink to the sea bed, where the male seizes the female and inserts one of his long "claspers" – modified pelvic fins – into her genital opening. He then pumps a mixture of seawater and sperm along a groove in the clasper and into the female's oviduct. The whole procedure can last up to 40 minutes. A few weeks later, the female begins laying individual eggs, each within a tough protective case.

Banded pipefish
Lengthy dance
SPECIES *Dunckerocampus dactyliophorus*
SIZE 10–20 cm (4–8 in) **DISTRIBUTION** Coastal waters and reefs in the tropical Indian and western Pacific oceans

Slender, eel-like pipefishes swim together for hours in a protracted nuptial dance. Closely related to seahorses (see above), pipefishes have the same elongated snouts and bony, segmented body armour. The males also have the same reproductive role, retaining the females' eggs in a brood pouch beneath the body until they hatch. The banded pipefish is one of the most striking species, with its wasplike yellow and black bands and vivid red tail. Each male claims a territory in a favoured patch of water, often in a tide pool or reef lagoon. In the early morning, a mature female that is ready to mate may enter the male's territory to attract his attention. The male then courts her, entwining his body with hers for two hours or more as they swim. Finally, the female transfers her eggs to the male's brood pouch, where they are fertilized and start to develop into young pipefishes. The system ensures that the eggs are well protected, but once they are born the baby fishes fend for themselves.

Matching pair Male and female banded pipefish look almost identical, so like many animals they must display their sexual identity by the way they behave rather than relying on their appearance.

Red-legged salamander
Special delivery
SPECIES *Plethodon shermani* **SIZE** 8–13 cm (3¼–5 in)
DISTRIBUTION Woodland in eastern USA

Like other amphibians, salamanders and newts must lay their eggs in water or very damp places. However, many salamanders mate on land, using a method that is quite unlike that of other vertebrates. The male's sperm is transferred to the female in a capsule called a spermatophore, which is placed on the ground for her to gather up. To ensure she collects the sperm package, most species have a complex courtship ritual. The male red-legged salamander releases an enticing pheromone that attracts the female. She then straddles his tail and he leads her in a circular "tail walk", stopping at intervals to anoint her snout with scent from a gland beneath his chin. Eventually he stops to deposit his spermatophore on the ground, before guiding her forwards just far enough to take it into her oviduct.

Seductive scent A red-legged salamander male turns to place a dab of scent on the female's snout during a tail-walk courtship in Nantahala National Forest, North Carolina, USA. This species is one of the many lungless salamanders that absorb all their oxygen through their moist skin.

Cooling off The red flush of a male red-headed rock agama is triggered by hormones and the heat of the sun. At dusk, he reverts to a more discreet colour scheme, making him less conspicuous to predators. Despite this, a dominant male retains his high status as defender of a family group and their joint territory.

Red-headed rock agama
Push ups
SPECIES *Agama agama* **SIZE** 20–25 cm (8–10 in)
DISTRIBUTION Rocky grassland in Central Africa

Chameleons are not the only lizards that are able to change their skin colour. The red-headed rock agama, or rainbow lizard, is named for the way a dominant male's head flushes bright orange-red or magenta during the breeding season, forming a dramatic contrast with his electric-blue body. He emphasizes the transformation by performing energetic press-ups with his forelegs so that his glowing head bobs up and down. This both discourages less brilliantly coloured rivals and attracts females, for the vividness of the male's colours are a measure of his health and vigour.

Ardent glow A male red-headed rock agama bobs his head at a female to show off his dazzling nuptial colours and persuade her to mate. These lizards often perform their courtship displays on bare rocks beneath the scorching African sun.

Panther chameleon
Colour flush
SPECIES *Furcifer pardalis* **SIZE** 20–50 cm (8–19½ in)
DISTRIBUTION Tropical forest and scrubland of Madagascar and surrounding islands

Chameleons can contract or expand specialized colour cells in their skin in order to change colour rapidly. They use this ability to communicate with each other, and in many species, such as the panther chameleon, the males use sudden flushes of bright colour during courtship. If receptive, a female will allow a male to fertilize her eggs, using one of two organs known as hemipenes. But if the female has already mated, she discourages the male by turning dark brown or black.

Colourful moods Panther chameleons invariably have a white or pale stripe along their flanks, and broad vertical bands, but the contrast and colours can vary according to their moods.

Grass snake
Friendly persuasion

SPECIES *Natrix natrix* **SIZE** Up to 1.2 m (4 ft); rarely up to 2 m (6½ ft) **DISTRIBUTION** Damp habitats, grassland, and heathland in Europe, Asia, and northwest Africa

Most snakes rely on scent to find a partner. They use their forked tongues to pick up chemical signals that they analyse using an organ in the roof of the mouth. When a male grass snake locates a female, he follows her wherever she goes, and stimulates her by rubbing his chin along her back, flicking his tongue as he does so. If he is successful, they entwine their long bodies and mate.

Scaly caress Much smaller than his partner, a male grass snake tries to persuade a female to mate by caressing her with his chin. She will eventually lay up to 40 eggs in a warm place.

Firm grip The male common snapping turtle takes hold of the female with his claws and positions himself on her back in order to fertilize her eggs.

Common snapping turtle
Biting embrace

SPECIES *Chelydra serpentina* **SIZE** 20–46 cm (8–18 in) **DISTRIBUTION** Muddy ponds, streams, and swamps in USA and southern Canada

Notorious for its powerful bite, especially in its own defence, the snapping turtle is a strictly aquatic species that buries itself in the bottom mud of pools and streams to ambush its prey. It usually lives alone, but during the breeding season males and females come together for a rough courtship in which they bite each other and blow streams of bubbles. Eventually the male clambers on top of the female, gripping her shell with his claws. He curls his tail under her body until their vents meet, enabling him to fertilize her eggs.

Blue-footed booby
Look to the skies

SPECIES *Sula nebouxii* **SIZE** 76–84 cm (30–33 in)
DISTRIBUTION Breeds on eastern Pacific coasts and islands from Mexico to Peru, and Galapagos Islands, feeding at sea

Blue-footed boobies are ocean birds that breed in enormous coastal colonies, mainly on islands. The male selects a small nesting territory within the colony and parades around it, displaying to discourage rivals and advertising to females.

He spreads his wings, rotating them so their upper surfaces face forwards, raises his tail, and positions his bill straight up in a posture known as "sky-pointing". He also performs a stately dance, lifting his big blue feet alternately to draw attention to their vivid colour. If a female is impressed by his performance, she joins him to form a pair. The two birds maintain their bond by continuing to display to each other using the same ritual postures. They perform them before one bird leaves the nest to fly out to sea in search of food and then repeat them in greeting upon its return.

6,400
The number of pairs of blue-footed boobies that return to the volcanic Galapagos Islands to nest every year.

Sky-pointing The male booby's sky-pointing courtship display becomes part of a pair-bonding ritual that is performed by both birds.

Foot-tapping dance During its dancing display, a blue-footed booby raises each brightly coloured foot in turn with a high-stepping flourish.

CASE STUDY **THE BLUER THE BETTER**

Studies of breeding blue-footed boobies have shown that those with the bluest feet have more breeding success. Both sexes find intensely blue feet attractive, and a deeper colour may be a reliable indicator of general fitness. Foot colour tends to become duller with age, meaning that younger birds are preferred as mates.

Little tern
Bearing gifts

SPECIES *Sternula albifrons* **SIZE** 22–24 cm (8½–9½ in) **DISTRIBUTION** Nests on sand or gravel beaches on coasts of western Europe, eastern Asia, India, and Australia, and feeds at sea

Courtship displays of some male birds demonstrate that they are fit and healthy, and will pass on strong genes to their young. For females, selecting a good provider can be just as important, because if her young are not fed well enough, they will starve.

The males of some species display their skills during courtship by offering potential mates gifts of food. A male little tern offers a freshly caught fish. This both proves that he can catch fish, and also provides the female with welcome extra nutrition at a time when she needs it to produce eggs. If she accepts, he will keep feeding her until she lays her clutch of two or three eggs. Little tern pairs usually stay together for life.

female tern accepting fish

Fishy offering Having caught a fish by plunge-diving into the water from the air, a male little tern offers it to his mate without even landing. Such a display is a practical demonstration of his fitness and fishing skill – both important qualifications in a father.

Warning lights Females readily pair with males whose red spots are dyed black by researchers, suggesting that these markings function to discourage rivals rather than attract mates.

Red-winged blackbird
Flash of colour

SPECIES *Agelaius phoeniceus* **SIZE** 18–19 cm (7–7½ in)
DISTRIBUTION Wetland and farmland in North America and Central America

Dazzling courtship plumage can help a male bird win a mate, but it also makes him conspicuous to enemies. The red-winged blackbird avoids this by concealing his brilliant red shoulder patches beneath black plumage and flashing them only when he is defending a breeding territory. Males with larger red patches are more successful at holding territories.

This species is polygamous, with each successful male mating with many females. The females nest alone, so they are only interested in the male's fitness, as demonstrated by the vigour of his display.

Mutual display Paddling furiously, a courting pair of great crested grebes dances together on a lake, each holding its offering of waterweed gathered from below the surface.

Great crested grebe
Weed dance

SPECIES *Podiceps cristatus* **SIZE** 46–51 cm (18–20 in)
DISTRIBUTION Lakes, rivers, lagoons, and coastal waters in Europe, Asia, Africa, Australia, and New Zealand

In species where parental care is shared equally, the sexes often look alike. Some engage in complex and coordinated displays that allow both birds to show off their fitness and abilities as providers, as well as build a bond as a cooperative team.

Great crested grebes build their floating nests from water plants and, as part of their courtship, both male and female present each other with billfuls of waterweed (showing they can collect nesting material). This is the climax of a spectacular courtship ceremony. The birds rear up out of the water, breast to breast, paddling rapidly, and swinging their heads from side to side. The balletic effect of this "weed dance" is enhanced by their crests and cheek ruffs.

Other grebes have similar displays. The western grebe of North America engages in a dramatic "rushing" ceremony that involves both birds rising out of the water, and running across the lake surface side by side in a cloud of spray, their long necks arched in a graceful curve.

Water ballet **>>01** In one of many variations of the weed dance, one bird crouches in the water, while another dives and reappears with a billful of weed. **>>02** With powerful strokes of their lobed feet, the grebes push themselves up out of the water. **>>03** Breast to breast, they dance together on the surface, swivelling their heads from left to right. **>>04** The pair settle back down, but continue to shake and toss their heads to display their erected plumes.

>>01   >>02   >>03   >>04

Spoilt for choice During the breeding season, male great frigatebirds settle in trees on oceanic islands and perform an astonishing group courtship display. Whenever females fly over, the males spread their wings, toss their heads back, and inflate huge scarlet throat pouches while clacking their bills. Here a female has landed between two hopeful males.

Shake it Displaying peacocks do not stand still, but rapidly shiver their fan of feathers, making a rustling sound. The frequency of this "train-rattle" sound is exactly right to trigger a corresponding shiver in the head crest feathers of his intended mate, in case the colourful show was not enough to catch her attention.

Indian peafowl

Eye opener

SPECIES *Pavo cristatus* **SIZE** Male up to 2.3 m (7½ ft); female 86 cm (34 in)
DISTRIBUTION Forest and farmland in India, Pakistan, and Sri Lanka, and introduced worldwide

Famous for its breathtaking plumage displays, the Indian peafowl is often regarded as an emblem of masculine finery. The female, or peahen, is well equipped for her maternal role with discreet, cryptic coloration, but the peacock is resplendent in deep violet-blue and iridescent green, with extended upper tail coverts adorned with vivid "eyespots". These extended coverts normally trail behind the bird, but in display he erects and spreads them to form a spectacular, rustling fan. He often backs towards any receptive female, swinging around to confront her with the magnificence of his display before taking several steps back and bowing. If the peahen is impressed, she will join his harem of females, for like most male birds with highly ornamented plumage, the peacock is polygamous. He takes no part in rearing his young and being so conspicuous, would probably be a liability.

Dazzling display The stunning display of the peacock is a familiar sight, thanks to its introduction as an ornamental bird to parks and gardens all over the world. Domesticated peafowl are very tame, but wild birds are shy and elusive.

Raggiana bird-of-paradise

Tree dancing

SPECIES *Paradisaea raggiana* **SIZE** 33 cm (13 in)
DISTRIBUTION Tropical rainforest in eastern New Guinea

Few birds can match male birds-of-paradise for dazzling courtship displays. Their native tropical forests are rich in resources, so breeding females have little trouble finding food. They do not need help from the males, which are able to devote all their energies to displaying and trying to mate with as many females as possible.

Male raggiana birds-of-paradise display competitively, in groups that gather in traditional treetop display sites known as leks. They dance on perches to show off their glorious plumes, and by degrees they establish a hierarchy, with the most accomplished, energetic male occupying the best perch. This dominant male normally mates with most of the females that visit the lek, and it is likely that they choose him on the basis of his high status, rather than by judging the quality of his performance.

Flamboyant display The plumes of the male raggiana bird-of-paradise normally trail behind him, but he tosses them forwards in a flamboyant display to impress a female, as shown here.

Giant panda
On a roll
SPECIES *Ailuropoda melanoleuca* **SIZE** Up to 1.9 m (6¼ ft)
DISTRIBUTION Cool, damp, mountain bamboo forest in central and western China

The giant panda has become a symbol of endangered wildlife because of its extreme rarity. Since it often refuses to breed in captivity, it was once thought to be reluctant to breed in the wild. However, when they are left to their own devices, male and female pandas naturally live in overlapping ranges, and although they are generally solitary, they will find each other through scent marking to engage in a brief courtship and mating period in spring. Males may compete for access to a female, who spends her time high in a tree until the day she is ready to mate. When receptive, she backs up to her chosen suitor with her tail raised to entice him. She may roll onto her back, squirm, and reach up to him with her forepaws. This usually encourages the male to mate.

Rolling around A captive female giant panda at the Wolong giant panda reserve in China rolls seductively on her back, inviting the watching male to mate with her.

Common raccoon
Thrill of the chase
SPECIES *Procyon lotor* **SIZE** 65–100 cm (2–3¼ ft) **DISTRIBUTION** Forest, scrubland, and suburban areas in North and Central America, from southern Canada to Panama

Encounters between male and female mammals often involve an element of aggression until the two settle their differences and sparring turns to courtship. Among common raccoons, which are highly social animals, these exchanges are marked by angry growls and bursts of chattering, as the animals chase through the undergrowth. Eventually they may mate, and females often form temporary relationships with males during the breeding season. A few unrelated males often form a loose alliance and try to keep other males away, although the dominant or strongest males in any group generally mate with most of the females.

Aggressive play Male raccoons are heavier than females and tend to become more aggressive during mating season.

Black rhinoceros
Scent signals
SPECIES *Diceros bicornis* **SIZE** Up to 3 m (10 ft)
DISTRIBUTION Forest and wooded scrubland in sub-Saharan Africa

In common with most mammals, scent is vital to black rhinoceroses as they not only use it to locate food, mark territory, and identify both friends and enemies, but also to find breeding partners. A black rhinoceros has poor vision, but an excellent sense of smell, so it relies heavily on scent signals. When females come into season, they spray hormone-rich urine to attract males. The males often fight for the right to mate, and may inflict deadly injuries. The victors then proclaim their dominance by spraying urine, often charging back and forth in the process. This may give the male the confidence to approach a female, though she is likely to reject his initial advances. If successful, they will form a temporary bond before mating and parting.

Taking courage A dominant male sprays to mark his territory (left), and to build confidence for a mating attempt that may be rejected by the female (below, on the right).

Siamang
Singing swingers

SPECIES *Symphalangus syndactylus* **SIZE** 75–90 cm (30–35 in)
DISTRIBUTION Forest on Malay Peninsula and Sumatra

Many mammals use sound during courtship, but few are quite so vocal as the gibbons of Southeast Asia. These slender, agile, tree-living apes are famous for their loud, complex calls, which are often described as songs. Those of the siamang, the largest gibbon species, are given extra resonance and volume by a throat sac that inflates like a balloon, enabling their calls to carry for 2 km (1¼ miles) through the forest.

Young gibbons of both sexes sing to attract mates, and although they keep moving through the forest to find partners, the process may take several years. Eventually they form long-term pair bonds and defend a joint territory. Most species advertise this with loud duets, in which the songs of the male and female are quite different. A male siamang screams, while a female gives a series of booms and barks, although both sexes sometimes make all call types. Siamang pairs call together, but in many other species the sexes sing alternately, with the female taking the longest, loudest solos. Their young may join in too, in a family chorus.

CASE STUDY STRENGTHENING BONDS

Some researchers believe that singing in a duet reinforces the pair bonds between mated siamangs. However, the duets are most frequently performed near the boundaries of their territory, when the pair sense the presence of neighbouring groups that might trespass on their patch. By advertising the fact that they are in possession, they reduce the risk of a dangerous confrontation, while, at the same time, backing each other up and strengthening their relationship. So it seems likely that duetting is primarily territorial, but also helps maintain a bond that could be threatened by intruders.

Great call Amplified by its inflated throat sac, the song of this siamang will be heard and noted by all its neighbours. It calls mainly in the morning, especially if it becomes aware of another siamang family group.

Swift movement Gibbons are the only apes that habitually move through the forest canopy using their long, muscular arms. They can swing from branch to branch with astonishing speed and agility, and rarely make a false move.

California sea lion
Beach harem
SPECIES *Zalophus californianus* **SIZE** 1.8–2.1 m (6–7 ft)
DISTRIBUTION Breeds on Pacific shores of North and Central America, and the Galapagos Islands

Female sea lions must come ashore to give birth to pups, and during this time males take the opportunity to mate. Male California sea lions have the same breeding strategy as blackbucks (see right), attempting to control as many females as possible by claiming territories on the breeding beaches. They are much bigger than females, and compete with rivals by actual and ritualized fighting. Throughout this time, they dare not leave their territories to feed. A successful male controls an average of 16 females, courting each with barks and headshaking as he lumbers around her, nipping her shoulders and flanks. If the female is receptive, she responds by lying on her side, belly, or back and looking up at the male, encouraging him to mate with her.

A male California sea lion may go 27 days without food to defend his territory during the breeding season.

Blackbuck
Striking a pose
SPECIES *Antilope cervicapra* **SIZE** 1–1.5 m (3¼–5 ft)
DISTRIBUTION Open woodland to semi-desert in India and Bangladesh

Most hoofed grazing animals that live in open country associate in herds and do not form mated pairs. Rival males compete over females, and have evolved powerful bodies and horns for fighting or intimidating rivals. A male blackbuck has long spiral horns that lock with those of rivals during clashes to reduce the risk of serious injury. He claims a territory by driving away other males – usually with threats rather than active fighting – and tries to monopolize a harem of females. The male displays to both rivals and females using an imperious raised-head gesture with his horns held horizontal, and tries to head off straying females to keep them within his territory for as long as possible. If a female comes into season, and is therefore ready to mate, the male can detect the hormone change from chemical signals in her urine. This triggers a lip-curling flehmen response that is common to most grazing animals and carnivores, and which helps transfer the scent to the sensitive vomeronasal organ in the roof of the mouth. If the test is positive he will mate with the female, but takes no part in raising her young.

Posturing His upper lip curled back as he scents the hormones in a female's urine, a male blackbuck raises his head in a display of dominance.

Amazon river dolphin
Gifted suitor
SPECIES *Inia geoffrensis* **SIZE** Up to 2.5 m (8¼ ft)
DISTRIBUTION Slow-moving waters in Amazon and Orinoco river systems in South America

Most dolphins are marine animals – small, toothed whales that hunt fishes and squid in the open oceans. A few dolphin species, however, live in the fresh waters of large rivers. These river dolphins have long, slender snouts, mobile necks, and small eyes, and they navigate and hunt in cloudy river waters mainly by echolocation. The Amazon river dolphin, or boto, is usually solitary, living in the same stretch of river throughout the year, but in the rainy season the dolphins come together to breed. Rival males compete for access to females, often biting each other aggressively, and many males bear the scars of combat. Males initiate courtship by nibbling at the flippers or flukes of females, but some courtship displays involve the male picking up sticks, aquatic plants, or lumps of clay, and flourishing them at the females as if they were gifts, to impress them. These males also tend to be more aggressive than average, and because of this, or their gift-carrying, they are the most successful in terms of the number of females they mate with, and the number of young they father.

Making a splash >>01 A male Amazon river dolphin surfaces with a mass of waterweed gripped in his teeth. >>02 He prepares to display to a female watching from nearby. >>03 He tosses the weed around to create a splash, and to demonstrate his fitness.

>>01   >>02   >>03

Mating

Mating behaviour brings together sperm from the male and eggs from the female, so that fertilization can occur. In some animals, fertilization is external, occurring outside the female's body; in others, it is internal, the sperm being introduced into the female's body, usually by means of a specialized sexual organ.

Seasonal spawner Reef-living Christmas tree worms are sedentary animals, so males and females cannot meet to mate. Eggs and sperm are shed into the water and carried away by currents, eventually meeting to form larvae.

INTERNAL FERTILIZATION

Internal fertilization is advantageous in many ways. It enables mating and egg-laying to be separated in time and space, so that a female can lay her eggs at the optimum time, in a suitable place. For example, having mated, female newts lay their eggs one at a time, placing them around a pond and protecting each one by wrapping it in a leaf. It allows females to mate with several males before her eggs are fertilized, so that her young have diverse fathers, whose sperm must compete to fertilize her eggs. In mammals and many other animals, internal fertilization means that the young can develop inside the mother. Some animals use a sexual organ called a penis to transfer sperm, but many birds simply touch cloacae (genital openings), and many male amphibians transfer sperm in a capsule called a spermatophore.

During mating, a male dead leaf bush cricket passes sperm to the female in a spermatophore.

Female Alpine newts wrap each egg in a leaf to protect it from ultraviolet radiation.

EXTERNAL FERTILIZATION

External fertilization is often used by animals that cannot move about in search of a mate. It is most common in aquatic animals, where eggs and sperm are released into water. There is a risk when eggs are fertilized outside the body that some will fail to meet a sperm, so many species counter this by producing huge numbers of eggs and vast quantities of sperm. Among fishes and amphibians, external fertilization is sometimes associated with male parental care. This may be because, as the female lays the eggs before the male fertilizes them, he is left "holding the babies". For example, male sticklebacks and male midwife toads provide care and protection for the developing eggs.

HERMAPHRODITES

Hermaphrodites (see p.296) are in a happy position – each individual of the same species they meet is a potential mate. Mating is often reciprocal, with each partner giving sperm to the other during the same mating act. Some slugs try to protect the paternity of their offspring by biting off their partner's penis after mating; a slug without a penis cannot provide sperm and so cannot attract another partner. Hermaphrodites are common in invertebrates.

Sperm swappers Snails are hermaphrodites, and after an elaborate courtship, each snail inserts its long penis into the body of its partner to exchange sperm.

High mount A bull African elephant mounts a female. She is receptive for only a few days each year and only allows larger, dominant males to mount her.

suspended slug

male organ

everted organ extends

entwined male organs from both slugs

Sex on a rope In this series of photographs, two suspended leopard slugs can be seen extending their male organs, which meet and entwine. When they join, they form a spectacular flowerlike structure (right), and sperm is finally exchanged.

Giant Pacific octopus
Specialized tentacle

SPECIES *Enteroctopus dofleini* **SIZE** Historically with a radial arm span up to 9 m (30 ft), but now much smaller
DISTRIBUTION Coastal waters of northern Pacific Ocean to depths of 750 m (2,500 ft), from Japan to California

Leopard slug
Suspended sex

SPECIES *Limax maximus* **SIZE** Up to 20 cm (8 in)
DISTRIBUTION Near human habitation: gardens, yards, cellars; under logs, stones, vegetation. Native to Europe, introduced to North America, Asia, Africa, and Australasia

Like other slugs, leopard slugs are hermaphrodites – they possess both male and female sexual organs. But for leopard slugs, mating is a fascinatingly complex and prolonged process. Two slugs circle each other for up to two-and-a-half hours before they climb together to a secure place, often in a tree, some distance above the ground. There they both secrete a thick "rope" of mucus upon which they slowly lower themselves, until the rope is about 1 m (3 ft 3 in) long. They entwine their bodies in a graceful mid-air dance as they move down along the mucus rope. Then each slug "everts" (extends by turning inside-out) its male sexual organ from the back of its head. These sleek, blue-white organs become longer and eventually meet and entwine. Then each slug inserts a sperm sac (spermatophore) into the body of its partner. After mating, the leopard slugs climb back up the rope and go their separate ways.

Leopard slugs lay 20–100 eggs in damp, shady places – under logs, stones, and leaf litter. Tiny slugs hatch after 22 days and take two years to reach sexual maturity.

Male octopuses have one arm modified to enable them to pass sperm packages (spermatophores) over to the female to fertilize her eggs. This arm, known as a heterocotylus is used by the male during mating to insert spermatophores into the female's body cavity. In the giant Pacific octopus, spermatophores take the form of long strings and are stored by the female until needed. After roughly a month, the female retires to a rocky den and lays up to 100,000 eggs, which are attached to the roof. Unlike related cuttlefishes and squid, female octopuses protect their eggs against predators. The giant Pacific octopus incubates her eggs diligently for seven months, during which she does not eat so she can assiduously clean and aerate her eggs, creating currents by squirting water. Once the eggs hatch and the tiny young drift away, the mother dies.

Giant Pacific octopuses are predators, feeding on shrimps, crabs, shellfish, and fish. They live for three to five years.

Nudibranch
Right sided

SPECIES *Nembrotha purpureolineata* **SIZE** Up to 5 cm (2 in)
DISTRIBUTION Coral reefs in tropical Pacific waters

Like all nudibranchs (bottom-dwelling sea slugs), *Nembrotha purpureolineata* is a hermaphrodite, producing both eggs and sperm. Individuals do not fertilize their own eggs but come together in pairs to exchange sperm. The genital orifice is situated on the right side of the body and, to mate, two slugs position themselves head to tail in a way that allows their right sides to touch. Nudibranch eggs are laid in masses, often on the adults' food source. They are very noticeable to divers, as they are most often a bright white, yellow, or pink colour, and take the form of variously shaped ribbons, spirals, and coils.

"Nudibranch" means "naked gills", referring to the fact that these molluscs have gills on the outside of their soft bodies. While many species display an array of bright colours, others are well camouflaged. Distinctive colour patterns may serve to warn predators that a nudibranch is not good to eat or even toxic, but some mimic other toxic species, such as flatworms.

Sperm exchange The male sexual organs of these mating *Nembrotha purpureolineata* touch and fit together in order to allow each sea slug to transfer sperm to the other.

Fire ants
Mating flights
GENUS Solenopsis **SIZE** 1–6 mm (1/16–1/4 in) **DISTRIBUTION** Underground, in dry to moist soil across diverse range of habitats, including fields, woodland, and open ground, worldwide

Fire ants live in colonies with one or more queens, many males, fertile females (potential queens), and huge armies of sterile female workers. Mating occurs high up in the air during late spring or early summer. Fertile females and males partake in mass mating flights, after which the female seeks a suitable nesting site. Her wings come off, ready for her to change into a queen, then she buries herself and begins to lay eggs. She may live for several years, producing up to 1,500 eggs each day. The male dies soon after mating and becomes food for other ants and small birds.

Fighting for a female During a pause in a mating flight, these two male fire ants fight over the right to mate with a female. The winner will lose his life, as males die soon after mating.

Meeting halfway Earthworms mate on top of the soil, but do not completely leave their burrows as their tails remain in the soil during the process.

Common earthworm
Side by side
SPECIES Lumbricus terrestris **SIZE** Up to 25 cm (10 in) (extended body) **DISTRIBUTION** In soil, originally in Europe, now introduced to most parts of the world

For many hermaphrodites, mating involves two individuals exchanging sperm. On a mild, damp night, two worms come halfway out of their burrows, lie side by side with heads pointing in opposite directions, and secrete mucus to form a sheath that binds their bodies together. Their alignment allows a groove running along each body to come together with its counterpart, forming a tube for sperm to pass along. Mating takes up to four hours.

Ploughnose chimaera
Head lock
SPECIES Callorhinchus milii **SIZE** Up to 1.2 m (4 ft) **DISTRIBUTION** Deep, temperate coastal waters around New Zealand, southern and southeast Australia

Also known as elephant fishes or ghost sharks, ploughnose chimaeras are best known for the hoelike "nose" in front of the mouth, which they use to find food among sediment on the sea bed. They live at depths of 200 m (660 ft) or more, but move into shallow, inshore waters in order to mate and lay eggs. When mating, the male uses retractable claspers to help him grip the female to get into the right position. He has a single, club-shaped, spiny clasper on his forehead between the eyes, and a spoon-shaped pair of claspers armed with small, toothlike denticles just in front of the pelvic fins, which are used for copulation. These are inserted into the female's body to transfer sperm.

Soft leafvent anglerfish
Sex slaves

SPECIES *Haplophryne mollis* **SIZE** Male 3 cm (1¼ in), female 20 cm (8 in) **DISTRIBUTION** Deep in Atlantic, Pacific, and Indian oceans

In the dark ocean depths, a slow-moving animal such as the soft leafvent anglerfish rarely encounters a potential mate. The male, who is much smaller than the female, makes the most of any such opportunity, attaching itself to the female's body permanently. Over time, its teeth, jaws, eyes, and nostrils degenerate until it is little more than a testis attached to the female. Because it feeds off the female, the fused male is often described as a parasite, but the relationship is mutually beneficial – the female has a constant supply of sperm for her eggs. Neither males nor females mature sexually until the male attaches to the female. The tiny males can swim long distances and use their excellent sense of smell to find a female.

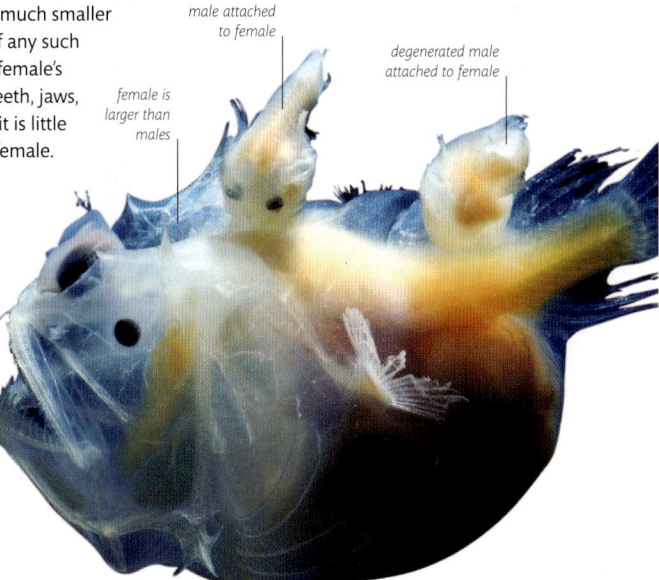

Male attachment This female anglerfish has two males attached to her skin. Like many deep-sea animals, leafvent anglerfishes live in total darkness and are largely transparent – adult females have no skin pigmentation. Many other deep-sea fishes are black.

Guppy
Multiple mates

SPECIES *Poecilia reticulata* **SIZE** Male 2.5–3.5 cm (1–1½ in); female 4–6 cm (1½–2¼ in) **DISTRIBUTION** Streams, ditches, pools in South America, West Indies (especially Trinidad); introduced to many parts of the world

Also known as millions fish, guppies occur in huge numbers. Both sexes mate with several partners (females prefer the more brightly coloured males). Having multiple partners benefits females – they produce more genetically diverse offspring, meaning there is a higher chance that at least some will survive in their variable environment. Unusually for bony fishes, females give birth to live young but they do not look after them after they are born.

Bright males Male guppies are colourful, with fan-shaped tails, while females are yellowish-grey. In captivity, there are many variants.

Small red-eyed damselfly
Sperm replacement

SPECIES *Erythromma viridulum* **SIZE** 3 cm (1¼ in) **DISTRIBUTION** In ponds, lakes, and ditches with floating vegetation in southern Europe and Africa; expanding into northern Europe

In order to mate with a female, the male damselfly grasps her by the neck with the pincers at the end of his long abdomen, then carries her to a suitable spot on some vegetation. He keeps hold of her during mating and she curves her abdomen forwards so its tip engages with his genitalia. He then inserts his penis into her genital opening to first remove sperm that may be left there from previous matings, before transferring his own sperm, contained in a spermatophore (sperm sac) to a secondary sexual organ located under the front end of his abdomen, which he uses to pass the spermatphore on to her. After mating, the pair fly off, in the same "tandem" position, to water. Here, the female lays her eggs on submerged plants. The male continues to hold her until she has finished.

In tandem The male clasps the female firmly by the neck as she holds her genital opening to his genitalia, forming a mating "wheel" (above). To lay eggs, the male supports the female on the water's surface (left).

ANATOMY **SPECIALIST TOOL**

The male damselfly has an elaborate penis that has evolved the ability to remove or push aside sperm from previous mating partners found in the female, thus increasing his own chances of fertilizing the largest proportion of her eggs. The penis is equipped with hooks or scrapers, and covered with hairs that are used to remove the sperm. The part of the penis that is inserted into the female is called the aedeagus, and its structure varies between species. In some damselflies, it is used simply to push sperm from previous couplings to one side, in others, to remove it altogether. Some species insert liquid to wash sperm out.

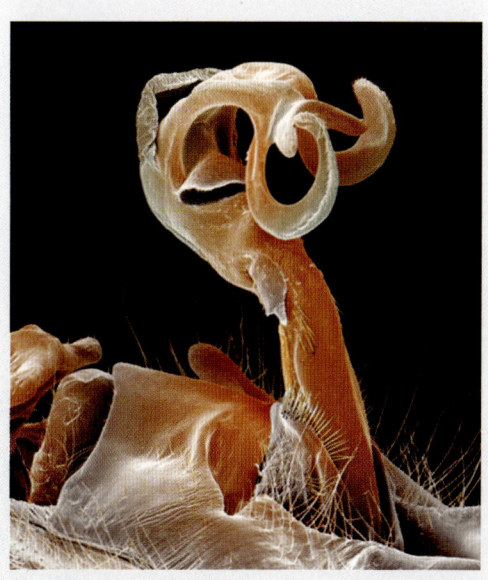

Holding on European common toads gather in vast numbers in spring to breed in ponds. Males greatly outnumber females and have to fend off other males. To mate, a male climbs on to a female's back, grasping her with his strong forelimbs in a position known as amplexus. The male holds on for several days until the female spawns, while trying to repel rivals.

Red-spotted newt
Tail waving

SPECIES *Notophthalmus viridescens* **SIZE** 7–10 cm (2¾–4 in), female slightly larger than male **DISTRIBUTION** Ponds, lakes, ditches, and slow-moving streams in eastern USA and southeast Canada

The breeding season for red-spotted newts occurs in late winter and early spring. When a male encounters a female, he waves his tail to attract her. The female, who is full of eggs waiting to be fertilized, responds by approaching him, but if she does not, the male leaps on her and clasps her around the neck with his muscular hind limbs. This allows him to keep waving his tail at her, and also to rub his cheek glands against her snout to expose her to an alluring pheromone. When she finally responds, he dismounts, moves away, and deposits a spermatophore (sperm sac), often at the bottom of a pond. The female follows him and picks it up in her genital opening, allowing the sperm to fertilize her eggs.

Strong legs During the breeding season, the hind limbs of the male red-spotted newt become enlarged. Their inside surfaces are covered in deeply textured patches that improve the male's grip on the female when mounting her.

Nuptial pads The male has "nuptial pads" (hard areas of skin) on the forefingers, allowing him to grip the female firmly when he has mounted her.

Natterjack toad
Hopping on

SPECIES *Epidalea calamita* **SIZE** Up to 10 cm (4 in), female larger than male **DISTRIBUTION** In open habitats where soil is sandy, in western and central Europe. Rare in Britain

Unlike male common toads (see p.338), natterjack males ignore paired couples and look for a mate of their own. At night, they gather around ponds and call loudly, creating a chorus that can be heard by females up to 2 km (1¼ miles) away. Females approach, and a male jumps on a female's back to mate. Only large males can call loudly for a long time, so small males cluster around them like satellites and attempt to intercept approaching females. Where natterjack populations are large, calling males attract so many satellites males that calling becomes an ineffective mating strategy. Males then abandon calling and simply go searching for females to mate with.

European common frog
Long embrace

SPECIES *Rana temporaria* **SIZE** Up to 11 cm (4½ in), female larger than male. **DISTRIBUTION** All kinds of habitats with nearby water, in Europe and northwest Asia

European common frogs spawn in the spring. When a male encounters a female, he clasps her in a strong embrace known as amplexus, pushing the horny pads on his thumbs firmly into her chest. Some pairs remain in amplexus for days, until the weather is warm enough for spawning. When it is, all mating pairs in the pond deposit their spawn simultaneously in the same place. Depending on her size, a female produces a clutch of 700–4,500 eggs. As soon as she does, the male sheds sperm to fertilize them, then releases the female. Males typically outnumber females. A male that fails to find a mate may perform "clutch piracy" – he finds a fresh clutch of eggs, embraces it as he would a female, and sheds sperm onto it to fertilize any unfertilized eggs. Clutch piracy is highly successful. One study found that a single clutch contained a mixture of eggs fertilized by four males, including the male that was in amplexus with the female who produced the clutch.

Worth the wait The male European common frog rides on the female's back, clinging on and waiting for just this moment, when she releases a clutch of eggs. He then fertilizes them immediately.

Communal spawning This mating pair of common frogs is swimming in a sea of frogspawn that has been released simultaneously by all the females in the pond. Within this mass, the temperature is higher than elsewhere in the pond, allowing fertilized eggs to develop quickly.

Komodo dragon
Gentle approach

SPECIES *Varanus komodoensis* **SIZE** 2–3 m (6½–9¾ ft)
DISTRIBUTION Grassland and lowland forest on Indonesian islands of Komodo and Flores and others in between

Male Komodo dragons fight to establish territories where they are visited by females. If approached by a male, the female is initially hostile, repelling his advances aggressively with her teeth and claws. So he advances cautiously. He sniffs her to determine if she is ready to mate, then he lightly scratches her back and licks her, using this gentle contact to gain her trust. If she accepts him, he climbs onto her back and inserts one of a pair of male sexual organs into her genital opening. Sometimes, long-term pair bonds are formed between a female and male – an unusual pattern among reptiles. The female lays around 20 eggs, either in a burrow or in the deserted nest of a scrub fowl.

Pinned down Once he is certain that the female will submit to his amorous advances, the male Komodo dragon clasps hold of her firmly, then uses his powerful tail to lift up her tail, allowing him to mate with her.

Western whip snake
Tails entwined

SPECIES *Hierophis viridiflavus* **SIZE** Up to 1.5 m (5 ft) **DISTRIBUTION** Dry, open, well-vegetated habitats in Europe, from France to Italy

In early spring, western whip snakes are ready to mate very soon after they emerge from hibernation. Males begin to look for females, and travel from hibernation sites to their summer habitats to find them. Fast-moving and agile, these snakes may travel up to 3 km (2 miles) in this search, and fight with other males for access to females, each lashing at the other with its tail. The successful male then twists his tail around the female during copulation. As with all snakes, the male has a pair of male sexual organs, which he inserts one at a time into the female's cloaca (the orifice leading to her reproductive organs). A few weeks later, in early to mid summer, the female lays 4–15 elongated eggs. The eggs hatch approximately six to eight weeks after being laid.

Whip embrace A male western whip snake grasps the female in his jaws while wrapping his tail around hers to bring their cloacae together for mating.

Common garter snake
Waiting game

SPECIES *Thamnophis sirtalis* **SIZE** 46–130 cm (18–43 in)
DISTRIBUTION Grassland, scrubland, chaparral, and forest, usually near water, in North America

In the northern part of their range, common garter snakes hibernate in huge numbers in communal dens. Males emerge from hibernation first and wait at the den for the females to appear. The result is an orgy in which many males struggle to mate with each female. After mating, the male produces a secretion, which quickly hardens to form a mating plug in the female's genital opening, preventing other males from inseminating her. Once mating is over, the snakes disperse to their feeding areas, and females give birth later in the year to live young, usually 12–18, occasionally more.

98 The maximum number of young ever recorded in a litter of common garter snakes.

Looking for a mate Common garter snakes form "mating balls" around females. As the females emerge from hibernation, up to 100 males surround each one, running their chins along her back and releasing pheromones to attract her. She will select just one of the males to mate with.

Careful coupling For all his attentiveness, a male goshawk must keep his guard up around his mate, as she is considerably larger and more powerful than him.

Red-necked phalarope
Role reversal
SPECIES *Phalaropus lobatus* **SIZE** 20 cm (8 in), female larger than male **DISTRIBUTION** Open seas around northern Europe, Canada, and Russia, breeding around lakes and pools in tundra

These aquatic birds spend most of their lives at sea and even mate in the water, only coming back to the shore to build nests in which they rear their young. Phalaropes are unusual among birds in the role reversal they display – the female is larger and more brightly coloured than the male. She is also the aggressive partner, and establishes a breeding territory, while the male alone incubates the eggs and feeds the young. Sometimes a female is polyandrous, leaving her mate and looking for a new male once she has laid her eggs.

Water lovers Unlike other seabirds, red-necked phalaropes prefer to copulate in the water itself, out at sea, rather than on land or on a perch.

Northern goshawk
Male attention
SPECIES *Accipiter gentilis* **SIZE** 48–69 cm (19–27 in), female larger than male **DISTRIBUTION** Broad-leaved and coniferous forest in North America, Europe, and Asia

Goshawks are monogamous. The male is very attentive to the female while she is laying her eggs. He rarely leaves her side and mates with her frequently – for each clutch of eggs, a pair will mate between 500 and 600 times. Diligent mate-guarding in this way reduces the chances of the female laying eggs that have been fathered by another male.

Mid-air mating >>01 The male closes in on the female from behind. >>02 The female signals her readiness to mate by raising her wings, and the male approaches. >>03 The male moves himself into the mating position, directly above the female. >>04 The female raises her tail while the male lowers his, and the cloaca (the orifice that leads to the reproductive organs) of each bird meets the other's briefly. All this occurs while they are flying at high speed.

Common swift
On the wing
SPECIES *Apus apus* **SIZE** 16–17 cm (6½ in) **DISTRIBUTION** Europe and Asia, winters in Africa. Entirely aerial, nests in buildings and on cliffs

Fast and acrobatic fliers, common swifts spend their lives in the air. Unlike other birds, they even mate while flying, and their mating is one of the fastest of couplings in the animal kingdom. Typically, they mate early in the morning on sunny days, often in groups – they breed in colonies of about 30–40 pairs. Pairs stay together over successive breeding seasons, and both male and female share in nest building (which is done using only materials caught in the air) and caring for the young, with each bird flying great distances to catch insect food on the wing. But while swifts are usually monogamous, they do occasionally mate with birds that are not their partners. Genetic studies of swift chicks have revealed that 4.5 per cent are not the offspring of the mother's partner.

>>01 >>02 >>03 >>04

Brown antechinus
Fatal mating
SPECIES *Antechinus stuartii* **SIZE** 80–120 cm (32–48 in) **DISTRIBUTION** Forest with thick ground cover in eastern Australia

The brown antechinus, a species of marsupial mouse, has a short and very stressful life. Normally solitary, brown antechinuses gather to breed in large communal nests when they are around 11 months old. Males and females form pairs, but the male has to work extremely hard to prevent other males from mating with his partner. He guards her and mates with her frequently but, despite his strenuous efforts, most litters (generally of around 4–12 young) are fathered by more than one male. The male brown antechinus puts so much effort into his mating activity that his immune system suffers and breaks down. He dies shortly after his one and only mating season. Many female antechinuses also die after their very first breeding effort, although some of them manage to live for as long as two or three years.

Competitive sperm When a female brown antechinus mates with multiple males, it is the vigour of the actual sperm cells that determines which male fathers the most babies.

Bonobo
Social sex
SPECIES *Pan paniscus* **SIZE** 1–1.2 m (3¼–4 ft)
DISTRIBUTION Humid forest in Democratic Republic of Congo

Bonobos use sex in a variety of social contexts: to resolve conflicts; as a greeting; as reconciliation after a fight; to soothe youngsters; and in exchange for gifts of food. Rather then being purely a means of reproducing, sex is part of everyday life for bonobos. Captive studies reveal that individuals of all ages and of the same or opposite sex mate with each other and although mating behaviour occurs very frequently, females only reproduce young every five to six years. The studies suggest that frequent sexual activity is instrumental in resolving power struggles, and that bonobos live in very peaceful societies, with few aggressive encounters. Bonobos are increasingly rare in the wild.

Bonobos are highly sexually active and mate in a variety of different sexual positions.

Face to face Bonobos frequently mate face to face. This was thought to be unique among non-human primates, but gorillas have been observed in the same position.

Painful mating During mating, a male tiger grasps the female by the scruff of her neck with his powerful teeth. As with all cat species (as well as various other mammals), his penis is barbed, which makes sex painful for the female.

Tiger
Aggressive affair
SPECIES *Panthera tigris* **SIZE** 2–3.7 m (6½–12¼ ft)
DISTRIBUTION Wide range of habitats that provide good cover, water, and prey across Asia

Tigers are solitary, non-social animals. The only bonds that exist are those between a mother and her cubs, a relationship that lasts for just 18 months. When ready to mate, a female signals the fact to males by roaring, moaning, and scent-marking. Once a male is attracted, the pair snarl at each other, separating several times before gaining one another's trust. The female then grooms the male, nuzzling and licking him, and rolls on the ground, waving her paws in the air, before lying on her belly and presenting herself to him. The male mounts her in a knees-bent position to avoid crushing her with his weight, then roars and bites her neck. The female jumps up, snarls, and swipes at him as he dismounts.

HUMAN IMPACT **THE TIGER TRADE**

Once inhabiting areas across a huge range in Asia, tigers are now confined to a few small, protected zones. The primary cause of their decline is loss of habitat, but they are also hunted for their skins, and for a variety of body parts that are used in some traditional medicine and as aphrodisiacs.

Birth and Development

348
Life stories

364
Raising young

376
Play and learning

First breath A Nile crocodile takes a look at the outside world for the first time. Crocodile embryos develop within a toughened egg, nourished by yolk. In about three months, the embryo has grown from a single fertilized cell into a complex multicellular animal.

BIRTH AND DEVELOPMENT

Animal development is a lifelong process. Beginning at the point of fertilization, animals first grow and develop in a protected environment within their mother or inside an egg. After the event known as birth, young animals must learn and develop skills and behaviours required to support them throughout life.

THE EMBRYO

The development of the embryo is called embryogenesis. After fertilization, the zygote, or single cell, begins to divide rapidly, doubling in cell number with each division. Once around 100 cells exist, the embryo is known as a blastula, comprising an outer layer (the blastoderm), and an inner cavity filled with fluid (the blastocoel). The cells migrate to the inside of the blastula, forming different layers. At this point, the inside of the embryo starts to form, folding inwards to create the mouth and anus. The internal organs then begin to develop.

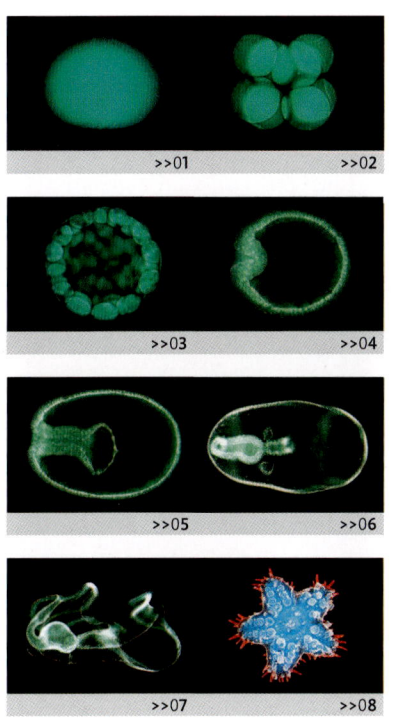

Starfish embryo development
>>01 The fertilized single cell. >>02 The cell rapidly divides, in a process known as cleavage. The stage shown has 8 cells. >>03 The starfish blastula, showing the outer layer and inner cavity. >>04 As the cells migrate within the blastula, various cell layers develop, and the mouth and anus begin to take shape. >>05 The gut starts to form. >>06 At this larval stage, the internal organs have begun to develop. >>07 The well-formed larva, viewed from the side. >>08 A fully-formed young starfish.

BIRTH

Birth is the process by which an animal leaves its mother's body and enters the world. This typically refers to animals that undergo a live birth, in contrast to hatching, when animals emerge from an egg outside the mother's body. Many animals carry their young within the uterus for a period of time before giving birth. This is known as the gestation phase, and its duration varies greatly between animals. Elephants, for example, have a very long gestation, carrying their offspring for 22 months prior to birth. To give birth, an animal goes through labour. This occurs by means of strong, rhythmic muscle contractions of the uterus, and, in mammals, is initiated by hormones. Across the animal kingdom, young animals emerge into the world at various stages – some are highly independent at birth, while others require extensive parental care for months or even years. The difference lies in the length of the gestation phase relative to the time taken for that animal to become fully independent. Precocial animals are those that are relatively mature and mobile from the point of hatching or birth – these include many bird species, such as ducks. Conversely, altricial animals, for example rats, are those that are born helpless. Their eyes are closed, they lack fur or feathers, and are dependent on their parents for an extended period of time.

GROWING UP

The process of animal development does not stop at birth. Many invertebrates and amphibians exhibit what is known as indirect development and, even after hatching, undergo radical changes in body form. During metamorphosis, these animals pass through various larval stages in order to change into their adult form. Direct development, in contrast, is when the young animal emerges as a miniature adult, although it may lack features such as hair, coloration, or sexual organs. This occurs in reptiles, birds, and mammals. Changes in body shape do still take place – sexual organs typically develop some time after birth – but essentially the juvenile resembles the adult form. Development is not just about physical form, however. Animals' brains develop throughout life, as they learn about the world around them, and form memories that are saved and drawn upon. While some behaviours may be instinctive, including courtship behaviour, reproduction, and nest building, many behaviours have to be learned, and are the result of life experience and observation.

REPRODUCTIVE METHODS

Oviparity Young develop inside eggs, nourished by yolk, with little or no development within the mother. Occurs in insects, amphibians, reptiles, fishes, and birds.

Viviparity Young develop inside the body of the mother, rather than within an egg. They are then delivered by live birth. Occurs in marsupials, for example.

Ovoviviparity Embryos grow inside eggs, which are retained within the female until they are about to hatch. Young feed on egg yolk. Often seen in sharks.

Placental mammals An advanced form of viviparity. Young develop inside the mother, nourished from her body via a placenta. The usual strategy among mammals.

Life stories

An animal's life story can be described in terms of the different stages and transitions in its life cycle and development, for example, from juvenile to adult, along with associated morphological, physiological, ecological, and behavioural changes. Sometimes, as in the case of parasites and parasitoids (which kill their hosts), the life cycle of an animal is dependent on that of others.

METAMORPHOSIS

Some young animals hatch as, or are born as, miniature versions of the adult. In other species, juveniles bear little resemblance to the adults; they live in different habitats and display different behaviours. Their young must undergo metamorphosis (see p.354) for their bodies to change into the mature form. Butterflies, for example, transform from leaf-munching caterpillars into nectar-drinking, winged adults. Other animals, besides insects, change in form during their life cycle. Jellyfish begin life as planktonic larvae, which then come to rest on the sea bed, before becoming free-swimming adults. Frogs and toads transform from aquatic tadpoles with gills and tails to terrestrial adults with lungs and limbs.

When ready to pupate, the caterpillar stops feeding. The caterpillar of the painted lady butterfly feeds on plants.

The caterpillar pupates inside a pupal case called a chrysalis, which is suspended from vegetation.

Grand finale Once pupation is complete, the adult painted lady butterfly emerges. The butterfly must wait for its brightly coloured wings to unfurl and expand before it can fly off to find a source of nectar and a mate, leaving behind the empty shell of the chrysalis.

From egg to beetle Beetles undergo complete metamorphosis. After hatching from the egg, the larva, or grub, passes through several stages as it grows, before pupating. Although from the outside there might appear to be little activity, inside the protective case of the pupa, the larval body structure is transforming into that of the adult beetle, which looks markedly different from the beetle larva.

EGG — EARLY STAGE LARVA — FINAL STAGE LARVA — PUPA — ADULT BEETLE

PARASITIC LIFE CYCLES

Parasites are dependent on one or more other species for the completion of their life cycle. Most live on (ectoparasites) or inside (endoparasites) the host animal, to which they cause varying degrees of harm. In the case of a parasitoid, it develops inside a host and usually causes death. In many parasitoids, such as parasitic wasps, it is the larval stage that is fatal to the host – the larva consumes its host from the inside. The adult, by contrast, is free-living. Some parasites have only one host and are said to have a direct life cycle; others have complex life cycles that require intermediate hosts for the larval stages, as well as primary hosts for the sexually reproductive adult stage. The eggs or larvae of many types of parasite can survive in the environment until they are able to infect a host.

Eaten alive Parasitoid phorid flies use their hooked ovipositors to place an egg into the head of a leafcutter ant. The fly's larva, or maggot, feeds on the host ant's body, eventually causing its death.

Nest invasion The common cuckoo is a brood parasite. The female lays her egg in the nest of a bird of another species, which then raises the chick as its own.

EARLY AND LATE DEVELOPERS

Across the animal kingdom, newborn offspring require different levels of parental care and take varying lengths of time to reach maturity. Among mammals, marsupials have the shortest gestation periods, relative to body size. Their young are born early on in their development, and continue to grow in their mother's pouch. Placental mammals give birth at a comparatively later stage in their offspring's development. However, there remains a vast spectrum between those that can stand and move at birth and those that are born blind and naked. The former are "precocial", and require relatively little parental care; the latter are "altricial", and entirely reliant on their parents for some time before becoming independent.

Helpless young Songbird chicks, like those of the American robin, are altricial. They stay in the nest after hatching and are cared for and fed by their parents for almost a fortnight.

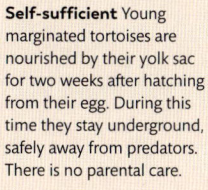

Self-sufficient Young marginated tortoises are nourished by their yolk sac for two weeks after hatching from their egg. During this time they stay underground, safely away from predators. There is no parental care.

precocial tortoise

yolk sac on underside

CASE STUDY **BREEDING LIKE RABBITS**

Some animals complete their life cycle very rapidly – they mature quickly and breed fast, but are often short-lived. Scientists refer to these animals as "r strategists", and the rabbit is a good example. Other animals, such as elephants, mature and breed slowly and live longer. Such animals are known as "K strategists". Although r strategists are often selected for in unpredictable environments and K strategists in more stable ones, in reality, many animals display both r and K traits. Green turtles, for instance, are long-lived and slow to mature, but they produce a large number of offspring.

Standing for survival >>01 Female wildebeest give birth to their calves in the centre of the herd. Around 80 per cent of the females calve during the same two- or three-week period. >>02 Newborn calves are very vulnerable to predators such as lions and hyenas, which follow the wildebeest migration. >>03 To have any chance of surviving, the calf must move with its mother. It is able to stand and run within minutes of being born.

>>01 >>02 >>03

Unwelcome guest
Leucochloridium paradoxum fluke

SPECIES *Leucochloridium paradoxum* **SIZE** 1.5 mm (1⁄16 in)
DISTRIBUTION Europe and North Africa

The *Leucochloridium paradoxum* fluke is an endoparasite, living inside and feeding on the bodies of birds, including crows, jays, sparrows, and finches. Larval worms first infect an intermediate host, the amber snail, which unsuspectingly eats the worm's eggs when it feasts on bird droppings. The eggs hatch inside the snail into first-stage larvae called miracidia, which inhabit the snail's digestive tract. These grow into sporocysts, saclike structures containing cercariae, the next larval stage of the worm's life cycle. Normally, the snails would avoid exposed, sunlit areas, but when infected by larval flukes they are attracted to bright sunlight and tend to climb to the top of grasses. This makes them more visible to birds, the flatworm's final host. Once ingested by a bird, the larvae develop into adult worms in the bird's intestine.

Amber snail host Brightly coloured, banded sacs of flatworm larvae extend into the snail's tentacles, where they pulsate, attracting the attention of birds, which eat the snail and become infected by the parasite.

Maturing into medusae Free-swimming ephyra larvae bud off from the polyp, taking up to a year to mature into medusae or adult jellyfish.

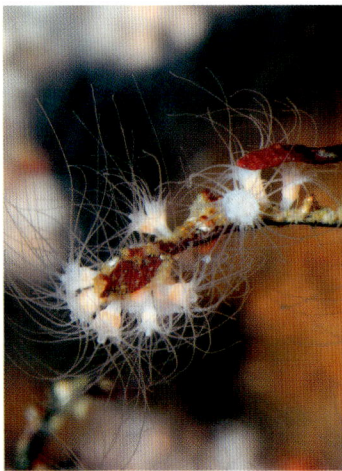

POLYP STAGE

Clear offspring
Garden snail

SPECIES *Cornu aspersum* **SIZE** Shell diameter 2.5–3.5 cm (1–1½ in) **DISTRIBUTION** Moist habitats in woods, hedgerows, parks, and gardens across western Europe, Mediterranean, North Africa, and Asia Minor

The offspring of garden snails are miniature, translucent versions of their parents. They hatch around two weeks after the eggs are laid in a hole in the ground. As the snail's body grows, so too does the shell, changing colour at the same time. They take two years to reach maturity, with a shell diameter of 1.5–2 cm (½–¾ in) after one year and 2.5–3.5 cm (1–1½ in) after the second.

Translucent hatchlings These young garden snails have delicate spiral shells that will grow and gain colour as the snails mature.

Changing shape
Moon jellyfish

SPECIES *Aurelia aurita* **SIZE** 5–40 cm (2–15½ in) **DISTRIBUTION** Warm, tropical, coastal waters of the Indian, Atlantic, and Pacific oceans

Also known as the common jellyfish, the moon jellyfish is a relatively simple organism with a complex, multi-stage life cycle. It alternates between the free-swimming medusa (bell-shaped jellyfish) and the sedentary polyp forms. The polyps are general feeders. They settle on the sea bed and use their tentacles to filter food from the water that flows past them. The adult jellyfish drift on the ocean currents and feed on copepods and phytoplankton that they trap using mucus and a fine fringe of stinging tentacles.

ANATOMY JELLYFISH LIFE CYCLE

Adult jellyfish reproduce sexually: males release sperm through their mouths into the sea, where they enter the mouth of a female and fertilize eggs in the female's gonads. The resulting embryos move to the arms around the mouth to develop before being released into the plankton as planula larvae. Eventually, the planula settles on the sea bed to form a scyphistoma polyp, which reproduces asexually to produce more polyps. The scyphistoma buds produce a strobila, or stack of immature ephyra larvae. As the stack grows, the ephyra furthest away from the base begin to mature and are released. These free-swimming ephyra larvae gradually mature into adult medusae, completing the life cycle.

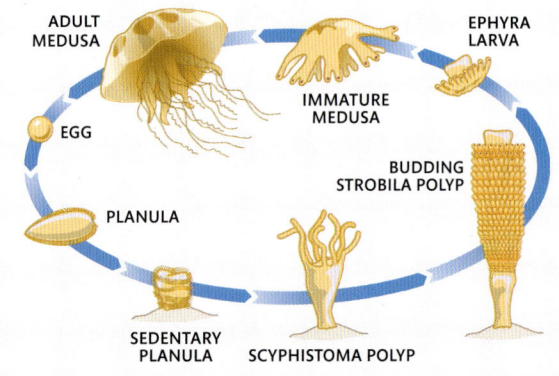

New armour
Slipper lobsters

FAMILY Scyllaridae **SIZE** Up to 30 cm (12 in)
DISTRIBUTION Wide distribution in warm oceans and seas, prevalent around the coast of Australia

Like other crustaceans, slipper lobsters have hard outer skeletons of chitin and calcium surrounding their bodies. This shell does not grow, so in order for the animal to increase in size it must shed its armour and grow it anew. In the larval stage they are planktonic (swimming and floating in open water) and may moult a dozen times before settling on a reef or rocky sea bottom. Young lobsters moult several times each year, then less often as they get older. Before moulting, they feed extensively, laying down fat stores. The lobster grows a soft new shell beneath the existing one, which cracks along lines of weakness to allow it to emerge. The lobster may eat its old shell to regain its valuable calcium content.

Emerging anew The slipper lobster's old shell fractures between the thorax and abdomen to allow the animal to pull itself out. The skin around the antennae, eyes, and gills remains intact. Depending on its size and age, a lobster may increase in weight by 6–24 per cent after each moult.

Emperor dragonfly
Shedding skin

SPECIES *Anax imperator* **SIZE** 8 cm (3¼ in) **DISTRIBUTION** Ponds and slow rivers in Europe, central Asia, North Africa, and the Middle East

The emperor dragonfly is an insect that undergoes incomplete metamorphosis during its development to the adult form. Its eggs hatch into aquatic larvae called nymphs, which undergo a series of moults, shedding their brown skin as they grow. Each successive larval stage resembles the one before and is known as an instar. In total, the emperor dragonfly spends around a year in this aquatic nymph stage. The predatory larvae grow and moult quickly during summer, and in autumn of the following year they moult into a final instar, which spends winter at the bottom of the pond or river in a state of diapause, or hibernation. Early the next summer, the final instar larva climbs out of the water and sheds its skin to emerge as a winged adult dragonfly. Adult dragonflies live for only a few weeks, hunting and becoming sexually mature before searching for mates. Male dragonflies patrol stretches of water, defending them against other males, while welcoming females. Male and female dragonflies mate on the wing, the male clasping the female behind the head with his abdomen in a characteristic "wheel" mating posture. Sperm is transferred from the male's primary genitalia to a secondary, or accessory, organ and, from there, to the female. Once the female lays the eggs, the dragonfly's life cycle is complete.

Laying eggs Once they have mated, female dragonflies use an ovipositor at the end of their abdomen to lay their eggs on vegetation floating in the water. The eggs hatch into a new generation of aquatic nymphs.

Facial mask The aquatic nymphs of dragonflies are voracious predators. They lie in ambush before capturing prey such as tadpoles (as here) or small fish with a grasping lower mouthpart called the facial mask.

Emergence When the nymph is ready to emerge, it climbs up a plant stem into the air and breaks out of its skin. After emerging, the dragonfly must wait for its wings to expand and harden before being able to fly.

Cluster of eggs Southern calamari squid (*Sepioteuthis australis*) lay their egg capsules in clusters on seagrass, sponges, or the sea bed in shallow, inshore waters. Each egg capsule can contain up to 10 fertilized eggs, but more usually holds three or four. Several females may add to the same cluster, resulting in an aggregation of up to 2,000 egg capsules.

Into the light >>01 The final stage nymph emerges from the ground and climbs a tree. >>02 Once attached to a leaf, the nymph begins to break free of its exoskeleton. >>03 The cicada gradually pulls itself out of its former skin. >>04 After emerging, it must wait for its wings to expand. >>05 The cicada's wings gradually harden. >>06 A newly moulted cicada is said to be "teneral" until its exoskeleton hardens.

Cicadas

Metamorphosis

FAMILY Cicadidae **SIZE** 2–15 cm (¾–6 in) **DISTRIBUTION** Woodland, worldwide except Antarctica

All insects undergo metamorphosis, with the exception of primitive wingless insects, such as silverfish. Metamorphosis, literally "transformation", refers to an animal's physical development from a larval body form to an adult one. There are two types of metamorphosis: gradual, or incomplete; and complete. Cicadas are an example of incomplete metamorphosis. The young insects superficially resemble the adults, but are wingless. As they feed and grow, cicadas pass through several developmental stages, called instars. They moult out of their exoskeletons between each instar, then a final moult reveals fully formed wings and the insects become sexually mature adults. Several other groups of insects also undergo incomplete metamorphosis, including grasshoppers, crickets, dragonflies (see p.351), and damselflies. In their adult form, these insects are sometimes called imagos, and the young are known as nymphs. Aquatic nymphs are referred to as naiads.

Insects that experience complete metamorphosis include beetles, butterflies (see p.348), bees, and flies. The changing form of their bodies during development is even more dramatic than in cicadas. Their larvae (variously called caterpillars, grubs, or maggots, according to the insect group to which they belong) also pass through several instars. They are often specialist feeders and may even be parasitic on other animals. Once they have finished feeding, the larvae pupate inside a cocoon or pupal case. During this time, they do not feed or move while their body undergoes a major transformation to the winged adult form.

There are over 3,000 species in the insect family Cicadidae

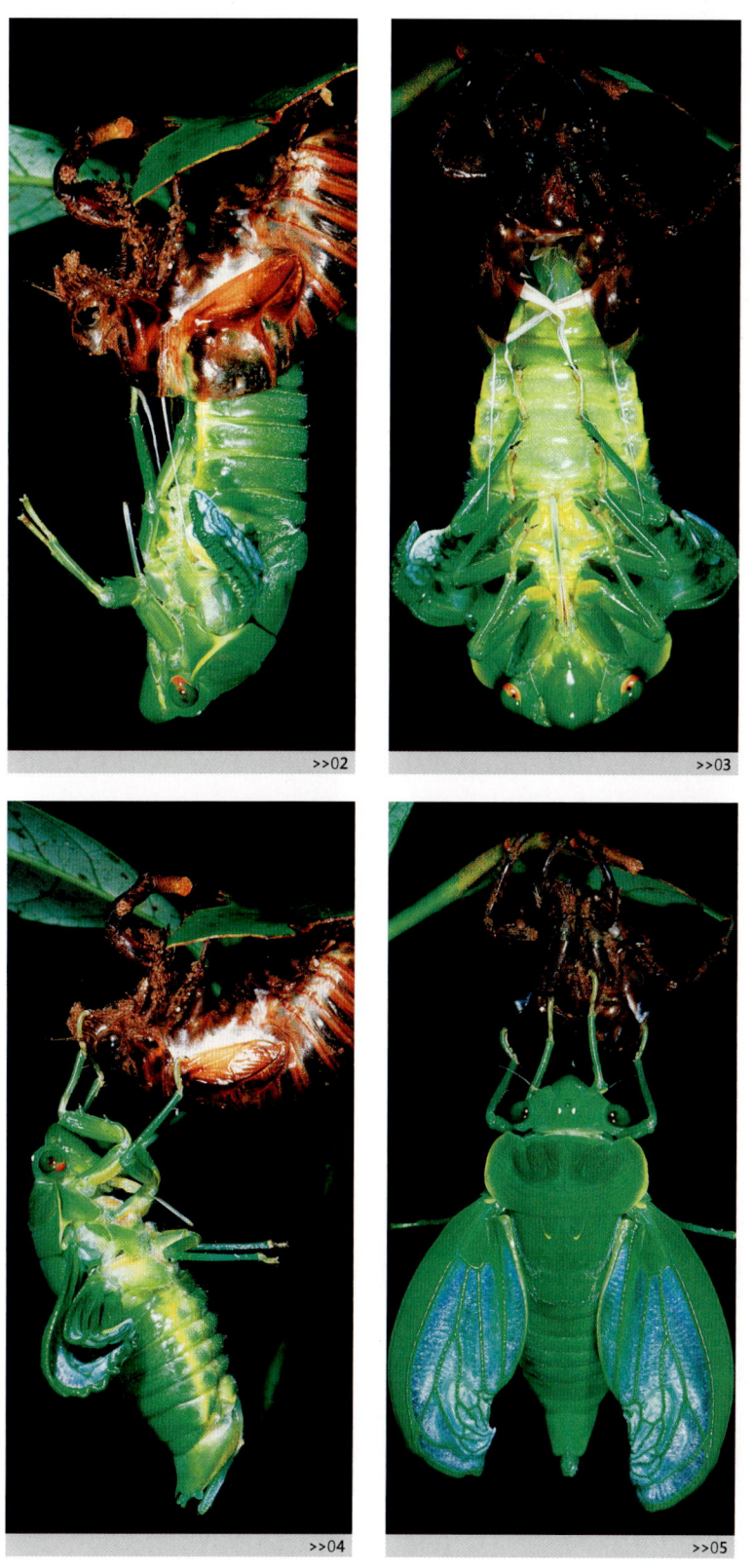

>>02

>>03

>>04

>>05

>>06

Periodical cicadas
Mass emergence

GENUS *Magicicada* **SIZE** 2.5–3 cm (1–1¼ in)
DISTRIBUTION Deciduous forests in the eastern USA

The periodical cicadas of North America are so-called because of their recurrent patterns of brood emergence. There are seven species, three with a 17-year life cycle and four with a 13-year life cycle, which means that every 17 or 13 years respectively a brood emerges from eggs that were laid and hatched 17 or 13 years previously. The nymphs spend the intervening years underground, going through various stages of development and feeding on juices from tree roots. Adult males mature to make a deafening chorus of noise, which attracts the females.

Emerging nymph When ready, the final-stage nymph digs a small tunnel through the ground to reach the surface. Unlike the adults, nymphs do not possess wings.

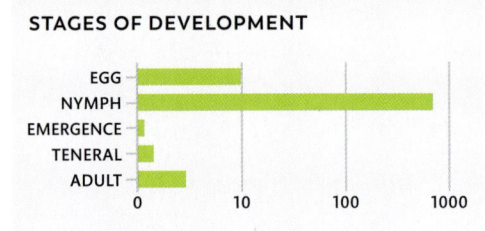

Cicada life span The total life span of the 17-year periodical cicada is 884 weeks. A massive 98 per cent of this time is spent underground as a nymph. At the teneral stage, the cicada is soft and pale.

Final moult Above ground, the final-stage nymph attaches itself to a tree and undergoes one final moult to become a winged adult. Initially, the adult is soft and pale, but it darkens as the exoskeleton hardens.

Green lacewing
Safety line

SPECIES *Chrysoperla carnea* **SIZE** 1.5–2 cm (½–¾ in)
DISTRIBUTION Herbaceous vegetation across North America, Europe, North Africa, and Asia

Green lacewing females each attach 400–500 eggs to leaves by thin silk threads. This keeps them out of the reach of insect predators, including their newly hatched siblings. Lacewing larvae are important predators of aphids, a crop pest, and they are widely used by horticulturalists as biological control agents.

Tsetse fly
Big baby

SPECIES *Glossina morsitans* **SIZE** 7–14 mm (¼–½ in)
DISTRIBUTION Savanna and woodland of Africa and Arabian Peninsula, south of the Tropic of Cancer

After mating, tsetse fly females retain a single fertilized egg in their uterus. There it hatches into a larva, which is fed on secretions from a modified gland. The larva passes through three larval instars (stages) in five days; the female then deposits it on the ground, into which it burrows to pupate. Pregnant flies feed on the blood of other animals in order to sustain their offspring.

Giving birth At birth, the tsetse fly larva is large and ready to pupate. It breathes through black lobes at its rear end.

Braconid wasps
Body snatcher

FAMILY Braconidae **SIZE** Up to 1.5 cm (½ in) **DISTRIBUTION** Worldwide

Braconid wasp larvae are parasitoids – parasites that ultimately cause the death of their host. In this case, the hosts are the larvae of other insects, often beetle grubs, fly maggots, or caterpillars. A female wasp places its eggs inside the body of another animal, using her long ovipositor. The eggs hatch into larvae that feed on the host's fluids and internal organs. Viruses may help the wasp larvae to evade detection by disabling the host's immune system. Larvae of some species of braconid wasp remain within the host's body to pupate, while others cut round holes and emerge through the skin, pupating while still attached to the host or moving away to pupate elsewhere. There are 12,000 described species of braconid wasp.

Cocooned caterpillar After the wasp larvae emerge from the body of their host, they wrap themselves in silk cocoons to undergo their final transformation to adult wasps.

Blotchy swell shark
Translucent home
SPECIES *Cephaloscyllium umbratile* **SIZE** 1.2 m (4 ft)
DISTRIBUTION Subtropical rocky reefs of the western Pacific Ocean from Japan to the South China Sea

The blotchy or Japanese swell shark is an egg-laying (oviparous) fish. After mating, the female produces pairs of eggs, one from each oviduct. Each egg becomes enclosed in a tough egg case, or "mermaid's purse", as it passes through the female shark's reproductive tract. Safe within the egg case, the embryo has its own food source – a sac of protein-rich yolk. However, some embryos may be eaten by predatory snails, which use their horny radula ("tongue") to cut through the egg case. When the young shark is ready to emerge, after up to 12 months, it uses a double row of toothlike structures on its back to help break its way out of its egg case.

Blotchy swell sharks are at one end of the shark reproductive spectrum, with little or no embryonic development occurring within the mother. At the other end are sharks that form a very close link with their developing embryos. Some produce a sort of uterine milk called histrotroph to nourish their young, while others have a placenta through which nutrients can pass from the mother's blood to her developing offspring, which are born live.

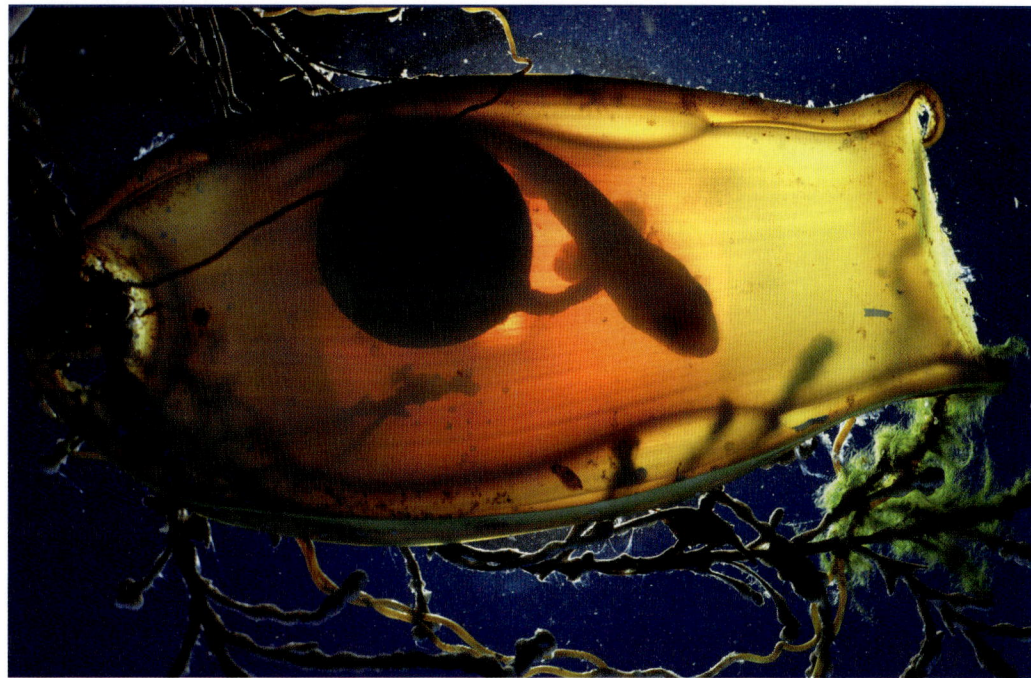

Mermaid's purse The embryos of blotchy swell sharks are held within tough egg cases that are anchored to seaweed or rocks using long tendrils. The light shining through this egg case reveals the yolk sac attached to the embryo.

Spiny dogfish
Food store
SPECIES *Squalus acanthias* **SIZE** 0.8–1.5 m (2½–5 ft)
DISTRIBUTION Coastal and shelf waters worldwide except the north Pacific

Also known as the spurdog or piked dogfish, the spiny dogfish gives birth to a litter of 2–11 live pups after a lengthy gestation of 18–24 months. It is an ovoviviparous shark, meaning that the eggs are retained inside the female, the embryos nourished by their attached egg sacs, until the young are fully developed and ready to be born. Sharks show a broad range of reproductive strategies. The embryos of some species, for example the sandtiger shark, feed inside the mother on her unfertilized eggs or by cannibalizing their siblings.

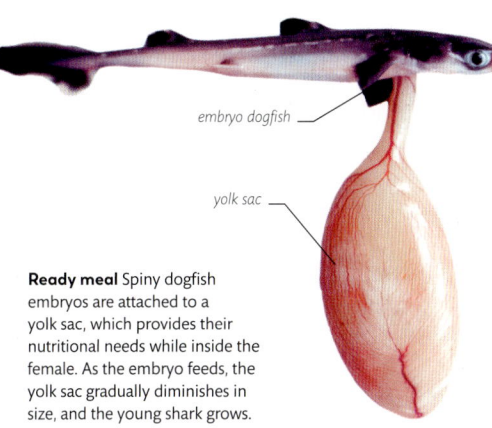

embryo dogfish
yolk sac

Ready meal Spiny dogfish embryos are attached to a yolk sac, which provides their nutritional needs while inside the female. As the embryo feeds, the yolk sac gradually diminishes in size, and the young shark grows.

Lemon sole
Face migration
SPECIES *Microstomus kitt* **SIZE** 20–70 cm (8–28 in)
DISTRIBUTION Stony and rocky sea beds of northeast Atlantic to a depth of 200–400 m (660–1,300 ft)

Adult lemon sole are bottom-dwelling (benthic) flatfishes, but they do not emerge from the egg that way. Their planktonic eggs develop into pelagic larval fishes, meaning they swim in open water. Gradually, the young fishes start to swim on their sides, flatten out, and eventually settle on the sea bed. In order to avoid having one eye looking at the sand, the lemon sole's left eye migrates around to the right side of its body. This new upper side of the body becomes elaborately pigmented, while the underside remains white. Lemon sole often partly bury themselves in the sandy substrate, so they are camouflaged and less visible to predators. When they swim, they do so close to the bottom, on their sides, and by flexing their body. Other flatfishes all undergo the same process but some species, such as turbot and brill, are "left-eyed", which means that the right eye moves around to the left side of the body. The metamorphosis from upright to flatfish is controlled by a thyroid hormone, which also controls metamorphosis in amphibians. Other fishes that live on the sea bed may be flat, but from top to bottom, so they do not undergo this dramatic transformation to lie on their sides.

Eyes to the right Lemon sole are right-eyed, meaning that the left eye moves over to the right side of the fish's body. Some species, for example the summer flounder (*Paralichthys dentatus*), are left-eyed, and the right eye migrates to the left side of the body.

ANATOMY TURNING HEADS

At 10 days old, the larval lemon sole swims upright and has a bilaterally symmetrical body and a relatively large skull, which will later become compressed as the face is distorted. Metamorphosis begins after 13 days: the left eye starts to migrate over the top of the head to the right side of the body. The transformation is complete after 35 days. Both eyes are on the right side, which is the adult lemon sole's upper surface and is now distinctly patterned.

TEN DAYS

THIRTEEN DAYS

THIRTY-FIVE DAYS

Laying eggs A female rosy bitterling approaches a freshwater mussel, ready to insert her long ovipositor into the mussel's gill cavity through its exhalant siphon. A male follows, ready to release his sperm next to the mussel's inhalant siphon.

Rosy bitterling
Surrogate mother

SPECIES *Rhodeus ocellatus* **SIZE** 4–8 cm (1½–3¼ in) **DISTRIBUTION** Inland waters, such as ponds, creeks, and reservoirs. Native to eastern Asia; introduced elsewhere

Bitterlings depend on a relationship with mussels for their reproduction. Before breeding, female bitterlings grow an egg-laying tube, or ovipositor, which is 5–6 cm (2–2¼ in) long, behind their anus. The female hangs vertically in the water before inserting her ovipositor into a mussel, laying two or three eggs into the mussel's body cavity. The male bitterling then fertilizes the eggs by shedding his sperm into the flow of water being drawn into the shell by the mussel's siphon. When the baby bitterlings hatch they remain in the safety of the bivalve's shell for a period of several weeks, eventually emerging through the mussel's siphon. A female bitterling lays eggs several times over a number of weeks, so a mussel can contain young at various stages of development.

Surinam toad
Protective skin

SPECIES *Pipa pipa* **SIZE** 10–17 cm (4–6½ in) **DISTRIBUTION** Ponds and swamps of South America and Trinidad

The tadpoles of the Surinam toad live within their mother's skin while they grow. During mating, the male toad grasps the female around her hind legs. The pair flips repeatedly in the water and each time the female releases up to 10 eggs that fall onto the male's belly, where they are fertilized. From there, they are transferred onto the female's back, where they sink into the skin, forming pockets, over the next few hours. In total, around 100 eggs are laid. The tadpoles hatch and complete their development within the mother's skin, which protects the eggs and tadpoles, keeping them safe from predators and ensuring they are kept moist. Even though they are not required for swimming, the tadpoles temporarily have tails. The tail helps each tadpole to obtain sufficient oxygen by increasing its surface area of moist skin.

Egg protection The eggs sink into honeycomblike skin on the female's back and become encased in a cystlike structure covered with a horny lid.

Hatching toadlets The fully-formed young toads emerge from their mother's back after 12–20 weeks, usually when the female moults her skin.

Transforming tail The tails of immature frogs (froglets) gradually disappear at the same time as other metamorphic changes are occurring.

European common frog
Total metamorphosis

SPECIES *Rana temporaria* **SIZE** Up to 11 cm (4½ in), female larger than male **DISTRIBUTION** Damp habitats, ponds, and ditches of Europe and northwest Asia, except Portugal, much of Spain, Italy, and most of Greece

European common frogs, like most frogs, toads, and other amphibians, begin their lives as aquatic tadpoles, but later transform into terrestrial adults. Their entire metamorphosis is governed by a thyroid hormone. Some frogs, such as the common coqui, lack a tadpole stage, instead hatching from their eggs as tiny frogs. Tadpole metamorphosis is flexible, depending on environmental conditions. For example, low temperatures and low food supply slow growth rates and delay metamorphosis.

LIFE STORIES 359

Male carers Male Mallorcan midwife toads carry their eggs in strings wrapped around their ankles, keeping them safe from attack. Mating occurs in May and June; eggs are carried until they hatch into tadpoles.

Mallorcan midwife toad
Fatherly concern
SPECIES *Alytes muletensis* **SIZE** 4 cm (1½ in)
DISTRIBUTION Endemic to the Spanish island of Mallorca. Lives in small streams in limestone gorges

All five species of midwife toad share a common behaviour – it is the male toad rather than the female that cares for the eggs. During mating, the female lays her eggs, which are simultaneously fertilized by the male. He then winds them around his legs to protect them from predators. When they are ready to hatch, he lowers the eggs into a pool for the tadpoles to emerge. The Mallorcan midwife toad was believed to be extinct until a tiny population was discovered in 1980. A captive breeding programme is helping the toad's recovery.

CASE STUDY **PREDATOR EFFECT**
Predatory viperine snakes (*Natrix maura*) were introduced to Mallorca around 2,000 years ago and pose a threat to midwife toads. Biologists have noticed differences in form between tadpoles that are exposed to these predators and those that are not. Tadpoles that share pools with one of these snakes tend to be leaner, with longer tails, narrower fins, and deeper tail muscles, allowing them to swim faster than tadpoles that do not coexist with a snake and tend to be fatter.

NON-PREDATOR-EXPOSED TADPOLE

PREDATOR-EXPOSED TADPOLE

Albino axolotl Albinos are relatively common among captive axolotls. Wild axolotls tend to be a mottled brown-green colour.

From water to land >>01 In spring, female common frogs lay batches of gelatinous eggs (frogspawn) in water. >>02 Six days after fertilization, the eggs hatch into tiny tadpoles that have tails and gills. >>03 After 6–9 weeks, they develop hind legs, and their gills are replaced by lungs, so they must swim at the water's surface to breathe. They then develop forelegs and their tales slowly disappear until, finally, metamorphosis is complete. They attain sexual maturity in three years.

Emperor angelfish
Colour change
SPECIES *Pomacanthus imperator* **SIZE** 40 cm (15½ in)
DISTRIBUTION Coral reefs of the Pacific and Indian oceans

Emperor angelfishes undergo a spectacular transformation as they mature. Their coloration and patterning change so markedly over a period of about two years that juveniles were first thought to belong to another species. The change may help immature angelfishes to avoid aggression from territorial adult male angelfishes, to which they might otherwise appear to pose a threat.

ADULT EMPEROR ANGELFISH

JUVENILE EMPEROR ANGELFISH

Axolotl
Permanent juvenile
SPECIES *Ambystoma mexicanum* **SIZE** 20–43 cm (8–17 in)
DISTRIBUTION Historically found in two lakes near Mexico City, one of which is no longer present. Endangered in the wild

The axolotl is a type of salamander that never grows up. It is "neotenic" or "paedomorphic", meaning that it retains larval features into adulthood and sexual maturity. It is permanently aquatic and has feathery gills for extracting oxygen from the water. It also has juvenile skin and fins on its tail to help it swim. Axolotls become sexually mature at around one year of age. The male deposits a packet of sperm or spermatophore on the lake bed via his cloaca, and the female then picks up the spermatophore to fertilize her eggs. Axolotls can transform into adult salamanders if they have hybridized with tiger salamanders or they can be induced to metamorphose by exposure to hormones or high iodine levels.

HUMAN IMPACT **FIGHTING AGEING**
The axolotl has the ability to regrow lost limbs, an attribute that has been studied with the hope that it could lead to breakthroughs in human medicine and therapies. One area of study has yielded results in laboratory mice. Gene therapy based on axolotl research allows mice to live up to 25 per cent longer and protected the mice against a variety of diseases. The hope is that the same science will form the basis of therapies that could extend human life.

Egg-laying female The female lays her eggs into a hole she has dug in the sand of a traditional nesting beach. When she has finished laying, she covers the eggs over and returns to the sea. The hatchling turtles emerge 40–75 days later.

Green turtle
Rapid egg production
SPECIES *Chelonia mydas* **SIZE** Up to 1.5 m (5 ft)
DISTRIBUTION Tropical and subtropical seagrass beds and open water in Atlantic and Indo-Pacific oceans

A female green turtle may lay up to nine clutches of eggs in a single breeding season, each clutch numbering between 100 and 200 eggs. She may not breed again for several years. Many turtle nests are destroyed by scavengers, such as dogs, coatis, and vultures, and they are also threatened by man's activities. Hatchlings are vulnerable to seabirds and crabs on the beach, and sharks and dolphins in the water. The high rate of egg production helps to offset the high rate of mortality suffered by the eggs and hatchling turtles, ensuring that at least a few individuals survive to adulthood.

short, beaked head

paddlelike flippers

Late bloomer Green turtles are long-lived animals that may take up to 50 years to reach sexual maturity.

Malleefowl mound Males tend their mound fastidiously during incubation, maintaining its temperature at 33–34°C (92–93°F) by adding and removing layers of soil. They test the mound's temperature by probing it with their bills.

Emperor penguin
Paternal instinct
SPECIES *Aptenodytes forsteri* **SIZE** 1.1 m (3½ ft)
DISTRIBUTION Pack ice, coastal islands, and waters around Antarctica

The only penguin species to reproduce during the Antarctic winter, male emperor penguins withstand some of the harshest conditions on Earth while incubating their eggs. Most emperor penguin colonies breed on stable pack ice, selecting sheltered areas where walls of ice or icebergs offer some protection against the bitter wind.

Emperor penguins are ready to breed at around three years of age. After laying their single egg in May or June, female penguins leave for the ocean to feed and replenish the energy lost in egg production. The males are left to take care of the egg for over two months, during which they do not feed and they lose around a third of their body weight by metabolizing fat to keep warm. The females return from the sea when their eggs are about to hatch. They regurgitate fishes and squid for their new offspring and switch places with the male so that he can go to feed. Occasionally, the egg hatches before the female comes back and the male produces a protein-rich secretion to feed the chick for a few days. For the next 45–50 days after hatching, the parents take turns to go on foraging trips and care for their young chick. Initially they may have to walk 50–120 km (30–75 miles) to reach the open ocean at the edge of the pack ice, but as the Antarctic summer progresses and the ice melts, this distance gradually reduces. The young penguins remain in crèches until they are 150 days old, when they leave the ice and head for the ocean.

Close colony Males huddle together to ride out the Antarctic winter. They may not see the sun for two months, temperatures can plunge to –45°C (–49°F), and blizzards may blow at up to 200 kph (124 mph).

Malleefowl
Decaying nest
SPECIES *Leipoa ocellata* **SIZE** 60 cm (23½ in)
DISTRIBUTION Semi-arid scrub and low eucalyptus woodland in southern Australia

Male malleefowl build large mounds of decaying vegetation and sand in which the females lay their eggs. The males use their feet to scrape out a large depression, which they then fill with plenty of organic matter. They turn the vegetation over after rain to encourage decay, which generates heat; the mound is also warmed by the sun. The female lays her eggs at 5–17 day intervals. Clutch sizes are highly variable but an average clutch will have between 15 and 20 eggs. These are laid in a chamber within the mound, which is then covered with a layer of sand. Hatching one at a time, the young mallee fowl dig their way out of the mound. They receive no parental care whatsoever, nor have any contact with their siblings, and are able to fly and fend for themselves within a single day.

Hoatzin
Tree climbing
SPECIES *Opisthocomus hoazin* **SIZE** 65 cm (26 in)
DISTRIBUTION Swamps, riverine forest, and mangroves in the Amazon Basin and Orinoco Delta in South America

The hoatzin is a noisy bird that breeds in trees overhanging water, laying two to three eggs in a stick nest. If threatened, the nestlings throw themselves out of their nest into the water below. Young hoatzins have two claws on each wing that act as hooks to help them cling onto vegetation, and they use these to climb back up the tree once the threat has passed. Hoatzins are unusual in feeding wholly on leaves. They possess a greatly enlarged crop in their gut, where the leaves' digestion is aided by bacterial fermentation. The evolutionary history of the hoatzin is far from clear. They have been variously linked to gamebirds, cuckoos, and African turacos, but modern taxonomy places them closest to the cranes and rails.

Hanging on The wing claws are lost when the birds moult into their adult plumage and are able to fly up into the trees rather than climb up. Even as adults, hoatzins are poor fliers and tend to clamber around their arboreal habitat in a clumsy manner.

ANATOMY **BROOD PATCH**
The male emperor penguin incubates the egg on top of his feet, in contact with a bare fold of skin called the brood patch. This allows the adult penguin's body heat to reach the delicate egg more efficiently. The fold of skin extends down over the top of the egg to keep it warm and safe. The male incubates the egg like this for 65 days. Once it hatches, the chick also takes refuge beneath the brood patch until it is able to withstand the cold. Many other bird species also develop a brood patch, and the feathers shed from the area are used as nest-lining material.

March of the penguins Male emperor penguins can still walk with the egg incubating in the brood patch. As their legs are set far back, penguins are efficient, graceful swimmers, but can look ungainly on land.

Red-necked wallaby
Protective pouch

SPECIES *Notamacropus rufogriseus* **SIZE** 70–105 cm (28–41 in) **DISTRIBUTION** Coastal scrub, bush, and eucalyptus forest in eastern and southeastern Australia

The gestation period of a red-necked wallaby lasts just 33 days, after which the foetus is born when still fairly undeveloped. Within minutes of birth, it makes its way to a pouch on its mother's belly to continue its development. Soon after the birth, the female mates again. The resulting embryo remains in a suspended state called "embryonic diapause" for up to eight months. It is then born within 30 days of the first joey leaving the pouch. A female may therefore have a young-at-foot, which she continues to feed, a joey in the pouch, and an embryo in utero at the same time.

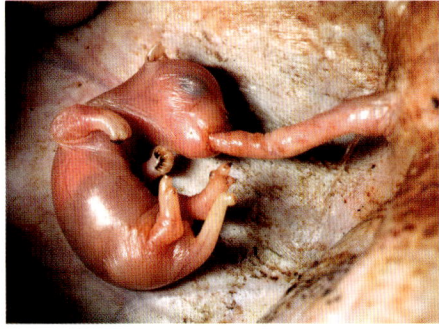

Wallaby suckling Newborn wallabies are about 1.5 cm (½ in) long. They crawl through their mother's fur to the pouch, where they latch on to one of four teats and suckle on their mother's milk for four months.

Joey in the pouch At around five months old the young wallaby starts to peek out of the pouch and, by six months it can hop in and out. At eight months, the joey is too large for the pouch but stays close to its mother.

Short-beaked echidna
Egg-laying mammal

SPECIES *Tachyglossus aculeatus* **SIZE** 30–45 cm (12–17½ in) **DISTRIBUTION** Forest, desert, and meadows in Australia; coastal and highland regions of southwestern New Guinea

The short-beaked echidna is one of only five species of extant mammal that lays eggs. The others are three species of long-beaked echidna and the platypus. They are known collectively as monotremes, a reference to the single common opening for the urinary, defecatory, and reproductive tracts. As in birds and reptiles, this opening is called the cloaca.

After a period of gestation, during which the single fertilized egg is nourished in the oviduct, female short-beaked echidnas lay the egg into a specially developed pouch at the rear of their abdomen; the platypus lays up to three eggs in a burrow. The young echidna remains in the pouch for two to three months. Since the mother has no teats, the young suckles milk from a patch of skin on the mother's belly called the areola; this is also the case with long-beaked echidnas and the platypus. Echidnas are slow breeders, maturing at five or more years old and producing only one young every two to six years. They can live to be 45 years old.

Strong digger All echidnas are adapted to digging, with short limbs and strong claws. As well as burrowing, they dig for ants and termites, using their sensitive snouts as a guide.

covered in stiff spines

elongated snout

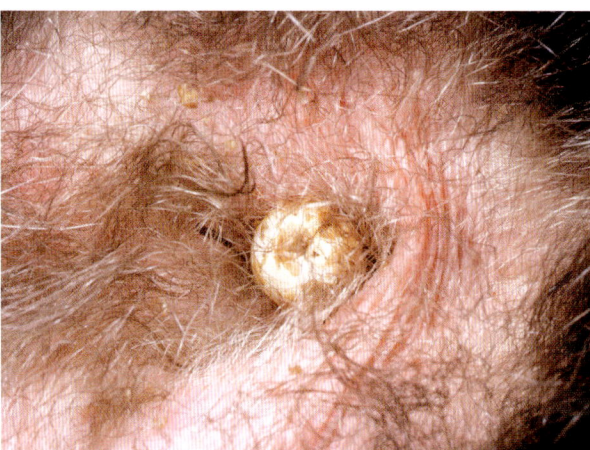

Egg in pouch A leathery egg is laid directly into the female's pouch from the cloaca after 21–28 days of gestation. The young echidna uses its egg tooth to hatch around 10 days later.

Young in burrow When the young echidna, or puggle, becomes too big to remain in the pouch, the female leaves it in a burrow. She allows it to suckle until it is six months old. It reaches independence after one year.

European badger
Sociable clan

SPECIES *Meles meles* **SIZE** 56–90 cm (22–35 in)
DISTRIBUTION Across Europe and Asia. Setts located in woods and forests; badgers forage in adjacent fields

A badger sett or burrow is home to a social group or "clan" of up to 12 badgers, comprising a dominant breeding pair and their subordinate offspring. The breeding pair may mate any time between late winter and midsummer, but implantation of the resulting embryos is delayed for up to ten months. The embryos are eventually triggered to implant and continue their development according to changing day length and temperature. Around seven weeks after the implantation of the embryos, in February or March, between two and six blind young are born. They open their eyes at about one month of age and suckle for up to three months. Although they are independent and can disperse at seven to eight months of age, the females in particular often stay with their parents for longer.

Sociable home Each sett has a breeding chamber, lined with dried vegetation, where the cubs are born and remain until they are old enough to venture outside. They often spend time playing or grooming one another.

Giraffe
Only child

SPECIES *Giraffa camelopardalis* **SIZE** 4.7–5.5 m (15½–18 ft) tall
DISTRIBUTION Savanna, grassland, and open woodland, particularly with acacia, in sub-Saharan Africa

Female giraffes usually have one offspring every 20–30 months. Gestation lasts around 15 months and the young are typically born between May and August. For the first week, the mother stands guard and feeds close to her resting baby during the day and nurses it at night. After three to four weeks, the pair will join the herd and the young giraffe is then sometimes cared for in a crèche with other young. Each female takes it in turn to mind the crèche while the other females feed. The young are fully weaned at between 12 and 16 months of age, but females do not breed until they are at least five and males at least seven years old. Giraffe herds contain animals of all ages, although males generally move between herds, searching for receptive females.

2.4 m The length of an adult giraffe's neck; it contains seven elongated vertebrae.

HUMAN IMPACT **POACHING**

It is illegal to kill giraffes in many African countries. However, they are illegally killed for their hides, meat, and tails. The long, hair-tipped tails are made into fly swats, good-luck bracelets, and thread for sewing, and the hide is used to make buckets or shields. Hunting has not yet had a disastrous effect on giraffe populations, but it is a cause for concern. Many other animals are also killed illegally for meat or other products, for example elephants for their ivory tusks and leopards for their fur.

Newborn giraffe Giraffes give birth while standing or walking. Within 20 minutes of birth, the newborn, which is up to 2 m (6½ ft) tall, is able to stand and suckle.

Raising young

Reproduction is a costly process. It takes time and resources, may influence an animal's chances of survival, and affects its future reproductive fitness. Parents must do whatever they can to maximize their offspring's chances of survival. Different animals approach the issue of caring for their young in a host of different ways.

Cub care Male tigers play no role in raising their young. The female nurses them, teaches them to hunt, and remains with them for two years until they are independent. She can then reproduce again.

PARENTAL CARE

Parental care is a behavioural strategy aimed at increasing the chances of a parent's offspring reaching adulthood. Not all animals care for their young (most egg-layers, except birds, simply lay their eggs and leave), but there are many that do take an active role. This effort is costly – it takes time, is often risky, and detracts from an animal's ability to produce further offspring. A parent must decide whether to invest in its current offspring, or to save its investment for the future.

Biparental care Frigatebird chicks fledge at around six months, yet their parents feed them for two years, which is the longest period of post-fledging care of any bird.

Reptilian care Only around 3 per cent of reptiles exhibit parental care. Viper mothers are one of the few groups that do look after their young, guarding the eggs or tiny snakes against predators.

CAREGIVERS

Although it may be in all animals' interests for their offspring to receive parental care, different species have different approaches to raising their young. For species that use internal fertilization, the male cannot guarantee his paternity and often has more to gain by deserting the female and finding new mates. The female, in contrast, has little choice but to care for her eggs until the point of laying or birth. For species with external fertilization, such as fish, the reverse is often true. The female lays the eggs, which are then fertilized by the male. He must take responsibility if he wants to guarantee his paternity and ensure his eggs survive. Some species show joint or biparental care, while a few leave their young in the care of other, often unrelated, individuals.

LENGTH OF CARE

How long a parent cares for its young is determined by several factors. Longer periods of care result in larger offspring with higher chances of survival. However, this level of investment decreases the number of broods a parent can produce in a lifetime, and may also place the parent at greater risk of predation. Evolution favours strategies that maximize an individual's reproductive output over its lifetime. Some parents simply care for their young prior to birth, keeping the eggs safe until they hatch. Others remain with their young after birth, guarding their brood or feeding them until they can feed themselves. Prolonged periods of parental care occur in some mammals and birds – most commonly in long-lived, large-brained, social animals, which need time to grow and learn the skills necessary for survival.

Koala cuddle Koala joeys stay close to their mothers for one year, until they are weaned.

Family herd Elephants have large brains, live in complex social groups, and have long lifespans. When a new calf is born, the whole group helps to care for it and keep it safe.

Safety in numbers Dominant female goosanders commonly form crèche systems, which may include the offspring of other birds. Greater numbers help reduce the chances of their own young being taken by predators.

Six-rayed starfish
Sticking close
SPECIES Leptasterias hexactis **SIZE** Up to 5 cm (2 in)
DISTRIBUTION Rocky, intertidal zone of the northeast Pacific region, from California to Alaska

Unlike many starfish, which release their eggs and sperm into the water and allow the eggs to develop without their care, this tiny starfish takes an active role in brooding its young. When a female six-rayed starfish is ready to spawn, she arches her body and stands on the tips of her arms to form a brood chamber. She then releases up to 1,500 large, yolky eggs (relatively few for a starfish), which she catches and holds beneath her body using her sticky tube feet. For around two months, the female broods the developing embryos and, subsequently, the tiny juveniles. As these are beneath her mouth, she cannot feed during this time. Towards the end of the brooding

Standing on tiptoes When the female is ready to brood, she searches for a safe location, such as the underside of a rock. She attaches herself using her tube feet.

time, the young starfish begin to move around on their own, having developed tube feet after about 40 days. They eventually crawl away from the mother to begin an independent life.

Nursery web spider
Protective web
SPECIES Pisaura mirabilis **SIZE** Up to 1.5 cm (½ in) **DISTRIBUTION** Widespread throughout Britain, Europe, Russia, China, and North Africa

The nursery web spider is named for the impressive structure it weaves in order to keep its immature young safe. Mating occurs in early spring. To avoid being attacked by the female and distract her attention while mating occurs, the male presents her with a gift of a wrapped insect. The female produces hundreds of eggs, which are held together in large white egg sacs. Initially, the female carries these in her jaws and pedipalps, or "feelers". When the eggs are about to hatch, she builds a tentlike nest and places the egg sacs within. Once the eggs hatch, they are contained inside the nest and the female stands guard outside, defending her young from predators for a week or more, until they can survive on their own. Although they are famous for their webs, these spiders do not weave traps during the rest of the year, preferring to hunt on foot and catch their prey using stealth.

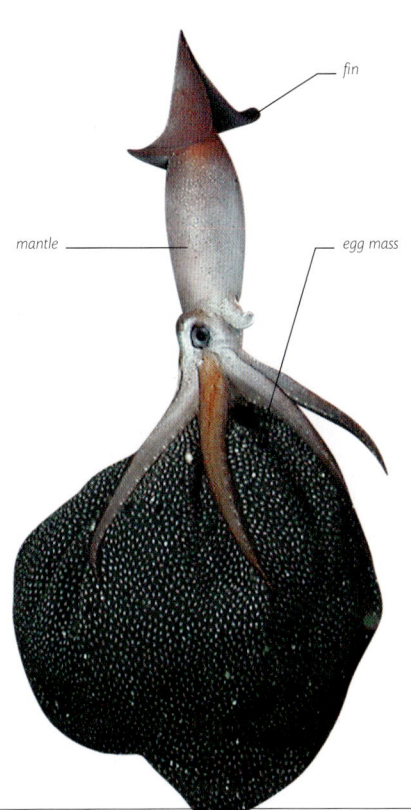

Clawed armhook squid
Double size
SPECIES Gonatus onyx **SIZE** Mantle 14 cm (5½ in)
DISTRIBUTION Abundant throughout the Atlantic and Pacific in mid- to deep waters

The clawed armhook squid lives in relatively deep water, between depths of about 1,000 m (3,280 ft) and 2,500 m (8,200 ft), although at times it can be found much nearer the surface. At depth, the female produces an enormous black mass of approximately 2,000–3,000 eggs. The egg mass is so long that it effectively doubles the body size of this tiny squid. It is suspended from hooks under the mother's arms. She cares for her eggs without eating anything for several months until they are ready to hatch.

Mother's burden A female clawed armhook squid with a huge egg mass. This photograph was taken by a robotic submarine operated by the Monterey Bay Aquarium Research Institute.

Safe house This nursery web spider has built its protective web on a young fern plant. The young spiders huddle together in a mass at the centre of the web, while their mother keeps watch for predators.

Giant Pacific octopus
Maternal sacrifice
SPECIES Enteroctopus dofleini **SIZE** 4.5–9 m (14¾–30 ft)
DISTRIBUTION On the continental shelf of the North Pacific, to depths of around 750 m (2,500 ft)

Females of the giant Pacific octopus (the largest octopus in the world) make the ultimate sacrifice for their young. When they are ready to reproduce, they find a rocky den and lay up to 100,000 eggs. Over the next seven or more months, they carefully tend, clean, and aerate the eggs until they hatch. Like other octopus species, females do not feed at all during this time and die shortly after the young emerge.

Protected nursery This giant Pacific octopus has attached her precious strings of eggs to the roof of her den. She remains with them, chasing off would-be predators, until they hatch, by which time she is very weak. She dies soon afterwards.

Potter wasp
Living larder

SUBFAMILY Eumeninae **SIZE** Up to 3 cm (1¼ in)
DISTRIBUTION Widespread distribution, including Australia, North America, South America, Asia, Africa, and Europe

Potter wasps are solitary wasps that live independently, without the social interactions seen in many other wasp species. A lone female seeks out a male to mate with, before setting off to build a nest. Nests are usually based around a pre-existing hole in a wall or rock, at the open end of which the female constructs a potlike cell. This is typically constructed from soil or chewed up leaves, held together with saliva and shaped like a small ball or vase with a single opening. The female wasp lays one or multiple eggs into individual brood cavities within the nest. Having laid her eggs, she leaves the nest to collect food for her young to eat once they have hatched. The mother hunts for caterpillars, which she paralyses by stinging them. She transports the caterpillars back to her nest, holding them upside-down using her middle set of legs. As soon as the cell's brood chambers are lined with food, she seals the door, using the same building materials to keep the cell watertight. After a few days, the larva hatches and emerges from its burrow to a welcoming larder full of fresh food. Once the nest is provisioned, the female wasp plays no further role in her offspring's care or development.

Fresh meal Caterpillars are paralysed by the female, not killed, to prevent them rotting before the larvae have had their feed. Potter wasps get their name from the small, pot-shaped structures that they build as their nests.

Jumping spider
Mother's milk

SPECIES *Toxeus magnus* **SIZE** 6.6 mm (¼ in) (average adult length)
DISTRIBUTION Relatively widespread in tropical and subtropical parts of Southeast Asia

Some jumping spiders show exceptional and prolonged maternal care. Mothers nurse their offspring with a creamy, white milk-like fluid, which looks similar to mammalian milk and contains fat, sugar, and about four times as much protein as cows' milk. This fluid is indispensible to newborn spiders and enables them to grow extremely fast. Spiderlings begin hunting for food about 20 days after hatching but are not weaned until they are 40 days old. During that time they consume a mix of insects and spider milk. Even at 20 days old, spiderlings that are orphaned are much less likely to survive than those with mothers. Scientist think the nutritious liquid may be made from unfertilized eggs that are recycled by the mother.

Nursing spider This female jumping spider is of a species of jumping spider that mimics the appearance of black ants found within their range.

Maternal care also influences the sex ratio among the offspring. When mothers are present in the nest after 20 days, most of the offspring that survive into adulthood are female. This is beneficial to the population as more females means more offspring. Moreover, mother spiders allow daughters to return to the nest after they become adults but attack sons that try to come home.

Large blue butterfly
Honey trap

SPECIES *Phengaris arion* **SIZE** Caterpillar 1.3 cm (½ in), adult wingspan 5 cm (2 in) **DISTRIBUTION** Widespread in Europe; became extinct in the UK in 1979 but reintroduced in 1983

The young caterpillar of the large blue butterfly brings the kiss of death to its unsuspecting hosts. It puts itself up for "adoption" by producing a sweet, honeylike substance from a gland at the rear of its body. This lure attracts the ant *Myrmica sabuleti*, which "adopts" the caterpillar for its nectar and takes it back to its nest. Once inside, the caterpillar acquires the red ant's scent, mimics the ant's sound, and readily provides honey for the nest. The unsuspecting ants are wooed by their visitor and fail to notice the caterpillar busily feasting on their eggs and larvae.

Ulterior motive The butterfly larva has succeeded in enticing an ant to carry it back to its nest; once in the nest it will consume ant larvae.

Parent bug
Maternal care

SPECIES *Elasmucha grisea* **SIZE** 7 mm (¼ in) **DISTRIBUTION** Birch woodland throughout Europe

Insects that lay a single clutch are more likely to defend their eggs than those that have several clutches. Female parent bugs live up to their name by standing guard over their single clutch of offspring, fiercely defending them from parasites and predators. Some females may even work together – a simple form of social behaviour. Females that work together tend to have better reproductive success than those that work alone.

On guard A female parent bug defends her brood from predators with body jerks, wing fanning, and releasing defensive odours.

RAISING YOUNG 367

Jawfishes
Mouth brooding

FAMILY Opistognathidae **SIZE** Up to 51 cm (20 in)
DISTRIBUTION Shallow reef areas of the Atlantic, Indian, and Pacific oceans

Jawfishes are a common family of marine fishes containing four genera, all of which share certain behavioural as well as physical traits. The most obvious physical characteristics are large, forward-facing eyes and a gaping mouth. Jawfishes use their mouths to dig their homes, to catch prey, and to threaten predators that venture too close to their territories. They also use them in an unusual way during the breeding season. Males hover above females, flashing their body coloration as a signal that they are ready to spawn. Receptive females enter the male's burrow and deposit their eggs; they then leave, taking no other role in the care of their offspring. The male fertilizes the eggs, then scoops them into his mouth where he broods them until they hatch. He aerates the eggs by moving them around in his mouth. As they mature, the eggs become less sticky and start to break apart. He increases the amount he aerates them until, after 7–10 days, they are ready to hatch and disperse. From this point, the young jawfishes are fully independent.

Jawfishes live in burrows, which they excavate by filling their large mouths with sand.

Oral incubation Jawfishes are aptly named for the method they use to brood and protect their offspring. This male from an *Opistognathus* species is keeping watch from his burrow with a mouthful of developing eggs.

African bullfrog
Water retention

SPECIES *Pyxicephalus adspersus* **SIZE** 25 cm (10 in)
DISTRIBUTION Near waterways, rivers, and streams of Central, eastern, and southern Africa

For much of the year, the African bullfrog lives in desert, which is dry for almost 10 months. To protect its moist skin from the harsh conditions, it hides in an underground burrow. In December or January, the rains finally arrive, forming puddles on the arid earth. The frogs soon emerge to spawn in these oases: females deposit their eggs, then leave the male to fend for the brood. With such a short-lived rainy season, the life cycle of the bullfrog must be rapid. The eggs hatch into tadpoles after just two days. But summer storms are sporadic, and the tadpoles' watery world soon dries out. The father, in addition to guarding his brood, must make sure the young stay moist. As one puddle dries, he searches out alternative areas, digging channels between the puddles and herding his young to safer ground. He watches over his offspring for around three weeks, until they metamorphose.

Sergeant major damselfish
On duty

SPECIES *Abudefduf saxatilis* **SIZE** 23 cm (9 in)
DISTRIBUTION Tropical and subtropical reefs in Atlantic Ocean

Damselfishes may be small, but they are among the boldest characters on coral reefs. Males defend nest sites (usually a rock or coral head), illustrating their dominance by turning near black in colour and displaying aggressively to potential challengers. After a brief courtship, during which males and females chase each other, the female deposits up to 200,000 salmon-red eggs. The male releases sperm to fertilize them, then defends and aerates the brood until the eggs hatch into tiny larvae and disperse.

Defending the brood The scientific name of this fish loosely translates as "father living among the rocks". The eggs are laid upon rocky nest sites guarded by the males.

Rescue mission As the sun beats down on their nursery pool, shrinking it by the second, an African bullfrog male hurriedly bulldozes an escape channel through the claylike ground for his tadpoles. The new pool will provide temporary safety.

4,000 The number of tadpoles in an African bullfrog brood. Males sometimes cannibalize their own young.

strong limbs for digging · *moist skin*

Sharp senses The African bullfrog has a good sense of smell, sight, and hearing, which is useful in the breeding season when communicating with loud, roarlike calls.

Alpine newt
Individual wrapping

SPECIES *Triturus alpestris* **SIZE** Up to 12 cm (4½ in) **DISTRIBUTION** Forested, mountainous regions of central Europe

Alpine newts live at high altitudes, where the atmosphere is thin and solar radiation levels are high. To protect their offspring from damaging ultraviolet light, female newts carefully wrap their larvae in leaves, forming tiny sunshades to shield them from harm. Many amphibians are sensitive to ultraviolet radiation. They can quickly suffer damage to their delicate skin, and exposure to the rays may cause death. This is particularly so during the egg and larval stages, before pigmentation has developed and when mobility is restricted.

Sunshade Tiny leaves shield Alpine newt larvae from the damaging effects of the sun's ultraviolet rays.

Risky ride Although crocodiles have large teeth and extremely strong jaws, they lift their young offspring with remarkable care. The journey from their nest to the water's edge is one of the most perilous the youngsters have to make.

>>01

>>02

>>03

Parental care >>01 The female Nile crocodile watches and stands guard as her offspring hatch out of their eggs and scramble up the bank towards her.
>>02 This young crocodile is struggling to break through the tough outer shell of its egg, so its mother assists, using her sharp teeth with amazing gentleness.
>>03 The female carries the hatchlings in her jaws as she swims, keeping them safe from predators. The head of a baby crocodile can be seen peering out from between its mother's teeth.

Gular pouch A crocodile has an elastic throat pouch that it uses to carry its young and hold prey. A flap of skin at the back prevents water from entering the lungs when feeding underwater.

Nile crocodile
Gentle touch

SPECIES *Crocodylus niloticus* **SIZE** 3.5–6 m (11½–20 ft) **DISTRIBUTION** Waterways throughout tropical and southern Africa and Madagascar

Although the Nile crocodile has a fierce reputation, it shows very gentle qualities when it comes to rearing its young. The female crocodile lays a clutch of about 50 eggs near water, in a nesting chamber approximately 50 cm (19½ in) deep in a sandy river bank. Once a female has found a suitable nesting site, she will revisit the same site every time she breeds. For the next three months, she guards the nest, defending it from flooding and scavengers, such as the Nile monitor. Crocodile eggs have a tough shell, which makes hatching difficult. If a juvenile gets trapped, the mother lifts the egg into her mouth, softly rolling it in her teeth in order to crack the shell and release the offspring. Once the young crocodiles hatch, they call to their mother using tiny chirps. She carefully digs into the hole, lifts them out, and carries them to the water in her jaws. If threatened, the female lowers one or more young into her gular, or throat pouch, for protection. Hatchlings are about 30 cm (12 in) long at birth, and they stay with their mother for the first two years. Nile crocodiles tend to be solitary, and the young live in burrows to avoid suffering the extreme heat of their natural habitat.

Monitor lizards
Air-conditioned nursery

GENUS *Varanus* spp. **SIZE** Up to 75 cm (30 in)
DISTRIBUTION Africa, India, China, and throughout Southeast Asia to Australia

Some monitor lizards inhabit savanna and other arid areas where temperatures can soar and the heat of the sun sucks moisture from any living thing. Breeding in these habitats usually happens during the rainy season. Female monitor lizards often lay their eggs in old or active termite mounds. The benefit of this is that, within the mound, environmental conditions are fairly constant. In addition, the termite inhabitants will actually repair and protect the mound (and the eggs within it) from marauding ants or predators. When monitor hatchlings emerge, they dig themselves out of the mound and disperse into the bush. From this point, the young lizards are fully independent.

Desert home Hatchling savanna monitor lizards cling to the outside of the termite mound from which they have emerged. In desert conditions, these mounds provide a safe haven for eggs, with constant levels of temperature and humidity.

Timber rattlesnake
Maternity ward

SPECIES *Crotalus horridus* **SIZE** 1.5 m (5 ft)
DISTRIBUTION Deciduous forest of eastern USA

Female timber rattlesnakes show maternal care of their young, and may even show kin cooperation, preferring to cooperate with their sisters while caring for their young. The rattlesnakes mate in summer and autumn, but the sperm is stored until the following spring. The live young are born the following August. Newborns have been observed climbing onto their mother to rest in her coils, which may assist with thermoregulation and offer protection against predators. They remain with their mother for around seven to ten days after birth and may even follow her scent trail to find suitable dens in which to hibernate.

Intensive care Female timber rattlesnakes do not feed during pregnancy or while caring for their offspring. They breed, on average, every three to four years, and each litter usually contains six to ten young.

Crash diet Male emus are such dedicated parents that they may lose one-third of their body weight by not feeding while brooding their clutch of eggs.

Emu
Male incubation

SPECIES *Dromaius novaehollandiae* **SIZE** 2 m (6½ ft) high
DISTRIBUTION Common across mainland Australia

In may, the male emu begins to construct a nest using sticks and bark. The female lays the eggs and leaves, often in search of another male. For the next eight weeks the male incubates the eggs without eating or even drinking, carefully turning them around ten times per day. Once they hatch, the chicks stay with their father even after they are fully grown at six months old.

Southern rockhopper penguin
Penguin crèche

SPECIES *Eudyptes chrysocome* **SIZE** 52 cm (20½ in) high **DISTRIBUTION** Rocky shorelines of the Southern Ocean islands

When it comes to breeding, rockhopper penguins like to do it en masse. Hundreds of thousands of pairs nest together on rocky slopes, with each pair returning to the same nesting area every year. Large numbers make it possible to always have someone on guard, watching for predators. Rockhoppers lay two eggs, the first much smaller than the second. In most cases, only this second egg is incubated, and this may mean the species is evolving towards only producing one egg per brood, as some other larger penguin species do. Incubation takes around 33 days, worked as shared shifts between the male and female. Once the egg hatches, the male cares for the hatchling while the female provides food. After 25 days, both parents join in the feeding runs, leaving their offspring in crèches, under the vigilant gaze of the other adults present.

Black-necked grebe
Back brooding

SPECIES *Podiceps nigricollis* **SIZE** 34 cm (13½ in)
DISTRIBUTION Widespread water bird found in every continent except Australia and Antarctica

Even before hatching, young black-necked grebes call to solicit care from their parents. Adult pairs build nests using mounds of leaves and aquatic plants. Into this, the female lays three to four creamy white eggs, which both parents take turns to incubate for around 22 days. One or two days before hatching, the embryo grebes begin to call to their parents, indicating when the egg needs to be turned or cooled. Once they emerge, the chicks stay in the nest for two days before transferring to the back of one of the parent birds, where they are back-brooded. They stay in this floating nest for around ten days. During this time, the parents protect the chicks by shielding them with their wings.

Under the wings The small head of a chick is just visible poking out from under one of its parent's wings. Each parent can comfortably accommodate two chicks at a time.

Clinging tight Orangutans are the largest tree-dwelling mammals, yet at birth they weigh just 1.5 kg (3¼ lb). Females carry their young continually for the first year, and even juveniles aged two years will ride on their mother's back. They suckle from their mother for around four years, and remain with her until they are seven or eight years old, sleeping in her nest.

Group care Babysitters tend to associate with one particular pup, feeding and grooming it regularly.

Banded mongoose
Babysitting
SPECIES *Mungos mungo* **SIZE** 55–60 cm (21½–23½ in)
DISTRIBUTION Grassland and woodland throughout central and eastern Africa

Banded mongoose females form strong bonds with other closely related females and work as a group to raise their young. They reach sexual maturity at around nine months of age and usually produce litters of two to six offspring. Breeding females are assisted by helpers of both sexes, although this is costly to the helper and maintained by the pups, who aggressively monopolize their chosen helper.

Tree pangolin
Tail riding
SPECIES *Manis tricuspis* **SIZE** 35–60 cm (14–23½ in)
DISTRIBUTION Forests of western and central Africa

Pangolins are solitary animals, coming together only when both sexes are in breeding condition. Females give birth to a single young after a gestation period of 150 days. The newborn's scales are initially very soft, but harden after a few days. Pangolins have an unusual parental behaviour: the juvenile is carried on the female's tail, piggyback style, until it is ready to wean at about three months old. It remains with the mother for a further two months, until it is prepared for full independence. If the baby is threatened, mother pangolins roll up around their young, forming a tight, protective ball with the offspring in the middle.

Grappling hooks Tree pangolins have strong claws to aid with climbing and to attack ants' nests. Babies also use them to hold tight to their mothers' tails.

Tightly packed colony Female bats leave their young behind when they go out to forage. The close packing of baby bats helps them to stay warm while the female is away.

Mexican free-tailed bat
Warm nursery
SPECIES *Tadarida brasiliensis* **SIZE** 9 cm (3½ in)
DISTRIBUTION Caves of western and southern USA, Mexico, Central America, Chile, and Argentina

Mexican free-tailed bats form the largest colonies of any mammal in the world. Different roosts are occupied at different times by the two sexes, depending on the breeding cycle and time of year. Maternity roosts can number many millions. In this dense mass of bats, the mother recognizes her offspring by its unique smell and pip-like call. The young bats are weaned after five or six weeks. They join the adults in migrating from the summer roosts in Texas, USA, to the winter roosts in Mexico.

Lesser white-toothed shrew
Caravanning
SPECIES *Crocidura suaveolens* **SIZE** 5–7 cm (2–2¾ in)
DISTRIBUTION Europe, Japan, and North Africa; absent in Britain except the Channel Islands and the Isles of Scilly

The lesser white-toothed shrew is a prolific breeder, producing four or five litters per year of one to six young each time. Babies wean at around 22 days. The female nests under logs or stones; if the nest is disturbed, she will move her young to safer ground. When forced to move locations, the young display "caravanning" behaviour, forming a chain by grasping the tail of the animal in front.

In convoy Young shrews follow their mother to safety by forming a line, holding onto the tail of the animal in front with their teeth.

Beluga whale
Keeping warm
SPECIES *Delphinapterus leucas* **SIZE** 3–5 m (9¾–16½ ft)
DISTRIBUTION Arctic and sub-Arctic marine areas

Beluga whales are an Arctic species, typically living in freezing waters along ice floes. In summer, females migrate to shallow bays and estuaries to deliver their single calf. The water in such areas is usually much warmer than the open sea. This means the young do not waste energy on simply keeping warm, and can instead use it to grow and build up fat reserves. Beluga milk contains as much as 30 per cent fat. Mothers suckle the young for up to 24 months, from nipples that are hidden in skin folds on the abdomen. The calf can swim independently from birth, but will often ride on its mother's back, or follow her slipstream, until it gains strength.

Immature coloration Belugas are social animals and usually travel in groups. The calves stand out with their grey skin, which changes to white as they mature.

Polar bear
Protective mother
SPECIES *Ursus maritimus* **SIZE** 2.5 m (8¼ ft) **DISTRIBUTION** Sea ice and coastal areas throughout Arctic regions (circumpolar)

Polar bears are typically solitary, males and females coming together to mate for just a few days in late winter or early spring. Pregnant females overwinter in dens dug into the snow, within a few kilometres of the coastline where, after just two months of pregnancy, they produce two (occasionally three) tiny cubs. The cubs are born covered in fur, but with their eyes closed, and may weigh only 600 g (1¼ lb). The female remains in the den, nursing her cubs until April. By the time the young family emerges, the cubs may be 10–15 kg (22–33 lb) in weight. They stay with their mother for the next two or three years, during which time she provides for them, teaching them to hunt, and protecting them from harm.

Cold comfort Polar bears spend much of their time sleeping or roaming the ice in search of seals. Adults are good swimmers, but small cubs drown easily. For this reason, young families stay on solid ice.

Family affair All members of the group, most of which are older offspring of the dominant pair, work to ensure that young pups are given enough food.

Giant river otter
Fishing lesson
SPECIES *Pteronura brasiliensis* **SIZE** 1.5–1.8 m (5–6 ft)
DISTRIBUTION Rivers, lakes, and creeks of South America

Giant river otters live in communal dens in the river bank, centred around a dominant breeding pair. Females usually give birth in the dry season, bearing between one and five pups. All members of the family play a role in raising the young, teaching them to hunt by bringing them injured fishes. This training begins at around three months and can be carried out by any adult. The young are weaned at nine months and may remain with the group for a further two years, before leaving to set up a group of their own.

Moose
Fiercely protective
SPECIES *Alces alces* **SIZE** 2.5–3.2 m (8¼–10½ ft)
DISTRIBUTION Deciduous forest of North America, northern Europe, and Russia

Moose are typically solitary animals, the only bonds being between a mother and her young. Mating occurs in September and October, with males fighting for access to mates. Females carry the young for around eight months before finding a quiet, secluded spot to give birth. They usually deliver one calf (rarely, twins). Young moose are gangly and weak and make easy targets for bears or wolves. However, females aggressively defend their young, rearing up on their hind legs or pounding potential predators with their hooves. Many choose to live near human civilization, where there are fewer wolves. Moose calf survival rates are poor – in some areas, only 20 per cent make it through the first year, although those that do reach adulthood may live as long as 25 years. Calves stay with the mother for a whole year, until she calves again the following breeding season.

Facing attack Bears and wolves are the biggest predators of young moose. The young quickly gain weight, and can swim and run within a few days of birth, but their chances of survival remain low.

Play and learning

Learning is the way in which animals develop the knowledge and skills they need for survival. Young animals have much to learn about their environment – how to find food, avoid predators, and interact with others. It is a lifelong process and every animal must adapt its behaviour as a result of individual experience.

Monkeying around Young olive baboons play together on a branch. Social primates are some of the most playful animals. They have an extended juvenile phase, when they must learn about the environment and the social conventions of their group.

SIMPLE LEARNING

Simple learning occurs when an animal's response to a repeated stimulus changes in the absence of any consequence. The major form of this is habituation, when an animal begins to ignore a stimulus following repeated exposure to it. For example, birds will initially take fright at a scarecrow but, over time, learn that it is harmless and stop responding to it. Habituation helps animals to filter out unimportant information from their environment.

CASE STUDY IMPRINTING

Chicks of some species instinctively follow the first large moving object they see after hatching and "imprint" on this object. In hand-rearing situations, such as with this common crane chick, a puppet may be used to help the chick imprint on the correct species.

ASSOCIATIVE AND OBSERVATIONAL LEARNING

Associative learning is when an animal's behavioural response becomes associated with a particular stimulus, by means of operant or classical conditioning. In operant conditioning, an animal learns the consequences (whether positive or negative) that result from an action, and therefore modifies its behaviour to account for these. In cases of classical conditioning, a behavioural response is taught to be associated with a neutral stimulus – a process that is usually reinforced with a reward. In the wild, many animals also learn by observation, watching the way in which others behave and using that knowledge to adapt their own behaviour.

Voice recognition Rockhopper penguin chicks and parents learn each other's calls so that they can find one another within their huge, riotous crèches when the parent comes back with food for the chicks.

Copycat Oystercatcher chicks watch their mother feeding. By copying her behaviour, they learn to find food themselves.

PLAY

Play is the name given to activities that have no obvious purpose, but may help to improve an animal's physical fitness, or help it to practise skills such as hunting. It is most often seen in mammals and some birds, and is especially common in the young, which suggests a link with learning. Some animals play with inanimate objects, carrying them around or pouncing on them like prey. Others play with members of their family, engaging in play fighting or wrestling. Predators may also play with their prey. Play can be risky, exposing the animal to predation; it also consumes energy, so must somehow benefit an animal in terms of its future behaviour.

Dolphins are extremely playful animals, often performing in spectacular group acrobatics.

Tiger cubs engage in play fights, gaining the speed and agility they will need as territorial animals.

Panda cub play has no clear purpose, but seems to provide huge enjoyment.

PLAY AND LEARNING 377

International student A marsh warbler embellishes its song by mimicking calls of other birds (up to 84 different species), many of which are learned in its African wintering grounds.

Marsh warbler
Learning the tune
SPECIES *Acrocephalus palustris* **SIZE** 13 cm (5 in)
DISTRIBUTION Low vegetation and thickets, usually near water; breeds in temperate Europe and western Asia, winters in southeast Africa

Marsh warblers learn their own songs as well as mimicking the calls of other birds. They develop almost their full repertoire in the first year of life. Many young songbirds have to learn their songs. There is great variation, but the general form involves a sensitive phase, during which the birds memorize songs they hear, refining an in-built "auditory template", against which they try to match their songs. This practice period, or "subsong", is very variable and quiet. Next comes "plastic song", which is flexible, but louder and more normal, until finally it crystallizes into "full song".

Masked booby
No fear
SPECIES *Sula dactylatra* **SIZE** 80–90 cm (31–35 in)
DISTRIBUTION Tropical and subtropical islands in Pacific and Caribbean

Young animals learn through experience – in adventures inspired by curiosity and by testing their luck. Boobies get their name from the Spanish word "bobo" meaning "stupid fellow", which is a reference to the comical expressions and gullible behaviour that made them easy hunting targets for sailors in the past. They inhabit isolated islands with few predators, and so have not learned fearfulness. Their young retain an inherent sense of curiosity for their surroundings, which makes them entertaining and endearing to observe.

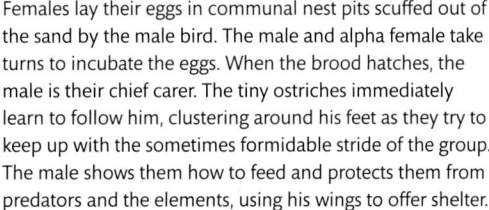

Learning from experience A young masked booby chick displays its fascination with a scarlet land crab that it has found lurking near its nest. This sense of natural curiosity will soon teach the young bird that crabs can deliver quite a pinch.

Common ostrich
Following footsteps
SPECIES *Struthio camelus* **SIZE** 1.7–2.8 m (5½–9¼ ft)
DISTRIBUTION African savanna

Ostriches live a nomadic life, roaming in groups of up to 50 birds. During the breeding season, males fight for a harem of two to seven females with which they mate. Females lay their eggs in communal nest pits scuffed out of the sand by the male bird. The male and alpha female take turns to incubate the eggs. When the brood hatches, the male is their chief carer. The tiny ostriches immediately learn to follow him, clustering around his feet as they try to keep up with the sometimes formidable stride of the group. The male shows them how to feed and protects them from predators and the elements, using his wings to offer shelter.

CASE STUDY CRECHES

Ostrich crèches are made up of the chicks of many females and are cared for by one or more male birds. Several females will deposit their large, white eggs in a communal nest, but only the alpha (first-paired) female will work with the male to incubate them, and she will often place her own eggs in optimum positions in the centre of the nest. Once hatched, the brood of up to 40 young form crèches. Having fought fiercely over mating, the male ostriches must cooperate to raise their young and teach them how to feed. When two males meet, their chicks instinctively group together to form a larger crèche.

Feeling broody The male and alpha female of an ostrich group take responsibility for raising chicks, and are often seen surrounded by young birds. Sometimes they steal chicks from other birds to add to their own brood, invariably targeting younger chicks. These are more likely to be taken by predators if the family is attacked, thus sparing the pair's own genetic offspring.

Surf's up A gentoo penguin surfs a wave as it returns to a beach in the Falkland Islands. Such frolics look like tremendous fun, but this behaviour also serves a more serious purpose. By launching themselves from the water and landing far up the beach, penguins avoid being battered by waves or falling prey to predators that can lurk in the water beneath them.

Red-necked wallaby
Combat skills

SPECIES *Macropus rufogriseus* **SIZE** 70–105 cm (28–41 in)
DISTRIBUTION Coastal scrub, bush, and eucalyptus forest in eastern and southeastern Australia

Juvenile wallabies learn to fight from an early age. Fights between adults can be brutal, involving sparring with their long, clawed forepaws, or sitting back on their tail to kick the opponent with their hind legs. For juveniles, fighting is all about play and learning, and they are prepared to adjust their fighting skills in order to allow the play to continue for as long as possible. Evidence suggests that young males vary the strength of their play fights depending on the relative age of their opposition. When encounters involve a younger male, the older wallaby will self-handicap itself, by standing in a flat-footed way and pawing with less aggression than it would with a tougher rival. This aim of this is to prolong the encounter, providing more fun for all concerned.

Play fights Through play, male wallabies develop fighting skills that allow them to challenge or maintain dominance within the group.

Bornean orangutan
Fun lovers

SPECIES *Pongo pygmaeus* **SIZE** 90–100 cm (35 in–3¼ ft)
DISTRIBUTION Forest canopy in Borneo

The name orangutan is Malay for "person of the woods" and is appropriate to this creature's love of swinging around in the treetops. Agile climbers, Bornean orangutans use their long arms to carry them from branch to branch in search of fruit, nuts, and bark. In the wild, they are largely solitary animals. The main social contact occurs between a mother and her young. Newborns cling tightly to their mother's abdomen for the first year; they depend on and are fed by their mothers for the five years of life, and take another couple of years to become fully independent. When artificially forced into groups (for rehabilitation purposes, for example), young orangutans are some of the most gregarious, fun-loving primates of all. Juvenile males and females engage in hours of playful social activity, such as wrestling, tickling, chasing, rolling, and swinging. Wrestling tends to occur more often between males, where the two competitors push each other to the ground and tumble over each other. Chases are enjoyed by both males and females. As the young orangutans age, the time they spend in such activities declines and they have less and less interest in social activities.

Juvenile frolics Wrestling may serve as practice for the time when males have to defend territories and fight for access to females.

Japanese macaque
Snowball fight

SPECIES *Macaca fuscata* **SIZE** 50–65 cm (19½–26 in)
DISTRIBUTION Subtropical to subarctic forest in Japan (excluding Hokkaido)

Snow monkeys, or Japanese macaques, are the most northerly-living primates, except for humans, and many live in areas that are snow-covered for at least one-third the year. They are famous for their bathing habits – many of them use hot thermal springs to keep warm. Others have learnt to wash the grain fed to them by humans to wash away sand particles, which is a skill that was developed by one bright female and has been passed on from generation to generation. But perhaps the most endearing learned behaviour is making snowballs. Young macaques carefully form clumps of snow using their hands and opposable thumbs before rolling them along the floor in play.

Snow man Just like human children, Japanese macaque babies make and throw snowballs. It is not clear how they learned this behaviour, yet whole groups of macaques engage in it as a social activity, seemingly just for fun.

Coyote
Rough and tumble

SPECIES *Canis latrans* **SIZE** 1–1.6 m (3 ft 3 in–5¼ ft)
DISTRIBUTION Throughout much of North America

Like all dogs, coyotes are territorial animals that maintain strict dominance rankings within their packs, but they do take part in bouts of harmless social play throughout their lives, starting from just a few days after birth. When trying to engage one another in play, coyotes use subtle signals to show that their intentions are not aggressive. Play behaviour in canids can appear very much like aggressive behaviour, involving biting and shaking the head rapidly from side to side. When such behaviour is punctuated by regular signals such as "bows" (dropping the forequarters to the ground while the hind legs stand tall), the coyote shows that it is only looking for some rough and tumble. The "bow" signal states "I want to play – the actions I have made, and am about to make, are for fun". This same bowing behaviour is seen in dogs and wolves, though their play fights are generally less aggressive than those of young coyotes. To prolong social play with a weaker or younger individual, a strong coyote will refrain from biting as hard as it is able to, and will play less vigorously than its strength allows for.

Early learning Pups live in their dens until 6–10 weeks old. By the time they emerge, they have already learned many of the social signals used to communicate with the group.

Playing hunter Young lion cubs stalk their mothers' black-tassled tails before pouncing on them, practising the skills they need to become successful hunters.

Lion
Pouncing practice

SPECIES *Panthera leo* **SIZE** 1.6–2.5 m (5¼–8¼ ft)
DISTRIBUTION Grassy plains and savanna in sub-Saharan Africa

For a young lion, learning to hunt is a basic requirement for survival, and begins early on in life. The cub has a lot to learn. Adult lions typically hunt in groups, stalking and tracking their chosen prey. Because they hunt in exposed spaces, lions must be able to coordinate their actions precisely and work well as a team. Lion cubs begin their training at around three months of age, chasing and stalking anything around them that moves. They are soon practising "the kill" on half-dead or young small prey, which the mother brings back to them. By the end of their first year, most cubs are able to join the pride in stalking and chasing prey and, after two years, they are proficient hunters in their own right.

Brown bear
Play fighting

SPECIES *Ursus arctos* **SIZE** 1.7–2.8 m (5½–9¼ ft)
DISTRIBUTION Forest and open landscapes in North America and Eurasia

Bear cubs spend much time play fighting and scrambling around with their siblings. Through such harmless fun, cubs practise fighting skills essential for survival in later life. In the wild, the biggest danger to cubs comes from other bears. If another bear threatens her young, a female bear quickly shoos her cubs up a nearby tree to escape attack, drawing on their climbing skills. Older bears can no longer climb, so must be able to fight to defend themselves and their territories. Social play fighting sometimes continues into adulthood.

Playmates and toys Bear cubs will play with siblings, or even with animals of another species, and will also use inanimate objects in their play.

Killing practice The young Thomson's gazelle may be the same size as these cheetah cubs, but the cubs must learn how to handle large prey if they are to survive. Female cheetahs help their young to learn by bringing back small or injured prey. The cubs can practise chasing and killing – developing the skills they will need to perfect for independent life.

Group bonding This group of otters is playing in the melting snow next to a stream. North American river otters live in family-based groups of a mother and her offspring. Male otters tend to be solitary.

CASE STUDY **TOBOGGANING**

Observing river otters in the wild is fascinating. One of their most comical behaviours is "tobogganing". Otters of all ages will frequently slide down muddy banks or snow-caked slopes, sometimes finishing in the river below. They slide on their bellies, tucking their feet up to create a streamlined shape. The function of this particular behaviour is not known – some researchers believe it is a form of locomotion, associated with travel but nothing more. Others see tobogganing as play behaviour, undertaken for no reason other than the pure pleasure of the slide.

North American river otter
Forever young

SPECIES *Lontra canadensis* **SIZE** 0.9–1.3 m (3–4¼ ft)
DISTRIBUTION Waterways and coastal areas in North America

Many animals play during their early years but abandon play behaviours in later life. North American river otters, like other otters, are unusual because their games continue beyond adolescence and throughout their adult lives. These playful creatures tumble and wrestle with one another and enjoy playing with inanimate objects. They like diving for rocks, rolling around, and playing "tag" or "follow the leader". Otters repeatedly "toboggan" down slopes, creating slides by following the same tracks each time (see panel, right). They seem to take enormous enjoyment in these capers and spend much time in play. The role of play in otter life and society is unclear. It may be a way of reinforcing social bonds within a group, practising certain skills, such as hunting, or it could be a form of exercise. Otters are highly active and intelligent animals, so perhaps for them, play is simply a way of killing time in an engaging and entertaining manner.

Dusky dolphin
Group gymnastics

SPECIES *Lagenorhynchus obscurus* **SIZE** 2–2.1 m (6½–7 ft)
DISTRIBUTION Coastal areas in southern hemisphere: New Zealand, South Africa, South America

Dusky dolphins are gregarious animals and regularly form large pods of up to 1,000 individuals. They are famous for their spectacular acrobatics. These agile swimmers are frequently observed leaping clear out of the water, twisting, turning, side-slapping, back-flipping, and creating a noisy, splashing display. The precise function of these behaviours within dolphin society is unclear. Some scientists believe they play a role in communication within the group (see p.429), signalling the presence of shoals of fish to feed on, and indicating the group should split up or come together. Others think they are associated with herding prey, an activity that dolphins perform as a coordinated group. Leaping out of the water to dive back in may be a way of dislodging parasites, or it could be nothing more than a form of play, or it may help deprive the fish they are hunting of oxygen.

Leaping for joy The dusky dolphin performs its acrobatics with unbounded enthusiasm throughout its 25-year lifespan.

Orca
Surfing for seals

SPECIES *Orcinus orca* **SIZE** 5–8 m (16½–26 ft)
DISTRIBUTION Common in all oceans and seas

For a whale, getting stranded on the shore can be fatal. Yet some orcas, or killer whales, intentionally beach themselves in the pursuit of land-living prey. In Patagonia, several orca pods have learned to surf waves onto beaches to grab unsuspecting seals from along the shoreline. Female orcas coax their young to follow in this dangerous game. To start with, the reluctant calves shadow their mothers, watching from the safety of the water. The females then push their offspring onto the beaches as a form of training.

African bush elephant
Trunk training

SPECIES *Loxodonta africana* **SIZE** 5.5–7.5 m (18–24½ ft)
DISTRIBUTION Open grassland, scrub, woodland, and occasionally desert in Africa south of the Sahara

Knowledge is passed down through the generations in elephant families. Calves often play with adults, who teach them vital skills to equip them for life, such as how to make good use of one of their most important assets – the trunk. To a baby elephant, a trunk must be both a confusion and a delight. Until around five months, it often falls over its trunk and has little idea of its use or function. An elephant's trunk contains up to 40,000 muscles, and it takes observation of others and practice to learn how to control this versatile appendage.

Splashing around Young elephants particularly enjoy playing in water. This has the added benefit of helping to keep them cool.

Drinking practice Because it uses its mouth to drink its mother's milk, a young calf doesn't know how to use its trunk for drinking. Adults use the trunk to squirt water into their mouths, but babies lie down to drink through their lips. It is only by watching others in the herd that they learn what a trunk can do.

American bison
Head butting

SPECIES *Bison bison* **SIZE** 3 m (9¾ ft)
DISTRIBUTION National parks, some prairies, and woodland in North America

The bison's solid, muscular head and neck are used to shove or head butt opponents and win the favour of females. A bull with its head lowered is a menacing spectacle. Female bison and their young herd together, forming "playgroups" that allow calves to socialize with each other. After around two months, the calves start to develop their distinctive shoulder humps and horns, which they use in play fights, honing the skills that ultimately serve in the ruts adult males undertake during the breeding season.

Play fighting Through play fights and learning to head butt opponents and solid objects, calves build strength in their muscles and develop their fighting skills.

Society

Island life These Cape gannets (*Morus capensis*) have gathered in a guano-encrusted colony to breed. Both parents incubate their egg by wrapping their feet around it. The fluffy off-white chick stays in the colony until it fledges at about three months of age.

SOCIETY

Very few animals spend their entire lives in isolation from others, and some of the most spectacular displays of behaviour occur when animals come together. Group living provides a host of advantages to an animal, but these benefits often come with challenges such as sharing resources and fitting in with social structures.

SOLITARY AND GROUP LIVING

Some animals remain alone for most of their lives, apart from during brief periods to mate or rear offspring. When food, water, or other environmental resources necessary for survival are scarce, or if an animal's predators and natural enemies are particularly good at finding grouped animals, it can pay to live alone. However, individual animals across many species form attachments with others (either within their own or with different species). The size of these groups can range immensely, from single pairs of long-term mating partners (in which the partnership is sustained long after the breeding season has finished) to vast colonies of thousands or even millions of individuals, within which each individual animal can face intense competition with its neighbours for space and resources.

WHY ANIMALS ARE SOCIAL

Because so many animals spend at least some of their life in social groups, social behaviour must provide considerable advantages to group members. If there are greater benefits to be had than if an animal lived alone, social behaviour will be favoured by natural selection. Many studies have examined the advantages of living in groups, which differ from species to species, according to the animals' life histories. Most of these reasons focus around group membership enhancing an individual animal's survival, either by reducing its risk of being preyed upon, or increasing its chances of successfully finding food. At the same time, group living confers reproductive advantages, both as a source of potential mates (and information about rivals) and as an extended childcare system.

GROUP COMPOSITION

The structure of groups differs vastly between species. In some, a group consists of a large mix of males and females of many different ages and ranks, while in others, all the members of a group will be of the same sex, age, or size. Exactly which individuals are found in a particular group changes over time. In some species, group membership is ephemeral, changing over the course of hours or days. Other species form groups that may be maintained for weeks or years, leading to intense prolonged relationships between the group members.

Constant companions Social insects such as hornets divide up their breeding and colony duties to such an extent that it would be impossible for them to live in isolation from their nest mates.

REASONS TO BE SOCIAL

Movement Travelling long distances uses lots of energy. Some birds and fish can take advantage of their travelling companions, riding their neighbour's slipstream to reduce their energy needs.

Hunting and feeding Coordinated social hunting means that groups can capture prey that is difficult to catch alone. Having many pairs of eyes also means that poorly distributed food is more likely to be found.

Defence Social animals reduce the time they spend scanning for predators, as vigilance is shared among the group. The individual risk of predation is reduced as the group grows.

Health benefits Although diseases can be caught from contact with others, forming groups also reduces health problems, for example it minimizes the attacks each group member receives from biting flies.

Breeding Many species collect together in groups for mating, where animals can both see and be seen by potential partners. Raising offspring is easier if others help with defence and food provision.

Saving energy In cold environments, hard-won energy is constantly lost as heat. Many social animals huddle together at low temperatures, in order to insulate and share each other's body heat.

Pecking order If raised intensively, chickens will aggressively maintain hierarchies, whereas their jungle-fowl ancestors (above) live in peaceful groups, as birds quickly learn who is dominant.

SOCIAL STATUS

The members of most social groups are not equal to each other. Instead, they operate systems in which high-ranking, dominant individuals have priority access to resources such as food, shelter, and mates, whereas low-ranking, subordinate individuals have fewer benefits. Possibly the best-known form of hierarchy is the "pecking order" seen in chickens. This involves unfamiliar birds fighting to assess which individual is dominant. The fights quickly lead to an established hierarchy, with each bird knowing its place. Once determined, there is little need for further aggression.

COALITIONS

Working alone means that none of the benefits gained have to be shared with others, but often single individuals don't have the power or stamina to gain or defend resources. In numerous socially living mammals, males can breed only if they control the access to harems of females, and the only way to gain this control is to fight incumbent males for it. This is difficult if there is a large imbalance of strength between the males, and one way around this is for males to form coalitions, in which several individuals gang up to attack the harem owner together. Other coalitions can form to defend territories and hunt difficult prey.

Backing down This juvenile baboon (centre), is being disciplined by an older member of the troop. It is risky for youngsters to challenge dominant adults and they usually show submissive behaviour to avoid conflict.

COOPERATION

The degree to which animals cooperate varies widely between species. It can be strongly dependent upon kinship, where helping close relations favours the survival of the cooperator's genes. The length of time group members stay together also plays a part, as this affects the likelihood of a favour being repaid by the recipient in the future. In some cooperatively breeding species, where group members are often closely related, division of labour is often seen, with different animals performing distinct roles within the group. This is particularly extreme in social insects and naked mole-rats (right), where only a few individuals breed.

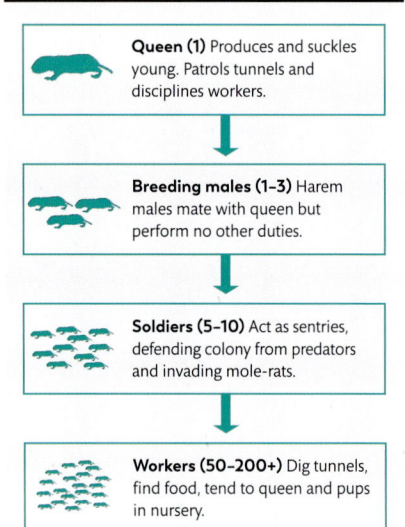

Queen (1) Produces and suckles young. Patrols tunnels and disciplines workers.

Breeding males (1–3) Harem males mate with queen but perform no other duties.

Soldiers (5–10) Act as sentries, defending colony from predators and invading mole-rats.

Workers (50–200+) Dig tunnels, find food, tend to queen and pups in nursery.

WARFARE

The increased strength that results from cooperation and the formation of coalitions means that groups can compete with others for access to resources. Launching attacks on neighbours is a good way to gain additional territory, and both good coordination and large group size confers distinct advantages to attacking groups. The ensuing battles are often short and violent. However, some species of sweat bee engage in extensive colonial wars, in which hundreds or thousands of individuals meet near potential nest sites and grapple with each other in fierce battles lasting for days.

Colonial aggression A few invertebrates, such as some species of sweat bees, will engage in aggression towards other colonies, often resulting a many casualties for both sides.

Group memory Female elephants tend to stay in the same social groups for their entire life. This means that maintained information about migration routes and the location of water and foraging sites can be held by a group over long periods of time.

SOCIETY 391

Reef variants This reef is dominated by soft mushroom and leather corals. A single colony of hardbrain coral is visible tucked between the mushroom corals.

Tentacle numbers The soft coral *Clavularia* has especially large polyps that are only loosely connected and so the characteristic eight tentacles can be seen with the naked eye.

Soft corals (tropical)
Competing corals

ORDER Alcyonacea **SIZE** Polyps mostly tiny but some up to 2 cm (¾ in) tall; colonies up to 1.5 m (5 ft) wide **DISTRIBUTION** Tropics

The hard structure of a coral reef is built up mainly by colonies of stony corals (see p.301), but many other coral types also crowd in to fill the available spaces. Soft corals belong to a different, related group known as octocorals, in which the individual polyps in a colony have eight tentacles. As their name suggests, the majority of soft corals do not secrete a hard skeleton, although they do contain individual slivers of calcium carbonate (sclerites) that provide support. Fast-growing leathery and fleshy species can shade out light-reliant hard corals and release chemicals that stunt or kill their neighbours. Soft corals of many species can quickly overgrow badly damaged hard coral reefs and may completely change the ecology. High-speed photography has revealed that static hard corals fight each other using their stinging tentacles and by spilling out their guts to digest tissue.

Social spider
Close-knit family

SPECIES Agelena consociata **SIZE** 4–9 mm (³⁄₁₆–⅜ in) **DISTRIBUTION** Rainforest in Gabon, Africa

Despite their antisocial reputation, several species of spider display communal living. *Agelena consociata* will share a nest and web. This is often connected to nearby webs and individual spiders move freely throughout the groups of webs. Larger individuals construct the web and the structures necessary for trapping prey. All the spiders cooperate in capturing prey that falls into the sheets of silk, with up to 25 spiders required to subdue some of the larger items. Up to 40 spiders have been observed feeding simultaneously from the same item of prey.

Web community Social spiders weave large sheets of silk for prey to fall into. Within the sheets are many retreats that lead to one or more communal nests, concealing eggs or young spiderlings.

Waiting game An *Agelena consociata* spider stands poised, ready to dart out and pounce on any prey that will fall into the dense silky sheeting of the web.

Drone The stingless male drones are solely involved with mating, which occurs away from the nest. Drones don't perform any useful duties within the nest, and they are vastly outnumbered by the workers.

Worker Most of the bees in a colony are female workers. They typically live for about six weeks, and perform a wide variety of different duties within the nest during that time. They are not able to reproduce.

Queen Usually, a nest contains a single queen. When new queens are needed (if the colony becomes too big or the queen, too old) they are produced by feeding larvae laid in special comb cells exclusively with royal jelly.

SOCIETY 393

Huddled masses Outside their nest, honey bees are only encountered in large numbers when they swarm and hunt for a new place to live. When swarming, the worker bees surround the queen, and are docile and non-aggressive. Gorged on honey, the bees carefully regulate swarm temperature, and those on the outside of the swarm may be much colder than those in the centre.

Honey bee
Workers unite

SPECIES *Apis mellifera* **SIZE** 1 cm (⅜ in) (worker), 2 cm (¾ in) (queen)
DISTRIBUTION Native to Africa, Europe, and Middle East. Domesticated worldwide

A mature honey bee nest is formed of between 20,000 and 100,000 closely related female workers, which all share the nest's single queen as their mother. As a worker ages, she moves through a range of jobs. Her duties start inside the nest, where she cleans, tends to the queen and developing pupae, and builds the hive's waxy comb. She then moves on to riskier jobs outside the nest, such as defending against attack, and foraging.

Worker honey bees are vital pollinators in many environments, and collect sugar-rich nectar and protein-rich pollen from flowers in exchange for their pollination services. On returning to the nest, they are able to describe the location of good foraging sites to other foragers by performing a circular, buzzing "waggle dance" (see p.431) on the surface of the comb. This dance conveys detailed information about the distance to the site and its angle away from the nest.

CASE STUDY DEMOCRATIC DECISION-MAKING

When a colony needs a new nest site, it sends hundreds of scouts out to look for suitable locations. Scouts hunt independently, and initially return with lots of possible options. If a scout finds a good site, it dances on the swarm's surface, pacing out the dimensions of the cavity, to recruit other scouts to visit their find – a stronger dance signals a better site. Over time, through comparison and disagreement, more scouts are recruited into favouring the best site available. When the number of scouts favouring one site reaches a critical threshold, they signal to the swarm and move it to the site that was chosen by a consensus vote.

Swarming When a colony gets too crowded, the queen and half of the workers leave the nest and form a dense mass on a nearby tree. They then sit quietly while scouts search for a new nest site.

In the grip of the enemy The ant in the centre is being attacked by fighters from a rival nest. Despite the prolonged battles, only a tiny fraction of the workers that fight will be killed or seriously injured.

Pavement ant
Turf wars

SPECIES *Tetramorium immigrans* **SIZE** 2–4 mm (1/16–3/16 in)
DISTRIBUTION Native to Europe, introduced throughout North and Central America

"Ant wars" can sometimes be seen in urban areas, where brown masses of fighters form on pavements. Swarms of hundreds or thousands of the small, dark brown workers lock in combat for hours at a time, tumbling, biting, and pulling one another, while new recruits are guided to the mêlée along freshly laid odour trails. These are usually contests between adjacent colonies in the vicinity of their territorial boundaries (see p.107).

6½ The number of weeks the longest recorded battle raged between pavement ant colonies.

Slave-making ant
Slave labour

SPECIES *Formica sanguinea* **SIZE** 7 mm (¼ in)
DISTRIBUTION Europe and temperate forest regions of Asia. Other closely related species are found in the Americas

At first sight, the nests of slave-making ants appear to be a harmonious mixture of different ant species. However, the extra species present are slaves held in thrall by the nest-owning ants. As well as hunting for food, scouts also look for the nests of these other species. When a suitable colony is found, platoons of raiding soldier ants are sent out to attack it. The raiders return home carrying stolen pupae, which are raised as slaves to work in the colony.

Carried away Slave-making ants kidnap ants of other species, in this case the captive is a silky ant (*Formica fusca*).

Whitespotted eagle rays
Eating together

SPECIES *Aetobatus narinari* **SIZE** Wingspan 3 m (9¾ ft)
DISTRIBUTION Atlantic Ocean, in tropical and subtropical waters to depths of about 80 m (260 ft)

Unlike bottom-living rays and skates, eagle rays spend most of their time swimming and may form large shoals in open water during the non-breeding season. Travelling shoals may consist of a hundred or more fishes and are often found swimming close to the surface. Small groups may splash and make agile leaps out of the water, possibly to help remove parasites. When foraging, eagle rays are often encountered swimming gracefully over the surface of reefs, sand, and mud. They may occasionally enter estuaries and tidal rivers when hunting prey. This endangered species is threatened by over-fishing.

Spotted swimmers Whitespotted eagle rays (named for the distinctive spots that adorn their dark dorsal side) are often seen swimming together in groups.

Spiny dogfish
Segregated shoals

SPECIES *Squalus acanthias* **SIZE** 0.8–1.5 m (2½–5 ft)
DISTRIBUTION Cooler to warm temperate coastal shelf waters worldwide

Spiny or piked dogfish is one of only a few species of shark known to regularly form segregated groups depending upon their size, sex, and stage of development. Groups can be found containing only juveniles (of both sexes), immature females, mature males, or mature (and often pregnant) females. Mature females may prefer to be away from males in order to avoid multiple energy-draining copulations. Females are able to store sperm for long periods of time. Sometimes very large shoals can occur, as dogfish form dense aggregations at good feeding grounds.

Easy target While there is usually safety in numbers, aggregating into huge groups makes spiny dogfishes an easy target for fisheries. Numbers are now a fraction of what they once were.

Own protection Barracudas are efficient predators, but juveniles and adults of smaller barracuda species are vulnerable to larger predators. Circling behaviour provides an all-around lookout.

Sawtooth barracuda
In the round

SPECIES *Sphyraena putnamae* **SIZE** 80–90 cm (31–35 in)
DISTRIBUTION Lagoons and reefs in tropical and subtropical regions of Pacific and Indian oceans

Barracudas are often encountered in open water, swimming in large shoals. These shoals may take the shape of balls, spirals, or even doughnuts, where each individual barracuda curves in a large circle as it swims. Complicated group patterns like these are found in many animals that aggregate in large groups; when flocks of birds and shoals of fish contain hundreds or thousands of members, the group appears to move as one, where every individual seems to change to a new agreed direction instantaneously. Rather than being directed by a few leading individuals, these complex patterns can come from each animal paying attention to its immediate neighbours. So, although a doughnut shape looks complicated to form and maintain, no group coordination is needed: all each barracuda needs to do is adjust its own speed and heading in response to the fish next to it.

Synchronized swimming These Indian mackerel are swimming with their mouths wide open to filter feed on plankton in the water. Mackerel swim in huge, closely coordinated shoals, in which each fish positions itself with similarly sized fishes and synchronizes its movement with that of its neighbours. The entire shoal can appear to change direction simultaneously.

Spectacled caiman
Nest protection
SPECIES *Caiman crocodilus* **SIZE** 1.8–2 m (6–6½ ft)
DISTRIBUTION Forests and wetlands from southern Mexico to northern Argentina. Introduced to Florida and Cuba

During the breeding season, spectacled caimans construct large nests on river banks, piling a large mound of soil, wood, and leaf litter in an area cleared of vegetation. Several different females may lay their eggs within this mound, which is then guarded by both males and females while the eggs are developing. Young caimans vocalize both before and after hatching. This could be to alert the attending parents, who provide assistance to the hatchlings in leaving their shells. Juveniles then stay in crèches for over a year before they become independent. While in the crèche, an adult caiman – not necessarily their parent – keeps a defensive eye on them.

Social group The spectacled caiman has the largest range of the South American species and will often occur together in groups of varying ages and sizes.

Green iguana
Leaving together
SPECIES *Iguana iguana* **SIZE** 1.2–1.5 m (4–5 ft)
DISTRIBUTION Tropical rainforest in Central and Southern America and on Caribbean islands. Introduced to Florida

Although they do not show parental care, female green iguanas often nest communally, which means that large numbers of hatchlings emerge together. As well as diluting the predation risk faced by individual hatchlings, emerging at the same time means that a communal effort can be made to dig out of the natal burrow – an arduous process that can take up to seven days. Once free, the juveniles then disperse to their future home ranges in the same groups they emerged with, and can be found sleeping together. Juveniles of this species are able to distinguish their relations. This may involve recognizing faecal scent or body odour.

Blending in The iguanas' green skin makes them inconspicuous in their favoured surroundings. They are specialist leaf eaters and spend most of the day inactive.

HUMAN IMPACT SHRINKING RANGE
Penguin populations are in serious trouble. The majority of penguins rely on krill for much of their nutrition. Krill in turn rely on winter ice for breeding sites, and for the algae growing on the underside of the ice sheets. Rising sea temperature means that there is less krill to go round. Some penguins also need to haul out onto pack ice to moult. If birds swim too far before they find solid ice, they drown.

King penguin
Vast colonies
SPECIES *Aptenodytes patagonicus* **SIZE** 85–95 cm (33–37 in) **DISTRIBUTION** Southern Indian Ocean (the Falklands, Macquarie Islands, Îles Crozet, Heard Island, and Marion Island)

During the breeding season, king penguins can form vast colonies on beaches and snow-free valleys near the sea. The colonies are segregated, and breeders tend to be separated from non-breeders. Despite the potential pressure for space and resources, there is little antagonistic behaviour seen within the colony. Pairs defend small territories, but their spacing keeps them just outside of their immediate neighbours' pecking range. In a breeding pair, both parents incubate and brood the chick, which will take around nine months to fledge. As it gets older, the chick is left with a creche of other youngsters, watched over by just a few adults within the colony for long periods, while its parents forage for food.

King colony This immense colony of breeding king penguins is interspersed with groups of fluffy brown juveniles.

SOCIETY

Ostrich
Shared nests
SPECIES *Struthio camelus* **SIZE** Height 1.7–2.8 m (5½–9¼ ft)
DISTRIBUTION Savanna regions of southern Africa

Although the nests defended by territorial male ostriches are only incubated by the guardian male and a single female, they can contain the eggs of up to 18 different females, sired by multiple fathers. Ostriches engage in a unique form of cooperative breeding, where females within a group may lay their eggs in a large number of different nests. However, a nest can only contain a finite amount of eggs. Although around 40 eggs are laid in a nest, only around 20 can be successfully incubated. Females are able to identify their own eggs and eject those laid by intruders. On hatching, chicks from multiple parents are cared for in crèches.

Whooper swan
Pecking order
SPECIES *Cygnus cygnus* **SIZE** 1.4–1.8 m (4½–6 ft)
DISTRIBUTION Large stretches of water, wetlands, and rivers throughout northern Europe and Asia

Swan song Whooper swans communicate with loud bugling calls but also body movements, with the most restless birds being the first to fly and stimulating the others to join them.

In the autumn, whooper swans fly long distances down from their Arctic breeding grounds to southerly wintering sites. Membership of the groups found on these wintering sites can be very stable, and groups are generally made up of closely related birds. Both group size and kinship are important in social hierarchy formations: large family groups will dominate small families, and groups composed of relatives will have a higher social status than groups of unrelated individuals. Each year, group composition changes slightly as older swans die and young males mature. This means that males have to fight, lunging and sparring for dominance within a group.

Cannon fodder Ostrich parents will rather forcibly adopt younger chicks from other pairs. The smaller, weaker adoptees are then more likely than the adoptive parents' own chicks to be taken by predators if the brood is attacked.

Dance troupe For lesser flamingos, impressing a mate in front of your friends takes on a whole new dimension. Groups of tens to hundreds of birds gather and march back and forth in formation, raising and lowering their bills. During the peak of the breeding season, a lake may be filled with many dance convoys, all travelling in different directions.

Terns
Flocking together

Subfamily Sterninae **size** 36–50 cm (14–20 in)
distribution Near coastal and inland water worldwide

Most species of tern are highly gregarious birds, and can form flocks of tens or hundreds, often from a mixture of species. Non-breeding birds develop white foreheads, replaced with solid black caps at the start of the breeding season. Young terns remain with their parents for weeks or months after fledging, perfecting the difficult task of plunge-diving for fish. Some terns migrate with their parents and stay with them for much of the winter.

Although they sometimes hunt alone, terns often have a better success rate at finding food when they are in a flock – the birds usually catch more fishes than if they are hunting alone. However, there is competition for the good fish within the flock, and on average each fish caught will be smaller than if the tern fed alone.

Ready to go Terns breed in colonies, but remain gregarious through autumn migration and through winter. Seen here is a mixed flock of yellow-billed royal terns (*Thalasseus maximus*) and black-billed sandwich terns (*T. sandvicensis*).

Crows of a feather Many corvids (members of the crow family) are gregarious, but few choose to nest in such close proximity as rooks do.

Rook
Communal nests

species *Corvus frugilegus* **size** 41–49 cm (16–19½ in)
distribution Open country or pasture with woods or clumps of trees across most of Europe, Middle East, and breeds as far east as Russia and China

Rooks are garrulous, intelligent, and highly social birds. From February onwards, they build nests communally in large groups, called "rookeries", at the tops of trees. Within these noisy assemblages, breeding pairs defend a small area of space around their nest. Rookeries are remarkably stable from year to year, and rooks fight for ready-built nests at the beginning of the breeding season, as the existence of an old nest may be a good indicator of how well chicks will survive at the site.

Outside the nesting season, rooks from different colonies roost together. These roosts can consist of enormous numbers of resting rooks: at one Scottish roost 65,000 birds were recorded.

American cliff swallow
Close neighbours

species *Petrochelidon pyrrhonota* **size** 13 cm (5 in)
distribution Open farmland, towns, and mountainous areas. Breed throughout North America, migrating to southern South America in winter

Breeding colonies of cliff swallows can consist of up to several hundred pairs of birds. They build gourd-shaped nests by cementing hundreds of small pellets of mud to the eaves of buildings, bridges, and other vertical structures. Nests may be reused from year to year, if they can be easily repaired. One advantage of living in such a close-knit colony is that if a swallow is having trouble finding food by itself, it can turn to its neighbours for help.

All it has to do is identify a successful forager returning to the colony, and then follow it when it goes back out to find food. It is debatable whether successful foragers are intentionally leading others to good sites, but every colony member can benefit from the pooled information about food sources that is collected by successful birds.

Packed in Cliff swallow nests are often stuck to each other, but each nest is a self-contained ball of dried mud, which is built up in layers and has one small entrance.

Red-billed quelea
Feeding frenzy
SPECIES *Quelea quelea* **SIZE** 12.5 cm (5 in)
DISTRIBUTION Most non-rainforest areas of sub-Saharan Africa

Nesting colonies of this species of weaver bird can extend over hundreds of acres, and hold millions of individuals, making it the most abundant wild bird species in the world. It is also known as "locust bird". It is nomadic, following the rains over hundreds of kilometres to find grass seeds that are ready to eat. When a flock moves into fields of seed crops, such as millet or sorghum, the birds will strip them bare, leading to severe counter-measures by farmers, who kill about 200 million queleas a year.

Drinking up A flock of thousands of red-billed queleas quench their thirst en masse. The birds drink from the water's surface while still in flight.

Sibling harmony Unlike most small birds, which disperse after breeding, long-tailed tits spend many months living in close-knit family groups.

Long-tailed tit
Sharing warmth
SPECIES *Aegithalos caudatus* **SIZE** 14 cm (5½ in)
DISTRIBUTION Throughout Europe and Asia

During the winter, noisy packs of dozens of these tiny birds are a common sight in north European woodlands as they pass through trees and bushes in messy waves. Non-migratory, these birds manage to find enough food in harsh, cold environments. Being highly active in low temperatures means that high levels of energy are spent, but long-tailed tits minimize the amount they lose as heat. As well as having fluffy plumage, these birds huddle together in little groups during the night and periods of the day when they are not active. Forming a huddle means that birds retain heat, but the middle of the huddle is much warmer than the outside. During roost formation, birds will try to get into the centre, and more subordinate individuals frequently end up stuck on the outside in the cold.

Naked mole-rat
Cooperative colony
SPECIES *Heterocephalus glaber* **SIZE** 14–18 cm (5½–7 in)
DISTRIBUTION Hot, dry regions of East Africa: Somalia, central Ethiopia, and northern and eastern Kenya

Often compared to social insects such as ants and bees, naked mole-rats have a social system that is unique among mammals. Living in colonies of up to 250 closely related invididuals, reproduction is delegated to a single breeding female (commonly called the queen). The other members of the colony do not breed, instead they tend to the pups produced by the queen. When a queen dies, the next female in line takes over, her body growing larger as it adapts to become reproductive.

Tunnels provide extra living space for an expanding colony and are vital for accessing the edible parts of underground tubers and roots, which are the mole-rat's staple diet. Smaller workers excavate tunnels by chiselling at the walls with their teeth. Chains of mole-rats form to clear out the dirt produced by the digging, shovelling it along from one mole-rat to another, until it is finally kicked up and out of the tunnels into an expanding volcanolike pile by one of the larger workers.

Excavation A worker naked mole-rat gouges away at a tunnel wall with its enormous incisors.

CASE STUDY KIDNAPPING

Some of the older, larger mole-rats in a colony act as soldiers. In addition to defending themselves against predators, mole-rats sometimes launch takeovers on neighbours, either occupying their tunnels, or making off with pups. These kidnapped pups are raised as slaves, and grow up as workers in the new colony. This behaviour favours larger colonies over smaller ones.

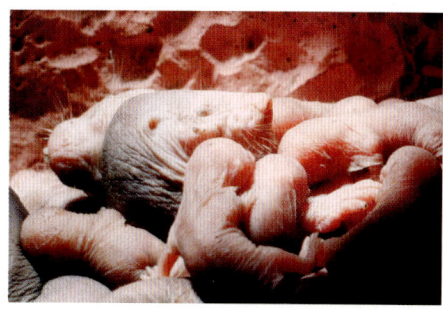

Nursery This queen is suckling her young, which will also be tended to by the colony's workers. Worker females have non-functional ovaries, apparently because of hormonal suppression.

Ring-tailed lemur
Dominant females
SPECIES *Lemur catta* **SIZE** 43 cm (17 in)
DISTRIBUTION Forest in southwestern Madagascar

Primate societies often centre on dominant males or breeding pairs, but male ring-tailed lemurs are submissive and females get first access to food and priority grooming. This total female dominance is rare in mammals, although is found in a few other lemurs and in spotted hyenas. Although daughters normally stay with their mothers, they do not always inherit their mother's social rank.

Moving on Young males will leave their natal groups when they are sexually mature, and subsequently migrate between other groups every one to three years.

Barbary macaque
Adoptive father
SPECIES *Macaca sylvanus* **SIZE** 50–70 cm (19½–28 in) **DISTRIBUTION** Forests in northern Africa, and a small population on Gibraltar

Male barbary macaques provide intensive childcare, often carrying, grooming, and playing with infants and babies. Although they often focus their care on a single infant, they are seldom its father or even have a close genetic relationship to it. Barbary macaques live in mixed troops of between ten and 100 individuals, and males must vie for the attention of females. However, the solicitous care of an infant does not seem to increase a male's chances of mating with its mother. Instead, males may expend energy caring for unrelated babies as a social networking tool to form coalitions with other males.

Possibly family An adult male and juvenile macaque huddle together, but it is highly likely that these two monkeys are not closely related.

Olive baboon
Female solidarity
SPECIES *Papio anubis* **SIZE** 60–74 cm (23½–29 in) **DISTRIBUTION** Widespread throughout equatorial Africa

Olive baboons live in closely knit troops of up to 150 predominantly female adults and juveniles. On maturing to adulthood, males usually leave the troop that they were born into, spending time in several different troops during their lifetime, while females tend to stay within the same group for their entire life. Females within a troop are very closely related, and immediate relatives, including aunts and nieces as well as mothers and daughters, tend to stick together within the troop. Troop dominance hierarchies are very stable and are passed down. The daughters of a high-ranking dominant female inherit their mother's status; the youngest daughter inherits the highest rank, giving her priority access to food, and making her offspring more likely to survive. When not in breeding condition, females still associate with males, and can form long-lasting friendships, grooming, foraging, and travelling together, and defending each other against aggression from other troop members.

Baboon troop A maned male sitting next to a juvenile enjoys a moment's peace (bottom left), while the remainder of the troop rest in the clearing or forage on vegetation in the surrounding trees.

CASE STUDY
BABOON STRESS

Like humans, baboons live in social groups, and have leisure time to devote to social interactions. Hormonal responses that are normally generated by immediate dangers, such as predators, can be caused over longer periods by a dominant bully. So, like humans, baboons suffer from diseases linked to chronic stress. Grooming is one way of lowering stress levels.

Lion
Gentlemen's agreement

SPECIES *Panthera leo* **SIZE** 1.7–1.9 m (5½–6¼ ft) **DISTRIBUTION** Found in reserves in southern Africa, and the Gir Forest, India

When a male lion takes over a pride (group) of females, usually after a vicious battle with the previous incumbent male, his first act is to kill all the young cubs, especially targeting the males. This brings the females into heat, and means that the male can then sire offspring of his own, whose survival depends on his ability to defend his position in the pride. This breeding strategy means that male lions are often at risk of severe injury, whether they control a pride or are trying to usurp a resident male. Some lions get around this risk by forming a coalition with other males. Although paternity is shared, forming a coalition means that the pride is better defended and increases cub survival.

Double strength Male lions form coalitions of different sizes. Coalitions of two or three lions are often unrelated, but males in larger coalitions tend to be close kin.

Pride mothers Lions live in prides of 4–12 lionesses and their cubs. Lionesses frequently cooperate in hunting, which allows them to kill large, fast-moving prey.

Bad neighbours Territorial competition is an important facet of chimpanzee social life. Males stay in their birth groups and may engage in warfare with neighbours.

Common chimpanzee
Border patrol

SPECIES *Pan troglodytes* **SIZE** 73–95 cm (29–37 in) **DISTRIBUTION** Forested habitats in equatorial Africa

Chimpanzees are one of the most territorial of primate species. The males in a group are closely related and, although they compete vigorously for dominance and access to females, they also cooperate to defend the territory, regularly banding together to conduct border patrols. In some western populations, both males and females actively participate in territorial defence. Moving quietly and warily as they near the edge of their territory, some individuals silently climb trees to scan the adjacent land. If they see a large group of outsiders, they start calling and crashing through the vegetation in dramatic displays of intimidation. If there is an imbalance between the two groups, the stronger party may attack and even kill members of the smaller group, thereby expanding their territory. Only females that are in season are tolerated and may transfer between communities.

CASE STUDY **CANNIBALISM**

Raiding male chimpanzees are known to commit infanticide, and on several occasions they have been observed eating their victims. The reasons for cannibalism are unclear, but infanticide may cause the dead infant's mother to return to a breeding state more quickly. In a reserve at Gombe in Tanzania, an adult female and her daughter were also seen to steal and eat babies from females within their own community.

Steller sea lion
Coastal colony

SPECIES *Eumetopias jubatus* **SIZE** 2.3–2.8 m (7½–9¼ ft) **DISTRIBUTION** Pacific coastal regions of USA, Canada, Russia, Japan, and China

Usually found on isolated rocky beaches, rookeries (colonies) of Steller sea lions can be composed of hundreds of individuals. These sea lions normally return to the beach they were born on when they are ready to breed. At the start of the breeding season, the larger males haul themselves onto land and establish a territory to defend. Females arrive a few days later and, after giving birth to a pup, usually mate with the male who "owns" the territory. This means that males have to constantly tend to their territory and vigorously defend it from potential usurpers. Consequently, males defending territories are unable to go to sea to feed and instead rely on huge blubber reserves for nutrition.

2 months The length of time male Steller sea lions fast during the breeding season.

Basking site Steller sea lions form noisy rookeries at haul-out sites when they are resting and during the breeding season.

Safely surrounded A cub peers inquisitively out from the safety offered by three of its clan members. Cubs continue to suckle until they are over a year old.

Spotted hyena
Communal den
SPECIES *Crocuta crocuta* **SIZE** 1–1.5 m (3¼ ft–5 ft)
DISTRIBUTION Desert fringe and savanna in central and southern Africa

Social hierarchies are an important part of a spotted hyena's life from birth. These carnivores live in clans that are dominated by an alpha female and her relatives, and a pup's social position is inherited from its mother, with the youngest daughter outranking her older sisters. Indeed, social rank is reflected in multiple differences in gene expression (epigenetics). For instance, low-ranking individuals have weaker immune systems and are better adaptation to long-distance foraging trips. Females give birth to pups in isolation and then, two to six weeks later, transfer them to communal nursery dens. Pups may attempt to suckle from females other than their mother, which is discouraged. Communal dens serve as a social hub for the clan and non-breeders often drop by to check up on their clan mates. This means that the pups are integrated into the clan's social structure and know their place in the pecking order from a very early age.

Meerkat
Shared responsibility
SPECIES *Suricata suricatta* **SIZE** 25–35 cm (10–14 in)
DISTRIBUTION Dry open plains in southern Africa

These highly social carnivores live in societies where childcare is a shared responsibility. After birth, pups stay in the burrow they were born in for around three weeks, and are suckled by helpers (often young, unmated females), while their mothers forage for food. When the pups are old enough to leave the burrow, they stick with the foraging group and are fed small items of prey by helpers.

Team players A female meerkat suckles pups, which may or may not be her own.

Mustang
Family herd
SPECIES *Equus caballus* **SIZE** 2.1 m (7 ft), with a huge amount of variation in domesticated breeds **DISTRIBUTION** Patchy distributions of feral horses throughout the world. Domesticated breeds found worldwide

Wild and feral horses like the mustangs found on North America's plains and deserts typically live in small, permanent family groups made up of one male (stallion), one to three females (mares), and their offspring. Stallions tend to remain with the same mares over long periods of time. This long pair-bond may be a defensive mechanism, as stallions will vigorously defend their harems against intruders and predators. Dispersal occurs when mature offspring of both sexes leave the group, with young males (and deposed older stallions) forming bachelor herds. Bonds are maintained through behaviours like mutual grooming. Herds form when several family groups come together, and can contain hundreds of animals. Herding horses travel around together, and also graze or rest as a group.

2,000 BCE

When wild horses were first domesticated. Fewer than 33,000 free-roaming mustangs remain in North America.

Stampede A herd of mustangs running through the desert in Wyoming, USA. Much variation exists in coat colour within these feral populations, which indicates their domestic origin.

Bactrian camel
Walking the line
SPECIES *Camelus bactrianus* **SIZE** 3 m (9¾ ft)
DISTRIBUTION Restricted to three areas of desert in southern Mongolia and northwest China

Nearly extinct in the wild, bactrian camels have been widely domesticated. Their ability to cope with arid, desert conditions and extreme temperature differences allows them to inhabit regions inaccessible to other animals. Fat is stored in the two humps on the back. These adaptations allow them to travel for long periods of time without food. Camels are nomadic rather than territorial, and during the mating season, gatherings can reach over 100, but normally social family groups consist of up to 30 animals. When moving over large distances to find food, the members of a group form a linear travelling party, or "caravan", in which a dominant male acts as the leader.

Camel caravan A small group of camels travels in a characteristic line along a ridge in the Gobi Desert. The camels sport thick fur to combat the cold.

HUMAN IMPACT **TERRITORY LOSS**
Critically endangered, the wild bactrian camel has been reduced to three small regions in central Asia. Its habitat has been lost to mining, industry, and nuclear testing. Every year, camels in protected regions are shot when they migrate into areas where they are in competition with livestock.

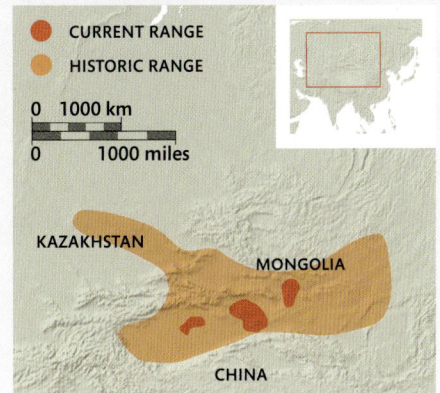

Ready to rumble In both matriarch-led and bachelor herds, elephants use low-frequency infrasound to communicate, including the distinctive "let's go" note from the leader telling the group when to leave an area.

African bush elephant
Mothers and daughters
SPECIES *Loxodonta africana* **SIZE** 4–5 m (13–16½ ft)
DISTRIBUTION Open grassland, scrub, woodland, and occasionally desert, in Africa south of the Sahara

Large herds containing hundreds or thousands of African elephants form during times of drought, but more typically elephants collect in smaller family groups of around 10 or 20 related individuals. Small herds are matriarchal: an older dominant female controls the herd, and frequently remains in the position until her death, when her eldest daughter usually assumes the role of matriarch. Family groups may join together in loose herds, but the matriarch controls and vetoes group membership. At puberty, males are ejected from their herd and form separate small bachelor herds. Adult males may be solitary but remain in contact with nearby groups through infrasound, which travels over 10 km (6 miles).

Spinner dolphin
Group greetings
SPECIES *Stenella longirostris* **SIZE** 1.5–3.5 m (5–11½ ft)
DISTRIBUTION Tropical and warm temperate waters of Atlantic, Pacific and Indian oceans

These gregarious dolphins are often found in pods (groups) containing hundreds of individuals. Pod membership is fluid, and changes regularly as smaller groups join and leave. When they are not resting, spinner dolphins are often very noisy, producing a huge range of whistles and clicks: individual dolphins may have signature whistles that enable them to be identified by others. When reuniting after long separations, spinner dolphins greet each other with lots of social interaction and vocalizations.

Group spin These dolphins are known for their unique spinning aerial leaps, with up to seven rotations at a time. When one spins, others join in, suggesting a social function for this behaviour.

Social intelligence Female coatis' brains have larger frontal cortexes than those of males, reflecting the greater complexity and challenges of group living.

Ring-tailed coati
Girl group
SPECIES *Nasua nasua* **SIZE** 0.7–1.3 m (2¼–4¼ ft) **DISTRIBUTION** Rainforest regions of South America, as far south as northern Argentina

The racoonlike coati is an agile arboreal forager, and has ankles that can face backwards, enabling it to run up and down trees. Male coatis are generally solitary and tend to forage alone, but females live in small groups of five to ten individuals. When it is time to breed, females move away from the group, but rejoin later, along with their new infants.

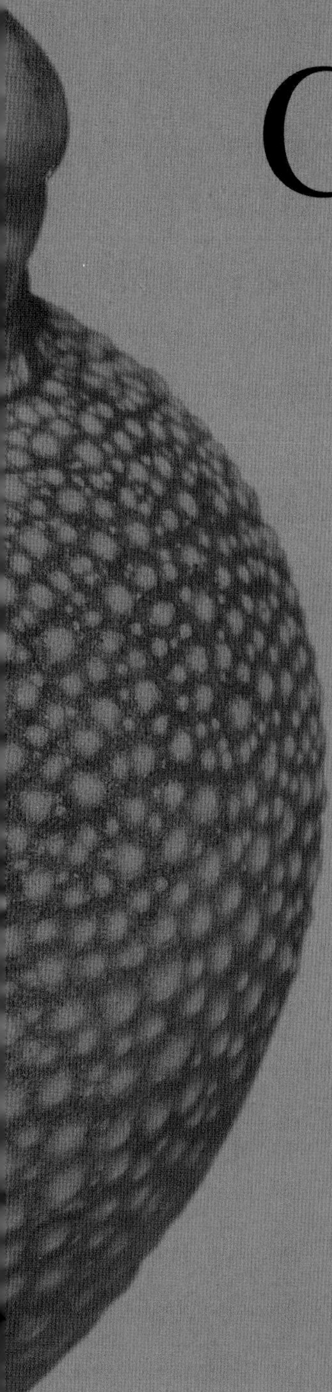

Communication

412
Pheromones and smell

416
Visual signals

424
Sound

430
Touch, vibration, electricity

Team call Like many animal signals, howling serves several functions, including declaring a pack's territory and strength, rallying pack members, and showing solidarity. When one wolf howls, the rest of the pack join in, at varying pitches, to create the impression of as large a pack as possible.

COMMUNICATION

A diversity of signals allow animals to communicate with their own species, enabling them to find mates, cooperate, and avoid conflict. The natural world is full of communication networks, from minute vibrations and electrical impulses, to cocktails of chemicals, colourful displays, and spectacular sounds.

Friendly signals Common between social animals, such as these young olive baboons, tactile signals are often used for reassurance and to maintain bonds.

WHAT IS COMMUNICATION?

Communication involves the transfer of information between animals, usually of the same species, with specialized signals. These signals tend to have evolved from aspects of behaviour, biology, or appearance that have become exaggerated, or "ritualized", to convey information. The leaping of a gazelle, for example, provides incidental information about its fitness and agility to a predator, but when the leaping is ritualized into a display of exaggerated movements, it becomes an active signal of fitness. This is not a fixed process, and some incidental aspects of appearance or behaviour may be halfway to being formal signals. The diversity of signals reflects that of animals, their environments, and the information they need to convey.

WHY ANIMALS COMMUNICATE

While the ways in which animals communicate are extremely diverse, the reasons for communication are fairly straightforward – finding a suitable mate, raising offspring, defending resources or a mate against rivals, and cooperation. The most fundamental of these is to find a mate of the right species, and a great many animals have their own courtship signals. These may be vocal, pheromonal, visual, tactile, acoustic, electric, or a combination of these. Some courtship signals, such as the bonding displays of many monogamous birds, offer information about the quality of a mate or cement long-term bonds. Parent–offspring signals, such as contact calls or begging, are used by animals with a long or intense period of parental care, particularly birds and mammals. Competition over mates, territory, or resources is another reason to communicate. Most aggressive signals actually reduce the need to fight. Showing off your size and strength by chest beating, like a silverback gorilla, can deter rivals, while marking territorial boundaries further reduces conflict. Those animals living in groups, however, tend to have the most complex communication. Close-knit groups often have signals that maintain cohesion, uphold social order, and enable cooperation, but even casual groups may have signals for danger, or to bring individuals together.

TALKING A FOREIGN LANGUAGE

Communication usually occurs within a species, but there are good reasons for inter-species communication. The most common examples of this are between prey and predators. In an attempt to avoid being eaten, some prey species signal to predators that they are dangerous, or extremely agile. Prey species also benefit from understanding and reacting to the alarm calls of others. An unusual example of inter-species communication is the greater honeyguide, which leads people to hives and feeds on the wax and larvae once the honey has been harvested by humans.

The "stotting" display of the springbok tells predators that it is fit, healthy, and most likely hard to catch.

CHANNELS OF COMMUNICATION

Chemical Used across the animal kingdom, chemical signals are particularly common among invertebrates. They are usually aimed at a general audience rather than a particular individual.

Visual Used by all groups of animals, visual communication is less developed in nocturnal and burrowing animals. It includes colours and markings, body language, and bioluminescence.

Acoustic Used by arthropods and vertebrates, acoustic signals travel through air or water. They are made by a voice box, or by mechanical means, such as rubbing together body parts.

Vibration Mainly used by arthropods but also by some vertebrates, vibration includes pressure waves that travel through wood or the ground, made by banging, tapping, or low-frequency infrasound.

Electric Known to be used by only two groups of fish, electricity is only effective in water, over a very short range. Electrical discharge patterns are produced by a special electric organ.

Tactile Used at close range before mating, or in social species that live close together, tactile messages are simple and usually friendly, and include tapping in insects and embracing in mammals.

Pheromones and smell

The word pheromone comes from Greek and means "carrier of excitement". Pheromones are chemicals released by animals that trigger a behavioural change or developmental reaction in another member of their species. In invertebrates, even tiny concentrations can produce dramatic effects, while the response of vertebrates is often more subtle.

SEA ANEMONE

HONEY BEE QUEEN

WEEVIL

AN ANCIENT LANGUAGE

Chemical signals were probably the earliest form of communication, and today the majority of animals communicate mostly or entirely with their use (with the seeming exception of birds). Pheromones are the main form of invertebrate communication, and social insects such as termites coordinate their activities with complex chemical vocabularies. Arthropods use sensory hairs on their exoskeleton, or on their antennae, to detect pheromones, while vertebrates employ a vomeronasal organ, or an olfactory membrane.

Potent aphrodisiac Female emperor moths produce a powerful attractant from a gland at the tip of their abdomen.

11km The distance a male emperor moth has been known to track the pheromone plume of a female.

Sensitive to scent Moths are very precise in detecting the composition of pheromones. The male ceanothus moth uses the thousands of hairlike sensilla on its antennae to detect tiny quantities of female sex attractant.

TYPES OF PHEROMONES

There are two main types of pheromone – primers and releasers. Primers produce a physiological change in the recipient: queen bees, for example, employ them to suppress the sexual development of workers. Releaser pheromones cause a behavioural response, and are of four main types – sex attractants, alarm signals, recruitment or aggregation signals, and marker or territorial pheromones. Once released, a pheromone has a physical existence apart from the animal that produced it, and can be carried huge distances by air currents, or deposited on the ground or a plant to be picked up later. Signals that need to carry long distances, act quickly, or switch on and off, like alarm pheromones, tend to be highly volatile and unstable. Those used for longer-term communication, such as territorial markers, are heavier, more stable compounds that may be active for days or weeks.

Pheromone types *Anthopleura elegantissima* (top) uses a "releaser" pheromone as a warning to others to retract their vulnerable tentacles; honey bee queens (centre) control workers with a "primer and releaser" system; and cabbage seed weevils (bottom) use "marker" pheromones.

SIGNPOSTING THE ENVIRONMENT

Many animals live in a landscape of smells that are as prominent to them as signposts are to humans. Chemical messages are unique in that they can be left behind like a note or calling card, and are often used by animals that are widely dispersed, or need to defend a large area. Many ants leave odour trails to mark the route to a food source. These "trail pheromones" may only last minutes, because the information is only valid for a short time. Territorial markings, however, tend to be long-term and some, such as those of hyenas, can persist for weeks.

Scent marking Animals such as this female ring-tailed lemur (who marks her troop's territory with an anal gland) use specialized glands for scent marking. Other animals mark territory with urine or dung.

CASE STUDY MASS BROADCAST

Researchers decipher insect pheromones by separating out the constituent compounds and testing their effects. The "queen pheromone" of the honey bee allows a single queen to exert precise control over thousands of workers. It induces workers to release a pheromone that causes them to swarm around and protect her, as dramatically demonstrated by this human lure, who holds a vial of queen pheromone.

PHEROMONES AND SMELL 413

Common earthworm
Alarm signal
SPECIES *Lumbricus terrestris* **SIZE** Up to 25 cm (10 in) **DISTRIBUTION** Soil in Europe; introduced across North America and western Asia

As it moves, an earthworm produces mucus that helps it to slide through its burrow, and binds the soil of the burrow walls together to prevent them from caving in. If under attack, the worm secretes considerably more mucus, and adds an alarm pheromone to it. Other worms ignore normal mucus, but if they detect just a drop of mucus with this pheromone, they move rapidly away from the danger.

Attractive to some Many predators spit out worms covered in alarm mucus, but some, such as this fire salamander and the red-sided garter snake, are attracted by it.

Orchid bee
Perfume gift
SPECIES *Euglossa* species **SIZE** 0.8–3 cm (5/16–1 1/4 in) **DISTRIBUTION** Tropical and subtropical forest from New Mexico to Argentina

Apart from humans, orchid bees are the only animals known to blend fragrances into perfumes. Males collect scents from orchids, which they store in special leg pouches. They also collect ingredients from other flowers, fruits, tree sap resin, rotten wood, and even faeces, to add depth and complexity to their scent. During courtship, the male transfers this concoction to the base of its wings and hovers around the female, wafting it at her. It is believed that the female orchid bee finds a complex perfume most attractive.

Extracting essential oils This orchid bee deposits a fatty substance onto an orchid to extract the scent oils – like the *enfleurage* methods perfumers once used. In return, the flower is pollinated. A packet of the orchid's pollen is seen stuck on the bee's back.

Queen butterfly
Toxic love
SPECIES *Danaus gilippus* **SIZE** Wingspan 7–8 cm (2 3/4–3 1/4 in) **DISTRIBUTION** Open sunny areas, including pastures, dunes, waterways in southern USA, West Indies, Central and South America to Argentina

This butterfly, like many others, uses pheromones to attract mates. The males use the alkaloid lycopsamine, obtained from the plants they feed on, to make a pheromone that attracts females to mate with them. Lycopsamine is highly toxic to humans, causing damage to the skin and liver with repeated exposure. In their caterpillar form these insects eat toxic plants, and these chemicals protect them and the adults they go on to become.

Weaver ant
Chemical language
SPECIES *Oecophylla longinoda* **SIZE** Workers average 6 mm (1/4 in) **DISTRIBUTION** Tropical forest and woodland in sub-Saharan Africa

The weaver ant has a highly sophisticated chemical communication system. For instance, foragers leave a trail pheromone to guide others to food and, if recruiting ants to fetch food, they touch them with their antennae, transferring the food's odour to persuade them to follow. If they encounter an intruder, foragers return for reinforcements and transfer an alarm pheromone to other ants, comprising four chemicals: the first commands "pay attention"; the second says "look for the intruder"; the third stimulates aggression; and the fourth sounds the attack.

Pine engraver beetle
Chemical broadcast
SPECIES *Ips pini* **SIZE** 2–6 mm (1/16–1/4 in) **DISTRIBUTION** Pine forest in southeastern, western, and northern USA into Canada

The power of pheromones is all too evident in the damage wrought by engraver beetles and their relatives. Once a beetle has settled on a pine tree (usually one that is already stressed) it sends out a pheromone summoning others to come to the tree to eat and mate, which involves boring into the tree. New arrivals join in the chemical broadcast so that, with each successive wave of newcomers, the signal gets stronger, producing a mass attack that can overwhelm and kill even a healthy tree. The tree contributes to its own downfall – the pheromone is produced using chemical substances extracted from the tree itself.

Beetle get together Pine engraver beetles are usually attracted to dead or stressed pine trees, but during periods of drought they will also feed on and breed in healthy trees.

Living bridge Weaver ants live in colonies in trees and here a group of ants are holding onto one another to create a bridge that members of the colony can use to reach a new feeding ground on a neighbouring tree.

Magnificent tree frog
Irresistible scent
SPECIES *Ranoidea splendida* **SIZE** 10.5 cm (4¼ in)
DISTRIBUTION Caves, rock crevices, close to human habitation; limited range in northwestern Australia

The male sex pheromone of the magnificent tree frog is the first to be discovered in frog and toad species. The substance, called splendipherin, reaches a peak during the breeding season. The female is immediately responsive to this compound when she detects it in water, altering her posture, becoming more alert, and moving towards the source.

Under my skin Male frogs are known to attract mates by calling, but the magnificent tree frog also attracts females with a chemical, produced in glands at the front and rear of its head, that is secreted through the skin.

West Indian manatee
Aquatic scent marks
SPECIES *Trichechus manatus* **SIZE** 2.5–4.5 m (8¼–14¾ ft)
DISTRIBUTION Shallow coastal water, estuaries, rivers, and lagoons in southeastern USA to northeastern South America and Caribbean

Dispersed manatees may use underwater scent marks to pass on information. On arriving at the mouth of the Crystal river in Florida in October, some individuals rub up against prominent stones or submerged logs, rubbing with genitals, eyes, armpits, and chin – all spots where glandular secretions occur. They use the same sites each year and, if a rubbing post disappears, they find a new object nearby. Females rub more than males, perhaps to advertise their sexual receptivity to roaming males.

Seductive scent A female manatee in oestrus can attract dozens of interested males, probably through scent signals. Communication at closer quarters is through vocalizations and touch.

Desert iguana
Visible smell
SPECIES *Dipsosaurus dorsalis* **SIZE** 40 cm (15½ in) **DISTRIBUTION** Dry, sandy desert and scrubland, in rock crevices and creosote bush in southwestern USA, northwestern Mexico

The strongest scents are volatile, which means they can change from liquid to vapour. But as these scents do not last in hot conditions, desert iguanas use "stable" scents to mark their territories. These last for days, but are not strong. However, iguanas' scent marks reflect ultraviolet light which other iguanas can see clearly. By investigating these, a desert iguana can tell who has been in its territory. Relatives, neighbours, and potential mates are tolerated, but the scents of strange males prompt an immediate aggressive reaction.

Making a mark On the underside of each thigh, the desert iguana has a row of pores that leave a twin trail of scent over the rocks and dirt wherever it goes, allowing this small animal to lay claim to a large territory.

Stand tall Female dwarf mongooses are more interested in scent marks that are placed higher up, as this indicates that the marker is a larger animal and thus may be a more intimidating rival.

Dwarf mongoose
Team players
SPECIES *Helogale parvula* **SIZE** 18–28 cm (7–11 in)
DISTRIBUTION Common in savanna, preferably with numerous termite mounds for refuge, in East and southern Africa

Mingling odours is a common way for groups of animals to maintain solidarity. The dwarf mongoose is intensely social, and both related and unrelated individuals in a pack help to raise the young of the alpha pair (usually the oldest male and female). Pack members jointly scent-mark objects in their home range, especially near the den, by rubbing an anal gland on a vertical surface, with an anal drag (often preceded by lifting a hind leg) on a horizontal surface, or by performing a handstand with treading motions to release scent into the air. They also anoint other members of the pack, including offspring, by rubbing them with anal and cheek-gland secretions to label them as part of the team.

European otter
Signposting the way
SPECIES *Lutra lutra* **SIZE** 55–90 cm (21½–35 in) **DISTRIBUTION** Rivers, lakes, estuaries, and sheltered rocky coasts in Europe, Asia, and northern Africa

Otters leave piles of faeces or "spraints" on prominent rocks and logs to advertise their territory and mark their possession of resources. Although solitary animals for the most part, the territories of males and females overlap and spraint marks allow them to build up a map of the movements of their neighbours. In the Shetland Islands and areas of northern Scotland, otters forage exclusively at sea, but still need fresh water to drink. Here, piles of spraint are built up into highly noticeable signposts by generations of otters. One spraint station leads to another, so that otters newly returned to land are never far from a series of stations leading them to fresh water.

Surprisingly sweet Otter faeces may contain fish scales and bones from their last meal, but are often described as smelling like newly mown hay or jasmine tea. With age, they fade in colour but retain a sweet, musky scent.

White rhinoceros
Information depots
SPECIES *Ceratotherium simum* **SIZE** 1.7–1.8 m (5½–6 ft) **DISTRIBUTION** Grassland with trees and water in southern and East Africa; once widespread, now in scattered populations

White rhinoceroses are the most social of all rhinoceroses. Females and their young associate in groups of up to 14 animals. Adult males, however, are solitary. The dominant bulls are territorial and regularly mark their territory by wiping their horns on bushes or on the ground, then scrape-marking with all four feet, and finally by spraying the spot three to five times with urine. Patrolling males urine-mark about ten times an hour. They also maintain 20–30 middens (dunghills), usually on the boundaries of their territory, where they always defecate, using slow, deliberate kicks before and after defecating to spread out the pile over a wider area, and carry its scent on their feet. Females, calves, and non-territorial males add their own deposits to the heap (without kicking), as though showing their allegiance. The piles become such conspicuous features of the landscape that other animals also use them as message stations for posting their own scent messages.

Frequent pastings A hyena pauses two or three times per square km (per one-third of a square mile) to mark its territory with anal secretions.

Two-tone pasting A hyena secretes a white territory-claiming paste, then a black one to communicate with other pack members.

Brown hyena
Two-part message
SPECIES *Parahyaena brunnea* **SIZE** 1.3 m (4¼ ft) **DISTRIBUTION** Dry savanna and desert in southwest and southern Africa, including Skeleton Coast

Brown hyenas live in clans of four to fourteen individuals who typically forage alone, but share a communal den. They mark their huge home ranges by pasting grass stems with anal-pouch secretions, especially in the heart of their range. At one time, 20,000 pastings may exist across a home range of 235–480 square kilometres (90–185 square miles).

The brown hyena deposits two different secretions in turn, one above the other. A white pomade lasts for more than a month and probably functions to establish and maintain territorial rights. The second, a black watery secretion, fades within hours. It is likely that this is addressed to other clan members, telling them who has passed that way and how long ago, so that they can avoid foraging in areas that have already been covered.

Red-sided garter snake
Chemical masquerade
SPECIES *Thamnophis sirtalis parietalis* **SIZE** 38–91 cm (15–36 in) **DISTRIBUTION** Grassland, scrubland, chaparral, forest, usually near water, across northern USA and into Canada

As many as 100 male red-sided garter snakes (a subspecies of the common garter snake) may descend upon a female in response to a pheromone she secretes, forming a writhing mass of bodies called a "mating ball". Each male tries to court the female by rubbing his chin along her back and positioning himself so he is ready to mate with her. At last one will succeed, mate, then mark the female with another pheromone to deter further suitors. Some males, however, produce small amounts of the female pheromone. This distracts other males, who start to court these disguised males, enabling the masqueraders to get into an advantageous position and win the female. This highly successful deception allows them to achieve 70 per cent of all matings.

The race for a mate On emerging from hibernation, there is intense competition between males, as the female red-sided garter snake will only mate with one male in a year. By attracting other males to get close, the masqueraders also warm up more quickly than their rivals. This explains why this behaviour is less common in the more southerly-living subspecies of the common garter snake.

Visual signals

Vivid patterns, elaborate ornaments, specialized postures, and facial expressions make bold and instant statements. For almost all creatures, visual signals are the fastest way of sending a message. But there are distinct disadvantages, too – they only work at close range and can sometimes draw unwanted attention.

UNIFORMS AND BADGES
Distinctive colours and patterns identify animals to their own kind and to species they interact with, which is important when several related species live in the same habitat. The sexes of a species may look different, and traits that suggest vigour (an elaborate tail or impressive antlers, for instance) can become exaggerated as species evolve. Some markings act as badges of social status. The black bib of the sparrow is a status symbol. The larger the bib, the higher the rank.

Professional perk Fish that might otherwise eat this cleaner wrasse recognize its distinctive blue-striped pattern as that of the fish that rids them of parasites and dead tissue.

BODY LANGUAGE
Some body language is universal. Animals make themselves appear as large as possible to seem more of a threat, and attract attention by waving arms or other appendages. When attracting a mate, postures help to display desirable traits – the courtship dances of many birds display their plumage to full effect, for example. Among social mammals in particular, postures or gestures can communicate much information, and larger monkeys and apes go a step further, using a range of facial expressions.

Male mandrill Surging hormones produce intense colours in this primate, indicating status. Facial expressions convey more immediate information.

LIGHT SHOWS
Some nocturnal animals and those that live in darkness are bioluminescent (they emit light), which is common in fishes, jellyfish, crustaceans, and squid that live in the deep ocean. The most abundant vertebrate on Earth may, indeed, be a bioluminescent genus of fishes called bristlemouths (*Cyclothone*). Light signals help find mates, avoid predators, and lure in prey. Some tiny crustaceans are able to synchronize their flashes to produce breathtaking light shows.

Sparkling lights Among the most spectacular of underwater light shows is the spinning wheel of light produced by some jellyfish.

INTERMITTENT SIGNALS
Some visual signals can be switched on and off to provide specific information. Many animals change their appearance when ready to breed, but sudden visual signals can be even more noticeable. Abruptly raising crown feathers, extending flaps of skin, swishing tails, or flashing coloured patches can signal aggression, attract a mate, sound the alarm, or keep a group together.

Instant colour Most of the time, the brightly coloured flap of skin under the brown anole lizard's neck is folded away to avoid attracting attention from predators. But it can be displayed quickly whenever necessary.

VISUAL SIGNALS **417**

Jumping spiders
Dancing for a partner

SPECIES *Maevia inclemens* **SIZE** Male 5–7 mm (³⁄₁₆–¼ in), female 7–10 mm (¼–⅜ in) **DISTRIBUTION** Throughout eastern and northern USA

Male jumping spiders of the species *Maevia inclemens* come in two forms, or morphs, each with its own distinctive courtship display. The tufted type begins his display 9 mm (⅜ in) from the female and waves his legs in the air, while the grey type gets to within 3 mm (⅛ in) of a female before crouching low and sidling back and forth with his first two pairs of legs pointed forwards in a triangular shape. Scientists hypothesize that the two male morphs evolved through natural selection as alternative strategies that stimulate different fields of the female visual range.

Jumping spiders have excellent vision and can see ultraviolet light. Males in many of the tropical species have brightly coloured hair and hair tufts, often conspicuous in ultraviolet light, which are displayed as part of their elaborate courtship rituals.

Shake a leg To attract a female, this tufted male jumping spider waves his first pair of legs vigorously while swinging his abdomen from side to side.

Porcelain fiddler crab
Giant claw

SPECIES *Austruca annulipes* **SIZE** 2–3 cm (¾–1¼ in) **DISTRIBUTION** Intertidal mud flats, salt marshes, and mangroves in South and East Africa, Asia

The male porcelain fiddler crab has a colossal claw that can weigh up to 40 per cent of the crab's body weight. It is used both to intimidate other males and wave at passing females to entice them into their burrows to mate. Some fiddler crabs wave their signal arms in unison – a useful ploy to attract distant females. Competition is intense and males often cluster around a female. With her 360-degree vision, she has a wrap-around view of waving claws to choose from. Both claw size and wave rate demonstrate vigour and attract females. Some crabs cheat – if a male loses his claw, he grows a flimsy fake, which takes less energy to wave yet impresses females.

Hopeful wave A male porcelain fiddler crab waves his extra-large claw to attract the attention of a female.

Ostracods
Light show

SPECIES *Cypridina* species **SIZE** Average ¹⁄₁₆ in (1 mm), up to 1¼ in (3 cm) **DISTRIBUTION** Marine, brackish, and fresh water worldwide

After dark, these tiny crustaceans perform amazing light shows. They use light as a means of protection, releasing brilliant puffs of bioluminescent material to startle predators. The light is produced when one chemical (a luciferin) is oxidized by means of an enzyme (a luciferase). Ostracods also use light to communicate with each other. Males move rapidly through the water, painting dotted trails of blue light to attract females. Each species has its own light-show pattern – it may be very short or very long, and move upwards, downwards, laterally, or obliquely, much like patterns traced with a sparkler.

Seed shrimps Resembling tiny clams, ostracods are actually crustaceans, as are the antennae-bearing copepods in the bottom-left corner of this image.

Genji firefly
Flashing lights

SPECIES *Nipponoluciola cruciata* **SIZE** 1–2 cm (⅜–¾ in) **DISTRIBUTION** Along riverbanks and waterways in Japan

Fireflies are beetles that produce a glowing light that is used to flash messages. The yellowish light is produced by a chemical reaction involving proteins called luciferins, an enzyme catalyst, oxygen, and energy from food. After dark in summer, male genji fireflies fly and flash in a distinctive fashion to attract females. Other males are also drawn to these flashes and gradually synchronize their pattern to create swathes of pulsing light. Females follow these signals, emitting an irregular pattern of flashes of their own. On encountering a female, a male perches on a branch, changes his flash pattern, and approaches her in order to mate.

Sending signals A female Genji firefly perches on a leaf, emitting flashes of light to attract a male's attention.

Grey reef shark
Threat postures

SPECIES *Carcharhinus amblyrhynchos* **SIZE** Up to 1.7 m (5½ ft) **DISTRIBUTION** Coral reefs and atolls throughout Indo-Pacific Ocean, including Red Sea

Several species of shark use body language as a warning. When threatened, the grey reef shark produces exaggerated swimming movements, such as rolling, zigzagging, and spiralling up and down in the water, and also adopts an S-shaped posture, lifting its snout, arching its back, dropping the pectoral fins, and bending its body to one side.

Group feeding Grey reef sharks are sociable creatures. They gather in groups on the edges of reefs where they feed on fishes, squid, and crustaceans. Their numbers have declined and they are under threat in some areas.

In intense displays, a shark adopts an exaggerated posture and swims in a compressed S-shaped pattern or even in a figure of eight. The more intense the display, the more likely the shark feels threatened enough to attack.

Butterflyfishes
Different uniforms

FAMILY Chaetodontidae **SIZE** 7–15 cm (2¾–6 in) is usual, some species up to 30 cm (12 in)
DISTRIBUTION Coral reefs in all tropical waters, but largest number in western Pacific and Indian Ocean

When closely related species live in the same habitat, distinctive markings act as a uniform, making individuals conspicuous to their own kind. Butterflyfishes share the same basic body shape but have bold patterns in shades of blue, yellow, black, white, orange, and red. Identified on this reef (see right) are the bannerfish, with its long dorsal fin and stripes; the millet or lemon butterflyfish, with its yellow fin and black spot; and the chevron butterflyfish, with its pale body chevrons.

Now you see me... Up close, markings help to identify species of butterflyfish, but at only 1–2 m (3¼ ft–6½ ft) they break up the outline of the fish and hide the eye to camouflage them.

Panamanian golden frog
Sign language

SPECIES *Atelopus zeteki* **SIZE** 35–50 cm (14–19½ in) **DISTRIBUTION** Streams in rainforest and cloud forest in western-central Panama. Extinct in wild, few hundred in captivity

Although it calls like other frogs, this frog's native habitat is near noisy waterfalls, so it has developed a system of waving. When two males compete for territory or females, they each raise a bright yellow forearm and sometimes a foot, until one backs down. Males also wave away females that don't appear ready to mate, but allow fertile females to enter their territory unhindered. However, fertile females turn the tables and wave aggressively at males. If one approaches despite her warning, she mates with him, but does not if he is intimidated. So in this case, waving seems to be a way of testing the male's resolve.

The last wave The Panamanian golden frog is now extinct in the wild because of an outbreak of chytridiomycosis, a particularly virulent fungal disease that is sweeping through Panama.

Frilled lizard
Frilly display

SPECIES *Chlamydosaurus kingii* **SIZE** Up to 90 cm (35 in) **DISTRIBUTION** Hot, dry forest in northern Australia and southern Papua New Guinea

During the breeding season, the male frilled lizard performs displays to claim territory. He lashes his tail against the bark of a tree to produce audible thumps, then raises his upper body in a push-up, following up with a series of partial raises of his magnificent frill. Such displays are performed most frequently in the morning and are not usually directed at any particular individual, but if another male doesn't take heed of the warnings and strays too close, a furious battle ensues. Prior to combat, the males fan out their frills to the maximum and open their mouths, exposing a pink or yellow lining, before lunging at each other head-on, interlocking jaws. Both sexes also employ the full frill display when cornered, or when handled by humans. One was reported displaying in response to a car travelling some 50 m (165 ft) away.

Using its assets Relative to its size, the frilled lizard has one of the largest visual displays of any animal. The huge flap of skin attached to its neck can be fanned out into a most dramatic Dracula-like collar some 30 cm (12 in) across.

Great crested newt
Handstand

SPECIES *Triturus cristatus* **SIZE** Up to 15 cm (6 in) **DISTRIBUTION** Pools and ponds across northern Europe, from Britain to Urals

Like many newts and salamanders, the great crested newt communicates using both visual signals and pheromones. On encountering a female during the breeding season, the male performs a handstand while waving its tail in the air like a flag and wafting an attractive chemical substance towards her. If he is successful, this persuades the female to accept the sperm packet that he drops on the floor of the pond at the end of his display. She picks it up in her cloaca (the chamber into which the genital tract opens) and, a few days later, starts to lay up to 300 eggs; using her hind legs, she carefully wraps each egg in a leaf in order to protect it.

Look at me During this impressive handstand, the male shows off his crest and striped tail, which he waves to a potential mate.

Northern gannet
Bowing and pointing
SPECIES *Morus bassanus* **SIZE** 89–102 cm (35–39¾ in)
DISTRIBUTION North Atlantic. Oceanic, often well offshore, but breeds on sea cliffs

These seabirds live in noisy, crowded colonies where nest sites are at a premium. Defence of nests can lead to vicious fights that may result in severe injury, such as the loss of an eye. But gannets manage to avoid many disputes using a range of ritualized visual signals. "Bowing", which is performed repeatedly, seems to be a significant signal of ownership. Standing in its nest, the gannet "bites" the ground at its feet, with wings slightly raised from its body and tail pointing upwards. This develops into proper bowing, with head inverted and bill to feet, and wings arched open. This conspicuous movement, accompanied by a loud call, seems to provide a way of reinforcing ownership of the nest without having to involve overt aggression. Breeding pairs of gannets work together closely to raise their chicks, and negotiate parental duties using a clear visual dialogue. When one bird is relieved of incubation duties by the other and is about to take flight, it will signal this intention by "skypointing". Often both will do this simultaneously, but neither will leave until the newly arrived bird shows willingness to stay by lowering its head. Only then will the other bird depart, safe in the knowledge that the nest remains protected. At the changing of the guard the pair greet each other by "fencing" with their bills, calling, and bowing.

Bickering Nests of compacted grass, seaweed, and droppings are often reused year after year and are defended fiercely. Stretching forwards with bill open, and ritualized sparring by jabbing bills at neighbours, are common.

Claiming territory The bird to the right in this picture asserts its claim to its nest site by showing a mild form of "bowing" towards a neighbouring pair. Territorial displays may be performed by either sex, but are always directed at birds of their own sex.

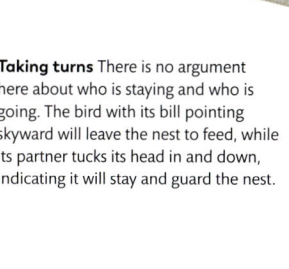

Taking turns There is no argument here about who is staying and who is going. The bird with its bill pointing skyward will leave the nest to feed, while its partner tucks its head in and down, indicating it will stay and guard the nest.

COMMUNICATION

Ruffled feathers In response to the male's "alighting display", the female (on the left) raises her plume and mantle feathers, indicating readiness to defend her nest and chicks.

Regal display Spreading his scarlet diadem to the full, a male may try to impress a female by waving his head rapidly so that the feathers quiver.

Grey heron
Mixed messages

SPECIES Ardea cinerea **SIZE** 90–98 cm (35 in–3¼ ft)
DISTRIBUTION Rivers, lakes, marshes, and estuaries in Europe, Asia, and sub-Saharan Africa, including Madagascar

Grey herons build nests of sticks gathered by males and arranged by females. Even in a well-established pair, each is possessive of its personal space. Meetings at the nest can be tense, with birds adopting a range of hostile postures, such as the "arch neck" and "forward stretch", while raising their crests and body plumes, before settling down amicably.

Royal flycatcher
Crowning glory

SPECIES Onychorhynchus coronatus **SIZE** 16.5–18 cm (6½–7 in)
DISTRIBUTION Most tropical and subtropical forest from Mexico to Brazil

Usually inconspicuous in the forest, both sexes of the royal flycatcher have a concealed crest that can be raised into a magnificent fan-shaped crown, which is used in both courtship and aggressive encounters. Under threat, a bird may open its crest slowly and wave its head from side to side while opening its mouth. It has been suggested that the crown mimics a large gaping mouth, intensifying an aggressive message.

White-winged chough
Blowing the whistle

SPECIES Corcorax melanorhamphos **SIZE** 49–68 cm (19½–27 in) **DISTRIBUTION** Mostly on ground in wetter areas of open forest and woodland throughout eastern and southeastern Australia

These birds live in family groups of 4–20, comprising a breeding pair and their offspring. To find food, they must search through leaf litter, and can only raise chicks if all group members assist in this arduous task. In return for helping to feed their siblings, juveniles pick up important skills and earn a chance to inherit the territory. But when times are hard, hungry juveniles have been observed faking the gesture of giving food to chicks and eating it themselves later on. In order to keep all members of the group in line, a policing system has been developed, so that any bird caught cheating is publicly identified by being subjected to a spectacular "shaming" display, in which the whistle-blower puffs up its feathers, waves its tail slowly and, at the same time, opens and closes its bill. A struggling family in need of more helpers may attempt to lure an unrelated, naive juvenile away from its own family by treating it as though it were their own offspring.

Boggling with indignation The culmination of the white-winged chough's "shaming" display is "boggling", in which the eyes bulge out of their sockets. These two shocking scarlet orbs create a striking finale.

Blue tit
Open mouthed

SPECIES Cyanistes caeruleus **SIZE** 10.5–12 cm (4¼–4½ in)
DISTRIBUTION Deciduous and mixed woodland and gardens throughout Europe, Middle East, parts of Asia, and northwest Africa

Blue tits raise broods of up to 10 chicks in cup-shaped nests, and both parents carry out the gargantuan task of feeding their young 100 food items (mostly caterpillars) each per day. In order to solicit food from their parents, nestlings perform vigorous postural displays, flapping their wings while calling loudly, and opening their bills to reveal brightly coloured mouths. They beg more intensely when hungry, but also in competition with their nest mates. So, the larger the brood, the more insistently the nestlings beg, even if their harried parents provision them at the same rate. Such gaping displays are common among nestlings of many species of birds.

Highly visible Unlike humans, most birds can see reflected UV light. Research shows that nestling gapes reflect UV light, especially from the flanges (rims), creating contrast with their background for maximum visibility.

Yawn threat A huge gape of 150° displays razor-sharp lower canines, used for fighting, that can be up to 50 cm (19½ in) long. This threat may be accompanied by water scooping, lunging, head shaking, rearing, roaring, and grunting.

Hippopotamus
Weapons on display

SPECIES *Hippopotamus amphibius*
SIZE 3.3–3.4 m (10¾–11¼ ft) **DISTRIBUTION** Grassland and scrubland near wallows, lakes, and rivers in West, Central, East, and South Africa

When foraging at night, hippos tend to be solitary, but when wallowing in water during the day, they spend time in herds comprising 15–20 individuals. These may be either bachelor males or territorial bulls with females and their young. Territorial bulls tolerate other bulls so long as they behave submissively, but hippos have a short fuse and can be highly aggressive, especially in the dry season when wallows dry up. Serious injuries are common. Ritualized threat displays, in which bulls throw back their heads and yawn widely, reduce instances of fighting. The slightest disturbance in a wallow can set off a wave of yawning and wheeze-honking.

Sun-tailed monkey
Follow the leader
SPECIES *Allochrocebus solatus* **SIZE** 50–70 cm (19½–28 in)
DISTRIBUTION Very limited distribution in lowland tropical rainforest in Gabon

Primates' tails are designed to give them balance when leaping through the canopy or purchase while moving, but many species also use them to signal to other members of their group. Sun-tailed monkeys live in rainforest, travelling in troops of 5–15 individuals. Very little sunlight penetrates to the forest floor, so a bold signal is needed to keep the group together. This is provided by the white tail with its orange tip. The dominant male keeps his tail vertical, the orange tip flicking like a banner as he leads his group through the shadowy, dense undergrowth.

Colourful surprise Despite its striking appearance, this beautiful monkey was only discovered in 1988 and remains one of the least-studied species of primates in the world.

Common chimpanzee
Expressive gestures
SPECIES *Pan troglodytes* **SIZE** 73–95 cm (29–37 in) **DISTRIBUTION** Gallery forest, rainforest, and woodland savanna across equatorial Africa. Once widespread, but now severely reduced

Chimpanzees' bodies and faces act like billboards advertising their intentions. Because they live in multi-male communities, males are constantly vying for power and access to females. Dramatic displays by high-ranking males help to make them appear as large and as intimidating to other chimps as possible.

Strike a pose During conflicts, an adult male chimpanzee bristles his hair (called "pilorection") and may well stand on two legs while swaying back and forth and shaking a branch. He then follows this by crashing through the surrounding vegetation in a dramatic charging display, which may be accompanied by slapping the ground, dragging branches, and hurling rocks.

Chimpanzees reach out to each other with arm outstretched and palm upwards in a gesture used to beg for food, ask for reassurance, appease a dominant individual, or in reconciliation. Or they may approach a dominant animal while bobbing and bowing in an exaggerated manner, or crouch and present their backs in a pose similar to a female presenting before mating.

Pout The flexibility of chimps' lips allows for a range of facial expressions. A pout expresses anxiety, frustration, or distress, and is often used by infants.

Fear grin This important, non-threatening signal given by a nervous individual can help diffuse an explosive situation, and may well share an origin with the human smile.

Play face This relaxed face is used in play, sometimes exaggerated by head shaking, especially when older individuals approach timid youngsters to play.

Hooded seal
Blowing balloons

SPECIES *Cystophora cristata* **SIZE** 2.2–2.5 m (7¼–8¼ ft) **DISTRIBUTION** Far North Atlantic, especially off Greenland. Breeds on heavy pack ice

Male hooded seals compete for females during the breeding season with bizarre aggressive displays. In early adulthood, males develop an enlargement of the nasal cavity that hangs down in front of their upper lip. This is inflated to form a black "hood". The nostril lining can be blown out to form a large red balloon, which the seal may display both on land and in the water.

Red signal As a sign of aggression, the lining of one nostril is forced out through the opposite nostril, blowing up the nasal membrane like a red balloon that makes a variety of attention-grabbing sounds when shaken.

White-tailed deer
Tail raising

SPECIES *Odocoileus virginianus* **SIZE** 1.5–2 m (5–6½ ft) **DISTRIBUTION** Forested habitats of all kinds from southern Canada to northern South America

While scent plays a key role in communication between deer, many species also use visual signals. When fleeing from danger, white-tailed deer use their large white tails as a flag to warn the rest of the herd and keep it together, while simultaneously notifying the predator that it has been spotted. Males use a range of postures in hostile situations, such as standing on their hind legs and pawing with the forelegs, or presenting a broadside view of their bodies in order to appear as large as possible.

Multi-modal signals White-tailed deer use auditory, visual, and scent signals, with each individual making a unique range of sounds.

Grey wolf
Body language

SPECIES *Canis lupus* **SIZE** 1–1.5 m (3¼–5 ft) **DISTRIBUTION** Forest, taiga, tundra, desert, plains, and mountains in North America, Europe, Middle East, and Asia

A wolf pack comprises a dominant pair and their adult offspring, all working as a team to hunt, defend territory, and raise pups. There is a strict dominance hierarchy, but a constant dialogue of body language largely prevents aggression. A raised tail and ears assert dominance, while lowering the tail is a sign of submission. Tails are such important communication devices that many members of the dog family, including jackals, foxes, and dingoes, have a black or white tail tip to make tail movements conspicuous.

If it feels challenged, a dominant wolf may raise its hackles and add a direct threat by drawing back its upper lips to expose powerful canines. To diffuse the tension, the subordinate responds by cowering, lowering its tail, and sometimes rolling over to expose its belly.

As with words, signals can be combined to produce many different and complex meanings. If it thinks an attack is imminent, a low-ranking wolf may give a mixture of signals: crouched with its tail low and ears flattened, but snarling and with the hair on its neck erect, indicating that it is submissive, but also willing to defend itself.

Combining signals This snarl could indicate aggression, but if combined with signals such as a tucked-in tail and pinned-back ears, it expresses defensive submission.

Status signal The wolf to the left indicates his dominance by standing tall, with his tail and ears raised. The subordinate individual, to the right, cowers with tail tucked under and ears back in a clearly submissive posture.

HUMAN IMPACT
WILD INSTINCTS

Dogs retain much of their wolf ancestry and use many of the same signals. Despite centuries of domestication, many wolf-pup behaviours remain. The "play/prey bow", seen here, is an invitation to play and may have evolved from a crouched hunting posture. The dog raises its bottom and may wag its tail to signal friendly intention before pouncing.

Sound

As sound travels quickly, it is a highly effective and versatile way to communicate. Animals produce an amazing array of sounds for a wide variety of reasons, from the simple mating chirps of crickets to the defensive communal howls of coyotes, and the sophisticated vocabulary of chimpanzees to the minute alarm calls of ants. Sounds can carry simple or complex messages over very short or incredibly long distances.

MAKING A NOISE

Audible displays are enormously diverse. Amphibians, reptiles, birds, and mammals can all make vocal sounds by expelling air from the lungs, which then passes a vibrating mechanism and one or more resonating chambers. However, there are many other ways in which animals generate sound. Some fishes expel air from their swim bladders, while others scrape parts of their gills together. Arthropods commonly use stridulation (rubbing together different body parts), and some snap membranes or vibrate their wings. Vertebrates that cannot vocalize often produce sounds by other means, such as drumming on trees or snapping their wing feathers.

Projecting sound Common chimpanzees (above) greet other members of the troop with individual "pant-hoots". Male dainty green tree frogs (left) amplify their mating calls through their vocal sacs.

SOUND AND ENVIRONMENT

Low-pitched sound travels furthest because it can pass through obstacles without being scattered. Forest animals, therefore, tend to have deeper calls, while animals in open environments have higher-pitched calls. Temperature and wind are also significant. At dawn, the air is cooler and there is less wind, so birdsong will carry up to 20 times further than at noon. Liquids have a much higher density than gases, and so sound travels four times faster in water than in the air, making effective long-distance communication possible.

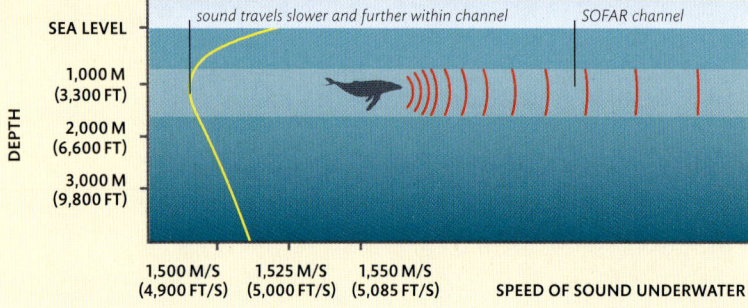

Sound trap The SOFAR (sound fixing and ranging) channel is a layer of the ocean located at a depth of about 1,000 m (3,300 ft). Sound travels at its slowest across the SOFAR channel. Sound waves emitted in this channel are trapped and can travel for hundreds of kilometres.

Vocal virtuoso The vocal skills of birds surpass that of all other animals. This corn bunting produces a remarkable song that sounds like a jangling set of keys. The extraordinary effect of the cold morning air makes the song almost visible to us.

DECODING SIGNALS

Vocal calls are designed to carry specific information. Low-pitched, short sounds often communicate simple, assertive messages. Calls that contain varied volume and pitch may encode more complex information, but do not carry as well. This is the reason that contact calls often start with an introduction of low notes to draw attention, like tapping a glass before a speech. Many animal alarm calls are quite similar. They tend to be short, high-pitched, and fade quickly, making them hard for a predator to locate.

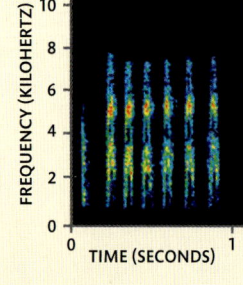
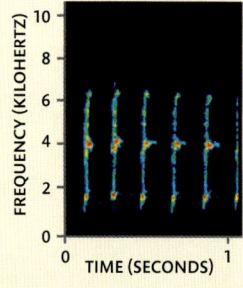
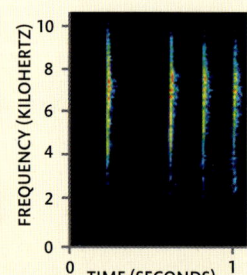

Calling for backup These sonograms show the similar mobbing calls of (from left to right) a song thrush, a blackbird, and a robin. While alarm calls are purposefully difficult to locate, these sharp notes act like a universal distress call, and are easy for allies to locate the caller.

King baboon spider
Hostile hissing
SPECIES *Pelinobius muticus* **SIZE** 12–20 cm (4½–8 in)
DISTRIBUTION Dry scrubland of eastern Central Africa

The second largest of all African spiders, king baboons are impressively powerful hunters. They can tackle prey at least as large as themselves, including scorpions, other spiders, frogs, reptiles, and even the chicks of ground-nesting birds. They are aggressive and, like several other large spiders, can produce a raspy hissing sound to warn off potential attackers. In an impressive display, they bare their fangs and rear up on their hind legs, then stridulate by rubbing the femora of the first and second pairs of legs together. This motion produces an audible hiss, which the spider will continue to make until the threat has passed.

Common field grasshopper
Country music
SPECIES *Chorthippus brunneus* **SIZE** 1.8cm–2.4 cm (⅝–1 in)
DISTRIBUTION Widespread in dry grassy habitats throughout Europe, Asia, and North Africa

Mature field grasshoppers appear in late June to July, sunning themselves in the morning before becoming active. To attract females, males stridulate by rubbing their hind legs against their forewings. This action produces a series of short, monotonous chirps, which are repeated every two seconds. Rivals in the vicinity respond in order to maintain spacing, calling back and forth in a chorus. A tympanal membrane, located in the middle ear, detects the sound and is sensitive to changes in pulse rates and durations, but not to the frequency. Different grasshopper species have different stridulation frequencies, but in each, the tympanum is probably tuned to one specific frequency, making them almost "deaf" to each other's songs.

ANATOMY **STRIDULATION**
Many insects and other arthropods produce sounds by stridulating – rubbing one part of the body (the scraper) against another part of the body that is finely ridged (the file). Grasshoppers rub their hind legs, which have a row of small "pegs" (shown below), against the veins of the forewings. Crickets rub their forewings together, while many beetles, spiders, and ants (see leaf-cutter ants, below), use hairs and filelike structures to click, rasp, squeak, and snap.

Leg rubbing The inner side of the male's femur has small, peglike projections for the purpose of stridulating. The field grasshopper is distinctive as it has relatively few pegs compared to other species.

Oyster toadfish
Courting cacophony
SPECIES *Opsanus tau* **SIZE** 30–40 cm (12–15½ in)
DISTRIBUTION Shallow, rocky waters along Atlantic coast of North America from the West Indies to Cape Cod

These strange bottom-dwellers produce a unique deep hum during the breeding season by contracting special muscles against their swim bladder, which acts like a drum. The muscles can contract nearly 200 times a second, creating a sound so penetrating that it has been known to keep inhabitants of houseboats awake at night. After building a nest of debris, males make their incredible foghorn sound. This attracts females, who swim into the nest to lay their large, adhesive eggs. They depart quickly, leaving the male to fertilize and care for the eggs and also care for the young that will hatch.

Safe lair This toadfish is keeping watch outside his lair and may be calling to attract a mate. Fleshy flaps on his head hide his large mouth, ready to engulf passing prey.

Leaf-cutter ant
Dinner bell
SPECIES *Atta cephalotes* **SIZE** 0.5–1.6 cm (³⁄₁₆–½ in) (depending on caste) **DISTRIBUTION** Forests throughout warmer regions of Central and South America

Most ant species are capable of producing high-pitched squeaks that are just audible to human ears. They do this by rubbing a scraper on their waist against ridges on the surface of their abdomen. Leaf-cutter ants cut and carry leaf fragments, which are used for cultivating fungus gardens, from which they feed. When the ants encounter a particularly desirable plant, they "sing" to call others in the vicinity. The more nutritious the leaf, the more intense the singing. If workers are trapped by a nest collapse, they can also squeak to summon help. Ants sense the sound through vibrations in their legs, but they may also be able to detect "nearfield" airborne sounds through the sense organs located on their antennae.

Hitching a ride As the heavily-laden "mediae" (larger workers) carry leaf fragments back to the nest, they "sing" to attract tiny "minim" workers. These smaller workers hop on board the leaves, protecting the mediae from parasitic phorid flies.

American bullfrog
Deep voice

SPECIES *Rana catesbeiana* **SIZE** 9–15 cm (3½–6 in)
DISTRIBUTION Streams, ponds, and swamps in Canada, USA, and Mexico. Also introduced elsewhere

Many male frogs and toads produce loud croaks or "advertisement calls" during the breeding season, which serve a dual function of attracting females and intimidating other males. The dominant frequency of the call is related to a male's size and fighting ability and studies have shown that, in many species, females prefer deep voices. Male American bullfrogs produce a particularly loud call, typically consisting of three to six vibrant bass croaks. The volume they are able to generate is due to their resonating external eardrums, which amplify their calls by up to 98 per cent. Males gather around ponds and call in choruses, which attract both females and other males to the mating site. As females are only receptive for brief periods of time, competition is intense.

Visible vibration The deep call the bullfrog generates is similar to the bellow of a bull, hence its name. The reason for the loudness of the call is that the sound from the bullfrog's vocal chords is amplified by their large vocal sac, and then resonated by their eardrums. These eardrums visibly vibrate when the bullfrog calls.

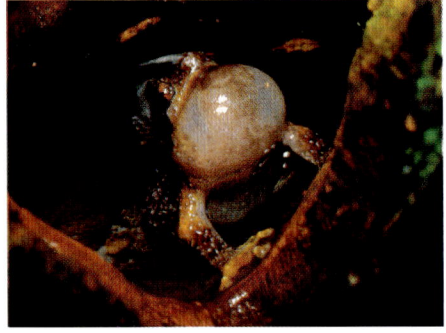

Calling for attention Males call from inside tree holes or artificial holes in posts. Tracking the source of the call is very difficult for humans but, presumably, not for females of the species.

Tokay gecko
Loud mouth

SPECIES *Gekko gecko* **SIZE** 20–35 cm (8–14 in) **DISTRIBUTION** Mainland and islands of Southeast Asia and extreme southern China. Introduced elsewhere

Most reptiles are either mute or can only produce extremely limited sounds, but geckos are a remarkable exception. This is probably because they are mostly active at night, when visual signals are not that useful. Tokay geckos are solitary and particularly fierce in the defence of their territory. They are capable of producing an abrupt, loud bark, or *ga* sound during conflicts and may attack rivals and other species alike, inflicting a severe bite. During the breeding season in early spring, males can be heard regularly giving the distinctive "advertisement call" for which they are named. First they produce a series of rattles increasing in intensity and then a series of 4–11 bi-notes that sound like *to-kay*.

Gape display As well as calling, male tokays use this "gape display" to intimidate rivals, showing an expanse of red tongue and black throat. Their bright colours may be the reason they are valued in the pet trade.

Treehole frog
Natural amplification

SPECIES *Metaphrynella sundana* **SIZE** 2.5 cm (1 in)
DISTRIBUTION Rainforests of Malaysia and Thailand

Treehole frogs are the only animals known to tune their calls to the acoustics of their surroundings. They breed in tree cavities in rainforests and when a male colonizes a new hole, he calls to attract a female. He emits a series of calls to "sample" the hole's acoustic properties, adjusting his pitch with each successive call to try and reach the resonant frequency of the cavity. The vocal range of individuals varies, as do the tree holes themselves, but when a male finds a hole that suits his voice, he ups his calling rate. The "resonance effect" amplifies his call by an extraordinary 10–15 decibels.

Ruddy duck
Blowing bubbles

SPECIES *Oxyura jamaicensis* **SIZE** 35–40 cm (14–15½ in)
DISTRIBUTION Marshy lakes and ponds throughout most of North America; also spread across much of Europe

The male North American ruddy duck attracts a mate by blowing bubbles – or so it seems at first glance. In fact, he has an air sac concealed under his breast feathers, which are dense enough to trap the air between them. As part of his extraordinary display, the male starts beating a vigorous drum roll on his breast with his bill, which releases the air trapped by the feathers and produces a spurt of bubbles on the surface of the water in front of him. Females are attracted by the combination of the visual bubbling display, the slapping sound, and the croak of the male's air sac deflating.

SOUND 427

King penguin
Voice recognition
SPECIES *Aptenodytes patagonicus* **SIZE** 90 cm (35 in)
DISTRIBUTION Breed on sub-Antarctic islands and Falklands. Forage in Southern Ocean

King penguins huddle together in huge colonies for protection against the freezing blizzards of the sub-Antarctic. Chicks learn the calls of their parents within the first month of their lives. Soon after this, the parents go to sea and bring food back for their young. On their return, parents and chicks are able to recognize each other's calls out of the thousands. Despite the cacophony, they can pick out familiar calls in the same way people can hear their name in a hub of conversation. This is known as the "cocktail-party" effect.

Finding family King penguin chicks face the challenge of locating their parents by recognizing and responding to their calls in a colony of tens of thousands.

CASE STUDY **CRACKING THE CODE**
Researchers have conducted playback experiments and manipulated different parts of the king penguin's calls in order to determine how they recognize each other. They found chicks responded only to the bass frequencies, which travel best through an intervening wall of bodies. Just the first quarter of a second of the parent's call is enough for recognition, and the parents continue to make the call every few seconds. It is only when the parent is around 11 m (36 ft) away that the chick will recognize and localize the call.

tail braced against tree for added stability

Red-naped sapsucker
Precise percussion
SPECIES *Sphyrapicus nuchalis* **SIZE** 18–22 cm (7–8½ in)
DISTRIBUTION Forested areas of mountain ranges of western North America

Woodpeckers are unusual among birds as they employ something other than their syrinx (vocal organs) or wings as instruments to generate sound. Red-naped sapsuckers hammer their bills in split-second repetitions against trees to declare their territory. Dead trees are a vital resource for nesting, feeding, and roosting, and by hammering on dead wood the birds advertise their presence. They also appear to pick their instruments carefully, drumming in locations that produce louder, longer-lasting sounds. Woodpeckers that live in urban environments sometimes learn to drum on other more resonant materials, such as metal chimney pots or gutters, to generate an even more attention-grabbing territorial "song".

Revealing sound Recent sonographic research makes it possible to identify the sex and emotional state of this red-naped sapsucker from the way it drums.

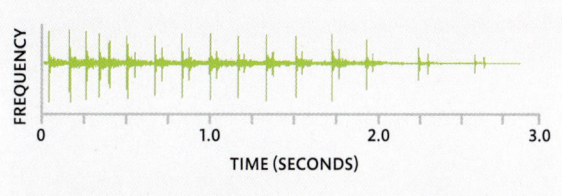

SAPSUCKER SONOGRAM
Each species of woodpecker has its own drumming pattern. This sonogram is of a yellow-bellied sapsucker. Its sequence lasts 3–4 seconds and has a relatively slow tempo, with double beats that slow down during the last part of the drum.

Bare-faced go-away bird
Telling tales
SPECIES *Corythaixoides personatus* **SIZE** 48–51 cm (19–20 in)
DISTRIBUTION Common in savanna woodland in eastern and southern Africa

These noisy, gregarious birds have earned their remarkable name from their distinctive alarm calls that sound a bit like the word *go-away*. The bare-faced go-away bird makes a bleating *go-ha* sound as well as a *ko-wo ko-wo* call, which is repeated by other members of the group. The white-bellied go-away bird has a penetrating *grr'waa grr'waa* call and the grey go-away bird makes a nasal *gwair* sound. From their vantage point in trees, go-away birds are able to see predators approaching before animals on the ground do, and many species have learned to pay heed to their alarm calls. This is often annoying to hunters, as their target is alerted long before the hunter gets close.

Bare-faced cheek The bare-faced go-away bird calls with a series of impulsive wild ringing chuckles, as well as a bleating *go-ha* when disturbed.

Venezuelan red howler monkey
Dawn chorus
SPECIES *Alouatta seniculus* **SIZE** 45–70 cm (17½–28 in)
DISTRIBUTION Wet and seasonal forest of northern South America

The vocalizations of howler monkeys are among the loudest of any mammal, thanks to a highly developed hyoid bone in their throats, which allows the various sounds to reverberate. Every morning at dawn, they produce a chorus of calls that carry for several kilometres through the rainforest. Howler monkeys don't maintain exclusive territories – they actually share their range with other troops. By announcing their presence at dawn and whenever they move, each troop informs their neighbours of their location and so avoids running into each other and competing over food.

Back off Female howler monkeys may pursue mating opportunities with males outside their own group, and so the howling by the group's dominant male may also serve as mate-guarding behaviour.

Gunnison's prairie dog
Sophisticated alarms
SPECIES *Cynomys gunnisoni* **SIZE** 30–32 cm (12–12½ in)
DISTRIBUTION High mountain valleys and plateaus of southern Rocky Mountains in USA, especially Four Corners area of Arizona, New Mexico, Colorado, and Utah

Gunnison's prairie dogs have one of the most sophisticated alarm systems in the animal kingdom. These small rodents require different escape strategies to evade their many predators. Like vervet monkeys, they have alarm calls that refer to specific predators. A bark to warn of a human intrusion sends the whole coterie to their burrows; with a hawk-elicited bark, animals look up, but only those in the flight path bolt. A coyote-elicited bark makes them run to the lip of their burrows and watch the predator. Callers can give even more detail, describing the animal's colour, approach speed, whether it is a known individual, and other attributes.

Friendly warning Prairie dogs live in groups called "coteries". They warn each other of danger, but only some predators cause them to scurry into their tunnel networks – an alarm call warning of an approaching dog, for example, triggers a milder response than one signalling a coyote.

Contact calls Chimpanzees use pant hoots to maintain contact between dispersed members of a community. These vocalizations can travel several kilometres through the rainforest.

Common chimpanzee
Wide vocabulary
SPECIES *Pan troglodytes* **SIZE** 73–95 cm (29–37 in)
DISTRIBUTION Gallery forest, rainforest, and woodland savanna across equatorial Africa

Chimpanzees' vocabulary may include as many as 390 different vocalizations. When food is concentrated they gather in large groups, but much of the time they forage in small groups or alone. Each individual has a distinctive "pant hoot" and responds very differently to the pant hoots of others, depending on who they are and what they are up to. Different types of pant hoot are used in different contexts. For example, a pant hoot with a long wailing climax is associated with plentiful food. They also use a range of screams when threatened. To enlist support, abrupt *waa* barks are given during conflicts and a loud *wraaa* in response to danger. One of the most significant social vocalizations is the pant grunt. Low-ranking chimpanzees make these breathy grunts when approaching those of high rank. In a male leadership contest, one may scream or run away, but the battle is not over until formally conceded by deferential pant grunts.

CASE STUDY
KNOCKING ON WOOD

Chimpanzees drum on the roots of large trees, pounding the buttress with their hands and feet. Adult males often drum and give deep roaring pant hoots while travelling, drumming on trees along their route to show their direction of travel. When trying to locate others, they may drum on the same tree several times, pausing in between to listen for a response.

Variety performance Bottlenose dolphins communicate with each other by using a wide range of squeaks and as many as 186 different whistles. They also use clicks to echolocate their prey.

Bottlenose dolphin

Signature whistles

SPECIES *Tursiops truncatus* **SIZE** 1.9–4 m (6¼–13 ft)
DISTRIBUTION Tropical and warm temperate seas worldwide

Bottlenose dolphins are highly social animals, but do not live in stable groups. Instead, they have a "fission-fusion" society in which group membership constantly changes. These dolphins are remarkable vocal learners and demonstrate faculties of cognition matched only by primates and corvids. To keep in touch with its group, or pod, each dolphin develops its own high-frequency signature whistle by the age of about two. However, they remain flexible and when males form an alliance, their individual whistles may gradually converge to produce a team call. In addition to signature whistles, researchers have identified a wide range of other whistles, 20 of which are commonly used. Flat-toned whistles are used when socializing, while "sine" whistles that rise and fall are used when travelling.

Perfect playmate Rats vary individually in how much they enjoy and engage in social play. Groups of rats with similar levels of playfulness are more harmonious than those with a mismatch.

Rats

Expressing joy

SPECIES *Rattus* sp. **SIZE** Up to 21cm (8⅓in)
DISTRIBUTION Worldwide

Researchers have discovered that some rats enjoy playing and may even take pleasure in certain forms of human contact. When the researchers recorded rats with specialized microphones, it was found that rats produce ultrasonic giggles, well above human hearing, when tickled. Giggles and hopping movements, referred to as "joy jumps", were also triggered when the rats played together. The researchers found that the rats particularly liked to play games of hide-and-seek.

Coyote

Community voices

SPECIES *Canis latrans* **SIZE** 75–85 cm (30–33 in)
DISTRIBUTION Various habitats in North and Central America

Coyotes live in packs of two to seven, but usually travel alone while foraging. Separated pack members will call back and forth to keep in touch. Bouts of calling almost always include both howls and a number of high-pitched barks. Long, pure-toned howls carry further and provide more complex information, while abrupt barks are used for estimating each other's distance. A combination of the two calls allows them to closely coordinate their movements and cooperate in the defence of their territory. The latter is essential as incursions by other coyotes can result in the death of the breeding pair's pups. Mountain coyote voices are deeper in tone than those of lowland dwellers and tend to be more voluminous.

The howl of a coyote reveals information about their identity, sex, and even their motivational state.

Night caller A coyote howl consists of a series of high-pitched yelps followed by a long siren wail, usually heard around dawn or dusk, but also through the night. The well-known barking chorus may sometimes be the work of only one coyote due to their ability to use different intonations.

Touch, vibration, electricity

The delicate vibrations travelling through a spider's web, or the electrical exchanges of fish living in murky waters, belong to sensory realms that we are only just beginning to probe thanks to advances in technology. Tactile signals, although familiar, are also not well understood because they are often hard to quantify.

Sniffing out food This fox cub sniffs and licks its mother's mouth to sense what she may have eaten and persuade her to regurgitate it.

TOUCH

Touch is a very direct, immediate, and persuasive way of communicating: lionesses, for example, nip their cubs as a reprimand, and chimpanzees embrace to show solidarity. It is only effective, however, over a very short range, and so tends to be used by social species living in close proximity, by parents and offspring, or by mating animals. Insects, arachnids, and crustaceans all communicate with touch, but it is most developed among mammals and birds that have long periods of parental care. Various forms of tactile contact between parents and young have become "ritualized", and been adopted by adults as well. For example, adult wild dogs lick the faces of fellow pack members in a friendly signal derived from pups begging for food, while grooming among adult primates probably stems from mothers cleaning their offspring.

Feline affection Licking and grooming keep offspring clean, and have evolved to show affection between adults of many social mammals, such as these lions.

ELECTRICITY

All animals produce a very faint electrical field around them, created by minute currents that carry signals through the body, but as yet only fishes, monotremes, and a few amphibians are known to harness this. Most are aquatic, because water is a good conductor of electricity. Fish sense their environment by picking up electrical signals with receptors along their lateral line, and a few, such as electric rays, use this as a weapon. However, as yet only the gymnotiforms of South America and the mormyrid fishes of Africa are known to use bursts of electrical discharge to communicate.

Turning it off and on In the aba *(Gymarchus niloticus)*, brief interruptions in an otherwise steady electrical discharge are a threat signal; longer breaks indicate submission.

VIBRATION

Until recently, the number and variety of animals that broadcast messages using vibrations travelling through the ground, mud, vegetation, spiders' webs, or water has been uknown. The earliest land animals almost certainly felt vibrations in the ground long before they could hear airborne sounds. Technology, such as laser beams and geophones, can now detect minute vibrations and seismic signals, respectively.

Diverse media Thorn bugs (top) send alarm signals as vibrations through plants. The golden mole (centre) uses ground vibrations to communicate. Male water striders (bottom) tap the water to attract mates.

TOUCH, VIBRATION, ELECTRICITY 431

Bush telegraph The southern green stink bug produces signals by sitting on a leaf or plant stem and vibrating its abdomen against the surface. These vibrations travel along the stem, radiating through the plant, into the roots, and across to other plants at speeds of 30–100 m (98–330 ft) per second.

Southern green stink bug
Feeling the vibes
SPECIES Nezara viridula **SIZE** Up to 1.5 cm (½ in)
DISTRIBUTION Originally from Ethiopia, now widespread crop pest in Europe, Asia, Africa, North and South America

In early summer, male southern green stink bugs, or shield bugs, produce wafts of pheromones to attract females, who fly towards the source. However, pinpointing the male's precise location is difficult, so when the female gets close, she lands on a leaf and starts to vibrate. An introductory pulse is followed by an intense burst over a narrow frequency range and then a burst over a broader range. After a five-second pause, she repeats the pattern. The vibrations travel through the plant and the male "listens" with his feet, stopping at junctions and straddling two stems to gauge the direction of the strongest signal. During the pauses in the female's call, he responds with a regular rhythm of five or so pulses of his own, which encourage her to continue singing until they find each other. If a female is not receptive to mating, she gives a low burst of vibrations and the male stops courting.

Wasp spider
Vibrating web
SPECIES Argiope bruennichi **SIZE** Male 5 mm (³⁄₁₆ in), females up to 2 cm (¾ in) **DISTRIBUTION** Webs near ground in open grassy habitats in many parts of Europe, Asia, the Middle East, and North Africa

The male wasp spider courts the female by drumming on her web with the palps (pair of appendages near the mouth) and abdomen, or by inserting a "mating thread" into her web and jerking it. The frequency and rhythm of the signal identify him as the right species, and suppresses the female's hunting instincts, albeit temporarily, in order to mate with him.

Final fling Unfortunately for the male wasp spider, copulation is likely to be his final act as, in almost all cases, the female will eat him afterwards.

Western honey bee
Waggle dance
SPECIES Apis mellifera **SIZE** 0.3–2.5 cm (⅛–1 in)
DISTRIBUTION Well-vegetated, flower-rich areas worldwide

Map dance As the scout dances, appearing to re-enact her journey in miniature, her sisters gather around her and follow her through her movements.

Bees share information about the location of flowers using one of the most exceptional forms of communication in the animal kingdom – the "waggle dance". Scouts return to the nest and inform their sisters of the distance to, and direction of, a rich patch of flowers. They do this by dancing up and down the vertical wall of the honeycomb.

The scout performs a "straight run" while waggling its body from side to side 15 times per second, and vibrating its wings. It then turns to the left, circles back to the starting point, performs another straight run, then turns to the right this time and circles back, repeating the pattern to create a figure of eight. The distance of the flowers is given by the duration of the straight run and the number of waggles – the further away the flowers, the longer the straight run and the slower the tempo of the waggles. The direction of the flowers is given according to the angle of the straight run in relation to the sun's position. The bees do not have to see the sun since they can perceive polarized light, which tells them the sun's direction.

Giving directions A vertical straight run by a scout represents flowers located in line with the sun. Those located at an angle to the right or left of the sun are disclosed by a corresponding angle to the right or left of vertical during the straight run.

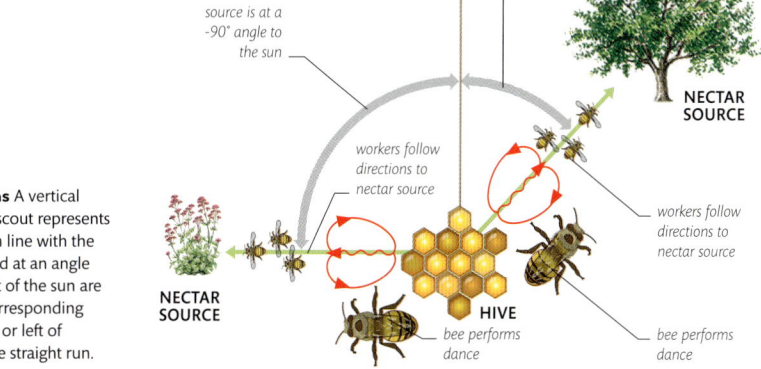

Shore ant
Tandem running

SPECIES *Temnothorax albipennis* **SIZE** 3–5 mm (⅛–³⁄₁₆ in)
DISTRIBUTION Rock crevices, hollow nuts, and other fragile preformed cavities in coastal western Europe

In addition to pheromones, many ants communicate using vibration and touch. The shore ant uses "tandem running" to lead a nest mate along an odour trail from the nest to a newly discovered food source. The recruit frequently taps the front runner with its antennae as they go, to indicate that it is following. If it falls behind and the tapping stops, the leader adjusts its pace. It takes the leader much longer to get to the food in this way, and involves two-way feedback, suggesting that tandem running is an example of teaching in animals.

Ghost knifefishes
Jamming frequencies

SPECIES *Apteronotus* species **SIZE** 18–130 cm (7 in–4¼ ft) **DISTRIBUTION** Rivers and streams in Central and South America

Ghost knifefishes live in loosely associated groups at the bottom of rivers and streams where they hunt at night for insect larvae and small crustaceans. They produce a weak electrical field and, in each group, one male advertises his dominance by giving out the highest rate of electrical discharge – 900 pulses per second. The others have lower signalling rates and adjust them when passing each other to avoid causing interference. However, during a challenge, a rival will shift his frequency to match that of the dominant male, as though trying to jam his signal. The dominant male may zap his rival with a burst of high-frequency charge (up to 1,000 hertz) but if the rival continues to imitate his frequency, the two males will fight, sometimes spending an entire night locked jaw to jaw.

Electric vision An organ in the fish's tail produces an electrical field. Sensors across the body pick up distortions in that field, allowing the fish to "see" its environment.

Alligator
Making waves

SPECIES *Alligator mississippiensis* **SIZE** 3–5 m (9¾–16½ ft)
DISTRIBUTION Fresh, slightly brackish water swamps, lakes, rivers in southeastern USA, especially Everglades in Florida

Alligators are acutely sensitive to splashes and movement in the water, and use this attribute both to communicate and catch prey. This offers a tremendous advantage to an animal that inhabits murky water. In early spring, male alligators establish breeding territories and warn away rivals using head slaps and bellows. The bellow consists of two parts. First, the bull vibrates, producing low-frequency "infrasound", which is followed by the audible bellow lasting three to four seconds. While an audible bellow can carry a kilometre (half a mile) to the human ear, the vibration can travel even further in still waters. It is thought that both the frequency and power of these inaudible signals are related to size, so that males can immediately assess their chances against a displaying rival.

Bellowing seems to alert other bulls and members of the opposite sex to the bellower's presence. During courtship, both the male and female bellow, as well as touch snouts, cough, and swim together – a complex ritual that can last for more than an hour before the pair eventually mate.

River dance The bull alligator raises its head and tail out of the water, waves the tail back and forth, inflates its throat, and emits a low-frequency sound so powerful, it makes the water dance along its back.

ANATOMY **VIBRATION SENSORS**

The thousands of little black dots sprinkled across the alligator's face, especially around the jaws, are known as dome pressure receptors (DPRs). Disturbances of the water surface create pressure waves that are detected by highly sensitive DPRs, allowing the creature to sense potential prey and pick up vibrational signals from other alligators.

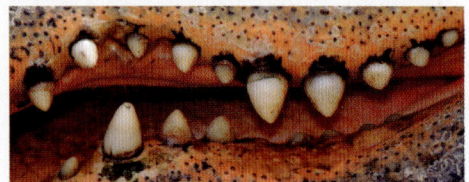

TOUCH, VIBRATION, ELECTRICITY 433

Red-and-green macaw
Preening feathers
SPECIES *Ara chloropterus* **SIZE** Up to 1 m (3¼ ft)
DISTRIBUTION Tropical forest in eastern Central America and northeastern South America

Macaws can live more than 40 years and usually pair for life. A close bond between partners appears to be essential in rearing young successfully – offspring stay with their parents, learning from them until they are three years old, despite being fully grown at six months. During large gatherings in fruit trees or at clay licks (riverbanks rich in minerals) families tend to stick together and, in between feeding, they cavort and play, regurgitate food for each other, and preen each other, all of which strengthen bonds.

Expressing affection Preening helps to keep the feathers of the red-and-green macaw clean and free of parasites, but it also reinforces familial bonds. In fact, when parents stop preening their offspring it's a way of indicating to them that it's time for them to leave home.

Plains zebra
Back scratching
SPECIES *Equus quagga* **SIZE** 2.2–2.5 m (7¼–8¼ ft)
DISTRIBUTION Grassland in eastern and southern Africa

Like horses, plains zebras are non-territorial; the one-male harems and bachelor herds coexist relatively peacefully. Closely related individuals engage in social grooming, during which two zebras nibble and scrape at the other's neck and back with their lips and incisors. Within the herd, mares and their foals and siblings groom most frequently, and low-ranking individuals groom higher-ranking members, which may help to appease aggression.

Back to front By standing nose to tail, zebras can groom each other's backs simultaneously and also keep a look out for danger in both directions.

Common chimpanzee
Staying close
SPECIES *Pan troglodytes* **SIZE** 73–95 cm (29–37 in)
DISTRIBUTION Gallery forest, rainforest, and woodland savanna across equatorial Africa

Highly tactile, chimpanzees embrace, kiss, reach out with open palms for reassurance, or touch other chimps back to give it. Much of their time is spent on grooming, which plays a key role in communication (its function has been compared with that of human gossip). Grooming may occur in pairs or groups, and reveals a lot about the relationships between individuals. Low-ranking chimpanzees frequently groom those of higher rank to appease them or curry favour, and the dominant alpha male is often at the hub of a grooming group. Grooming is also a way in which males establish political coalitions. The alpha male may even groom allies to win support.

Cultural differences In Tanzania's Mahale Mountains, chimps like these use the "handclasp" when grooming in pairs, unlike their neighbours in Gombe, who rest an arm on a branch or hold it up when having an armpit groomed.

Family ties Infant chimpanzees are in close physical contact with their mothers for their first five years. A mother grooms her offspring judiciously during the early years, and older youngsters learn to return the favour.

Kissing On meeting, chimps sometimes kiss, and youngsters frequently embrace and carry infants around. Adults also embrace to show solidarity when excited or frightened, especially during conflicts.

Banner-tailed kangaroo rat
Fancy footwork
SPECIES *Dipodomys spectabilis* **SIZE** 10–15 cm (4–6 in) **DISTRIBUTION** Arid parts of New Mexico, south-central Arizona, and west Texas into Mexico

Banner-tailed kangaroo rats communicate by thumping out messages from their burrows using their enormous hind feet. Each individual advertises its territory with a unique pattern. Neighbours, which are often extended family members, recognize each others' signatures and respond with their own. If a stranger is heard, the foot drumming becomes increasingly vigorous, and they may even approach and challenge the intruder in a foot-drumming contest. Foot-drumming is also used to signal alertness to potential predators.

Big foot The kangaroo rat has huge, four-toed hind feet that are almost half its body length. It drums with the tips of both hind feet, while balancing on its tail and fore feet.

KANGAROO RAT COMMUNICATION

Footdrums are grouped into short bursts called footrolls. Several of these form a sequence. These traces show the foot-drumming signature of four rats. Each has a distinct number of footrolls per sequence.

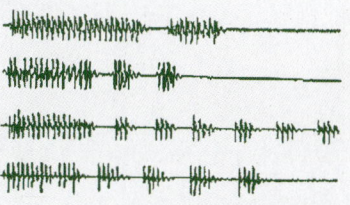

Foot vibrations Elephants can communicate over long distances with "infrasound". Deep rumbles that carry more than 3.25 km (2 miles) in the air and generate seismic waves that may travel three times that distance through the ground. Elephant feet and trunks contain pressure-sensitive nerve endings that detect such infrasonic (inaudible) vibrations.

CASE STUDY
ELEPHANT NAMES

Scientists have discovered that within two herds in Kenya, elephants used sounds to identify each other. Elephants use a wide variety of sounds to communicate, including some deep rumbles that are inaudible to human hearing. Using an AI algorithm, biologists analysed recordings of elephant herds in Kenya's Samburu National Reserve and Amboseli National Park and observed that individual elephants would respond to specific sounds made by other members of the herd, as though they were responding to a name.

TOUCH, VIBRATION, ELECTRICITY 435

Close kinship Bonds between mothers and daughters are strong, but all females within a family group lavish physical attention on youngsters and may cross-suckle each other's infants. The matriarch, recognizable as the largest cow, is the central figure and is responsible for the welfare of the entire family.

African bush elephant
Keeping in touch

SPECIES *Loxodonta africana* **SIZE** 5.5–7.5 m (18–24½ ft) **DISTRIBUTION** Open grassland, scrub, woodland, and occasionally desert, in Africa south of the Sahara

Related elephant females and their young live in close-knit families. When they grow beyond about 10 individuals they divide in two but remain close, and these "bond groups" often meet. Males leave the group at adolescence and travel in bachelor herds or alone, but join females when sexually active, or when large herds gather. Within this fluid society, relationships are complex and elephants use a wide vocabulary, including touch, to communicate.

At close quarters, touch is a very direct, immediate, and persuasive form of expression. A mother often reassures her young calf by embracing it with her trunk or rubbing it with her foot, steers it by gripping its tail and moving it ahead of her, or disciplines it with a slap. Courting elephants touch each other and entwine trunks, and related females reach out to greet each other, or rest their trunks amicably on each other.

Greeting ceremony After even a short separation, related cows reach out their trunks as they meet. It seems that the lower-ranking cow puts its trunk in the other's mouth, like a calf sampling food from its mother's mouth.

Link to life Almost from birth, a calf uses its trunk to explore its environment through touch and smell, and to hang on to its mother when on the move. This ensures that it doesn't get separated from her and also lets its mother know that it is still with her.

Intelligence

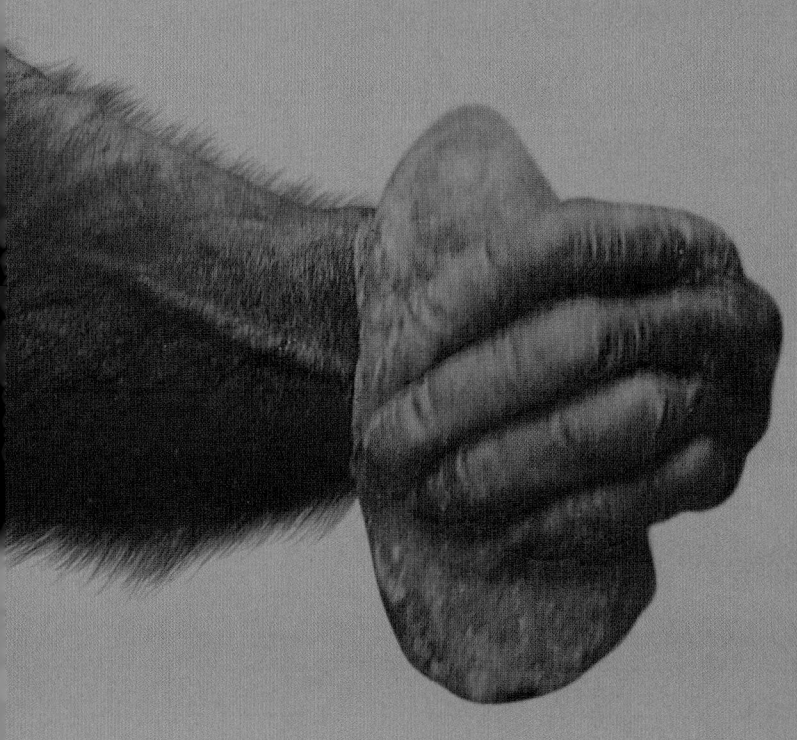

Lost in thought It is hard to know what another human is thinking, let alone another species. But this bonobo (*Pan paniscus*), seemingly lost in thought, is likely to be preoccupied with a fairly sophisticated calculation given that she has a large brain and is among our closest living relatives.

INTELLIGENCE

How do you define intelligence? One view is that it is the ability to solve problems. An animal's life is full of problems, such as finding food, escaping from predators, staying healthy, navigating the world about them, finding a mate, and raising young. The problem for us when we try to assess how clever animals are, is that it is hard to avoid believing that the most intelligent animals are those most similar to ourselves.

IMPORTANCE OF BRAIN SIZE

In general, the larger an animal's brain, the more intelligent the species. However, the overall size of the animal itself is important. For instance, the average human brain is 2 per cent of its body weight, yet the brain of a sperm whale, which weighs around 78 kg (172 lb), is only 0.002 per cent of its body weight. Another factor to consider with intelligence and brain size is how many neurons there are in the brain and how many connections there are between them. The greater the number, the higher the level of intelligence. The size of the cortex (the outer, wrinkled layer of the brain present in many animals) usually relates to social intelligence and, in primates, frequently corresponds with the intricacy of their relationships. Highly social animals have a higher ratio of cortex to brain. Despite this general rule, there is evidence of the ability to acquire and apply knowledge among some animals with minuscule brains (see fringed jumping spider, p.442) that may require us to revise our understanding of intelligence.

Instinctive return Female Atlantic ridley turtles (*Lepidochelys kempii*) take 10 to 12 years to mature, but will then instinctively return to the beach they were born on when it is time to lay their eggs.

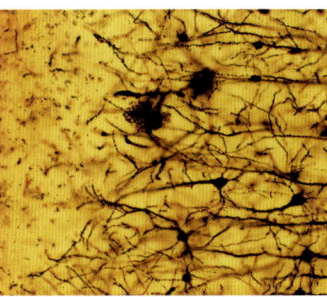

Biological wiring Neurons are cells found in the brain and spinal cord that process and transmit information when electrically stimulated. Neurotransmitter chemicals transfer information across gaps between the neurons.

INSTINCT AND LEARNING

When assessing intelligence, it is necessary to distinguish between behaviour that is innate, or instinctive, and that which is learned. Many animals have instinctive rules for complex behaviour, which can appear intelligent. For instance, solitary wasps make a burrow for their young and catch and paralyse grubs for their larvae to feed on when they hatch. But if the wasp is prevented from carrying out any of these steps, it will continue regardless – an indicator of limited intelligence. Most animals show a balance between instinctive and learned behaviours. Even an animal as simple as an earthworm can show learned behaviour, as the English naturalist Charles Darwin noted more than a century ago, when he observed them "choosing" what kind of leaves to use to block their tunnels. Often it is difficult for us to determine how much of an animal's behaviour is instinctive and how much is learned. A salmon instinctively returns to its river of birth to spawn, but it must also learn the smell of its home and other landmarks. The fish must therefore also have a chemical memory and an in-built ability to navigate.

TYPES OF LEARNING

The ability to learn from experience is judged to be a key intelligence indicator. A number of species are capable of an important form of learning – category learning. This is the ability to categorize events or objects using rules. In the wild this ability makes sense: an animal needs to be able to categorize what is or isn't a predator, and what is or isn't edible. It has been demonstrated through observation and experiments that animals learn in several different ways (see below). Humans have used the aptitude of some animals to teach them skills either for entertainment or for work.

DIFFERENT WAYS TO LEARN

Habituation The animal learns to ignore frequent, unimportant stimuli that do not indicate a predator or food. For instance, rabbits may become used to or "habituated" to road traffic noise.

Conditioning This occurs when natural behaviour is linked to another event. A dog salivates when it sees meat. If a bell is rung at the same time, the dog may learn to salivate when it hears the bell.

Operant conditioning This is used by humans to train animals by modifying their natural behaviour. Such training often consists of rewarding desired behaviour and/or punishing unwanted behaviour.

Observational learning This is learning in which an animal watches another and adopts its behaviour. Intelligent, social animals often learn by observing one another, or sometimes by watching other species.

Trial and error This involves repeated attempts to solve a problem until successful. Chimpanzees may use a twig to fish for termites (observational learning), but work out how long the twig should be by trial and error.

Spontaneous learning This occurs when an animal is able to work out how to solve a problem without trial and error, watching other individuals, or by being taught. It is seen in humans, but rarely in other species.

Time for reflection Animals that can recognize themselves in a mirror are thought to have some form of self-awareness. This Celebes crested macaque is examining its reflection in an old car wing mirror.

PROBLEM SOLVING

Most of an animal's problem-solving ability is focused on the search for food. A number of species, such as Clark's nutcracker, have the capacity to form mental maps. These birds store around 33,000 pine nuts across an area of 400 square km (154 square miles) during the autumn. It's a prodigious feat to remember the location of all their hidden caches. Other species use mental maps to navigate immense distances – elephants in the Namibian desert frequently travel 70 km (44 miles) a day to find food and water. Another sophisticated

Tool-use culture A group of orangutans in Sumatra use tools, such as sticks, to ram holes in termite nests, flush out ants from their nests, or to poke honey from hives.

Counting cormorants In China and Japan there is a traditional form of fishing that uses cormorants to catch fish. The birds are allowed to eat every eighth fish and show their ability to count by refusing to dive until allowed their reward.

type of problem solving is to use tools. Only a handful of species are able to do this. The carrion crow, one of the most accomplished tool users among birds, has been observed using tools in a laboratory, and tiny cameras attached to the birds have also recorded this ability in the wild. One of the animal kingdom's most expert tool users, the chimpanzee, fishes for insects with twigs and uses stone hammers and anvils to smash open palm nuts.

CULTURE AND SELF-AWARENESS

Once thought of as a uniquely human trait, some animal species seem to exhibit rudimentary cultural behaviour: they can learn by copying one another so that a group will develop behaviour that is passed on from one generation to another. This kind of culture may not be seen in other groups of the same species. For instance, orangutans in Sumatra are adept tool-users and yet other populations of these apes do not use as many tools, or else use tools for different purposes. Theory of mind, the ability to understand that another individual can think, was also thought to be exclusive to humans. But it is now known that some species can use deception, which requires a sophisticated understanding of another animal's thought processes. Others have a capacity for self-awareness: the test scientists use is whether they recognize themselves in a mirror.

Capacity for concealment Some scrub jays are able to deceive others. If they are seen hiding their food by other jays, they will hide it somewhere else. "Innocent" birds – those who have not stolen another bird's cache – will not do this.

Purple flatworm
Sense of direction

SPECIES *Pseudoceros ferrugineus* **SIZE** 2 cm (³⁄₄ in)
DISTRIBUTION Tropical coral reefs in the Red Sea, Indian and Pacific oceans, and off the east coast of South Africa

Although they are primitive creatures, flatworms have a brain and nervous system and are capable of learning. Experiments carried out in the 1920s revealed that terrestrial flatworms can remember the location of buried food. They can even be trained to remember the route through a simple maze. In one experiment, flatworms were put into a double T-maze, a simple maze with a choice of turning left or right with food at one end. The worms remembered the route 90 per cent of the time. This is a good adaptation for finding food, but has not been demonstrated in marine flatworms like this one.

Graceful swimmer If threatened, this marine flatworm will swim away with elegant undulations of its flat body.

Mop head The body of this worm is hidden away safely inside its tube. Only its extended mop head of tentacles is visible. The tentacles trap drifting plankton and the food then passes down to the worm's mouth.

Giant feather duster worm
Light sensitive

SPECIES *Eudistylia polymorpha* **SIZE** 25 cm (10 in) **DISTRIBUTION** Tidal pools on the Pacific coast of North America from Alaska to San Diego

These worms are distinguished by their mass of featherlike gills that collect food and also act as gills. They are sensitive to changes in light levels and to vibrations and will instantly withdraw into their tube at a sudden change in background light levels or if they detect vibrations from movement in the surrounding area. This is an adaptive response – a shadow might indicate the approach of a predator. However, these animals can learn not to respond when light levels change in a regular and constant way, indicating that they can become habituated to non-threatening changes in their environment.

Veined octopus
Problem solving

SPECIES *Amphioctopus marginatus* **SIZE** Head diameter 5 cm (2 in)
DISTRIBUTION Coastal waters around Sulawesi, Indonesia

The veined octopus uses large shells found on the sea bed to hide inside or creates a fortress with a number of smaller shells. It has also been known to hide inside coconut shells. If there is no shell available, this octopus has evolved the unusual trick of walking bipedally along the ocean floor. It uses the outer edges of two of its back arms, rolling the sucker edge along the ground as if tiptoeing backwards, and wraps the other six arms tightly around its body. This disguises the shape of the octopus and helps it avoid predators. Octopuses are considered to be among the most intelligent of all invertebrates, able to distinguish shapes and patterns as well as solve simple problems. The veined octopus feeds predominantly on crabs; some species look for lobster traps and prize out their hapless prey.

CASE STUDY **BOTTLE OPENER**

In laboratory experiments, common octopuses (*Octopus vulgaris*) have learned how to open jars to scoop out a shrimp or crab trapped inside. Part of their skill is due to their dexterity, but it is also a result of their distributed brain power: they have "mini brains", or ganglia, in each of their arms, which can operate independently of their brain to some extent.

Similar species The mimic octopus (*Thaumoctopus mimicus*) can mimic other species by changing colour and body shape. It seems to choose which species to mimic according to the threat it wishes to deter.

Protective shell This veined octopus has made its own den inside a shell on the sea bed. From the safety of its protective "walls", the octopus can lie in wait for its favoured prey of small crabs and shrimps.

Fringed jumping spider
Web of deceit

SPECIES *Portia fimbriata* **SIZE** Legspan up to 1 cm (⅜ in)
DISTRIBUTION Tropical forests of Africa, Asia, Australia

This tiny spider has a brain smaller than a pinhead, yet hunts a wide variety of web-building spiders that are much larger than itself, and shows a remarkable capacity to plan ahead and develop new strategies to trick its quarry. For common prey, the fringed jumping spider uses instinctive hunting tactics, but can alter its strategy, using trial and error, against unfamiliar prey or in unusual situations. It has excellent eyesight and when it sees prey it determines which strategy is best. Because it is camouflaged to look like a fragment of leaf litter, it may sit in the web in order to fool the resident spider (web-building spiders often have poor eyesight) into coming over to tidy up, at which point the jumping spider leaps on the resident from behind and delivers a lethal bite. Another method used to lure victims is to move to the edge of their web and pluck the threads with its legs to mimic the courtship signals of that species or the struggles of an insect trapped in the web. If that doesn't work, it will try different vibrations, repeating any pattern that induces the resident spider to move towards it, and quickly learns from experience which vibration works best. In laboratory experiments, the fringed jumping spider has been observed using this kind of trial-and-error hunting to successfully prey on spiders it would never have encountered in its evolutionary history.

> Six lateral eyes provide this spider with a **360°** field of vision.

Trial and error If it comes across the web of an unfamiliar prey, the fringed jumping spider vibrates the silk randomly until it finds a signal that attracts its victim.

Homespun Golden orb-weaver spiders, like this one, spin webs up to 1.5 m (5 ft) wide. A width of under 3 m (9¾ ft) is average for this family of spiders, but Darwin's bark spider makes the biggest web of any species; its webs can be up to 24 m (79 ft) wide and are large enough to span rivers.

Orb-weaver spiders
Planning the web

FAMILY Araneidae **SIZE** Up to 5 cm (2 in) **DISTRIBUTION** Widespread globally, except for polar regions and Greenland

Spiders are a very ancient and successful lineage. Around a third of spiders make orb webs – beautiful geometric traps that are perfectly tailored to fit a specific place. Orb spiders can adapt the size and structure of their webs depending on how much silk they have remaining in their silk glands, to ensure they do not run out of silk midway through the job. But they can also adapt their web according to weather conditions and the size of local prey, learning from near misses, and laying down more silk if their prey escapes. This suggests that they can not only create mental maps to create their webs, but can also fine-tune their constructions according to past experience.

Army ant
Swarm intelligence

SPECIES *Eciton burchellii* **SIZE** 3–12 mm (⅛–½ in)
DISTRIBUTION Tropical forests of Central and South America

Army ants on the warpath can be an astonishing sight: up to 200,000 ants drive through the forest at 20 m (66 ft) per hour forming a column 15 m (49 ft) in length and 1–2 m (3¼–6½ ft) wide. With their ferocious bite and venomous sting, army ants are able to overpower any insect and small vertebrate they find in their path. The colony as a whole shows clever behaviour, a phenomenon that scientists have dubbed "swarm intelligence". No ant general tells the colony when to start the raid or decides in which direction they should travel, yet the raids are precisely timed and the swarm moves in what appears to be a highly disciplined manner. It seems that each ant responds to chemical markers left by other ants and makes a few simple decisions on the direction it will take. Collectively these decisions make the colony function as a unit. Other ant species show similar collective intelligence.

Army on the move Cooperation is the key to success for army ants. They will overcome virtually any obstacle in their path, for example, by forming bridges over gaps or plugging small holes with their bodies to help fellow ants across.

INTELLIGENCE

Pest control The mosquitofish has been widely introduced around the world to help control mosquitoes, as it eats their aquatic larvae and other tiny invertebrates. Sadly, the ploy has failed and the fish itself has become a pest.

Eastern mosquitofish
Counting fish
SPECIES *Gambusia holbrooki* **SIZE** 4–7 cm (1½–2¾ in)
DISTRIBUTION Lakes and rivers in North America; widely introduced elsewhere

Many animals can tell whether one amount is larger than another and some fish species are able to discern whether one shoal is bigger than another. In the wild, this is a useful adaptive response since there is safety in numbers. However, mosquitofishes have been shown to be able to distinguish the size of groups more accurately. Female mosquitofishes prefer to be with the largest shoal and when researchers gave fish in an aquarium a choice of which group to join, they regularly chose a shoal of four fishes in preference to one of three, and a shoal of three over one of two.

French grunt
Fish school
SPECIES *Haemulon flavolineatum* **SIZE** 15–25 cm (6–10 in)
DISTRIBUTION Reefs in western Atlantic from Bermuda to the Gulf of Mexico and Brazil

One definition of culture is a set of behaviours that are specific to a particular group, and are passed on to different groups or generations through learning. This seems to occur among French grunts. When a group of these fishes is moved from one location to another, they adopt the schooling and migratory behaviour patterns (such as the best routes to feeding grounds) of fishes of the same species in their new home. Resident groups of French grunts seem to include a "teacher" fish. When the teacher is removed, the new arrivals do not adopt the behaviour of the residents. It seems, therefore, that the French grunts are truly learning, rather than behaving by instinct or responding to the new environment.

Following the teacher French grunts gather in specific spots in Caribbean coral reefs before moving off to feed. Older individuals lead the migration to feeding spots and young fish learn from them where to go.

Widespread Native to freshwaters along the west coast of North America, this colourful trout has been introduced all over the world, often for angling purposes. It is also widely farmed for food.

Rainbow trout
Bad memories
SPECIES *Oncorhynchus mykiss* **SIZE** Up to 1.2 m (4 ft)
DISTRIBUTION Temperate fresh waters worldwide

Studies of rainbow trout seem to have disproved the myth that fishes do not have the brain power to feel emotions and suffer pain. They have pain receptors that respond to chemicals, heat, and pressure. When rainbow trout suffer painful stimuli, such as being injected with bee venom, they react as a mammal would, rubbing the afflicted area and breathing rapidly. They can also remember painful or stressful experiences. Studies have shown that fishes that have previously been caught make distress sounds when they next see a fish hook or net. Rainbow trout also show nervous and fearful behaviour when faced with a novel object – a useful response to have in the wild.

Corn snake
Finding shelter
SPECIES *Pantherophis guttatus* **SIZE** 1.2–1.8 m (4–6 ft)
DISTRIBUTION Farmland, woodland, rocky hillsides in central and southeastern USA

Scientists have often regarded snakes as unintelligent because they are unable to remember how to negotiate a maze. However, it has been discovered that corn snakes are capable of learning as long as the task makes sense to them – such as finding a dark place to shelter in the heat of the day. Corn snakes were put in a large tub with eight holes cut in the bottom. One, marked with a brightly coloured card, led to a hidden shelter. The snakes quickly learned which hole led to their hiding place, to which they rapidly retreated when a bright light was shone at them.

Day shelter Corn snakes and related species rely on the ability to find places in which to hide and shelter during the day, when they are inactive.

Running the gauntlet Crossing single-file might seem to make each individual zebra more vulnerable to attack from the waiting Nile crocodiles, but it has survival advantages – they can see better on all sides and can move freely without bumping into each other.

Nile crocodile
Waiting in line

SPECIES *Crocodylus niloticus* **SIZE** 3.5–6 m (11½–20 ft)
DISTRIBUTION Waterways throughout Africa and western Madagascar

Crocodiles normally hunt alone, waiting submerged in water, in order to ambush their prey. However, in some places they have learned to hunt semi-cooperatively, which indicates a certain level of intelligence. In parts of Africa, Nile crocodiles have learned the regular crossing points across a river so that they can trap migrating animals, such as wildebeest or zebras. They assemble and line up near these sites to wait for their prey, and seem to act in concert to make a kill.

Socially, crocodiles lead relatively complex lives and relate to one another more like birds and mammals do, rather than reptiles. Most crocodile species have an extensive communication system using gestures, smell, and vocalizations. For instance, a head-slap on the water, jaw snapping, and tail thrashing all signal dominance, while head raising is a gesture of submission. Crocodiles have an acute sense of smell but their chemosensory communication is not well understood. Adults will come to the rescue of juveniles if they hear their distress calls, even if they are not their own.

Green heron
Using bait

SPECIES *Butorides virescens* **SIZE** 35–45 cm (14–17½ in)
DISTRIBUTION Wetlands of North and Central America

The green heron is a patient and effective hunter. As in most herons, its normal mode of feeding is to stand motionless with its neck drawn in, staring into the water. If it spots prey, it makes a sudden, precise lunge with its thick, sharp bill. At other times, it will disturb the riverbed with its feet to stir up invertebrates, fishes, and frogs, which it can then snap up. However, the most interesting technique in the feeding repertoire of the green heron is its use of bait to lure prey to the surface. This bird employs a variety of lures, including mayflies, feathers, nuts, and even bread, probably scavenged from humans or their rubbish. Other heron species have also been seen to use this technique to fish, but not all individuals within a species use it, and the origins of the behaviour are not known. They have learned an association between putting out the bait and seeing fish or other prey come to the surface to investigate.

Laying the bait >>01 A green heron has selected a nut as bait. >>02 It lays the bait on the water surface and waits motionless until a fish or small animal comes closer to investigate. >>03 The heron swiftly attacks and succeeds in seizing its target, a small fish.

>>01   >>02   >>03

INTELLIGENCE 445

Grey parrot
Learning languages
SPECIES *Psittacus erithacus* **SIZE** 33 cm (13 in)
DISTRIBUTION Secondary rainforest of West and Central Africa

One of the most intelligent species of bird, the grey parrot is thought to have developed its impressive communication skills as a result of its habit of living in large flocks and feeding co-operatively in the wild. Most of the research on parrot intelligence, however, has come from studies of captive animals. Grey parrots can mimic and remember a large number of human words and, taking the use of language a significant stage further, are also able to understand the meaning of some words, demonstrating this ability by using them appropriately. They are thought to have the same level of understanding as a five-year-old human child, with the emotional acuity of a two-year-old.

Words and concepts
One grey parrot named Alex learned to identify 50 different objects, distinguish seven colours and five shapes, and understood concepts such as bigger, smaller, same, different, and zero. Alex died relatively young for this long-lived species, so the full extent of his potential linguistic ability was never known.

Alex, the grey parrot, learned and remembered 150 words.

Rock pigeon
Long memory
SPECIES *Columba livia* **SIZE** 29–33 cm (11½–13 in)
DISTRIBUTION Widespread and common throughout Europe; also occurs in Africa, North America, South America, and Asia

As well as having excellent eyesight and the capacity to remember hundreds of images for long periods of time, the rock pigeon is also able to discriminate between different classes of object using abstract concepts (see panel, right). Domestic pigeons also have an extraordinary capacity for homing: being able to return to their nest from considerable distances. A combination of factors contribute to this remarkable ability: recognition of major visual landmarks, use of an internal magnetic compass, and – probably what they rely on most – a memory of the signature smell of the area where they live.

City birds Domestic pigeons have adapted very well to urban habitats and will gather in large groups where humans also congregate, such as parks and city squares.

CASE STUDY **ART CRITICS**
Pigeons are renowned for their ability to distinguish between and categorize objects. In one study they were trained to discriminate between individual paintings by Picasso and Monet, the famous Cubist and Impressionist painters. They then generalized this ability to tell the difference between specific paintings by these two artists, to the ability to recognize paintings by these artists that they had not seen before, showing that they had learned the difference between a Cubist and an Impressionist painting. The same scientists trained both human students and pigeons and found that their ability to tell Van Gogh from Chagall paintings that they had not seen before was remarkably similar. Because it would be nearly impossible to devise a simple rule to distinguish a Monet from a Picasso, it has been suggested that pigeons have a similar ability to humans for categorizing objects or understanding abstract concepts.

Trained pigeons have also shown a better-than-human ability to appraise medical ultrasound scans, identifying the micro-calcifications that are an early sign of breast cancer.

Japanese macaques
Clean culture
SPECIES *Macaca fuscata* **SIZE** 50–65 cm (19½–26 in) **DISTRIBUTION** Subtropical to subarctic forest in Japan (excluding Hokkaido)

Japanese macaques have been studied in the wild for over 50 years, longer than most other non-human primates. They lead complex social lives, living in groups of around 30, but sometimes up to 100, individuals. These monkeys have a rudimentary form of culture, picking up new behaviours from each other. For example, they have learned how to make tiny snowballs in their hands and then roll them along the ground to create larger ones. This behaviour does not seem to have a purpose other than enjoyment, but in some troops this playful behaviour has spread rapidly. Other forms of culturally transmitted behaviour include, famously, the habit among one troop of Japanese macaques on the island of Koshima of washing their food in the sea (see panel, opposite). Another troop developed the habit of taking warming baths in the hot springs of their home territory.

Females have a strict matrilineal dominance hierarchy, though typically an alpha male is in overall control. Often, new behaviours that are taken up by the troop are initiated by the females. Other distinctive features of Japanese macaque troops include regional differences in their vocalizations, or "accents", particularly for calls relating to food items, which they use to notify others of a particularly delicious find.

Carrion crow
Nut cracker
SPECIES *Corvus corone* **SIZE** 47–52 cm (18½–20½ in) **DISTRIBUTION** Open country and urban areas in Europe and Asia

Crows are among the most adept tool users of the bird world and, in Japan, carrion crows have taken this ability a stage further by using vehicles to crack nuts (see below). A similar species, the New Caledonian crow (*Corvus moneduloides*) has been observed in the wild making and using a variety of tools fashioned from grass stems and twigs – for example, to extract grubs from rotting wood. Studies have confirmed the highly sophisticated tool-making abilities of the New Caledonian crow. One individual joined four short hollow sticks by inserting the end of one into the next, to create a pole long enough to reach through a narrow gap and pull out a treat.

Car crushing When cars stop at a red light, carrion crows place nuts on the road. As the lights change, the cars drive over the nuts, and crack them open. Later the birds can retrieve their nuts and access the kernel inside.

Long-tailed manakin
Dance class
SPECIES *Chiroxiphia linearis* **SIZE** 12.5 cm (5 in) **DISTRIBUTION** Subtropical or tropical dry or moist lowland forest throughout Central America

All species of manakin are lek maters. At a lek the males perform an elaborate courtship in front of females, and the male who shows the most impressive display is able to mate with the greatest number of females. Normally lekking involves males competing with other males, but long-tailed manakin males actually cooperate during their display. Usually, two males, a dominant "alpha" male and a subordinate "beta" male, will form a partnership that can last for years. When there are females present, the males display with elaborate jumps, leapfrogging, and "butterfly" flights. The alpha male, who is normally the oldest, mates with the females. The evolutionary advantage of this altruistic behaviour for the beta male is that he learns how to court females more effectively, following a form of apprenticeship. He will eventually replace the dominant male when he dies.

Follow my lead The male long-tailed manakins summon the female by calling. They then leapfrog backwards over a branch and make a butterfly like flight. Once both males have performed, the dominant male will continue the butterfly flight on his own and then mate with the female if she is receptive.

INTELLIGENCE 447

Macaque sauna To keep warm in temperatures often below -15°C (5°F), a troop of Japanese macaques sits in hot springs. The behaviour was started by females and copied until the whole troop was having hot baths.

Follow my leader Even though these "snow monkeys" are the most northerly living primates in the world, they hate deep snow. In Japan's Nagano Prefecture at an altitude of 800 m (2,600 ft), as much as a metre of snow can fall in a single night. One monkey will often lead the way, creating a path through the snow, which the others follow, eventually creating a network of snowy trails.

CASE STUDY WASHING POTATOES

Two new cultural practices were taken up by a troop of Japanese macaques in Koshima. Instead of using her hands to brush the sand off sweet potatoes offered to her on the beach, a female called Imo started dipping them in the nearby river. Her immediate family soon copied her, followed by the rest of the troop. Imo then started dipping her potato in the sea, biting it, and dunking it again – presumably because she liked the salty taste – and the others began to copy her. Later she took to washing wheat. She would pick up a handful and toss it in the water. The wheat floated on the surface, where she could easily scoop it up free from sand. Again, the rest of the troop followed her example.

Tufted capuchin
Tool kit

SPECIES *Cebus apella* **SIZE** 36–42 cm (14–16½ in) **DISTRIBUTION** Variety of forest types in northern South America

Capuchin monkeys are considered among the most intelligent species of monkey because of their use of tools in laboratory conditions. Tufted capuchins in the wild in the Caatinga forests of Brazil have been observed using stones to crack open seeds, and branches to dig for tubers. But the most common form of tool use recorded was the use of stones for digging; the monkeys pounded the earth with the stone with one hand while scraping away the soil with the other. An unusual practice observed among capuchins in the wild is to rub millipedes across their fur. The insects' bitter body fluid acts as a natural insect repellent. This behaviour is similar to "anting", seen in birds, whereby they rub ants over their bodies. The ants squirt formic acid, which drives out parasites. Being able to use "tools" in this way could indicate that these monkeys appreciate the link between cause and effect, a skill that human infants also develop.

Cracking the problem >>01 A tufted capuchin selects a large rock to use as a hammer to crack a nut. >>02 The monkey lifts the rock over the nut that is placed on a stone anvil. >>03 It pounds the nut to break the shell. >>04 The monkey can now get at the edible part inside the shell.

Common chimpanzee
Master toolmaker

SPECIES *Pan troglodytes* **SIZE** 73–95 cm (29–37 in) **DISTRIBUTION** Gallery forest, rainforest, and woodland savanna across equatorial Africa

Chimpanzees exhibit several behaviours that are thought to be key indicators of intelligence, including their sophisticated use of tools. For example, at Gombe National Park, Tanzania, the chimpanzees have been observed to scrunch up handfuls of leaves and dip this "sponge" into pools of water that have collected in tree hollows. They then squeeze the leafy sponge into their mouths to drink. When one chimp started using moss instead, this more efficient method quickly spread to other individuals and groups. Approximately nine types of tool use have been documented in chimpanzees, including the use of sticks to extract insects from their nests. Different groups often use completely different tools and techniques to accomplish the same goals, and resist switching methods unless there is a clear advantage to a new idea. This demonstrates a form of culture that is passed on from one generation to the next.

Various studies have shown that chimpanzees can learn sign language. They can also learn how to count and do simple mathematics, such as addition and subtraction. Chimpanzees can recognize their reflections in a mirror, indicating some level of self-awareness. Some studies suggest that they have "theory of mind" – the ability to understand what another individual might be thinking.

Although chimpanzees are mainly vegetarian, these apes also eat other animals, usually monkeys, for which they hunt co-operatively. Chimpanzees live in large hierarchical social groups. One male is dominant, but other males may form variable coalitions to oust him or to keep him in "power". Their society is more fluid than that of most monkeys; chimpanzees will form friendships and alliances rather than always inheriting their rank. They are one of the few animal species capable of deception, often attempting to trick each other to obtain food or matings. Like most social animals, chimpanzees can be extremely violent.

A variety of tools Chimpanzees have been documented using many different types of tools, from the use of a stone as a nutcracker (above) to the use of a long stick as an arm extension to retrieve a banana from the water (right). The latter tool was found to be necessary because chimpanzees dislike entering large bodies of water (although they sometimes play in the shallows).

CASE STUDY UNDERSTANDING SIGNS AND SYMBOLS

The bonobo (*Pan paniscus*) is the only other species in the genus to which the common chimpanzee belongs. In a study of language learning at Georgia State University, USA, two bonobos, Kanzi (pictured right) and Panbanisha, were taught to point to keys on a keyboard labelled with symbols of a variety of familiar objects and concepts to obtain food or initiate actions. Pressing the keys also produced the word sounds, which the bonobos also learned. Kanzi is said to know more than 3,000 spoken word meanings and, more recently, he has even learned how to play the video game Minecraft.

Termite fishing This chimpanzee has extracted termites – a favourite meal among chimpanzees – from their nest by sticking a twig into a hole in the mound. Chimpanzees use a similar technique to "fish" for ants using grass stems. As in humans, individuals exhibit a preference for using their left or their right hand for these manual tasks.

Are animals self-aware? Whether or not animals other than humans have a consciousness is a subject of much debate. There is solid evidence that chimpanzees are self-aware to some degree and that their concept of self enables them to understand the outcome of their actions and how these affect other individuals. Moreover, they can put themselves in another individual's place and recognize the other's goals and intentions.

Bornean orangutan
Watch and learn

SPECIES *Pongo pygmaeus* **SIZE** 90–100 cm (35 in–3¼ ft)
DISTRIBUTION Forest canopy in Borneo and Sumatra

Although orangutans lead relatively solitary lives, they are very adaptable primates and can copy behaviour they have seen in other orangutans or even humans. One orangutan was involved in a number of experiments, including one that showed that he could imitate 90 per cent of the body movements that were performed in front of him. They also use tools, such as twigs, to poke out insects in trees and branches and to chisel open termite nests. For orangutans, leaves come in useful for a wide range of things – for example, for cleaning themselves, as a napkin when eating messy food, or as gloves to handle prickly durian fruits. They have even been known to use pitcher plants as cups and drink from them. In captivity, orangutans have been taught to use a rudimentary language system with keys representing up to six items of food, and can mimic the varying pitch of human speech, producing new sounds that are not known in wild orangutans.

CASE STUDY SELF MEDICATION
In 2024, an adult male Sumatran orangutan was the first wild animal ever observed to use a plant with known medical properties to treat a wound. He applied a paste of chewed-up leaves, like a poultice. The leaves were from a plant known locally as akar kuning (*Fibraurea tinctoria*), which has medicinal properties including pain relief and antibacterial action. After a few days the wound had fully closed.

All-weather protection Most animals construct nests, but orangutans go a step further, using leaves to make a rain shelter or sun shade, or by creating an "artistic" nest lining from twigs placed with the leafy end sticking outward.

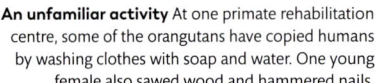

An unfamiliar activity At one primate rehabilitation centre, some of the orangutans have copied humans by washing clothes with soap and water. One young female also sawed wood and hammered nails.

Sea otter
Thinking ahead

SPECIES *Enhydra lutris* **SIZE** Up to 1.4 m (4½ ft)
DISTRIBUTION Coastal water of the North Pacific

The sea otter is one of only a few mammals that use tools. Able to power its swimming with its strong hind-limbs alone, its forelimbs are free to manipulate objects. Its diet consists of a wide range of molluscs and crustaceans, as well as fishes and sea urchins, and it often uses stones to knock shellfish from rocks. It may need to use a force equivalent to 4,000 times its own body weight. It also uses stones to break open shellfish. A sea otter may balance a stone on its chest and pound the shellfish against it, or use two stones at once, one as a hammer and one as an anvil. It often keeps the same stone during a feeding session, which may well imply that it can think ahead, anticipating using it in the future. Although they forage on their own, sea otters usually rest in large groups. When resting, they prevent themselves from drifting out to sea by wrapping themselves in kelp to anchor them to the sea floor, and they will also wrap captured live crabs in kelp to eat later.

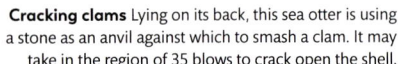

Cracking clams Lying on its back, this sea otter is using a stone as an anvil against which to smash a clam. It may take in the region of 35 blows to crack open the shell.

INTELLIGENCE 453

California sea lion
New tricks

SPECIES *Zalophus californianus* **SIZE** 1.8–2.1 m (6–7 ft)
DISTRIBUTION Coastal water of the eastern Pacific from British Columbia, Canada, to Mexico

In the wild, Californian sea lions are long-lived, social creatures. They travel great distances to breeding and feeding areas and remember their locations. Long known for their ability to learn tricks (see panel, right), their intelligence levels have also been tested scientifically. Scientists have discovered that sea lions have exceptionally good long-term memories, recalling concepts they were tested on up to ten years previously. Sea lions have also been taught gestures to represent words – mainly objects such as balls and rings, as well as colours. So, for instance, one sea lion could understand complex commands such as "fetch the small black ball". Sea lions have also been shown to recognize similarities in pictures.

An enquiring mind Sea lions are flexible and highly motivated learners, able to quickly switch concepts and to use multi-modal learning (for example, linking a particular sound with an object).

HUMAN IMPACT PERFORMANCE ARTIST

Humans have exploited the intelligence of sea lions for many decades. They have long been major attractions in amusement parks and circuses, where they have been trained to catch balls, run up ladders, and honk horns. They have also been taught how to paint, using their mouths to hold brushes, an activity that prevents boredom in captive environments. The sea lion shown here is said to be able to write Chinese characters. The US military have also attempted to utilize their intelligence coupled with their underwater skills to counter enemy divers.

Bottlenose dolphin
Spongy protection

SPECIES *Tursiops truncatus* **SIZE** 1.9–4 m (6¼–13 ft) **DISTRIBUTION** Temperate, tropical, and subtropical coastal waters

Highly social, big-brained animals, bottlenose dolphins live in groups, called pods, of around 12 individuals. In the wild they can show altruism, helping sick or injured dolphins, as well as being compassionate towards other species. Bottlenose dolphins in Shark Bay, Australia, have started using marine sponges as tools. They balance the sponges on the ends of their noses to protect their delicate beak when ferreting out prey buried in the sea floor. This innovative technique was discovered by one female and spread throughout the population, allowing each individual the opportunity to exploit a new food source.

Scientists have taught dolphins sign language using hand and arm signals. They can still follow these commands when their trainer is on a television screen, showing that they understand the images as representations of the real world.

Wild boar
Hungry minds

SPECIES *Sus scrofa* **SIZE** 0.9–1.1 m (3–3½ ft)
DISTRIBUTION Woodlands of Europe, North Africa, and Asia

Pigs have good long-term memories. In the wild, their food is unevenly distributed, which means that they have to remember where the good foraging areas are. The ancestor of domestic pigs, wild boar are social animals, able to recognize individuals and their rank, and have a complex system of communication with grunts and squeaks that are used in different contexts. There is some evidence that they can learn from watching one another. Researchers suggest that, thanks to this skill, combined with their memory and problem solving abilities, pigs of all species are cleverer than dogs, and possibly equivalent to primates in intelligence. Scientists have tested their memory by training pigs to learn the meaning of simple words and phrases. When presented with them several years later, the pigs could still remember the instructions.

Watch and learn Pigs can follow pointed directions from a human to find food, and also show theory of mind, recognizing that other pigs have different knowledge to themselves.

Endless love With bonds that can persist over many decades, it is no surprise that these highly social and intelligent animals deeply feel the loss of family members.

Asian elephant
Burying the dead

SPECIES *Elephas maximus* **SIZE** 2.4–2.8m (8–9¼ft)
DISTRIBUTION Grassland and forests throughout India and Southeast Asia

In the first report of its kind, Asian elephants have been documented burying their dead calves. The calves were found in drainage ditches on tea-growing estates in north Bengal in India in 2024. Examination of footprints and dung at the sites showed that elephants of all ages had contributed to the burials. While it is possible that the calves might have fallen into the ditches and died, the fact that they were covered over with mud, and the pattern of the bruising on their bodies, suggests that their bodies had been dragged or carried long distances to the site. African bush elephants (*Loxodonta africana*) have been observed covering dead bodies with vegetation, and later returning to the locations, but the Asian elephants involved in the burials in this study generally avoided returning to the sites and used alternative pathways.

Glossary

abdomen
The belly of a vertebrate or the hind part of the body of an arthropod.

adaptation
Any inherited feature of an animal's structure or behaviour that helps fit it to its environment and lifestyle; also, the evolutionary process giving rise to such features.

advertisement
Any behaviour by an animal that functions to announce its presence. Advertisement is often used by males, both to warn off other males and to attract females. See also *song*.

aestivation
A bodily state similar to hibernation but occurring typically in the summer – to avoid dry conditions, for example.

aggregation
A non-social gathering of animals, occurring, for example, if many animals arrive independently to feed at a food source. See also *congregation*.

algae
Any of a variety of simple photosynthetic life forms, including both single-celled species and larger forms, such as seaweeds. As the main food-producers in the oceans, algae are vital to marine food chains. See also *plankton*, *protists*.

alpha, beta, gamma
In animal behaviour, terms that apply to the position of an individual within its social group. An alpha male (and/or alpha female) is the dominant member of the group. Beta individuals are the next most dominant, while gamma individuals occupy a lower position in the group's hierarchy.

altruism
Behaviour that benefits others at one's own expense, such as a parent putting itself at risk to defend its offspring. It is argued that true altruism cannot exist in animals since natural selection would weed it out, and that most apparent altruism can be explained as kin selection. See also *kin selection*.

ambush predator
Any predator whose main feeding strategy is to stay in one place and wait for suitable prey to approach. Also known as a sit-and-wait predator.

amniote
A reptile, bird, or mammal. The term derives from the fact that the embryo of these animals develops within a fluid-filled sac called an amnion. This occurs either inside an egg (as is the case in most reptiles and birds) or in a uterus (as is the case in most mammals).

anadromous
Of fishes: living most of their lives at sea but entering rivers to breed. See also *catadromous*.

anisogamy
A condition in which the sex cells (gametes) are of two different kinds. Anisogamy occurs in all animals, with sperm cells (smaller) produced by males, and egg cells (larger) produced by females. Hermaphrodites produce both sperm and eggs. See also *gamete*.

apex predator
A predator at the top of its food chain, hunted by no other animal.

aposematic
Of colours and patterns on an animal: designed to warn potential predators that the animal is poisonous or otherwise dangerous.

appeasement
Any set of behaviours designed to deflect aggression coming from another member of the same species.

appendage
A limblike structure, especially of an arthropod, which may be modified as legs, gills, swimming organs, or in other ways.

appetitive behaviour
Any behaviour of an animal when seeking a particular goal (not necessarily food), as distinct from its behaviour when the goal is actually reached.

arachnids
The group of arthropods that includes scorpions, spiders, mites, and relatives. See also *arthropods*.

arthropods
A major group (phylum) of invertebrate animals with jointed legs and a hard outer skeleton. Arthropods include insects, arachnids, and crustaceans. There are more species of arthropods than species of all other animals groups put together.

asexual reproduction
Reproduction that does not involve sex. Examples include splitting or fragmenting the body, budding off new individuals from a larger "parent", or forming specialized reproductive structures, such as spores. See also *parthenogenesis*.

autonomic nervous system
The part of the nervous system in vertebrates that deals with involuntary processes, such as controlling the body's glands and the muscles of the gut. In mammals it is further divided into the sympathetic nervous system, which tends to prepare the body for "fight or flight", and the parasympathetic nervous system, which acts to bring the body back to normal.

axon
A cablelike extension of a nerve cell (neuron) along which electrical signals are transmitted away from the cell.

bachelor group
A group formed by males of the same species that have no sexual partners. In lions, for example, young males may team up in a bachelor group to displace another dominant male.

Batesian mimicry
See *mimicry*.

behaviourism
An approach to analysing human and animal behaviour, most influential in the early to mid-20th century. Its theories focused strictly on external behaviour patterns and the links between them, avoiding discussion of "unobservable" phenomena, such as mental states.

benthic
Associated with the sea floor, or the bottom of a lake or river.

beta
See *alpha, beta, gamma*.

bioluminescence
The production of light by living organisms.

biome
A large-scale land ecosystem, or set of ecosystems, whose main characteristics are determined by climate. Deserts and tropical rainforests are both examples of biomes.

bivalves
Aquatic molluscs, such as clams, mussels, and oysters, that have a shell made up of two halves joined by a hinge. Most bivalves move slowly or not at all, and are filter feeders. See also *filter feeding*, *molluscs*.

bonding
The formation and maintenance of a strong, mutually helpful relationship between two or more members of the same species. It includes pair bonding, the attachment between male and female formed in monogamous species.

bony fishes
The group that includes most of the world's fish species, except for cartilaginous fishes (sharks, rays and their relatives) and jawless fishes (hagfishes and lampreys). See also *cartilaginous fishes*, *jawless fishes*.

brachiation
A method of movement characteristic of apes, such as gibbons, in which the body is swung through the trees by the arms.

brackish
Saltier than fresh water, but less salty than ocean water.

bryozoans
Small colonial sea-living animals, also called moss animals, that live attached to surfaces such as seaweed fronds. They are filter feeders. See also *filter feeding*.

caching
See *hoarding*.

calcareous
Made of or containing the mineral calcium carbonate; chalky.

camouflage
Colours or patterns that cause an animal to resemble its environment, so that it is not noticed by potential predators or prey (or both). See also *mimicry*.

cartilaginous fishes
A group of fishes, including sharks, rays, skates, and chimaeras, that have skeletons made of cartilage, not bone. See also *bony fishes, jawless fishes*.

catadromous
Of fishes: living most of their lives in fresh water but migrating to the sea in order to breed. Eels are an example. See also *anadromous*.

caudal
Relating to the tail or posterior part of an animal.

central nervous system (CNS)
The brain and spinal cord of vertebrates, as distinct from the nerves supplying the rest of the body. Also, similar concentrations of nerve tissue in some invertebrates.

cephalopods
A group of predominantly swimming molluscs that includes squid, cuttlefish, octopuses, and nautiluses. They have large brains and display complex behaviour. See also *molluscs*.

cephalothorax
The front part of the body of some arthropods (arachnids and crustaceans) when not obviously divided into a separate head and thorax. See also *thorax*.

cerebellum
Part of the rear of the brain in vertebrates, responsible for coordinating the details of complex body movements.

cerebral hemispheres
Paired outgrowths of nervous tissue at the front of the brain in vertebrates. They reach their greatest size and importance in mammals, where they are the main regions integrating behaviour and processing information.

chemoreception
The ability to detect particular chemical substances, a fundamental ability common to all animals. Taste and smell are forms of chemoreception.

chitin
A tough, horny substance that is the main material of arthropod exoskeletons. See also *exoskeleton*.

chromosome
One of a number of structures found in the cells of all animals and plants, each consisting of a single DNA molecule combined with various proteins. A single chromosome may contain thousands of different genes, and between them they contain the animal's genome. There is an identical set of chromosomes in nearly all the cells of the body. See also *DNA, gene, genome, protein*.

circadian rhythm
An internal physiological rhythm in animals with a time period of about a day. It can be thought of as an internal "biological clock", kept accurate by reference to outside events such as day and night.

circannual rhythm
An internal physiological rhythm with a period of about a year.

clade
A group of species consisting of all the evolutionary descendants of a given ancestor. Mammals are a clade, for example. Reptiles, however, are not a clade unless birds are included within them, since birds are descended from dinosaurs, which are reptiles. Cladistics is the approach to classification that seeks to use only clades to classify organisms, and to avoid using other terms.

cnidarians
A major group (phylum) of aquatic invertebrate animals with simple bodies bearing tentacles armed with stinging cells that surround a single opening (mouth). Cnidarians include corals, sea anemones, and jellyfish, and are often colonial.

colonial
Of an animal: living in colonies. A colony can consist of separate individuals, as with ant colonies, or animals joined by strands of living tissue, as is the case of many marine invertebrates, such as corals. Individuals may be specialized for different roles, such as feeding, reproduction, and defence, in which case the colony may behave more like a single individual.

commensalism
Living in close association with an animal of another species, for example by sharing its burrow, without either helping or damaging it. See also *mutualism, symbiosis*.

communication
Processes in which an animal gives out information intended to influence the behaviour of another animal. Most communication is between animals of the same species, and can relate to social life, reproduction, territorial disputes, or other aspects of life. Communication between different species often involves deceit. See also *deceit, display, scent marking, song, vocalization*.

conflict (internal)
The state of being torn between conflicting motivations, such as between attacking and fleeing. An animal often demonstrates internal conflict by resorting to a displacement activity such as grooming. See also *displacement activity, motivation*.

congregation
Any genuine, intentional social gathering of animals, as distinct from a mere aggregation. See also *aggregation, flocking, herding, shoaling*.

consciousness
Roughly, being aware that one exists and of one's physical sensations and feelings. Consciousness probably exists in a number of other animals as well as in humans, although it is difficult to prove either way. Behavioural scientists are also interested in self-consciousness (for example, whether an animal is aware that it is one particular chimpanzee among others).

convergent evolution
The phenomenon in which unrelated organisms have evolved to look similar as a result of being adapted to similar environments or ecological niches. For example, the marsupial mice in Australia look similar to mice found elsewhere, but are not related.

copulation
The sex act in which sperm cells are deposited within the body of a partner, usually by a penis or equivalent structure. Copulation is most common in land animals, where the alternative of releasing unfertilized sex cells into the water is not available. In some hermaphrodite animals, each partner deposits sperm within the other. See also *spermatophore*.

countershading
A type of camouflage pattern in which an animal is typically darker above and lighter beneath. It tends to counter the effect of shadows, making the animal more difficult to see.

crèche
A group formed by the young of several mothers, usually looked after by several adults. The young of penguins and of some mammals form crèches.

crustaceans
The dominant group of arthropods (jointed-legged invertebrates) found in the oceans. Crustaceans include crabs, lobsters, shrimp, and barnacles. See also *arthropods*.

cultural transmission
The passing on of behaviour patterns from one animal to another through learning, rather than via the animals' genes. Knowledge of migration routes in birds and mammals is often passed on by cultural transmission.

deceit
A process in which an animal sends misleading information to others. A bird pretending to be injured in order to lure a predator from its nest is an example. See also *mimicry*.

delayed implantation
The phenomenon found in some mammals here the development of a fertilized egg is put "on hold" at an early stage, before implantation (attachment of the embryo to the wall of the uterus) has taken place. Implantation may be delayed for months, allowing young to be born at a time more suitable to both mother and baby. See also *uterus*.

dendrite
A branchlike outgrowth of a nerve cell (neuron) that carries incoming electrical signals to that cell. A neuron usually has many dendrites.

desiccation
The process or result of losing moisture content; drying up.

detritus
The decaying fragments of dead organisms. A detritivore is an animal that feeds on detritus.

diapause
A period, which may last for months, in which development or growth is suspended; the term is commonly used in the context of insect eggs or pupae.

dispersal, dispersion
(1) The phenomenon in which animals or animal groups leave their birth area for another area. Dispersal usually involves a one-way trip, in contrast to migration. Depending on the species, it is often only young males or young females that disperse. An explosive spread of a species, for instance as a result of a population explosion and food shortages, is called an irruption. See also *migration, nomadic*. **(2)** Dispersion also refers to the static pattern of an animal population in its environment, for example whether it is regularly spaced out or clumped together in small areas.

displacement activity
An activity such as preening, when carried out not for its own sake but at a time when the animal is in a state of conflict between opposing motivations, such as attacking or fleeing. See also *conflict, motivation*.

display
A form of visual communication in which an animal uses body postures, movements, and particular patterns on its body to communicate, usually to another member of the same species. The behaviour is typically stereotyped for a given species, and the purposes can include courtship and threat.

disruptive coloration
Colour patterns on an animal, often bold stripes and blotches, that disguise its shape; a form of camouflage.

DNA
Short for deoxyribonucleic acid, a very long molecule made up of small individual units. DNA is found in the cells of all animals and other living things; the order of the small units "spells out" the genetic instructions (genes) of the animal. See also *chromosome, gene, genome*.

dominance
Phenomenon in group-living animals in which some members of the group have a higher status than others. Dominant animals have more access to resources such as food and mates. Which animal becomes dominant may be settled by actual fighting or by ritualized displays, or in some species status may be inherited.

dorsal
Relating to the back or upper surface of an animal. See also *ventral*.

echinoderms
A major group (phylum) of marine invertebrates that includes starfish, brittle stars, sea urchins, and sea cucumbers. Echinoderms have bodies arranged in parts rather like the spokes of a wheel (so-called "radial symmetry"). They use a unique system of hydraulic "tube feet" for moving or capturing prey (or both).

echolocation
A method of locating and characterizing nearby objects used by dolphins, bats, and some other animals, that involves emitting sounds and interpreting their echoes.

ecosystem
Any community of organisms considered together with the interactions between them and their associated physical environment.

ectoparasite
A parasite that lives on the outside of an animal. A louse is an example. See also *endoparasite, parasite*.

ectothermic
Deriving body heat mainly from the environment, for example by basking in the sun's rays. See also *endothermic*.

emotion
A complex term that can refer to the subjective feeling of being angry, fearful, or happy, for example, and also the bodily and behavioural changes associated with such feelings. Animal behaviour experts usually focus on the latter, which are easier to measure and assess.

endoparasite
A parasite that lives within an animal, rather than on the animal's outside surface. See also *ectoparasite, parasite*.

endoskeleton
An internal skeleton, such as the bone skeleton of vertebrates. Unlike an exoskeleton, this type of skeleton is able to grow along with the rest of the body. See also *exoskeleton*.

endothermic
Deriving body heat mainly from internal chemical reactions, rather than from the environment. The main endothermic animal groups (birds and mammals) are also homeothermic, meaning that they keep their bodies at a constant temperature. See also *ectothermic*.

enzyme
Any of a large variety of different molecules (nearly always proteins) that promote a particular chemical reaction in the body.

ethology
The scientific study of animal behaviour, especially in relation to how animals live under natural conditions.

eusocial
A term applied to highly organized animal societies, such as those of ants and termites. In colonies of eusocial animals there is typically a single breeding female (the queen), with other non-breeding workers and sometimes "soldiers" serving the colony's interests.

evolution
In its straightforward modern definition, evolution is simply any change in the average genetic makeup of a population of living things between one generation and the next. By this definition, evolution is an observed fact for many species, both in the wild and in laboratories. What is often called "the theory of evolution" is based on the idea, supported by various lines of evidence, that such genetic change is not random but is largely the result of natural selection, and that the operation of such processes over time can account for the huge variety of species found on Earth. See also *natural selection*.

evolutionary psychology
An academic approach to psychology that seeks to explain psychological phenomena as functional adaptations that have arisen during evolution. See also *adaptation*.

exogamy
Breeding outside one's own social group. In animals this is commonly achieved by young females or young males (depending on the species) leaving their original group and joining another one.

exoskeleton
A skeleton found on the outside of an animal. The term is mainly used in relation to insects and other arthropods. Exoskeletons combine support with body protection. See also *arthropod, endoskeleton*.

experimental psychology
An academic approach to psychology based upon experiments, in contrast to pre-20th century philosophical approaches. Experimental psychologists have traditionally studied animals in isolated laboratory conditions, in contrast to ethologists. See also *behaviourism, ethology*.

fertilization
The union of a male and female sex cell (in animals, a sperm and an egg cell) as the first step in the production of a new organism by sexual reproduction. In external fertilization, common in marine animals, eggs and sperm are released into the sea to meet by chance, while in internal fertilization, the male transfers sperm directly into the female's body.

filter feeding
Feeding by collecting and separating small food particles from the environment. When the food particles are suspended in water, it is also called suspension feeding. Collecting and sieving small particles from mud and sand is called deposit feeding.

fission–fusion society
A type of animal society in which a larger group splits into smaller groups for some purposes (for example, feeding) and comes together for others (such as sleeping or migration). Examples include many monkeys, apes, and dolphins.

fitness
In evolutionary theory, "fitness" is the sum total of the qualities that give an individual an increased chance of leaving descendants. What makes an animal "fit" can include features such as a male peacock's tail that may be inconvenient for daily life, but helps to attract females to mate with, and thus results in the male peacock having more offspring.

flash coloration
A form of defence in which a normally hidden pattern or colour, such as eyespots, is suddenly revealed when the animal is under threat, possibly startling a potential predator.

fledging
Of a young bird: in the process of developing feathers big enough to fly with. A fledgling is a young bird that has just reached the stage of being able to fly.

flocking
Group-forming behaviour in birds, corresponding to herding in mammals and shoaling in fishes. Its functions may include group defence through "safety in numbers" and more accurate direction-finding during migration. See also *aggregation, herding, shoaling*.

foraging
Activities concerned with seeking and obtaining food.

frugivorous
Fruit-eating.

gamete
A sex cell (in animals, either a sperm cell or an unfertilized egg cell). Gametes typically contain just one copy of each of the body's chromosomes (the structures that, between them, carry the genes), whereas normal body cells have two copies. When sperm and egg combine during fertilization, the two-copy condition is restored. See also *chromosome, meiosis*.

gamma
See *alpha, beta, gamma*.

gastropods
The group of molluscs that includes snails and slugs. See also *molluscs*.

gene
A length of a DNA molecule that contains a particular genetic instruction. Many genes are blueprints for making particular proteins; others have a role in controlling other genes. Between them, the thousands of different genes in the body provide the instructions for a single cell to grow into an adult, and for many essential activities of the body to be carried out. Nearly every cell of an animal's body contains an identical set of its genes.

gene pool
Each of the thousands of different genes in the body may come in several varieties: the "gene pool" of a population or species of animal is a measure of the variety in their genes. If animals are highly inbred, their gene pool may be smaller, meaning that they have less genetic variety to cope with unexpected challenges, such as new diseases.

genome
The complete set of genes of a given species of animal or other living thing. The human genome, for example, is thought to contain about 20,000–25,000 different coding genes, which issue instructions to make protein.

genotype
The genetic make-up of a particular organism. Identical twins, for example, have the same genotype because they share identical versions of all their genes. See also *phenotype*.

gestation
Pregnancy. In animals that produce live young, the gestation period is the time between fertilization and birth of the young.

gizzard
A region of the gut in which food is ground down before digestion. Many animals have gizzards, including birds and some worms.

gonad
Any organ that produces gametes (sex cells). It may be an ovary, a testis, or both at once. See also *ovary, testis*.

grooming
Behaviours that keep body coverings, such as fur or feathers, in good condition. In social animals, individuals may groom each other for secondary reasons such as appeasement. See also *appeasement, displacement activity*.

habituation
The phenomenon in which an animal reacts less and less to a repeated stimulus, such as a noise or a shadow overhead, if no harm follows. Habituation is a simple form of learning.

harem
In animal behaviour, a group of females controlled by a single dominant male, who will defend them against other males trying to mate with them. Harems occur in many species of deer and antelope, for example. See also *polygamy*.

herding
A term used for group-forming behaviour in mammals, especially large plant-eating species such as deer and antelope. Large herds are most common in open habitats that lack hiding places, where many eyes make it easier to spot predators. See also *aggregation, flocking, shoaling*.

hermaphrodite
An animal that is both male and female at some point in its life. Species that are both sexes at once are called simultaneous hermaphrodites. There are also sequential hermaphrodites, which start out as males and become females later, or vice versa. Some species change sex repeatedly.

hibernation
A state in which the bodily processes of some animals are drastically slowed down in winter, with the animals becoming completely inactive. The term is mainly applied to mammals and birds that let their temperatures fall close to those of their surroundings. Less drastic inactive states are called dormancy, while similar states occurring for short periods are called torpor. See also *aestivation*.

hoarding
The practice of hiding food items for later use. An animal may either hide its food in a single "larder" (caching), or in small amounts in different locations (scatter hoarding).

homeostasis
The maintenance of stable conditions within the body, for example in terms of chemical balance and temperature.

home range
The area in which an animal carries out most of its activities. A home range may or may not also be a territory. See also *territory*.

hormone
A circulating chemical messenger produced by one part of the body that affects other organs or parts.

hydroids
A group of simple aquatic animals (cnidarians) that grow as small, branching colonies attached to rocks or seaweed. See also *cnidarians*.

imitation
The ability to observe and copy what another animal does. See also *mimicry*.

imprinting
A type of learning that occurs during a "sensitive period" in the early life of many birds and mammals, whereby the young animal forms an attachment to a particular object, treating it as a parent. While in nature it would attach to its real parent, in captivity young animals can imprint on humans or even inanimate objects. See also *sensitive period*.

infrared
Radiation similar to light but with a longer wavelength. It is invisible to humans and most animals, although it can be detected as "radiant heat".

infrasound
Sound that is too low in pitch for humans to hear, but is used for communication by some other animals.

innate
Inborn, in contrast to being learned or acquired from the environment.

insectivorous
Insect-eating.

insight
In animal studies, a term used especially in relation to learning and problem solving: an animal is said to have insight if it solves a problem by understanding its nature, rather than by trial and error, for example.

instinct
Any unlearned, genetically inherited ability enabling an animal to act in a particular way – for example, nest-building in most birds is instinctive.

intelligence
An ability to think and solve problems in a way that involves understanding, and is not completely automatic or pre-programmed. Although some animal species appear to be more intelligent than others, it is difficult to devise tests to compare the intelligence of different animals in an unbiased way.

intraspecific
Within a species, or between members of the same species.

invertebrate
Any animal without a backbone. Of the 30 or so major groups (phyla) that animals are classifed into, vertebrates (animals with a backbone) form only a part of one phylum; all the rest are invertebrates.

irruption
See *dispersal*.

isolation call
A call emitted by the young of some animals when separated from their parent(s) that tends to bring the parent to their aid.

isolation mechanism
Any feature of anatomy, physiology, behaviour, or the environment that serves to prevent members of different animal species or populations from breeding with each other.

iteroparous
Breeding repeatedly as adults, as compared with once only. See also *semelparous*.

Jacobson's organ
An extra organ of smell, also called the vomeronasal organ, located in the roof of the mouth in most land vertebrates (although apparently not primates). When snakes flicker their tongues, for example, they are transferring molecules from the air to be detected by this organ.

jawless fishes
Two groups of primitive fishes, lampreys and hagfishes, that branched off the line of fish evolution before jaws had evolved. See also *bony fishes*, *cartilaginous fishes*.

kinesis
A form of behaviour in which animals move more quickly in unsuitable habitats, thus tending to end up in suitable locations without directly seeking them. An example is woodlice or sowbugs, which are more active in dry, well-lit environments that are less suitable for them. See also *taxis*.

kin selection
A form of natural selection in which a genetic trait spreads if it benefits enough of an individual animal's relatives (which share many of the s ame genes with it), even if the individual itself leaves no direct descendants. Kin selection is thought to explain the existence of apparently unselfish behaviour in some animals. See also *altruism*.

K-strategist
A species that competes with others by becoming dominant in a stable ecosystem over the longer term. K-strategist animals are typically larger, invest more energy in body growth than reproduction, and have longer life histories than the contrasting r-strategist species. See also *r-strategist*, *strategy*.

language, animal
True language is sometimes defined as requiring grammatical rules and a wide vocabulary, so that new messages never encountered before can be sent and understood. In this sense, some animals such as chimpanzees do appear to show language abilities, in addition to communication skills in the broader sense. See also *communication*.

larva
A young stage of an animal, when completely different in form from the adult. Caterpillars and tadpoles are examples.

learning
Gaining information or acquiring new skills as a result of experience. Learning in an animal may take place in various ways, such as by trial and error, observation, or insight. See also *habituation*, *imprinting*, *maturation*.

lek system
A mating system that involves males gathering communally and competing for the attention of females by performing displays, building mounds, or undertaking other "show-off" activities. Species that use lek systems include many birds, such as peacocks, and some species of antelope. See also *mating system*, *display*.

lineage
Any branch on an evolutionary "family tree", consisting of a species or group plus its forebears, traced back to an original ancestor. See also *clade*.

mangrove swamp
A forestlike ecosystem found on many sandy and muddy coastlines in the tropics, and based on the growth of salt-water-tolerant mangrove trees.

mantle
In molluscs, the layer of tissue, originally forming the upper surface of the animal, that secretes the mollusc's shell. See also *molluscs*.

mating system
The typical pattern of mating behaviour for any particular species. Different mating systems include monogamy (a single male and female paired together, either for life or a single season), promiscuity (in which both sexes have multiple partners), and polygyny (one male with several females). The term also includes the methods by which individuals compete for partners, such as the lek system. See also *lek system*, *polygamy*.

matrix
A term used in various different senses, often with the meaning of "surrounding substance". In bone, cartilage, and other connective tissues, the term refers to the non-cellular supporting material in which the cells are embedded.

maturation
The situation of new features or behaviours appearing as an animal grows older, especially behaviours that are inborn and do not depend on learning. See also *learning*.

medusa
One of the two main body forms of cnidarians. Unlike the other form (polyp), medusas are wide and saucer-shaped, as well as usually free-floating and able to swim. A jellyfish is an example of a medusa. See also *cnidarians*, *polyp*.

meiosis
The way in which a cell nucleus divides during the process of making sex cells (gametes). Unlike in normal cell division, the cells formed as a result of meiosis contain only half the number of chromosomes found in the original cell. See also *chromosome*, *gamete*, *mitosis*.

memory
Scientists distinguish between various types of memory, including semantic memory (knowledge of facts), episodic memory (memory for personal events), and procedural memory (memory for how to do things, such as riding a bicycle) as well as between long-term and short-term memory. Studies of the brain have confirmed that these are real distinctions, with different types of memory associated with distinct areas of the brain.

metabolism
The sum total of all the chemical reactions taking place in the body.

metamorphosis
A process in which an animal's body undergoes a major change in structure between the young stage and adult. Metamorphosis occurs in many species, including crabs, starfish, frogs, and butterflies. In insects, complete metamorphosis involves a total change in shape during a resting phase, called a pupa. During incomplete metamorphosis, a series of smaller changes occur each time the animal moults.

metapopulation
Any population of organisms that is made up of a number of smaller, semi-isolated subpopulations scattered throughout a given area. Many animal species exist naturally as metapopulations.

migration
A regular, often annual, large-scale movement of animals of a particular species from one region to another and back again, often connected with seeking food or breeding sites. See also *dispersal*, *nomadic*.

mimicry
The phenomenon in which one species of animal has evolved to look very similar to another unrelated animal; the assumption is that the mimicking animal gains benefit from the resemblance, especially via predators avoiding it. Where a harmless animal mimics a dangerous or poisonous one, it is called Batesian mimicry; where two or more dangerous species resemble each other, Mullerian mimicry. See also *imitation*.

mitosis
The process by which chromosomes are copied and shared out during normal cell division. The two cells that are produced during mitosis have the same number of chromosomes as the original cell. See also *chromosome*, *meiosis*.

mobbing
The harassing of a predator by a group of its potential prey, for example of a hawk by a group of small birds.

molluscs
A major group (phylum) of invertebrate animals that includes the gastropods (snails and slugs), bivalves (clams and relatives), and cephalopods (octopuses, squid, and relatives). Molluscs are soft-bodied and typically have hard shells, though some subgroups have lost their shell during their evolution.

montane
Relating to mountains, and especially to upland habitats where trees can still grow – that is, habitats lying below the tree line.

morph
A distinctive form of a species that displays a visual or behavioural difference to other populations of the same species.

motivation
A mental or bodily condition (or both) within an animal causing it to do something; also, the goal towards which the animal's activity is aimed. See also *conflict*.

Mullerian mimicry
See *mimicry*.

musth
A phenomenon in which some male animals (especially elephants and camels) become aggressive at a particular time of year. Musth is caused by increased male sex hormones and is related to the breeding cycle.

mutualism
A close relationship between two different species in which both benefit.

natural selection
The evolutionary process by which the environment favours the fittest individuals in a given population, weeding out those that are less fit. Since fitness is partly inherited, this should result in a population or species changing genetically over time and (other things being equal) becoming better adapted to their environment. See also *fitness*.

neoteny
See *paedomorphosis*.

nerve net
A netlike arrangement of individually connected nerve cells (neurons), without a central brain. Some simple invertebrate animals rely only on nerve nets, but still show quite sophisticated behaviour.

neuron
A nerve cell. A simple neuron consists of a rounded cell body, branchlike outgrowths called dendrites that carry incoming electrical signals to the neuron, and a single cablelike extension, called an axon, that transmits outgoing messages. In practice, however, many neurons are more complex than this.
See also *dendrite*.

neurotransmitter
Any of various chemical substances released by nerve cells that stimulate other nerve cells or muscles. Drugs such as antidepressants often work by affecting the amounts of different neurotransmitters active in the brain. See also *neuron*, *synapse*.

niche
Roughly, the ecological role that an animal or other living thing plays; also the role itself (for example "small, tree-living insect-eater"). Ecological theory says that no two species can occupy exactly the same niche, because one should out-compete the other.

niche splitting
The phenomenon in which an animal takes over part of the niche of another animal. For example, an invading bird species may outcompete a native bird when hunting insects low down in a tree, but the native bird may still be at an advantage when hunting higher up; the original niche therefore becomes "split".

nomadic
Of an animal: wandering widely and irregularly as part of its lifestyle (for example, in response to food shortages), as distinct from undertaking regular migrations. See also *migration*.

oestrous cycle
A regular cycle that occurs in the bodies of non-pregnant female mammals: the length of the cycle varies from days to months depending on the species. Each cycle includes a short period called oestrus, or being "in heat", where the female is fertile and sexually receptive. The menstrual cycle of women and other female primates is a modified oestrous cycle, but with sexual receptivity not limited to a short period.

omnivore
Literally, "eating all". An animal whose natural diet includes a wide variety of animal and vegetable food.

ontogeny
The development of any life form from individual cell up to adult.

operculum
A term with various applications in zoology, all related to the original Latin meaning of "covering" or "lid". It can mean: the horny or calcareous disc used by many snails to shut themselves into their shells; the flaps that cover the gills of bony fishes and tadpoles; or any of various other structures. An opercular cavity is the space beneath the operculum of a fish or tadpole.

opposable
Of a thumb or other digit: able to be pressed against other digits of the same hand or foot, allowing objects to be grasped.

orientation
Accurately keeping track of one's direction or position in the environment. Different animals have different ways of orientating themselves (often using more than one at a time). Examples include counting the number and angle of the steps they take (some ants), observing the sun, moon, and stars, and detecting the Earth's magnetic field. See also *migration*.

ovary
An organ in female or hermaphrodite animals that produces egg cells. It usually has other functions such as producing sex hormones that affect the animal's body.

oviduct
A tubelike anatomical structure that conveys eggs from an animal's ovary. In mammals, the oviduct is highly modified, with part of it expanded to form the uterus, or womb.

oviparous
Producing eggs, as distinct from live young. See also *ovoviviparous*, *viviparous*.

ovipositor
An egg-laying tube extending out from the body of some female animals, especially in insects.

ovoviviparous
Producing eggs that are allowed to hatch within the female's body, so that live young are produced. See also *oviparous*, *viviparous*.

paedomorphosis
Also called *neoteny*, an evolutionary trend in which a larval or juvenile stage becomes sexually mature, and no longer develops into the original "adult"; also, the retention of formerly juvenile characteristics into adulthood.

parasite
Any organism that lives in or on the body of a organism and feeds off it for an extended period. See also *ectoparasite*, *endoparasite*.

parasitoid
An animal that, while a larva, feeds on or inside another animal, usually killing this host, before emerging to become a mature, free-living adult. Most parasitoids are insects.

parasympathetic nervous system
See *autonomic nervous system*.

parthenogenesis
Literally "virgin birth". Reproduction from an unfertilized egg cell. Females of some invertebrates, such as aphids, produce young parthenogenetically only during the summer months, when food is abundant. A few species always reproduce in this way, and form all-female populations. Unfertilized parthenogenetic eggs typically already contain two copies of each chromosome. See also *gamete*.

pelagic
Associated with the waters of the open ocean, distant from both the shore and the sea bottom.

phenotype
The sum of the observable characteristics of an individual organism. For example, identical twins, having the same genetic makeup (genotype), may not look identical because of differences in diet or other aspects of lifestyle. See also *genotype*.

pheromone
An odour produced to communicate with others of the same species – to attract the opposite sex, for example.

phylogeny
The pattern of evolutionary history of a species or group of species, or of an individual feature such as the eye. Phylogenetic classification uses methods such as cladistics to classify animals based on their evolutionary history. See also *clade*.

phylum (pl. phyla)
The highest-level grouping in the classification of the animal kingdom. Each phylum has a unique basic body plan. Molluscs, arthropods, and echinoderms are examples of phyla.

placenta
A fleshy structure, rich in blood vessels, that develops on the wall of the uterus during pregnancy in most mammals. It connects the growing embryo to the mother and allows nutrition and waste products to pass between the two. A similar structure is found in some other animals such as sharks.

plankton
Marine or freshwater life-forms living in open water that cannot swim strongly and so drift with the currents.

play
Activities that are not immediately useful, but are seemingly done just for fun. They are associated mainly with young animals, and usually interpreted as being useful in practising skills for later life, or for learning about the environment.

polarized light
Light waves that all vibrate in one particular direction or plane. Some animals can detect polarized light coming from the sun or sky, helping them to navigate.

polygamy
Any mating system in which males or females or both have multiple sex partners. The term is sometimes used specifically to mean a system where one male controls and mates with a number of females, which is more strictly called polygyny. Where only females have multiple partners it is called polyandry; where both sexes do, promiscuity. See also *mating system*.

polyp
One of two main body forms of cnidarians (the other form being a medusa). A sea anemone or coral animal is a polyp. Polyps are typically tubular in form and attached at their base. See also *cnidarians, medusa*.

prehensile
Capable of grasping. The tails of many monkeys are prehensile, for example.

problem solving
Achieving a particular goal when the method of doing so is not immediately obvious. See also *insight, intelligence*.

proteins
Molecules found in the body, consisting of long, folded strands made up of small units called amino acids. Proteins are vital to life, and there are thousands of different kinds. Nearly all enzymes are proteins, as is the horny substance that makes up hair and nails. See also *enzyme*.

protists
A wide grouping of often unrelated, mainly microscopic organisms, traditionally classified as a single kingdom. Protists are single-celled, and include algal forms, which photosynthesize, and protozoans, which do not. Their cells contain nuclei, like the cells of animals and plants, but unlike those of bacteria. See also *algae*.

reflex
An involuntary response in the nervous system to certain stimuli, for example the "knee-jerk" response in humans. Some reflexes, called conditioned reflexes, can be modified by learning.

reproductive investment
The amount of effort – in terms of time or food resources, for example – that parents devote to reproduction, or to their individual offspring.

respiration
(1) Breathing. (2) Also called cellular respiration, the biochemical processes within cells that break down food molecules to provide energy, usually by combining the food molecules with oxygen.

ritualization
An evolutionary process whereby an activity originally done for practical reasons – for example, grooming – comes to acquire a secondary function in communication. Many animal displays contain ritualized versions of other behaviours.

r-strategist
A species that survives and competes by devoting itself to prolific reproduction ("r") rather than to large body size. Such species typically have short life cycles and do well in less stable environments. See also *K-strategist, strategy*.

ruminant
A mammal such as a cow, antelope, or deer with a stomach in several compartments. The first compartment, the rumen, contains micro-organisms that partially digest the animal's usually grassy diet, whose food value would not otherwise be available to the animal.

rut
The breeding season of deer, often occurring in the autumn. The rut, or rutting season, is marked by intense rivalry between males. It often involves roaring ("rut" is an old word for roar) and fighting. The term may also be applied to the breeding seasons of other hoofed mammals.

satellite male
A male animal living unobtrusively within the territory of a larger or more dominant male, seeking the opportunity to mate with females that are attracted by the dominant animal.

scavenger
An animal that feeds by eating the remains of other animals, such as those killed and left by a predator.

scent marking
The deposition of odours by an animal onto the environment, or sometimes onto itself or another animal. The odours are usually produced by specialized scent glands. They may be used to mark territory, but can also have other functions such as creating "landmarks" to follow after dark.

search image
A "mental picture" that predatory animals seem capable of developing, which helps them recognize a particular prey species.

selfish-gene theories
Evolutionary theories emphasizing that the individual genes of an organism may tend to favour their own spread, rather than any overall "good" of the individual, or of the secies as a whole. See also *altruism, kin selection*.

semelparous
Programmed to breed only once before dying. Examples include salmon, octopuses, and many insects. See also *iteroparous*.

sensitive period
A period in the life of a young animal in which it is particularly receptive to learning certain skills or information, such as details of its parents' bird song, in a young bird. See also *imprinting*.

sexual dimorphism
The condition in which the males and females of a species differ obviously in appearance (for example, in colour, shape, or size).

sexual selection
A type of natural selection in which a feature has developed solely because of its advantages in furthering sexual reproduction. The two main types are male rivalry – resulting, for example, in the evolution of large antlers in male deer for fighting each other with – and female choice, in which features such as the male peacock's tail have apparently evolved because they attract females. In both cases, the features may be a nuisance or disadvantage for the rest of the animal's lifestyle.

shoaling
The tendency of many fish species to gather together in large groups. Also known as schooling, the shoaling is probably done for a number of reasons, including confusing a predator trying to pick out one individual target among many. Shoals formed by sea mammals, such as dolphins, tend to have other functions, such as cooperative hunting. See also *aggregation, flocking, herding*.

social insects
Insects that live in colonies in complex societies. The main social insects are wasps, bees, ants, and termites. See also *eusocial*.

sociobiology
The study of the biological bases of social behaviour, especially in an ecological and evolutionary context.

song
In studies of birds, "song" refers to a specific kind of communication distinct from other bird calls. The main purposes of bird songs, which are usually uttered by males, are thought to be territorial defence against rivals and attraction of a mate. See also *vocalization*.

spermatophore
A protective package containing sperm, produced by some animals including octopuses and spiders. Depending on the species, it is either transferred directly to the female or left for her to pick up.

sperm competition
Literally, the competition between sperm (of different males) to fertilize a female's egg cells within her body. Sperm competition is thought to be the evolutionary force behind many features of animals, such as the size of the testes in different species.

spiracle
In some fishes, an opening behind the eye that lets water flow into the gills. In insects, an opening on the thorax or abdomen that lets air into the tracheal system.

sporocyst
A non-moving larval stage in some parasitic worms. Several embryos grow within each sporocyst, each developing into the next larval stage – part of the process in which one egg gives rise to many adult worms.

strategy
As used in biology, an overall pattern of living shaped by evolution that helps an organism to survive (more fully, evolutionary strategy); it does not imply conscious thought. Different animals typically have different strategies: see for example *K-selection*, *r-selection*.

stress
An altered bodily state in an animal, especially a vertebrate, resulting from exposure to threatening or painful stimuli. Stress typically involves changes in the body's hormones and alterations in the animal's behaviour.

supernormal stimulus
A stimulus greater than anything of its kind found in nature. For example, a male butterfly may find an unnaturally large model female more attractive than the real thing.

symbiosis
A close living relationship between two species, that may benefit both animals involved, or may be more exploitative. See also *commensalism*, *mutualism*, *parasite*.

sympathetic nervous system
See *autonomic nervous system*.

synapse
A close contact between two nerve cells (neurons) allowing information to be passed between them. Synapses can either be electrical (the information is transmitted electrically) or chemical (chemicals called neurotransmitters are released from one neuron and stimulate the next). See also *neuron*, *neurotransmitter*.

syrinx
The sound-producing organ of birds. In contrast to the larynx of mammals, the syrinx is situated at the bottom of the trachea (windpipe).

tactile
Relating to touch.

taxis
A directed movement of an animal towards a particular place. See also *kinesis*.

teneral
A term applied to a newly emerged adult insect in which the outer covering (exoskeleton) is still soft and the colours are yet to develop fully.

territory
A particular area or section of habitat defended by an animal or group of animals against rivals, usually of the same species. See also *home range*.

testis
An organ in male or hermaphrodite animals that produces sperm cells. It usually has other functions such as producing sex hormones, which affect the animal's own body.

thorax
The chest region of land vertebrates, containing the heart and lungs; also the middle body division of insects and other arthropods.

threat display
A form of display performed by an animal that is threatening aggression. The threat may be directed against members of the same species or against other species. See also *display*.

tool
An external object, such as a twig, used by an animal for a particular purpose. Some bird and mammal species regularly use tools, and may trim or alter them to make them more effective.

trachea
The windpipe of vertebrates; also, any of the air tubes in insects and other land arthropods.

tunicates
A group of mainly filter-feeding marine invertebrates related to backboned animals (vertebrates). They include both attached forms (sea squirts) and others that drift in the plankton.

ultrasound
Sound too high in pitch for humans to hear, although other animals may be able to hear it.

ultraviolet
Radiation similar to light but with a shorter wavelength. It is invisible to humans but can be seen by other animals, including many insects and birds.

unken reflex
A defensive posture adopted by many frogs and other amphibians, in which brightly colored skin, usually on the underside, is exposed to warn a predator that the animal is distasteful.

uterus
In mammals, the enlarged part of the female reproductive tract in which the young develop before birth.

ventral
Relating to the lower surface or belly of an animal. See also *dorsal*.

vertebrate
Any animal with a backbone, including amphibians, reptiles, birds, mammals, and fishes. See also *invertebrate*.

viviparous
Giving birth to live young, especially when nourished by a placenta or similar structure, rather than developing from eggs hatched within the female's body. See also *oviparous*, *ovoviviparous*, *placenta*.

vocalization
Uttering sounds by means of a vocal organ, such as the larynx of mammals and the syrinx of birds. Animals also make use of non-vocalized sounds, for example the drumming of woodpeckers. See also *song*, *syrinx*.

vomeronasal organ
See *Jacobson's organ*.

worms
Any of various, usually non-swimming, invertebrate animals that are long, slender, and flexible, and lack shells. There are several major groups (phyla) of worms, including flatworms, roundworms, and segmented worms, such as earthworms and their relatives.

Index

Page numbers in **bold** indicate illustrated references.

A

Abudefduf saxatilis **368**
Acanthostega **17**
Acanthurus
   leucosternon **156**
Accipiter gentilis **342**
Acinonyx jubatus **203**
acorn woodpecker **158**
acoustic signals, communication 411
Acrocephalus palustris **377**
Acropyga sauteri 228
Adelphobates galactonotus **253**
adders **304**
   Peringuey's desert **103**, **194-5**
   African puff **288**
Aegithalos caudatus **140**, **403**
Aeoliscus strigatus **272**
aerodynamics, wings **60**
aestivation 103
Aetobatus narinari **394**
African blue tailed skink **254**
African bombardier beetle **249**
African buffalo **161**, **299**
African bullfrog **368**
African bush elephant **385, 407, 434-5**, 453
   trunks **385**
   family groups **407**,
   keeping in touch **434-5**
   communication 435
   touch **435**
African elephant **263**
   aggression **263**
African foam grasshopper **249**
African forest elephant **112-3**
African harrier-hawk **166**
African land snail **88**
African mound-building termites **134**
African puff adder **288**
African white-backed vulture **222**
African wild dog **206-7**, **208**
afrotherian mammals 39
Agama agama **324-5**
agamas
   red-headed rock **324-5**
   southern rock **78-9**
Agelaius phoeniceus **326**
Agelena consociata **391**
aggression, territorial **107, 110-11**, 263
agriculture, dung beetles 220
Ailuropoda melanoleuca **160, 331**
air-conditioning, in termite mounds **134**
alarm calls 411, 424
albatrosses 61
   black-browed **108-9, 221**
   snowy **123**
   southern royal **306**
Alcedo atthis **198-9**
Alces alces **307, 375**
alien introductions 252
allergies, dust mites 219
Alex, grey parrot **445**
allied cowrie **264**
alligator **69, 432**
Alligator mississippiensis **432**
alligator snapping turtle **189**
Allochrocebus solatus **422**
allomerus ant **181**
Allomerus decemarticulatus **181**
Alopex lagopus **203**
Alouatta seniculus **428**
Alpheus randalli **248**
Alpine newt **334, 369**
Alytes
   muletensis **359**
Amazon river dolphin **212, 333**
Amazonian giant centipede **179**
amber snail **350**
Amblotherium **18**
Amblyeleotris yanoi **248**
Amblyornis inornatus **140**
Amblyrhynchus cristatus **156-7**
Ambystoma
   mexicanum **359**
   tigrinum **304**
American bison **385**
American bullfrog **426**
American cliff swallow **402**
American cockroach **220**
American eel 120
American lobster **163**
American moon moth **68**
American oystercatcher **173**
American robin **20, 349**
amniotes 29
amphibians
   classification **23, 29, 32-3**
   communication 424
   courtship 320
   defences 67
   evolution 17-19
   gills **75**
   mating 300, 334
   metamorphosis 358-9
   respiration 65
   warning colours **245**
Amphioctopus marginatus **441**
Amphiprion ocellaris **251**
amplexus 136, **338-9**, 340
ampullae of Lorenzini **96**, 183, 221
Amur tiger **111**
anatomy **42-71**
   body coverings **64-7**
   burrowing, slithering and sliding **58-9**
   climbing and leaping **56-7**
   feathers **70**
   flying and gliding **60-61**

anatomy contd.
   fur, hair, and bristles **71**
   scales **68-9**
   skeletons and muscles **44-51**
   swimming **62-3**
   walking and running **54-5**
Anax
   imperator **351**
   junius **118**
   parthenope **179**
Anaxyrus cognatus **304**
Andean cock-of-the-rock **317**
Andean condor **61, 108**
Anderson's spiny crocodile newt **252**
Androctonus crassicauda **248**
anemonefish, false clown **251**
anemones 46, **230, 296, 412**
   cloak **248**
   jewel **297**
angelfishes, emperor **327**
anglerfish, soft leafvent **337**
Anguilla
   anguilla **120**
   rostrata 120
anguimorph lizards 35
Anguis fragilis **316**
animals, definition 13
anole lizards **416**
   ground **314-5**
Anomalops katoptron **282**
Anser indicus **123**
Antarctic sea urchin **152**
anteaters
   giant **202**
antechinus, brown **342**
Antechinus stuartii **342**
antelopes 57
antennae **86, 412**
Antennarius striatus **183**
Anthopleura elegantissima **412**
Antilope cervicapra **333**
antlers
   deer **318**
   flies **312-3**
antlion larva, giant **180**
ants 260
   allomerus ant **181**
   army ant **442**
   carpenter ants **230**
   colonies 106
   communication 413
   defences 244
   driver ants **181**
   fire ants **336**
   honeypot ant **154-5**
   leaf-cutter ant **425**
   Malaysian giant ant **106-7**
   Myrmica sabuleti **366**
   pavement ant **394**
   slave-making ant **394**
   red wood ant **281**
   sound production 93
   weaver ants **130, 135, 413**
Aotus **436**
apes *see* primates

aphid galls **105**
aphids **154-5, 228, 230, 296**
   poplar petiole gall **105**
Apis
   cerana 181, **281**
   mellifera **135, 153, 392-3, 431**
aposematic coloration 253
Aptenodytes
   forsteri **360-61**
   patagonicus **398-9, 427**
Apteronotus **432**
Apteryx
   australis lawryi **193**
Apus
   apus **342**
Ara chloropterus **167, 433**
arachnids
   communication 430
Arachnocampa tasmaniensis **181**
Archaeopteryx **18**
archerfish, banded **183**
Archimylacris **17**
architects, animal **130-43**
archosaurs 29, 34
Arctic fox **203, 276-7**
Arctic tern 116
Ardea cinerea **236, 420**
Argiope
   aurantia **133**
   bruennichi **431**
Argonauta nodosus **132**
argonaut, knobby 132
   see also paper nautilus
Argyroneta aquatica **132**
Aristotle's lantern **152**
armadillo lizard **254**
armadillos **50**, 68
   three-banded **260**
armhook squid, clawed **365**
armour, defences **245**
army ant **442**
arthropods
   classification 24, **26-7**
   communication 411, 424
   evolution 16
   eyes **88-9**
   joints 45
   sense of smell 86
   skeletons 47
   sound production 93
   touch receptors 84
Artibeus lituratus **160**
asexual reproduction 295, **296**
Asian elephant **453**
   burying the dead **453**
Asian giant hornet **181**, 248, **281**
Asian tiger leech **231**
Asiatic honey bee **281**
assassin bug **173**
associative learning 376
Atelopus
   zeteki **418**
Atlantic flying fish **250**
Atlantic ridley turtle **439**

Atlantic salmon 116
Atta cephalotes **425**
Aurelia aurita **350**
Australian sleepy lizard 300
Austruca annulipes **417**
autarchoglossans 35
axolotl **359**
aye-aye **56**, 95, **215**

B

baboon spider, king **425**
baboons 321, **390**, **404**
    olive **300**, **376**, **404**, **411**
bacteria 13
    decomposers 218
Bactrian camel **71**, **407**
badger **112**, **363**
    European **112**
    Meles meles **112**, **363**
Balaenoptera
    musculus **168**
baleen whales **162**, 173
Balistoides viridescens **106**
balling, defence **260**, **281**, **282**
bamboo lemur, golden **77**
banded archerfish **183**
banded hornet, greater **90–91**
banded mongoose **239**, **374**
banded pipefish **323**
banner-tailed kangaroo rat **78**, **433**
bar-headed goose 116, **123**
bar-tailed godwit 116, **124**
    tracking **124**
Barbary macaque **404**
bare-faced go-away bird **427**
barn owl **60–61**, **93**, 170
barn swallow 116, **125**
barnacles **228**
barracuda
    blackfin **62–3**
    sawtooth **395**
basal laceration **296**
basilisk lizard, plumed **257**
basking shark **165**
bat-eared fox **93**
Batesian mimicry **265**
bats
    canyon bat **209**
    common vampire bat **239**
    echolocation 83, **94–5**, **170**, **209**
    Egyptian fruit bat **94**
    fishing bat **210–11**
    frog-eating bat 300
    great fruit-eating bat **160**
    greater horseshoe bat **209**
    Honduran white bat **143**
    lesser horseshoe bat **94**
    Mexican free-tailed bat **288**, **374**
    speed 53
    straw-coloured fruit bat **128**
    whiskered bat **79**
Bdelloida **299**

bdelloid rotifer **299**
beaked whale, Cuvier's **75**
beaks *see* bills
bearded dragons **69**, **166**
    eastern **166**
bears
    black **104**
    brown **169**, **381**
    polar 104, **130**, **162**, **173**, 203, **226–7**, **279**, 321, **374–5**
beaver **71**, 130, **141**
    North American 141
bee-eaters
    carmine **136**
    European **198**, **320–21**
bees 355
    Asiatic honey bee **281**
    honey 97, **135**, **153**, **181**, **228**, **392–3**, **412**
    orchid **413**
    sweat **390**
    western **431**
beetles **348**, 354
    African bombardier **249**
    burying **220**
    dung **220**
    European rhinoceros **311**
    furniture **150**
    Hercules **311**
    pine engraver **413**
    rhinoceros **47**
    soldier **163**
Belostomatidae **180**
beluga whale **279**, **375**
Bengal tiger **111**, **264**
Bibio March fly **19**
bigfin reef squid **63**
bilaterians 24
bills
    adaptations **159**
    wading birds **197**
    as weapons 172
binocular vision **88**
bioluminescence 186, **282**, **411**, 416
birdfeeder **159**
bird-eating spider **248**
birds **36–7**
    bill adaptations **159**
    birds of prey 172
    breathing **75**
    brood parasites **349**
    classification 23, **28–9**, 34, **36–7**
    communication **424**, 430
    courtship 320, 416
    defences 282–3
    digestive system **77**
    echolocation 95
    evolution **18–19**
    feathers **65**, **70**
    flight **60–61**
    flocking **283**
    hearing 92, **93**
    learning **376**
    magnetoreception 97
    mating 300, 334
    migration **116–7**, 123–5

birds contd.
    preening **70**, **433**
    scaly legs 68
    skeletons **51**
    skin 66
    soaring **61**
    songs 424
    swimming 62, 63
    syrinx **93**
    temperature regulation 65
    tools **446**
    urine 78
    vibration receptors 85
    vision 89
    wading birds **197**
birds-of-paradise
    raggiana **330**
birth and development **344–63**
bison, American **385**
Bison bison **385**
Bitis peringueyi **194–5**
bitterling, rosy **358**
bivalves **49**, 58, 59, 84, **173**, 217, 310
black and yellow garden spider **133**
black-backed jackal **83**
black bear **104**
black-browed albatross **108–9**, **221**
black egret **197**
    see also black heron
black grouse **295**
black heron **197**
black mamba 170
black-necked grebe **371**
black rat **117**
black rhinoceros **244–5**, **331**
black-spotted porcupinefish **251**
black-tailed prairie dog **142**
black widow spider **320**
blackbirds 116, **424**
    red-winged **326**
blackbuck **333**
blackfin barracuda **62–3**
blastula 13
Bleeker's parrotfish **251**
blood
    circulation **76**
    clotting 239
blotchy swell shark **357**
blowpipe darts, poison from frogs 253
blubber 65, 66
blue butterflies, large **366**
blue-chested hummingbird **158**
booby
    blue-footed **78**, **326**
    masked **377**
blue-footed booby **78**, **326**
blue-ringed octopus 244, **247**
blue shark **120**
blue tit 103, **420**
blue whale **168**
blue wildebeest 116, **129**
bluefin tuna 123
bluegill sunfish **314**

bluehead wrasse **303**
bluestreak cleaner wrasse **235**, **416**
boa, Central American **189**
Boa imperator **189**
boar, wild **162**, **168**, **453**
bobtail squid **268**
body coverings **64–7**
body language 416, 423
body systems **72–81**
    brains and nerves **80–81**
    breathing **74–5**
    circulation **76**
    digestive system **77**
    hormones 81
    temperature control **78–9**
Bohadschia argus **246**
bombardier beetle, African **249**
Bombina variegata **252**
bonnethead shark **299**
bonobo **343**, **438**, **449**
bony fishes
    buoyancy 62
    classification 30
bony skeletons **50–51**
bony vertebrates, classification 28
boree moth **120**
Bornean flat-headed frog **74**
Borneo horned frog **274**
Bothriechis nigroadspersus **275**
boto **212**, **333**
bottlenose dolphin **67**, **94**, **319**, **429**, **453**
bowerbirds
    satin **308**
    Vogelkop **140**
box jellyfish **174**
box turtle, eastern **254**
boxer crab **230**
boxfishes **245**
brachiation **57**
braconid wasps **356**
Braconidae **356**
Bradypus variegatus **112**, **279**
brain **80–81**
    development 347
    hearing 93
    intelligence **439**
    senses 83
Brazilian tapir **76**
Brazilian tree frog, Izecksohn's **165**
breathing **74–75**
breeding *see* sex and reproduction
brent goose **151**
brine shrimps **103**
bristlemouth **416**
bristles **71**
brittlestars **48**
broadclub cuttlefish **268–9**
bronze whaler shark **184–5**
brood parasites **349**
brood patches, penguins **361**
brown antechinus **342**
brown bear **169**, **381**
brown hare **81**
brown hyena **86**, **415**

brown-throated three-toed sloth **112**, **279**
brown trout **187**
browsers 150
bubble-nets, whales **214**
budding, asexual reproduction **296**
buffalo, African **161**, **289**
Bufo
  bufo **122**, **252**
bullfrogs
  African **368**
  American **426**
buntings
  corn **424**
buoyancy, swimming **62**
Buphagus africanus **237**
Burchell's zebra **116**
Burhinus vermiculatus **258-9**
Burmese python **59**
burrowing **58-9**
  prairie dogs **142**
burrowing toad, Mexican **32**
burying beetles **220**
bush crickets
  dead leaf **334**
bush elephant, African **385, 407, 434-5**, 453
bush viper **65**
bustard, great **167**
Buthus occitanus **322**
Butorides virescens **444**
butterflies
  cabbage white butterfly **152**
  evolution **14-15**
  Indian leafwing butterfly **264**
  large blue butterfly **366**
  large tiger butterfly **265**
  metamorphosis **348**
  migration **119**
  monarch butterfly 116, **119**, **150**
  painted lady **348**
  queen butterfly **413**
  scales **68**
  speckled wood butterfly **308**
  spicebush swallowtail butterfly **267**
  zebra longwing butterfly **302**
butterflyfishes **418**
  longnose **273**
buzzard, common **282**

C

cabbage seed weevil **412**
cabbage white butterfly **152**
caching food **148**, 151
caddis flies 130
caecilians 32
Caenorhabditis elegans **296**
Caiman crocodilus **398**
caimans 64
  spectacled **398**
calamari squid, southern **352-3**
calcium, chalky skeletons 48-9

Calidris pugnax **317**
California condor 108
California flying fish **61**
California ground squirrel **261**
California grunion **302**
California sea lion **333**, **453**
calleta silkmoth **131**
Calliactis palliata **248**
calling frogs 32
Callorhinchus milii **336**
Cambrian period 16
camels 54
  Bactrian **71**, **407**
Camelus
  bactrianus **407**
camouflage **264-79**
Camponotus festinus **107**
cancer, detection by dogs 86
candiru **235**
cane toad **67**, 117, **252**
Canis
  latrans **381, 428**
  lupus **423**
cannibalism 105, 170, 405
Cantharidae 163
canyon bat **209**
Cape gannet **196, 239, 388**
Cape legless skink **69**
Cape mole-rat **85**
Cape pangolin **260**
Cape porcupine **260-61**
capercaillie, western **306**
capuchin, tufted **447**
carbon dioxide 13, 73, 74-5, 218
Carboniferous period 17
Carcharhinus amblyrhynchos **417**
Carcharodon carcharias **182**
caribou **126-7**
  see also reindeer
carmine bee-eater **136**
carnivores 170
  classification 38
  feeding 147, 148
  sense of smell 86
  teeth **172**
  weapons **244**
carpenter ants **230**
carrion crow **282, 440, 446**
cartilage 45, **50**
cartilaginous fishes
  classification 28, 31
  scales **68**
  swimming 62
Cassis cornuta **175**
Castor canadensis **141**
category learning 439
caterpillars **47**, **150**, **366**
  legs 54
  metamorphosis **348**, 355
  skin **66**
  mimicry 265
  "woolly" **71**
catfishes **122**
  electric **96**
  glass **272**
  striped **282**

cats 117
  claws **244**
catsharks, leopard **249**
caudal luring **194**
cave swiftlets **95**, 131
ceanothus moth **412**
Cebus apella **447**
Celebes crested macaque **440**
cells 13
  chromatophores 264, **268**
  division **293**
  embryo **347**
  nerve **80**
  sensory **81**
  sexual reproduction **293**
Cenozoic era 19
centipedes 54
  Amazonian giant **179**
Central American boa **189**
cephalopods
  shells 49, 62
  swimming **63**
  sight 170
  camouflage 264
Cephaloscyllium umbratile **357**
Ceratotherium simum 23, **415**
Cervus elaphus **318**
Chaetodontidae **418**
Chalcosoma mollenkampi **311**
chalky skeletons **48-9**
chameleons 56, **88**
  Madagascan short-horned **308**
  panther **190-91**, **324**
  Parson's **264**
Charadrius
  semipalmatus **278**
cheetah
  backbone 54
  learning to hunt **382-3**
  speed **52**, 170, **203**
Cheilopogon melanurus **250**
Cheiracanthus 17
Chelonia mydas **305, 360**
Chelonoidis niger **157, 314**
Chelydra serpentina **325**
chemicals
  chemosensory organs 170
  communication 86, 87, 411
  pheromones 87, 320, 412-5
chicken **390**
chimaera, ploughnose **336**
chimpanzee
  cannibalism 405
  common **142, 215, 405, 422, 428, 433, 448-51**
  communication **424, 428**
  cooperative hunting **172**, **215**
  facial expressions **422**
  feeding **162**
  grooming **71**, **433**
  hands and feet **56**
  infanticide **309**
  intelligence 439, **450-51**
  night nests **142**
  territory 405
  tools 151, 440, **448-9**

chinstrap penguin **102**
Chiromantis xerampelina **136**
Chironex fleckeri **174**
Chiroxiphia
  linearis **446**
chitin 45, 47
chitons **49**
Chlamydosaurus kingii **418**
Chlorurus
  bleekeri **251**
chordates, classification 25
Chorthippus
  brunneus **425**
chough, white-winged **420**
Christmas Island red crab **118**
Christmas tree worm **246, 334**
chromatophore cells **269**
chromosomes, sexual reproduction 293
Chrysiptera cyanea **156**
Chrysoperla carnea **356**
chum salmon **121**
cicadas **301, 354-5**
  periodical **356**
Cicadidae **301, 354-5**
cichlids
  featherfin **131**
  red/Guayas **314**
  shell-brooding **136**
Ciconia ciconia **137**
cigarfish **284-5**
circulation **76**
clades 14
cladograms **22-3**
clams **173**
  giant **298**
Clark's nutcracker 159, 440
classes, classification 21
classical conditioning 376
classification 20-23
  diagrams **24-39**
  groups **24-39**
  phylogenetic classification 22-3
claws
  defences **244**
  meerkats **286**
  as weapons **172**
clawed armhook, squid **365**
cleaner shrimp **229**
cleaner wrasse, bluestreak **235, 416**
clearwing moths **272**
cleavage 347
cliff swallows, American **402**
climbing **56**
cloak anemone **248**
clones 296
cnemidophorus lizards **295**
coevolution 15
cooperative hunting 148, **172, 215**
coal tit 103
coalitions 390
coatis
  ring-tailed **407**
  white-nosed **168**
cobra, Mozambique spitting **255**

cock-of-the-rock, Andean **317**
cockroach, American **220**
coconut crab **75**
  see also robber crab
cod 68
coelacanth **69**
"cold-blooded" animals 53
colonies
  ants **106**
  bats **374**
  bees **392-3**
  black-browed albatross 109
  common wasp 135
  courtship in 321
  hard corals 132
  prairie dogs **142**
  weaver ants 135
colour
  camouflage 264, 265
  changing 203, 264, **268-9**, 278
  colour vision **89**
  visual signals 416
  warning colours **245**
Columba livia **445**
commensalism 228
Commiphora 161
common buzzard **282**
common chimpanzee
  communication **422**, **424**, **428**
  hands and feet **56**
  grooming **71**, **433**
  nesting **142**
  hunting **215**
  territory **405**
  touch **433**
  intelligence **448-51**
common crane **376**
common dolphin **212**
  long-beaked 239
common earthworm **53**, **219**, **336**, **413**
common field grasshopper **425**
common kingfisher **198-9**
common limpet **105**
common lionfish **250**
common ostrich **259**, **377**
common pondskater **180**
common potoo **279**
common praying mantis **178-9**
common raccoon **226**, **331**
common side-blotched lizard **107**
common starling **283**
common swift **342**
common vampire bat **239**
communication 408-35
  boggling **420**
  electricity 430
  pheromones and smell 412-5
  shaming **420**
  sounds 424-9
  touch 430, 433-5
  vibrations 430, 432, 435
  visual signals 411, **416-23**
community camouflage 265

competition
  hunting and feeding 148
  sexual reproduction 295
  sexual rivalry **308-19**
complete metamorphosis 348, 354
compound eyes **88-9**
Compsognathus **18**
conditioning 376, 439
condors
  Andean **61**, **108**
  California 108
Condylura cristata **215**
cone cells, vision **89**
cone shells **175**
Conidae **175**
Connochaetes taurinus **129**
convergent evolution 15
cookiecutter shark **234**
cooperation 390
  hunting 148, **172**, **215**
cooperative pseudoscorpion **181**
copper shark **184-5**
coqui frog **304**
coral grouper **228-9**
corals 246
  bleaching 301
  evolution 16
  hard coral **132**, **301**
  mushroom coral **391**
  polyps **46**, **77**, **132**
  reefs **132**, **391**
  soft coral **391**
Corcorax melanorhamphos **420**
cormorants **62**, **440**
corn bunting **424**
corn snake **443**
Corucia zebrata **157**
corvids **402**
Corvus
  corone **282**, **446**
  frugilegus **402**
  moneduloides 446
Corynactis viridis **297**
Corythaixoides personatus **427**
Cosmophasis umbratica **301**
conotoxin 175
cottony cushion scale insect **296**
countershading 264
counting ability 440
courtship 320-33, 411, 416
cowries
  allied **264**
  spindle 264
coyotes **148**, **170**, **381**
  bow 381
  mountain **429**
crabs **44**, **54**, 149
  boxer **230**
  coconut **75**
  Christmas Island red **118**
  hermit **131**
  horseshoe 219
  Leach's hermit **248**
  porcelain fiddler **417**
  Sally lightfoot **232-3**, **310**
  sand bubbler **219**

shore **149**, **173**
spider **47**, **266**
spiny spider **281**
cranes
  common **376**
  whooping **125**
craniates 25
creosote bush katydid **77**
crested macaque, Celebes **440**
Cretaceous–Paleogene extinction 19
Cretaceous period 18-19
crickets 354-5, 425
  dead leaf bush **334**
  mole **300**
Crocidura suaveolens **375**
crocodiles **116**, **243**
  evolution 14
  hunting **188**, **444-5**
  Nile crocodile **188**, 258, **346**, **368-9**, **444-5**
  skin 68, **69**
  young **346**, **368-9**
crocodile newt, Anderson's spiny **252**
crocodilians 34
Crocodylus
  niloticus **188**, **368-9**, **444-5**
Crocuta crocuta **226**, **406**
crossbill, red **159**
Crotalus
  atrox **255**
  horridus **371**
  mitchellii **316**
crown-of-thorns starfish **48**, **49**
crows
  carrion **282**, 440, **446**
  New Caledonian 446
crustaceans
  classification 26
  communication 430
  shells 47, **245**
cryptobranchians 33
"cuckoo spit" 65
cuckoo, common **349**
cultural behaviour 440
curlew **197**
cuticle 45, **47**
cuttlefish
  broadclub cuttlefish **268-9**
  buoyancy 62
  colour changes 264, **268-9**
  eyes **88**
  giant cuttlefish **174**, **310**
  jet propulsion 63
Cuvier's beaked whale **75**
Cyanistes caeruleus **420**
Cyclosa insulana **178**
Cygnus
  cygnus **399**
  olor **316**
Cynognathus **18**
Cynomys
  gunnisoni **428**
  ludovicianus **142**
Cypridina **417**
Cystophora cristata **423**

D

dainty green tree frog **424**
Dama dama **279**
dams, beavers 130, **141**
damselfish, sergeant major **368**
damselflies 75, **339**, 354-5
  small red-eyed **336-7**
Danaus
  gilippus **413**
  plexippus **119**
dance flies **322**
dances
  bees **431**
  courtship **321**, 416
dancing white lady spider **105**
dark wood-owl **265**
Darwin, Charles 14, 219, 439
Darwin's frog **274**
Dasyatis brevicaudata **303**
Daubentonia madagascariensis **215**
day octopus **247**, **269**
dead leaf bush cricket **334**
death
  feigning **245**, **258**
  burying 453
decapods 26
deception **264-9**, 440
  camouflage 171, 203, 243, **264-9**
decomposers 218
decoy spider **178**
deer
  fallow **279**
  red **318**
  white-tailed **423**
defences **242-89**
  armour **245**
  balling **260**, **281**, **282**
  camouflage **264-9**
  changing colour 264, **268-9**, 278
  confusing predators 243
  group defence 280-89
  hiding 243
  inflation **251**
  mimicry **265**, **266**, **267**, **274**
  skin 67
  social behaviour 389
  survival strategies **245**
  tail shedding **254**
  weapons and threats **244-63**
  see also poisons
Deinopis subrufa **175**
Delphinapterus leucas **279**, **375**
Delphinus delphis **212**
Dendrobates tinctorius **253**
Dendrobatidae **253**
Dermatophagoides pteronyssinus **219**
Dermochelys coriacea **122**
desert adder, Peringuey's **137**, **194-5**
desert iguana **414**
desert locust 116, **152**
desman 55
Desmodus rotundus **239**
detritivores 147, **148**
deuterostomes 25

devil
    Tasmanian **226**
    thorny **243**
Devonian period 17
diadectosalamandroidei 33
diamondback rattlesnake, western **255**
diapsids 34
Dicerorhinos sumatrensis 22
Diceros bicornis 23, **331**
Dictyophorus cuisinieri **249**
diet *see* feeding
digestive systems **77**
    ruminants **161**
digger wasp **104**
dikkop, water **243**, **258–9**
dimorphism, sexual 295, 308, 320
Dinomyrmex gigas **107**
dinosaurs
    evolution 18–19
    extinction 19
    scales 68
Diocerorhinus sumatrensis 23
Diodon hystrix **251**
Diomedea
    epomorphora **306**
    exulans **123**
    melanophris **403**
diopsid flies **311**
Dipodomys spectabilis **433**
Dipsosaurus dorsalis **414**
disruptive patterning, camouflage 264
divergent evolution 15
diving, breath-holding **74–5**
DNA **15**
    genetic diversity 13
    phylogenetic classification 22
dogfishes
    spiny **357**, **394**
dogs
    African wild dog **206–7**, **208**, 430
    body language **423**
    brain **81**
    sense of smell 86
dolphins
    Amazon river dolphin **212**, **333**
    bottlenose dolphin **67**, **94**, **319**, **429**, **453**
    common dolphin **212**
    defences 244
    dusky dolphin **384**
    echolocation **94**, 171, 333
    killer whale **212–3**, **384**
    long-beaked common dolphin **239**
    play **376**
    skeletons 51
    skin 67
    social groups 280
    spinner dolphin **407**
Dorylus **181**
double banded plover **278**
Douglas fir glow worm **302**
dove, ring-necked **300**
draco 50

Draco volans **255**
dragon, Komodo **188**, **296**, **341**
dragonflies **60**, **179**, **292**, 354–5
    common whitetail **105**
    emperor **351**
    green darner **118**
    lesser emperor, nymph **179**
driver ants **181**
Dromaius novaehollandiae **371**
Dryocopus pileatus **137**
duck-billed platypus **96**, **202**
duck, ruddy **426**
dugong **161**, **307**
Dugong dugon **161**, **307**
Dunckerocampus dactyliophorus **323**
dung beetles **220**
dunnock **316**
dusky dolphin **384**
dust mite, European house **219**
dwarf mongoose **288**, **414**
Dynastes hercules **311**

E

eagle ray, whitespotted **394**
eagle, white-tailed **192–3**
ears and hearing 83, **92–3**, 170
    animals lacking ears 85
    owls 198
    "true ear" 178
earthworms 46
    common **53**, **219**, **336**, **413**
eastern bearded dragon **166**
eastern box turtle **254**
eastern mosquitofish **443**
eastern newt **274**
eastern tiger salamander **304**
ecdysozoa 24
Echeneis naucrates **234**
echidna, short-beaked **96**, **362**
echinoderms
    chalky skeletons 48, **49**
    classification 25
Echinotriton andersoni **252**
echolocation 83, **94–5**, 170, **209**
Eciton burchelli **442**
ecosystems, decomposers 218
ecotype, orcas 213
ectoparasites 349
Ectophylla alba **143**
eels
    American 120
    electric **96**
    European 116, **120**
    garden **187**
    moray **102**
    mosaic moray **186**
egg-laying mammals 38
eggs
    amphibians 46, 358–9
    birds 361
    evolution of shells 14
    fertilization **293**, 321, **334**, 347
    insects 356, **367**

eggs contd.
    mating **334**
    parasites 349
    parthenogenesis 13
    reptiles **346**
    temperature and **294**
egrets, black **197**
    see also black heron
Egretta ardesiaca **197**
Egyptian fruit bat **94**
Egyptian vulture **66**
Eidolon helvum **128**
elasmobranchs 31
Elasmucha grisea **366**
electric catfish 96
electric eel **96**
electric ray **96**, 430
electricity
    communication 411, 430–35
    as defence 244
    electrogenesis **96**
    electrolocation 96, 186
    electroreception 83, **96**, **182**
    sensing **183**
Eleonora's falcon 116
elephant seals **76**, **319**
    northern **318**
elephantnose fish **96**, **186**
elephants
    African bush elephant **385**, **407**, **434–5**, 453
    aggression **263**
    Asian elephant **453**
    burying the dead 453
    communication 434–5
    dung **151**
    eyes **82**
    family groups 407, 434–5
    forest elephant **112–3**
    gestation 347
    hearing 83, 92
    keeping in touch **434–5**
    learning 385
    mating **334**
    memory **390**
    raising young **364**
    reproduction 349
    skin **66–7**
    teeth **150**
    temperature control **79**
    trunks **385**
    tusks 244
Elephas maximus **453**
Eleutherodactylus coqui **304**
elf owl **131**
embryo 13, 347
emperor angelfish **327**
emperor dragonflies **351**
    lesser emperor, nymph **179**
emperor moths **86**, **412**
emperor penguin **103**, **360–61**
Empis
    opaca **322**
    tessellata **322**
emu **371**
Enchelycore ramosa **186**

endocrine system 81
endoparasites 349
energy
    energy-efficient locomotion 57
    energy-saving behaviour 389
    food chains and webs **147**, **218**
    food production 13
    from plants 150–51
    maintenance 196
    recycling 218
    life chemicals and processes 73
enfleurage 413
engraver beetle, pine **413**
Enhydra lutris **452**
Enteroctopus dofleini **335**, **365**
enzymes 77
Epidalea calamita **340**
epigenetics 406
Episyrphus balteatus **322**
Eptatretus burgeri **220**
Equidae 23
Equus
    caballus **406**
    quagga **433**
Eremitalpa granti **202**
Eretmochelys imbricata **165**
Erithacus rubecula **20**, **109**
Eryon **18**
Erythromma viridulum **336–7**
Estonioceras **16**
euarchontoglires 39
eucaridans 26
Eudistylia polymorpha **441**
Eudyptes chrysocome **371**
Euglossa **413**
Eumeninae **367**
eumetazoa 24
Eumetopias jubatus **405**
Eurasian oystercatcher **197**
Eurasian sparrowhawk **61**
Eurasian water shrew **86**
European badger **112**
    Meles meles **112**, **363**
European bee-eater **198**, **320–21**
European common frog **341**, **358**
European common toad **122**, **252**, **338–9**
European eel 116, **120**
European hornet **248**
European mole **58–9**, **143**
European otter **415**
European rabbit **306**
European rhinoceros beetle **311**
European robin **20**, **109**, 116
Eurypyga helias **259**
euteleosts 30
evolution **14–19**
    classification and 25
    sexual 295
    sexual rivalry and 308
excretion 67, 76, 78
exoskeletons 45, **47**
expressions, facial **416**, **422**
external fertilization 321, 334

extinction
    major events 16–19
extreme habitats **102**
eye spots **243**
eyelash viper **173**, **275**
eyes and vision 82, **88–9**
    compound eyes **88–9**
    flatfishes **357**
    frogs **187**
    infrared light **189**
    predators 170
    snakes **69**

F

facial expressions **416**, **422**
    chimpanzees **422**
facial recognition 440
fairywrens
    white-winged **306**
Falco peregrinus **192**
falcons
    Eleonora's 116
    peregrine 170, **192**
fallow deer **279**
false clown anemonefish **251**
families, classification 21
family hunting 204–5
fangs, defences **244**
fangtooth fish **103**
fat-tailed lemur **79**
fat-tailed scorpion **172**
    Arabian **248**
favosites coral **16**
feather duster worms 246
    giant **441**
feather star **65**
featherfin cichlid **131**
feathers **65**, **70**
    flight **60**
    preening **70**, **433**
feeding
    caching food **148**, 151
    decomposers 218
    digestion **77**
    energy **73**
    feeding relationships **228–39**
    food chains and webs **147**, 170, **218**
    foraging 148–9
    hunting **146–9**
    omnivores **162–9**
    partnerships **228–39**
    predation **170–217**
    scavenging **218–27**
    social behaviour 389
    see also carnivores; herbivores
feet
    blue-footed booby **326**
    climbing **56**
    moles **143**
    primates **56**
    webbed **55**, **63**
Felis serval **262**

fertilization
    eggs **293**, 321, 347
    external fertilization 321, 334
    internal fertilization 334
fiddler crab, porcelain **417**
field grasshopper, common **425**
fig wasps **311**
fighting, sexual rivalry 308–9
filefishes **265**
    edible mimic **265**
filter feeding
    baleen whales 162
    molluscs 162
    sharks 165
finch, woodpecker **15**
fins **62**
fire ants **336**
fire-bellied newt **66**
fire salamander **413**
fireflies **308**
    Genji **417**
fishes
    breathing 74
    camouflage **245**
    classification 22, 28, **30–31**
    communication 416, 425, 430
    courtship 321
    defences 244, **245**
    electroreception **96**, 430
    elephantnose **96**, **186**
    evolution 16–19
    fangtooth **103**
    fertilization of eggs 334
    fins **62**
    gills **75**
    hearing 92
    home ranges 104
    lateral line **84**
    lobe-finned **22**, 28, 30
    migration 117
    scales **68**, **69**, 245
    shoals **62**, **84**
    skeletons **50**, **51**
    swimming **62–3**
    vision 88, 89
fishing, long-line 123
fishing bat **210–11**
fishing spider **176–7**
flamingos, lesser **400–01**
flashlightfish, splitfin **282**
flatfishes, eyes **357**
flatworms
    circulatory system **74**
    excretory system 78
    marine flatworms **74**
    movement 59
    purple flatworm **441**
    reproduction **296**
fleas **57**
flehmen response **87**
flicker, northern **131**
flies 96, **113**, **205**, 387
    Bibio March **19**
    dance **322**
    diopsid **311**

flies contd.
    goat **312**
    house 60, **80**, **173**
    moose **312**
    phorid **349**
    stag **312–3**
    tsetse **356**
flight *see* flying
flocks, flying in **283**, **403**
flounder, Mediterranean 273
flowers, nectar guides **89**
fluid balance 78
flukes
    Leucochloridium paradoxum **350**
flycatchers, royal **420**
flying 53, **60–61**
    feathers **60**, **70**
    in flocks **283**
    non-stop flying **124**
flying fishes
    Atlantic **250**
    California **61**
flying frog, Wallace's **61**
flying gurnard **250**
flying lemurs 53, 61
flying lizard 61, **255**
flying possum 61
flying squirrels 53, 61
foam grasshopper, African **249**
foam-nest frog, grey **136**
food *see* feeding
food chains and webs **147**, 170, **218**
foot-drumming **433**
foraging strategies 148–9
Forcipiger flavissimus **273**
forest elephant, African **112–3**
formic acid 281
Formica
    fusca **394**
    rufa **281**
    sanguinea **394**
fossils **16–17**
four-eyed frog **254**
fowl, classification 36
fox sparrow 116
foxes 170, 218, **430**
    Arctic **203**, **276–7**
    bat-eared **93**
    red **113**, **262**
free-tailed bat, Mexican **288**, **374**
French grunt **443**
frigatebirds **364**
    great **328–9**
frilled lizard **50**, **418**
fringed jumping spider **442**
frog-eating bat 300
frogfish, hairy **183**
froghopper bug 65
froglet **358**
frogs **47–9**, 93
    African bullfrog **368**
    American bullfrog **426**
    Bornean flat-headed frog **74**
    Borneo horned frog **274**

frogs contd.
    classification 32–3
    coqui frog **304**
    courtship 320
    dainty green tree frog **424**
    Darwin's frog **274**
    European common frog **341**, **358**
    eyes **187**
    four-eyed frog **254**
    ghost **273**
    glass frogs **76**
    golden poison frog **253**
    grey foam-nest frog **136**
    harlequin poison dart frog **107**
    hearing **92**
    Izecksohn's Brazilian tree frog **165**
    magnificent tree frog **414**
    metamorphosis 348
    Panamanian golden frog **418**
    Perez's frog **187**
    poison frogs 245, **253**, 274
    red-eyed tree frog **88**
    strawberry poison frog **315**
    swimming **63**
    treehole frog **426**
    Verreaux's tree frog **320**
    Wallace's flying frog **61**
    water-holding frog **78**
    water lily frog **300**
Fromia **246**
frugivores 150
fruit bats
    Egyptian **94**
    straw-coloured **128**
fruit-eating bat, great **160**
fungi
    decomposers 218
    in termite mounds **134**
fungus gnat larva **181**
fur **71**
fur trade 71
fur seal **71**, **74–5**
Furcifer pardalis **324**
furniture beetle **150**

G

gaits **54**
Galapagos giant tortoise **157**, **314**
Galapagos penguin **235**
Galeocerdo cuvier **221**
galls, aphid **105**
Gambusia holbrooki **443**
gametes **293**
gannets
    Cape **196**, **239**, **388**
    northern **104**, **419**
ganoid scales 68
garden eel **187**
garden snail **59**, **350**
garden spider **104**
    black and yellow **133**
garpike 68, **69**

garter snakes
    common **341**
    red-sided **415**
gas exchange 13
gastropods
    movement 95
    shells **85**
Gazella thomsoni **288**
gazelles 53, 203, 411
    Thomson's **288**, **382–3**
Gecarcoidea natalis **118**
geckos **56**
    giant leaf-tailed **275**
    Madagascan day **56**, **68**
    mossy leaf-tailed **274–5**
    mourning **299**
    tokay **426**
geese
    bar-headed 116, **123**
    brent **151**
Gekko gecko **426**
gemsbok **300**
genetics **14–15**, **22**
    courtship and 321
    gene flow **14–15**
    gene shuffling **15**
    genes 13, 15
    genetic drift **14**
    phylogenetic classification 22
    sexual reproduction 293
Genji firefly **417**
gentoo penguin **237**, **378–9**
gerenuk **13**, **150–51**
Gerris lacustris **180**
gestation periods 347, 349
    giraffe **363**
    red-necked wallaby **362**
    short-beaked echidna **362**
    spiny dogfish **357**
    tree pangolin **374**
gestures 416, **422**
ghost fish **273**
ghost knifefishes **432**
giant anteater **202**
giant antlion larva **180**
giant centipede, Amazonian **179**
giant clam **298**
giant cuttlefish **174**, **310**
giant feather duster worms **441**
giant hornets, Asian **181**, 248, **281**
giant leaf-tailed gecko **275**
giant Pacific octopus **247**, **365**
giant panda 77, **160**, **331**, **376**
giant petrel, southern **86**
giant river otter **375**
giant stick insect **266**
giant water bug **180**
gibbons **57**
    siamang **332**
gifts, courtship **320–21**, **322**
gills 65
    breathing **75**
    filter feeding sharks 165
Giraffa
    camelopardalis **161**, **319**, **363**

giraffes
    birth and development **363**
    feeding **151**
    flehmen response **87**
    poaching **363**
gizzard **77**
glands, endocrine system 81
glass catfish **272**
glass frogs **76**
gliding 53, **61**
Glossina morsitans **356**
glow worms 181, 334
    common **302**
    Douglas fir **302**
glucose 13
Gnathonemus petersii **186**
gnat larva, fungus **181**
goat fly **312**
goats 117
goby fish **248**
godwits **197**
    bar-tailed 116, **124**
golden bamboo lemur **77**
golden frog, Panamanian **418**
golden mole, Grant's **202**, **430**
golden poison frog **253**
golden seahorse **265**
Goliath grouper **284–5**
Gonatus onyx **365**
goosander **364**
goose *see* geese
Gorgasia maculata **187**
Gorilla
    beringei beringei **261**
gorillas **66**, 142, 411
    mountain **261**
goshawk, northern **342**
Graeophonus "spider" **17**
granivores 150
Grant's golden mole **202**, **430**
Grapsus grapsus **310**
grass snake **252**, **258**, **325**
grasshoppers 56, **92**, **181**, 354–5
    African foam **249**
    common field **425**
gravity
    gravitational detectors **84**
    movement and 53
gray whale 116, **227**
grazers 150
Great Barrier Reef **132**
great bustard **167**
great crested grebe **327**
great crested newt **418**
great frigatebird **328–9**
great fruit-eating bat **160**
great grey owl **198**, **265**
Great Plains toad **304**
great skua **237**
great white pelican **196**
great white shark **182**
    see also white shark
greater banded hornet **90–91**
greater honeyguide 411
greater horseshoe bat **209**

greater kudu **204–5**
grebes
    black-necked **371**
    great crested **327**
    western 327
green ants 135
    see also weaver ants
green crested lizard **264**
green darner dragonfly **118**
green heron **444**
green iguana **64**, **398**
green lacewing **356**
green stink bug, southern **431**
green tree python **189**
green turtle **305**, 349, **360**
grey foam-nest frog **136**
grey heron **147**, **236**, **420**
grey owl, great **198**, **265**
grey parrot **445**
grey plover **197**
grey reef shark **417**
grey wolf
    body language **423**
    feeding relationships **238**
    pack hierarchy **423**
    prey **126**
griffon vulture, Eurasian **222–3**
grooming **71**, 404, **433**
ground anole **314–5**
ground squirrel, California **261**
group defences 280–89
group hunting 196
group living 389
groupers
    coral **228–9**
    Goliath **284–5**
    tiger **235**
grouse
    black **295**
    red 278
    willow **278**
grunion, California **302**
grunts, French **443**
Grus
    grus **60**, **290**
guayas cichlid 314
gulls 61
Gunnison's prairie dog **428**
guppy **337**
gurnards
    flying **250**
gymnotiforms 430
Gyps fulvus **222–3**

H

habitats **103**
habituation, learning 376, 439
Haemadipsa picta **231**
Haematopus ostralegus **197**
haemolymph 76, 78
Haemulon flavolineatum **443**
hagfishes **22**, 30, **66**
    Japanese **220**

hair **71**
    irritant hairs 244
    touch receptors **84**
hairy frogfish **183**
Haliaeetus albicilla **192–3**
hamerkop **136**
hammerhead 136
hammerhead shark, scalloped **183**
hands, primates **56**
Hapalochlaena **247**
Haplophryne mollis **337**
hard coral **132**, **301**
harlequin poison dart frog **107**
harrier-hawk, African **166**
Harris's hawk **136**
Hawaiian monk seal **62**
hawk wasp, tarantula **231**
hawks
    Harris's **136**
    red-backed **172**
hawksbill turtle **165**
health benefits, social behaviour 389
hearing *see* ears and hearing
heart **76**
hedgehog 171, **229**
Heliconia 143
Heliconius charithonia **302**
Heliobatis **19**
Helix aspersa **350**
helmet shells, horned **175**
Helogale parvula **288**, **414**
Hennig, Willi 22
herbivores
    defences **244**
    feeding 147, 148, **150–61**
    food chains 170
Hercules beetle **311**
herding, pectoral 214
hermaphrodites 293, 296, 298, 299, 334, 335
hermit crabs **131**
    Leach's **248**
herons
    black **197**
    green **444**
    grey **147**, **236**, **420**
Herrerasaurus **18**
Heterocephalus glaber **403**
Heterodontus francisci **323**
hexapods 27
hibernation 79, 103
hierarchies 390
Hierophis viridiflavus **341**
Himalayas, flying over **123**
Hippocampus
    abdominalis **323**
    bargibanti **273**
hippopotamus **280**
    feeding **160**
    skin **66**
    visual signals **421**
Hippopotamus amphibius **160**, **421**
Hirtella physophora **181**
hirudin 231
Hirundo rustica **125**
history 16–19

INDEX

hoatzin **361**
holometabola 27
Homarus
  americanus **163**
home ranges 103, **104**
  see also territories
Homo sapiens, evolution **19**
Honduran white bat **143**
honey bees
  Asiatic honey bee **281**
  colonies **153**, **392-3**
  communication **431**
  feeding **153**
  fertilization of plants **228**
  honeycomb **135**
  Japanese honey bee, population 181
  magnetoreception 97
  pheromones **412**
  predators 181
  western **431**
honeycomb **135**, **153**
honeydew 230
honeyguides, greater 411
honeypot ant **154-5**
hooded seal **423**
hoofed mammals 54
  classification 38-9
  defences **244**
  pronking **57**
Hoploteryx **19**
hormones 81
horn shark **323**
hornbills
  southern ground **88**
horned frogs
  Borneo **274**
horned helmet shell **175**
horned lizards
  Texas **254**
horned viper **69**
hornets **389**
  Asian giant **181**, **248**, **281**
  European **248**
  greater banded **90-91**
horns, rhinoceroses **244-5**
horny skeletons **47**
horses 54
  mustang **150**, **406**
horseshoe bats
  greater **209**
  lesser **94**
horseshoe crab **219**
hosts, parasites **229**, **349**
house fly 60, **80**, **173**
house martin **125**
house sparrow 14
hoverflies **88-9**
  marmalade **322**
howler monkeys, Venezuelan red **428**
humans
  brains **439**
  and elephants 263
  evolution **19**
  human-assisted migration 117

humans contd.
  nervous system **81**
  shark attacks 182
hummingbirds 15, 79, **150**
  blue-chested **158**
  sparkling violet-ear **61**
humpback whale **128-9**, **214**
hunger 147
hunting *see* predation
Hydra **80**, **297**
Hydra vulgaris **297**
Hydrosaurus **256-7**
hydroskeletons **46**
Hydrurga leptonyx **200-01**
hyenas **172**, 412
  brown **86**, **415**
  spotted **224-5**, **226**, **406**
hyloides 32
Hystrix africaeaustralis **260-61**

I

ibex **308-9**
Ichthyosaurus communis **18**
Idotea 264
Iguana iguana **398**
iguanas 34
  desert **414**
  green **64**, **398**
  marine **69**, 149, **156-7**, **232-3**
imagos 354
immune system 76
impala 57, **208**
imprinting **376**
incomplete metamorphosis **354-5**
Indian leafwing butterfly **264**
Indian mackerel **396-7**
Indian peafowl **330**
Indian rhinoceros 22, **23**, **262**
Indri lemur **56**
infanticide 309, 405
infrared light **189**
infrasound 83, 411
Inia geoffrensis **212**, **333**
inland taipan **189**
insects
  breathing 74
  classification 27
  communication 412, 430
  compound eyes **88-9**
  evolution 16-19
  flight **60**
  hearing 92
  legs 54
  mating 334
  metamorphosis 348, **351**, **354-5**
  mimicry 265
  movement 53
  muscles 45
  sound production 93
  stridulation 93, 425
  vibration receptors 85
  vision 89

instars 354, 356
instinct 347, 439
intelligence **436-53**
  sea lion 453
intermittent signals 416
internal fertilization 334
invertebrates
  body systems **73**
  breathing **74**
  burrowing 59
  classification 24
  communication 411, 412
  evolution 16-19
  legs 54
  muscles **45**
  nervous systems **80**
  number of species 13
  scales 68
  water skeletons 45, **46**
Ips pini **413**
irritant hairs, defences **244**
Isistius brasiliensis **234**
Ixodes ricinus **231**
Izecksohn's Brazilian
  tree frog **165**

J

jackal, black-backed **83**
Jacobson's organ **87**
jaguar **171**
Japanese hagfish **220**
Japanese honey bee, population 181
Japanese macaque **380**, **446-7**
Javan rhinoceros 22, **23**
jawed vertebrates, classification 28
jawfishes **367**
jawless fishes 17-19
jaws
  leopard seals **200**
  lions **205**
  moray eels **186**
  as weapons **172**
jays **151**
  western scrub **440**
jellyfish
  box jellyfish **174**
  hydroskeleton **46**
  jet propulsion 63
  life cycle 348, **350**
  moon jellyfish **350**
  sea-nettle jellyfish **72**
jet propulsion **63**
jewel anemone **297**
joints **45**
jumping spiders **47**, **178**, **366**, **417**
  fringed **442**
  kerengga ant-like **310**
  ornate **301**
Jurassic period 18

K

kangaroo rats 53, **78**
  banner-tailed **78**, **433**
  communication **433**
kangaroos **53**, 57
  red **70**
katydids **266**
  creosote bush **77**
  lichen-mimic **266**
kea **166**
keratin
  feathers 70
  hair 71
  scales 68
  skin 66, 67
kerengga ant-like jumper **310**
kidneys 78
killer whale **212-3**, **384**
killifishes, mangrove **299**
killing techniques **173**
king baboon spider **425**
king penguin **398**, **427**
kingdoms, classification 13, 21
kingfishers, common **198-9**
kiwi, Stewart Island brown **193**
kleptoparasitic attack **236**
knifefishes **96**
  ghost **432**
knobby argonaut 132
  see also paper nautilus
koala
  feeding **150**, **159**
  home ranges **108**
  raising young **364**
Komodo dragon **188**, **296**, **341**
krill 173, 398
Kryptolebias marmoratus **299**
Kryptopterus bicirrhis **272**
kudu, greater **204-5**

L

Labroides dimidiatus **235**
laceration, basal **296**
lacewings
  green **356**
ladybirds **60**
Lagenorhynchus obscurus **384**
Lagopus lagopus **278**
lampreys **22**, 30
  sea **234**
Lamprologus callipterus **136**
Lampyridae **302**
Lampyris noctiluca **302**
land snail, African **88**
language
  mammals 448, **449**
  parrots 445
Lanius collurio **198**
Lapland owl **265**
large blue butterfly **366**
large tiger butterfly **265**

larvae
 fungus gnat **181**
 giant antlion **180**
 metamorphosis 347, 355
 parasites 349
lateral line **81**, **84**, 280, 430
laurasiatherians 38
Leach's hermit crab **248**
leaf-cutter ant **425**
leaf insects **299**
leaf-tailed geckos
 giant **275**
 mossy **274-5**
leaf-cutter ant **425**
leafwing butterfly, Indian **264**
leafy seadragon **273**
leaping **56**, 57
learned behaviour 347, 439
learning and play 376–85
 lobtailing 214
 spatial learning **104**
leatherback turtle **122**
leeches
 Asian tiger **231**
 medicinal **231**
legs
 climbing and leaping **56-7**
 number of 54
 swimming 62, **63**
 walking and running **54-5**
Leipoa ocellata **361**
leks 300
 bird-of-paradise, raggiana **330**
 diopsid fly **311**
 dugong **307**
 gemsbok **300**
 ruff **316**
 western capercaillie **306**
lemming, Norway **125**
Lemmus lemmus **125**
lemon sole **357**
Lemur catta **404**
lemurs
 fat-tailed **79**
 flying 53, 61
 golden bamboo **77**
 Indri **56**
 ring-tailed **404**, **412**
lenses, eyes **89**
leopard **85**, **148-9**
leopard catshark **249**
leopard sea cucumber **246**
leopard seal **200-01**
leopard slug **335**
Lepidochelys kempii **439**
Lepidodactylus lugubris **299**
lepidosaurs 29, 34
Lepidotus **18**
Lepomis macrochirus **314**
Leptasterias hexactis **365**
Lessepsian migration 117
lesser flamingo **400-01**
lesser horseshoe bat **94**
lesser white-toothed shrew **375**
Leucochloridium paradoxum **350**
Leuconotopicus borealis **258**

Leucorchestris arenicola **105**
Leuresthes tenuis **302**
Libellula lydia **105**
lice **228**
 sea 121
lichen-mimic katydid **266**
life, kingdoms 13
ligaments 57
light
 bioluminescence 186, **282**, **411**
 and colour changes **278**
 vision **88-9**
Limax maximus **335**
limbs *see* legs
Limosa lapponica **124**
limpets 59, **245**
 common **105**
Limulus polyphemus **219**
Linnaeus, Carl **20**
lion **204-5**
 cannibalism 170
 coalitions **405**
 communication **430**
 hunting **204-5**, **289**
 infanticide **309**
 learning **381**
 speed 170
 territory **78**
lionfish, common **250**
little tern **326**
little weaver **139**
live-bearing mammals 38
live sharksucker **234**
lizards 54
 anguimorph lizards 35
 anole lizard **416**
 armadillo lizard **254**
 basilisk lizard **256**
 classification 34, 35
 climbing 56
 Cnemidophorus lizard **295**
 common side-blotched lizard **107**
 eggs **294**
 flying lizard 61, **255**
 frilled lizard **50**, **418**
 green crested lizard **264**
 Jacobson's organ **87**
 Jesus lizard **256**
 monitor lizard **258**, **370**
 moulting **68**
 plumed basilisk lizard **257**
 sailfin lizards **256-7**
 scales 68, 69
 Australian sleepy lizard 300
 temperature control **79**
 Texas horned lizard **254**
 walking 54
lobe-finned fishes **22**, 28, 30
Lobophyllia **301**
lobsters
 American **163**
 Caribbean spiny **118**
 slipper **350**
lobtailing, bubble-nets **214**
locomotion 53
locust, desert 116, **152**

lodges, beavers **141**
long-beaked common dolphin **239**
long-tailed manakin **446**
long-tailed tit **140**, **403**
longitudinal fission **297**
longnose butterflyfish **273**
Lontra canadensis **384**
loosejaw, stoplight **186**
lophotrochozoa 25
Loxia curvirostra **159**
Loxodonta
 africana **263**, **385**, **407**, **434-5**, 453
 cyclotis **112-3**
Lucida cruciata **417**
luciferin 282, 302, **417**
luciferase **417**
lugworm **77**
Lumbricus terrestris **219**, **336**, **413**
lungs **75**
lures, predation **171**
luring, caudal 194
Lutra lutra **415**
Lycaon pictus **208**
lymph system 76

M

Macaca
 fuscata **380**, **446-7**
 sylvanus **404**
macaques
 Barbary **404**
 Celebes crested **440**
 Japanese **380**, **446-7**
macaw, red-and-green **167**, **433**
mackerel, Indian **396-7**
Macrochelys temminckii **189**
macroevolution 14
Macropus
 rufus **70**
Macrotermes **134**
Madagascan day gecko **56, 68**
Madagascan short-horned
  chameleon **308**
Maevia inclemens **417**
maggots **219**, 354
Magicicada **356**
magnetoreception 83, **97**
magnificent tree frog **414**
Maja brachydactyla **281**
Majidae **266**
mako sharks **97**
 shortfin 170
Malacosteus niger **186**
Malaysian giant ant **106-7**
malleefowl **360**, **361**
Mallorcan midwife toad **359**
Malurus
 leucopterus **306**
mamba, black 170
mammals
 armour 50
 breathing 75
 classification **23**, 28, **38-9**

mammals contd.
 communication 424, 430
 courtship 320, 321, 416
 defences **244**
 echolocation **94-5**
 evolution 15, 18–19
 excretion 78
 fur **71**
 gestation periods 349
 grooming **71**
 hearing **92**
 hibernation **79**
 hoofed mammals 38, 39, 54, **244**
 Jacobson's organ **87**
 mating 300
 movement 54
 muscles 45
 placental 38, 347, 349
 sense of smell 86
 skin **66**
 swimming 62
 temperature regulation 65
 tool using 447, 448, 452
 touch receptors **84**
 vision 89
manakins, long-tailed **446**
manatees
 West Indian **414**
mandarin fish **88**
mandrill **89**, **416**
mangrove killifish **299**
Manis tricuspis **374**
mantis, praying **320**
 common **178-9**
Mantis religiosa **178-9**
mantis shrimps **89**, 244
 peacock **310**
maps, mental 117, 440
Marabou stork **218**
marginated tortoise **349**
marine flatworms **74**
marine iguana
 feeding 149, **156-7**
 feeding relationships **232-3**
 scales **69**
marine turbellarian **74**
marking territories **104**, **111**
marlin **221**
marmalade hoverfly **322**
marsh tit **159**
marsupials 347
 classification 38
 gestation periods 349
martins 130
 house **125**
 purple **131**
masked booby **377**
mates, attracting 300
mating 320, **334-43**
Mawsonites **16**
mealy bugs 228
medicine
 blood clotting compounds 239
 fighting ageing 359
 leeches **231**
 self medication 452

Mediterranean flounder 273
meerkat **286-7**, **406**
megamouth shark **165**
Megaptera novaeangliae **128-9**, **214**
meiosis **293**
Meissner's corpuscles **84**
Melanerpes formicivorus **158**
Meles meles **112**, **363**
memory 390, 439
mental maps 117, **440**
Mephitis mephitis **262**
Merops
  apiaster **198**
  nubicoides **136**
Mesozoic era 18-19
metabolism, and movement 53
metamorphosis 347, **348**
  amphibians 358-9
  cicadas **354-5**
  insects **351**, **357**
Metaphrynella sundana **426**
Metopaster **19**
Mexican burrowing toad **32**
Mexican free-tailed bat **288**, **374**
Mexican red-kneed tarantula **56**
mice **86**, **321**
microevolution 14
micrognathozoans 24
Microstomus kitt **357**
midshipman, plainfin **303**
midwife toads 334
  Mallorcan **359**
migration 103, **116-29**
  birds 123-5
  butterflies **119**
  eels **120**
  gene flow **14-15**
  whales **128**
millions fish **337**
millipedes 53, **54**
mimic octopus **441**
mimicry 265, **266-7**, **270-71**, 445
Minecraft 449
Mirounga angustirostris **318**
mites, European house dust **219**
mole cricket **300**
mole-rats 93
  Cape **85**
  naked 53, **58**, 390, **403**
molehills **143**
moles
  European **58-9**, **143**
  Grant's golden **202**, **430**
  star-nosed **84**, **215**
molluscs
  classification 25
  movement 58, 59
  predation 173
  shells 48, **49**, 65, 245
monarch butterfly 116, **119**, **150**
mongooses
  banded **239**, **374**
  dwarf **288**, **414**
monitor lizards **258**, **370**
  savanna **370**

monk seal, Hawaiian **62**
monkey-tailed skink **157**
monkeys
  brains **438**
  communication **416**
  sun-tailed monkey **422**
  tufted capuchin monkey **447**
  Venezuelan red howler monkey **428**
  vision 89
monocular vision **88**
monogamy **300**
moon jellyfish **350**
moon moth, American **68**
moon snail **173**
moorhen **309**
moose **307**, **375**
moose fly **312**
moray eels **66**
  mosaic **186**
Morelia viridis **189**
mormyrid fish 430
Morus
  bassanus **419**
  capensis **196**, **388**
mosaic moray eel **186**
mosquitofish, eastern **443**
mosquitos **92**, **228**
mossy leaf-tailed gecko **274-5**
mother-of-pearl 49
moths **68**, 92
  boree **120**
  calleta silkmoth **131**
  ceanothus **412**
  clearwing **272**
  emperor **86**, **412**
  peppered **14**
  saturniid **270-71**
  sphinx **74**
motion detectors 84
moulting 65
  feathers 70
  metamorphosis **351**, 354, **356**
mountain coyote **429**
mountain gorilla **261**
mourning gecko **299**
mouse *see* mice
mouth-brooding fishes **367**
movement 13, **52-63**
  burrowing, slithering and sliding **58-9**
  climbing and leaping **56-7**
  flying and gliding **60-61**
  hydroskeletons 46
  jet propulsion **63**
  muscles 45
  sidewinding 59, **194**
  social behaviour 389
  swimming **62-3**
  walking and running **54-5**
Mozambique spitting cobra **255**
mud, wading birds **197**
mudskipper **53**
mullet, striped red **220**
Mullus surmuletus **220**
multicellular animals 13
Mungos mungo **374**

murex **49**
  venus comb **246**
Murex pecten **246**
Muricella 273
murmuration **283**
muscles **45**, 46
mushroom coral **391**
muskox 172
mussels **149**, 358
mustang **150**, **406**
mutations, evolution **15**
mute swan **131**, **316**
mutualism 15, 228
Myrmarachne plataleoides **310**
myriapods 26
Myrmecophaga tridactyla **202**
Myrmica sabuleti 366

N

naiads 179
Naja
  mossambica **255**
naked mole-rat 53, **58**, 390, **403**
names 20
Namib desert sidewinding adder **194-5**
  see also Péringuey's desert adder
Nasua
  nasua **407**
  narica **168**
Natrix
  helvetica **258**
  maura 359
  natrix **325**, **357**
natterjack toad **340**
natural selection **14**
nautilus **49**, **62**
  estonioceras **16**
  paper **132**
navigation
  fishes 430
  insects 442
  magnetoreception **97**
  mental maps 440
  migration **117**
nectar guides 89
nematode worm **46**, **296**
Nembrotha purpureolineata **335**
neoaves 37
Neogene period 19
neognaths 36
neoptera 27
nerves **80-81**
  senses 83
Nestor notabilis **166**
net-casting spider, rufous **175**
neurons 80
neuropterids 27
New Caledonian crow 446
newts 33, 54, **75**, **321**, 334,
  Alpine **334**, **369**
  Anderson's spiny crocodile **252**

newts contd.
  eastern **274**
  fire-bellied **66**
  great crested **418**
  red-spotted **340**
  smooth **321**
Nezara viridula **431**
Nicrophorus **220**
night
  nocturnal predators 170
Nile crocodile **188**, **258**, **346**, **368-9**, **444-5**
  hunting **188, 444-5**
  young **346, 368-9**
nitrogen 218
nocturnal predators 170
nomenclature 20
Norops humilis **314-5**
North American beaver 141
North American river otter **384**
northern elephant seal **318**
northern flicker **131**
northern gannet **104**, **419**
northern goshawk **342**
northern raccoon **226**
Norway lemming **125**
Notophthalmus viridescens **340**
nudibranch **335**
numeracy, mammals 449
nursery web spider **365**
nutcracker, Clark's 159, **440**
nutrients, recycling 218
nutrition *see* feeding
Nyctibius griseus **279**
nymphs
  dragonfly, lesser emperor **179**
  giant water bugs **180**

O

oak trees, food chains **148**
observational learning 376, 439
oceans, sound in **424**
Ochrogaster lunifer **120**
Octopus
  cyanea **247**
  vulgaris **441**
octopuses **46**, 63
  blue-ringed **244**, **247**
  common **441**
  day **247**, **269**
  giant Pacific **247**, **365**
  mimic **441**
  paper nautilus **132**
  veined **441**
Odocoileus virginianus **423**
Odontodactylus scyllarus **310**
Oecophylla **135**
  longinoda **413**
  smaragdina 107
oilbird 95
Olenellus **16**

olive baboon
  communication **411**
  troops **300**, **404**
ommatidia, compound eyes **88–9**
omnivores 147, **162–9**
Oncorhynchus
  keta **121**
  mykiss **443**
  nerka **121**
Onychorhynchus coronatus **420**
Oophaga histrionicus **107**
Oophaga pumilio **253**, **315**
operant conditioning, learning 376, 439
Opisthocomus hoazin **361**
Opistognathus **367**
opossum, Virginia **245**
opportunism **162**, **171**
Opsanus tau **425**
orangutan
  nests 142, **452**
  tool-using **440**
  young **372–3**, **380**
orapel **275**
orb-weaver spiders **442**
  golden **442**
orb-web spiders **133**
orca **212–3**, **384**
  see also killer whale
orchid bees **413**
Orcinus orca **213–4**, **384**
orders, classification 21
Ordovician period 16
Ordovician–Silurian extinction 16
ornate jumping spider **301**
Ornithorhynchus anatinus **202**
oropendolas 258
Oryctes nasicornis **311**
Oryctolagus cuniculus **306**
osprey **192–3**
ostracods **417**
ostrich
  breeding **377**, **399**
  common **259**, **377**
  kicking 244, 259
  running **54**
  speed 54, **259**
  temperature control **109**
Otis tarda **167**
Otospermophilus beecheyi **261**
otters **71**
  European **415**
  giant river **375**
  North American river **384**
  sea **173**, **452**
Ouroborus cataphractus **254**
oviparity **347**
oviviparity 379
owls **77**
  barn **60–61**, **93**, **170**
  dark wood **265**
  elf **131**
  great grey **198**, **265**
  hearing **93**
  Lapland **265**
oxpecker, yellow-billed **237**

oxygen 13, 74–5, 136–7, 299
Oxyura jamaicensis **426**
Oxyuranus microlepidotus **189**
oyster toadfish **425**
oystercatchers **376**
  American **173**
  Eurasian **197**

P

pack hunting 206–7
Pagurus prideaux **248**
painted lady butterfly **348**
paintings
  pigeons recognize **445**
pair bonds 300, 332
Paleogene period 19
Paleozoic era 16–18
Palpares immensus **180**
Pamphobeteus **248**
Pan
  paniscus **343**, **438**, **449**
  troglodytes **143**, **215**, **422**, **428**, **433**, **448–9**
Panamanian golden frog **418**
panarthropodia 24
pandas, giant 77, **160**, **331**, **376**
Pandion haliaetus **192–3**
pangolins 68
  Cape **260**
  Temminck's **68**, **260**
  tree **374**
pant-hooting, chimpanzees **428**
panther chameleon **190–91**, **324**
Panthera
  leo **204–5**, **381**, **405**
  leo persica 205
  tigris **110–11**, **343**
Pantherophis guttatus **443**
Panulirus argus **118**
paper nautilus **132**
paper wasp **131**
Papilio
  troilus **267**
  zagreus **265**
Papio anubis **404**
Parabuteo unicinctus **196**
Paradisaea raggiana **330**
Parahyaena brunnea **415**
parasites 229
  flukes 350
  and host's behaviour 243
  life cycles 349
  parasitoids 348
  reproduction 300
  tapeworms 67, 300
Parastrellus hesperus **209**
Paratemnoides nidificator **181**
parent bug **366**
parental care 349, 364
parrotfishes, Bleeker's **251**
parrots 300
  grey **445**
Parson's chameleon **264**

parthenogenesis 13, 266, 293, 296
Parus palustris **159**
Patella vulgata **105**
patterns
  camouflage 264
  recognition **445**
  visual signals **416**
pavement ant **394**
Pavo cristatus **330**
peacock mantis shrimp **310**
peacock worm **163**
peafowl, Indian **330**
pecking order **390**
pectoral herding 214
Pelecanus
  onocrotalus **196**
pelicans **235**
  great white **196**
Pelinobius muticus **425**
Pelobatrachus nasuta **274**
Pelophylax perezi **187**
Pemphigus populitransversus **105**
penguins 15, **102**, **398**
  blubber 66
  chinstrap penguin **102**
  colonies **398**
  emperor penguin **103**, **360–61**
  Galapagos penguin **235**
  gentoo penguin **237**, **378–9**
  king penguin **398–9**, **427**
  rockhopper penguin **280**, **371**, **376**
  swimming 63
  temperature regulation **79**
penis 334, **337**
peppered moth **14**
Pepsis heros **231**
perch 68
perching birds 37
perchlike fishes 31
percomorphs 31
peregrine falcon 170, **192**
perennibranchians 33
Perez's frog **187**
Peringuey's desert adder **103**, **194–5**
periodical cicadas **356**
Periplaneta americana **220**
permanent camouflage 264
Permian period 17
Permian–Triassic extinction 16, 18
petrels, southern giant **86**
Petrochelidon pyrrhonota **402**
Petromyzon marinus **234**
phalarope, red-necked **342**
Phalaropus lobatus **342**
Phascolarctos cinereus **108**, **159**
Phasma gigas **266**
Phengaris arion **366**
pheromones 87, 320, **412–5**
Philetairus socius **140**
phorid fly **349**
phosphorus 218
photosynthesis 13
Phrynosoma cornutum **254**
phyllid leaf insects **267**
Phyllidae **267**

phylogenetic classification 14, 22–3
phylum, classification 21
Physalaemus nattereri **254**
physiology *see* body systems
Phytalmia
  alcicornis **312**
  cervicornis **312–3**
  mouldsi **312**
piddock **58**
Pieris brassicae **152**
pigeons **97**, 300
  rock **445**
pigs 150, **453**
pikas **280**
pike **62**
piked dogfish **357**
  see also spiny dogfish
pileated woodpecker **137**
pine engraver beetle **413**
pineapple fish **69**
Pipa pipa **358**
pipefish, banded **323**
piranhas **164**
Pisaura mirabilis **365**
placental mammals 38, 347, 349
placoid scales **68**, **69**
plaice **273**
plainfin midshipman **303**
plains zebra **433**
plankton 104, 397
plants
  feeding on 150–61
  mutualism 228
  photosynthesis 13
  toxins in **150**, 151
platypus, duck-billed **96**, **202**
play and learning 376–85
Plethodon shermani **324**
Pleuronectes platessa **273**
Ploceus 139
  cucullatus **139**
  luteolus **139**
  velatus **138–9**
Plotosus lineatus **282**
ploughnose chimaera **336**
plovers
  double banded **278**
  grey **197**
  semipalmated **278**
plumed basilisk lizard **257**
poaching
  elephants 263
  giraffes **363**
Podiceps
  cristatus **327**
  nigricollis **371**
Poecilia reticulata **337**
Pogona barbata **166**
poison frogs 245, **253**, 274
  golden **253**
  harlequin **107**
  strawberry **315**
poisons
  stinging cells **174**
  titan triggerfish 106
  venomous spines 244

polar bear 203, 279, **374-5**
  breeding 321, **375**
  dens **130**
  feeding **162**, **173**, **226-7**
  home ranges 104
  hunting 162, **226-7**
polarized light 89, **431**
polyandry 309
Polyboroides typus **166**
Polyerata amabilis **158**
polyps, coral **46**, **77**, **132**
Pomacanthus
  imperator **359**
Pompeii worm **103**
pondskater, common **180**
Pongo pygmaeus **380**, **452**
poplar petiole gall aphid **105**
porcelain fiddler crab **417**
porcupinefishes **69**
  black-spotted **251**
porcupines
  Cape **260-61**
Porichthys notatus **303**
Poroderma pantherinum **249**
porpoises 94, 170
Portia fimbriata **442**
possums, flying 61
posture, courtship 416
pot-belly seahorse **323**
potoo, common **279**
potter wasps **366**
powder blue surgeonfish **156**
prairie dogs
  black-tailed **142**
  Gunnison's **428**
praying mantis **320**
  common **178-9**
Precambrian period 16
predation **146-9**, **170-217**
  bubble-nets **214**
  communication 411
  cooperative hunting 148, **172**, **215**
  group hunting 196
  effects on tadpoles **359**
  electrogenesis **96**
  family hunting 204-5
  killing techniques **173**
  pack hunting 206-7
  social behaviour 389
  wave-hunting **213**
  wave-washing **213**
  weapons **172**
  see also defences
preening, feathers **70**, **433**
prey species
  communication 411
  see also predation
primates
  brachiation **57**
  classification **39**
  communication 416, **422**, **428**
  hands and feet **56-7**
  vision 89
Prionace glauca **120**
problem solving **440**

Procyon lotor **226**, **331**
projectiles, defences 244
pronghorn **75**
pronking **57**
Prosqualodon **19**
protection, body coverings 65
protists 13
Prunella modularis **316**
Pseudoceros ferrugineus **441**
Pseudociccidae rhizoecinae 228
pseudoscorpion, cooperative **181**
Pseudotriton ruber **274**
Psittacus erithacus **445**
ptarmigan, willow **278**
Pteraspis rostrata **17**
Pterodactylus **18**
Pterois volitans **250**
Pteronura brasiliensis **375**
pterosaurs 18
Pterotus obscuripennis **302**
puff adder, African **288**
purple flatworm **441**
purple martin **131**
purple sea urchin **301**
pygmy seahorse 264, **273**
pythons
  Burmese **59**
  green tree **189**
Pyxicephalus adspersus **368**

Q

queen butterfly **413**
quelea, red-billed **403**
Quelea quelea **403**
quills, porcupine **260**

R

rabbits **349**, **439**
  European **306**
raccoon, common **226**, **331**
raccoon, northern **226**
raft spider **85**, **295-5**
raggiana bird-of-paradise **330**
rainbow lizard **324-5**
  see also red-headed rock agama
rainbow trout **443**
rainbowfishes **68**
Ramphastos toco **158**
Rana
  catesbeiana **426**
  temporaria **340**, **358**
Rangifer tarandus **126-7**
Ranoidea splendida **414**
ranoides 33
ratites 36
rats **429**
  banner-tailed kangaroo **78**, **433**
  black **117**
  joy jumps **429**

rattlesnakes **69**
  rattles **93**, **255**
  speckled **316**
  timber **371**
  western diamondback **255**
Rattus **429**
raven **149**
  common **238**
Ray, John 20
ray-finned fishes **22**, **28**, **30**
rays 17-19, **22**, 68
  electric **96**, **430**
  electroreception **96**
  whitespotted eagle **394**
razor shell **59**
razorfish **272**
recycling
  dung beetles **220**
  scavengers **218-27**
red-and-green macaw **167**, **433**
red-backed hawk **172**
red-backed shrike **173**, **198**
red-billed quelea **403**
red blood cells **73**, 76
red cichlid **314**
red-cockaded woodpecker **258**
red crab, Christmas Island **118**
red crossbill **159**
red deer **318**
red-eyed damselfly, small **336-7**
red-eyed tree frog **88**
red fox **113**, **262**
red-headed rock agama **324-5**
red-kneed tarantula, Mexican **56**
red-legged salamander **324**
red light, bioluminescence 186
red mullet, striped **220**
red-necked phalarope **342**
red-necked wallaby **362**, **380**
red salamander **274**
red-sided garter snake **415**
red-spotted newt **340**
red-winged blackbird **326**
red grouse 278
red wood ant **281**
redshank **197**
reef shark, grey **417**
reef squid, bigfin **63**
reef stonefish **272**
reefs, coral **132**, **391**
reindeer **126-7**
  see also caribou
relationships, feeding **228-39**
remora 234
reproduction *see* sex and reproduction
reptiles
  classification **23**, **28**, **29**, **34-5**
  communication 424
  eggs **294**
  evolution 14, 16-19
  hearing 92
  parental care 264
  scales **68**, **69**, 245

reptiles contd.
  skeletons 50
  skin 66
  vision 89
respiration
  breathing **74-5**
  through body coverings 65
retina 83, **89**
Rhincodon typus **164-5**
rhinoceros beetle **311**
  European **47**
Rhinoceros
  sondaicus 22, 23
  unicornis 22, 23, **262**
rhinoceroses **23**, **54**
  black **244-5**, **331**
  Indian 22, **23**, **262**
  Javan 22, **23**
  Sumatran 22, **23**
  white **415**
Rhinolophus
  ferrumequinum **209**
Rhodeus ocellatus **358**
ridley turtle, Atlantic **439**
ring-necked dove **300**
ring-tailed coati **407**
ring-tailed lemur **404**, **412**
rivalry, sexual **308-19**
river dolphins
  Amazon **212**, **333**
river otters
  giant **375**
  North American **384**
robber crab **75**
  see also coconut crab
robins **424**
  American **20**, **349**
  European **20**, **109**, 116
rock agamas
  red-headed **324-5**
  southern **78-9**
rock pigeon **445**
rockhopper penguin **280**, **371**, **376**
rod cells, vision **89**
rodents
  classification 39
  sense of smell 86
Roman snail **80**
rook **402**
rose-snapper, spotted 229
roseate spoonbill **70**
rosy bitterling **358**
rotifers, bdelloid **299**
round scad **284-5**
roundworms **46**
royal albatross, southern **306**
royal flycatcher **420**
royal tern **402**
ruddy duck **426**
ruff **317**
rufous net-casting spider **175**
ruminants, digestive system **161**
running **54-5**
Rupicola peruvianus **317**

S

Sabella pavonina **163**
safari ants **181**
    see also driver ants
Sagittarius serpentarius **193**
sailfin lizards **256-7**
sailfishes 170
salamanders 32, 33, 54, 74
    axolotl **359**
    eastern tiger **304**
    fire **413**
    red **274**
    red-legged **324**
    tiger **54**, **304**
salema, white **84**
saliva, vampire bats 239
Sally lightfoot crab **232-3, 310**
Salmo trutta **187**
salmon 169, **234**, 439
    Atlantic 116
    chum **121**
    sockeye **121**
salt balance 78
Salticidae **178**
sand adder **194-5**
    see also Péringuey's desert adder
sand bubbler crab **219**
sandfish **58**
sandwich tern **402**
sapsucker, yellow-bellied **427**
Sarcophilus harrisii **226**
sardine **196**, **239**
Sargasso Sea **120**
Sargassum fish 265
Sargassum seaweed 265
satellite
    bar-tailed godwit **124**
    tracking 120, **122**, **124**
    ruff, male **317**
satin bowerbird **308**
saturniid moths **270-71**
savanna monitor lizard **370**
sawtooth barracuda **395**
scad, round **284-5**
scale insect, cottony cushion **296**
scales 66, **68-9**, 245
scaleworms 68
scalloped hammerhead shark **183**
scallops **84**
Scarabaeus **220**
scavengers 147, **218-27**
scent, marking territories **104, 111**
Schistocerca gregaria **152**
Schmidt, Johannes 120
scleroglossans 35
Scolopendra gigantea **179**
Scopimera inflata **219**
Scopus umbretta **136**
scorpionfish 272
scorpions
    Arabian fat-tailed **248**
    fat-tailed **172**
    yellow **322**
scrub jay, western **440**

scutes 50, 68, **69**
Scyllaridae **350**
sea anemones *see* anemones
sea cow *see* dugong
sea cucumbers **46, 49**
    leopard **246**
sea fans 264, **266**, 273
sea lamprey **234**
sea lice 121
sea lions
    California **333, 453**
    Steller **405**
sea-nettle jellyfish **72**
sea otter **173, 452**
sea slugs 75, **335**
sea snakes 62, 245
sea squirts **67**
sea urchins **49, 175**
    Antarctic **152**
    purple **301**
sea whips 264
seadragons
    leafy **273**
seahorses **50**, 62, **83**
    golden **265**
    pot-belly **323**
    pygmy 264, **273**
seals 147, **182**
    blubber 66, 227
    elephant seal **76, 319**
    evolution 15
    fur **71**
    fur seal **71, 74-5**
    Hawaiian monk seal **62**
    hooded seal **423**
    leopard seal **200-01**
    northern elephant seal **318**
    skin 66
    swimming 63
    wave-hunting by orca **213**
    wave-washing **213**
seaweed, *Sargassum* 265
secretarybird **193**
self-awareness 440, **450-51**
self medication 452
semipalmated plover **278**
senses 13, **82-97**
    detecting prey 170
    echolocation **94-5**
    electroreception **96**
    hearing **92-3**
    magnetoreception **97**
    taste and smell **86-7**
    touch and vibration **84-5**
    vision **88-9**
Sepia
    apama **174, 310**
    latimanus **268-9**
Sepioteuthis australis **352-3**
sergeant major damselfish **368**
Serrasalmus **164**
serval **262**
sex and reproduction 13, **292-343**
    asexual reproduction **293, 296**
    birth and development
        346-85

sex and reproduction contd.
    courtship 320-33, 411, 416
    diversity 295
    and evolution 295, 308, 364
    finding a mate **300-07**
    longitudinal fission **297**
    mating 300, **334-43**
    raising young 349, **364-75**
    sexual dimorphism **295**, 320
    sexual reproduction 293, 295
    sexual rivalry **308-19**
    social behaviour 289
    temperature and **294**
sharks 50
    basking shark **165**
    blotchy swell shark **357**
    blue shark **120**
    bonnethead shark **299**
    bronze whaler shark **184-5**
    classification **22**
    cookiecutter shark **234**
    defences against 280
    electroreception 96, **97**
    evolution 17-19
    filter feeding 165
    great white shark **182**
    grey reef shark **417**
    horn shark **323**
    mako shark **97**
    megamouth shark **165**
    nervous system **80-81**
    sandtiger shark 357
    scales **68, 69**
    scalloped hammerhead shark **183**
    shortfin mako shark 170
    swimming **62**
    teeth **221**
    tiger shark 170, **221**
    tracking 120
    whale shark **66, 164-5, 234**
    white shark **182**
sharksucker, live **234**
shearwater, sooty 116
sheep tick **231**
shell-brooding cichlid **136**
shells
    crustaceans 26
    defences **245**
    evolution of shelled eggs 14
    molluscs 48, **49**, 65
    tortoises 65
    turtles 51
shield bugs 245
shipworm **58**
shoals, fishes **62-3, 84, 184-5, 280, 282, 395**
shore crab **149, 173**
short-beaked echidna **96, 362**
short-horned chameleon,
    Madagascan **308**
short-tail stingray **303**
shortfin mako shark 170
shoveller **70**
shrews 95
    Eurasian water **86**
    lesser white-toothed **375**

shrikes, red-backed **173, 198**
shrimps **174**
    brine **103**
    cleaner **228-9**
    mantis **89**, 244
    peacock mantis **310**
    snapping **248**
siamang **57, 332**
side-blotched lizard, common **107**
sidewinders **59, 194**
sidewinding adder, Namib desert
    194-5
sifaka, Verreaux's **56**
sight *see* eyes and vision
signals
    communication 411
    courtship 320
    intermittent 416
    visual **416-23**
    see also sounds
silkmoth, calleta **131**
Silurian period 16
silverfish 354
silversides **280**
six-rayed starfish **365**
skeletons **45-51**
    bony skeletons **50-51**
    chalky skeletons **48-9**
    horny skeletons **47**
    joints **45**
    muscles **45**
    water skeletons 45, **46**
skin **65-7**
    breathable skin 74
    defences 67
    scales **68-9**
    touch receptors **84**
skinks 58
    Cape legless **69**
    blue tailed, African **254**
    monkey-tailed **157**
skuas, great **237**
skulls 51
    giraffes **319**
    jaws **172**
    leopard seal **200**
    snakes **85**
    weapon **172**
    woodpecker **137**
skunk, striped **262**
slave-making ant **394**
sleepy lizard, Australian 300
slipper lobster **350**
sloths
    brown-throated three-toed **112, 279**
slow-worm **316**
slugs **59**, 334
    leopard **335**
small red-eyed damselfly
    336-7
smell, sense of 83, 86, 170
    pheromones 86, 87, 281, 320,
        412-15
    scent-marking territories **104, 111**
smooth newt **321**

Smutsia temminckii **260**
snails **81**, **197**, **334**
    African land snail **88**
    amber snail **350**
    garden snail **59**, **350**
    moon snail **173**
    movement 53, **59**
    reproduction 296
    Roman snail **80**
    shells 48, **49**
snake starfish **48**
snakes **103**
    adder **304**
    African puff **288**
    Batesian mimicry 265
    black mamba 170
    bush viper, African **65**
    central American boa **189**
    classification 34, 35
    common garter snake **341**
    corn snake **443**
    eyelash viper **173**, **275**
    eyes 69
    fangs **244**
    feeding 173
    grass snake **252**, **258**, **325**
    green tree python **189**
    horned viper **69**
    inland taipan **189**
    Jacobson's organ **86**, **87**
    lure 171
    moulting **68**
    movement 53, **59**
    Mozambique spitting cobra **255**
    Péringuey's desert adder **103**, **194–5**
    raising young **364**
    rattlesnakes **69**, **93**, **255**
    red-sided garter snake **415**
    scales **68**, **69**
    sea snakes 62, 245
    sidewinding **194**
    skeleton **51**, **85**
    skulls **172**
    speckled rattlesnake **316**
    temperature 170
    timber rattlesnake **371**
    vibration receptors **85**
    viperine snake 359
    western diamondback rattlesnake **255**
    western whip snake **341**
snapping shrimp **248**
snapping turtles
    alligator **189**
    common **325**
snow monkey **380**, **447**
snowy albatross **123**
soaring **61**
sociable weaver **140**
social spider **391**
society **388–407**
sockeye salmon **121**
soft coral **391**
soft leafvent anglerfish **337**
soldier beetles **163**

sole, lemon **357**
Solenopsis **336**
solitary living 389
song thrush **424**
songbirds
    classification 37
sooty shearwater 116
sounds
    alarm calls 411, 424
    communication 424–9, **433**
    courtship 330, 332
    echolocation 83, **94–5**
    hearing **92–3**
    infrasound 83
    mimicry 445
    multi-modal **423**
    production 93
    train-rattle 330
southern brown kiwi 193
    see also Stewart Island brown kiwi
southern calamari squid **352–3**
southern giant petrel **86**
southern green stink bug **431**
southern ground hornbill **88**
southern masked weaver **138–9**
southern rock agama **78–9**
southern rockhopper penguin **280**, **371**, **376**
    see also rockhopper penguin
sparkling violet-ear hummingbird **61**
sparrowhawk, Eurasian **61**
sparrows 416
    fox 116
    house 14
spatial learning **104**
spawning grounds, eels **120**
species
    classification 20–1
    communication 411
    evolution 15
    numbers of 13
    speciation 15
speckled rattlesnake **316**
speckled wood butterfly **308**
spectacled caiman **398**
speed
    predators 170
    primates 57
    speed to energy ratio 53
sperm
    cells 13
    courtship 321
    external fertilization 334
    internal fertilization 334
    mating 334–43
    sexual reproduction **292**, 296
sperm whale **94**, 439
spermatophore 321, 322, 324, 334, 335, 337, 340
Spheniscus mendiculus **235**
sphinx moths **74**
Sphyraena putnamae **395**
Sphyrapicus nuchalis **427**
Sphyrna
    lewini **183**
    tiburo **299**

spicebush swallowtail butterfly **267**
spider crabs **47**, **266**
    spiny **281**
spiders **56**, 74
    bird-eating spider **248**
    black and yellow garden spider **133**
    black widow spider **320**
    dancing white lady spider **105**
    decoy spider **178**
    fishing spider **176–7**
    fringed jumping spider **442**
    garden spider **104**
    jumping spiders **47**, **178**, **366**, **417**
    kerengga ant-like jumper **310**
    king baboon spider **425**
    mexican red-kneed spider **56**
    nursery web spider **365**
    orb-weaver spiders **442**
    orb-web spiders **133**
    ornate jumping spider **301**
    raft spider **85**, **295–5**
    rufous net-casting spider **175**
    sexual dimorphism 320
    social spider **391**
    tarantula spiders **170**, **244**, **248**
    vibration receptors 85
    wasp spider **431**
    water spider **132**
    webs 171
spindle cowrie 264
spines **244**
spinner dolphin **407**
spiny dogfish **357**, **394**
spiny lobster, Caribbean **118**
spiny-rayed fishes 31
spiny spider crab **281**
spiracles **74**
Spirobranchus
    giganteus 246
splitfin flashlightfish **282**
spontaneous learning 439
spoonbills, roseate **70**
spotted hyena **224–5**, **226**, **406**
spotted rose-snapper 229
springbok **57**, **411**
spurdog **357**
    see also spiny dogfish
Squalicorax **19**
Squalus acanthias **357**, **394**
squid **49**, 62
    bigfin reef **63**
    bioluminescence 416
    bobtail **268**
    clawed armhook **365**
    skin 269, **268**
    southern calamari **352–3**
squirrels, California ground **261**
    see also flying squirrels
stag fly **312–3**
star-nosed mole **84**, **215**
starfish
    common starfish **173**
    crown-of-thorns starfish **48**, **49**
    embryo development **347**

starfish contd.
    feeding 173
    limb regeneration **246**
    movement **54**
    six-rayed starfish **365**
    snake starfish **48**
starlings **162**
    common **283**
statocysts **84**
status
    social behaviour 390
    visual signals 416
stealth, predators 171
Steller sea lion **405**
Stenaptinus insignis **249**
Stenella longirostris **407**
Stercorarius skua **237**
Sterechinus neumayeri **152**
Sterninae **402**
Sternula albifrons **326**
Stewart Island brown kiwi **193**
stick insects
    giant **266**
sticklebacks **334**
    three-spine **321**
stinging cells, jellyfish **174**
stingrays 19
    short-tail **303**
stink bug, southern green **431**
stomach
    porcupinefish **251**
    ruminants **161**
stonefishes, reef **272**
stoplight loosejaw **186**
storks 61
    Marabou **218**
    white **137**
stotting **288**, **411**
    see also pronking
straw-coloured fruit bat **128**
strawberry poison frog **315**
streaked tenrec **95**
stress, in baboons 404
stridulation 93, 424, 425
striped catfish **282**
striped red mullet **220**
striped skunk **262**
Strix
    nebulosa **198**
Strongylocentrotus purpuratus **301**
Struthio camelus **259**, **377**, **399**
sturgeon 68
Sturnus vulgaris **283**
subterranean predators 170
Suez Canal, Lessepsian migration 117
Sula
    dactylatra **377**
    nebouxii **326**
Sumatran rhinoceros 22, **23**
sun-tailed monkey **422**
sunbittern **259**
sunfishes, bluegill **314**
supermales, wrasses **303**
surgeonfishes 244
    powder blue **156**

Suricata suricatta **286-7**, **406**
Surinam toad **358**
survival strategies **245**
Sus scrofa **168**, **453**
swallowing, with eyes **187**
swallows 53, 61
    American cliff **402**
    barn 116, **125**
swallowtail butterfly,
    spicebush **267**
swans
    mute **131**, **316**
    whooper **399**
swarming 152, 393
sweat bee **390**
swell shark, blotchy **357**
swiftlet, cave **95**, 131
swifts **61**
    common **342**
swim bladder **62**, 92
swimming **62-3**
symbiosis **228**
Symphalangus syndactylus **332**
Synanceia verrucosa **272**
Synanthedon **272**
Syncerus caffer **161**, **289**
synovial fluid 45
Systema Naturae 20
syrinx, birds **93**

T

Tachyglossus aculeatus **362**
Tadarida brasiliensis **288**, **374**
tadpoles **136**, **170**, 348, **351**, **358-9**, **368**
tailorbird **130**
tails
    shedding **254**
    swimming 62
taipan, inland **189**
talons **172**
Talpa europaea **143**
tapeworms **67**, **300**
tapirs 23, 76
tarantula hawk wasp **231**
tarantula spiders **170**, **244**, **248**
    red-kneed, Mexican **56**
tarpon **280**
Tasmanian devil **226**
taste, sense of 83, **86-7**
taxonomy **20-21**, 22
teeth 244
    carnivores **172**
    defences 244
    elephants **150**
    hunting 147, 151
    leopard seal **200**
    lions **205**
    omnivore 162
    sea lamprey **234**
    sharks **69**, **221**, **234**
Teleopsis dalmanni **311**
teleosts 30

Temminck's pangolin **68**, **260**
Temnothorax albipennis **432**
temperature 53, 68, 103
    and sex **295**
    control of 65, **78-9**
    sensors 83, 170
    sound 424
    tolerance **281**
tendons 57
tenrecs 95
    streaked **95**
termite mounds **131**, **134**, **202**, **370**
termites **131**, **202**, **228**, **448-9**
    African mound-building **134**
terns **402**
    Arctic 116
    little **326**
    royal **402**
    sandwich **402**
Terrapene carolina **254**
territories 103, **104-15**
    aggression 104, 106, **110-11**
    boundaries **104**
    overlapping **112**
    scent-marking **104**, **111**
    seasonal variation **109**
    see also colonies
Tetramorium immigrans **394**
Tetrao urogallus **306**
tetrapods 14, 36, 28, 29, 30
Tettigoniidae **266**
Texas horned lizard **254**
Thalassarche melanophris **108-9**, **221**
Thalasseus
    maximus **402**
    sandvicensis **402**
Thalassoma bifasciatum **303**
Thamnophis
    sirtalis **341**
    sirtalis parietalis **415**
Thaumoctopus mimicus **441**
thermals, soaring on **61**
thermoreceptors (temperature sensors) 83, 170
Thomson's gazelle **288**, **382-3**
thorn bug **267**, **430**
thorny devil **243**
three-banded armadillo **260**
three-spine stickleback **321**
thrush, song **424**
Thysanostoma loriferum **416**
ticks 228, **229**, **231**
    sheep **231**
tiger butterfly, large **265**
tiger leech, Asian **231**
tiger salamander **54**, **304**
tiger salamander, eastern **304**
tiger shark 170, **221**
tigers
    Amur tiger **111**
    Bengal tiger **111**, **264**
    claws 244
    eyes **88**
    hunting 173

tigers contd.
    mating 87, **343**
    play **376**
    raising young **364**
    skeleton **50-51**
    territories **110-11**
timber rattlesnake **371**
Tinbergen, Niko 104
titan triggerfish **106**
tits
    blue 103, **420**
    coal 103
    long-tailed **140**, **403**
    marsh **159**
toadfishes
    oyster **425**
toads **32**, 348
    cane **67**, 117, **252**
    European common **122**, **252**, **338-9**
    Great Plains **304**
    Mallorcan midwife **359**
    midwife **334**
    Mallorcan midwife **359**
    natterjack **340**
    Surinam **358**
    yellow-bellied **252**
toco toucan **158**
tokoeka 193
    see also Stewart Island brown kiwi
tokay gecko **426**
Tolypeutes tricinctus **260**
tongues
    Jacobson's organ **86-7**
    taste buds **86**
tools, use of 15, 151, 215, **440**, **446-9**, 452, 453
tooth spirals, heliocoprion **17**
toothed whales **94**, 170
torpor 79
tortoises 51, 65, **245**
    Galapagos giant **157**, **314**
    marginated **349**
    tortoiseshell", 165
toucans, toco **158**
touch, sense of 83, 84, 170
    communication 411, 430, **434-5**
    courtship 321
    hair and 71
toxins, in plants **150**, 151
Toxotes jaculatrix **183**
Trachops cirrhosus 300
Trachylepis quinquetaeniata **254**
tracking
    bar-tailed godwit **124**
    sharks 120
    turtles **122**, **305**
tree ants 135
    see also weaver ants
tree frogs 55
    dainty green **424**
    Izecksohn's Brazilian **165**
    magnificent **414**
    red-eyed **88**
    Verreaux's **320**

tree pangolin **374**
treehole frog **426**
trees
    drumming on 424, 428
    in food chains **148**
trial and error, learning 265, 439
Triassic–Jurassic extinction 18
Triassic period 18
Trichechus manatus **414**
Tridacna gigas **298**
triggerfish, titan **106**
trilobites, olenellus **16**
triton trumpet **48**
Triturus
    alpestris **369**
    cristatus **418**
trout **69**, 97
    brown **187**
    rainbow **443**
trumpet, triton **48**
tsetse fly **356**
tufted capuchin **447**
tuna **62**
    bluefin 123
tunnelling **58**
turbellarian, marine **74**
Turdus migratorius **20**
turkey vulture **222**
turnstone **197**
Tursiops truncatus **319**, **429**, **453**
turtles
    alligator snapping turtles **189**
    classification 28, 34
    common snapping turtle **325**
    eastern box turtle **254**
    eggs **295**
    evolution 14, **18**
    green turtle **305**, **349**, **360**
    hawksbill turtle **165**
    leatherback turtle **122**
    ridley turtle, Atlantic **439**
    scute 68
    shells **51**
    swimming 63
    tracking **122**, **305**
tusks, elephants 244
tympanic ears 92
Tyrannosaurus rex **19**

U

ultraviolet 420
    glow **301**
    vision 83, 89
Umbonia crassicornis **267**
umbrella bird **197**
    see also black heron
urine 78
    marking territories 78, **111**, **331**
Uroplatus sikorae **274-5**
Ursus
    arctos **169**, **381**
    maritimus **226-7**, **374-5**

V

Vachellia 161
vampire bat, common **239**
Vandellia cirrhosa **235**
Varanus **370**
  komodoensis **188**, **341**
veined octopus **441**
Venezuelan red howler monkey **428**
venom *see* poisons
venus comb murex **246**
Verreaux's sifaka **56**
Verreaux's tree frog **320**
vertebrae **50-51**
vertebrates
  body systems **73**
  burrowing 59
  circulation 76
  classification 15, 22-3, 24, **28-9**
  communication 411, 412, 424
  evolution 14, 16-19
  eyes **89**
  Jacobson's organ **87**
  joints 45
  muscles **45**
  nervous systems 81
  number of species 13
  scales **68**
  sense of smell 86
  skeletons **50-51**
  touch receptors 84
Vespa
  crabro **248**
  mandarina **181**
  tropica **90**
Vespula vulgaris **135**
vibrations
  communication 411, 430, 431, 432, 434
  hearing 92
  receptors 85
village weaver 130, **139**
Vipera berus **304**
viperine snake 359
vipers
  bush **65**
  eyelash **173**, **275**
  horned **69**
virgin birth 296
Virginia opossum **245**
vision *see* eyes
visual signals, communication 411, **416-7**
viviparity 347
vocalizations 93
Vogelkop bowerbird **140**
vomeronasal organ **86**, **87**, 412
Vulpes vulpes **113**
Vultur gryphus **108**
vultures 61, 104
  African white-backed **222**
  Egyptian **66**
  griffon, Eurasian **222-3**
  Old World vultures 222
  turkey **222**

W

waders 70
bills **197**
"waggle dance", bees **431**
walking **54-5**
wallaby, red-necked **362**, **380**
Wallace's flying frog **61**
walrus **65**, **66**, **216-7**
warfare 390
"warm-blooded" animals 53, 65
warning colours **245**
warthog **206-7**, **239**
washing food **447**
wasps **47**
  braconid **356**
  common **135**
  digger **104**
  fig **311**
  paper **131**
  parasitic 349
  potter **366**
  tarantula hawk **231**
wasp spider **431**
water
  movement in 53
  sound in **424**
  walking on **256-7**
  water balance 78
water bug nymph, giant **180**
water dikkop **243**, **258-9**
water flea 13
water-holding frog **78**
water lily frog **300**
water shrew, Eurasian **86**
water skeletons 45, **46**
water spider **132**
water strider **430**
waterfowl 36
waterproofing feathers 70
wave-hunting, orca **213**
wave-washing **213**
waxwings **70**
weapons
  defences **244**
  predators **172**
weaver ants **130**, **135**, **413**
weaver birds
  little **139**
  red-billed quelea **403**
  sociable **140**
  southern masked **138-9**
  village 130, **139**
webbed feet **63**, **202**
webs, spiders **133**, **171**
weever fish **244**, 273
weevils, cabbage seed **412**
West Indian manatee **414**
western capercaillie **306**
western diamondback rattlesnake **255**
western grebe 327
western honey bee **431**
western scrub jay **440**
western whip snake 341
Westlothiana lizzae **17**
whale shark **66**, **164-5**, **234**
whales 280
  baleen **162**, 173
  barnacles **228**
  beluga whale **279**, **375**
  blubber 66
  blue whale **168**
  classification 22, 38
  Cuvier's beaked whale **75**
  echolocation 94, 170
  evolution 15, 19
  gray 116, **227**
  humpback whale **128-9**, **214**
  killer **212-3**, **384**
  lice **228**
  migration **128**
  skeletons 51
  skin **66**
  southern right whale **162**
  sperm whale **94**, 439
  rorqual whale 116
  toothed whale **94**, 170
whip snake, western **341**
whiskered bat **79**
whiskers **71**, 84, **85**, **86**
white-backed vulture, African **222**
white-bearded wildebeest **129**
white-nosed coati **168**
white pelican, great **196**
white rhinoceros **415**
white salema **84**
white shark **182**
white stork **137**
white-tailed deer **423**
white-tailed eagle **192-3**
white-toothed shrew, lesser **375**
white-winged chough **420**
white-winged fairywren **306**
whitespotted eagle rays **394**
whitetail dragonfly, common **105**
whooper swan **399**
whooping crane **125**
wild boar **162**, **168**, **453**
wild dog, African **206-7**, **208**, 430
wildebeest **280**, **349**, **444**
  blue 116, **129**
  white-bearded **129**
willow grouse **278**
willow ptarmigan **278**
wings
  birds **60-61**
  butterflies and moths **68**
  feathers **70**
  insects **60**
wolves
  body language **423**
  feeding relationships **238**
  grey wolf **238**, **423**
  howling **114-5**, **410**
  pack hierarchy **423**
  prey **126**
wombat **67**
wood-owl, dark **265**
woodlice **47**, 53, **148**, **218**
woodpecker finch **15**
woodpeckers
  acorn woodpecker **158**
  pileated woodpecker **137**
  red-cockaded woodpecker **258**
  shock absorbers **137**
  yellow-bellied sapsucker **427**
worm casts **77**
worms
  anatomy 45, **46**
  Christmas tree worm **246**, **334**
  excretion 67, 78
  feather duster worm **246**
  giant feather duster worm **441**
  peacock worm **163**
  nematode worm **46**, **296**
  Pompeii worm **103**
  respiration 65
  see also earthworms
wrasses **416**
  bluehead **303**
  bluestreak cleaner **235**
wren **93**

X

Xenohyla truncata **165**

Y

yak **103**
yellow-bellied sapsucker **427**
yellow-bellied toad **252**
yellow-billed oxpecker **237**
yellow scorpion **322**
yolk sac **349**, **357**

Z

Zalophus californianus **333**, **453**
zebra longwing butterfly **302**
zebras **91**
  Burchell's zebra **116**
  camouflage **264**
  defences **244**, **280**
  flehmen response **87**
  movement **55**
  plains **433**
  predators **444-5**
zygote 13, 293, 347

Acknowledgments

For this edition, the publisher would like to thank Saumya Agarwal, Ekta Chadha, Abhijit Dutta, Debjyoti Mukherjee , Arshti Narang, and Anjali Sachar for text assistance; and Manpreet Kaur and Vagisha Pushp for aditional picture research.

For previous editions:
Dorling Kindersley would like to thank the following people for their help in the preparation of this book: Dawn Techow, Anna Pikovsky, and Udayan Chattopadhyay at the American Museum of Natural History for their help in co-ordinating the project; Peter Laws for early design work; Jack Metcalf for administrative assistance; and Helen Gilks, Daniel Gilpin, and Rachelle Macapagal.

Charlotte Uhlenbroek would like to thank: Ben Anderson and Simon McCreadie for help with research; Julian Partridge of Bristol University and Bridget Waller of the University of Portsmouth for comments on the text; Dan Rees, for his support and patience; and Sheila Abelman for being a wonderful agent and helping to get this project off the ground.

For their help in supplying images, **Laura Barwick** would like to thank: all at DK Image Library; Martin Copeland and Jenny Baskaya for their in-house support; Rebecca Sodergren and Sarah Hopper for picture research cover; and, in particular, all the researchers at the main contributing agencies who helped turn over every stone to find the very best pictures for this title.

Sources for the illustrations listed below are as follows: **p.75** Cuvier's beaked whale diving graph: Peter Tyack et al, *Journal of Experimental Biology*, Vol. 209, p.4238; **p.85** Seismic signalling in mole rats: "Seismic signal transmission between burrows of the Cape mole-rat," P. M. Narins, O. J. Reichman, J. U. M. Jarvis, and E. R. Lewis, *Journal of Comparative Physiology*, 170:13-21, 1992; **p.93** Timelags in sound reception: www.nature.com/nature/journalv417/n6886/images/417322a-f1.2jp; **p.94** Echolocation in sperm whales: http://palaeo.gly.bris.ac.uk/Palaeofiles/whales/odontoceti.htm; **p.95** Echolocation by Australian cave swiftlets: "Hearing and echolocation in the Australian grey swiftlet", Roger B. Coles, Masakazu Konishi, and John D. Pettigrew, *Journal of Experimental Biology* 129, 365-371, 1987; **p.107** Territorial boundaries of the Malaysian giant ant: "Territoriality in the Malaysian giant ant Camponotus gigas," Martin Pfeiffer and Karl E. Linsenmair, *Journal of Ethology Volume* 19, Number 2, 75-85, December 2001; **p.117** Body fat and migration in birds: *The Complete Encyclopedia of Birds and Bird Migration*, Christopher M. Perrins and Jonathan Elphick, 2003, p.26; **p.162** Intenstine length in starlings: F. Harvey Pough, Christine M. Janis, and John B. Heiser, *Vertebrate Life*, p.461; **p.182** Attacks by great whites: "Graphs of white shark attacks and percentage of fatal attacks by decade" (web publication), International Shark Attack File, Florida Museum of Natural History, University of Florida; **p.186** Pharyngeal jaws in moray eels: "Raptoral jaws in the throat help moray eels swallow large prey," Rita S. Mehta and Peter C. Wainwright, *Nature* 449, 79-82, 6 September 2007; **p.209** Western pipistrelle attack sequence: "Echolocation by insect-eating bats," Hans-Ulrich Schnitzler and Elizabeth K.V. Kalko, *BioScience* July 2001/Vol.51 No.7; p.241 Echo recognition in greater horseshoe bats: "Classification of insects by echolocating greater horseshoe bats," G. von der Emde and H-U. Schnitzler, *Journal of Comparative Physiology*, August 1990/Vol. 167 No.3; **p.214** Lobtail feeding in humpback whales: "Culture in whales and dolphins," L. Rendell and H. Whitehead, *Behavioural and Brain* Sciences 24 (2); **p.278** Plumage change in the willow ptarmigan: "Cryptic behaviour in moulting hen willow ptarmigan lagopus l. lagopus during snow melt," Johan B. Steen, Kjell Einar Erikstad, and Karsten Høidal, *Ornis Scandinavica*, Vol. 23, No.1 (Jan.-Mar., 1992), pp.101-104; **p.433** Kangaroo rat sonogram: J.A. Randall, Acoustic Society of America.

The publisher would like to thank the following for their kind permission to reproduce their photographs:

(Key: a-above; b-below/bottom; c-centre; f-far; l-left; r-right; t-top)

2-3 naturepl.com: Christophe Courteau. **4-5 National Geographic Image Collection:** Norbert Rosing. **7 naturepl.com:** Tui De Roy. **8-9 stevebloom.com. 10-1 naturepl.com:** Kim Taylor. **12 Ardea:** Jean Paul Ferrero (fcla). **FLPA:** Colin Marshall (br). **Getty Images:** James Balog (ftl); Bill Beatty (fclb); Ralph Lee Hopkins/National Geographic (crb); Jeff Lepore (bl). **naturepl.com:** Willem Kolvoort (fcra); Michel Roggo (cra); Jeff Rotman (fbl). **Gastone Pivatelli:** (clb). **Science Photo Library:** Gilbert S. Grant (fcrb). **SeaPics.com:** (tr) (cla). **stevebloom.com:** (tl) (fbr) (ftr). **13 Ardea:** Jean Michel Labat (clb). **Corbis:** Paul Souders (cr). **naturepl.com:** Nick Garbutt (crb). **Photolibrary:** Phototake Inc (tr). **Alex Wild/myrmecos.net:** (cra). **14 DK Images:** Jerry Young (bl) (bc). **15 Alamy Stock Photo:** Rolf Nussbaumer (br). Ardea: D. Parer & E. Parer-Cook (cr). **18 DK Images:** Colin Keates (c) Dorling Kindersley, Courtesy of the Natural History Museum, London (cra) (crb). **19 DK Images:** Colin Keates (c) Dorling Kindersley, Courtesy of the Natural History Museum, London (crb). **20 Alamy Stock Photo:** Nordic Photos (cb). **Shutterstock:** Michael J Thompson (bl). **21 Alamy Stock Photo:** Terry Whittaker (br/tworhino). **Photolibrary:** Mary Plage/OSF (br). Shutterstock: Stephane Angue (cb); John Carleton (cra); EcoPrint (crb/black rhino); Jan Gottwald (crb); Volker Kirchberg (tr); Snowleopard1 (crb/indian rhino); Elena Talberg (br/rhinos); Chris Turner (cr). **22 Alamy Stock Photo:** blickwinkel (cla). **Science Photo Library:** Peter Scoones (cr); Sinclair Stammers (br). **SeaPics.com:** (tl). **Shutterstock:** Ian Scott (ca) (cra). **23 Klaus Lang & WWF Indonesia:** (bl). **naturepl.com:** Rod Williams (clb). **Shutterstock:** Ziga Camernik (cl); Luis Louro (fcl); Victor Soares (c). **40-1 Getty Images / iStock:** E+ / assalve. **42-3 Getty Images / iStock:** Grafissimo. **44 National Geographic Image Collection:** David Doubilet. **46 naturepl.com:** AFLO (bc); Jurgen Freund (cl) (bl); Jeff Rotman (fbl) (br); Sinclair Stammers (tr). **47 FLPA:** Reinhard Dirscherl (c). **Science Photo Library:** Susumu Nishinaga (tr). **48 Photolibrary:** Tobias Berhard/OSF (tr); Howard Hall/OSF (ca). **48-49 naturepl.com:** Jeff Rotman (bl). **49 DK Images:** Steve Gorton/Oxford University of Natural History (tc). **Photolibrary:** David Fleetham/OSF (br). **Science Photo Library:** Eye of Science (cl); M. I. Walker (tr). **50 Science Photo Library:** Steve Gschmeissner (clb); Susumu Nishinaga (cl). **51 naturepl.com:** Mark Payne-Gill (tc); Jose B. Ruiz (tl); Dave Watts (tr). **52 NHPA/Photoshot:** Martin Harvey. **53 Ardea:** Bill Coster (clb); Ken Lucas (cb). **naturepl.com:** Staffan Widstrand (bc). **Photolibrary:** David M Dennis/OSF (bc). . **54 Alamy Stock Photo:** imagebroker/Alamy (c). **Ardea:** Gavin Parsons (bl). **FLPA:** Mitsuaki Iwago/Minden Pictures (bc). **Getty Images:** Piotr Naskrecki/Minden Pictures (cl). **Sharon Heald:** (cb). **55 naturepl.com:** Ingo Arndt (crb).**shahimages.com :** Anup and Manoj Shah. **56 Alamy Stock Photo:** A & J Visage (br). **FLPA:** Mark Moffett/Minden Pictures (clb). **Science Photo Library:** Claude Nuridsany & Marie Perennou (cl); Andrew Syred (c). **56-7 Nick Garbutt. 57 naturepl.com:** Philippe Clement (cr). **NHPA/Photoshot:** Stephen Dalton (cra). **58 Alamy Stock Photo:** blickwinkel (tr) (cra). **naturepl.com:** David Shale (ca). **Still Pictures:** F. Hecker (tc). **58-9 NHPA/Photoshot:** Guy Edwardes. **59 naturepl.com:** Philippe Clement (tr). **NHPA/Photoshot:** Roy Walker (cla) (ca). **60 FLPA:** Michael Durham/Minden Pictures (ca). **naturepl.com:** Kim Taylor (tr). **60-1 naturepl.com:** Kim Taylor. **61 naturepl.com:** Todd Pusser (c); Gabriel Rojo (br); Markus Varesvuo (bc). **NHPA/Photoshot:** Stephen Dalton (cra). **62 FLPA:** B. Borrell Casals (cr); Colin Marshall (bc). **naturepl.com:** Michael Pitts (bl). **63 FLPA:** Chris Newbert/Minden Pictures (t). **naturepl.com:** Georgette Douwma (crb); Nature Production (clb) (bl). **64 stevebloom.com. 65 Alamy Stock Photo:** Andre Seale (cl). **Getty Images:**-Michael D. Kern (c). **66 Ardea:** Ken Lucas (bl). **naturepl.com:** Doug Perrine (c); Premaphotos (cl). **NHPA/Photoshot:** Martin Harvey (crb). **66-7 NHPA/Photoshot:** Martin Harvey. **67 Corbis:** Stuart Westmorland (br). **Getty Images:** David Burder (c); Tim Laman/National Geographic (bc). **68 Corbis:** Gallo Images (cra). **naturepl.com:** Premaphotos (fcl); Doug Wechsler (cl). **69 Alamy Stock Photo:** Arte Sub (fbl); Chris Mattison (fcra). **Corbis:** Robert Pickett (br); Jeffrey L Rotman (fclb); Paul Souders (cra); Winfried Wisniewski/Zefa (fbr). **Chris Mattison Nature Photographics:** (crb). **naturepl.com:** Georgette Douwma (bl); Tony Phelps (cr); Jeff Rotman (fcl). **NHPA/Photoshot:** Image Quest 3-D (tr); Mark O'Shea (c). **Photolibrary:** OSF (cl). **Science Photo Library:** Eye of Science (fcla). **70 FLPA:** Winfried Wisniewski/Foto Natura (bl). **Shutterstock.com:** Rick Thornton (cra). **Markus Varesvuo:** Markus Varesvuo/birdphoto.fi (crb). **71 Alamy Stock Photo:** franzfoto.com (bl); Nearby (ca). **Corbis:** Gallo Images (bc); Staffan Widstrand (tr). **NHPA/Photoshot:** Kevin Schafer (c). **Science Photo Library:** British Antarctic Survey (tc). **72 Science Photo Library:** Gilbert S. Grant. **74** Alamy Stock Photo: Scott Camazine (bc). David Bickford: (cl). **naturepl.com:** Jurgen Freund (tr). **Science Photo Library:** Microfield Scientific Ltd (cb). **74-5 Corbis**: Paul Souders. **75 Ardea:** B. Moose Peterson (br). **FLPA:** Chris Newbert/Minden Pictures (cra); Ariadne Van Zandbergen (clb). **76 Thomas Marent:** (clb). **naturepl.com:** Peter Bassett (br). **Photolibrary:** Phototake Inc/OSF (ca). **Science Photo Library:** Professors PM Motta & S Correr (tr); Dr Linda Stannard, UCT (cra). **77 FLPA:** Frans Lanting (bc); Mark Moffett/Minden Pictures (cb). **Photolibrary:** Satoshi Kuribayashi/OSF (tr). **78 Alamy Stock Photo:** Images of Africa Photobank (bc); Michael J. Kronmal (clb). **Ardea:** D. Parer & E. Parer-Cook (cl). naturepl.com: Mary McDonald (ca). **78-9 FLPA:** Ariadne Van Zandbergen. **79 Alamy Stock Photo:** Steve Bloom Images (tr). **FLPA:** Frans Lanting (crb). **naturepl.com:** Hans Christoph Kappel (br). **80 Alamy Stock Photo:** Phototake Inc (ca). **Science Photo Library:** Dr John Zajicek (tl). **80-1 Science Photo Library:** D. Roberts. **81 Alamy Stock Photo:** Phototake Inc (ca). **naturepl.com:** Gary K. Smith (br). **Science Photo Library:** Thierry Berrod, Mona Lisa Production (tl); H. Raguet/Eurelios (bl). **82 stevebloom.com. 83 naturepl.com:** Philippe Clement (bl); Andy Sands (cl). **Science Photo Library:** D. Roberts (br). **84 naturepl.com:** Brandon Cole (bl). **Photolibrary:** Rodger Jackman/OSF (crb). Science **Photo Library:** Steve Gschmeissner (cr); Susumu Nishinaga (cl); Rod Planck (cla). **85 naturepl.com:** Geoff Dore (ca); Anup Shah (cb). **NHPA/Photoshot:** Peter & Beverly Pickford (cra). **86 Corbis:** Fritz Polking (crb). **naturepl.com:** Dave Bevan (ca); Andy Sands (cb). **NHPA/Photoshot:** Anthony Bannister (cl). **Photolibrary:** Owen Newman/OSF (bc); Phototake Inc/OSF (c). **86-7 FLPA:** Derek Middleton. **87 naturepl.com:** Christophe Courteau (ca); Tony Heald (ca). **88 Alamy Stock Photo:** Martin Harvey (clb); Mike Veitch (cl). **naturepl.com:** Mark Carwardine (ca); Nick Garbutt (fclb); Alan James (fcl); Toby Sinclair (cb). **Christian Ziegler:** (c). **88-9 Corbis:** Visuals Unlimited. **89 Alamy Stock Photo:** blickwinkel (cr); imagebroker (ca). **Science Photo Library:** Leonard Lessin (bl) (bc); Omikron (tr). **90-1 Getty Images / iStock:** Abdul Latif. **92 Alamy Stock Photo:** Marrin Dembinsky Photo Associates (clb). **Science Photo Library:** J. C. Revy (crb). **92-3 Tony Heald. 93 FLPA:** Tim Fitzharris/Minden Pictures (fbr). **naturepl.com:** Premaphotos (bc); Shattil & Rozinski (br). **94 Ardea:** Augusto Stanzani (bl). naturepl.com: Doc White (cl). **94-5 Ardea:** Jean Paul Ferrero. **95 Alamy Stock Photo:** Danita Delimont (bc). **NHPA/Photoshot:** A. N. T. Photo Library (cr). **96 Ardea:** Pat Morris (cra). **FLPA:** Norbert Wu/Minden Pictures (bc). **naturepl.com:** Dave Watts (tl). **96-7 Photolibrary:** Chris & Monique Fallows/Apex Predators/OSF. **97 Alamy Stock Photo:** David Hosking (br). **NHPA/Photoshot:** Martin Harvey (crb). **Science Photo Library:** Catherine Pouedras (cb). **98-9 Getty Images:** Moment Open / Jim Cumming. **100 Getty Images:** Photodisc / Manoj Shah. **102 Corbis:** Frans Lanting. **103 Alamy Stock Photo:** Mark Conlin (br/fish); Gallo Images (br/side winding snake); Juniors Bildarchiv (cr). **imagequestmarine.com:** Peter Batson (crb). **Photolibrary:** Mary Plage/OSF (br/yak). **Science Photo Library:** Geroge Steinmetz (br/soda flats). **104 Alamy Stock Photo:** Steve Bloom Images (cb); Holmes Garden Photos (br). **naturepl.com:** George McCarthy (l). **105 Alamy Stock Photo:** Natural Visions (cl). **Ardea:** Tom & Pat Leeson (bl). **Thomas P Peschak/thomaspeschak.com:** (tc). **H. A. (Joe) Pase III, Lufkin , TX:** (crb) (br). **106 Alamy Stock Photo:** Wolfgang Polzer (bl). **NHPA/Photoshot:** Michael Patrick O'Neill (br). **106-7 Ch'ien C. Lee:** (t). **107 FLPA:** Larry West (bc). **Thomas Marent:** (bl). **108 Alamy Stock Photo:** Rodney Hyett (bl). **NHPA/Photoshot:** John Shaw (clb). **Photolibrary:** Tui De Roy/OSF (tr). **108-9 Andy Rouse Wildlife Photography:** (b). **109 Getty Images:** Geoff du Feu (tr). **110-1 shahimages.com :** Anup and Manoj Shah. **111 naturepl.com:** Anup Shah (br); Klein & Hubert (bl). **112 fogdenphotos.com :** M & P Fogden (cla). **Getty Images / iStock:** E+ / DamianKuzdak (cra). **112-3 naturepl.com:** James Aldred (b). **113 naturepl.com:** Laurent Geslin (cla); David Kjaer (tr); Ian Redmond (br). **114-5 Dr. Elliot McGucken / McGucken Fine Art. 116** Alamy Stock Photo: Steve Bloom Images (br). **116-7 Photolibrary:** John Downer/OSF. **117 Alamy Stock Photo:** Terry Whittaker (br). **Corbis:** Jonathan Blair (bl). **118 Tom Biegalski:** Tom Biegalski/TTBphoto.com (cr). **naturepl.com:** Jurgen Freund (tc) (cra); Doug Perrine (bl).. **119 FLPA:** Frans Lanting (t). **Thomas Marent:** (bl). **120 Ardea:** Don Hadden (tc). **naturepl.com:** Doug Perrine (cr); David Shale (crb). **SeaPics.com:** (clb). **121 National Geographic Image Collection:** Paul Nicklen (fbl). **naturepl.com:** Michel Roggo (bl). **Photolibrary:** Daniel Cox/OSF (ca). **SeaPics.com:** (bc) (br). **122 FLPA:** Frans Lanting (cl) (c). **naturepl.com:** Michael Hutchinson (tr); George McCarthy (ca); Doug Perrine (clb); Ralph Pace (br). **Photolibrary:** Olivier Grunewald/OSF (br). **123 Alamy Stock Photo:** Nature PL (cla). **Getty Images:** Jason Edwards (cb). **Splashdowndirect.com:** Dave Hansford/Greenpeace (br). **124 USGS photo by Robert Gill:** (br). **naturepl.com:** Mike Read (t). **Miranda Shorebird Centre:** (clb). **125 Alamy Stock Photo:** blickwinkel (bl). **FLPA:** Cyril Ruoso/JH Editorial (cr). **naturepl.com:** Tom Hugh-Jones (cra). **Mark Trabue:** (tl). **126-7 FLPA:** Michio Hoshino/Minden Pictures. **127 National Geographic Image Collection:** Paul Nicklen (cr); Maria Stenzel (br). **naturepl.com:** Jeff Turner (bl). **128 Kieran Dodds/kierandodds.com:** (tr). **NHPA/Photoshot:** A.N.T. Photo Library (cl). **128-9 FLPA:** Reinhard Dirscherl (b). **129 naturepl.com:** Anup Shah (cr). **NHPA/Photoshot:** Jonathan & Angela Scott (tl). **130 Alamy Stock Photo:** Peter Arnold, Inc (cla). **FLPA:** Gerry Ellis/Minden Pictures (cr). **naturepl.com:** Gertrud & Helmut Denzau (cl). **130-1 National Geographic Image Collection:** Michael S. Quinton. **131 Alamy Stock Photo:** blickwinkel (cr). **Ardea:** Pascal

Goetgheluck (cb). **FLPA:** Mitsuhiko Imamori/Minden Pictures (tr). **naturepl.com:** Jane Burton (crb); John Cancalosi (cra); Georgette Douwma (ca); Tom Vezo (bc). **NHPA/Photoshot:** T. Kitchin & V. Hurst (br). **132 FLPA:** Fred Bavendam/Minden Pictures (clb). **naturepl.com:** Michael Pitts (cl). **Photolibrary:** Neil Bromhall/OSF (cb). **133 Alamy Stock Photo:** Lawrence Stepanowicz (t). **134 Alamy Stock Photo:** AP Photo / Victor R. Caivano (br). **Corbis:** Anthony Bannister (cla); Frans Lanting. **135 Alamy Stock Photo:** James Berry (tc); Margaret Welby (ca). **FLPA:** Mark Moffett/Minden Pictures (clb); Pete Oxford/Minden Pictures (cr); Krystyna Szulecka (crb). **Photolibrary:** Densey Clyne/OSF (bl). **136 fogdenphotos.com:** M & P Fogden (tr) (cra). **NHPA/Photoshot:** Martin Harvey (bl). **Photolibrary:** Mark Deeble & Victoria Stone/OSF (cla). **Shutterstock.com:** Dave Montreuil (bc). **137 naturepl.com:** Jose B. Ruiz (c). **Photolibrary:** Ifa-Bilderteam GmbH/OSF (bc). **138-9 FLPA:** Jim Brandenburg/Minden Pictures. **139** naturepl.com: Dietmar Nill (cb). **Photolibrary:** Juniors Bildarchiv/OSF (br). **140 FLPA:** David Hosking (bl); Winfried Wisniewski (br); Konrad Wothe/Minden Pictures (cla). **naturepl.com:** William Osborn (tc). **141 FLPA:** Jim Brandenburg/Minden Pictures (b). **142 FLPA:** Jim Brandenburg/Minden Pictures (tc); Cyril Ruoso/JH Editorial (br). **naturepl.com:** Jen Guyton (clb). **143 Thomas Marent:** (cla). **Photolibrary:** Juniors Bildarchiv/OSF (clb); OSF (br). **144-5 Shutterstock.com:** Rudi Hulshof. **148 Alamy Stock Photo:** Lambie Brothers (bl). **Ardea:** Mary Clay (cr). **148-9 Denver Bryan:** (t). **149 Alamy Stock Photo:** Adrian Sherratt (crb). **150 Corbis:** M & P Fogden (cl); Momatiuk-Eascott (cb). **FLPA:** Nigel Cattlin (clb). **Photolibrary:** Animals Animals/Earth Sciences/OSF (bl). **Shutterstock:** Kitch Bain (c). **150-1 Corbis:** DLILLC. **151 FLPA:** Richard Brooks (ca); Jurgen & Christine Sohns (bl). **NHPA/Photoshot:** Anthony Bannister (clb). **152 Alamy Stock Photo:** Philip Dalton (cr); Maximillian Weinzierl (tr). **Corbis:** Juan Medina/Reuters (c). **Getty Images:** Norbert Wu/Minden Pictures (tl). **Photolibrary:** London Scientific Films (bl). **153 Corbis:** Andreas Lander/dpa (cla). **Getty Images:** Bill Beatty (b). **PunchStock:** Digital Vision (tr). **154-5 Alex Wild/myrmecos.net:** Alex Wild/myrmecos.net. **156 imagequestmarine.com:** Roger Steene (cla). **Science Photo Library:** Georgette Douwma (cra). **156-7 FLPA:** Tui De Roy/Minden Pictures (br). **157 Alamy Stock Photo:** David Hosking (bl); Nature PL (cl). **FLPA:** Tui De Roy/Minden Pictures (cla). **NHPA/Photoshot:** Daniel Heuclin (cra). **Still Pictures:** Tom Vezo (ca). **158 FLPA:** S & D & K Maslowski (t). **fogdenphotos.com :** M & P Fogden (br). **naturepl.com:** Staffan Widstrand (bl). **159 Alamy Stock Photo:** Arco Images (bl). **Ardea:** Jean Paul Ferrero (crb); Duncan Usher (tc). **naturepl.com:** David Tipling (tr). **NHPA/Photoshot:** Stephen Krasemann (c). **160 Getty Images:** Taylor S. Kennedy/National Geographic (clb). **Photolibrary:** Mark Hamblin/OSF (br). **Christian Ziegler:** (tr). **161 Alamy Stock Photo:** AfriPics.com (cl). **naturepl.com:** Jurgen Freund (bl). **NHPA/Photoshot:** Ernie James (cr). **162 Alamy Stock Photo:** MJ Photography (clb); Panorama Media Ltd (ca); A & J Visage (cra). **Jean-Jacques Alcalay:** (tr). **163 naturepl.com:** Sue Daly (clb). **Photolibrary:** Paul Kay/OSF (tl). **Science Photo Library:** Dr John Brackenbury (br). **SeaPics.com:** (br). **164 NHPA/Photoshot:** Mark Bowler (cb). **Photolibrary:** Rodger Jackman (br). **164-5 SeaPics.com:** (t). **165** FLPA: Minden Pictures (bl). **naturepl.com:** Alan James (tr). **Photolibrary:** Animals Animals/Earth Sciences/OSF (cla). **SeaPics.com:** (cra). **Still Pictures:** Reinhard Dirscherl/WaterFrame (br). **166 FLPA:** Fritz Polking (cr). **Photolibrary:** OSF (cla). **167 FLPA:** S Charlie Brown (bc); Tui De Roy/Minden Pictures (br); Frans Lanting (tr). **naturepl.com:** David Kjaer (bl). **168 Alamy Stock Photo:** Roger Bamber (tr). **Ardea:** Stefan Meyers (tl). **Corbis:** Joe McDonald (ca). **FLPA:** M & P Fogden/Minden Pictures (bl). **naturepl.com:** Doc White (cr). **169 Corbis:** Joe McDonald (cla). **Still Pictures:** Klein J.- L & Hubert M.-L/Biosphoto (b). **170 Alamy Stock Photo:** Steve Bloom Images (bl). **FLPA:** M & P Fogden/Minden Pictures (c). **171 FLPA:** Gerry Ellis/Minden Pictures (cra). **naturepl.com:** Meul/ARCO (crb); Rod Williams (bc). **172 FLPA:** Martin B Withers (crb). **NHPA/Photoshot:** Daniel Heuclin (br). **172-3 FLPA:** Jim Brandenburg/Minden Pictures (t). **173 Alamy Stock Photo:** WildPictures (tr). **FLPA:** Pete Oxford/Minden Pictures (cr). **naturepl.com:** Alan James (bl); Steven Kazlowski (crb); Constantinos Petrinos (fclb); Mike Read (cb); Lynn M. Stone (bc); Dave Watts (br); Doug Wechsler (cra). **NHPA/Photoshot:** Mark Bowler (cl). **174 FLPA:** Fred Bavendam/Minden Pictures (bl). **National Geographic Image Collection:** David Doubilet (tc). **175 Photolibrary:** Densey Clyne/OSF (cr). **SeaPics.com:** (tl) (ftr) (tc) (tr). **seashell-collector.com:** David Touitou (br). **176-7 naturepl.com:** Ingo Arndt. **178 Photolibrary:** Satoshi Kuribayashi/OSF (cla); Phototake Inc/OSF (tr). **179 FLPA:** Mitsuhiko Imamori/Minden Pictures (c) (cr) (fcr). **Tim Green:** (tr). **Science Photo Library:** Christian Laforsch (tr). **180 naturepl.com:** Kim Taylor (clb). **NHPA/Photoshot:** Anthony Bannister (bc). **Still Pictures:** Thierry Montford BIOS (tr). **181 Alamy Stock Photo:** Nature Picture Library / Simon Colmer (clb). **Getty Images:** vinisouza128 / 500px (tr). **Natural Visions:** Andrew Henley (cla). **Jerome Orivel, CNRS:** (c) (cr). **Photolibrary:** Satoshi Kuribayashi/OSF (cr). **182 Chris & Monique Fallows/Apexpredators.com:** (bc) (bl) (br) (r). **183 naturepl.com:** Doug Perrine (cl). **NHPA/Photoshot:** Stephen Dalton (cra). Photolibrary: Kathie Atkinson/OSF (bl). **SeaPics.com:** (crb). **184-5 Thomas P Peschak/thomaspeschak.com. 186 Ardea:** Jean Michel Labat (bc). **imagequestmarine.com:** Peter Herring (clb). Photolibrary: Tobias Bernhard/OSF (tl). **187 naturepl.com:** Kim Taylor (clb). **NHPA/Photoshot:** B Jones & M Shimlock (tr). **Photolibrary:** Paulo De Oliveira/OSF (br). **188 FLPA:** Cyril Ruoso/JH Editorial (cra). **Photolibrary:** Mauritius Die Bildagentur Gmbh/OSF (tl). **Winfried Wisniewski:** (b). **189 Getty Images:** Christian Ziegler/Minden Pictures (bl). **naturepl.com:** Michael D. Kern (tc). **NHPA/Photoshot:** Ken Griffiths (cr); Daniel Heuclin (c). **Photolibrary:** Brian P. Kenney (br). **David Wright:** (tr). **190-1 NHPA/Photoshot:** Stephen Dalton. **192 Ardea:** John Daniels (bc); Clem Haagner (tc). **FLPA:** Tui De Roy/Minden Pictures (cr). **192-3 Mart Smit/martsmit.nl:** (c). **193 FLPA:** John Watkins (bl). **194 Ardea:** M. Watson (bl). **Corbis:** M & P Fogden (cb). **NHPA/Photoshot:** Anthony Bannister (clb). **194-5 Ardea:** Thomas Dressler. **196 naturepl.com:** Vincent Munier (cl); Tom Vezo (tc). **SeaPics.com:** (br). **197 Alamy Stock Photo:** Westend 61 (tc). **FLPA:** Wendy Dennis (br); Frans Lanting (tr) (bl). **198 Alamy Stock Photo:** Alan Tunnicliffe (ca); Malcolm Schuyl (cl). **Ardea:** Karl Terblanche (bl). **naturepl.com:** Dave Watts (bc). **198-9 naturepl.com:** Charlie Hamilton-James. **199 naturepl.com:** Charlie Hamilton-James (fbl) (bl) (bc) (br). **200-1 National Geographic Image Collection:** Paul Nicklen. **201 National Geographic Image Collection:** Paul Nicklen (br) (bl). **www.skullsunlimited.com:** (bc). **202 FLPA:** Jurgen & Christine Sohns (c). **fogdenphotos.com :** M & P Fogden (br). **naturepl.com:** Richard du Toit (crb); Dave Watts (tr). **203 National Geographic Image Collection:** Norbert Rosing (cl) (c) (cr). **stevebloom.com:** (t). **204 Alamy Stock Photo:** Chris McLennan (clb). **NHPA/Photoshot:** Martin Harvey (bl) (c) (br). **204-5 NHPA/Photoshot:** Martin Harvey. **205 naturepl.com:** Martin Dohrn (br). **206-7 Shutterstock.com:** Lars Royal. **208 National Geographic Image Collection:** Chris Johns (b). **209 FLPA:** Michael Durham/Minden Pictures (tl). **Frank Greenaway:** (bc). **210-1 naturepl.com:** Christian Ziegler. **212 naturepl.com:** Mark Carwardine (cb) (bl); Doug Perrine (tc); **SeaPics.com:** (tr) **212-3 Ardea:** Francois Gohier. **214 National Geographic Image Collection:** Ralph Lee Hopkins (bl). **naturepl.com:** Brandon Cole (t). **215 FLPA:** Dembinsky Photo Ass (bl); Frans Lanting (tr). **naturepl.com:** Barrie Britton (tc); Anup Shah (cr). **216-7 Göran Ehlmé. 218 Alamy Stock Photo:** blickwinkel (bc). **naturepl.com:** Bruce Davidson (br); Anup Shah (tl). **NHPA/Photoshot:** Daniel Heuclin (c). **Still Pictures:** H. Schmidbauer (cr). **219 Alamy Stock Photo:** Jon Massie (br). **FLPA:** Nigel Cattlin (ca); Frans Lanting (tr). **Science Photo Library:** Eye of Science (cl). **Frances Dipper:** (br). **220 Alamy Stock Photo:** Robert Fried (cra). Kurt Jay Bertels: (tl). **FLPA:** Mark Moffett/Minden Pictures (cr); André Skonieczny/Imagebroker (fcl). **naturepl.com:** Neil Bromhall (cl) (c); Brent Hedges (cb); Nature Production (br); Jose B. Ruiz (bl). **Science Photo Library:** Barbara Strnadova (tr). **221 Alamy Stock Photo:** imageBROKER.com GmbH & Co. KG / Arco Images / TUNS (bc). **naturepl.com:** Pete Oxford (br). **SeaPics.com:** (cl) (cr). **222-3 Juan Manuel Hernández. 222 naturepl.com:** Ron O'Connor (br); Lynn M. Stone (bl). **Still Pictures:** Sylvain Cordier/Biosphoto (cra). **224-5 naturepl.com:** Christophe Courteau. **226 naturepl.com:** Michael Durham (cl); Anup Shah (cb); Dave Watts (tc). **226-7 Howie Garber/WanderlustImages.com. 228 FLPA:** Frans Lanting (c); Mark Newman (ca); Colin Marshall (br) NHPA/Photoshot: N A Callow (bl). **229 Photolibrary:** Les Stocker/OSF (bc). **Still Pictures:** Darlyne A. Murawski (br). **228-9** SeaPics.com. **230 Alamy Stock Photo:** Gerry Bishop: (tl). **Oceanwide Images:** Gary Bell/oceanwideimages.com (bl). **231 Alamy Stock Photo:** blickwinkel (tr) ; Martin Harvey (cr). **Corbis:** Anthony Bannister (tl). **FLPA:** Mark Moffett/Minden Pictures (clb) (bl). **Photoshot:** Newscom (br). **232-3 FLPA:** Minden Pictures/Tui De Roy. **234 Alamy Stock Photo:** blickwinkel (ca) (crb); Jeff Rotman (bl). **Getty Images:** Bill Curtsinger/National Geographic (cr). **iStockphoto.com:** Anne de Haas (tl). **235 Alamy Stock Photo:** blickwinkel (br). **Photolibrary:** Max Gibbs (Goldfish Bowl)/OSF (cla). **Still Pictures:** Klein/WaterFrame (cra). **236 Photoshot:** Bence Mate. **237 Alamy Stock Photo:** Danita Delimont (cr); Imagestate (ca); Mike Lane (tl). **Getty Images:** Beverly Joubert/National Geographic (br). **238 FLPA:** Jim Brandenburg/Minden Pictures (b). **239 naturepl.com:** Nick Gordon (crb); Anup Shah (bl). **NHPA/Photoshot:** Daniel Heuclin (br). **SeaPics.com:** (tl) (ca). **240-1 Dreamstime.com:** Farinoza. **242 Getty Images:** John & Lisa Merrill. **243 Alamy Stock Photo:** Matthew Doggett (cl). **naturepl.com:** Anup Shah (br). **244 Alamy Stock Photo:** E. R. Degginger (bl). **FLPA:** Mitsuaki Iwago/Minden Pictures (tl); Mike Lane (cla). **NHPA/Photoshot:** Roger Tidman (clb). **SeaPics.com:** (cl). **244-5 Alamy Stock Photo:** Danita Delimont. **245 FLPA:** Simon Litten (br). **Thomas Marent:** (t). **naturepl.com:** Martin Gabriel (cb); Pete Oxford (bc); Phil Savoie (crb); Claudio Velasquez (cra). **246 Getty Images:** Fred Bavendam/Minden Pictures (cr). **naturepl.com:** Constantinos Petrinos (tl). **Scubazoo.com:** Roger Munns (bl) (bc). **imagequestmarine.com:** Roger Steene (br). **247 imagequestmarine.com:** Mark Blum (tc). **Photolibrary:** David Fleetham/OSF (b). SeaPics.com: (cr). **248 Getty Images:** Heidi & Hans-Jurgen Koch/Minden Pictures (tr). **imagequestmarine.com:** Valda Butterworth (cr); Jim Greenfield 2004 (br); Roger Steene (cl). **NHPA/Photoshot:** Joe Blossom (tl). **Still Pictures:** Eichaker Xavier/Biosphoto (cr). **249 Tom Eiser, Cornell University:** (cra). **Getty Images:** Piotr Naskrecki/Minden Pictures (cla). **Thomas P Peschak/thomaspeschak.com:** (b). **Photolibrary:** Satoshi Kuribayashi/OSF (tc). **250 Alamy Stock Photo:** Anthony Pierce (clb). **FLPA:** Reinhard Dirscherl (bl). **imagequestmarine.com:** Peter Parks (cla). **SeaPics.com:** (cra). **251 naturepl.com:** Doug Perrine (clb). **SeaPics.com:** (br). **252 Alamy Stock Photo:** Jack Picone (bc). **Edmund D. Brodie, Jr.:** (cl). **naturepl.com:** Christophe Courteau (t) (tc) (ca) (c); George McCarthy (crb); Mark Payne-Gill (bl). **253 FLPA:** ZSSD/Minden Pictures (t). **Thomas Marent:** (cb) (bl). **naturepl.com:** Nick Gordon (br). **254 Corbis:** Rod Patterson (crb). **Edmund D. Brodie, Jr.:** (cla). **naturepl.com:** John Cancalosi (clb). **Photolibrary:** Animals Animals/Earth Sciences/OSF (bc); Waina Cheng (cl). **Still Pictures:** Ed Reschke (tr) (ca). **255 Alamy Stock Photo:** Jean-Paul Ferrero / Auscape (tl); Phototake Inc (br). **Ardea:** Pascal Goetgheluck (tr); Jean Paul Ferrero (cl). **National Geographic Image Collection:** Joel Sartore (bl). **NHPA/Photoshot:** Anthony Bannister (cr). **256 Joe McDonald:** (bl). **NHPA/Photoshot:** Stephen Dalton (fbl). **256-7 NHPA/Photoshot:** Stephen Dalton Production. **258 naturepl.com:** Markus Varesvuo (c). Barry Mansell (tr) **258-9 FLPA:** Peter Davey (b). **259 naturepl.com:** Tony Heald (tl) **FLPA:** Flip De Nooyer/Foto Natura (cr). **260 naturepl.com:** Mark Payne-Gill (fcl) (c) (cl) (cr). **NHPA/Photoshot:** Nigel Dennis (tl). **260-1 Getty Images:** J. Sneesby/B. Wilkins (b). **261 National Geographic Image Collection:** Peter G. Veit (tl). **naturepl.com:** George McCarthy (cr). **262 Corbis:** John Conrad (tl); Martin Harvey (br). **Getty Images:** (bl). **263 Afripics.com:** Daryl Balfour (b). **Alamy Stock Photo:** Kitch Bain (tr). **264 Alamy Stock Photo:** Nick Hardwick (cr). **DK Images:** Philip Dowell (ca). **FLPA:** Frans Lanting (bc) (br). **naturepl.com:** E. A. Kuttapan (tr). **SeaPics.com:** (cl). **264-5 National Geographic Image Collection:** Tim Laman. **265 FLPA:** Michael Quinton/Minden Pictures (br). **naturepl.com:** Georgette Douwma (cr); David Shale (crb). **José Roberto Peruca:** (tc). **Still Pictures:** Francois Gilson/Biosphoto (cra). **266 FLPA:** Frans Lanting (c); Chris Newbert/Minden Pictures (tc). **Getty Images:** Patricio Robles Gil/Minden Pictures (cr). **naturepl.com:** Pete Oxford (bl). **267 Getty Images:** Jeff Lepore (br). **Thomas Marent:** (c). **NHPA/Photoshot:** James Carmichael Jr (bl). **Senckenberg, Messel Research Department, Frankfurt a. M. (Germany) :** (cra). **268 268-9 NHPA/Photoshot:** Trevor McDonald. **SeaPics.com:** (bl) (bc) **269 Lydia Mäthger (permission from Biology Letters) :** (bl) (bc). **270-1 Art Wolfe. 272 FLPA:** Reinhard Dirscherl (cb). **naturepl.com:** Dave Bevan Photography (cra). **Photolibrary:** Waina Cheng (br). **SeaPics.com:** (tl). **273 FLPA:** Fred Bavendam/Minden Pictures (cl). **naturepl.com:** Sue Daly (cb). **Photolibrary:** David Fleetham/OSF (t). **SeaPics.com:** (br). **274 FLPA:** Gerry Ellis/Minden Pictures (tr). **fogdenphotos.com :** M & P Fogden (cra). **Nick Garbutt:** (cr). **naturepl.com:** Doug Wechsler (cl). **274-5 Thomas Marent:** (b). **275 Alamy Stock Photo:** Martin Harvey (cla). **Corbis:** M & P Fogden (tr). **Thomas Marent:** (br). **naturepl.com:** Pete Oxford (cla). **276-7 Anna Henly Photography. 278 Ardea:** Tom & Pat Leeson (ca). **FLPA:** Thomas Mangelson/Minden Pictures (tl); Chris Schenk/Foto Natura (clb). **naturepl.com:** Peter Reese (bc). **279 naturepl.com:** Sue Flood (crb); Paul Johnson (ca); Pete Oxford (tl); Philippe Clement (clb). **Photolibrary:** David Fleetham/OSF (br). **280 Alamy Stock Photo:** Steve Bloom Images (b). **Corbis:** D. Robert & Lorri Franz (tr). **Getty Images:** Mike Kelly (tc); Peter Lilja (cla). **281 Alamy Stock Photo:** Andrew Darrington (bl). **FLPA:** D. P. Wilson (cla); Konrad Wothe/Minden Pictures (br). **Getty Images:** Mark Moffett/Minden Pictures (cl). **A.Stabentheiner/H.Kovac/S.Schmaranzer:** (cra) (cr) (fcr) (fcra). **Wikipedia, The Free Encyclopedia:** (tr). **282 Alamy Stock Photo:** Duncan Usher (crb). **Ardea:** Valerie Taylor (cra) (cr). **FLPA:** Fred Bavendam/Minden Pictures (cla) (tc). **283 José Luis Gómez de Francisco:** (b). **Manual Presti:** (cra) (cr) (crb). **284-5 Alamy Stock Photo:** Chris Gug. **286-7 National Geographic Image Collection:** Mattias Klum; **Getty Images:** Mattias Klum/National Geographic (bc). **287 Getty Images:** Mattias Klum/National Geographic (cr) . **NHPA/Photoshot:** Nigel Dennis (bl). **288 Corbis**: Steve Kaufman (tr). **Getty Images:** Stone / Paul Souders (br). **naturepl.com:** Bruce Davidson (bl); Rolf Nussbaumer (ca). **289 FLPA:** Pete Oxford/Minden Pictures (cla) (ca) (cra). **National Geographic Image Collection:** Beverly Joubert (b). **290 naturepl.com:** Tui De Roy. **292 naturepl.com:** Bernard Castelein. **294-5 Photoshot:** Andy Newman/Woodfall Wild Images. **295 Alamy Stock Photo:** blickwinkel (cl). **naturepl.com:** Michael Pitts (cr). **296 Alamy Stock Photo:** Holt Studios International Ltd (cl). Ardea: Steve Hopkin (b). **Corbis:** Visuals Unlimited (fcl). **imagequestmarine.com:** Valdimar Butterworth (cl). **Reuters:** Phil Noble (tr). **Science Photo Library:** Sinclair Stammers (c). **297 FLPA:** Fritz Siedel (tl); D. P. Wilson (cl). **SeaPics.com:** (clb). **Still Pictures:** Joel Bricout/Biosphoto (tc). **298 Ardea:** D. Parer & E. Parer-Cook. **SeaPics.com:** (cl). **299 Alamy Stock Photo:** Chris Mattison (br). **Ben Chapman:** (cr). **naturepl.

com: Willem Kolvoort (tl). **SeaPics.com:** (bc). **D. Scott Taylor:** (tr). **300 FLPA:** M & P Fogden/Minden Pictures (ca); Frans Lanting (b); Albert Visage (cla). **naturepl. com:** Hanne & Jens Eriksen (tc). **301 FLPA:** Norbert Wu/Minden Pictures (tr). **Getty Images:** Piotr Naskrecki/Minden Pictures (br). **naturepl.com:** Kim Taylor (cb). **PA Photos:** Matthew L. M. Lim & Daiqin Li (c). **Scubazoo.com:** Matthew Oldfield (cl). **302 FLPA:** Michael Durham/Minden Pictures (t). **Brian Kenney:** (clb). **naturepl.com:** Kim Taylor (cr). **303 Ardea:** Ken Lucas (cr). **Anthoni Floor / seafriends.org:** (bl). **Blue Planet Archive** (tl). **304 Alamy Stock Photo:** Peter Arnold Inc (bc). **FLPA:** Paul Hobson (bl). **fogdenphotos.com :** M & P Fogden (tc). **naturepl. com:** Rolf Nussbaumer (cl). **NHPA/Photoshot:** James Carmichael Jr (cl). **305 Tasha L. Metz/seaturtle.org:** (cr). **Photolibrary:** David Fleetham/OSF (t). **SeaPics. com:** (bl). **306 Ardea:** M. Watson (br). **Chris Gomersall Photography:** (cra). **FLPA:** Neil Bowman (cr) (cra); Konrad Wothe/Minden Pictures (bl). **naturepl.com:** Jorma Luhta (tl). **SeaPics.com:** (bc). **307 Ardea:** D. Parer & E. Parer-Cook (br). **FLPA:** Michio Hoshino/Minden Pictures (c). **SeaPics.com:** (bc). **308 FLPA:** Mitsuaki Iwago/Minden Pictures (cb); Frans Lanting (cla). **Photolibrary:** Satoshi Kuribayashi/ OSF (bc). **308-9 naturepl.com:** John Cancalosi. **309 naturepl.com:** Nature Production (c). **NHPA/ Photoshot:** Jonathan & Angela Scott (crb); Alan Williams (cra). **Photolibrary:** Clive Bromhall/OSF (bc). **310 FLPA:** Mark Moffett/Minden Pictures (br) (bl); Chris Newbert/Minden Pictures (cl). **National Geographic Image Collection:** Jozsef Szentpeteri (bl). **naturepl.com:** Georgette Douwma (tl). **NHPA/ Photoshot:** Karl Switak (tr). **311 FLPA:** B. Borrell Casals (c); Mark Moffett/Minden Pictures (br). **naturepl.com:** Nick Garbutt (cl). **NHPA/Photoshot:** Anthony Bannister (bl). **Photolibrary:** M & P Fogden/OSF (t). **312 FLPA:** Mark Moffett/Minden Pictures (ca) (bl) (cl). **312-3 FLPA:** Mark Moffett/Minden Pictures. **314 FLPA:** Mark Newman (bl). **NHPA/Photoshot:** Linda Pitkin (tc). **SeaPics.com:** (tc). **314-5 fogdenphotos. com :** M & P Fogden (b). **315 fogdenphotos.com :** M & P Fogden (tr). **316 FLPA:** Jim Brandenburg/Minden Pictures (bl). **naturepl.com:** Rupert Barrington (cla); Kim Taylor (tc). **naturepl.com:** Barrie Britton (c); **317 Ardea:** M. Watson (tl) (br). Pete Oxford (clb). **318 FLPA:** Tim Fitzharris/Minden Pictures (bl); Cyril Ruoso/ JH Editorial (tr); Jan Vermeer/Foto Natura (tc). **319 FLPA:** Mark Newman (bl). **naturepl.com:** Terry Andrewartha (br). **SeaPics.com:** (tl) (tc). **www. skullsunlimited.com:** (cr). **320 Lydia Fucsko/ lydiafucsko.com:** (cl); **Science Photo Library:** James H. Robinson (tr). **naturepl.com:** Jose B. Ruiz (crb) (br). **320-1 Ardea:** Duncan Usher. **321 naturepl.com:** Bengt Lundberg (crt). **Photolibrary:** OSF (clt); **Photolibrary:** Mark Hamblin/OSF (tr). **322 FLPA:** Richard Becker (bl). **naturepl.com:** Meul/ARCO (br). **Premaphotos Wildlife:** Ken Preston-Mafham (tc). **Photolibrary:** Joaquin Gutierrez Acha/OSF (tr). **323 Oceanwide Images:** Rudie Kuiter/oceanwideimages. com (tc). **SeaPics.com:** (cl) (tr) (cb). **324 Alamy Stock Photo:** Ainars Aunins (tc). **Photolibrary:** David M Dennis/OSF (cla). **FLPA:** Ingo Arndt/Foto Natura (bl). **324-5 Ulrich Doering. 325 Alamy Stock Photo:** John Cancalosi (crb). **naturepl.com:** Solvin Zankl (bl). **326 FLPA:** Frans Lanting (c). **Nick Garbutt:** (cra). **naturepl. com:** Pete Oxford (tc); Artur Tabor (bl); Tom Vezo (cr). **327 Photolibrary:** Eliott Neep/OSF (bl) (bcl) (bcr) (br). **rspb-images.com:** Chris Knights (r). **328-9 FLPA:** Tui De Roy/Minden Pictures. **330 Chris Mattison Nature Photographics:** (tl). **National Geographic Image Collection:** Jason Edwards (tr). **naturepl.com:** Phil Savoie (br). **331 Ardea:** Stefan Meyers (cra). **Corbis:** Tom Brakefield (tl). **FLPA:** David Hosking (cr). **Sharon Heald:** (b). **332 FLPA:** Mark Newman (l); Terry Whittaker (cr). **naturepl.com:** Wegner/ARCO (cra). **333 National Geographic Image Collection:** Joel Sartore (tl). **NHPA/Photoshot:** Ernie James (c). **Photolibrary:** Tony Martin/OSF (bl) (bc) (br). **334 Alamy Stock Photo:** Luigi Carta (tr). **FLPA:** Silvestris Fotoservice (c). **naturepl.com:** Premaphotos (crb). **Photolibrary:** Martyn Colbeck/OSF (bl). **Science Photo Library:** Dr George Beccaloni (ca). **335 FLPA:** Fred Bavendam/Minden Pictures (ftr). **naturepl.com:** Constantinos Petrinos (br). **David Nelson:** (ftl) (tc) (tl) (tr). **336 FLPA:** Robin Chittenden (tl). **naturepl.com:** Doug Perrine (cra). **Photolibrary:** OSF (ca). **336-7 Thomas Endlein:** (b). **337 Ardea:** Jean Michel Labat (cra). **naturepl.com:** Meul/ARCO (bc). **Photolibrary:** Clive Bromhall (c). **Science Photo Library:** Andrew Syred (br). **338-9 Getty Images:** Universal Images Group / Education Images / David Tipling. **340 FLPA:** B. Borrell Casals (cra); Derek Middleton (bl). National Geographic Image Collection: George Grall (cl). **naturepl.com:** Willem Kolvoort (br). **341 Ardea:** Steve Downer (t). **Dreamstime.com:** Chris Hill (br). **NHPA/ Photoshot:** Alberto Nardi (bl). **342 Auscape:** C. Andrew Henly (br). **Graham Catley:** (fcl) (c) (cl) (cr). **FLPA:** Neil Bowman (ca). **naturepl.com:** Jorma Luhta (tr). **NHPA/Photoshot:** Alan Williams (tl). **343 Alamy Stock Photo:** Terry Whittaker (br). **FLPA:** Cyril Ruoso/ JH Editorial (tr). **naturepl.com:** Anup Shah (cl). **344 Getty Images / iStock:** Janugio. **346 Getty Images:** Anup Shah/Image Bank. **347 Science Photo Library:** Science Source (fcla) (cla) (fcl) (cl) (clb) (fclb) (bl) (fbl). **348 FLPA:** Michael Durham/Minden Pictures (cl) (c). **348-9 FLPA:** Michael Durham/Minden Pictures. **349 Alamy Stock Photo:** ARCO Images GmbH (bl). **FLPA:** Sumio Harada/Minden Pictures (ca). **naturepl.com:** Ingo Arndt (clb); Anup Shah (bc) (br). **NHPA/ Photoshot:** George Bernard (ca); Stephen Dalton (tr). **350 Alamy Stock Photo:** blickwinkel / Hecker (tr). **Anthoni Floor / seafriends.org:** (bl). **Christian Fuchs:** (tl). **naturepl.com:** Kim Taylor (c). **SeaPics. com:** (tc). **351 Alamy Stock Photo:** NaturePics (br). **naturepl.com:** Ross Hoddinott (t). **NHPA/Photoshot:** Stephen Dalton (bl). **352-3 FLPA:** Reinhard Dirscherl. **354 Thomas Marent:** (l). **355 Thomas Marent:** (c), (cl) (clb) (cb) (r). **356 FLPA:** Nigel Cattlin (cl). **fogdenphotos.com** : M & P Fogden (b). **Getty Images:** National Geographic (tc). **National Geographic Image Collection:** Darlyne A. Murawski (tl). **naturepl.com:** Kim Taylor (cr). **357 Jose Castro:** (bl). **National Geographic Image Collection:** David Doubilet (tr). **SeaPics.com:** (br). **358 Alamy Stock Photo:** Vincent Premel / Biosphoto (cra). **Corbis:** David A. Northcott (c). **Thomas Marent:** (br). **naturepl.com:** Kim Taylor (tl). **359 Alamy Stock Photo:** Albert Lleal / Minden Pictures (tl). **Conservation International:** Robin Moore (ca). **FLPA**: Foto Natura Stock (cl) (clb); Reinhard Dirscherl (bl). **naturepl.com:** Doug Wechsler (cb); George McCarthy (bl); Jane Burton (tr). **360 Ardea:** Hans & Judy Beste (cra). **naturepl.com:** Doug Allan (bc); Matthew Maran (tl). **Photolibrary:** Kathie Atkinson/OSF (tr). **360-1 naturepl.com:** Doug Allan. **361 FLPA:** Foto Natura Stock (tr). **Getty Images:** Pete Oxford/Minden Pictures (br). **362 Ardea:** D. Parer & E. Parer-Cook (bl) (cr). **NHPA/Photoshot:** Kevin Schafer (tr). **Still Pictures:** Regis Cavignaux/Biosphoto (tc). **363** Christophe Couteau: (clb). naturepl.com: Andrew Cooper (tc); Anup Shah (br). **364 Corbis:** M & P Fogden (c); Christophe Karaba/epa (tr). **FLPA:** Michael Gore (bl); Winfried Wisniewski/Foto Natura (cr). **Sharon Heald:** (br). **naturepl.com:** John Cancalosi (cb). **365 FLPA:** Phil McLean (br). **2002 MBARI:** (cl). **SeaPics.com:** (tc) (bc). **366 Ardea:** Alan Weaving (tr). **FLPA:** Heinz Schrempp (bl). **Getty Images:** John Bernard Triumfante / 500px (c). **Natural Visions:** Jeremy Thomas (br). **367 Photolibrary:** Pacific Stock/OSF (b). **368 naturepl. com:** Mark Payne-Gill (cl). **SeaPics.com:** (tc). **368-9 naturepl.com:** Anup Shah. **369 Alamy Stock Photo:** Digital Vision (clb). **Ardea:** M. Watson (cla). **naturepl. com:** Anup Shah (cl). **photographersdirect.com:** AfriPics Images (cr). **SuperStock:** Rene Krekels / Minden Pictures (t). **370 Photolibrary:** Alan Root/OSF. **371 FLPA:** Tui De Roy/Minden Pictures (cl); Adri Hoogendijk/Foto Natura (br). **naturepl.com:** John Cancalosi (ca); Dave Watts (tr). **372-3 FLPA:** Frans Lanting. **374 Ardea:** Nick Gordon (c). **Bat Conservation International:** Merlin D. Tuttle (tr). **naturepl.com:** Anup Shah (tl); Tom Mangelson (b). **375 Ardea:** Tom & Pat Leeson (c). **FLPA:** Flip Nicklin/ Minden Pictures (tr); Michio Hoshino/Minden Pictures (br). **NHPA/Photoshot:** Daniel Heuclin (cla). **376 Ardea:** Jagdeep Rajput (bl). **FLPA:** Gerry Ellis/Minden Pictures (bc). **naturepl.com:** Doug Perrine (fbl); Anup Shah (tl); Tom Vezo (cr); Carol Walker (c). **NHPA/ Photoshot:** Joe Blossom (tr). **377 Alamy Stock Photo:** imagebroker (br). **FLPA:** Neil Bowman (tl); Andrew Forsyth (bc). **Photolibrary:** Aldo Brando/OSF (ca). **378-9 NHPA/Photoshot:** Andy Rouse. **380 FLPA:** R P Lawrence (tc); Fritz Polking/Foto Natura (br); Inga Spence (bl). **381 Ardea:** Jean Michel Labat (clb); Tom & Pat Leeson (t). **Suzi Eszterhas Photography:** (br). **382-3 naturepl.com:** Anup Shah. **384 Ardea:** Francois Gohier (crb). brandoncole.com: Brandon Cole (bc). **FLPA:** Michael Quinton/Minden Pictures (tl). **Cathy & Gordon ILLG/advenphoto.com:** (cr). **385 Suzi Eszterhas Photography:** (bc). **FLPA:** Gerry Ellis/ Minden Pictures (cra); Frants Hartmann (cla). **386 Dreamstime.com:** Anekoho. **389 Alamy Stock Photo:** Ryan Ayre (fcrb); blickwinkel (cra); Holt Studios International Ltd (fcr); Michael Patrick O'Neill (clb/fish); Top-Pics TBK (bl/lions). **Getty Images:** Tohuku Color Agency (fbr/birds). **Shutterstock:** Craig Hosterman (cl). **390 Alamy Stock Photo:** Penny Boyd (tl); dbimages (tr). **Getty Images:** Mitch Reardon/Riser (b). **391 FLPA:** J. W. Alker/Imagebroker (cra). **Frances Dipper:** (tl). **Pauline Montecot:** (bl) (br). **392-3 FLPA:** Pete Oxford/Minden Pictures. **393** Hugh Schermuly: (br). **394 Alamy Stock Photo:** Stephen Frink (bl). **naturepl.com:** Kim Taylor (cr). **SeaPics.com:** (br). **Alex Wild/myrmecos.net:** Alex Wild (tc). **395 Photolibrary:** Tobias Bernhard/OSF. **396-7 Béla Násfay. 398 Getty Images:** Roy Toft/National Geographic (cra); Harald Sund/Photographers Choice (bl). **Photolibrary:** Konrad Wothe/OSF (tl). **398-9 FLPA:** Suzi Eszterhas/Minden Pictures (b). **399 Corbis:** Keren Su (tl). **naturepl.com:** Anup Shah (cra). **400-1 naturepl.com:** Jose B. Ruiz. **402 Alamy Stock Photo:** Tom Uhlman (crb). Mark Newman (tl); Tom Vezo/ Minden Pictures (br). **naturepl.com:** Chris Gomersall (cl). **403 Arto Juvonen/Birdfoto.fi:** (cl). **naturepl. com:** Neil Bromhall (crb) (br); Bruce Davidson (tl). **404 Alamy Stock Photo:** Cyril Ruoso / Minden Pictures (tr). **FLPA:** David Hosking (b). **NHPA/Photoshot:** David Higgs (cr). **Still Pictures:** A & J Visage (tl). **405 Alamy Stock Photo:** Worldfoto (cl). **FLPA:** Tim Fitzharris/Minden Pictures (br). **Getty Images:** Manoj Shah/Stone (cla). naturepl.com: Karl Ammann (tr). **NHPA/Photoshot:** David Higgs (cr). **406 FLPA:** Jurgen & Christine Sohns (tl); Yva Momatiuk & John Eastcott/ Minden Pictures (b). **Still Pictures:** MCPHOTO (cr). **407 Alamy Stock Photo:** blickwinkel (crb). **FLPA:** Frans Lanting (tr). **naturepl.com:** Huw Cordey (cl); Doug Perrine (bl). **408-9 Shutterstock.com:** EcoPrint. **410 Corbis:** Daniel J. Cox. **411 naturepl.com:** Francois Savigny (fbr). **412 Alamy Stock Photo:** Michael Patrick O'Neill (tr). **FLPA:** Nigel Cattlin (cr). **naturepl.com:** Mark Brownlow (br); Pete Oxford (cb). **Photolibrary:** Keith Porter/OSF (ca). **Science Photo Library:** Stuart Wilson (bl). **413 Alamy Stock Photo:** Maximillian Weinzierl (tl). **Ardea:** Chris Martin Bahr (clb). **FLPA:** Mark Moffett/Minden Pictures (br). **fogdenphotos. com** : M & P Fogden (tr). **Premaphotos Wildlife:** Ken Preston-Mafham (cl). **414** M. Watson (cr). **fogdenphotos.com :** M & P Fogden (tc). **NHPA/ Photoshot:** Jonathan & Angela Scott (crb). **Still Pictures:** Reinhard Dirscherl/WaterFrame (bl). **415 Ardea:** Francois Gohier (bl). **Alamy Stock Photo:** Nick Greaves (tc). **FLPA:** Gerald Lacz (c). **naturepl.com:** Solvin Zankl (cl). **Ingrid Wiesel/Brown Hyena Research Project:** (tr). **416 Alamy Stock Photo:** Arco Images GmbH (bl); Isita Image service (r); Peter Llewellyn (L) (bc). **Science Photo Library:** Tim & Alistair Lionel (c). **SeaPics.com:** (cla). **417 Ardea:** Peter Steyn. **FLPA:** Mark Moffett/Minden Pictures (tl). **Natural Visions:** Peter David (cl). **naturepl.com:** Nature Production (cr); Doug Perrine (b). **418 Ardea:** Jean Paul Ferrero (br). **fogdenphotos.com :** M & P Fogden (clb). **SeaPics.com:** (tr). **419 Ardea:** John Daniels (tc). **Getty Images:** Norbert Rosing/National Geographic (ca). **Still Pictures:** S. Weber (r). **420 Alamy Stock Photo:** Octavio Campos Salles (tr). **FLPA:** John Hawkins (cla). **Photolibrary:** Kathie Atkinson/ OSF (bl). **421 naturepl.com:** Pete Oxford (tr). **stevebloom.com. 422 Alamy Stock Photo:** Jeff Minter (bl). **NHPA/Photoshot:** David Higgs (tr); Martin Harvey (fbl). **Photolibrary:** Clive Bromhall/OSF (bc) (br). **423 Ardea:** Duncan Usher (b). **FLPA:** Mark Raycroft/Minden Pictures (br). **naturepl.com:** Doug Allan (tc). **Still Pictures:** BIOS Bios (c). **424 Alamy Stock Photo:** Steve Bloom Images (ca). **FLPA:** M & P Fogden/Minden Pictures (cl). **Gastone Pivatelli:** (r). **425 Ardea:** Pat Morris (bl). **Corbis:** Anthony Bannister/Gallo Images (tl). **fogdenphotos.com :** M & P Fogden (bc). **naturepl.com:** Meul/ARCO (cra); Kim Taylor (c). **426 Getty Images:** Tom Hopkins/Aurora (tl). **Björn Lardner:** (cl). **naturepl.com:** Gary K. Smith (bc). **Shutterstock.com:** kamnuan (cr). **427 Ardea:** Sid Roberts (bl). **Corbis:** Theo Allofs (tc). **NHPA/ Photoshot:** Tony Crocetta (br). **Photolibrary:** Konrad Wothe/OSF (cra). **428 Alamy Stock Photo:** Amazon Images (cl); Arco Images GmbH (clb); Rick & Nora Bowers (c). **naturepl.com:** Anup Shah (br). **429 Alamy Stock Photo:** Alaska Stock LLC (bc). **FLPA:** Flip Nicklin/Minden Pictures (tr). **naturepl.com:** David Tipling (clb). **430 Ardea:** Pat Morris (c). **FLPA:** Tim Fitzharris/Minden Pictures (tl); Pete Oxford/Minden Pictures (tr/thorn bug). **fogdenphotos.com :** M & P Fogden (tr/golden mole). **naturepl.com:** Anup Shah (b); Kim Taylor (cra). **431 Alamy Stock Photo:** Simon de Glanville (tl). **FLPA:** Richard Becker (bl). **naturepl. com:** Kim Taylor (tr). **432 Ardea:** Brian Bevan (tr). **naturepl.com:** Niall Benvie (crb); Steven David Miller (b). **Tom Richardson/Nigel Franks:** (tl). **433 FLPA:** Jurgen & Christine Sohns (tl). **fogdenphotos.com :** M & P Fogden (br). **shahimages.com :** Anup and Manoj Shah (bl) (bc). **Still Pictures:** H. Brehm (cra); Cyril Ruoso/Biosphoto (cl). **434 naturepl.com:** Anup Shah (br). **434-5 FLPA:** Gerry Ellis/Minden Pictures. **435 Alamy Stock Photo:** Images of Africa Photobank (crb). **naturepl.com:** Anup Shah (bl). **436-7 Alamy Stock Photo:** Avalon.red / Martin Harvey. **438 stevebloom. com. 439 Getty Images:** Bill Curtsinger/National Geographic (ca). **Science Photo Library:** CNRI (fcl). **440 FLPA:** Jurgen & Christine Sohns (c). **naturepl. com:** George McCarthy (br); Solvin Zankl (t). **441 Ardea:** Becca Saunders (tc). **imagequestmarine.com:** Michael Aw (bl). **National Geographic Image Collection:** Robert Sisson (crb). **naturepl.com:** Constantinos Petrinos (br). **SeaPics.com:** (tr). **442 Alamy Stock Photo:** Joseph creamer (tr). **FLPA:** Mark Moffett/Minden Pictures (cl). **naturepl.com:** Premaphotos (b). **443 naturepl.com:** Doug Perrine (c); Michel Roggo (tr). **Photolibrary:** Animals Animals/ Earth Sciences/OSF (br); Brian P. Kenney/OSF (tl). **444 National Geographic Image Collection:** Robert Sisson (bl) (bc) (br). **444-5 FLPA:** Suzi Eszterhas/ Minden Pictures. **445 Ardea:** Steve Hopkin (bc). **naturepl.com:** Lynn M. Stone (cra). **446 naturepl. com:** Miles Barton (bl). **Photoshot:** Marie Read/ Woodfall Wild Images (bc). **446-7 naturepl.com:** Ingo Arndt (tc). **447 FLPA:** Pete Oxford/Minden Pictures (crb) (bc) (br) (cb). **Yukihiro Fukuda:** (tr). **naturepl. com:** Miles Barton (cra). **448 FLPA:** Cyril Ruoso/JH Editorial (bc). **Still Pictures:** Cyril Ruoso/Biosphoto (bl). **448-9 naturepl.com:** Anup Shah. **449 National Geographic Image Collection:** Michael K. Nichols (bc). **450-1 stevebloom.com. 452 Ardea:** Tom & Pat Leeson (b). **Getty Images:** - / SUAQ Foundation / AFP (cla). **naturepl.com:** Andrew Murray (tr); Anup Shah (ca). **453 Alamy Stock Photo:** Pravine Chester (crb). **483 FLPA:** Reinhard Dirscherl (tl). **Getty Images:** APF (br). **naturepl.com:** Hugh Pearson (cr).)

Cover images: *Front:* Thanks to the Spanish photographer Jesús Frías, for his photograph that is used on the cover of this book; *Spine:* **Dreamstime. com:** Leopold Brix

Endpaper images: *Front and Back:* **Alamy Stock Photo:** blickwinkel / E. Teister